CENTRAL STATISTICAL OFFICE

Indexes to the Standard Industrial Classification

Revised 1980

London: Her Majesty's Stationery Office

© Crown copyright 1981

First Published 1981

Fourth impression 1987

ISBN 0 11 620001 4

PREFACE

The aim of this booklet is to provide a list of typical products or activities for each heading of the Standard Industrial Classification Revised 1980 as well as an index of the headings under which different activities appear in the Classification.

The first index, the Numerical index, lists each heading of the Standard Industrial Classification followed by a list of characteristic activities included within that heading.

In the second index these activities have been arranged in alphabetical order. Alongside each is the heading to which the activity is classified. These activities may be known under different names. Some activities have been classified in the Alphabetical index under several alternative titles but it has obviously not been possible to list all variations.

Both Indexes also include references to the Standard Industrial Classification Revised 1968 and to the General Industrial Classification of Economic Activities within the European Communities, more commonly known as NACE. These are included to assist users of the classification but it must be borne in mind that when the Standard Industrial Classification Revised 1968 was devised less detailed information was available which made it difficult to allocate some activities. NACE lacks a comprehensive index so these references are, therefore, the Central Statistical Office's interpretation of that classification. In some cases reference could only be made to Group level but in most cases reference is to the Sub-group level of NACE.

Central Statistical Office
Great George Street
London
SW1P 3AQ

August 1981

CONTENTS

	Page
Preface	3
Standard Industrial Classification Revised 1980	
Part 1 Numerical index	5
Part 2 Alphabetical index	95

PART 1

NUMERICAL INDEX

SIC 1980	Activity	SIC 1968	NACE
0100/1	Arable farming and livestock production		
	Angora rabbit breeding	001/1	01
	Animal rearing for production of serum	001/1	01
	Arable farming	001/1	01
	Bee keeping	001/1	01
	Cattle farming	001/1	01
	Dairy farming	001/1	01
	Egg hatchery	001/1	01
	Farmer's wife (if engaged primarily in farm work); farming and stock-rearing	001/1	01
	Farming (undefined)	001/1	01
	Flax growing	001/1	01
	Fur farming	001/1	01
	Game bird farming	001/1	01
	Grazing	001/1	01
	Hop growing	001/3	01
	Horse breeding	001/1	01
	Hunting commercial	001/2	01
	Milk Marketing Board cattle breeding centres	001/1	01
	Osier growing	001/1	01
	Pig farming	001/1	01
	Potato growing	001/1	01
	Poultry farming	001/1	01
	Ranching	001/1	01
	Sheep agisting (grazing)	001/1	01
	Sheep farming	001/1	01
	Small holding	001/1	01
	Stockbreeding and farming	001/1	01
	Stud farming	001/1	01
	Sugar beet growing	001/1	01
	Teasel growing	001/1	01
	Willow growing	001/1	01
	Withy growing	001/1	01
0100/2	Horticulture		
	Allotment farming	001/3	01
	Bulb growing	001/3	01
	Cider apple growing	001/3	01
	Farmer's wife (if engaged primarily in farm work); market gardening, fruit, flower and seed growing	001/3	01
	Flower growing	001/3	01
	Fruit growing (all)	001/3	01
	Glasshouse crop growing	001/3	01
	Herb growing	001/3	01
	Horticulture	001/3	01
	Market gardening	001/3	01
	Mushroom growing (cultivated)	001/3	01
	Nurseryman	001/3	01
	Ornamental tree and shrub growing	001/3	01
	Seed growing (not farming)	001/3	01
	Tomato growing	001/3	01
	Vegetable growing (except potatoes)	001/3	01
	Vine yards	001/3	01
	Watercress growing	001/3	01
0100/3	Agricultural and Horticultural services		
	Agricultural contracting	001/2	01
	Bait production	001/2	01
	Crop and grass drying plant operation by contractor	001/2	01
	Crop spraying by contractor	001/2	01
	Fencing by agricultural contractor	001/2	01
	Landscape gardening	001/3	01
	Mole catching by contractors	001/1	01
	Rabbit destroying and trapping on agricultural land	001/2	01
	Rat destroying and trapping on agricultural land	001/2	01
	Rodent destroying and trapping on agricultural land	001/2	01
	Thatching	001/2	01
	Threshing by contractor	001/2	01
	Vermin destroying and trapping on agricultural land	001/2	01
0200	Forestry		
	Charcoal burning	002	02
	Fern collecting, cutting, gathering	002	02
	Forestry	002	02
	Forestry Commission	002	02
	Furze collecting, cutting, gathering	002	02
	Heath collecting, cutting, gathering	002	02
	Moss collecting, cutting, gathering	002	02
	Reed collecting, cutting, gathering	002	02
	Tree nursery (not fruit or ornamental trees)	002	02
	Treefelling (by forestry owners)	002	02
	Wood logging etc, within forestry site	002	02
0300/1	Commercial sea fishing		
	Cockle gathering	003/1	03
	Fisherman—crofter	003/1	03
	Fishing—line	003/1	03
	Fishing—sea	003/1	03
	Fishing—shellfish	003/1	03
	Kelp collecting, cutting and gathering uncultivated	002	03
	Mussel gathering	003/1	03
	Oyster fishery	003/1	03
	Periwinkle gathering	003/1	03
	Salmon netting	003/1	03
	Seaweed collecting, cutting and gathering (uncultivated)	002	03
	Share fisherman	003/1	03
	Shrimping	003/1	03
	Whaling	003/1	03
	Winkle gathering	003/1	03
0300/2	Commercial fishing in inland waters		
	Fish breeding	003/2	03
	Fish farming (including hatcheries)	003/2	03
	Fish hatchery (freshwater)	003/2	03
	Fish hatchery (sea)	003/1	03
	Fishing (freshwater)	003/2	03
	Fishing (inland water)	003/2	03
	Fishing (rivers)	003/2	03
	Laver gathering (cultivated)	002	03
	Salmon and trout fishery (hatchery)	003/2	03
1113	Deep coal mines		
	Coal mine (deep or drift)	101	111.1
	Coal mining (not opencast)	101	111.1
	Coal preparation	101	111.1
	Coal washing	101	111.1
	Colliery	101	111.1
	Mines' rescue station	101	111.1
	National Coal Board; central workshop	101	111.1
	National Coal Board; coal stocking	101	111.1
	National Coal Board; colliery road transport	101	111.1
	National Coal Board; dirt disposal	101	111.1
	National Coal Board; engineering establishment	101	111.1
	National Coal Board; internal railway	101	111.1
	National Coal Board; Mining Research Establishment	876	940
	National Coal Board; plant pool	101	111.1
	National Coal Board; pumping station	101	111.1

SIC 1980	Activity	SIC 1968	NACE
1114	Opencast coal working		
	Coal recovery (from old dumps etc.)	500	111.1
	National Coal Board, opencast executive	500	111.1
	Opencast coal contractor	500	111.1
	Opencast coal disposal point	500	111.1
	Opencast coal site	500	111.1
1115	Manufacture of solid fuels		
	Briquette, solid fuel, manufacturing	261/2	111.2
	Coal tar (crude) from manufactured fuel plants manufacturing	261/2	111.2
	Ovoid, solid fuel, manufacturing	261/2	111.2
	Patent fuel manufacturing	261/2	111.2
	Solid smokeless ovoids and briquettes, preparation of	261/2	111.2
1200	Coke ovens		
	Ammoniacal liquor (from coke oven) manufacturing	261/1	120
	Benzole, crude, (from coke ovens) manufacturing	261/1	120
	Coal tar, crude, (from coke ovens) manufacturing	261/1	120
	Coal: carbonization	261/1	120
	Coke oven gas manufacturing	261/1	120
	Foundry coke manufacturing	261/1	120.2
	Hard coke manufacturing	261/1	120
	Hard coke breeze manufacturing	261/1	120
	Metallurgical coke manufacturing	261/1	120.2
	Sulphate of ammonia (from coke ovens) manufacturing	261/1	120.2
1200/1	Colliery coke ovens	261/1	120
1200/2	Iron and steel industry coke ovens	261/1	120
1200/3	Other coke ovens	261/1	120
1200/4	Low temperature carbonization plants		
	Low temperature carbonization solid fuel (not ovoids or briquettes) manufacturing	261/2	120.3
1300	Extraction of mineral oil and natural gas		
	Butane extraction (from natural gas)	104	132
	Crude oil exploration	104	134
	Crude oil extraction	104	131
	Drilling contractor for off-shore oil or gas well	104	502.3
	Exploration for gas or oil	104	134
	Floating drilling rig operation (for petroleum or natural gas exploration or production)	104	134
	Gas (natural) production well	104	132
	Gas off-shore pipeline laying	104	502.7
	Geological surveying for petroleum or natural gas (not geological consultancy)	104	134
	Methane extraction (from natural gas)	104	132
	Mineral oil extraction	104	131
	Natural gas condensates separation	104	132
	Natural gas exploration	104	134
	Natural gas production well	104	132
	Off-shore pipeline installation (from oil or gas well)	104	502.7
	Off-shore pipeline operating (natural gas)	104	132
	Off-shore pipeline operating (oil)	104	131
	Oil off-shore pipeline laying	104	502.7
	Oil pipeline terminal operating (for petroleum)	104	131
	Oil platform operation	104	131
	Oil production well or platform operating	104	131
	Oil shale mine	104	133
	Oil shale retorting	104	133
	Oil stabilisation plant operating	104	131
	Petroleum exploration	104	134
	Propane extraction (from natural gas)	104	132
	Seismic surveying for petroleum	104	134
	Separation terminal operation, natural gas	104	132
	Test well (petroleum) drilling	104	502.3
	Well drilling (petroleum)	104	502.3
	Well logging	104	134
1401	Mineral oil refining		
	Aviation spirit manufacturing	262	140.1
	Aviation turbine fuel manufacturing	262	140.1
	Bitumen manufacturing	262	140.1
	Burning oil manufacturing	262	140.1
	Butane manufacturing	262	140.1
	Chemical feedstock manufacturing	262	140.1
	Crude oil refining	262	140.1
	Derv manufacturing	262	140.1
	Diesel oil manufacturing	262	140.1
	Fuel oil manufacturing	262	140.1
	Gas oil manufacturing	262	140.1
	Grease (at refineries) manufacturing	262	140.1
	Industrial benzole manufacturing	262	140.1
	Industrial spirit (from petroleum) manufacturing	262	140.1
	Insulating oil (at refineries) manufacturing	262	140.1
	Kerosene manufacturing	262	140.1
	Lubricating oil (at refineries) manufacturing	262	140.1
	Marine diesel oil manufacturing	262	140.1
	Medicinal paraffin manufacturing	262	140.1
	Motor spirit manufacturing	262	140.1
	Naphtha (LDF.) manufacturing	262	140.1
	Paraffin manufacturing	262	140.1
	Paraffin wax manufacturing	262	140.1
	Petrol manufacturing	262	140.1
	Petroleum coke manufacturing	262	140.1
	Petroleum feedstock manufacturing	262	140.1
	Petroleum gas manufacturing	262	140.1
	Petroleum grease (at refineries) manufacturing	262	140.1
	Petroleum jelly, crude, (at refineries) manufacturing	262	140.1
	Petroleum product (at oil refineries) manufacturing	262	140.1
	Petroleum refining	262	140.1
	Process oil refining	262	140.1
	Propane manufacturing	262	140.1
	Refinery gas manufacturing	262	140.1
	Shale oil refining	262	140.1
	Tail gas manufacturing	262	140.1
	Technical white oil manufacturing	262	140.1
	Transformer oil (at refineries) manufacturing	262	140.1
	Vaporizing oil manufacturing	262	140.1
	White spirit manufacturing	262	140.1
	Wide cut gasoline manufacturing	262	140.1
1402	Other treatment of petroleum products (excluding petrochemicals manufacture)		
	Blending of mineral oil	263	140.2
	Cutting oil manufacturing	263	140.2
	Hydraulic oil (outside refineries) formulation	263	140.2
	Insulating oil (outside refineries) formulation	263	140.2

SIC 1980	Activity	SIC 1968	NACE
	Lubricating grease (outside refineries) formulation	263	140.2
	Lubricating oil (outside refineries) formulation	263	140.2
	Penetrating oil manufacturing	263	140.2
	Petroleum grease (outside refineries) formulation	263	140.2
	Petroleum jelly (outside refineries) formulation	263	140.2
	Strap paste for transmission belts manufacturing	263	140.2
	Transformer oil (outside refineries) formulation	263	140.2
1520	Nuclear fuel production		
	Nuclear fuel manufacturing	271/3	152
	Plutonium processing	271/3	152
	Spent nuclear fuel re-processing	271/3	152
	Uranium, enriched, manufacturing	271/3	152
	Uranium, natural, production	271/3	152
1610/1	Public electricity supply		
	Electricity Board	602	161
	Electricity Council	602	161
	Electricity production and distribution	602	161
	Electricity showroom	602	161
	Generating Board	602	161
	Generating station (public supply)	602	161
	Hydro-electric power station (public supply)	602	161.2
	Hydro-electricity Board	602	161
	Nuclear power station (public supply)	602	161.3
	Power station (public supply)	602	161
1610/2	Other electricity generation, separately identifiable		
	Generating station (other than public supply)	602	161
	Hydro-electric power station (not for public supply)	602	161.6
	Power station (not for public supply)	602	161
1620	Public gas supply		
	Benzole (crude; from gas works) manufacturing	601	162.1
	Coal tar (crude; from gas works) manufacturing	601	162.1
	Gas coke manufacturing	601	162.1
	Gas Corporation	601	162
	Gas showroom	601	162
	Gas works	601	162.1
	Natural gas booster/compression site	601	162.2
	Natural gas distribution	601	162.2
	Natural gas storage	601	162.2
	Sulphate of ammonia (from gas works) manufacturing	601	162.1
	Town gas distribution	601	162.2
	Town gas production	601	162.1
1630	Production and distribution of other forms of energy		
	Compressed air production and distribution	not classified	163
	District heating plant	602	163
	Hot water production and distribution	602	163
	Hydraulic power production and distribution	603/2	163
	Steam production and distribution	602	163
1700	Water supply industry		
	National Water Council	603/1	170
	River management	603	170
	Water authority (headquarters and water supply)	603/1	170
	Water company	603/2	170
	Water conservation	603	170
2100	Extraction and preparation of metalliferous ores		
	Copper ore and concentrate extraction and preparation	109/2	212
	Haematite quarry	109/1	211
	Iron ore calcining	109/1	211.2
	Iron ore crushing	109/1	211.2
	Iron ore mine or quarry	109/1	211
	Iron ore preparation	109/1	211.2
	Iron ore sintering	109/1	211.2
	Iron ore washing	109/1	211.2
	Lead mining	109/2	212.1
	Lead ore and concentrate extraction and preparation	109/2	212
	Mining of non-ferrous metal ore	109/2	212.1
	Quarrying of non-ferrous metal ore	109/2	212.1
	Silver ore and concentrate extraction and preparation	109/2	212
	Tin mining	109/2	212.1
	Tin ore and concentrate extraction and preparation	109/2	212
2210	Iron and steel industry (as defined in the European Coal and Steel Community Treaty of Paris 1951)		
	Bar, steel, (semi-finished) manufacturing	311/2	221.1
	Basic slag, uncrushed, manufacturing	313	221.1
	Beam, rolled steel, manufacturing	311/2	221.1
	Billet, steel, manufacturing	311/2	221.1
	Blackplate manufacturing	311/2	221.2
	Blast furnace gas manufacturing	311/2	221.1
	Bloom, steel, manufacturing	311/2	221.1
	Coil, wide, hot-rolled (other than coil classed as a finished product), manufacturing	311/2	221.1
	Crude steel manufacturing	311/2	221.1
	Electrical sheet steel coated and uncoated, manufacturing	311/2	221.1
	Ferro-manganese, high carbon, manufacturing	311/2	221.1
	Fish-plate (railway) steel, manufacturing	311/2	221.1
	Flat, steel, hot rolled, manufacturing	311/2	221.1
	Galvanised sheet, steel, manufacturing	311/2	221.2
	Girder, steel, manufacturing	311/2	221.1
	Heavy section, steel, 80mm and over, manufacturing	311/2	221.1
	Hoop, steel, hot-rolled, manufacturing	311/2	221.1
	Ingot, steel, manufacturing	311/2	221.1
	Iron, directly reduced manufacturing	313/2	221.1
	Iron, pig, manufacturing	313	221.1
	Iron, refined manufacturing	313/2	221.1
	Iron, wrought, manufacturing	311/1	221.1
	Joist, steel, manufacturing	311/2	221.1
	Liquid steel (primary) manufacturing	311/2	221.1
	Plate, steel, manufacturing	311/2	221.1
	Rail (railway), steel, manufacturing	311/2	221.1
	Rod, steel, hot-rolled, manufacturing	311/2	221.1
	Section, steel manufacturing	311/2	221.1
	Sheet, steel (organic coated) manufacturing	311/2	221.2
	Sheet, steel, cold-rolled under 3mm, manufacturing	311/2	221.1

SIC 1980	Activity	SIC 1968	NACE
	Sheet, steel, hot-rolled, manufacturing	311/2	221.1
	Slab, steel, manufacturing	311/2	221.1
	Sleeper (railway), steel, manufacturing	311/2	221.1
	Soleplate, (railway) steel, manufacturing	311/2	221.1
	Spiegeleisen manufacturing	311/2	221.1
	Steel strip for tinplate manufacturing	311/2	221.1
	Steel strip, hot-rolled, manufacturing	311/2	221.1
	Terneplate manufacturing	311/2	221.2
	Tinplate manufacturing	311/2	221.2
	Tube round, steel, manufacturing	311/2	221.1
	Tube square, steel, manufacturing	311/2	221.1
	Tube strip, steel, hot-rolled, manufacturing	311/2	221.1
	Universal plate 150mm and over (steel) manufacturing	311/2	221.1
	Wire rod, steel, manufacturing	311/2	221.1
2220	Steel tubes		
	Conduit, steel, manufacturing	312	222
	Electrical conduit, steel, manufacturing	312	222
	Fittings for tubes and pipes (steel) manufacturing	312	222
	Flexible tube, steel, manufacturing	312	222
	Gas pipe, steel, manufacturing	312	222
	Junction box, steel, manufacturing	312	222
	Pipe fittings, steel, manufacturing	312	222
	Pipe, steel, manufacturing	312	222
	Rectangular hollow section, steel, manufacturing	312	222
	Scaffold tube, steel, manufacturing	312	222
	Seamless tube, steel, manufacturing	312	222
	Steel cylinder, for compressed or liquefied gas, manufacturing	312	222
	Steel tube, welded, manufacturing	312	222
	Steel tube, wrought, manufacturing	312	222
	Tube fittings, steel, manufacturing	312	222
	Tube, steel, manufacturing	312	222
2234	Drawing and manufacture of steel wire and steel wire products		
	Bale tie, steel, manufacturing	394	223.4
	Barbed wire (steel) manufacturing	394	223.4
	Carpet wire (ferrous) manufacturing	394	223.4
	Iron wire manufacturing	394	223.4
	Piano wire manufacturing	394	223.4
	Reinforcing fabrication of steel wire for concrete, manufacturing	394	223.4
	Scaffold tie (of ferrous wire) manufacturing	394	223.4
	Steel reinforcement for concrete manufacturing	394	223.4
	Steel upholstery spring manufacturing	399/4	223.4
	Steel wire cable manufacturing	394	223.4
	Steel wire fabric manufacturing	394	223.4
	Steel wire nail manufacturing	394	223.4
	Steel, wire netting manufacturing	394	223.4
	Upholstery components from steel wire manufacturing	394	223.4
	Wire fencing (steel) manufacturing	394	223.4
	Wire rope manufacturing	394	223.4
2235	Other drawing, cold rolling and cold forming of steel		
	Bright steel bar manufacturing	311/2	223.2
	Corrugated iron manufacturing	311/2	223.3
	Drawn steel, cold, other than steel wire, manufacturing	311/2	223.1
	Hoop, steel, cold rolled, manufacturing	311/2	223.2
	Rod, steel, cold drawn, manufacturing	311/2	223.1
	Section, steel, cold formed, manufacturing	399/12	223.3
	Shape, steel, cold drawn, manufacturing	311/2	223.1
	Steel angle, cold formed manufacturing	311/2	223.3
	Steel strip, cold rolled, manufacturing	311/2	223.2
	Steel, cold forming of	399/12	223.3
	Steel, cold rolling of	311/2	223.2
2245/1	Primary and secondary aluminium and aluminium alloys unwrought		
	Aluminium refining	321	224.1
	Aluminium smelting	321	224.1
	Aluminium, unwrought, manufacturing	321	224.1
	Billet, aluminium, manufacturing	321	224.1
	Extrusion ingot, aluminium, manufacturing	321	224.1
	Foundry alloy, aluminium, manufacturing	321	224.1
	Foundry ingot, aluminium, manufacturing	321	224.1
	Hardener, aluminium, manufacturing	321	224.1
	Notched bar, aluminium, manufacturing	321	224.1
	Remelt ingot, aluminium, manufacturing	321	224.1
	Rolling ingot and slab, aluminium, manufacturing	321	224.1
	Wirebar, aluminium, manufacturing	321	224.1
2245/2	Rolled, drawn, extruded and other semi-manufactured aluminium products		
	Aluminium conductor steel reinforced cable manufacturing	394	224.3
	Angle, aluminium, manufacturing	321	224.1
	Bar, aluminium, manufacturing	321	224.1
	Blank, aluminium, manufacturing	321	224.1
	Cable, sheathing, aluminium, manufacturing	321	224.3
	Cable, uninsulated, of aluminium, manufacturing	321	224.3
	Circle, aluminium, manufacturing	321	312.2
	Continuous cast rod, aluminium, manufacturing	321	224.3
	Corrugated plate, sheet or strip, aluminium, manufacturing	321	224.3
	Deoxidiser, aluminium, manufacturing	321	224.1
	Disc, aluminium, manufacturing	321	312.2
	Drawn product, aluminium, manufacturing	321	224.3
	Extruded section, aluminium, manufacturing	321	224.3
	Extruded tube, aluminium, manufacturing	321	224.3
	Extrusion, aluminium, manufacturing	321	224.3
	Flake, aluminium, manufacturing	321	224.3
	Foil stock, aluminium, manufacturing	321	224.3
	Foil, aluminium, (not put up as packaging product) manufacturing	321	224.3
	Forging bar, aluminium, manufacturing	321	224.3
	Hollow section, aluminium, manufacturing	321	224.3
	Paste, aluminium, manufacturing	321	224.3

SIC 1980	Activity	SIC 1968	NACE
	Pipe fittings, aluminium, manufacturing	321	224.3
	Pipe, aluminium, manufacturing	321	224.3
	Plate, aluminium, manufacturing	321	224.3
	Powder, aluminium, manufacturing	321	224.3
	Rod, aluminium, manufacturing	321	224.3
	Rolled product, aluminium, manufacturing	321	224.3
	Section, aluminium, manufacturing	321	224.3
	Sheet, aluminium, manufacturing	321	224.3
	Slug, aluminium, manufacturing	321	224.3
	Solid section, aluminium, manufacturing	321	224.3
	Strands for cable, aluminium, manufacturing	321	224.3
	Strip, aluminium, manufacturing	321	224.3
	Tube fittings, aluminium, manufacturing	321	224.3
	Wire strand, aluminium, manufacturing	394	224.3
	Wire, aluminium, manufacturing	394	224.3
2246/1	Primary and secondary copper and copper based alloys unwrought		
	Billet, copper, manufacturing	322	224.1
	Blister copper manufacturing	322	224.1
	Bloom, copper, manufacturing	322	224.1
	Brass billet manufacturing	322	224.2
	Brass ingot manufacturing	322	224.2
	Brass slab manufacturing	322	224.2
	Brass, unwrought, manufacturing	322	224.2
	Bronze, unwrought, manufacturing	322	224.2
	Cadmium copper, unwrought, manufacturing	322	224.2
	Continuous cast rod, copper manufacturing	322	224.1
	Copper matte manufacturing	322	224.2
	Copper refining	322	224.1
	Copper smelting	322	224.1
	Copper, unwrought, manufacturing	322	224.1
	Cupro-nickel, unwrought, manufacturing	322	224.2
	Delta metal, unwrought, manufacturing	322	224.2
	Electrolytic copper manufacturing	322	224.1
	Fire refined copper manufacturing	322	224,1
	German silver, unwrought, manufacturing	322	224.2
	Gun metal, unwrought, manufacturing	322	224.2
	Ingot, copper, manufacturing	322	224.1
	Manganese bronze, unwrought, manufacturing	322	224.2
	Master alloys of copper manufacturing	322	224.2
	Naval brass, unwrought, manufacturing	322	224.2
	Nickel silver manufacturing	322	224.2
	Primary copper manufacturing	322	224.1
	Red metal, unwrought, manufacturing	322	224.2
	Secondary copper manufacturing	322	224.1
	Slab, copper, manufacturing	322	224.1
2246/2	Rolled, drawn, extruded and other semi-manufactured copper and copper alloy products		
	Bar, copper, manufacturing	322	224.2
	Brass bar manufacturing	322	224.2
	Brass circle manufacturing	322	312.2
	Brass disc manufacturing	322	312.2
	Brass foil manufacturing	322	224.2
	Brass pipe and pipe fittings manufacturing	322	224.2
	Brass powder manufacturing	322	224.2
	Brass rod manufacturing	322	224.2
	Brass section manufacturing	322	224.2
	Brass sheet manufacturing	322	224.2
	Brass strip manufacturing	322	224.2
	Brass tube manufacturing	322	224.2
	Coil, copper, manufacturing	322	224.2
	Copper circle manufacturing	322	312.2
	Disc, copper, manufacturing	322	312.2
	Drawn products, copper, manufacturing	322	224.2
	Extruded products, copper, manufacturing	322	224.2
	Flake, copper, manufacturing	322	224.2
	Foil, copper, manufacturing	322	224.2
	Pipe blank, copper, manufacturing	322	224.2
	Pipe fittings, copper, manufacturing	322	224.2
	Pipe, copper, manufacturing	322	224.2
	Powder, copper, manufacturing	322	224.2
	Rod, copper, manufacturing	322	224.2
	Rolled products, copper, manufacturing	322	224.2
	Section, copper, manufacturing	322	224.2
	Semi-manufactures, copper, manufacturing	322	224.2
	Sheet, copper, manufacturing	322	224.2
	Stranded wire, copper (uninsulated) manufacturing	394	224.2
	Strip, copper, manufacturing	322	224.2
	Tube blank, copper, manufacturing	322	224.2
	Tube fittings, copper, manufacturing	322	224.2
	Tube shell, copper, manufacturing	322	224.2
	Tube, copper, manufacturing	322	224.2
	Wire product, copper, uninsulated, manufacturing	394	224.2
	Wire rod, copper, manufacturing	322	224.2
	Wire, copper, uninsulated, manufacturing	394	224.2
2247/1	Other base non-ferrous metals		
	Antifriction metal manufacturing	323	224.2
	Antimony manufacturing	323	224.1
	Arsenic manufacturing	323	224.1
	Beryllium manufacturing	323	224.1
	Bismuth manufacturing	323	224.1
	Britannia metal manufacturing	323	224.2
	Cadmium manufacturing	323	224.1
	Chromium manufacturing	323	224.1
	Cobalt manufacturing	323	224.1
	Continuous cast rod, other base non-ferrous metal manufacturing	323	224.1
	Ferro-alloy manufacturing	323	224.2
	Germanium manufacturing	323	224.1
	Lead manufacturing	323	224.1
	Magnesium manufacturing	323	224.1
	Magnolia metal manufacturing	323	224.2
	Manganese manufacturing	323	224.1
	Molybdenum manufacturing	323	224.1
	Nickel manufacturing	323	224.1
	Pewter manufacturing	323	224.2
	Radium manufacturing	323	224.1
	Solder manufacturing	323	224.2
	Sterio metal manufacturing	323	224.2
	Tantalum manufacturing	323	224.1
	Tin manufacturing	323	224.1
	Titanium manufacturing	323	224.1
	Tungsten manufacturing	323	224.1
	Type metal manufacturing	323	224.2
	Vanadium manufacturing	323	224.1

SIC 1980	Activity	SIC 1968	NACE
	White metal manufacturing	323	224.2
	Wolfram manufacturing	323	224.1
	Zinc manufacturing	323	224.1
	Zirconium manufacturing	323	224.1
2247/2	Precious metals		
	Bullion, gold and silver, manufacturing	396	224.1
	Gold manufacturing	396	224.1
	Iridium manufacturing	323	224.1
	Palladium manufacturing	323	224.1
	Platinum group metals manufacturing	396	224.1
	Platinum manufacturing	396	224.1
	Rhodium manufacturing	396	224.1
	Silver manufacturing	396	224.1
2310/1	Slate quarrying and mining		
	Slate mine or quarry	102/2	231.1
2310/2	Stone quarrying and mining		
	Basalt mine	102/1	231.2
	Blackstone quarry	102/1	231.2
	Blue pennant stone quarry	102/1	231.2
	Chert quarry	102/1	231.2
	Dolomite mine or quarry	102/1	239.3
	Flagstone quarry	102/1	231.2
	Flint bed, pit or quarry	102/1	231.2
	Freestone mine or quarry	102/1	231.2
	Granite quarry	102/1	231.2
	Igneous rock quarry	102/1	231.2
	Limestone mine or quarry	102/1	231.2
	Marble quarry	102/1	231.2
	Ragstone quarry	102/1	231.2
	Road stone pit or quarry	102/1	231.2
	Rubbing stone mine, pit or quarry	102/1	231.2
	Sandstone mine, pit or quarry	102/1	231.2
	Sett quarry	102/1	231.2
	Stone pit or quarry	102/1	231.2
	Whinstone quarry	102/1	231.2
2310/3	Chalk quarrying and mining		
	Chalk pit or quarry	103	231.3
2310/4	Extraction and dredging of sand, pebbles and gravel		
	Gravel pit	103	231.4
	Pebble dredging	103	231.4
	Sand pit	103	231.4
	Shingle dredging	103	231.4
2310/5	Gypsum quarrying and mining		
	Alabaster mine	109/4	231.2
	Anhydrite mine or quarry	109/4	231.6
	Gypsum mine or quarry	109/4	231.6
2310/6	Extraction of clay, kaolin and marl		
	Ball clay mine or opencast working	103	231.7
	China clay pit	103	231.7
	China stone mine	103	231.7
	Clay pit	103	231.7
	Fireclay mine or quarry	103	231.7
	Fuller's earth pit	103	231.7
	Marl pit	103	231.5
	Pipeclay pit	103	231.7
	Potters' clay mine or quarry	103	231.7
2330	Salt extraction and refining		
	Brine pit	109/3	233.2
	Rock salt manufacturing	109/3	233.2
	Salt mine	109/3	233.2
	Salt works	109/3	233
	Sea salt manufacturing	109/3	233
	White salt manufacturing	109/3	233
2396	Extraction of other minerals, not elsewhere specified		
	Alum mine	109/4	239.4
	Barytes mine	109/4	239.4
	Celestite pit	109/4	239.4
	Diatomite bed	109/4	239.4
	Earth colours extraction	103	239.4
	Fluorspar mine	109/4	239.4
	Ganister extraction	109/4	239.4
	Graphite Mine	109/4	239.4
	Iron pyrites extraction (not for iron production)	109/4	239.1
	Jet mine	109/4	239.4
	Mica mine	109/4	239.4
	Ochre pit	103	239.4
	Peat cutting and digging	109/4	239.5
	Potash mine	109/4	232
	Quartz quarry	109/4	239.4
	Semi-precious stones extraction	109/4	239.4
	Silica stone extraction	109/4	239.4
	Talc mine or quarry	109/4	239.4
	Witherite mine	109/4	239.4
2410	Structural clay products		
	Blue brick manufacturing	461/2	241
	Brick, clay, manufacturing	461/2	241
	Brick, engineering, manufacturing	461/2	241
	Brick, quarry floor, manufacturing	461/2	241
	Building brick, unglazed, manufacturing	461/2	241
	Cable conduit, clay, manufacturing	461/2	241
	Chimney liner (clay) manufacturing	461/2	241
	Chimney pot (clay) manufacturing	461/2	241
	Clay building brick manufacturing	461/2	241
	Drainpipes and fittings (clay) manufacturing	461/2	241
	Flag (clay) manufacturing	461/2	241
	Floor quarry and tile (clay) unglazed manufacturing	461/2	241
	Flooring block (clay) manufacturing	461/2	241
	Flue tile (clay) manufacturing	461/2	241
	Hearth tile (clay), unglazed, manufacturing	461/2	241
	Hollow partition (clay) manufacturing	461/2	241
	Paving tile (clay), unglazed, manufacturing	461/2	241
	Roofing tile (clay), unglazed, manufacturing	461/2	241
	Wall tile (clay), unglazed, manufacturing	461/2	241
2420	Cement, lime and plaster		
	Agricultural lime processing manufacturing	469/2	242.2
	Aluminous cement manufacturing	464	242.1
	Anhydrite plaster manufacturing	469/2	242.3
	Blue lias lime kiln	469/2	242.2
	Building plaster manufacturing	469/2	242.3
	Calcareous cement manufacturing	464	242.1
	Cement manufacturing	464	242.1
	Gypsum plaster manufacturing	469/2	242.3
	Hydrated lime manufacturing	469/2	242.2
	Hydraulic lime manufacturing	469/2	242.2
	Keene's cement manufacturing	469/2	242.3
	Mortar manufacturing	469/2	242.2
	Plaster of paris manufacturing	469/2	242.3
	Portland cement manufacturing	464	242.1
	Quicklime manufacturing	469/2	242.2
	Slaked lime manufacturing	469/2	242.2

SIC 1980	Activity	SIC 1968	NACE
2436	Ready-mixed concrete		
	Ready-mixed concrete manufacturing	469/2	243.6
	Ready-mixed wet mortars manufacturing	469/2	243.6
2437	Other building products of concrete, cement or plaster		
	Asbestos building board manufacturing	469/2	243.1
	Asbestos cement building board manufacturing	469/2	243.1
	Asbestos cement pipe manufacturing	469/2	243.1
	Asbestos cement product manufacturing	469/2	243.1
	Breeze block manufacturing	469/2	243.2
	Brick, sand lime, manufacturing	469/2	243.4
	Cast concrete product manufacturing	469/2	243.2
	Cast stone units, precast concrete, manufacturing	469/2	243.2
	Cement product manufacturing	469/2	243.2
	Cement-based paint manufacturing	464	255
	Cement-wood product manufacturing	469/2	243.2
	Cladding wall panels, precast concrete, manufacturing	469/2	243.2
	Concrete block manufacturing	469/2	243.2
	Concrete brick manufacturing	469/2	243.2
	Concrete dry-mix manufacturing	469/2	243.2
	Concrete pipe manufacturing	469/2	243.2
	Concrete/Terrazzo floor and wall tile manufacturing	469/2	243.2
	Flagstone, precast concrete, manufacturing	469/2	243.2
	Floor units, precast concrete, manufacturing	469/2	243.2
	Gulley, concrete, manufacturing	469/2	243.2
	Gypsum plaster products, manufacturing	469/2	243.3
	Kerb and edging, pre-cast concrete, manufacturing	469/2	243.2
	Pitch-fibre pipes and fittings, manufacturing	469/2	243.1
	Plaster tile manufacturing	469/2	243.3
	Plasterboard manufacturing	469/2	243.3
	Post, precast concrete, manufacturing	469/2	243.2
	Pre-cast concrete products manufacturing	469/2	243.2
	Pre-stressed concrete products manufacturing	469/2	243.2
	Prefabricated buildings and components, concrete, manufacturing	469/2	243.2
	Pressure pipe, pre-stressed concrete, manufacturing	469/2	243.2
	Pylon, precast concrete, manufacturing	469/2	243.2
	Railway sleeper, pre-cast concrete, manufacturing	469/2	243.2
	Reinforced concrete products manufacturing	469/2	243.2
	Roof units, precast concrete, manufacturing	469/2	243.2
	Roofing tile, precast concrete, manufacturing	469/2	243.2
	Structural wall panels, precast concrete, manufacturing	469/2	243.2
	Tube, concrete, manufacturing	469/2	243.2
2440	Asbestos goods		
	Asbestos carding	429/1	244
	Asbestos cloth manufacturing	429/1	244
	Asbestos engine packing manufacturing	429/1	244
	Asbestos felting	429/1	244
	Asbestos mixing	429/1	244
	Asbestos moulding	429/1	244
	Asbestos packing (woven) manufacturing	429/1	244
	Asbestos sheet and sheeting (woven) manufacturing	429/1	244
	Asbestos sock manufacturing	429/1	244
	Asbestos spinning	429/1	244
	Asbestos weaving	429/1	244
	Board, asbestos, manufacturing	429/1	244
	Boiler packing, asbestos, manufacturing	429/1	244
	Brake lining, asbestos, manufacturing	429/1	244
	Carded fibre, asbestos, manufacturing	429/1	244
	Clutch lining, asbestos, manufacturing	429/1	244
	Composition, asbestos, manufacturing	429/1	244
	Gasket, asbestos, manufacturing	429/1	244
	Insulation, asbestos, manufacturing	429/1	244
	Joints, asbestos, manufacturing	429/1	244
	Lagging rope, asbestos, manufacturing	429/1	244
	Millboard, asbestos, manufacturing	429/1	244
	Panel, asbestos, manufacturing	429/1	244
	Paper, asbestos, manufacturing	429/1	244
	Paste, asbestos, manufacturing	429/1	244
	Pipe covering section, asbestos, manufacturing	429/1	244
	Processed fibre, asbestos, manufacturing	429/1	244
	Ring, asbestos, manufacturing	429/1	244
	Rope lagging, asbestos, manufacturing	429/1	244
	Sheeting, non-woven asbestos/rubber, manufacturing	429/1	244
	Tape, asbestos, manufacturing	429/1	244
	Tile, asbestos, (woven) manufacturing	429/1	244
2450/1	Ground and processed minerals		
	Asphalt manufacturing	469/2	245.1
	Chalk, ground, manufacturing	469/2	245.1
	China clay, ground, manufacturing	469/2	245.1
	Coated roadstone manufacturing	469/2	245
	Coated tarmacadam manufacturing	102	245
	Dolomite, ground manufacturing	469/2	245.1
	Flint grit manufacturing	469/1	245.1
	French chalk manufacturing	469/2	245.1
	Limestone, ground, manufacturing	469/2	245.1
	Road metal (crushed and processed) manufacturing	469/2	245.1
	Stone chippings manufacturing	469/2	245.1
	Stone dust manufacturing	469/2	245.1
	Whiting and prepared chalk manufacturing	469/2	245.1
2450/2	Slate products		
	Slate polishing	469/2	245.2
	Slate slab and sheet cutting and preparation	469/2	245.2
	Slate tile manufacturing	469/2	245.2
	Slate working	469/2	245.2
2450/3	Building, ornamental and funerary stonework		
	Building stone, decorated, manufacturing	469/2	245

SIC 1980	Activity	SIC 1968	NACE
	Funerary stonework manufacturing	469/2	245.4
	Granite working	469/2	245.3
	Kerbstone (not concrete) manufacturing	469/2	245.3
	Limestone working	469/2	245.3
	Litho stone working	469/2	245.3
	Marble masonry working	469/2	245.4
	Millstone and grindstone cutting	469/2	245.3
	Monumental stonework manufacturing	469/2	245.4
	Mosaic cube manufacturing	469/2	245.4
	Paving slab manufacturing	469/2	245.3
	Paving stone manufacturing	469/2	245.3
	Stone working	469/2	245.3
2450/4	Other non-metallic mineral products		
	Bituminous and flax felts, for roofing and damp proof courses, manufacturing	469/2	245
	Carbon product (not carbon copying paper or electrical carbon) manufacturing	469/2	245.5
	Expanded vermiculite manufacturing	469/2	245.5
	Foamed slag manufacturing	469/1	245.5
	Graphite product (other than block and crucible) manufacturing	469/2	245.5
	Mica goods, manufacturing	469/2	245.5
	Mica slab and sheet processing	469/2	245.5
	Mineral insulation product manufacturing	469/2	245.5
	Mineral wool manufacturing	469/2	245.5
	Moss litter manufacturing	499/2	495.3
	Peat product (e.g. briquette, pot or for chemical use) manufacturing	469/2	245.5
2460	Abrasive products		
	Abrasive bonded disc, wheel and segment manufacturing	469/1	246.1
	Abrasive cloth manufacturing	469/1	246.3
	Abrasive grains, artificial, manufacturing	469/1	246
	Abrasive paper manufacturing	469/1	246.3
	Abrasives, bonded, manufacturing	469/1	246.1
	Agglomerated abrasives manufacturing	469/1	246.1
	Aluminium oxide abrasive grain manufacturing	469/1	246
	Artificial corundum abrasive grain manufacturing	469/1	246
	Boron carbide abrasive grain manufacturing	469/1	246
	Coated abrasives manufacturing	469/1	246
	Diamond impregnated disc and wheel manufacturing	469/1	246.2
	Disc, abrasive (bonded), manufacturing	469/1	246.1
	Emery cloth manufacturing	469/1	246.3
	Emery paper manufacturing	469/1	246.3
	Emery wheel manufacturing	469/1	246.1
	Flint cloth manufacturing	469/1	246.3
	Flint paper manufacturing	469/1	246.3
	Garnet abrasives manufacturing	469/1	246
	Glass paper manufacturing	469/1	246.3
	Grinding paste manufacturing	469/1	256.7
	Grindstones of bonded abrasives manufacturing	469/1	246.1
	Hones, bonded, manufacturing	469/1	246.1
	Millstones of bonded abrasives manufacturing	469/1	246.1
	Oilstones, bonded, manufacturing	469/1	246.1
	Organic bonded abrasives manufacturing	469/1	246.1
	Polishes, abrasive, manufacturing	469/1	256.7
	Polishing stones of bonded abrasives manufacturing	469/1	246.1
	Pumice stones, bonded, manufacturing	469/1	246.1
	Rouge, jeweller's, manufacturing	469/1	246
	Sandpaper manufacturing	469/1	246.3
	Segment, bonded abrasive, manufacturing	469/1	246.1
	Sharpening stones of bonded abrasives manufacturing	469/1	246.1
	Silicon carbide abrasive grain manufacturing	469/1	246.1
	Vitrified bonded abrasives manufacturing	469/1	246.1
	Wheel, abrasive (bonded), manufacturing	469/1	246.1
2471/1	Flat glass not further worked		
	Antique glass manufacturing	463/1	247.1
	Blown glass manufacturing	463/1	247.1
	Cast glass manufacturing	463/1	247.1
	Drawn sheet glass manufacturing	463/1	247.1
	Figured glass manufacturing	463/1	247.1
	Flat glass manufacturing	463/1	247.1
	Float glass manufacturing	463/1	247.1
	Mirror glass manufacturing	463/1	247.1
	Plate glass manufacturing	463/1	247.1
	Rolled glass manufacturing	463/1	247.1
	Tinted glass manufacturing	463/1	247.1
	Window glass (not cut to size) manufacturing	463/1	247.1
	Wired glass manufacturing	463/1	247.1
2471/2	Flat glass further worked		
	Coloured glass manufacturing	463/1	247.6
	Glass mirror suitable for motor vehicle (not further assembled) manufacturing	463/1	247.6
	Laminated glass manufacturing	463/1	247.6
	Leaded light manufacturing	463/1	247.6
	Multiple insulating glass manufacturing	463/1	247.6
	Safety glass manufacturing	463/1	247.6
	Stained glass manufacturing	463/1	247.6
	Toughened glass manufacturing	463/1	247.6
	Window glass (cut to size) manufacturing	463/1	247.6
	Windscreen (glass) manufacturing	463/1	247.6
2478	Glass containers		
	Ampoule, glass, (hygienic and pharmaceutical) manufacturing	463/2	247.7
	Carboy, glass, manufacturing	463/2	247.2
	Glass bottle manufacturing	463/2	247.2
	Glass bottle stopper manufacturing	463/2	247.2
	Glass container manufacturing	463/2	247
	Glass container made from tubing, (hygienic and pharmaceutical), manufacturing	463/2	247.7
	Jar, glass, manufacturing	463/2	247.2
	Pot, glass, manufacturing	463/2	247.2
	Stopper, glass, manufacturing	463/2	247.2
	Syphon, glass, manufacturing	463/2	247.7
	Tubular glass container manufacturing	463/2	247.7
	Vial manufacturing	463/2	247.7
	Waste glass resulting from glass container manufacture	463	247
2479/1	Domestic and ornamental glassware		
	Bowl, glass, manufacturing	463/1	247
	Culinary glassware manufacturing	463/1	247

SIC 1980	Activity	SIC 1968	NACE
	Domestic glassware manufacturing	463/1	247
	Drinking glass manufacturing	463/1	247
	Glass ovenware manufacturing	463/1	247
	Glass tableware manufacturing	463/1	247
	Heat resisting glassware for cooking purposes manufacturing	463/1	247
	Kitchenware, glass, manufacturing	463/1	247
	Lead crystal tableware manufacturing	463/1	247
	Ornament, glass, manufacturing	463/1	247.4
	Stemmed drinking vessel, glass, manufacturing	463/1	247
	Tumbler, glass, manufacturing	463/1	247
2479/2	Glass envelopes and illuminating glassware		
	Bulb, glass, manufacturing	463/1	247.4
	Envelope (glass) for light bulbs and electronic valves manufacturing	463/1	247.4
	Glass parts of electric lamps and electronic valves manufacturing	463/1	247.4
	Globe, glass, manufacturing	463/1	247.4
	Illuminating glassware manufacturing	463/1	247.4
	Lamp chimney, glass, manufacturing	463/1	247.4
	Lamp glass manufacturing	463/1	247.4
	Lens of coloured glass for rail and road signals (not optically worked) manufacturing	463/1	247.4
	Shade, glass, manufacturing	463/1	247.4
	Signalling glassware manufacturing	463/1	247.4
	Tube, glass, (for electric light) manufacturing	463/1	247.4
	Well and bulkhead glass manufacturing	463/1	247.4
2479/3	Glass tubing and scientific glassware		
	Ball, glass, manufacturing	463/1	247.4
	Bar, glass, manufacturing	463/1	247.4
	Burette, glass, manufacturing	463/1	247.7
	Desiccator, glass, manufacturing	463/1	247.7
	Glass ball, bar, rod and tube for processing manufacturing	463/1	247.4
	Glass tubing manufacturing	463/1	247.4
	Graduated glassware manufacturing	463/1	247.4
	Hygienic glassware (other than container) manufacturing	463/1	247.7
	Laboratory glassware (not container) manufacturing	463/1	247.4
	Marble, glass, manufacturing	463/1	247.4
	Pharmaceutical glassware (other than container) manufacturing	463/1	247.4
	Pipette, glass, manufacturing	463/1	247.7
	Rod, glass, manufacturing	463/1	247.4
	Tank, glass, manufacturing	463/1	247
	Test tube manufacturing	463/1	247.7
	Volumetric glassware manufacturing	463/1	247.7
2479/4	Glass fibre and glass fibre products		
	Board, glass fibre manufacturing	463/1	247.5
	Chopped roving and strand, glass fibre, manufacturing	463/1	247.5
	Felt, glass fibre, manufacturing	463/1	247.5
	Flock, glass fibre, manufacturing	463/1	247.5
	Glass wool manufacturing	463/1	247.5
	Insulating material, glass fibre, manufacturing	463/1	247.5
	Loose glass fibre manufacturing	463/1	247.5
	Mat, glass fibre, manufacturing	463/1	247.5
	Mattress, glass fibre, manufacturing	463/1	247.5
	Sheet, glass fibre, manufacturing	276/1	247.5
	Slab, glass fibre, manufacturing	463/1	247.5
	Thermal and sound insulating material, glass fibre, manufacturing	463/1	247.5
	Tissue, glass fibre, manufacturing	463/1	247.5
2479/5	Other glass products		
	Absorption drum, glass, manufacturing	463/1	247.4
	Accumulator and cell case (glass) manufacturing	463/1	247.4
	Architectural glass manufacturing	463/1	247.4
	Ballotini manufacturing	463/1	247.4
	Basement light, glass, manufacturing	463/1	247.4
	Bead, glass manufacturing	463/1	247.4
	Blank for corrective spectacle lens manufacturing	463/1	247.4
	Brick, glass manufacturing	463/1	247.4
	Bulb for vacuum flask inner manufacturing	463/1	247.2
	Button, glass, manufacturing	463/1	247.4
	Catseye reflector manufacturing	463/1	247.4
	Clock and watch glass manufacturing	463/1	247.4
	Electrical insulator, glass, manufacturing	463/1	247.4
	Enamel glass manufacturing	463/1	247.4
	Fancy articles and goods, glass, manufacturing	463/1	247.4
	Gauge glass manufacturing	463/1	247.4
	Glass in the mass manufacturing	463/1	247
	Industrial glassware (not container) manufacturing	463/1	247.4
	Lens, pressed or moulded, unworked, (not of coloured glass for traffic signals) manufacturing	463/1	247.4
	Mosaic cube manufacturing	463/1	247.4
	Moulded glassware manufacturing	463/1	247.4
	Multicellular glass block manufacturing	463/1	247.4
	Optical glass manufacturing	463/1	247.4
	Pavement light manufacturing	463/1	247.4
	Powder, glass manufacturing	463/1	247.4
	Prism, pressed or moulded, unworked, manufacturing	463/1	247.4
	Spectacle glass manufacturing	463/1	247.4
	Sunglass blank manufacturing	463/1	247.4
	Tile, glass manufacturing	463/1	247.4
	Vacuum flask (complete) manufacturing	463/2	247.4
	Vacuum flask inner manufacturing	463/1	247.2
	Vacuum jar manufacturing	463/2	247.4
	Waste glass resulting from glass product (other than glass container) manufacture	463	247
	Watch glass manufacturing	463/1	247.4
2481	Refractory goods		
	Alumina brick manufacturing	461/1	248.1
	Bauxite brick manufacturing	461/1	248.1
	Block, graphite, manufacturing	461/1	248.1
	Boiler block manufacturing	461/1	248.1
	Brick, magnesite, manufacturing	461/1	248.1
	Brick, refractory, insulating, manufacturing	461/1	248.1
	Brick, silica, manufacturing	461/1	248.1
	Brick, sillimanite, manufacturing	461/1	248.1
	Castable, refractory, manufacturing	461/1	248.1
	Casting pot manufacturing	461/1	248.1
	Cement, dolomite, manufacturing	461/1	248.1
	Cement, fireclay, manufacturing	461/1	248.1
	Cement, high alumina, manufacturing	461/1	248.1
	Cement, refractory jointing, manufacturing	461/1	248.1
	Cement, silica and siliceous, manufacturing	461/1	248.1
	Chrome brick manufacturing	461/1	248.1
	Chromite brick manufacturing	461/1	248.1
	Crucible, fireclay or graphite, manufacturing	461/1	248.1

SIC 1980	Activity	SIC 1968	NACE
	Dolomite brick manufacturing	461/1	248.1
	Firebrick and shape manufacturing	461/1	248.1
	Fireclay crucible manufacturing	461/1	248.1
	Furnace block and pot manufacturing	461/1	248.1
	Ganister brick manufacturing	461/1	248.1
	Gas mantle ring and rod manufacturing	461/1	248.1
	Gas retort and kiln lining manufacturing	461/1	248.1
	Graphite crucible manufacturing	461/1	248.1
	Graphite retort manufacturing	461/1	248.1
	High alumina brick manufacturing	461/1	248.1
	Hollow-ware, refractory, manufacturing	461/1	248.1
	Kiln lining manufacturing	461/1	248.1
	Magnesite brick and moulding manufacturing	461/1	248.1
	Magnesite-chrome brick manufacturing	461/1	248.1
	Magnesite-chrome shape manufacturing	461/1	248.1
	Mouldable, refractory, manufacturing	461/1	248.1
	Moulding, magnesite, manufacturing	461/1	248.1
	Muffle (refractory product) manufacturing	461/1	248.1
	Plumbago crucible manufacturing	461/1	248.1
	Radiant for gas and electric fire manufacturing	461/1	248.1
	Ramming material, refractory, manufacturing	461/1	248.1
	Refractory brick manufacturing	461/1	248.1
	Refractory cement manufacturing	461/1	248.1
	Refractory goods manufacturing	461/1	248.1
	Retort, fireclay, silica and siliceous manufacturing	461/1	248.1
	Shape, chrome-magnesite, manufacturing	461/1	248.1
	Silica mould manufacturing	461/1	248.1
	Siliceous brick manufacturing	461/1	248.1
	Steel moulders' composition manufacturing	461/1	248.1
	Tunnel oven refractory manufacturing	461/1	248.1
2489/1	Glazed earthenware tiles		
	Art tile, earthenware (glazed), manufacturing	462/2	248.3
	Biscuit tile manufacturing	462/2	248.3
	Decorative tile, earthenware (glazed), manufacturing	462/2	248.3
	Earthenware tile, glazed, manufacturing	462/2	248.3
	Enamelled tile, glazed, manufacturing	462/2	248.3
	Encaustic tile manufacturing	462/2	248.3
	Fireplace tile, glazed, manufacturing	462/2	248.3
	Glazed fireplace brick manufacturing	462/2	248.3
	Mosaic tile, glazed, manufacturing	462/2	248.3
	Ornamental tile, earthenware (glazed), manufacturing	462/2	248.3
	Tesselated pavement tile, glazed, manufacturing	462/2	248.3
	Tesserae, earthenware, manufacturing	462/2	248.3
	Tile, glazed, manufacturing	462/2	248.3
	Wall tile, glazed, manufacturing	462/2	248.3
2489/2	Ceramic sanitary ware		
	Bidet (ceramic, fireclay etc.) manufacturing	462/2	248.5
	Sanitary ware, ceramic, manufacturing	462/2	248.5
	Sanitary ware, fireclay, manufacturing	462/2	248.5
	Sanitary ware, vitreous china, manufacturing	462/2	248.5
	Urinal (ceramic, fireclay etc.) manufacturing	462/2	248.5
	Wash basin or sink (ceramic, fireclay etc.) manufacturing	462/2	248.5
	Water closet bowl (ceramic, fireclay etc.) manufacturing	462/2	248.5
2489/3	Domestic china and other pottery		
	Art pottery manufacturing	462/3	248
	Brown stone pottery manufacturing	462/3	248.6
	Cup and saucer, china or porcelain, manufacturing	462/3	248.7
	Domestic ceramic ware manufacturing	462/3	248.6
	Earthenware, domestic, manufacturing	462/3	248.6
	Furniture, ceramic, manufacturing	462/3	248.6
	Jet ware (pottery) manufacturing	462/3	248.6
	Kitchenware, ceramic, manufacturing	462/3	248
	Ornamental ceramic ware manufacturing	462/3	248
	Rockingham ware manufacturing	462/3	248.6
	Samian ware manufacturing	462/3	248.6
	Stoneware, domestic, manufacturing	462/3	248.6
	Tableware, ceramic, manufacturing	462/3	248
	Terracotta ware manufacturing	462/3	248.6
2489/4	Other ceramic goods		
	Agricultural ceramic ware, manufacturing	462/3	248.9
	Bacteria bed tile manufacturing	461/2	248
	Bat, ceramic, manufacturing	462/3	248.9
	Ceramic packaging product manufacturing	462/3	248.9
	Electrical fittings and furniture, ceramic, manufacturing	462/1	248.8
	Flower pot, clay, manufacturing	461/2	248.9
	Industrial ceramic product, non-refractory, manufacturing	462/3	248.9
	Insulating component, ceramic, (electrical) manufacturing	462/1	248.8
	Insulator, ceramic, manufacturing	462/1	248.8
	Kiln furniture manufacturing	462/3	248.9
	Laboratory ceramic product, non-refractory, manufacturing	462/3	248.9
	Pillar, ceramic, manufacturing	462/3	248.9
	Prop, ceramic, manufacturing	462/3	248.9
	Saggar manufacturing	462/3	248.9
	Stilt, ceramic, manufacturing	462/3	248.9
2511	Inorganic chemicals except industrial gases		
	Acid, inorganic, manufacturing	271/1	251
	Alkali manufacturing	271/1	251
	Aluminium compounds (excluding bauxite and abrasives) (not put up as water treatment chemicals or preparations) manufacturing	271/1	251
	Alums manufacturing	271/1	251
	Ammonia manufacturing	271/1	251
	Ammonium compounds (excluding ammonium nitrate, sulphate and phosphate) manufacturing	271/1	251
	Bromine and bromides manufacturing	271/1	251
	Calcium and calcium compounds manufacturing	271/1	251
	Calcium carbide manufacturing	271/1	251
	Carbon manufacturing	271/1	251
	Carbon black manufacturing	271/1	251
	Carbon decolouring or other activating (except wood charcoal) manufacturing	271/1	251

SIC 1980	Activity	SIC 1968	NACE
	Carbon disulphide manufacturing	271/1	251
	Charcoal, activated and unactivated (other than wood charcoal) manufacturing	271/1	251
	Chlorine and chlorides manufacturing	271/1	251
	Chromium compounds (excluding prepared pigments) manufacturing	271/1	251
	Fluorine, hydrofluoric acid and fluorides manufacturing	271/1	251
	Halogen and halides (inorganic) manufacturing	271/1	251
	Hydrochloric acid manufacturing	271/1	251
	Hydrogen peroxide manufacturing	271/1	251
	Hydrosulphite manufacturing	271/3	251
	Iodine and iodides manufacturing	271/1	251
	Iron compounds manufacturing	271/1	251
	Iron oxide, synthetic, manufacturing	277	251
	Lead compounds manufacturing	271/1	251
	Magnesium compounds manufacturing	271/1	251
	Manganese oxide manufacturing	271/1	251
	Metallic compounds (inorganic) manufacturing	271/1	251
	Nitric acid and nitrates manufacturing	271/1	251
	Oxygen compounds of non-metals (excluding carbon dioxide) manufacturing	271/1	251
	Peroxides (inorganic) manufacturing	271/1	251
	Pesticide chemical, inorganic, (excluding formulated preparations) manufacturing	271/1	251
	Phosphorous compounds (excluding phosphatic fertiliser) manufacturing	271/1	251
	Potassium compounds manufacturing	271/1	251
	Radio-active isotopes (other than of uranium, thorium or plutonium) manufacturing	271/3	251
	Sodium and sodium compounds (not put up as water treatment chemicals or preparations) manufacturing	271/1	251
	Sulphur manufacturing	271/1	251
	Sulphuric acid manufacturing	271/1	251
	White lead (not in paste form) manufacturing	271/1	251
	Zinc compounds manufacturing	271/1	251
	Zinc oxide manufacturing	277	251
2512	Basic organic chemicals except specialised pharmaceutical chemicals		
	Acetone manufacturing	271/2	251
	Acids (organic) and their esters and halogenated, nitrosated and sulphonated derivatives manufacturing	271/2	251
	Acrylonitrile manufacturing	271/2	251
	Alcohols (synthetic) manufacturing	271/2	251
	Aldehyde manufacturing	271/2	251
	Amines manufacturing	271/2	251
	Anthracene manufacturing	271/2	251
	Aromatic hydrocarbons manufacturing	271/2	251
	Benzene manufacturing	271/2	251
	Butadiene manufacturing	271/2	251
	Citric acid manufacturing	271/2	251
	Coal tar naphtha manufacturing	271/2	251
	Creosote manufacturing	271/2	251
	Cresylic acid manufacturing	271/2	251
	Cumene manufacturing	271/2	251
	Cyclic hydrocarbons manufacturing	271/2	251
	Cyclohexane manufacturing	271/2	251
	Epoxides manufacturing	271/2	251
	Esters (but not polyesters) manufacturing	271/2	251
	Ethane diol (excluding anti-freeze mixtures) manufacturing	271/2	251
	Ethanol (synthetic) manufacturing	271/2	251
	Ethylene manufacturing	271/2	251
	Ethylene glycol (excluding anti-freeze mixtures) manufacturing	271/2	251
	Formaldehyde manufacturing	271/2	251
	Halogenated derivatives of hydrocarbon manufacturing	271/2	251
	Heterocyclic compounds manufacturing	271/2	251
	Hydrocarbons (not fuels) manufacturing	271/2	251
	Hydrocarbons sulphonated, nitrated or nitrosated derivatives manufacturing	271/2	251
	Ketones manufacturing	271/2	251
	Lactones manufacturing	271/2	251
	Melamine manufacturing	271/2	251
	Methanol manufacturing	271/2	251
	Naphthalene manufacturing	271/2	251
	Pesticide chemical, organic (excluding formulated preparations) manufacturing	271/2	251
	Phenol manufacturing	271/2	251
	Phthalic anhydride manufacturing	271/2	251
	Pitch manufacturing	271/2	251
	Propylene manufacturing	271/2	251
	Propylene oxide manufacturing	271/2	251
	Pyridine base manufacturing	271/2	251
	Styrene manufacturing	271/2	251
	Tar acids manufacturing	271/2	251
	Toluene manufacturing	271/2	251
	Urea (not for use as a fertiliser) manufacturing	271/2	251
	Vinyl acetate manufacturing	271/2	251
	Xylene manufacturing	271/2	251
2513	Fertilizers		
	Ammonium nitrate (not for explosives) manufacturing	278	251
	Ammonium phosphate manufacturing	278	251
	Ammonium sulphate manufacturing	278	251
	Artificial manure manufacturing	278	251
	Basic slag (ground) manufacturing	278	251
	Compound fertilizer manufacturing	278	251
	Fertilizer manufacturing	278	251
	Lawn sand manufacturing	278	256.8
	Lime (ammonium nitrate) manufacturing	278	251
	Nitrogenous straight fertilizer manufacturing	278	251
	Phosphatic straight fertilizer manufacturing	278	251
	Potassic straight fertilizer manufacturing	278	251
	Superphosphate manufacturing	278	251
	Urea (for use as a fertilizer) manufacturing	278	251
2514	Synthetic resins and plastics materials		
	ABS (acrylonitrile-butadiene-styrene) polymers manufacturing	276/1	251
	Acrylic resins manufacturing	276/1	251
	Acrylonitrile-butadiene-styrene (ABS) polymers manufacturing	276/1	251
	Alginates manufacturing	276/1	251
	Alkyd resins manufacturing	276/1	251

SIC 1980	Activity	SIC 1968	NACE
	Aminoplastic resins manufacturing	276/1	251
	Casein resins manufacturing	276/1	251
	Cellulose acetate manufacturing	271/2	251
	Cellulose ester and ether ester manufacturing	271/2	251
	Cellulose nitrate manufacturing	279/3	251
	Co-polymers (plastics) manufacturing	276/1	251
	Condensation, polycondensation and polyaddition products (plastics material) manufacturing	276/1	251
	Cresylic resins manufacturing	276/1	251
	Dispersions of synthetic resin manufacturing	276/1	251
	Emulsions of synthetic resin manufacturing	276/1	251
	Epoxide resins manufacturing	276/1	251
	Extrusion compounds (plastics) manufacturing	276/1	251
	Melamine resin manufacturing	276/1	251
	Moulding compounds, plastics, manufacturing	276/1	251
	Phenolic resins manufacturing	276/1	251
	Polyamide compounds manufacturing	276/1	251
	Polyesters manufacturing	276/1	251
	Polyethylene manufacturing	276/1	251
	Polypropylene manufacturing	276/1	251
	Polystyrene manufacturing	276/1	251
	Polytetra fluorethylene (PTFE) manufacturing	276/1	251
	Polyvinyl acetate manufacturing	276/1	251
	Polyvinyl chloride manufacturing	276/1	251
	PTFE (polytetra fluoroethylene) manufacturing	276/1	251
	Resins for paint manufacturing	276/1	251
	Resins, synthetic, manufacturing	276/1	251
	Silicones manufacturing	276/1	251
	Siloxanes manufacturing	276/1	251
	Synthetic resin adhesive, unformulated, manufacturing	276/1	251
	Thermoplastic resins manufacturing	276/1	251
	Thermosetting resins manufacturing	276/1	251
	Urea formaldehyde resins manufacturing	276/1	251
2515	Synthetic rubber		
	Rubber, synthetic, manufacturing	276/2	251
2516	Dyestuffs and pigments		
	Acid dye manufacturing	277	251
	Alizarine dye manufacturing	277	251
	Aniline dye manufacturing	277	251
	Azoic dye manufacturing	277	251
	Basic dye manufacturing	277	251
	Chromium pigment manufacturing	277	251
	Colour lake manufacturing	277	251
	Colours for food and cosmetics manufacturing	271/3	251
	Colours in dry, liquid or paste form manufacturing	277	251
	Crushed pigment colours manufacturing	277	251
	Direct dye manufacturing	277	251
	Disperse dye manufacturing	277	251
	Dye manufacturing	277	251
	Dyes (for food, drink and cosmetics) manufacturing	271/3	251
	Dyes modifed for dyeing acrylic fibres manufacturing	277	251
	Fluorescent brightening agent manufacturing	277	251
	Lake (pigment) manufacturing	277	251
	Laundry blue manufacturing	229/2	259.4

SIC 1980	Activity	SIC 1968	NACE
	Mineral colours manufacturing	277	251
	Mordant dye manufacturing	277	251
	Ochres (pigments) manufacturing	277	251
	Optical bleaching agent manufacturing	277	251
	Pigment, synthetic organic, manufacturing	277	251
	Solvent dye manufacturing	277	251
	Sulphur dye manufacturing	277	251
	Synthetic dyestuffs manufacturing	277	251
	Titanium dioxide manufacturing	277	251
	Toner (pigment) manufacturing	277	251
	Vat dye manufacturing	277	251
	Vegetable tanning and dyeing extracts manufacturing	277	251
2551	Paints, varnishes and painters' fillings		
	Acrylic paint manufacturing	274	255
	Alkyd paint manufacturing	274	255
	Aluminium paint manufacturing	274	255
	Anti-corrosive paint manufacturing	274	255
	Artists' colours manufacturing	274	255
	Bituminous paint manufacturing	274	255
	Cellulose paint manufacturing	274	255
	Cellulose varnish manufacturing	274	255
	Ceramic colours manufacturing	271/3	255
	Ceramic glaze manufacturing	271/3	255
	Chlorinated rubber based paint manufacturing	274	255
	Distemper manufacturing	274	255
	Electrocoats paint manufacturing	274	255
	Emulsion paint manufacturing	274	255
	Enamel manufacturing	274	255
	Epoxy paint manufacturing	274	255
	French polish manufacturing	274	255
	Lacquer manufacturing	274	255
	Lead paint manufacturing	274	255
	Marine paint manufacturing	274	255
	Metal pre-treatment paint manufacturing	274	255
	Metallic paint manufacturing	274	255
	Nitrogen resin type paint manufacturing	274	255
	Oleo resinous paint manufacturing	274	255
	Paint (not cement based) manufacturing	274	255
	Polyester paint manufacturing	274	255
	Polyurethane paint manufacturing	274	255
	Primer paint manufacturing	274	255
	Putty manufacturing	274	255
	Sealing and filling compounds (painters') manufacturing	274	255
	Shellac varnish manufacturing	274	255
	Ships' bottom composition manufacturing	274	255
	Stain manufacturing	274	255
	Thinners manufacturing	274	255
	Varnish manufacturing	274	255
	Vinyl paint manufacturing	274	255
	Vitreous enamel frits manufacturing	271/3	255
	White lead (in paste form) manufacturing	274	255
	Wood stain manufacturing	274	255
	Zinc paint manufacturing	274	255
2552	Printing ink		
	Flexographic ink manufacturing	279/5	255
	Gravure ink manufacturing	279/5	255
	Letterpress ink manufacturing	279/5	255
	Lithographic ink manufacturing	279/5	255
	News ink manufacturing	279/5	255
	Printers' varnish manufacturing	279/5	255

SIC 1980	Activity	SIC 1968	NACE
	Printing ink manufacturing	279/5	255
	Screen process ink manufacturing	279/5	255
2562	Formulated adhesives and sealants		
	Acrylic adhesive manufacturing	279/2	256.2
	Adhesive coating manufacturing	279/2	256.2
	Adhesive paste manufacturing	279/2	256.2
	Anaerobic adhesive manufacturing	279/2	256.2
	Bituminous sealants manufacturing	279/2	256.2
	Bone glue manufacturing	279/2	256.2
	Casein based adhesive manufacturing	279/2	256.2
	Cellulose based adhesive manufacturing	279/2	256.2
	Cross-linking adhesive manufacturing	279/2	256.2
	Cyanoacrylate adhesive manufacturing	279/2	256.2
	Dextrin based adhesive manufacturing	279/2	256.2
	Emulsion adhesive manufacturing	279/2	256.2
	Epoxide adhesive manufacturing	279/2	256.2
	Gelatine manufacturing	279/2	256.2
	Glue manufacturing	279/2	256.2
	Gum manufacturing	279/2	256.2
	Hot melt adhesive manufacturing	279/2	256.2
	Mountant manufacturing	279/2	256.2
	Oil based sealants manufacturing	279/2	256.2
	Polyester adhesive manufacturing	279/2	256.2
	Polyurethane adhesive manufacturing	279/2	256.2
	Polyvinyl acetate (and co-polymer) adhesive manufacturing	279/2	256.2
	Resorcinal formaldehyde adhesive manufacturing	279/2	256.2
	Rubber-based adhesive manufacturing	279/2	481.2
	Sealants manufacturing	279/2	255
	Size, decorators', manufacturing	279/2	256.2
	Starch based adhesive manufacturing	279/2	256.2
	Synthetic resin adhesive manufacturing	279/2	256.2
	Urea formaldehyde adhesive manufacturing	279/2	256.2
2563	Chemical treatment of oils and fats		
	Acyclic (fatty) alcohols manufacturing	275	256.3
	Fat splitting and distilling	275	256.3
	Fatty acid manufacturing	275	256.3
	Fatty amines and quaternary ammonium salts manufacturing	275	256.3
	Glycerol manufacturing	275	256.3
	Oleic acid manufacturing	275	256.3
	Oleine manufacturing	275	256.3
	Stearic acid manufacturing	275	256.3
	Stearine manufacturing	275	256.3
2564	Essential oils and flavouring materials		
	Compound flavour (blended flavour concentrates) manufacturing	271/3	256.4
	Essential oils and essences (other than turpentine) manufacturing	271/3	256.4
	Natural material used in flavours or perfumes manufacturing	271/3	256.4
	Perfume compounds (blended perfume concentrates) manufacturing	271/3	256.4
	Perfumery and flavour chemicals (synthetic) manufacturing	271/3	251
2565	Explosives		
	Ammonium nitrate (explosives) manufacturing	279/3	256.5
	Amorce manufacturing	279/3	256.5

SIC 1980	Activity	SIC 1968	NACE
	Black powder manufacturing	279/3	256.5
	Blasting powder manufacturing	279/3	256.5
	Chlorate explosive manufacturing	279/3	256.5
	Cordite manufacturing	279/3	256.5
	Detonating fuse manufacturing	279/3	256.5
	Detonator manufacturing	279/3	256.5
	Dynamite manufacturing	279/3	256.5
	Electric detonator manufacturing	279/3	256.5
	Explosive manufacturing	279/3	256.5
	Firelighter manufacturing	499/2	256.5
	Firework manufacturing	279/3	256.5
	Flint (for lighters) manufacturing	399/12	256.5
	Fuse (for explosives) manufacturing	279/3	256.5
	Gelignite manufacturing	279/3	256.5
	Guncotton manufacturing	279/3	256.5
	Gunpowder manufacturing	279/3	256.5
	Incandescent mantle manufacturing	499/2	256.5
	Incendiary composition manufacturing	279/3	256.5
	Match manufacturing	279/3	256.5
	Nitro-glycerine manufacturing	279/3	256.5
	Perchlorate explosive manufacturing	279/3	256.5
	Percussion cap manufacturing	279/3	256.5
	Propellant powder manufacturing	279/3	256.5
	Pyrotechnics manufacturing	279/3	256.5
	Signal rocket manufacturing	279/3	256.5
	TNT (trinitrotoluene) manufacturing	279/3	256.5
	Trinitrotoluene (TNT) manufacturing	279/3	256.5
2567	Miscellaneous chemicals for industrial use		
	Acetylene manufacturing	271/2	256.1
	Activated earths manufacturing	271/1	256.7
	Anti-freeze mixtures, excluding pure ethylene glycol, manufacturing	271/3	256.7
	Anti-knock compounds manufacturing	271/3	256.7
	Anti-rust preparations manufacturing	271/3	256.7
	Brewing preparations (excluding yeast) manufacturing	271/3	256.8
	Carbon dioxide manufacturing	271/1	256.1
	Chemicals specially prepared for laboratory use manufacturing	271/3	256.7
	Desiccants (chemical) manufacturing	271/3	256.7
	Factice manufacturing	271/3	256.7
	Finings manufacturing	271/3	256.8
	Fire extinguishing chemicals manufacturing	271/3	256.7
	Flocculating agents (chemical) manufacturing	271/3	256.7
	Flux manufacturing	271/3	256.7
	Foundry bonding clays manufacturing	271/3	256.7
	Foundry core binder manufacturing	271/3	256.7
	Foundry facing manufacturing	279/1	256.7
	Foundry preparation manufacturing	279/1	256.7
	Fuel additive manufacturing	271/3	256.7
	Heat treatment salts manufacturing	271/3	256.7
	Hydrogen manufacturing	271/1	256.1
	Industrial catalyst manufacturing	271/3	256.7
	Industrial cleaning preparation manufacturing	271/3	256.7
	Lubricating oil additive manufacturing	271/3	256.7
	Metal treatment chemical manufacturing	271/3	256.7
	Nitrogen manufacturing	271/1	256.1
	Oil additive manufacturing	271/3	256.7
	Oxygen manufacturing	271/1	256.1
	Pickling preparations for metal treatment manufacturing	271/3	256.7
	Rare gas manufacturing	271/1	256.1
	Refined coal tar manufacturing	271/2	256.7
	Rosin size manufacturing	271/2	256.7

SIC 1980	Activity	SIC 1968	NACE
	Rubber processing chemicals manufacturing	271/3	256.7
	Spirit of turpentine manufacturing	271/3	256.7
	Stabilisers and extenders for PVC processing manufacturing	271/3	256.7
	Surface active chemical (excluding finished detergent and scouring powder) manufacturing	271/3	256.7
	Tanning agents (synthetic) manufacturing	271/3	256.6
	Textile chemical auxiliaries manufacturing	271/3	256.6
	Water treatment chemical manufacturing	271/3	256.7
	Wax manufacturing	279/1	256.7
	Wine making preparations (excluding yeast) manufacturing	271/3	256.8
	Wood tar chemical manufacturing	271/2	256.7
2568	Formulated pesticides		
	Acaricide manufacturing	279/4	256.8
	Anti-sprouting compound manufacturing	279/4	256.8
	Cattle dip manufacturing	279/4	256.8
	Fly paper manufacturing	279/4	256.8
	Formulated pesticide manufacturing	279/4	256.8
	Fruit dropping compound manufacturing	279/4	256.8
	Fruit setting compound manufacturing	279/4	256.8
	Fumigating block manufacturing	279/4	256.8
	Fungicide manufacturing	279/4	256.8
	Herbicide manufacturing	279/4	256.8
	Insecticide manufacturing	279/4	256.8
	Nematocide manufacturing	279/4	256.8
	Nicotine preparation manufacturing	279/4	256.8
	Plant hormone manufacturing	279/4	256.8
	Rodenticide manufacturing	279/4	256.8
	Seed dressing manufacturing	279/4	256.8
	Sheep dip manufacturing	279/4	256.8
	Soil fumigant manufacturing	279/4	256.8
	Weed killer manufacturing	279/4	256.8
2569	Adhesive film, cloth and foil		
	Adhesive labels of plastics or cellulose manufacturing	491/2	259.3
	Adhesive repair material manufacturing	not classified	not classified
	Adhesive tape manufacturing	491/2	259.3
	Cable cloth manufacturing	491/2	438.3
	Cellulose adhesive tape manufacturing	491/2	259.3
	Heat sensitive adhesive tape manufacturing	496	259.3
	Insulating tape (cloth) manufacturing	491/2	438.3
	Pressure sensitive adhesive tape manufacturing	491/2	259.3
	Varnished tape (insulating) manufacturing	491	438.3
	Water sensitive adhesive tape manufacturing	491	259.3
2570	Pharmaceutical products		
	Adhesive plaster and bandage (surgical) manufacturing	279/6	257
	Anaesthetics manufacturing	272	257
	Analgesics manufacturing	272	257
	Anti-infectives manufacturing	272	257
	Antibiotics manufacturing	272	257
	Antiseptics manufacturing	272	257
	Bandage (surgical) manufacturing	279/6	257
	Capsule (medicinal) manufacturing	272	257
	Confectionery (medicated) manufacturing	272	257
	Cotton wool and tissues manufacturing	279/6	257
	Cyclamates manufacturing	272	251
	Dental cement manufacturing	353/1	257
	Dental filling manufacturing	353/1	257
	Dietary food (pharmaceutical) manufacturing	272	423.5
	Disinfectant manufacturing	279/4	257
	Dressing, surgical manufacturing	279/6	257
	Drug manufacturing	272	257
	Embrocation manufacturing	272	257
	Gauze (surgical) manufacturing	279/6	257
	Hormone (not plant hormone) manufacturing	272	251
	Lint (surgical) manufacturing	279/6	257
	Lozenge (medicated) manufacturing	272	257
	Medicated dressings manufacturing	279/6	257
	Medicinal feed additives (veterinary) manufacturing	272	257
	Medicine manufacturing	272	257
	Mineral and pharmaceutical nutritional ingredients for food and feedingstuff manufacturing	272	not classified
	Ointment manufacturing	272	257
	Pharmaceutical chemicals manufacturing	272	251
	Pharmaceutical preparations manufacturing	272	257
	Pills, medicinal, manufacturing	272	257
	Saccharin manufacturing	272	259.4
	Saccharin tablet manufacturing	272	259.4
	Salines manufacturing	272	257
	Sera manufacturing	272	257
	Sheep and cattle dressings manufacturing	279/4	257
	Sticking plaster (surgical) manufacturing	279/6	257
	Sulphonamides manufacturing	272	251
	Suture, surgical, manufacturing	279/6	257
	Vaccine manufacturing	272	257
	Veterinary biologicals manufacturing	272	257
	Veterinary pharmaceuticals manufacturing	272	257
	Wadding (surgical) manufacturing	279/6	257
2581	Soap and synthetic detergents		
	Abrasive soap manufacturing	275	258.1
	Brushless shaving cream manufacturing	275	258.1
	Carpet soap manufacturing	275	258.1
	Detergent, soapless, (formulated) manufacturing	275	258.1
	Dog soap manufacturing	275	258.1
	Floor cleanser manufacturing	275	258.1
	Hard soap manufacturing	275	258.1
	Industrial soap manufacturing	275	258.1
	Liquid soap manufacturing	275	258.1
	Scouring powder manufacturing	275	258.1
	Shaving cream manufacturing	275	258.1
	Shaving soap manufacturing	275	258.1
	Soap manufacturing	275	258.1
	Soap chips manufacturing	275	258.1
	Soap flakes manufacturing	275	258.1
	Soap powder manufacturing	275	258.1
	Synthetic detergent manufacturing	275	258.1
	Textile soap manufacturing	275	258.1
	Toilet soap manufacturing	275	258.1
2582	Perfumes, cosmetics and toilet preparations		
	After-shave lotion manufacturing	273	258.2

SIC 1980	Activity	SIC 1968	NACE
	Anti-perspirant manufacturing	273	258.2
	Bath preparations manufacturing	273	258.2
	Colognes manufacturing	273	258.2
	Cosmetic manufacturing	273	258.2
	Dental cleansing preparation manufacturing	273	258.2
	Deodorant (personal) manufacturing	273	258.2
	Depilatory manufacturing	273	258.2
	Face powder or cream manufacturing	273	258.2
	Hair preparations manufacturing	273	258.2
	Hand cream manufacturing	273	258.2
	Lipstick manufacturing	273	258.2
	Make-up preparation manufacturing	273	258.2
	Manicure preparations manufacturing	273	258.2
	Nail preparation (cosmetic) manufacturing	273	258.2
	Perfume manufacturing	273	258.2
	Pre-shave lotion manufacturing	273	258.2
	Shampoo manufacturing	275	258.1
	Skin care preparations manufacturing	273	258.2
	Talcum powder manufacturing	273	258.2
	Tooth paste manufacturing	273	258.2
	Tooth powder manufacturing	273	258.2
2591	**Photographic materials and chemicals**		
	Cinematographic film (sensitized) manufacturing	279/7	259.1
	Clearing agents (photographic) manufacturing	279/7	259.1
	Developer (photographic) manufacturing	279/7	259.1
	Fixer (photographic) manufacturing	279/7	259.1
	Intensifier (photographic) manufacturing	279/7	259.1
	Photographic chemicals manufacturing	279/7	259.1
	Photographic film (sensitized) manufacturing	279/7	259.1
	Photographic plate (sensitized) manufacturing	279/7	259.1
	Sensitized cloth manufacturing	279/7	259.1
	Sensitized paper manufacturing	279/7	259.1
	Toner (photographic) manufacturing	279/7	259.1
2599	**Chemical products, not elsewhere specified**		
	Candle manufacturing	275	259.4
	Car polish manufacturing	279/1	259.2
	Cleaning powder (other than detergents and scouring powder) manufacturing	279/1	259.2
	Floor polish manufacturing	279/1	259.2
	Floor seal manufacturing	279/1	259.2
	Food preservative manufacturing	271/3	259.4
	Furniture polish manufacturing	279/1	259.2
	Household deodoriser manufacturing	279/4	258.2
	Impregnated cleaning and polishing cloth manufacturing	279/1	259.2
	Metal polish manufacturing	279/1	259.2
	Nightlight manufacturing	275	259.4
	Plate polish manufacturing	279/1	259.2
	Polish manufacturing	279/1	259.2
	Polishing paste and powder manufacturing	279/1	259.2
	Sanitary cleanser manufacturing	279/1	259.2
	Shoe dye manufacturing	279/1	259.2
	Shoe polish manufacturing	279/1	259.2
	Ski wax manufacturing	279/1	259.4
	Unrecorded magnetic tape manufacturing	364/3	259.4
	Wax products manufacturing	279/1	259.4

SIC 1980	Activity	SIC 1968	NACE
2600	**Production of man-made fibres**		
	Man-made fibre (not glass fibre) manufacturing	411	260
	Man-made fibre bulking (carried out in man-made fibre producing establishments)	411	260
	Man-made fibre crimping (carried out in man-made fibre producing establishments)	411	260
	Man-made fibre texturing (carried out in man-made fibre producing establishments)	411	260
	Man-made fibre twisting (carried out in man-made fibre producing establishments)	411	260
	Man-made fibre warping (carried out in man-made fibre producing establishments)	411	260
	Man-made fibre winding (carried out in man-made fibre producing establishments)	411	260
	Polyamide (man-made fibre) manufacturing	411	260
	Polyester (man-made fibre) manufacturing	411	260
	Staple fibre (acetate, synthetic or viscose) production	411	260
	Staple man-made fibre manufacturing	411	260
	Synthetic fibre manufacturing	411	260
	Tow, man-made, manufacturing	411	260
	Yarn, continuous filament, (man-made fibres) manufacturing	411	260
3111	**Ferrous metal foundries**		
	Bath, cast iron, manufacturing	313/4	311.1
	Boot and shoe tip and protector (malleable casting) manufacturing	313/4	311.1
	Boot last, iron, manufacturing	313/3	311.1
	Box irons, manufacture of iron castings for,	313/4	311.1
	Cast iron chair for railway track manufacturing	313/3	311.1
	Cast iron cistern manufacturing	313/4	311.1
	Cast iron cooker manufacturing	313/4	311.1
	Cast iron domestic hot water boiler manufacturing	313/4	311.1
	Cast iron fire bar manufacturing	313/3	311.1
	Cast iron floor plate manufacturing	313/4	311.1
	Cast iron grate manufacturing	313/4	311.1
	Cast iron grating manufacturing	313/4	311.1
	Cast iron hollow-ware manufacturing	313/4	311.1
	Cast iron paving manufacturing	313/4	311.1
	Cast iron pipe manufacturing	313/4	311.1
	Cast iron radiator manufacturing	313/4	311.1
	Cast iron rainwater gutter manufacturing	313/4	311.1
	Cast iron rainwater pipe manufacturing	313/4	311.1
	Cast iron range manufacturing	313/4	311.1
	Cast iron stove manufacturing	313/4	311.1
	Cast iron tunnel segment manufacturing	313/3	311.1
	Casting boxes, manufacture of iron castings for,	313/4	311.1
	Casting, grenade, manufacturing	313/3	311.1
	Casting, steel, manufacturing	311/2	311.1
	Ferrous casting manufacturing	313/3	311.1
	Ingot mould and bottom manufacturing	313/4	311.1
	Iron casting manufacturing	313/3	311.1

SIC 1980	Activity	SIC 1968	NACE	SIC 1980	Activity	SIC 1968	NACE
	Iron foundry	313	311.1		Bolt end manufacturing	393	313.1
	Malleable casting manufacturing	313/3	311.1		Coach screw manufacturing	393	313.1
	Pattern casting (ferrous) manufacturing	313/3	311.1		Cotter manufacturing	393	313.1
	Roll for rolling mill and rolling mill train (not machined) manufacturing	311/2	311.1		Cotter pin manufacturing	393	313.1
					Linch pin manufacturing	393	313.1
					Nail (not wire) manufacturing	393	316.9
					Nut manufacturing	393	313.1
3112	Non-ferrous metal foundries				Precision screw manufacturing	393	313.1
	Aluminium casting manufacturing	321	311.2		Rivet (bifurcated, tubular, etc.) manufacturing	393	316.9
	Aluminium die casting manufacturing	321	311.2		Screw, metal, all types, manufacturing	393	313.1
	Bell founding	399/12	311.2		Staple, (not wire), manufacturing	394	316.9
	Brass casting, ornamental,	399/12	311.2		Tack (not wire) manufacturing	393	316.9
	Britannia metal founding	323	311.2		Tubular rivet manufacturing	393	316.9
	Bronze founding (general)	322	311.2		Washer (metal) manufacturing	393	313.1
	Bronze founding (ornamental)	399/12	311.2				
	Casting, non-ferrous base metal, manufacturing	not classified	311.2	3137/2	Springs		
					Belleville washer manufacturing	399/4	313.2
	Copper or copper alloy die casting manufacturing	322	311.2		Coil spring (not motor vehicle suspension) manufacturing	399/4	313.2
	Die casting, non-ferrous base metal, manufacturing	not classified	311.2		Heavy wire manufacturing	394	313.1
					Lock washer manufacturing	399/4	313.2
	Founding, non-ferrous base metal	not classified	311.2		Ring spring manufacturing	399/4	313.2
					Spring presswork manufacturing	399/4	313.2
	Gravity casting non-ferrous base metal manufacturing	not classified	311.2		Spring washer manufacturing	399/4	313.2
					Torsion bar spring manufacturing	399/4	313.2
	Pressure die casting non-ferrous base metal manufacturing	not classified	311.2	3137/3	Non-precision chains		
					Chain (not articulated transmission) manufacturing	399/12	313.4
	Sand casting non-ferrous base metal, manufacturing	not classified	311.2		Chain, non-precision, manufacturing	399/12	313.4
					Skid chain manufacturing	399/12	313.4
					Stud link chain manufacturing	399/12	313.4
					Welded link chain manufacturing	399/12	313.4
3120	Forging, pressing and stamping			3138	Heat and surface treatment of metals, including sintering		
	Axle, steel, (railway and tramway) manufacturing	311/2	312		Anodising	399/11	313.5
	Closed die forging	399/5	312.1		Case-hardening	399/11	313.5
	Cold pressing (of base metals)	399/12	312.2		Electroplating	399/11	313.5
	Cold stamping (of base metals)	399/12	312.2		Enamelling metals (including vitreous enamelling)	399/11	313.5
	Die forging (ferrous metals)	399/5	312.1		Galvanising	399/11	313.5
	Drop forging (ferrous metals)	399/5	312.1		Gilding metals	399/11	313.5
	Drop stamping (base non-ferrous metals)	321, 322, 323	312.2		Grinding (metal finishing)	399/11	313.5
					Hot dip coating (metal finishing)	399/11	313.5
	Drop stamping (ferrous metals)	399/5	312.2		Japanning (metal finishing)	399/11	313.5
	Engineers' stampings and pressings (base non-ferrous metals) manufacturing	321, 322, 323	312.2		Lacquering (metal finishing)	399/11	313.5
					Metal spraying	399/11	313.5
					Plating (metal finishing)	399/11	313.5
	Engineers' stampings and pressings (ferrous metals) manufacturing	399/12	312.2		Polishing (metal finishing)	399/11	313.5
					Sintering of metals	399/11	313.3
	Expanded metal manufacturing	399/12	312.2		Stove painting	399/11	313.5
	Forging	not classified	312.1	3142	Metal doors, windows etc.		
					Casement, metal, manufacturing	399/2	314.2
	Hammer forging (steel)	311/2	312.1		Curtain walling, metal, manufacturing	399/2	314.2
	Heavy forging	311/2	312.1		Door frame, metal, manufacturing	399/2	314.2
	Hot pressing (ferrous metals) manufacturing	399/5	312.2		Door, metal, (other than safe door), manufacturing	399/2	314.2
	Hot stamping (ferrous metals)	399/5	312.2		Garden frame, metal, manufacturing	399/12	314.2
	Perforated metal manufacturing	399/12	312.2		Gate, metal, manufacturing	399/12	314.2
	Piercing of base metal	399/12	312.2		Glazing bar manufacturing	399/2	314.2
	Pressing of base metal	399/12	312.2		Grille, metal, (not cast) manufacturing	399/12	314.2
	Stamping of base metal	399/12	312.2		Hut, metal, manufacturing	341/4	314.1
3137/1	Bolts, nuts, screws, washers, rivets, etc.				Partitioning, metal, manufacturing	399/2	314.2
					Railing, metal, manufacturing	399/12	314.1
	Bifurcated rivet manufacturing	393	316.9		Shed, metal, manufacturing	341/4	314.1
	Bolt manufacturing	393	313.1		Skylight, metal, manufacturing	399/2	314.2
					Window frame, metal, manufacturing	399/2	314.2

SIC 1980	Activity	SIC 1968	NACE
3161/1	**Agricultural hand tools**		
	Adze manufacturing	391	316.1
	Agricultural knife manufacturing	392	316.1
	Axe manufacturing	391	316.1
	Fork, garden, manufacturing	391	316.1
	Garden trowel manufacturing	391	316.1
	Hatchet manufacturing	391	316.1
	Hoe manufacturing	391	316.1
	Horticultural knife manufacturing	391	316.1
	Matchet manufacturing	391	316.1
	Mattock manufacturing	391	316.1
	Pick manufacturing	391	316.1
	Pruning shears manufacturing	391	316.1
	Scythe manufacturing	391	316.1
	Secateurs manufacturing	391	316.1
	Shears, agricultural and horticultural manufacturing	391	316.1
	Shears, garden, manufacturing	391	316.1
	Sheep shears (not power) manufacturing	391	316.1
	Shovel manufacturing	391	316.1
	Sickle manufacturing	391	316.1
	Spade manufacturing	391	316.1
3161/2	**Other hand tools**		
	Auger and auger bit manufacturing	391	316.1
	Bench vice manufacturing	391	316.1
	Blow lamp manufacturing	391	316.1
	Bolt cropper manufacturing	391	316.1
	Brazing lamp manufacturing	391	316.1
	Builder's knife manufacturing	391	316.1
	Carpenter's drill manufacturing	391	316.1
	Case opener manufacturing	391	316.1
	Chisel, cold, manufacturing	391	316.1
	Chisel, wood, manufacturing	391	316.1
	Clamp manufacturing	391	316.1
	Cramp manufacturing	391	316.1
	Draw-knife manufacturing	392	316.1
	File manufacturing	391	316.1
	Glass cutter manufacturing	391	316.1
	Gouge, wood frame, manufacturing	391	316.1
	Hacksaw blade, hand tools, manufacturing	391	316.1
	Hammer manufacturing	391	316.1
	Handsaw manufacturing	391	316.1
	Industrial knife manufacturing	392	316.1
	Nippers manufacturing	391	316.1
	Pincers manufacturing	391	316.1
	Pipe cutter manufacturing	390	316.1
	Plane manufacturing	391	316.1
	Pliers manufacturing	391	316.1
	Rasp manufacturing	391	316.1
	Scraper manufacturing	391	316.1
	Screwdriver manufacturing	391	316.1
	Shave hook manufacturing	391	316.1
	Socket set manufacturing	391	316.1
	Spanner manufacturing	391	316.1
	Spoke-shave manufacturing	391	316.1
	Tension strapping tool manufacturing	391	316.1
	Tinman's snips manufacturing	391	316.1
	Tradesmen's knife manufacturing	392	316.1
	Trowel (not garden) manufacturing	391	316.1
	Wood-boring bit manufacturing	391	316.1
	Wrecking bar manufacturing	391	316.1
	Wrench manufacturing	391	316.1
3162/1	**Cutlery, spoons, forks and similar tableware**		
	Bayonet manufacturing	392	316.8
	Butter knife manufacturing	392	316.2
	Domestic cutlery manufacturing	392	316.2
	Electro-plated nickel silver cutlery manufacturing	392	316.2
	Fish-eater manufacturing	392	316.2
	Fork manufacturing	392	316.2
	Kitchen knife manufacturing	392	316.2
	Knife (cutlery) manufacturing	392	316.2
	Knife with folding blade manufacturing	392	316.2
	Ladle manufacturing	392	316.2
	Pinking shears manufacturing	392	316.2
	Pocket knife manufacturing	392	316.2
	Pruning knife manufacturing	391	316.2
	Scissors manufacturing	392	316.2
	Sheath knife manufacturing	392	316.2
	Silver plated cutlery manufacturing	392	316.2
	Spoon manufacturing	392	316.2
	Sword manufacturing	392	316.8
	Tailors' shears manufacturing	392	316.2
3162/2	**Razors and razor blades**		
	Razor (not electric) manufacturing	392	316.2
	Razor blade manufacturing	392	316.2
	Razor set manufacturing	392	316.2
	Safety razor manufacturing	392	316.2
3163	**Metal storage vessels (mainly non-industrial)**		
	Bin, metal, manufacturing	399/7	316.4
	Cistern, metal, manufacturing	399/7	316.4
	Coal bunker, metal, manufacturing	399/7	316.4
	Dustbin, metal, manufacturing	399/6	316.4
	Expansion tank manufacturing	399/6	316.4
	Fuel bunker, metal, manufacturing	399/7	316.4
	Galvanised tank manufacturing	399/7	316.4
	Oil storage tank, domestic, manufacturing	399/7	316.4
	Tank, storage, (domestic) manufacturing	399/7	316.4
3164/1	**Metal cans and boxes**		
	Aerosol can, metal, manufacturing	395	316.4
	Aluminium can and box manufacturing	395	316.4
	Aluminium collapsible tube (packaging) manufacturing	321	316.4
	Aluminium tubular container manufacturing	395	316.4
	Blackplate can manufacturing	395	316.4
	Can, metal, manufacturing	395	316.4
	Collapsible tube, metal, (for packaging) manufacturing	395	316.4
	Tin can and box manufacturing	395	316.4
	Tinned plate, sheet, strip (decorated etc., for box and other container) manufacturing	395	316.4
	Tubular container, metal, manufacturing	395	316.4
3164/2	**Metal kegs, drums and barrels**		
	Barrel, metal, manufacturing	399/7	316.4
	Cask, metal, manufacturing	399/7	316.4
	Churn, metal, manufacturing	399/7	316.4
	Drum, metal, manufacturing	399/7	316.4
	Keg, metal, manufacturing	399/7	316.4
	Milk churn, metal, manufacturing	399/7	316.4
	Reconditioning metal drum	399/7	316.4
3164/3	**Metallic closures**		
	Bottle top, metal, manufacturing	399/10	316.4
	Capsule metal, manufacturing	399/10	316.4
	Closure, metal, manufacturing	399/10	316.4
	Crown cork manufacturing	399/10	316.4

SIC 1980	Activity	SIC 1968	NACE
	Metallic closure manufacturing	399/10	316.4
	Pilfer-proof cap, metal, manufacturing	399/10	316.4
	Screw cap, metal, manufacturing	399/10	316.4
	Stopper, metal, manufacturing	399/10	316.4
3164/4	Foil packaging goods		
	Aluminium foil container manufacturing	395	316.4
	Aluminium foil laminate manufacturing	321	316.4
	Aluminium foil packaging goods manufacturing	395	316.4
	Container, foil, manufacturing	395	316.4
	Cooking foil (metal) manufacturing	321	316.4
	Foil packaging goods (metal) manufacturing	395	316.4
	Foil, decorated, embossed or cut to size (metal) manufacturing	321	316.4
	Kitchen foil (metal) manufacturing	321	316.4
	Laminates, metal foil with other materials, manufacturing	321	316.4
3164/5	Other packaging products of metal		
	Cable drum, metal, manufacturing	399/7	316.4
	Metal pallet manufacturing	399/12	316.4
	Roll, metal, for cable, hose, etc., manufacturing	399/7	316.4
	Stillage, metal, manufacturing	399/12	316.4
	Tensional steel strapping manufacturing	399/12	316.4
3165	Domestic heating and cooking appliances (non-electrical)		
	Boiler, oil, (domestic type) manufacturing	399/12	311.1
	Boiler, solid-fuel, (domestic type) manufacturing	399/12	311.1
	Commercial catering cooking appliance, non-electric, manufacturing	399/12	316.5
	Cooker, gas, manufacturing	399/9	316.5
	Cooker, oil, manufacturing	399/12	316.5
	Cooker, solid-fuel, manufacturing	399/12	316.5
	Domestic cooking appliance, non-electric, manufacturing	399/12	316.5
	Domestic heating appliance, non-electric, manufacturing	399/12	316.5
	Fire, gas, manufacturing	399/9	316.5
	Fire, oil, manufacturing	399/12	316.5
	Gas fired domestic cooking and heating appliance manufacturing	399/9	316.5
	Oil fired domestic heating and cooking appliance manufacturing	399/12	316.5
	Solid-fuel fired domestic heating and cooking appliance manufacturing	399/12	316.5
	Space heater, gas, manufacturing	399/9	316.5
	Space heater, oil, manufacturing	399/12	316.5
	Stove, gas, manufacturing	399/9	316.5
	Stove, oil, manufacturing	399/12	316.5
	Stove, solid fuel, manufacturing	399/12	316.5
	Water heater, gas, manufacturing	399/9	316.5
3166/1	Metal furniture		
	Bed head, metal, manufacturing	399/1	316.6
	Bedstead, metal, manufacturing	399/1	316.6
	Bookcase, metal, manufacturing	399/1	316.6
	Bunk bed, metal, manufacturing	399/1	316.6
	Cabinet, metal, manufacturing	399/12	316.6
	Chair, metal, manufacturing	399/1	316.6
	Coat stand, metal, manufacturing	399/1	316.6
	Desk tray, metal, manufacturing	399/1	316.6
	Desk, metal, manufacturing	399/1	316.6
	Drawer, metal, manufacturing	399/1	316.6
	Filing cabinet, metal, manufacturing	399/1	316.9
	Locker, metal, manufacturing	399/1	316.6
	Mattress support, metal, manufacturing	399/1	316.6
	Office furniture, metal, manufacturing	399/1	316.6
	Outdoor furniture, metal, manufacturing	399/1	316.6
	Plan chest, metal, manufacturing	399/1	316.6
	Racking, metal, manufacturing	399/1	316.6
	Seating, metal, (not for road vehicles or aircraft), manufacturing	399/1	316.6
	Shelving, metal, manufacturing	399/1	316.6
	Spring wire mattress manufacturing	399/1	316.6
	Table, metal, manufacturing	399/1	316.6
	Wardrobe, metal, manufacturing	399/1	316.6
3166/2	Safes, etc.		
	Cash box manufacturing	399/3	316.6
	Deed box manufacturing	399/3	316.6
	Night safe manufacturing	399/3	316.6
	Safe manufacturing	399/3	316.6
	Strong box manufacturing	399/3	316.6
	Strong room manufacturing	399/3	316.6
	Strongroom door manufacturing	399/3	316.6
3167	Domestic and similar utensils of metal		
	Baking dish, pan and tin, manufacturing	399/6	316.7
	Bucket, metal, manufacturing	399/6	316.7
	Butter dish, metal, manufacturing	392	316.7
	Candelabra, base metal, manufacturing	392	316.7
	Condiment set, metal, manufacturing	392	316.7
	Frying pan manufacturing	399/6	316.7
	Kettle, non-electric, manufacturing	399/6	316.7
	Milk pan manufacturing	399/6	316.7
	Omelette pan manufacturing	399/6	316.7
	Pressure cooker manufacturing	399/6	316.7
	Saucepan manufacturing	399/6	316.7
	Scourer (of metal) manufacturing	399/12	316.7
	Serving dish, base metal, manufacturing	392	316.7
	Steel wool (for domestic use) manufacturing	399/12	316.7
	Stewpan manufacturing	399/6	316.7
	Tableware, base metal, manufacturing	392	316.7
	Tea set, base metal, manufacturing	392	316.7
	Teapot, base metal, manufacturing	399/6	316.7
	Toast rack, base metal, manufacturing	392	316.7
	Tray, base metal, manufacturing	399/12	316.7
3169/1	Locks, etc.		
	Key manufacturing	399/3	316.3
	Key blank manufacturing	399/3	316.3
	Latch manufacturing	399/3	316.3
	Lock manufacturing	399/4	316.3
	Padlock manufacturing	399/3	316.3
3169/2	Needles, pins and other metal small-wares		
	Bag clasp manufacturing	399/8	316.9
	Bag frame manufacturing	399/8	316.9
	Buckle, metal, manufacturing	399/8	316.9
	Button, metal, manufacturing	399/8	316.9
	Collar stud manufacturing	399/8	316.9
	Cuff link manufacturing	399/8	316.9
	Drawing pin manufacturing	399/8	316.9
	Eyelet manufacturing	399/8	316.9

SIC 1980	Activity	SIC 1968	NACE
	Fastener, metal, manufacturing	399/8	316.9
	Hair grip and pin, metal, manufacturing	399/8	316.9
	Hook and eye manufacturing	399/8	316.9
	Knitting needle, metal, manufacturing	399/8	316.9
	Metal badge manufacturing	399/8	316.9
	Needle, metal, manufacturing	399/8	316.9
	Paper clip manufacturing	399/8	316.9
	Paper fastener manufacturing	399/8	316.9
	Pin manufacturing	399/8	316.9
	Press stud manufacturing	399/8	316.9
	Safety pin manufacturing	399/8	316.9
	Sewing needle manufacturing	399/8	316.9
	Slide fastener, metal, manufacturing	399/8	316.9
	Tiepin manufacturing	399/8	316.9
	Zip fastener, metal, manufacturing	399/8	316.9
3169/3	Base metal fittings and mountings for furniture, builders' joinery, leather and travel goods, not elsewhere specified		
	Bracket, base metal, manufacturing	399/12	316.3
	Carpet fittings, metal, manufacturing	399/8	316.3
	Catch, door and window, manufacturing	399/12	316.3
	Clothes hook manufacturing	399/12	316.3
	Curtain rail and runner, metal, manufacturing	399/12	316.3
	Door fittings, metal, manufacturing	399/12	316.3
	Furniture fittings, metal, manufacturing	399/12	316.3
	Hinge manufacturing	399/12	316.3
	Stair rod, metal, manufacturing	399/12	316.3
	Suitcase fittings, metal, manufacturing	399/12	316.3
	Wall mountings, metal, manufacturing	399/12	316.3
	Window fittings, metal, manufacturing	399/12	316.3
3169/4	Miscellaneous finished metal products, not elsewhere specified		
	Anchor manufacturing	399/12	316.9
	Art metal work manufacturing	399/12	319
	Basin, metal, manufacturing	399/12	316.7
	Bath, metal, (other than cast iron) manufacturing	399/12	316.7
	Crane hook manufacturing	399/12	316.9
	Domestic tap and stopcock manufacturing	399/12	328.8
	Fire extinguisher (hand held) manufacturing	339/9	328.9
	Grapnel manufacturing	399/12	316.9
	Hand truck, metal, manufacturing	399/12	316.9
	Ladder, metal, manufacturing	399/12	316.9
	Plumbing and pipe fittings, metal, (not cast), manufacturing	399/12	316.9
	Sanitary ware and fittings, metal, manufacturing	399/12	316.7
	Shackle manufacturing	399/12	316.9
	Sheet metal working manufacturing	399/12	319
	Shower cabinet (metal) manufacturing	399/12	316.7
	Sign plate, metal, manufacturing	399/12	316.9
	Sink, metal, (other than cast iron) manufacturing	399/12	316.7
	Steps, metal, manufacturing	399/12	316.9
	Stopcock, domestic, manufacturing	399/12	328.8
	Tap, domestic, manufacturing	399/12	328.8
	Trellis work, metal, manufacturing	399/12	316.9
	Wheelbarrow, metal, manufacturing	399/12	316.9
3204/1	Fabricated constructional steelwork: for buildings		
	Agricultural building steelwork manufacturing	341/4	314.1
	Aluminium structure (for building) manufacturing	341/4	314.1
	Commercial building steelwork manufacturing	341/4	314.1
	Distribution depot steelwork manufacturing	341/4	314.1
	Domestic building steelwork manufacturing	341/4	314.1
	Exhibition centre steelwork manufacturing	341/4	314.1
	Fabricated structural steelwork (for buildings) manufacturing	341/4	314.1
	Factory building steelwork manufacturing	341/4	314.1
	Glasshouse, metal framed, manufacturing	341/4	314.1
	Greenhouse, metal framed, manufacturing	341/4	314.1
	Hospital building steelwork manufacturing	341/4	314.1
	Portable building metalwork manufacturing	341/4	314.1
	Power station structural steelwork manufacturing	341/4	314.1
	Prefabricated building metalwork manufacturing	341/4	314.1
	Roof truss (metal) manufacturing	341/4	314.1
	School building steelwork manufacturing	341/4	314.1
	Steelwork (for buildings) manufacturing	341/4	314.1
	Steelwork for glass roofs manufacturing	341/4	314.1
	Structural steelwork (for buildings) manufacturing	341/4	314.1
3204/2	Fabricated constructional steelwork: for civil engineering works		
	Aluminium structure (for civil engineering) manufacturing	341/4	314.1
	Bridge steelwork manufacturing	341/4	314.1
	Column (fabricated structural steelwork) manufacturing	341/4	314.1
	Deck (oil platform) manufacturing	341/4	314.1
	Dock gates (steel) manufacturing	341/4	314.1
	Dock steelwork manufacturing	341/4	314.1
	Flooring systems (metal) manufacturing	341/4	314.1
	Harbour steelwork manufacturing	341/4	314.1
	Jetty steelwork manufacturing	341/4	314.1
	Module (oil platform) manufacturing	341/4	314.1
	Oil platform (structural) section manufacturing	341/4	314.1
	Plant support (fabricated steelwork) manufacturing	341/4	314.1
	Shuttering (steel) manufacturing	341/4	314.1
	Sluice gate (steel) manufacturing	341/4	314.1
	Tower (steel) manufacturing	341/4	314.1
	Tunnel steelwork manufacturing	341/4	314.1
	Viaduct steelwork manufacturing	341/4	314.1
3205/1	Boilers and boilerhouse plant		
	Boiler drum manufacturing	341/1	315.1
	Boilerhouse plant manufacturing	341/1	315.1
	Boilers and associated equipment and parts (not marine or central heating) manufacturing	341/1	315.1
	Economic boiler manufacturing	341/1	315.1
	Feed water heater (for boilers) manufacturing	341/1	315.1

SIC 1980	Activity	SIC 1968	NACE
	Firing plant for boilers etc. manufacturing	341/1	315.1
	Fuel economiser for boilers manufacturing	341/1	315.1
	Fuel handling equipment for boilers manufacturing	341/1	315.1
	Industrial air heater (for boilers) manufacturing	341/1	328.4
	Nuclear fired boiler (not marine) manufacturing	341/1	315.1
	Process heater manufacturing	341/2	324.1
	Shell boiler (not marine) manufacturing	341/1	315.1
	Vertical boiler (not marine) manufacturing	341/1	315.1
	Waste heat boiler manufacturing	341/1	315.1
	Water tube boiler (not marine) manufacturing	341/1	315.1
3205/2	Process plant fabrications		
	Column (process plant) manufacturing	341/5	324.1
	Condenser (steam) manufacturing	341/5	315.1
	Condenser (vapour not steam) manufacturing	341/5	324.1
	Cracker (process plant) manufacturing	341/5	324.1
	Evaporator manufacturing	341/5	324.1
	Heat exchanger manufacturing	341/5	324.1
	Nuclear fuel plant manufacturing	341/2	324.1
	Process pressure sphere manufacturing	341/5	315.2
	Process pressure vessel manufacturing	341/5	315.2
	Reactor column manufacturing	341/5	324.1
	Reactor vessel manufacturing	341/5	324.1
	Reformer manufacturing	341/5	324.1
3205/3	Other heavy fabricated steelwork in plate		
	Bunker (of heavy steel plate) manufacturing	341/5	314.1
	Chimney (steel) manufacturing	341/5	314.1
	Duct (of heavy steel plate) manufacturing	341/5	315.2
	Flotation vessel (of steel, for oil platform) manufacturing	341/5	314.1
	Jacket leg (of steel plate, for oil platform) manufacturing	341/5	314.1
	Module (tubular), for oil rig, manufacturing	341/5	314.1
	Monopod tower (of steel plate) manufacturing	341/5	314.2
	Oil platform fabrication (of steel plate), manufacturing	341/5	314.1
	Penstock (steel) manufacturing	341/5	315.2
	Piling (tubular welded) manufacturing	341/5	315.2
	Pipe (fabricated steel) manufacturing	341/5	315.2
	Process pipework manufacturing	341/5	315.2
	Silo (steel) manufacturing	341/5	314.1
	Storage tank (of heavy steel plate) manufacturing	341/5	315.2
	Water tower (of steel plate) manufacturing	341/5	315.2
3211/1	Soil preparation and cultivating machinery		
	Broadcaster (agricultural machinery) manufacturing	331	321.1
	Cultivator manufacturing	331	321.1
	Cultivator tine manufacturing	331	321.1
	Disc harrow manufacturing	331	321.1
	Drill, agricultural, manufacturing	331	321.1
	Farmyard manure spreader manufacturing	331	321.1
	Fertilizer distributor or broadcaster manufacturing	331	321.1
	Harrow manufacturing	331	321.1
	Planter, agricultural machinery, manufacturing	331	321.1
	Plough manufacturing	331	321.1
	Plough disc manufacturing	331	321.1
	Roller (agricultural machinery) manufacturing	331	321.1
	Tool bar, agricultural machinery, manufacturing	331	321.1
	Tractor hoe manufacturing	331	321.1
	Tractor plough manufacturing	331	321.1
	Transplanter, agricultural machinery, manufacturing	331	321.1
3211/2	Harvesting and threshing machinery		
	Bale handler (agricultural machinery) manufacturing	331	321
	Baler, hay and straw, manufacturing	331	321.1
	Combine harvester manufacturing	331	321.1
	Digger (elevator and shaker) manufacturing	331	321.1
	Forage harvester manufacturing	331	321.1
	Fruit picking and sorting machinery manufacturing	331	321.1
	Grain drier manufacturing	331	321.1
	Hay making equipment manufacturing	331	321.1
	Mower, agricultural, manufacturing	331	321.1
	Pick-up baler manufacturing	331	321.1
	Potato harvester and sorter manufacturing	331	321.1
	Root crop harvesting and sorting machinery manufacturing	331	321.1
	Silage making machine manufacturing	331	321.1
	Sugar beet harvester manufacturing	331	321.1
	Threshing machine manufacturing	331	321.1
	Vegetable harvesting and sorting machinery manufacturing	331	321.1
	Winnower manufacturing	331	321.1
3211/3	Dairy, feed processing and other agricultural machinery		
	Chemical dresser (seed), for farm use, manufacturing	331	321.1
	Conveyor, agricultural, manufacturing	331	321.1
	Elevator, agricultural, manufacturing	331	321.1
	Grain auger manufacturing	331	321.1
	Grinding mill, agricultural, manufacturing	331	321.1
	Hedgecutter (agricultural type) manufacturing	331	321.1
	Milking machine manufacturing	331	321.1
	Seed cleaner or pre-cleaner agricultural machinery) manufacturing	331	321.1
	Spraying machine (agricultural) manufacturing	331	321.1
3212	Wheeled tractors		
	Internal combustion engine, tractor, manufacturing	380	321.2
	Safety frame, tractor, manufacturing	380	321.2
	Skidded unit, tractor, manufacturing	380	321.2
	Tractor, half track, manufacturing	380	321.2
	Tractor, wheeled, manufacturing	380	321.2
	Wheeled and half-track tractor parts manufacturing	380	321.2

SIC 1980	Activity	SIC 1968	NACE
3221/1	Metal cutting machine tools		
	Boring machine (metal-cutting) manufacturing	332/1	322.1
	Broaching machine (metal-cutting) manufacturing	332/1	322.1
	Chemical process (metal-working) machine tool manufacturing	332/4	322.1
	Cutting machines (for metal) manufacturing	332/1	322.1
	Drilling machine (metal-cutting) manufacturing	332/1	322.1
	Electric discharge (metal-working) machine tool manufacturing	332/4	322.1
	Electro-chemical (metal-working) machine tool manufacturing	332/4	322.1
	Gear making or finishing (metal-cutting) machine manufacturing	332/1	322.1
	Grinding machine, metal-cutting, manufacturing	332/1	322.1
	Honing machine (metal-cutting) manufacturing	332/1	322.1
	Lapping machine (metal-cutting) manufacturing	332/1	322.1
	Laser cutting or welding (metal-working) machine tool manufacturing	332/4	322.1
	Lathe, (metal-cutting) manufacturing	332/1	322.1
	Machining centre (metal-working) manufacturing	332/1	322.1
	Metal cutting machine (numerically controlled) manufacturing	332/1	322.1
	Metal cutting machine tool manufacturing	332/1	322.1
	Milling machine (metal-working) manufacturing	332/1	322.1
	Physical process (metal-working) machine tool manufacturing	332/4	322.1
	Physico-chemical process welding machine (metal-working) manufacturing	332/4	322.1
	Planing machine (metal-cutting) manufacturing	332/1	322.1
	Sawing machine (metal-cutting) manufacturing	332/1	322.1
	Screwing machine (metal-cutting) manufacturing	332/1	322.1
	Shaping machine (metal-cutting) manufacturing	332/1	322.1
	Slotting machine (metal-working) manufacturing	332/1	322.1
	Spark erosion (metal-working) machine manufacturing	332/4	322.1
	Threading machine (metal-cutting) manufacturing	332/1	322.1
	Turning machine (metal-cutting) manufacturing	332/1	322.1
	Ultrasonic (metal-working) machine tool manufacturing	332/4	322.1
	Unit construction and transfer machine (metal-working) manufacturing	332/1	322.1
3221/2	Metal forming machine tools		
	Bending machine, metal-forming, manufacturing	332/2	322.1
	Draw bench (metal-forming) manufacturing	332/2	322.1
	Drawing machine (metal-forming) manufacturing	332/2	322.1
	Forging machine (metal-forming) manufacturing	332/2	322.1
	Forming machine, high energy rate, manufacturing	332/2	322.1
	Hydraulic press (metal-forming) manufacturing	332/2	322.1
	Mechanical press (metal-forming) manufacturing	332/2	322.1
	Numerically controlled (metal-forming) machine manufacturing	332/2	322.1
	Pneumatic press (metal-forming) manufacturing	332/2	322.1
	Press (metal-forming) manufacturing	332/2	322.1
	Punching machine (metal-forming) manufacturing	332/2	322.1
	Shearing machine (metal-forming) manufacturing	332/2	322.1
	Sheet metal forming machine manufacturing	332/2	322.1
	Swaging machine (metal-forming) manufacturing	332/2	322.1
3222/1	Hard tipped and other metal cutting tools		
	Bandsaw blades (for all materials) manufacturing	390	322.2
	Bit stock drill manufacturing	390	322.2
	Broach (for metal-working machine tools) manufacturing	390	322.2
	Circular saw (for all materials) manufacturing	390	322.2
	Diamond tipped tool manufacturing	390	322.2
	Die (for machine tools) manufacturing	390	322.2
	Die pellet manufacturing	390	322.2
	End mill manufacturing	390	322.2
	Hacksaw blade, for machines (for all materials), manufacturing	390	322.2
	Hard metal tipped tool manufacturing	390	322.2
	Knives for machines manufacturing	392	322.2
	Lathe tool manufacturing	390	322.2
	Machine tool manufacturing	390	322.2
	Milling cutter manufacturing	390	322.2
	Mining tool (bit) manufacturing	390	325.1
	Planer tool manufacturing	390	322.2
	Reamer manufacturing	390	322.2
	Saw blades for machines (including wood cutting) manufacturing	391	322.2
	Slitting saw manufacturing	390	322.2
	Threading die manufacturing	390	322.2
	Threading tap manufacturing	390	322.2
	Tip (for cutting tools) manufacturing	390	322.2
	Twist drill manufacturing	390	322.2
3222/2	Press tools		
	Die (press tool) manufacturing	390	322.2
	Mould (engineers' small tools) manufacturing	390	322.2
	Press tool manufacturing	390	322.2
3222/3	Other engineers' small tools		
	Drill chuck manufacturing	390	322.2
	Fixtures (engineers' small tools) manufacturing	390	322.2
	Jig manufacturing	390	322.2
	Lathe chuck manufacturing	390	322.2
	Tool holder manufacturing	390	322.2
	Work holder (engineers' small tools) manufacturing	390	322.2
3230/1	Textile machinery for processing fibres		
	Blowroom machinery (textile) manufacturing	335	323.1
	Carding machinery (textile) manufacturing	335	323.1

SIC 1980	Activity	SIC 1968	NACE
	Combing machinery (textile) manufacturing	335	323.1
	Cutting machinery (textile fibre) manufacturing	335	323.1
	Doubling machinery (textile) manufacturing	335	323.1
	Drawing machinery (textile) manufacturing	335	323.1
	Extruding machinery (textile) manufacturing	335	323.1
	Spinning machinery (textile) manufacturing	335	323.1
	Texturing and softening machinery (textile) manufacturing	335	323.1
	Twisting machinery (textile) manufacturing	335	323.1
	Winding machinery (textile) manufacturing	335	323.1
3230/2	Textile machinery for producing fabrics and carpets		
	Automatic stop motions (textile machinery) manufacturing	335	323.1
	Backing and curling machinery (carpet making) manufacturing	335	323.1
	Beaming machinery (textile) manufacturing	335	323.1
	Card tape reader (for textile machinery) manufacturing	335	323.1
	Carpet making machinery manufacturing	335	323.1
	Dobby (textile machinery) manufacturing	335	323.1
	Film reader (for textile machinery) manufacturing	335	323.1
	Hosiery knitting machinery manufacturing	335	323.1
	Jacquard (textile machinery) manufacturing	335	323.1
	Jacquard machinery (carpet making) manufacturing	335	323.1
	Knitting machine manufacturing	335	323.1
	Loom manufacturing	335	323.1
	Loom winder manufacturing	335	323.1
	Reaching-in machinery (textile) manufacturing	335	323.1
	Reeling machinery (textile) manufacturing	335	323.1
	Shuttle changing mechanism manufacturing	335	323.1
	Spooling machinery (carpet making) manufacturing	335	323.1
	Textile fabric making machinery manufacturing	335	323.1
	Tufting machinery (carpet making) manufacturing	335	323.1
	Warping machinery manufacturing	335	323.1
	Weaving machinery (loom) manufacturing	335	323.1
3230/3	Finishing and other textile machinery		
	Bleaching machinery (textile) manufacturing	335	323.1
	Calendering machinery (textile) manufacturing	335	323.1
	Coating machinery (textile) manufacturing	335	323.1
	Crabbing machinery (textile) manufacturing	335	323.1
	Cropping machinery (textile) manufacturing	335	323.1
	Curing machinery (textile) manufacturing	335	323.1
	Cutting machinery (textile fabric) manufacturing	335	323.1
	De-sizing machinery (textile) manufacturing	335	323.1
	Decatising machinery (textile) manufacturing	335	323.1
	Drying machinery (textile) manufacturing	335	323.1
	Dye cycle controller (textile machinery) manufacturing	335	323.1
	Dyeing machinery (textile) manufacturing	335	323.1
	Embossing machinery (textile) manufacturing	335	323.1
	Finishing machinery (textile) manufacturing	335	323.1
	Heat-setting machinery (textile) manufacturing	335	323.1
	Mercerising machinery (textile) manufacturing	335	323.1
	Milling machinery (textile) manufacturing	335	323.1
	Plaiting machinery (textile) manufacturing	335	323.1
	Printing machinery (textile) manufacturing	335	323.1
	Programmer (textile machinery) manufacturing	335	323.1
	Raising machinery (textile) manufacturing	335	323.1
	Rigging machinery (textile) manufacturing	335	323.1
	Scouring machinery (textile) manufacturing	335	323.1
	Shearing machinery (textile) manufacturing	335	323.1
	Shrinking machinery (textile) manufacturing	335	323.1
	Singeing machinery (textile) manufacturing	335	323.1
	Sizing machinery (textile) manufacturing	335	323.1
	Slitting machinery (textile) manufacturing	335	323.1
	Steaming machinery (textile) manufacturing	335	323.1
	Stentering machinery (textile) manufacturing	335	323.1
	Washing machine (textile) manufacturing	335	323.1
3230/4	Accessories for use with textile machinery		
	Bobbin (textile machinery accessory) manufacturing	335	323.1
	Comb (textile machinery accessory) manufacturing	335	323.1
	Cots (textile machinery accessory) manufacturing	335	323.1
	Dyesprings (textile machinery accessory) manufacturing	335	323.1
	Fallers (textile machinery accessory) manufacturing	335	323.1
	Healds (textile machinery accessory) manufacturing	335	323.1
	Pirns (textile machinery accessory) manufacturing	335	323.1
	Reed (textile machinery accessory) manufacturing	335	323.1
	Ring traveller (textile machinery accessory) manufacturing	335	323.1

SIC 1980	Activity	SIC 1968	NACE
	Roller (textile machinery accessory) manufacturing	335	323.1
	Shuttle (textile machinery accessory) manufacturing	335	323.1
	Sliver can (textile machinery accessory) manufacturing	335	323.1
	Spindle (textile machinery accessory) manufacturing	335	323.1
	Spool (textile machinery accessory) manufacturing	335	323.1
	Teasel rod (textile machinery accessory) manufacturing	335	323.1
	Thread guide (textile machinery accessory) manufacturing	335	323.1
3244/1	**Food and drink processing machinery**		
	Bakery machinery and oven manufacturing	339/7	324.1
	Beverage processing machinery manufacturing	339/7	324.1
	Biscuit making machinery and oven manufacturing	339/7	324.1
	Brewing machinery and plant manufacturing	339/7	324.1
	Cheese press manufacturing	339/7	324.1
	Chocolate and cocoa making machinery manufacturing	339/7	324.1
	Cider making machinery manufacturing	339/7	324.1
	Coffee processing machinery manufacturing	339/7	324.1
	Confectionery machinery manufacturing	339/7	324.1
	Cream separator (industrial) manufacturing	339/7	324.1
	Crusher (food or drink machinery) manufacturing	339/7	324.1
	Dairy machinery and plant (not agricultural) manufacturing	339/7	324.1
	Distilling machinery (for potable spirits) manufacturing	339/7	324.1
	Dough making machinery manufacturing	339/7	324.1
	Drink processing (including combined processing and packaging or bottling machinery) manufacturing	339/7	324.1
	Edible oil and fat processing machinery manufacturing	339/7	324.1
	Flour confectionery machinery manufacturing	339/7	324.1
	Food processing (including combined processing and packaging or bottling machinery) manufacturing	339/7	324.1
	Fruit juice preparation machinery manufacturing	339/7	324.1
	Grain processing machinery and plant manufacturing	341/2	324.1
	Meat processing machinery manufacturing	339/7	324.1
	Milk pasturisation plant manufacturing	339/7	324.1
	Milling (food processing) machine manufacturing	339/7	324.1
	Mustard processing machine manufacturing	339/7	324.1
	Oven (food processing) machine manufacturing	339/7	324.1
	Pastry roller (food preparation machinery) manufacturing	339/7	324.1
	Press (for food and drink manufacture) manufacturing	339/7	324.1
	Slaughterhouse machinery manufacturing	339/7	324.1
	Soft drink machinery manufacturing	339/7	324.1
	Sterilisation (for food and drink) equipment manufacturing	339/7	324.1
	Sugar confectionery making machinery manufacturing	339/7	324.1
	Sugar making and refining machinery manufacturing	339/7	324.1
	Tea processing machinery and plant manufacturing	339/7	324.1
	Vinegar processing machine manufacturing	339/7	324.1
	Wine making machinery manufacturing	339/7	324.1
3244/2	**Packaging and bottling machinery**		
	Baling press (not agricultural) manufacturing	339/8	324.2
	Bottle cleaning and/or drying machinery manufacturing	339/8	324.2
	Bottling machinery manufacturing	339/8	324.2
	Canning machinery manufacturing	339/8	324.2
	Capsuling machinery manufacturing	339/8	324.2
	Cartoning machinery manufacturing	339/8	324.2
	Case packing machinery manufacturing	339/8	324.2
	Closing machinery manufacturing	339/8	324.2
	Crating and de-crating machinery manufacturing	339/8	324.2
	Filling machinery manufacturing	339/8	324.2
	Labelling machinery (not for office use) manufacturing	339/8	324.2
	Packaging machinery manufacturing	339/8	324.2
	Packing machinery manufacturing	339/8	324.2
	Sealing machinery manufacturing	339/8	324.2
	Wrapping machinery manufacturing	339/8	324.2
3244/3	**Tobacco processing machinery**		
	Cigar making machinery manufacturing	339/9	324.1
	Cigarette making machinery manufacturing	339/9	324.1
	Tobacco processing machinery manufacturing	339/9	324.1
3245/1	**Chemical industry machinery**		
	Centrifuge (for chemical industry) manufacturing	339/9	324.1
	Chemical industry machinery (other than plant) manufacturing	339/9	324.1
	Crystalliser (for chemical industry) manufacturing	339/9	324.1
	Drying machine (for chemical industry) manufacturing	339/9	328.4
	Filtration equipment (for chemical industry) manufacturing	339/9	324.1
	Granulator (for chemical industry) manufacturing	339/9	324.1
	Industrial mixing equipment (for chemical industry) manufacturing	339/9	324.1
	Oil refining industry machinery (other than plant) manufacturing	339/9	324.1
	Petro-chemical industry machinery (other than plant) manufacturing	339/9	324.1
	Pulverising machinery (for chemical industry) manufacturing	339/9	324.1
	Size reduction equipment (for chemical industry) manufacturing	339/9	324.1

SIC 1980	Activity	SIC 1968	NACE
	Size separation equipment (for chemical industry) manufacturing	339/9	324.1
	Soap making machinery manufacturing	339/9	324.1
	Solvent extraction equipment (for chemical industry) manufacturing	339/9	324.1
	Solvent recovery equipment (for chemical industry) manufacturing	339/9	324.1
	Tableting and pelleting press (for chemical industry) manufacturing	339/9	324.1
3245/2	Furnaces and kilns		
	Blast furnace manufacturing	341/2	328.6
	Box furnace manufacturing	341/2	328.6
	Cement processing kiln manufacturing	341/2	328.6
	Direct arc furnace manufacturing	341/2	343.1
	Electric furnace manufacturing	341/2	343.1
	Electro-slag furnace manufacturing	341/2	343.1
	Forging furnace manufacturing	341/2	328.6
	Furnace (for strip processing line) manufacturing	341/2	328.6
	Heat treatment furnace manufacturing	341/2	328.6
	Induction furnace manufacturing	341/2	343.1
	Laboratory furnace manufacturing	341/2	328.6
	Lime processing kiln manufacturing	341/2	328.6
	Melting furnace manufacturing	341/2	328.6
	Re-heating furnace manufacturing	341/2	328.6
	Steelmaking furnace manufacturing	341/2	328.6
3245/3	Gas, water and waste treatment plant		
	Aeration plant (effluent treatment) manufacturing	341/2	324.1
	Air cleansing plant (not for air conditioning equipment) manufacturing	341/2	328.4
	Base exchange plant (water treatment) manufacturing	341/2	324.1
	Chlorination plant (water treatment) manufacturing	341/2	324.1
	Clarification plant (water treatment) manufacturing	341/2	324.1
	Comminution plant (effluent treatment) manufacturing	341/2	324.1
	De-aeration plant (water treatment) manufacturing	341/2	324.1
	Desalination plant (water treatment) manufacturing	341/2	324.1
	Dialysis plant (water treatment) manufacturing	341/2	324.1
	Dosing plant (water treatment) manufacturing	341/2	324.1
	Effluent treatment plant manufacturing	341/2	324.1
	Electrostatic precipitator manufacturing	341/2	343
	Gas cleansing plant manufacturing	341/2	328.4
	Grit extraction plant (effluent treatment) manufacturing	341/2	324.1
	Incinerator manufacturing	341/2	328.6
	Ion exchange plant (water treatment) manufacturing	341/2	324.1
	Pollution control plant, atmospheric, manufacturing	341/2	328.4
	Refuse disposal plant manufacturing	341/2	324.1
	Screening plant (effluent treatment) manufacturing	336	324.1
	Sedimentation plant (effluent treatment) manufacturing	341/2	324.1
	Settlement plant (water treatment) manufacturing	341/2	324.1
	Sewage treatment plant manufacturing	341/2	324.1
	Water softening plant manufacturing	341/2	324.1
	Water treatment plant manufacturing	341/2	324.1
3246	Process engineering contractors		
	Engineering contractor responsible for complete process plant	341/3	324
	Process engineering contractor	341/3	324
3251	Mining machinery		
	Borer (mining machinery) manufacturing	339/1	325.1
	Cage plant (mining) manufacturing	339/1	325.1
	Coal cutter manufacturing	339/1	325.1
	Coal plough manufacturing	339/1	325.1
	Coal preparation plant manufacturing	339/1	325.1
	Continuous miner manufacturing	339/1	325.1
	Conveyor, underground, (mining) manufacturing	339/1	325.1
	Crushing machine (mining) manufacturing	339/1	325.1
	Dinting machine (mining) manufacturing	339/1	325.1
	Hauling engine, stationary, (mining) manufacturing	339/1	325.1
	Heading machine (mining) manufacturing	339/1	325.1
	Loader (mining) manufacturing	339/1	325.1
	Mineral cutter manufacturing	339/1	325.1
	Mineral dressing plant manufacturing	339/1	325.1
	Pit bottom machinery manufacturing	339/1	325.1
	Powered roof support (mining) manufacturing	339/1	314.3
	Ranging drum shearer (mining) manufacturing	339/1	325.1
	Road ripper (mining) manufacturing	339/1	325.1
	Rock drilling machinery manufacturing	339/1	325.1
	Rocker shovel (mining) manufacturing	339/1	325.1
	Roof support, hydraulic, manufacturing	339/1	314.3
	Sinking machine (mining) manufacturing	339/1	325.1
	Skip plant (mining) manufacturing	339/1	325.1
	Stowing machine (mining) manufacturing	339/1	325.1
	Tunnelling machine (mining) manufacturing	339/1	325.1
	Winding machine (mining) manufacturing	339/1	325.1
3254/1	Earth moving equipment		
	Bucket (construction machinery) manufacturing	336	325.4
	Crawler loader manufacturing	336	325.4
	Crawler tractor manufacturing	336	325.4
	Dozer blade manufacturing	336	325.4
	Dragline excavator manufacturing	336	325.4
	Draglines, walking manufacturing	336	325.4
	Dump truck manufacturing	336	325.4
	Dumper manufacturing	336	325.4
	Earth leveller manufacturing	336	325.4
	Earth mover (construction equipment) manufacturing	336	325.4
	Excavator manufacturing	336	325.4
	Grab manufacturing	336	325.4
	Grader manufacturing	336	325.4
	Land clearing equipment machinery manufacturing	336	325.4
	Loading shovel manufacturing	336	325.4
	Powered barrow manufacturing	336	325.4

SIC 1980	Activity	SIC 1968	NACE
	Rear digger manufacturing	336	325.4
	Rear digger unit manufacturing	336	325.4
	Ripper manufacturing	336	325.4
	Rooter (not agricultural) manufacturing	336	325.4
	Scraper (earth moving equipment) manufacturing	336	325.4
	Tractor shovel manufacturing	336	325.4
	Tractor winch manufacturing	336	325.4
	Trencher manufacturing	336	325.4
3254/2	Equipment for concrete, crushing and screening, and road works		
	Asphalt laying plant manufacturing	336	325.4
	Asphalt processing plant manufacturing	336	325.4
	Concrete mixer manufacturing	336	325.4
	Concrete placing machinery manufacturing	336	325.4
	Crushing plant (not for mines) manufacturing	336	325.3
	Gritting machine manufacturing	336	325.4
	Pulverising plant (not for mines) manufacturing	336	325.3
	Road roller manufacturing	336	325.4
	Screening plant (not for mines) manufacturing	336	325.3
	Snow blower manufacturing	336	325.4
	Snow plough manufacturing	336	325.4
	Tar laying plant manufacturing	336	325.4
	Tar macadam laying plant manufacturing	336	325.4
	Tar macadam processing plant manufacturing	336	325.4
	Tar processing plant manufacturing	336	325.4
3254/3	Pile driving, well drilling and other construction equipment		
	Earth boring machine manufacturing	336	325.4
	Petroleum drilling equipment manufacturing	336	325.1
	Pile driving equipment manufacturing	336	325.4
	Well drilling equipment manufacturing	336	325.1
3255/1	Conveyors, aerial ropeways, hoists and handling plant		
	Aerial ropeway and cableway manufacturing	337/1	325.5
	Bucket wheel reclaimer manufacturing	337/1	325.5
	Cableway manufacturing	337/1	325.5
	Cableway excavator manufacturing	337/1	325.5
	Conveying plant (hydraulic and pneumatic) manufacturing	337/1	325.5
	Conveyor and feeder (not for agriculture or mining) manufacturing	337/1,	325.5
	Drag scraper manufacturing	337/1	325.4
	Elevator manufacturing	337/1	325.5
	Handling plant (hydraulic and pneumatic) manufacturing	337/1	325.5
	Hoist (hydraulic, mechanical and pneumatic), other than builders', hand operated and electric types, manufacturing	337/1	325.5
	Live storage rack manufacturing	337/1	325.5
	Overhead runway manufacturing	337/1	325.5
	Pallet hoist manufacturing	337/1	325.5
	Palletizer manufacturing	337/1	325.5
	Stacking machine manufacturing	337/1	325.5
	Suspension railway manufacturing	337/1	325.5
	Tipper manufacturing	337/1	325.5
3255/2	Cranes and transporters		
	Container handling crane manufacturing	337/2	325.5
	Crane manufacturing	337/2	325.5
	Dockside crane manufacturing	337/2	325.5
	Goliath type crane manufacturing	337/2	325.5
	Mobile crane manufacturing	337/2	325.5
	Special steelworks crane manufacturing	337/2	325.5
	Transporter manufacturing	337/2	325.5
	Travelling crane manufacturing	337/2	325.5
3255/3	Lifts and escalators		
	Escalator manufacturing	337/3	325.5
	Lift manufacturing	337/3	325.5
	Passenger conveyor manufacturing	337/3	325.5
3255/4	Lifting and winding devices		
	Builders' hoist manufacturing	337/4	325.5
	Capstan manufacturing	337/4	325.5
	Chain pulley block manufacturing	337/4	325.5
	Dock leveller manufacturing	337/4	325.5
	Hoist (electric, wire rope or chain) manufacturing	337/4	325.5
	Hoist (hand operated, pulley and sheave block) manufacturing	337/4	325.5
	Jacks (other than for motor vehicles) manufacturing	337/4	325.5
	Lorry loader manufacturing	337/4	325.5
	Motor vehicle jack manufacturing	337/4	325.5
	Motor vehicle lift manufacturing	337/4	325.5
	Pulley block manufacturing	337/4	325.5
	Scissor lift manufacturing	337/4	325.5
	Tailboard lift manufacturing	337/4	325.5
	Winch manufacturing	337/4	325.5
	Winding device manufacturing	337/4	325.5
	Windlass manufacturing	337/4	325.5
3255/5	Powered industrial trucks		
	Fork-lift truck manufacturing	337/5	325.5
	Industrial tractor manufacturing	337/5	325.5
	Industrial trucks, special purpose manufacturing	337/5	325.5
	Pallet truck manufacturing	337/5	325.5
	Rough terrain industrial trucks manufacturing	337/5	325.5
	Side loader manufacturing	337/5	325.5
	Stillage truck manufacturing	337/5	325.5
	Straddle carrier manufacturing	337/5	325.5
3261/1	Precision chains		
	Bicycle chain manufacturing	349/2	326.1
	Precision chain manufacturing	349/2	326.1
	Sprocket chain manufacturing	349/2	326.1
	Transmission chain manufacturing	349/2	326.1
3261/2	Plain bearings and bushes		
	Bush (for bearing) manufacturing	349/1	326.1
	Plain bearing manufacturing	349/1	326.1
3261/3	Other mechanical power transmission equipment including gears and gear boxes		
	Camshaft (not for motor vehicle etc. engine) manufacturing	349/3	326.1
	Clutch (not for motor vehicle etc.) manufacturing	349/3	326.1
	Crankshaft (not for motor vehicle etc. engine) manufacturing	349/3	326.1
	Flywheel (not for motor vehicle etc. engine) manufacturing	349/3	326.1
	Gear box (not for motor vehicle etc.) manufacturing	349/3	326.1

SIC 1980	Activity	SIC 1968	NACE
	Gear cutting (not for motor vehicle etc.)	349/3	326.1
	Geared motor unit manufacturing	361/3	326.1
	Mechanical power transmission plant manufacturing	349/2	326.1
	Pulley manufacturing	349/3	326.1
	Pulley wheel manufacturing	349/3	326.1
3262	Ball, needle and roller bearings		
	Ball bearing manufacturing	349/1	326.2
	Cylindrical roller bearing manufacturing	349/1	326.2
	Needle roller bearing manufacturing	349/1	326.2
	Roller bearing manufacturing	349/1	326.2
	Spherical roller bearing manufacturing	349/1	326.2
	Tapered roller bearing manufacturing	349/1	326.2
3275/1	Woodworking machinery		
	Chipboard press manufacturing	339/9	327.1
	Cutter (for wood) manufacturing	339/9	327.1
	Moulding machine (for wood etc.) manufacturing	339/9	327.1
	Planing machine (for wood) (not portable power) manufacturing	339/9	327.1
	Plywood press manufacturing	339/9	327.1
	Sanding and polishing machines for wood (not portable) manufacturing	339/9	327.1
	Sawing machine (for wood) manufacturing	339/9	327.1
	Veneer press manufacturing	339/9	327.1
	Woodworking machinery manufacturing	339.9	327.1
3275/2	Rubber and plastics working machinery		
	Blow moulding machine manufacturing	339/9	324.3
	Calender (for rubber or plastics working) manufacturing	339/9	324.3
	Extruder (for rubber or plastics) manufacturing	339/9	324.3
	Forming machine (for rubber or plastics) manufacturing	339/9	327.1
	Injection moulding machine manufacturing	339/9	324.3
	Mixing machine (rubber or plastics working) manufacturing	339/9	324.3
	Moulding machine (rubber or plastics working) manufacturing	339/9	327.1
	Plastics working machinery manufacturing	339/9	324.3
	Presses (rubber or plastics working) machinery manufacturing	339/9	327.1
	Pressure forming machine (for rubber or plastics) manufacturing	339/9	327.1
	Roll mill (for rubber or plastics) manufacturing	339/9	324.3
	Rubber working machinery manufacturing	339/9	324.3
	Thermo-forming machine manufacturing	339/9	324.3
	Transfer moulding press (for rubber or plastics) manufacturing	399/9	324.3
	Vacuum forming machine manufacturing	399/9	324.3
	Vulcanising machines (rubber and plastics working) manufacturing	339/9	327.1
3275/3	Leatherworking and footwear making and repairing machinery		
	Footwear making machine manufacturing	339/9	327.4
	Footwear repairing machine manufacturing	339/9	327.4
	Leather working machine manufacturing	339/9	327.4
3275/4	Paper making machinery		
	Board (except chipboard) making machine manufacturing	339/9	327.2
	Fourdrinier manufacturing	339/9	327.2
	Paper making machine manufacturing	339/9	327.2
	Pulp making machine manufacturing	399/9	327.2
	Stock preparation plant (paper or board) manufacturing	339/9	327.2
3275/5	Glass and brick making and similar machinery		
	Annealing lehr manufacturing	339/9	328.6
	Brickmaking machine manufacturing	339/9	325.3
	Cement block making machine manufacturing	339/9	325.3
	Ceramic making machine manufacturing	339/9	325.3
	Concrete block making machine manufacturing	339/9	325.3
	Electric lamp making machine manufacturing	339/9	325.3
	Forming machine (multi-head; glass working) manufacturing	339/9	325.3
	Glass making machine manufacturing	339/9	325.3
	Glass working machine manufacturing	339/9	325.3
	Grinding machine (for glass etc.) manufacturing	339/9	325.3
	Polishing machine (for glass) manufacturing	339/9	325.3
	Pottery making machine manufacturing	339/9	325.3
	Tile making machine (not plastics working) manufacturing	339/9	325.3
3275/6	Laundry and dry cleaning machinery		
	Dry cleaning machinery manufacturing	339/9	327.3
	Drying machine (for laundry or dry cleaner) manufacturing	339/9	327.3
	Flatwork machine (for laundry) manufacturing	339/9	327.3
	Ironing machine (non domestic) manufacturing	339/9	327.3
	Laundry machinery manufacturing	339/9	327.3
	Spotting table manufacturing	339/9	327.3
	Washing machine (laundry) manufacturing	339/9	327.3
3276	Printing, bookbinding and paper goods machinery		
	Blocking machine manufacturing	339/2	327.2
	Bookbinding machine manufacturing	339/2	327.2
	Cardboard box making machine manufacturing	339/2	327.2
	Carton making machine manufacturing	339/2	327.2
	Coating machine (bookbinding or paper working) manufacturing	339/2	327.2
	Collating machine (bookbinders') manufacturing	339/2	327.2
	Composing room equipment manufacturing	339/2	327.2
	Creasing machine (bookbinding) manufacturing	339/2	327.2
	Cutting machine (bookbinding) manufacturing	339/2	327.2

SIC 1980	Activity	SIC 1968	NACE
	Embossing machine (paper and board working) manufacturing	339/2	327.2
	Envelope making machine manufacturing	339/2	327.2
	Flexographic printing machine manufacturing	339/2	327.2
	Folding machinery (for paper and board not for office use) manufacturing	339/2	327.2
	Gathering machine (paper working) manufacturing	339/2	327.2
	Glueing machinery (bookbinders' etc.) manufacturing	339/2	327.2
	Gravure printing machine manufacturing	339/2	327.2
	Laminating machinery (paper working) manufacturing	339/2	327.2
	Letterpress printing machine manufacturing	339/2	327.2
	Matrice manufacturing	339/2	327.2
	Offset litho printing machine manufacturing	339/2	327.2
	Paper bag making machinery manufacturing	339/2	327.2
	Photoengraving machine manufacturing	339/2	327.2
	Photogravure machine manufacturing	339/2	327.2
	Photolitho machine manufacturing	339/2	327.2
	Printing machine or press manufacturing	339/2	327.2
	Ruling machinery (printers') manufacturing	339/2	327.2
	Scanner (printing machinery) manufacturing	339/2	327.2
	Sewing machinery (bookbinding) manufacturing	339/2	327.2
	Slitting machine (for paper) manufacturing	339/2	327.2
	Stitching machine (bookbinding) manufacturing	339/2	327.2
	Type setting machine manufacturing	339/2	327.2
3281/1	**Industrial internal combustion engines**		
	Agricultural machinery engine manufacturing	334/1	328.1
	Block (for industrial engine) manufacturing	334/1	328.1
	Carburettor (for industrial engine) manufacturing	334/1	328.1
	Combine harvester engine manufacturing	334/1	328.1
	Compression ignition engine (for industrial use) manufacturing	334/1	328.1
	Compressor engine manufacturing	334/1	328.1
	Construction equipment engine manufacturing	334/1	328.1
	Cylinder head (for industrial engine) manufacturing	334/1	328.1
	Diesel engine (for industrial use) manufacturing	334/1	328.1
	Fork lift truck engine manufacturing	334/1	328.1
	Fuel injection equipment (for industrial engine) manufacturing	334/1	328.1
	Fuel pump (for industrial engine) manufacturing	334/1	328.1
	Generator engine manufacturing	334/1	328.1
	Industrial engine (spark or compression ignition) manufacturing	334/1	328.1
	Lawn mower engine manufacturing	334/1	328.1
	Locomotive engine manufacturing	334/1	328.1
	Manifold (for industrial engine) manufacturing	334/1	328.1
	Parts of industrial engine manufacturing	334/1	328.1
	Petrol engine (industrial) manufacturing	334/1	328.1
	Railway vehicle engine manufacturing	334/1	328.1
	Spark-ignition engine (industrial) manufacturing	334/1	328.1
3281/2	**Marine engines**		
	Gas turbine (marine) manufacturing	370/2	328.1 and 328.2
	Marine engine manufacturing	370/2	328.1 and 328.2
	Non-propulsion engine, marine, manufacturing	370/2	328.1 and 328.2
	Propulsion engine, marine, manufacturing	370/2	328.1 and 328.2
	Slow speed diesel engine, marine, manufacturing	370/2	328.1
	Steam turbine, marine, manufacturing	370/2	328.2
3281/3	**Other prime movers**		
	Gas turbine (industrial engine) manufacturing	334/1	328.2
	Steam engine manufacturing	334/2	328.2
	Steam turbine (not marine or for electricity generation) manufacturing	334/2	328.2
3283/1	**Compressors**		
	Air compressor manufacturing	333/3	328.3
	Axial compressor manufacturing	333/3	328.3
	Centrifugal compressor manufacturing	333/3	328.3
	Exhauster manufacturing	333/3	328.3
	Gas compressor manufacturing	333/3	328.3
	Reciprocating compressor manufacturing	333/3	328.3
	Rotating compressor manufacturing	333/3	328.3
	Screw compressor manufacturing	333/3	328.3
	Vacuum pump manufacturing	333/3	328.3
3283/2	**Oil hydraulic equipment**		
	Accumulator for hydraulic equipment manufacturing	333/4	328.3
	Actuator for hydraulic equipment manufacturing	333/4	328.3
	Cylinder for hydraulic equipment manufacturing	333/4	328.3
	Filtration equipment for hydraulic equipment manufacturing	333/4	328.3
	Flowline assembly (hydraulic equipment) manufacturing	333/4	328.3
	Hydrostatic transmission manufacturing	333/4	328.3
	Intensifier (hydraulic equipment) manufacturing	333/4	328.3
	Motor for hydraulic equipment manufacturing	333/4	328.3
	Pump for hydraulic equipment manufacturing	333/4	328.3
	Reservoir (hydraulic) manufacturing	333/4	328.3
	Surge damper (hydraulic equipment) manufacturing	333/4	328.3
	Valve for hydraulic equipment manufacturing	333/4	328.3

SIC 1980	Activity	SIC 1968	NACE
3283/3	Pneumatic control equipment		
	Cylinder (pneumatic control equipment) manufacturing	333/4	328.3
	Filter (pneumatic control equipment) manufacturing	333/4	328.3
	Hydro-pneumatic device manufacturing	333/4	328.3
	Intensifier (pneumatic control equipment) manufacturing	333/4	328.3
	Motor (pneumatic) manufacturing	333/4	328.3
	Positioner (pneumatic control equipment) manufacturing	333/4	328.3
	Reservoir (pneumatic) manufacturing	333/4	328.3
	Tube coupling and equipment (pneumatic) manufacturing	333/4	328.3
	Valve for pneumatic control equipment manufacturing	333/2	328.3
3284/1	Refrigerating machinery		
	Cold storage equipment manufacturing	339/3	328.5
	Compressor (for refrigerator) manufacturing	339/3	328.5
	Condenser (for refrigerator) manufacturing	339/3	328.5
	Condensing unit (for refrigerator) manufacturing	339/3	328.5
	Display cabinet, refrigerated, manufacturing	339/3	328.5
	Evaporator (refrigeration machinery) manufacturing	339/3	328.5
	Food freezer (over 12 cu. ft.) manufacturing	339/3	328.5
	Ice cream conservator manufacturing	339/3	328.5
	Sectional coldroom manufacturing	339/3	328.5
	Service cabinet, refrigerated, manufacturing	339/3	328.5
3284/2	Space heating equipment		
	Boiler, central heating, manufacturing	339/4	311.1 or 315.1
	Calorifier manufacturing	339/4	328.4
	Cylinder, direct and indirect, space-heating equipment, manufacturing	339/4	328.4
	Heat emitter (space-heating equipment) manufacturing	339/4	328.4
	Radiant panel (space-heating equipment) manufacturing	339/4	328.4
	Radiator (space-heating equipment) manufacturing	339/4	328.4
	Warm air generator manufacturing	339/4	328.4
3284/3	Fans and other ventilating equipment		
	Fans, ventilating, manufacturing	339/4	328.4
	Ventilating unit manufacturing	339/4	328.4
3284/4	Air conditioning equipment		
	Air conditioning package manufacturing	339/4	328.4
	Air filter manufacturing	339/4	328.4
	Condenser (air or water cooled for air conditioning equipment) manufacturing	339/4	328.4
	Cooling tower (for air conditioning) manufacturing	339/4	328.4
	Dust collector (air conditioning equipment) manufacturing	339/4	328.4
	Fan coil unit (for air conditioning equipment) manufacturing	339/4	328.4
	Humidifier manufacturing	339/4	328.4
	Induction unit (air conditioning equipment) manufacturing	339/4	328.4
	Scrubber (air conditioning equipment) manufacturing	339/4	328.4
3284/5	Burners		
	Fuel (other than oil or gas) burner manufacturing	399/9	328.6
	Gas burner manufacturing	399/9	328.6
	Oil fuel burner manufacturing	349/3	328.6
3285/1	Scales and weighing machinery		
	Scales, domestic, manufacturing	339/5	316.7
	Scales, platform, manufacturing	339/5	328.9
	Scales, postal, manufacturing	339/5	328.9
	Scales, retail, manufacturing	339/5	328.9
	Spring balance manufacturing	339/5	328.9
	Weighbridge manufacturing	339/5	328.9
	Weighing machine manufacturing	339/5	328.9
	Weight (for weighing machine) manufacturing	339/5	316.9
3285/2	Portable power tools		
	Drill (powered), portable, manufacturing	339/6	343.1
	Electric portable power tool manufacturing	339/6	343.1
	Flexible shaft drive tool manufacturing	339/6	not classified
	Grinding tool (powered), portable, manufacturing	339/6	not classified
	Hammer (powered), portable manufacturing	339/6	not classified
	Hedge trimmer (powered), portable manufacturing	339/6	not classified
	Mining tool (powered), portable, manufacturing	339/6	325.1
	Pneumatic portable power tool manufacturing	339/6	328.3
	Portable power tool manufacturing	339/6	not classified
	Power tool, electric, portable, manufacturing	339/6	343.1
	Powered hammer, portable, manufacturing	339/6	not classified
	Rock drill (portable) manufacturing	339/6	325.1
	Sanding tool (powered), portable manufacturing	339/6	not classified
	Saw (powered), portable, manufacturing	339/6	not classified
3286/1	Industrial and commercial machinery and service equipment		
	Amusement (automatic slot) machine manufacturing	339/9	328.9

SIC 1980	Activity	SIC 1968	NACE
	Carpet shampoo appliance (not domestic electric) manufacturing	339/9	328.9
	Carpet sweeper manufacturing	339/9	328.9
	Dishwashing machine (commercial catering type) manufacturing	339/9	324.1
	Fire extinguishing apparatus (excluding hand operated chemical extinguishers) manufacturing	339/9	328.9
	Gaming (automatic slot) machine manufacturing	339/9	328.9
	Garage equipment and plant manufacturing	339/9	328.9
	Lawn mower manufacturing	339/9	321.1
	Mowers for lawns, parks and sportsgrounds manufacturing	339/9	321.1
	Sewing machine manufacturing	339/9	323.2
	Sprinkler (for fire extinguishing) manufacturing	339/9	328.9
	Testing machine and equipment manufacturing	339/9	328.9
	Vending machine manufacturing	339/9	328.9
3286/2	Machinery for foundries and rolling mills		
	Castings machines (for foundries) manufacturing	339/9	325.2
	Die-casting machine (for foundries) manufacturing	339/9	325.2
	Investment casting equipment manufacturing	339/9	325.2
	Mould (for foundry) manufacturing	339/9	325.2
	Mould preparation plant manufacturing	339/9	325.2
	Moulding machine manufacturing	339/9	325.2
	Rolling mill (for metals) manufacturing	339/9	325.2
	Sand handling, mixing, treatment or reclamation plant (for foundries) manufacturing	339/9	325.2
	Tube mill plant manufacturing	339/9	322.1
3286/3	Manufacture of other machinery and mechanical equipment not elsewhere specified		
	Battery making machine manufacturing	339/9	328.9
	Cable making machine manufacturing	339/9	328.9
	Metal spraying machine manufacturing	339/9	328.7
	Paint spraying machine manufacturing	339/9	328.3
	Rope making machine manufacturing	339/9	328.9
	Wire coiling machine manufacturing	339/9	322.1
	Wire rope making machine manufacturing	339/9	328.9
	Wire weaving machine manufacturing	339/9	322.1
3287	Pumps		
	Archimedian screw pump manufacturing	333/1	328.3
	Axial flow pump manufacturing	333/1	328.3
	Centrifugal pump manufacturing	333/1	328.3
	Channel impeller pump manufacturing	333/1	328.3
	Circulator pump manufacturing	333/1	328.3
	Delivery pump manufacturing	333/1	328.3
	Diaphragm pump manufacturing	333/1	328.3
	Dosing and proportioning pump manufacturing	333/1	328.3
	Ejector pump manufacturing	333/1	328.3
	Hand pump manufacturing	333/1	328.3
	Helical rotor pump manufacturing	333/1	328.3
	Jet pump manufacturing	333/1	328.3
	Lobe pump manufacturing	333/1	328.3
	Lubricating pump (not for internal combustion engine) manufacturing	333/1	328.3
	Metering pump manufacturing	333/1	328.3
	Petrol station pump manufacturing	333/1	328.3
	Positive displacement pump (reciprocating) manufacturing	333/1	328.3
	Pump (not hydraulic or for internal combustion engine) manufacturing	333/1	328.3
	Radial flow pump manufacturing	333/1	328.3
	Screw pump manufacturing	333/1	328.3
	Submersible motor pump manufacturing	333/1	328.3
	Vane pump manufacturing	333/1	328.3
3288	Industrial valves		
	Automatic process control valve manufacturing	333/2	328.8
	Ball valve manufacturing	333/2	328.8
	Butterfly valve manufacturing	333/2	328.8
	Check valve manufacturing	333/2	328.8
	Cock (industrial type) manufacturing	333/2	328.8
	Diaphragm valve manufacturing	333/2	328.8
	Gate valve manufacturing	333/2	328.8
	Globe valve manufacturing	333/2	328.8
	Parallel slide valve manufacturing	333/2	328.8
	Penstock valve manufacturing	333/2	328.8
	Plug valve manufacturing	333/2	328.8
	Reducing valve manufacturing	333/2	328.8
	Relief valve manufacturing	333/2	328.8
	Safety valve manufacturing	333/2	328.8
3289/1	Marine engineering		
	Boiler (marine engineering) manufacturing	370/2	315.1
	Bow thruster manufacturing	370	361
	Decompression chamber manufacturing	349/3	371.7
	Diving equipment (excluding breathing apparatus) manufacturing	349/3	371.7
	Hatch cover (mechanically operated) manufacturing	370	361
	Propeller (marine—built-up or machined casting) manufacturing	370	361
	Reduction gear (marine) manufacturing	370	326.1
	Stabilizer (ship's) manufacturing	370	361
	Steering gear (marine) manufacturing	370	361
	Stern gear manufacturing	370	361
	Trawl door manufacturing	370	361
3289/2	Precision components for engines and machinery not elsewhere specified		
	Cylinder insert manufacturing	349/3	328.9
	Cylinder liner manufacturing	349/3	328.9
	Gasket manufacturing	349/3	328.9
	Jointing (precision component) manufacturing	349/3	328.9
	Lubricator manufacturing	349/3	328.9
	Moulding box manufacturing	349/3	322.2
	Oil seal manufacturing	349/3	328.9
	Piston manufacturing	349/3	328.9
	Piston ring manufacturing	349/3	328.9
3289/3	Mechanical engineering work not elsewhere specified		
	Brazing equipment (gas) manufacturing	332/3	328.7

SIC 1980	Activity	SIC 1968	NACE
	Cutting torch manufacturing	332/3	328.7
	Points and crossings for railway track manufacturing	311/2	314.4
	Railway signalling equipment (mechanical) manufacturing	384	328.9
	Railway track equipment (mechanical) manufacturing	384	314.4
	Rolls of iron or steel manufacturing	349/3	328.9
	Scaffolding manufacturing	341/5	314.1
	Soldering equipment (gas) manufacturing	332/3	328.7
	Valves for tyres manufacturing	349/3	328.8
	Welding machines (gas) manufacturing	332/3	328.7
	Welding torch manufacturing	332/3	328.7
	Wires or rods (for gas welding, soldering or brazing) manufacturing	332/3	223.4
3290/1	Ordnance and small arms		
	Air gun manufacturing	342	328.9
	Air pistol manufacturing	342	328.9
	Air rifle manufacturing	342	328.9
	Automatic gun manufacturing	342	328.9
	Gun manufacturing	342	328.9
	Gun carriage, mounting or platform manufacturing	342	328.9
	Howitzer manufacturing	342	328.9
	Machine gun manufacturing	342	328.9
	Military carbine manufacturing	342	328.9
	Military rifle manufacturing	342	328.9
	Mortar (ordnance) manufacturing	342	328.9
	Pistol manufacturing	342	328.9
	Revolver manufacturing	342	328.9
	Sporting carbine manufacturing	342	328.9
	Sporting gun manufacturing	342	328.9
	Sporting rifle manufacturing	342	328.9
3290/2	Ammunition		
	Aircraft bomb manufacturing	342	328.9
	Ammunition manufacturing	342	328.9
	Artillery ammunition manufacturing	342	328.9
	Bomb fuse manufacturing	342	328.9
	Cartridge case manufacturing	342	328.9
	Cartridge primer manufacturing	342	328.9
	Fuse (for shells and bombs) manufacturing	342	328.9
	Grenade manufacturing	342	328.9
	Guided weapon warhead manufacturing	342	328.9
	Mine case and component manufacturing	342	328.9
	Mortar bomb manufacturing	342	328.9
	Shell case manufacturing	342	328.9
	Shell fuse manufacturing	342	328.9
	Torpedo manufacturing	342	328.9
3290/3	Tracked armoured fighting vehicles		
	Bridgelayer (tracked military) manufacturing	342	328.9
	Personnel carrier (tracked armoured fighting vehicle) manufacturing	342	328.9
	Recovery vehicle (tracked military type) manufacturing	342	328.9
	Tank (armoured fighting vehicle) (tracked) manufacturing	342	328.9
3301	Office machinery		
	Accounting machine manufacturing	338	330
	Address plate embossing machine manufacturing	338	330
	Addressing machine manufacturing	338	330
	Bank note counting machine manufacturing	338	330
	Binding machine manufacturing	338	330
	Bookkeeping machine manufacturing	338	330
	Calculating machine manufacturing	338	330
	Calculator, electronic, manufacturing	338	330
	Cash and credit card imprinting and embossing machine manufacturing	338	330
	Cash dispenser manufacturing	338	330
	Cash register manufacturing	338	330
	Cheque-writing and signing machine manufacturing	338	330
	Coin sorting and coin counting machine manufacturing	338	330
	Counting and dating machine manufacturing	338	330
	Data processing equipment (non-electronic) manufacturing	338	330
	Document handling machine manufacturing	338	330
	Document shredder manufacturing	338	330
	Duplicating machine (excluding copiers) manufacturing	338	330
	Franking machine manufacturing	338	330
	Invoicing machine manufacturing	338	330
	Labelling machine (for office use) manufacturing	338	330
	Laminating machine (for office use) manufacturing	338	330
	Letter-opening machine manufacturing	338	330
	Listing machine manufacturing	338	330
	Mail handling machine manufacturing	338	330
	Point of sale unit manufacturing	338	330
	Punched card machine (other than for computer use) manufacturing	338	330
	Shorthand writing machine manufacturing	338	330
	Tabulating machine manufacturing	338	330
	Ticket issuing machine manufacturing	338	330
	Ticket punch manufacturing	338	330
	Typewriter manufacturing	338	330
	Visible record computer (tabulator) manufacturing	338	330
3302	Electronic data processing equipment		
	Analogue computer manufacturing	366	330
	Central processing unit, computer, manufacturing	366	330
	Computer, electronic, manufacturing	366	330
	Computer peripheral equipment manufacturing	366	330
	Computer system manufacturing	366	330
	Control unit, computer, manufacturing	366	330
	Converter (for computers) manufacturing	366	330
	Data processing equipment, electronic (other than electronic calculators) manufacturing	366	330
	Digital computer manufacturing	366	330
	Hybrid computer manufacturing	366	330
	Memory store, computer, manufacturing	366	330
	Peripheral equipment (including card punches and verifiers) for computer uses, manufacturing	366	330
	Printer, computer, manufacturing	366	330
	Store, computer manufacturing	366	330
	Tape reader, computer, manufacturing	366	330

SIC 1980	Activity	SIC 1968	NACE
	Terminal unit, computer, manufacturing	366	330
	Visual display unit, computer, manufacturing	366	330
3410	Insulated wires and cables		
	Cable accessory, manufacturing	362	341
	Cable jointing material manufacturing	362	341
	Cable, insulated electrical, manufacturing	362	341
	Cable, telecommunication, manufacturing	362	341
	General wiring cable manufacturing	362	341
	Insulated wire manufacturing	362	341
	Mains (power distribution) cable (insulated) manufacturing	362	341
	Overhead line fitting manufacturing	362	341
	Ship wiring manufacturing	362	341
	Submarine cable manufacturing	362	341
	Telecommunication wire manufacturing	362	341
	Winding wire and strip manufacturing	362	341
3420/1	Machinery for generating and transmitting electric power		
	Alternator (not for vehicle) manufacturing	361/1	342
	Capacitor (for power factor improvement) manufacturing	361/1	342
	Choke and coil (for power) manufacturing	361/1	342
	Dynamo (not for vehicle) manufacturing	361/1	342
	Generator set manufacturing	361/1	342
	Generator, alternating current, manufacturing	361/1	342
	Generator, direct current, manufacturing	361/1	342
	Industrial transformer manufacturing	361/1	342
	Shunt and limiting reactor manufacturing	361/1	342
	Transformer (generator, transmission system and distribution) manufacturing	361/1	342
	Turbine for electricity generation manufacturing	361/1	328.2
	Turbo-alternator manufacturing	361/1	342
3420/2	Switchgear and control gear		
	Circuit breaker (power) manufacturing	361/2	342
	Electronic motor starting and controlling gear manufacturing	361/2	342
	Fuse and fusegear (power) manufacturing	361/2	342
	Switchgear (power) manufacturing	361/2	342
3420/3	Other basic electrical equipment		
	Armature repairing and rewiring	361/3	342
	Bus bar manufacturing	361/2	342
	Ceiling rose manufacturing	369/5	342
	Converting machinery, electrical, manufacturing	361/3	342
	Electric motor manufacturing	361/3	342
	Fuse (domestic type) manufacturing	369/5	342
	Fuse box (domestic type) manufacturing	369/5	342
	Fuse wire manufacturing	369/5	342
	Junction box manufacturing	369/5	342
	Lamp holder, electric, manufacturing	369/5	342
	Miniature circuit breaker manufacturing	369/5	342
	Moulded case circuit breaker manufacturing	361/3	342
	Overhauling of electrical machinery	361/3	342
	Plug, electric, manufacturing	369/5	342
	Rectifier plant manufacturing	361/3	342
	Rectifier, electric, (for power) manufacturing	361/3	342
	Socket, electric, manufacturing	369/5	342
	Switch, electric, manufacturing	369/5	342
	Traction motor (with or without associated control equipment) manufacturing	361	342
	Wiring accessories manufacturing	369/5	342
3432/1	Primary batteries		
	Dry battery (non-rechargeable) manufacturing	369/2	343.2
	Flash lamp battery manufacturing	369/2	343.2
	Primary battery manufacturing	369/2	343.2
	Torch battery manufacturing	369/2	343.2
3432/2	Secondary batteries		
	Accumulator (battery) manufacturing	369/3	343.2
	Car battery manufacturing	369/3	343.2
	Secondary battery manufacturing	369/3	343.2
	Traction battery (rechargeable) manufacturing	369/3	343.2
	Vehicle battery manufacturing	369/3	343.2
3433	Alarms and signalling equipment		
	Bell, electric, (other than telephone type) manufacturing	369/5	343.1
	Burglar alarm and system manufacturing	367/1	343.1
	Electric bell apparatus (other than telegraphic or telephonic) manufacturing	367/1	343.1
	Fire alarm and system manufacturing	367/1	343.1
	Indicator panel manufacturing	367/1	343.1
	Railway signalling equipment (electric) manufacturing	384	343.1
	Road traffic signalling equipment manufacturing	367/1	343.1
	Security alarms and systems manufacturing	367/1	343.1
	Traffic control equipment (for roads and inland waterways) manufacturing	367/1	343.1
3434	Electrical equipment for motor vehicles, cycles and aircraft		
	Alternator (for vehicle) manufacturing	369/1	343.1
	Coil, ignition, manufacturing	369/1	343.1
	Cycle dynamo lighting set manufacturing	369/1	343.1
	Cycle lamp manufacturing	369/1	343.1
	Dashboard instrument (electric) manufacturing	369/1	343.1
	Defrosting and demisting equipment (for vehicle) manufacturing	369/1	343.1
	Dynamo (for vehicle) manufacturing	369/1	343.1
	Electrical equipment (for vehicles and aircraft) manufacturing	369/1	343.1
	Horn, electric, manufacturing	369/1	343.1
	Ignition equipment (other than coils and magnetos) manufacturing	369/1	343.1
	Insulating fitting, other than ceramic (for vehicles and aircraft) manufacturing	369/1	343.1
	Lighting equipment (for vehicles) manufacturing	369/1	343.1
	Magneto manufacturing	369/1	343.1
	Measuring Instrument, indicating (electric) for vehicles and aircraft manufacturing	369/1	344

SIC 1980	Activity	SIC 1968	NACE
	Sparking plug manufacturing	369/1	343.1
	Starter motor (for vehicle) manufacturing	369/1	343.1
	Traffic indicator (for vehicle) manufacturing	369/1	343.1
	Voltage regulator (for vehicle) manufacturing	369/1	343.1
	Windscreen wiper manufacturing	369/1	343.1
3435	**Electrical equipment for industrial use, not elsewhere specified**		
	Battery charger manufacturing	361	343.1
	Brazing equipment (electric) manufacturing	368	343.1
	Carbon brush manufacturing	469/2	343.1
	Catering equipment (electric) manufacturing	368	343.1
	Cyclotron manufacturing	367/2	343.1
	Dielectric heating equipment (electric) manufacturing	367/2	343.1
	Electric cooking equipment (commercial catering) manufacturing	368	343.1
	Electrical carbon manufacturing	469/2	343.1
	Electrochemical apparatus (industrial) manufacturing	341/2	343.1
	Electrolytic chemical process plant manufacturing	341/2	343.1
	Electroplating equipment manufacturing	341/2	343.1
	Heating/melting equipment, electric (high frequency induction or dielectric) manufacturing	341/2	343.1
	Particle accelerator manufacturing	367/2	343.1
	Soldering equipment (electric) manufacturing	391	343.1
	Vacuum cleaner (industrial and commercial) manufacturing	368	343.1
	Welding electrode manufacturing	332/3	223.4
	Welding equipment (electric) manufacturing	332/3	343.1
3441	**Telegraph and telephone apparatus and equipment**		
	Bell (telephone type) manufacturing	363	344
	Data transmission link (line) manufacturing	363	344
	Dial (telephone) manufacturing	363	344
	Facsimile transmission apparatus manufacturing	363	344
	Line apparatus (carrier, duplex and repeater) manufacturing	363	344
	Picture transmitter	363	344
	Subscriber apparatus (telephone) manufacturing	363	344
	Switchboard, telecommunication, manufacturing	363	344
	Switching equipment (telegraph and telex) manufacturing	363	344
	Telegraph apparatus manufacturing	363	344
	Telephone manufacturing	363	344
	Telephone apparatus manufacturing	363	344
	Telephone dial manufacturing	363	344
	Telephone exchange equipment manufacturing	363	344
	Telephone handset manufacturing	363	344
	Teleprinter manufacturing	363	344
	Telewriter manufacturing	363	344
	Telex machine manufacturing	363	344
	Terminal equipment (telegraphic and data communication) manufacturing	363	344
	Transmission equipment (telephone and telegraph) manufacturing	363	344
3442	**Electrical instruments and control systems**		
	Actuator, electric, manufacturing	354/2	344
	Ammeter manufacturing	354/2	344
	Electric process control equipment manufacturing	354/2	344
	Electricity meter manufacturing	354/2	344
	Electronic counter manufacturing	354/2	344
	Electronic process control equipment manufacturing	354/2	344
	Electronic testing equipment manufacturing	354/2	344
	Electronic timer (not electronic clock or watch) manufacturing	354/2	344
	Exposure meter (electric) manufacturing	351	344
	Frequency converter (not power) manufacturing	354/2	344
	Frequency meter manufacturing	354/2	344
	Galvanometer manufacturing	354/2	344
	Instrument, electric, manufacturing	354/2	344
	Light meter (electric) manufacturing	351	344
	Nucleonic instrument manufacturing	354/2	344
	Numerical control and indication equipment for machine tools manufacturing	354/2	344
	Ohmmeter manufacturing	354/2	344
	Oscilloscope manufacturing	354/2	344
	Photo-electric exposure meter manufacturing	351	344
	Potentiometric recorder manufacturing	354/2	344
	Power supply unit for electronic applications manufacturing	354/2	344
	Radiation measuring and detection instrument manufacturing	354/2	344
	Recorder, electric, manufacturing	354/2	344
	Semi-conductor control equipment manufacturing	354/2	344
	Sensor for electric process control equipment manufacturing	354/2	344
	Signal generator manufacturing	354/2	344
	Telemetering instrument manufacturing	354/2	344
	Voltmeter manufacturing	354/2	344
	Wattmeter manufacturing	354/2	344
	Wave-form generator manufacturing	354/2	344
	X-ray diffraction or fluorescence apparatus manufacturing	354/2	344
3443	**Radio and electronic capital goods**		
	Aerial (non-domestic) manufacturing	367/2	344
	Airborne electronic equipment manufacturing	367/2	344
	Airfield control and approach aid (electronic) manufacturing	367/2	344
	Amplifier for broadcasting studio manufacturing	367/2	344
	Camera, television, manufacturing	367/2	344
	Cautery and light unit manufacturing	367/2	344
	Closed-circuit television equipment manufacturing	367/2	344
	Diathermy apparatus manufacturing	367/2	344
	Electro-medical equipment manufacturing	367/2	344
	Flight simulator, electronic, manufacturing	367/2	344

SIC 1980	Activity	SIC 1968	NACE
	Ground station (for relay satellite communication) manufacturing	363	344
	Hearing aid (electronic) manufacturing	367/2	344
	Monitoring equipment, radio and television, manufacturing	367/2	344
	Navigational aid, electronic, manufacturing	367/2	344
	Nucleonic apparatus, industrial, manufacturing	367/2	344
	Nucleonic apparatus, medical, manufacturing	367/2	344
	Pacemaker, electro-medical, manufacturing	367/2	344
	Public broadcasting equipment manufacturing	367/2	344
	Radar equipment manufacturing	367/2	344
	Radio communications equipment manufacturing	367/2	344
	Radio transmitter manufacturing	367/2	344
	Relay link apparatus manufacturing	367/2	344
	Relay, satellite, manufacturing	367/2	344
	Stimulator, electro-medical, manufacturing	367/2	344
	Teaching aid, electronic, manufacturing	367/2	344
	Telemetric equipment manufacturing	367/2	344
	Television closed-circuit equipment manufacturing	367/2	344
	Television transmitter manufacturing	367/2	344
	Trainer, electronic, manufacturing	367/2	344
	Transmitter, radio and television, manufacturing	367/2	344
	X-ray apparatus, industrial, manufacturing	367/2	344
	X-ray apparatus, medical, manufacturing	367/2	344
3444	Components other than active components, mainly for electronic equipment		
	Cabinet (for non-domestic electronic apparatus) manufacturing	364/3	344
	Capacitor (for electronic apparatus) manufacturing	364/3	344
	Circuit protection device, electronic, manufacturing	364/3	344
	Delay lines and networks manufacturing	364/3	344
	Dial for electronic apparatus manufacturing	364/3	344
	Enclosure and associated mounting component (for non-domestic electronic apparatus) manufacturing	364/3	344
	Ferrite part for electronic apparatus manufacturing	364/3	344
	Filter, electronic, manufacturing	364/3	344
	Inductor (electronic) manufacturing	364/3	344
	Knob for electronic apparatus manufacturing	364/3	344
	Microwave component (not tube) manufacturing	364/3	344
	Plug, electronic, manufacturing	364/3	344
	Printed circuit manufacturing	364/3	344
	Rack and mounting for electronic apparatus manufacturing	364/3	344
	Rectifier, selenium, manufacturing	364/3	344
	Relay, electronic and telecommunication, manufacturing	364/3	344
	Resistor manufacturing	364/3	344
	Solenoid (for electronic apparatus) manufacturing	364/3	344
	Switch (for electronic apparatus) manufacturing	364/3	344
	Terminal (for electronic apparatus) manufacturing	364/3	344
	Transformer (for electronic apparatus) manufacturing	364/3	344
3452	Gramophone records and pre-recorded tapes		
	Audio tape recording manufacturing	365/1	345.2
	Gramophone record (including blanks for cutting) manufacturing	365/1	345.2
	Pre-recorded tape manufacturing	365/1	345.2
	Video tape recording manufacturing	365/1	345.2
3453/1	Active components		
	Amplifying valve manufacturing	364/1	345.1
	Backward wave oscillator manufacturing	364/1	345.1
	Cathode ray tube manufacturing	364/1	345.1
	Cold cathode valve manufacturing	364/1	345.1
	Diode manufacturing	364/1	345.1
	Electron optical device manufacturing	364/1	345.1
	Integrated circuit manufacturing	364/2	345.1
	Integrated circuit (monolithic, hybrid and passive) manufacturing	364/2	345.1
	Klystron manufacturing	364/1	345.1
	Magnetron manufacturing	364/1	345.1
	Microcircuit manufacturing	364/2	345.1
	Microwave tube manufacturing	364/1	345.1
	Photo semi-conductor device manufacturing	364/1	345.1
	Photo-diode manufacturing	364/1	345.1
	Photo-electric cell manufacturing	364/1	345.1
	Piezo-electric crystal, manufacturing	364/1	345.1
	Quartz crystal manufacturing	364/1	345.1
	Rectifier, solid state, (not power) manufacturing	364/1	345.1
	Rectifying valve and tube manufacturing	364/1	345.1
	Semi-conductor (not power) manufacturing	364/1	345.1
	Solid-state circuit manufacturing	364/2	345.1
	Stabilizing valve manufacturing	364/1	345.1
	Television camera tube manufacturing	364/1	345.1
	Television picture tube manufacturing	364/1	345.1
	Thyratron manufacturing	364/1	345.1
	Thyristor manufacturing	364/1	345.1
	Transistor manufacturing	364/1	345.1
	Travelling wave tube manufacturing	364/1	345.1
	Tube, electronic, manufacturing	364/1	345.1
	Valve, electronic, manufacturing	364/1	345.1
3453/2	Sub-assemblies and components mainly for electronic consumer goods		
	Aerial, domestic, manufacturing	364/3	345.1
	Earphone manufacturing	364/3	345.1
	Gramophone accessory manufacturing	364/3	345.1
	Headset (not telecommunication type) manufacturing	364/3	345.1
	Loudspeaker manufacturing	364/3	345.1
	Magnetic recording head manufacturing	364/3	345.1
	Microphone manufacturing	364/3	345.1
	Pick-up arm and cartridge, for record player, manufacturing	364/3	345.1
	Record player accessory manufacturing	364/3	345.1
	Record playing mechanism manufacturing	364/3	345.1

SIC 1980	Activity	SIC 1968	NACE
	Stylus for record player manufacturing	364/3	345.1
	Tape deck (not for computer) manufacturing	364/3	345.1
	Television EHT transformer manufacturing	364/3	345.1
	Television scan coil manufacturing	364/3	345.1
	Tuner, radio and television (other than audio separates), manufacturing	364/3	345.1
3454/1	Electronic consumer goods		
	Amplifier (audio separate) manufacturing	365/2	345.1
	Audio separate manufacturing	365/2	345.1
	Dictating machine and accessory manufacturing	365/2	345.1
	Gramophone manufacturing	365/2	345.1
	Public address system manufacturing	365/2	345.1
	Radio receiving set manufacturing	365/2	345.1
	Radiogram manufacturing	365/2	345.1
	Record player manufacturing	365/2	345.1
	Sound recording and reproducing equipment manufacturing	365/2	345.1
	Stereo system manufacturing	365/2	345.1
	Tape player and recorder (audio and visual) manufacturing	365/2	345.1
	Television receiver manufacturing	365/2	345.1
	Tuner (audio separate) manufacturing	365/2	345.1
3454/2	Other electronic equipment not elsewhere specified		
	Electron microscope manufacturing	354/1	345.1
	Electronic equipment (miscellaneous, unspecified) manufacturing	367	345
	Proton microscope manufacturing	354/1	345.1
3460	Domestic-type electric appliances		
	Aquarium heater (electric) manufacturing	368	346
	Blanket, electric, manufacturing	368	346
	Clothes airer (electric) manufacturing	368	346
	Coffee percolator, electric, manufacturing	368	346
	Cooker, electric, manufacturing	368	346
	Deep freeze unit (domestic) manufacturing	368	346
	Dishwasher (domestic) manufacturing	368	346
	Domestic electrical appliance manufacturing	368	346
	Electricaire unit manufacturing	368	346
	Fan (non-industrial, electric) manufacturing	368	346
	Fan, electric, domestic, manufacturing	368	346
	Fire, electric, manufacturing	368	346
	Floor polisher, electric, manufacturing	368	346
	Food mixer, electric, manufacturing	368	346
	Freezer, domestic, manufacturing	368	346
	Gas lighter, electric, manufacturing	368	346
	Hair clipper, electric, manufacturing	368	346
	Hair dryer, electric, manufacturing	368	346
	Immersion heater, electric, manufacturing	368	346
	Iron, electric, manufacturing	368	346
	Ironing machine, electric, domestic, manufacturing	368	346
	Kettle, electric, manufacturing	368	346
	Percolator (electric) manufacturing	368	346
	Plate-warmer (electric) manufacturing	368	346
	Radiator, electric, manufacturing	368	346
	Razor, electric, manufacturing	368	346
	Refrigerator, electric and non-electric, domestic, manufacturing	368	346
	Shaver, electric, manufacturing	368	346
	Spin dryer manufacturing	368	346
	Storage heater manufacturing	368	346
	Toaster, electric, manufacturing	368	346
	Towel rail (electric) manufacturing	368	346
	Tumbler dryer (domestic) manufacturing	368	346
	Vacuum cleaner, domestic, manufacturing	368	346
	Washing machine, domestic, manufacturing	368	346
	Washing heater (domestic, electric) manufacturing	368	346
3470/1	Electric lamp bulbs and tubes		
	Discharge lamp manufacturing	369/4	347.1
	Electric light bulb manufacturing	369/4	347.2
	Flash lamp bulb manufacturing	369/4	347.1
	Fluorescent tube manufacturing	369/4	347.1
	Gas discharge lamp manufacturing	369/4	347.1
	Mercury vapour lamp manufacturing	369/4	347.1
	Neon tube manufacturing	369/4	347.1
	Photoflash bulb manufacturing	369/4	347.1
	Projector lamp manufacturing	369/4	347.1
	Sodium vapour lamp manufacturing	369/4	347.1
	Vehicle lamp (bulb and sealed beam unit) manufacturing	369/4	347.1
3470/2	Other electric lighting equipment		
	Advertising light manufacturing	369/4	347.2
	Arc lamp manufacturing	369/5	347.2
	Electric flash lamp case manufacturing	369/5	347.2
	Electric lighting fitting (other than glassware) manufacturing	369/5	347.2
	Electric torch manufacturing	369/5	347.2
	Miners' lamp manufacturing	369/5	347.2
	Portable lamp (electric) manufacturing	369/4	347.2
	Searchlight manufacturing	369/5	347.2
	Spotlight manufacturing	369/5	347.2
	Stage lighting manufacturing	369/5	347.2
3480	Electrical equipment installation		
	Electrical equipment installation	Not classified	348
3510/1	Passenger cars		
	Car (3 or 4 wheeled) manufacturing	381	351
	Electric car manufacturing	381	351
	Estate car manufacturing	381	351
	KD set, car, (at least 50 per cent of value of complete vehicle) manufacturing	381	351
	Station wagon manufacturing	381	351
	Taxi manufacturing	381	351
3510/2	Commercial vehicles		
	Ambulance manufacturing	381	351
	Armoured car manufacturing	381	351
	Battery-powered electric commercial vehicle manufacturing	381	351
	Breakdown lorry manufacturing	381	351
	Bus manufacturing	381	351
	Chassis with engine (commercial vehicle) manufacturing	381	351
	Coach, motor, manufacturing	381	351
	Crane lorry manufacturing	381	351
	Electrically powered commercial vehicle manufacturing	381	351

SIC 1980	Activity	SIC 1968	NACE
	Fire engine manufacturing	381	351
	Fire tender manufacturing	381	351
	KD set, commercial vehicle, (at least 50 per cent of value of complete vehicle) manufacturing	381	351
	Lorry manufacturing	381	351
	Mobile library (not trailer) manufacturing	381	351
	Mobile X-ray unit (not trailer) manufacturing	381	351
	Motor vehicle reconditioning	381	351
	Refrigerated lorry manufacturing	381	351
	Refuse disposal vehicle manufacturing	381	351
	Road tanker (not trailer) manufacturing	381	351
	Road tractor unit manufacturing	381	351
	Spraying lorry manufacturing	381	351
	Street sweeping lorry manufacturing	381	351
	Troop-carrier manufacturing	381	351
	Van, motor, manufacturing	381	351
3510/3	Motor vehicle engines		
	Internal combustion engine (motor vehicle) manufacturing	381	351
	Motor vehicle engine manufacturing	381	351
3521	Motor vehicle bodies		
	Body building, motor vehicle	381	352
	Bus body manufacturing	381	352
	Car body manufacturing	381	352
	Coach body manufacturing	381	352
	Commercial vehicle body manufacturing	381	352
	Fibre glass body shell (motor vehicle) manufacturing	496	352
	Lorry cab manufacturing	381	352
	Plastic body shell (motor vehicle) manufacturing	496	352
3522	Trailers and semi-trailers		
	Agricultural trailer (motor-drawn) manufacturing	381	352
	Chassis (for caravan) manufacturing	381	352
	Flat trailer (motor-drawn) manufacturing	381	352
	Freight container manufacturing	381	315.2
	Low loader (trailer) manufacturing	381	352
	Platform trailer (motor-drawn) manufacturing	381	352
	Road tractor trailer manufacturing	381	352
	Semi-trailer manufacturing	381	352
	Skeletal trailer (motor-drawn) manufacturing	381	352
	Tanker trailer (motor-drawn) manufacturing	381	352
	Trailer (motor-drawn) manufacturing	381	352
3523	Caravans		
	Caravan manufacturing	381	352
	Mobile bank (not self-propelled) manufacturing	381	352
	Mobile canteen (not self-propelled) manufacturing	381	352
	Motorised caravan manufacturing	381	351
	Permanent caravan (residential) manufacturing	381	352
	Special purpose caravan manufacturing	381	352
	Touring caravan manufacturing	381	352
3530	Motor vehicle parts		
	Anti-roll bar (motor vehicle) manufacturing	381	353
	Arm-rest (motor vehicle) manufacturing	381	353
	Axle (motor vehicle) manufacturing	381	353
	Belt, car, safety, manufacturing	381	353
	Brake and parts (not brake linings) (motor vehicle) manufacturing	381	353
	Cam-shaft (motor vehicle engine) manufacturing	381	353
	Cap, for petrol, oil or radiator (motor vehicle) manufacturing	381	353
	Carburettor and parts (motor vehicle) manufacturing	381	353
	Clutch and parts (motor vehicle) manufacturing	381	353
	Coupling for articulated motor vehicle manufacturing	381	353
	Crankshaft (motor vehicle engine) manufacturing	381	353
	Differential unit (motor vehicle) manufacturing	381	353
	Door (motor vehicle) manufacturing	381	353
	Drive shaft (motor vehicle) manufacturing	381	353
	Engine block, finished (motor vehicle) manufacturing	381	353
	Engine components including bearings (motor vehicle) manufacturing	381	353
	Exhaust system and component (motor vehicle) manufacturing	381	353
	Fuel tank (motor vehicle) manufacturing	381	353
	Gear box, manual or automatic (motor vehicle) manufacturing	381	353
	Half shaft manufacturing	381	353
	Heater (motor vehicle) manufacturing	381	353
	Independent suspension unit manufacturing	381	353
	KD sets for car and commercial vehicle (where value is less than half the value of complete assembled vehicle) manufacturing	381	353
	Lock (motor vehicle) manufacturing	381	316.3
	Mirror, interior and wing (motor vehicle) manufacturing	381	247.6
	Motor chassis and parts manufacturing	381	353
	Motor vehicle seat manufacturing	381	316.6
	Oil filter (motor vehicle) manufacturing	381	353
	Panel for motor vehicle bodywork (fibreglass, metal) manufacturing	381	353
	Parts of motor vehicle (not electric) manufacturing	381	353
	Propeller shaft (motor vehicle) manufacturing	381	353
	Pump and parts, non-electric for oil, gas, petrol, or water (motor vehicle) manufacturing	381	353
	Radiator (motor vehicle) manufacturing	381	353
	Radiator grill manufacturing	381	353
	Registration plate (motor vehicle) manufacturing	381	353
	Running gear (motor vehicle) manufacturing	381	353
	Shock absorber (motor vehicle) manufacturing	381	353

SIC 1980	Activity	SIC 1968	NACE
	Silencer (motor vehicle) manufacturing	381	353
	Steering equipment components (motor vehicle) manufacturing	381	353
	Suspension spring (motor vehicle) manufacturing	381	313.2
	Tipping gear (complete and parts, not hydraulic) (motor vehicle) manufacturing	381	353
	Track rod (motor vehicle) manufacturing	381	353
	Universal joint (motor vehicle) manufacturing	381	353
	Valve, engine (motor vehicle) manufacturing	381	353
	Wheel and hub (motor vehicle) manufacturing	381	353
	Window winding gear, not electric (motor vehicle) manufacturing	381	353
	Windscreen wiper (non-electric) manufacturing	381	353
3610/1	Sea-going and inland water vessels		
	Barge (river and sea-going) manufacturing	370/1	361
	Beacon (for shipping) manufacturing	370/1	361.1
	Bulk carrier (cargo ship) manufacturing	370/1	361.1
	Buoy (not plastics) manufacturing	370/1	361.2
	Cable ship manufacturing	370/1	361.1
	Caisson manufacturing	370/1	361.2
	Cargo ship manufacturing	370/1	361.1
	Coffer dam manufacturing	370/1	361.2
	Container ship manufacturing	370/1	361.1
	Conversions to ships	370/1	361.1
	Dredger manufacturing	370/1	361.1
	Drilling ship manufacturing	370/1	361.1
	Ferry manufacturing	370/1	361
	Fishing vessel manufacturing	370/1	361
	Fleet tender manufacturing	370/1	361.1
	Floating crane manufacturing	370/1	361.2
	Floating dock manufacturing	370/1	361.2
	Floating harbour manufacturing	370/1	361.2
	Hydrofoil manufacturing	370/1	361
	Landing stage (floating) manufacturing	370/1	361.2
	Lifeboat manufacturing	370/1	361.1
	Liferaft (not rubber inflatable) manufacturing	370/1	361.1
	Lighter (ship) manufacturing	370/1	361.2
	Lightship manufacturing	370/1	361.1
	Liner (ship) manufacturing	370/1	361.1
	Model of ship (made by shipbuilder) manufacturing	370/1	361.1
	Naval dockyard (shipbuilding and repairing)	370/1	361.1
	Naval ships (of all types) manufacturing	370/1	361.1
	Off-shore drilling rig (floating) manufacturing	370/1	361.1
	Off-shore support vessel manufacturing	370/1	361.1
	Passenger-cargo liner manufacturing	370/1	361.1
	Platform drilling rig manufacturing	370/1	361.1
	Pontoon manufacturing	370/1	361.2
	Refitting, ship	370/1	361
	Repairing ships	370/1	361
	Research vessel manufacturing	370/1	361.1
	Rigging for ships manufacturing	370/1	361
	Salvage vessel manufacturing	370/1	361.1
	Sea-going luxury yacht (of 100 gross tons or more) manufacturing	370/1	361.3
	Ship cementing	370/1	361
	Ship painting	370/1	361.4
	Ships' decking, manufacturing	370/1	361.1
	Ships' mast and spar manufacturing	370/1	361
	Sludge vessel manufacturing	370/1	361
	Submarine manufacturing	370/1	361.1
	Tanker (ship) manufacturing	370/1	361.1
	Trawler manufacturing	370/1	361.1
	Tug manufacturing	370/1	361.1
	Vehicle transport (ship) manufacturing	370/1	361
	Warship manufacturing	370/1	361.1
	Whaler manufacturing	370/1	361.1
3610/2	Pleasure boats and yachts		
	Boat kit (for assembly) manufacturing	370/1	361.3
	Canal cruiser manufacturing	370/1	361.3
	Canoe manufacturing	370/1	361.3
	Catamaran manufacturing	370/1	361.3
	Cleat (for pleasure boat) manufacturing	370/1	361.3
	Collapsible boat (not inflatable dinghy) manufacturing	370/1	361.3
	Houseboat manufacturing	370/1	361.3
	Mast and spar (for pleasure boat) manufacturing	370/1	361.3
	Power boats (of all types) manufacturing	370/1	361.3
	Punt manufacturing	370/1	361.3
	Refitting pleasure craft	370/1	361.3
	Repairing pleasure craft	370/1	361.3
	Rowing boat manufacturing	370/1	361.3
	Yacht (other than sea-going luxury yacht) manufacturing	370/1	361.3
3610/3	Shipbreaking		
	Shipbreaking	399/12	361.5
3620/1	Locomotives and parts		
	Diesel electric locomotive manufacturing	384	362.1
	Electric locomotive manufacturing	384	362.1
	Locomotive manufacturing	384	362.1
	Locomotive body manufacturing	384	362.1
	Locomotive bogie manufacturing	384	362.1
	Locomotive braking system manufacturing	349/3	362.1
	Locomotive chassis manufacturing	384	362.1
	Locomotive parts and accessories manufacturing	384	362.1
	Locomotive, diesel, manufacturing	384	362.1
3620/2	Other railway and tramway rolling stock and parts		
	Goods wagon (railway) manufacturing	385	362.2
	Luggage van, railway, manufacturing	385	362.2
	Passenger carriage, railway, manufacturing	385	362.2
	Post van, railway, manufacturing	385	362.2
	Railway and tramway rolling stock manufacturing	385	362.2
	Railway coach manufacturing	385	362.2
	Railway wagon manufacturing	385	362.2
	Railway wagon axle box and axle lubricator manufacturing	385	362.2
	Refrigerated wagon, railway, manufacturing	385	362.2
	Self-propelled railway car manufacturing	385	362.2
	Special purpose railway wagon manufacturing	385	362.2

SIC 1980	Activity	SIC 1968	NACE
	Tanker wagon, railway, manufacturing	385	362.2
	Test wagon, railway, manufacturing	385	362.2
	Workshop wagon, railway, manufacturing	385	362.2
3620/3	Repair of railway and tramway rolling stock		
	Railway locomotive repairing	384	362.3
	Railway rolling stock repairing	385	362.3
	Tramway rolling stock repairing	385	362.3
3633	Motor cycles and parts		
	Auto-cycle manufacturing	382	363.1
	Axle, motor cycle, manufacturing	382	363.2
	Engine, motor cycle, internal combustion, manufacturing	382	363.2
	Frame, motor cycle, manufacturing	382	363.2
	Gear box, motor cycle, manufacturing	382	363.2
	Handlebar, motor cycle, manufacturing	382	363.2
	Moped manufacturing	382	363.1
	Motor cycle manufacturing	382	363.1
	Motor cycle parts and accessories manufacturing	382	363.2
	Motor scooter manufacturing	382	363.1
	Motor tricycle frame manufacturing	382	363.2
	Pillion seat (for motor cycle) manufacturing	382	363.2
	Saddle, motor cycle, manufacturing	382	363.2
	Sidecar, motor cycle, manufacturing	382	363.2
	Tricycle, motor, and parts manufacturing	382	363.2
	Wheel, motor cycle, manufacturing	382	363.2
3634	Pedal cycles and parts		
	Bell (pedal cycle) manufacturing	382	363.2
	Bicycle (pedal) and parts manufacturing	382	363
	Crank wheel (pedal cycle) manufacturing	382	363.2
	Cycle and parts manufacturing	382	363
	Cyclometer manufacturing	382	363.2
	Free wheel (pedal cycle) manufacturing	382	363.2
	Gear (pedal cycle) manufacturing	382	363.2
	Handlebar (pedal cycle) manufacturing	382	363.2
	Pedal (for pedal cycle) manufacturing	382	363.2
	Pedal cycle frame manufacturing	382	363.2
	Pedal cycle parts and accessories manufacturing	382	363.2
	Pedal tricycle frame manufacturing	382	363.2
	Pump, tyre, (cycle type), manufacturing	382	363.2
	Tandem manufacturing	382	363.1
	Tricycle and parts manufacturing	382	363
	Tyre inflator (cycle type) manufacturing	382	363.2
	Wheel (pedal cycle) manufacturing	382	363.2
3640	Aerospace equipment manufacturing and repairing		
	Aero-engine parts and sub-assemblies manufacturing or repairing	383/2	364
	Aero-engine, all types, manufacturing or repairing	383/2	364
	Air conditioning equipment for aircraft manufacturing	383/4	364
	Air cushion vehicle manufacturing or repairing	383/3	364
	Aircraft brake (not brake lining) manufacturing or repairing	383/4	364
	Aircraft galley manufacturing	383/4	364
	Aircraft parts and sub-assemblies, not electric, manufacturing or repairing	383/4	364
	Aircraft propeller manufacturing or repairing	383/4	364
	Aircraft seat manufacturing	383/4	316.6
	Aircraft, complete, manufacturing or repairing	383/1	364
	Airframe manufacturing or repairing	383/1	364
	Airframe parts and sub-assemblies, not electric, manufacturing or repairing	383/4	364
	Airscrew manufacturing	383/4	364
	Airship manufacturing	383/1	364
	Anti-icing equipment and systems for aircraft manufacturing	383/4	364
	Auxiliary power unit for aircraft manufacturing	383/2	364
	Balloon (not toy) manufacturing	383/4	364
	Catapult (aircraft launching device) manufacturing	383/4	364
	De-icing equipment for aircraft manufacturing	383/4	364
	Ejector seat for aircraft manufacturing	383/4	364
	Escape chute for aircraft manufacturing	383/4	364
	Fuel pump for aero-engine manufacturing	383/2	364
	Glider manufacturing	383/1	364
	Ground effect vehicle manufacturing	383/3	364
	Ground equipment for spacecraft (excluding electronic or telemetric equipment) manufacturing	383/1	364
	Guided weapon manufacturing	383/1	364
	Guided weapon airborne delivery system manufacturing	383/1	364
	Guided weapon launching gear or launch control post manufacturing	383/1	364
	Helicopter manufacturing	383/1	364
	Hovercraft manufacturing	383/3	364
	Hydraulic equipment (aircraft) manufacturing	383/4	364
	Jet engine manufacturing or repairing	383/2	364
	Kite (not toy) manufacturing	383/4	364
	Launch vehicle for spacecraft manufacturing	383/1	364
	Missile (guided weapon) manufacturing	383/1	364
	Nozzle for gas turbine aero-engine manufacturing	383/2	364
	Parachute manufacturing	383/4	364
	Pneumatic equipment and systems for aircraft manufacturing	383/4	364
	Power control for aircraft manufacturing	383/4	364
	Propeller (aircraft) manufacturing	383/4	364
	Rocket (aerospace) manufacturing	383/2	364
	Rocket motor manufacturing	383/2	364
	Safety belt or harness for aircraft crew or passengers manufacturing	383/4	364
	Sailplane manufacturing	383/1	364
	Satellite manufacturing	383/1	364
	Spacecraft manufacturing	383/1	364

SIC 1980	Activity	SIC 1968	NACE
3650/1	Baby carriages and wheelchairs		
	Baby carriage manufacturing	494/2	365.1
	Bath chair manufacturing	494/2	365.2
	Bedfolder manufacturing	494/2	365.1
	Carry-cot manufacturing	473	365.1
	Children's carriage manufacturing	494/2	365.1
	Folding perambulator manufacturing	494/2	365.1
	Invalid carriage, manually propelled, manufacturing	494/2	365.2
	Perambulator manufacturing	494/2	365.1
	Push chair manufacturing	494/2	365.1
	Sun car manufacturing	494/2	365.1
	Wheel chair manufacturing	494/2	365.2
3650/2	Other vehicles		
	Chassis, (powered invalid carriage) manufacturing	382	365.2
	Handcart (not wooden) manufacturing	399/12	365.2
	Invalid car (body shell) manufacturing	382	365.2
	Invalid carriage (electrically propelled) manufacturing	382	365
	Invalid carriage (power operated) and parts manufacturing	382	365.2
	Steering column and gear (powered invalid carriage) manufacturing	382	365.2
	Trailer, horse-drawn, (not wooden) manufacturing	399/12	365.2
	Truck, horse-drawn, (not wooden) manufacturing	399/12	365.2
	Truck, manually propelled, (not wooden) manufacturing	399/12	365.2
3710	Measuring, checking and precision instruments and apparatus		
	Absorptiometer manufacturing	354/2	371
	Accelerometer manufacturing	354/2	371.2
	Active gauge manufacturing	390	371.5
	Altimeter manufacturing	354/2	371.3
	Apparatus for testing physical and mechanical properties of materials manufacturing	354/2	371.2
	Artificial horizon manufacturing	354/2	371.3
	Barometer manufacturing	354/2	371.2
	Compass (drawing) manufacturing	354/2	371.4
	Compass (magnetic) manufacturing	367/2	371.3
	Compressibility testing equipment manufacturing	354/2	371.2
	Counting instrument eg counter (non-electric) manufacturing	354/2	371.2
	Diving equipment (breathing apparatus only) manufacturing	349/3	371.7
	Drawing instrument manufacturing	354/2	371.4
	Elasticity testing equipment manufacturing	354/2	371.2
	Expansion meter manufacturing	354/2	371.2
	Flow measuring and control instrument (non-electronic) manufacturing	354/2	371.2
	Fluorimeter manufacturing	354/2	371.2
	Gas chromatograph manufacturing	354/2	371.2
	Gas meter manufacturing	354/2	371.1
	Geophysical instrument manufacturing	354/2	371.3
	Gunnery control instrument manufacturing	354/2	371.2
	Gyroscope manufacturing	367/2	371
	Hardness testing instrument manufacturing	354/2	371.2
	Hydrographic instrument and apparatus manufacturing	354/2	371.3
	Hydrological instrument manufacturing	354/2	371.3
	Instrument for educational or exhibition purpose manufacturing	354/2	371.6
	Instrument for testing physical and mechanical properties of materials manufacturing	354/2	371.2
	Level measuring and control instrument manufacturing	354/2	371.2
	Liquid supply meter manufacturing	354/2	371.1
	Magnetic compass manufacturing	367/2	371
	Mask and respirator (not medical) manufacturing	349/3	371.7
	Mathematical instrument and machine manufacturing	354/2	371.4
	Meteorological instrument manufacturing	354/2	371.3
	Meter (other than electricity meter and parking meter) manufacturing	354/2	371.1
	Micrometer manufacturing	390	371.5
	Mitre manufacturing	391	371.5
	Models for educational or exhibition purposes manufacturing	354/2	371.6
	Nautical instrument (not electronic) manufacturing	354/2	371.3
	Petrol pump meter manufacturing	354/2	371.1
	Porosimeter manufacturing	354/2	371
	Precision balance manufacturing	354/2	371.6
	Precision drawing instrument and machine manufacturing	354/2	371.4
	Pressure gauge manufacturing	354/2	371.2
	Pressure measuring and control instrument manufacturing	354/2	371.2
	Pressure switch manufacturing	354/2	371.2
	Pyrometer (non-electronic) manufacturing	354/2	371
	Rule (measuring) manufacturing	391	371.5
	Scientific laboratory instrument (non-electrical or non-optical) manufacturing	354/2	371.6
	Scientific model for educational and exhibition purposes manufacturing	354/2	371.6
	Spectrofluorimeter manufacturing	354/2	371.2
	Spectrometer manufacturing	354/2	371.2
	Speedometer manufacturing	354/2	371.2
	Spirit level manufacturing	391	371.5
	Static gauge manufacturing	390	371.5
	Stroboscope manufacturing	354/2	371
	Tachometer manufacturing	354/2	371.2
	Tape (measuring) manufacturing	391	371.5
	Temperature measuring and control instrument (non-electronic) manufacturing	354/2	371.2
	Thermometer manufacturing	354/2	371.2
	Thermostat manufacturing	354/2	371.2
	Velocity measuring instrument manufacturing	354/2	371.1
	Vernier gauge manufacturing	390	371.5
	Viscometer manufacturing	354/2	371.2
	Water meter, manufacturing	354/2	371.1
3720/1	Medical, surgical and veterinary equipment		
	Anaesthetic equipment manufacturing	353/1	372.2
	Aseptic hospital furniture manufacturing	353/1	372
	Autoclave manufacturing	353	372.2
	Catheter manufacturing	353	372.2
	Dissecting instrument manufacturing	353	372.2

SIC 1980	Activity	SIC 1968	NACE
	Hypodermic syringe and equipment manufacturing	353/1	372.2
	Medical instrument (non-optical) manufacturing	353	372
	Myograph manufacturing	353	372
	Opthalmic instrument manufacturing	354	372.1
	Optometer manufacturing	353	372.1
	Oxygen breathing equipment (medical) manufacturing	353	372.2
	Respirator and mask (medical) manufacturing	353/1	372.2
	Resuscitation equipment manufacturing	353/1	372.2
	Sterilising equipment (medical) manufacturing	353/1	372.2
	Surgical instrument manufacturing	353/1	372.2
	Veterinary equipment manufacturing	353/1	372.2
3720/2	Dental instruments and appliances		
	Brush, dental, manufacturing	493	372.3
	Chair, dental, manufacturing	353/1	372.3
	Cutter, dental, manufacturing	353	372.3
	Dental instrument manufacturing	353/1	372.3
	Dental laboratory instrument and equipment manufacturing	353	372.3
	Dental surgical instrument and equipment manufacturing	353	372.3
	Drill, dental, manufacturing	353/1	372.3
	Mirror, dental, manufacturing	353/1	372.3
3720/3	Orthopaedic appliances and artificial limbs etc.		
	Artificial eye manufacturing	353/1	372.4
	Artificial limb manufacturing	353/1	372.4
	Denture manufacturing	353	372.4
	Foot support manufacturing	353/1	372.4
	Instep support manufacturing	353/1	372.4
	Orthopaedic appliance (not footwear) manufacturing	353/1	372.4
	Surgical hosiery manufacturing	353/1	372.4
	Truss, surgical, manufacturing	353/1	372.4
3731	Spectacles and unmounted lenses		
	Contact lens manufacturing	353/2	373.1
	Dispensing opticians (wholesale)	354/1	373.1
	Filter, colour, (unmounted) manufacturing	354/1	373.1
	Goggles manufacturing	353/2	373.1
	Grating, (unmounted, optical) manufacturing	354	373.1
	Lens (unmounted) manufacturing	354/1	373.1
	Monocle manufacturing	353/2	373.1
	Optical element (unmounted) manufacturing	354/1	373.1
	Prism, (unmounted) manufacturing	354/1	373.1
	Spectacle frame manufacturing	353/2	373.1
	Spectacle lens manufacturing	353/2	373.1
	Spectacle mounts manufacturing	353	373.1
	Spectacles manufacturing	353/2	373.1
	Sunglasses manufacturing	353	373.1
3732	Optical precision instruments		
	Auto-correlator (optical) manufacturing	354/1	373
	Binocular manufacturing	354/1	373.2
	Correlator (optical) manufacturing	354/1	373
	Gunnery control instrument (optical) manufacturing	354	373.2
	Laser (excluding laser system) manufacturing	367/2	373
	Meteorological instrument (optical) manufacturing	354/1	373.2
	Microscope manufacturing	354/1	373.2
	Monocular manufacturing	354/1	373.2
	Nautical instrument (optical) manufacturing	354/2	373.2
	Optical density measuring equipment manufacturing	354/1	373.2
	Optical instrument and appliance (other than photographic goods and analytical instruments) manufacturing	354/1	373.2
	Optical projector (meteorological) manufacturing	354	373.2
	Optical surveying instrument manufacturing	354/1	373.2
	Photogrammetric equipment manufacturing	354	373.2
	Range-finder (optical) manufacturing	354/1	373.2
	Sextant manufacturing	354/1	373.2
	Spectrograph manufacturing	354/2	373.2
	Spectrophotometer manufacturing	354/2	373.2
	Surveying instrument (optical) manufacturing	354/1	373.2
	Telescope manufacturing	354/1	373.2
	Theodolite manufacturing	354/1	373.2
	Wedge (optical) manufacturing	354	373.2
3733	Photographic and cinematographic equipment		
	Camera (still and cine) manufacturing	351	373.3
	Cine camera manufacturing	351	373.3
	Cinema projector manufacturing	351	373.3
	Cinematographic equipment manufacturing	351	373.3
	Dark room equipment manufacturing	351	373.3
	Document copying equipment manufacturing	351	373.3
	Dyeline copying machine manufacturing	351	373.3
	Electrostatic copying machine manufacturing	351	373.3
	Enlarger, photographic, manufacturing	351	373.3
	Episcope manufacturing	351	373.3
	Grating (mounted) manufacturing	354	373.3
	Lens (mounted) manufacturing	354	373.3
	Microfilm equipment manufacturing	351	373.3
	Optical element (mounted) manufacturing	351	373.3
	Photographic instrument manufacturing	351	373.3
	Prism (mounted) manufacturing	354/1	373.3
	Projector (photographic or cinematographic) manufacturing	351	373.3
	Reducer (photographic) manufacturing	351	373.3
	Slide projector manufacturing	351	373.3
	Television camera lens manufacturing	354/1	373.3
	Xerographic copying machine manufacturing	351	373.3
3740	Clocks, watches and other timing devices		
	Alarm clock manufacturing	352	374
	Car clock manufacturing	352	374
	Case (clock and watch) manufacturing	352	374
	Chronometer manufacturing	352	374
	Clock manufacturing	352	374
	Clock (electric) manufacturing	352	374
	Instrument panel clock manufacturing	352	374
	Metronome (electronic or mechanical) manufacturing	352	374
	Movement (clock and watch), manufacturing	352	374
	Parking meter manufacturing	354/2	374

SIC 1980	Activity	SIC 1968	NACE
	Pocket timer manufacturing	352	374
	Pocket watch manufacturing	352	374
	Stop watch manufacturing	352	374
	Time clock manufacturing	352	374
	Time lock manufacturing	352	374
	Time recorder manufacturing	352	374
	Time switch manufacturing	369/5	374
	Timer (industrial) manufacturing	352	374
	Travelling clock manufacturing	352	374
	Watch manufacturing	352	374
	Watch case manufacturing	352	374
	Wrist watch manufacturing	352	374
4115	Margarine and compound cooking fats		
	Compound cooking fat manufacturing	229/1	411.5
	Margarine manufacturing	229/1	411.5
4116/1	Crude oils from fish and other marine animals		
	Fat of marine animals production	221	411.1
	Fish liver oil (unrefined) production	221	411.1
	Fish oil (crude) production	221	411.1
	Marine animal crude oils and fats production	221	411.1
	Unrendered and crude fats (marine animals) manufacturing	221	411.1
	Whale oil production	221	411.1
4116/2	Crude oils, cakes and meals from oilseeds and nuts		
	Benniseed crushing	221	411.3
	Castor seed crushing	221	411.3
	Copra (coconut) crushing	221	411.3
	Cotton seed crushing (including delinting or cleaning)	221	411.3
	Gingelly seed crushing	221	411.3
	Groundnut crushing	221	411.3
	Kapok seed crushing	221	411.3
	Kernel crushing	221	411.3
	Linseed crushing	221	411.3
	Mustard seed crushing	211	411.3
	Oil seed cake and meal manufacturing	221	411.3
	Oil seed crushing	221	411.3
	Palm kernel crushing	221	411.3
	Rape seed crushing	221	411.3
	Seed and nut crushing	221	411.3
	Sesame seed crushing	221	411.3
	Shea nut crushing	221	411.3
	Soya bean crushing	221	411.3
	Sunflower seed crushing	221	411.3
	Tung oil extraction	221	411.3
	Unrendered and crude fats (vegetable) manufacturing	221	411.3
4116/3	Treated vegetable, marine and animal oils and fats		
	Benniseed oil refining	221	411.4
	Castor oil processing	221	411.4
	Coconut oil refining	221	411.4
	Cod liver oil refining	221	411.4
	Cola oil refining	221	411.4
	Cotton seed oil refining	221	411.4
	Edible oil manufacturing	221	411.4
	Fish liver oil refining	221	411.4
	Gingelly oil refining	221	411.4
	Groundnut oil refining	221	411.4
	Herring oil refining	221	411.4
	Kapok seed oil refining	221	411.4
	Linseed oil refining	221	411.4
	Neatsfoot oil manufacturing	221	411.4
	Olive oil refining	221	411.4
	Palm kernel oil refining	221	411.4
	Palm oil refining	221	411.4
	Rape oil refining	221	411.4
	Sesame oil refining	211	411.4
	Shea butter manufacturing	221	411.4
	Soya bean oil refining	221	411.4
	Sperm oil refining	221	411.4
	Sunflower oil refining	221	411.4
	Technical tallow	221	411.4
	Vegetable oil refining	221	411.4
	Whale oil refining	221	411.4
4121	Slaughterhouses		
	Abattoir	810/2	412.1
	Hides and skins from animals (from abattoirs) production	810/2	412.1
	Meat chilling or freezing for human consumption	214/2	412.1
	Offal (edible) preparation (i.e. removal, freezing, packing etc.)	810/2	412.1
	Slaughterhouse	810/2	412.1
4122/1	Bacon and ham		
	Bacon curing	214/2	412.2
	Bacon smoking	214/2	412.2
	Ham boiling	214/2	412.2
	Ham cooking or preparing in bulk	214/2	412.2
	Ham curing	214/2	412.2
	Ham smoking	214/2	412.2
	Pork, salted or pickled, manufacturing	214/2	412.2
4122/2	Frozen meat products		
	Frozen meal based on meat manufacturing	214/1	412.2
	Meat pies and puddings (frozen) manufacturing	214/1	412.2
	Sausage roll (frozen) manufacturing	214/1	412.2
4122/3	Other processed and preserved meats		
	Beef extract manufacturing	214/2	412.2
	Beef paste manufacturing	214/2	412.2
	Beef pickling	214/2	412.2
	Black pudding making	214/2	412.2
	Blood pudding manufacturing	214/2	412.2
	Brawn manufacturing	214/2	412.2
	Calves' foot jelly manufacturing	214/2	412.2
	Cooked and preserved meat manufacturing	214/2	412.2
	Cooked polony manufacturing	214/2	412.2
	Haggis making	214/2	412.2
	Meat canning	214/2	412.2
	Pie, meat, (fresh or canned) manufacturing	214/2	412.2
	Pork pie manufacturing	214/2	412.2
	Potted meat manufacturing	214/2	412.2
	Preserved meat manufacturing	214/2	412.2
	Sausage manufacturing	214/2	412.2
	Sausage meat making	214/2	412.2
	Sausage roll (not frozen) manufacturing	214/2	412.2
	Tinned meat manufacturing	214/2	412.2
4123/1	Poultry slaughter		
	Chicken cuts, chilled, production in slaughterhouse	214/1	412.3
	Chicken cuts, fresh, production in slaughterhouse	214/1	412.3
	Chicken cuts, frozen, production in slaughterhouse	214/1	412.3

SIC 1980	Activity	SIC 1968	NACE
	Duck (fresh, chilled or frozen) slaughter and dressing	214/1	412.3
	Game bird, fresh, frozen or chilled, dressing or preparation	214/1	412.3
	Goose, fresh, chilled or frozen, slaughtering and dressing	214/1	412.3
	Poultry dressing	214/2	412.3
4123/2	Poultry meat products		
	Chicken paste manufacturing	214/2	412.3
	Chicken ready to eat meals manufacturing	214/1	412.3
	Poultry canning	214/2	412.3
	Poultry potting	214/2	412.3
4126/1	Fats and greases		
	Animal grease manufacturing	221	412.4
	Animal oil manufacturing	221	411.4
	Bone oil manufacturing	221	411.4
	Dripping manufacturing	221	412.4
	Edible tallow production	221	412.4
	Fat recovery (from knackers)	221	412.4
	Lanolin recovery (from knackers)	221	412.4
	Lard (from knackers) manufacturing	221	412.4
	Lard oil manufacturing	221	412.4
	Lard refining	214/2	412.4
	Oleo-stearine manufacturing	221	412.4
	Premier-jus manufacturing	221	412.4
	Suet manufacturing	221	412.4
4126/2	Processed guts and offals		
	Bladder processing	214/2	412.5
	Casing (sausage) production	214/2	412.5
	Edible offals (processed) production	214/2	412.5
	Sausage skins and casings (natural) manufacturing	214/2	412.5
	Tripe dressing	214/2	412.5
4126/3	Slaughtering other than for human consumption and other processing of animal by-products		
	Bile processing (by knackers)	214/2	412.5
	Bone boiling (by knackers)	221	412.4
	Bone crushing (by knackers)	221	412.4
	Bone degreasing (by knackers)	221	412.4
	Bone flour (from knackers) manufacturing	221	412.5
	Bone meal (from knackers) manufacturing	221	412.5
	Bone scraping (by knackers)	221	412.4
	Bone sorting (by knackers)	221	412.4
	Bones, raw (from knackers) production	899/7	412.5
	Bovine hides and skins production (from knackers)	899/7	412.1
	Bristles (from knackers) production	899/7	412.5
	Hair (animal by-products) from knackers production	899/7	412.5
	Hides and skins from animals production (from knackers)	899/7	412.1
	Hooves (from knackers) production	899/7	412.1
	Meat and bone meal (from knackers) manufacturing	221	412.5
	Meat meal (ground meat) manufacturing	221	412.5
	Rennet (not artificial) manufacturing	229/2	412.5
	Sterilized bone flour (not for fertilizers) manufacturing	221	412.5
	Unrendered and crude fat (from knackers) manufacturing	899/7	412.4
4130/1	Liquid milk and cream		
	Clotted cream manufacturing	215/2	413.1
	Creamery (not farm or retail shop)	215/2	413.1
	Double cream manufacturing	215/2	413.1
	Heat treatment of milk	215/1	413.1
	Homogenized milk production	215/1	413.1
	Milk homogenizing	215/1	413.1
	Milk sterilizing	215/1	413.1
	Milk ultra heat treatment	215/1	413.1
	Sterilized cream manufacturing	215/2	413.1
4130/2	Butter and cheese		
	Butter manufacturing	215/2	413.1
	Butter blending	215/2	413.1
	Butter milk manufacturing	215/2	413.1
	Butter oil manufacturing	215/2	413.1
	Butterfat manufacturing	215/2	413.1
	Cheese manufacturing	215/2	413.1
	Cream cheese manufacturing	215/2	413.1
	Milk products factory (butter and cheese)	215/2	413.1
	Processed cheese manufacturing	215/2	413.1
4130/3	Other milk products		
	Condensed milk manufacturing	215/2	413.2
	Desserts, with a milk base, manufacturing	229/2	413.2
	Dietetic food, with a milk base, manufacturing	215/2	413.2
	Dried milk manufacturing	215/2	413.2
	Evaporated milk production	215/2	413.2
	Infant food (milk based) manufacturing	215/2	413.2
	Invalid food (milk based) manufacturing	215/2	413.2
	Lactose manufacturing	215/2	413.1
	Malted milk production	215/2	413.1
	Milk powder manufacturing	215/2	413.2
	Preserved cream manufacturing	215/2	413.2
	Sweetened skimmed whey production	215/2	413.2
	Yoghourt manufacturing	215/2	413.1
4147/1	Freezing of fruit and vegetables		
	Fruit quick freezing	218/2	414.1
	Quick freezing of fruit and vegetables	218/2	414.1
	Vegetable quick freezing	218/2	414.1
4147/2	Pickling and preserving of fruit and vegetables in salt or oil		
	Chutney (pickle) manufacturing	218/3	414.3
	Fruit pickling	218/3	414.3
	Gherkin pickling	218/3	414.3
	Olive preserving in salt or brine	218/3	414.3
	Piccalilli production	218/3	414.3
	Pickle (including beetroot and onion) manufacturing	218/3	414.3
	Pickling of fruit	218/3	414.3
	Pickling of vegetables	218/3	414.3
	Vegetable pickling	218/3	414.3
4147/3	Jam, marmalade and table jellies		
	Candied peel manufacturing	218/1	421.2
	Crystallised fruit manufacturing	218/1	421.2
	Fruit jelly (preserve) manufacturing	218/1	414.6
	Fruit pulp manufacturing	218/1	414.5
	Homogenized fruit and vegetable manufacturing	218/3	414.5
	Jam manufacturing	218/1	414.6
	Jelly (table) manufacturing	218/1	423.6
	Jelly powder manufacturing	218/1	423.6
	Marmalade manufacturing	218/1	414.6
	Mincemeat manufacturing	218/1	414.6

SIC 1980	Activity	SIC 1968	NACE
	Strained fruit manufacturing	218/3	414.5
	Strained vegetable manufacturing	218/3	414.6
	Table jelly manufacturing	218/1	423.6
4147/4	Canning, bottling, drying, etc. of fruit and vegetables		
	Bottling of fruit and vegetables	218/3	414
	Canning of fruit and vegetables	218/3	414.6
	Dehydrating fruit for human consumption	218/3	414.6
	Dehydrating of vegetables for human consumption	218/3	414.6
	Dried fruit (except field dried) manufacturing	218/3	414.6
	Dried fruit cleaning	218/3	414.6
	Dried vegetable (except field dried) manufacturing	218/3	414.6
	Heat treatment of fruit and vegetables	218/3	414.6
	Potato flour manufacturing	218/3	423.8
	Vegetable dehydrating, for human consumption	218/3	414.6
4150/1	Fish: freezing		
	Crustaceans (freezing of)	214/1	415.1
	Fish cake (frozen) manufacturing	214/2	415.1
	Fish finger (frozen) manufacturing	214/2	415.1
	Fish product quick freezing	214/1	415.1
	Fish quick freezing	214/1	415.1
	Shellfish freezing	214/1	415.1
4150/2	Fish: other processing and preserving		
	Canning of fish	214/2	415.2
	Fish cake (fresh) manufacturing	214/2	415.2
	Fish curing (other than by distributors)	214/2	415.2
	Fish drying	214/2	415.2
	Fish paste manufacturing	214/2	415.2
	Fish processing (not freezing)	214/2	415.2
	Fish salting	214/2	415.2
	Kipper manufacturing	214/2	415.2
	Potted shrimp manufacturing	214/2	415.2
	Shellfish preserving (not freezing)	214/2	415.2
	Shrimp preserving (not freezing)	214/2	415.2
4160	Grain milling		
	Barley (blocked, flaked, puffed or pearled) processing	211/2	416.2
	Barley meal production	211/2	416.1
	Barley milling	211/2	416.1
	Bean grinding	211/2	416.2
	Bean milling	211/2	416.2
	Bean splitting	211/2	416.2
	Bran production	211/1	416.1
	Breakfast cereal (uncooked) manufacturing	211/2	416.2
	Flaked maize production	211/2	416.2
	Flour milling	211/1	416.1
	Grist milling	211/1	416.2
	Lentil splitting, grinding or milling	211/2	416.2
	Maize flour and meal production	211/1	416.1
	Miller (undefined)	211/1	416.1
	Oat flour and meal manufacturing	211/2	416.1
	Oat grinding, rolling, crushing or flaking	211/2	416.2
	Pea splitting, milling or grinding	211/2	416.2
	Rice cleaning	211/2	416.2
	Rice flaking	211/2	416.2
	Rice husking	211/2	416.2
	Rice milling	211/2	416.2
	Rice rolling	211/2	416.2
	Rye flaking	211/2	416.2

SIC 1980	Activity	SIC 1968	NACE
	Rye flour and meal manufacturing	211/2	416.2
	Rye milling	211/2	416.1
	Rye rolling	211/2	416.2
	Sago grinding	211/2	416.2
	Self-raising and patent flour manufacturing	211/1	416.1
	Semolina milling	211/1	416.1
	Soya bean grinding	211/2	416.2
	Soya bean milling	211/2	416.2
	Soya flour and meal manufacturing	211/2	416.2
	Tapioca grinding	211/2	416.2
	Wheat flake manufacturing	211/2	416.1
	Wheat milling	211/1	416.1
	Wheat offal manufacturing	211/1	416.1
4180	Starch		
	Arrowroot manufacturing	229/2	418.4
	Dextrin manufacturing	229/2	418.2
	Dextrose manufacturing	229/2	418.2
	Glucose manufacturing	229/2	418.3
	Laundry starch manufacturing	229/2	418.4
	Maize starch manufacturing	229/2	418.1
	Potato starch manufacturing	229/2	418.4
	Rice starch manufacturing	229/2	418.1
	Soluble starch manufacturing	229/2	418.2
	Starch manufacturing	229/2	418
	Warp starch manufacturing	229/2	418.4
	Wheat starch manufacturing	229/2	418.1
4196	Bread and flour confectionery		
	Bread baking (including rolls)	212	419.1
	Cake making	212	419.3
	Crumpet making	212	419.1
	Fancy pastry manufacturing	212	419.3
	Flour confectionery manufacturing	212	419.3
	Fruit cake baking	212	419.3
	Fruit loaf baking	212	419
	Fruit pie making	212	419.3
	Pancake making	212	419.3
	Pastry (including buns) making	212	419
	Pie, other than meat, manufacturing	212	419.3
	Pikelet making	212	419.3
	Sandwich cake baking	212	419.3
	Scone baking	212	419.3
4197	Biscuits and crispbread		
	Biscuit making	213	419.5
	Crispbread making	213	419
	Matzos making	213	419.1
	Oat cake manufacturing	213	419
	Rusk making	213	419.4
	Sausage filler, cereal, manufacturing	213	419.5
	Wafer making	213	419.5
4200	Sugar and sugar by-products		
	Beet pulp manufacturing	216	420.1
	Beet sugar manufacturing	216	420.1
	British Sugar Corporation	216	420.1
	Caramel (not sweets) manufacturing	216	420.3
	Castor sugar manufacturing	216	420.2
	Icing sugar manufacturing	216	420.2
	Invert sugar manufacturing	216	420.3
	Liquid sugar manufacturing	216	420
	Molasses manufacturing	216	420.1
	Powdered sugar manufacturing	216	420
	Sugar milling	216	420
	Sugar refining	216	420.2
	Syrup (sugar) manufacturing	216	420.3
	Treacle manufacturing	216	420.3
	White sugar manufacturing	216	420.2

SIC 1980	Activity	SIC 1968	NACE
4213	Ice cream		
	Ice cream (all flavours) manufacturing	215/3	421.3
	Ice cream powder manufacturing	229/2	421.3
	Water ices manufacturing	215/3	421.3
4214/1	Cocoa and chocolate		
	Chocolate manufacturing	217/1	421.1
	Chocolate confectionery manufacturing	217/1	421.1
	Chocolate couverture manufacturing	217/1	421.1
	Cocoa bean roasting and dressing	217/1	421.1
	Cocoa butter manufacturing	217/1	421.1
	Cocoa powder (drinking chocolate etc.) manufacturing	217/1	421.1
	Drinking chocolate manufacturing	217/1	421.1
	Milk chocolate manufacturing	217/1	421.1
	Milk cocoa manufacturing	217/1	421.1
4214/2	Sugar confectionery		
	Boiled sugar confectionery manufacturing	217/2	421.2
	Boiled sweet manufacturing	217/2	421.2
	Butterscotch manufacturing	217/2	421.2
	Caramel (sweets) manufacturing	217/2	421.2
	Chewing gum manufacturing	217/2	421.2
	Clear gum (confectionery) manufacturing	217/2	421.2
	Confectioner's novelty manufacturing	217/2	421.2
	Fondant manufacturing	217/2	421.2
	Jujube manufacturing	217/2	421.2
	Liquorice manufacturing	217/2	421.2
	Lozenge (not medicated) manufacturing	217/2	421.2
	Marshmallow manufacturing	217/2	421.2
	Marzipan sweets manufacturing	217/2	421.2
	Nougat manufacturing	217/2	421.2
	Nut and bean confectionery manufacturing	217/2	421.2
	Pastille manufacturing	217/2	421.2
	Pomfret (pontefract) cake manufacturing	217/2	421.2
	Spice making (in Yorkshire)	217/2	421
	Toffee manufacturing	217/2	421.2
	Turkish delight manufacturing	217/2	421.2
4221	Compound animal feeds		
	Compound animal feed manufacturing	219	422
	Dairy concentrate (animal feed) manufacturing	219	422
	Molassed feeding stuff (containing more than 30 per cent molasses) manufacturing	219	422
	Protein concentrate (animal food) manufacturing	219	422
4222/1	Pet foods		
	Bird food manufacturing	219	422
	Cat food manufacturing	219	422
	Dog biscuit manufacturing	219	422
	Dog food manufacturing	219	422
	Pet food (including canned) manufacturing	219	422
4222/2	Non-compound animal feeds and feeds supplements		
	Animal feed supplement manufacturing	272	422
	Dehydrating potatoes for animal feeding	219	422
	Fish meal manufacturing	219	422
	Non-compound animal feed and cattle feeding stuffs (excluding output of grain offals and oilseed cakes and meals) manufacturing	219	422
	Poultry grit manufacturing	219	422
	Synthetic protein, for animal feed, manufacturing	219	422
4239/1	Coffee and coffee substitutes		
	Coffee bag manufacturing	229/2	423.1
	Coffee blending	229/2	423.1
	Coffee essence and extract manufacturing	229/2	423.1
	Coffee grinding and roasting (not retail)	229/2	423.1
	Coffee/chicory essence and extract manufacturing	229/2	423.2
	Dandelion coffee manufacturing	229/2	423.2
	Decaffeinated coffee manufacturing	229/2	423.1
	Instant coffee manufacturing	229/2	423.1
	Liquid coffee manufacturing	229/2	423.1
4239/2	Tea		
	Seasoning manufacturing	229/2	423.3
	Soluble tea manufacturing	229/2	423.1
	Spice purifying manufacturing	229/2	423.3
	Tea bag manufacturing	229/2	423.1
	Tea blending	299/2	423.1
	Tea extract and essence manufacturing	229/2	423.1
4239/3	Potato crisps and other snack products		
	Potato crisp manufacturing	218/3	423.8
	Potato puff manufacturing	218/3	423.8
	Potato stick manufacturing	218/3	423.8
	Potato straw manufacturing	218/3	423.8
	Snack products, puffed or extruded (from farinaceous or proteinaceous material) manufacturing	218/3	423.8
4239/4	Infant and dietetic foods, starch and malt extract		
	Diabetic food manufacturing	229/2	423.5
	Dietetic food (excluding milk based) manufacturing	229/2	423.5
	Infant food (other than milk based) manufacturing	229/2	423.5
	Invalid food (other than milk based) manufacturing	229/2	423.5
	Malt extract manufacturing	229/2	423.5
	Yeast and vegetable extract manufacturing	229/2	423.8
4239/5	Sweets and puddings, cake mixtures, cornflour products and yeast		
	Aerating powder manufacturing	229/2	423.6
	Baking powder manufacturing	229/2	423.6
	Blancmange powder manufacturing	229/2	423.6
	Cake mixture manufacturing	229/2	423.6
	Canned pudding, including rice pudding, manufacturing	229/2	not classified
	Cornflour manufacturing	229/2	423.6
	Custard powder manufacturing	229/2	423.6
	Fruit pudding (canned) manufacturing	229/2	not classified
	Junket powder manufacturing	229/2	423.6
	Pudding mixture manufacturing	229/2	423.6
	Rice pudding (canned) manufacturing	229/2	not classified
	Yeast preparation	229/2	423.8

SIC 1980	Activity	SIC 1968	NACE
4239/6	Broths, soups, sauces and other relishes		
	Canned broth, containing meat or vegetables or both, manufacturing	218/3	423.7
	Canned soup, containing meat or vegetables or both, manufacturing	218/3	423.7
	Catsup manufacturing	218/3	423.7
	Ketchup manufacturing	218/3	423.7
	Mayonnaise manufacturing	218/3	423.7
	Mint sauce manufacturing	229/2	423.7
	Powdered broth, containing meat or vegetables or both, manufacturing	218/3	423.7
	Powdered soup, containing meat or vegetables or both, manufacturing	218/3	423.7
	Relish manufacturing	218/3	423.7
	Salad cream manufacturing	218/3	423.7
	Salad dressing manufacturing	218/3	423.7
	Sandwich spread manufacturing	218/3	423.7
	Sauce manufacturing	218/3	423.7
	Soup manufacturing	218/3	423.7
4239/7	Pasta products (including filled pasta)		
	Macaroni manufacturing	229/2	417
	Noodle manufacturing	229/2	417
	Ravioli manufacturing	229/2	417
	Spaghetti manufacturing	229/2	417
	Spaghetti canning	218/3	417
	Vermicelli manufacturing	229/2	417
4239/8	Breakfast cereals		
	Breakfast cereal manufacturing	211/2	423.8
	Cornflake manufacturing	211/2	423.8
	Puffed rice manufacturing	211/2	423.8
	Puffed wheat manufacturing	211/2	423.8
4239/9	All other foods, not elsewhere specified		
	Almond grinding	229/2	414.6
	Chicory root drying manufacturing	229/2	423.2
	Curry powder manufacturing	229/2	423.3
	Dried egg manufacturing	229/2	423.8
	Dried herbs (except field dried) manufacturing	218/3	423.3
	Egg drying	229/2	423.8
	Egg pickling	229/2	423.8
	Egg substitute manufacturing	229/2	423.8
	Flaked coconut (including desiccated but not sugared) manufacturing	229/2	414.6
	Forcemeat manufacturing	229/2	423.3
	Gravy manufacturing	229/2	423.3
	Gravy salt (not at salt mine or brine pit) manufacturing	229/2	423.3
	Ground pepper manufacturing	229/2	423.3
	Ground spice manufacturing	229/2	423.3
	Herb tea manufacturing	229/2	423.1
	Honey processing and packing	218/1	423.8
	Hop extract manufacturing	218/3	423.3
	Ice manufacturing	229/2	423.4
	Isinglass manufacturing	229/2	423.8
	Mustard manufacturing	229/2	423.3
	Nut food manufacturing	229/2	414.6
	Nut shelling, grinding and preparing	229/2	414.6
	Peanut butter manufacturing	229/2	423.7
	Pepper substitute manufacturing	229/2	423.3
	Salt preparation (not at salt mine or brine pit) manufacturing	229/2	423.3
	Seasoning manufacturing	229/2	423.3
	Spice purifying	229/2	423.3
	Stuffing manufacturing	229/2	423.3
	Vinegar (malt, spirit, wine, acetic acid) manufacturing	218/3	423.3
	Wine vinegar manufacturing	218/3	423.3
4240/1	Ethyl alcohol from fermentation (including denatured)		
	Bakers' yeast (from distillery) production	239/1	424.1
	Distillery draff production	239	424
	Ethyl alcohol (obtained by fermentation) manufacturing	271/2	424.1
	Fusel oil manufacturing	239	424
	Methylated spirits manufacturing	271/2	424.1
4240/2	Potable spirits		
	Aperitif, spirit based, manufacturing	239/1	424.3
	Cherry brandy production	239/1	424.3
	Gin distilling and rectifying	239/1	424.2
	Liqueur making	239/1	424.3
	Rum distilling	239/1	424.2
	Spirit distilling and compounding	239/1	424.2
	Vodka distilling	239/1	424.2
	Whisky blending	239/1	424.2
	Whisky distilling	239/1	424.2
4261/1	Wines based on concentrated grape must		
	British wine manufacturing	239/2	425.1
	Sherry production	239/2	425.1
	Tonic wine production	239/2	425.1
4261/2	Cider and perry		
	Apple pomace and pectin manufacturing	239/2	426
	Cider (alcoholic) manufacturing	239/2	426
	Perry manufacturing	239/2	426
4261/3	Fruit wines		
	Apple wine making	239/2	426
	Fruit wine manufacturing	239/2	426
	Wine, from fresh grapes, manufacturing	239/2	425
4270/1	Beer and other brewing products		
	Ale brewing	231	427.1
	Beer brewing	231	427.1
	Lager brewing	231	427.1
	Porter brewing	231	427.1
	Stout brewing	231	427.1
4270/2	Malt and malt products		
	Barley malting	231	427.2
	Malt and malt products manufacturing	231	427.2
4283/1	Mineral waters and soft drinks (carbonated and still)		
	Aerated water manufacturing	232	428.2
	Black beer brewing	232	428
	Carbonated soft drink manufacturing	232	428.2
	Cordial, (non-alcoholic), manufacturing	232	428.2
	Cream soda manufacturing	232	428.2
	Fruit cordial manufacturing	232	428.2
	Fruit squash manufacturing	232	428.2
	Fruit syrup manufacturing	232	428.2
	Ginger beer manufacturing	232	428.2
	Hop bitters manufacturing	232	428.2
	Lemonade powder manufacturing	232	428.2
	Low alcohol drink (not exceeding 2 degrees of proof) brewing	232	428.2
	Milk shake base manufacturing	232	428.2

SIC 1980	Activity	SIC 1968	NACE
	Mineral water bottling	232	428.1
	Non-alcoholic beer manufacturing	232	428.2
	Non-alcoholic cider manufacturing	232	428.2
	Non-alcoholic wine manufacturing	232	428.2
	Shandy manufacturing	232	428.2
	Soda water manufacturing	232	428.2
	Soft drink manufacturing	232	428.2
	Squash drink manufacturing	232	428.2
	Table water manufacturing	232	428.1
4283/2	Fruit and vegetable juices (concentrated and unconcentrated)		
	Fruit juice manufacturing	232	414.4
	Vegetable juice manufacturing	232	414.4
4290	Tobacco industry		
	Cheroot manufacturing	240	429
	Cigar manufacturing	240	429
	Cigarette manufacturing	240	429
	Cigarillo manufacturing	240	429
	Snuff manufacturing	240	429
	Tobacco (for use in pipes and rolled cigarettes) manufacturing	240	429
4310/1	Preparation of wool or hair fibres		
	Animal hair preparation	414/1	431.2
	Carded sliver (textiles industry) preparation	414/1	431.2
	Combers' shoddy (woollen industry) manufacturing	414/4	439.7
	Commission combing and slubbing (wool)	414/1	431.2
	Noils (woollen industry) manufacturing	414/1	431.2
	Recovered wool (mungo and shoddy) manufacturing	414/4	439.7
	Sliver dyeing (wool)	414/1	431.2
	Slubbing dyeing (wool)	414/1	431.2
	Topmaking (wool)	414/1	431.2
	Wool carbonising	414/1	431.2
	Wool carding	414/1	431.2
	Wool cleaning	414/1	431.2
	Wool combing	414/1	431.2
	Wool condensing	414/1	431.2
	Wool extracting	414/1	431.2
	Wool opening and willeying	414/1	431.2
	Wool recovery	414/4	439.7
	Wool scouring	414/1	431.2
	Wool sorting	414/1	431.2
	Wool topmaking	414/1	431.2
	Woollen rag carbonising	414/4	431.2
	Woollen rag carding	414/4	431.2
	Woollen rag garnetting	414/4	439.7
	Woollen rag grinding or pulling	414/4	439.7
	Woollen waste breaking	414/4	439.7
	Woollen waste, garnetting	414/4	439.7
	Woollen waste, grinding	414/4	439.7
	Woollen waste, opening and willeying	414/4	439.7
	Worsted carding	414/2	431.2
	Worsted waste grinding	414/4	431.2
4310/2	Spinning in the woollen and worsted industry		
	Alpaca and mohair spinning	414/2	431.3
	Botany spinning	414/5	431.3
	Camel hair spinning	414/2	431.3
	Carpet pile yarn (spun on the woollen, worsted and semi-worsted systems) manufacturing	414	431.3
	Fingering wool	414/5	431.3
	Knitting wool manufacturing	414/5	431.3
	Knitting worsted yarn manufacturing	414/2	431.3
	Knitting yarns of wool manufacturing	414/5	431.3
	Man-made fibre spinning on the woollen, worsted and semi-worsted systems	414	431.3
	Man-made fibre twisting on the woollen, worsted and semi-worsted systems	414	431.4
	Man-made fibre warping on the woollen, worsted and semi-worsted systems	414	431.3
	Man-made fibre winding on the woollen, worsted and semi-worsted systems	414	431.4
	Merino yarn spinning	414/2	431.3
	Mohair spinning	414/2	431.3
	Semi-worsted yarn spinning	414/2	431.3
	Spinning (woollen, worsted and semi-worsted systems) manufacturing	414	431.3
	Warp dressing, woollen	414/5	431.3
	Warp sizing and dressing (worsted)	414/2	431.3
	Woollen yarn, carding	414/5	431.3
	Woollen yarn, condensing	414/5	431.3
	Woollen yarn, reeling	414/5	431.3
	Woollen yarn, sizing	414/5	431.3
	Woollen yarn, spinning	414/5	431.3
	Woollen yarn, twisting	414/5	431.4
	Woollen yarn, warping	414/5	431.3
	Woollen yarn, winding	414/5	431.4
	Worsted yarn, reeling	414/2	431.3
	Worsted yarn, warping	414/2	431.3
	Worsted yarn, winding	414/2	431.4
	Worsted, doubling	414/2	431.3
	Worsted, spinning and twisting	414/2	431
4310/3	Weaving in the woollen and worsted industry		
	Alpaca weaving	414/3	431.5
	Bedford cord, worsted, weaving	414/3	431.5
	Blanket, woollen, manufacturing	414/5	431.5
	Bonded fabric (main fabric woven) manufacturing	414	431.5
	Bunting, woollen, manufacturing	414/5	431.5
	Camel hair weaving	414/3	431.5
	Cashmere weaving	414/3	431.5
	Coating, woollen, manufacturing	414/5	431.5
	Coating, worsted, weaving	414/3	431.5
	Coffin cloth manufacturing	414/5	431.5
	Damask, woollen, manufacturing	414/5	431.5
	Damask, worsted, weaving	414/3	431.5
	Dress goods, woollen, manufacturing	414/5	431.5
	Dress goods, worsted, weaving	414/3	431.5
	Flag, woollen, manufacturing	414/5	431.5
	Flannel manufacturing	414/5	431.5
	Frieze cloth manufacturing	414/5	431.5
	Furnishing fabric, woollen, manufacturing	414/5	431.5
	Furnishing fabric, worsted, weaving	414/3	431.5
	Imitation fur, woollen, manufacturing	414/5	431.5
	Man-made fibre weaving of fabrics from yarns spun on the woollen, worsted and semi-worsted system	414/5	431.5
	Mohair weaving	414/3	431.5
	Moquette, woollen, manufacturing	414/5	431.5
	Overcoating manufacturing	414/5	431.5
	Plush, wool, manufacturing	414/5	431.5
	Plush, worsted, weaving	414/3	431.5
	Press cloth manufacturing	414/5	431.5
	Shawl, not knitted, woollen manufacturing	414/5	431.5

SIC 1980	Activity	SIC 1968	NACE
	Suiting, woollen, manufacturing	414/5	431.5
	Suiting, worsted, weaving	414/3	431.5
	Taffeta, woollen, manufacturing	414/5	431.5
	Tapestry, woollen, manufacturing	414/5	431.5
	Travelling rug, woollen, manufacturing	414/5	431.5
	Tweed manufacturing	414/5	431.5
	Woollen and worsted product manufacturing	414	431
	Woollen cloth weaving	414/5	431.5
	Worsted weaving	414/3	431.5
4321/1	Spinning on the cotton system		
	Bobbin, cotton, manufacturing	412	432
	Core spun yard (cotton system) manufacturing	412	432.3
	Cotton carding	412	432.3
	Cotton combing	412	432.3
	Cotton drawing	412	432.3
	Cotton lap, sliver, rovings and other intermediate bobbin manufacturing	412	432
	Cotton opening	412	432.3
	Cotton sorting	412	432.3
	Cotton spinning	412	432.3
	Cotton warp manufacturing	412	432.3
	Cotton waste spinning	412	432.3
	Man-made fibre spinning on the cotton system	412	432.3
	Silk waste noil spinning	412	433.3
	Silk yarn manufacturing	412	433.3
	Spinning (cotton system)	412	432.3
	Waste yarn (cotton) manufacturing	412	432.3
	Yarn, cotton manufacturing	412	432.3
4321/2	Doubling and winding in the cotton industry		
	Carpet pile yarn (spun on the cotton system) manufacturing	412	432.4
	Cotton doubling	412	432.4
	Cotton fishing net yarn manufacturing	412	432.4
	Cotton reeling	412	432.4
	Cotton thread mill	412	432.4
	Cotton yarn doubling	412	432.4
	Cotton yarn twisting	412	432.4
	Cotton yarn warping	412	432.4
	Cotton yarn winding	412	432.4
	Embroidery cotton manufacturing	412	432.4
	Glass fibre spinning and doubling	412	432.4
	Glass fibre yarn manufacturing	412	432.4
	Glass fibre yarn, doubled, manufacturing	412	432.4
	Knitting yarns (of cotton) manufacturing	412	432.4
	Knitting yarns (of man-made fibres) manufacturing	412	432.4
	Man-made fibre twisting on the cotton system	412	432.4
	Man-made fibre warping on the cotton system	412	432.4
	Man-made fibre winding on the cotton system	412	432.4
	Sewing and embroidery yarn, cotton, manufacturing	412	432.4
	Sewing thread, cotton, manufacturing	412	432.4
	Silk thread manufacturing	412	433.4
	Silk twisting	412	433.4
	Silk warping	412	433.4
	Silk winding	412	433.4
	Thread (sewing and embroidery), cotton, manufacturing	412	432.4
	Tyre cord (cotton system) manufacturing	412	432.4
4322	Weaving of cotton, silk and man-made fibres		
	Apparel cloth (woven from yarns spun on the cotton system) manufacturing	413	432.5
	Bandage, cloth, weaving	413	432.5
	Bedford cord (not worsted) weaving	413	432.5
	Belting duck weaving	413	432.5
	Book cloth weaving	413	432.5
	Brocade weaving	413	432.5
	Bunting, cotton weaving	413	432.5
	Calico weaving	413	432.5
	Cambric weaving	413	432.5
	Casement cloth weaving	413	432.5
	Cellular cloth weaving (from yarn spun on the cotton system)	413	432.5
	Chenille manufacturing	413	432.5
	Chiffon weaving (from yarn spun on the cotton system)	413	432.5
	Chintz weaving (from yarn spun on the cotton system)	413	432.5
	Cloth (cotton and similar man-made fibre) manufacturing	413	432.5
	Corduroy weaving (from yarn spun on the cotton system)	413	432.5
	Corset cloth weaving (from yarn spun on the cotton system)	413	432.5
	Cotton flock manufacturing	413	432.5
	Cotton weaving	413	432.5
	Crepe, woven, manufacturing	413	432.5
	Cretonne weaving	413	432.5
	Damask (not woollen or worsted) weaving	413	432.5
	Denim weaving	413	432.5
	Downproof cloth weaving	413	432.5
	Dress fabric, woven (not wool), manufacturing	413	432.5
	Drill weaving (from yarn spun on the cotton system)	413	432.5
	Duck weaving	413	432.5
	Felt, cotton, weaving	413	432.5
	Filter cloth weaving	413	432.5
	Flag, cotton, weaving	413	432.5
	Flannelette weaving	413	432.5
	Furnishing fabric, woven (not wool or worsted), manufacturing	413	432.5
	Fustian weaving	413	432.5
	Gaberdine, cotton, weaving	413	432.5
	Gauze weaving	413	432.5
	Gingham weaving	413	432.5
	Glass fibre, woven fabric, manufacturing	413	432.5
	Haircord weaving	413	432.5
	Imitation fur, man-made fibre, manufacturing	413	432.5
	Interlining weaving (from yarn spun on the cotton system)	413	432.5
	Jeans cloth weaving	413	432.5
	Leno fabric weaving	413	432.5
	Man-made fibre weaving (from yarns spun on the cotton system)	413	432.5
	Moquette (not woollen) weaving	413	432.5
	Muslin weaving	413	432.5
	Organdie weaving	413	432.5
	Pique weaving	413	432.5
	Plush silk manufacturing	413	433.5
	Pocketing weaving	413	432.5
	Poplin weaving	413	432.5
	Poult weaving	413	432.5
	Print cloth weaving	413	432.5

SIC 1980	Activity	SIC 1968	NACE
	Printers' weaving	413	432.5
	Quilt weaving	413	432.5
	Sateen weaving	413	432.5
	Satin weaving	413	432.5
	Sheeting weaving (from yarn spun on the cotton system)	413	432.5
	Shirting weaving (from yarn spun on the cotton system)	413	432.5
	Silk, woven cloth manufacturing	413	433.5
	Taffeta (not woollen) weaving	413	432.5
	Tapestry (not woollen or worsted) manufacturing	413	432.5
	Ticking weaving	413	432.5
	Tie silk manufacturing	413	433.5
	Towelling weaving	413	432.5
	Tracing cloth weaving	413	432.5
	Twill weaving	413	432.5
	Tyre fabric (woven from yarn spun on the cotton system) manufacturing	413	432.5
	Veiling, silk, manufacturing	413	433.5
	Velvet manufacturing	413	432.5
	Velveteen manufacturing	413	432.5
	Voile weaving	413	432.5
	Wadding (from yarn spun on the cotton system) manufacturing	413	432.5
	Weaving (cotton and man-made fibres)	413	432.5
	Winceyette weaving	413	432.5
	Woven elastic over 30cm wide manufacturing	413	439.4
	Woven elastomeric over 30cm wide manufacturing	413	439.4
	Zephyr weaving	413	432.5
4336	Throwing, texturing, etc., of continuous filament yarn		
	Man-made fibre bulking (other than in man-made fibre producing establishments)	412	433.4
	Man-made fibre crimping (other than in man-made fibre producing establishments)	412	433.4
	Man-made fibre texturing (other than in man-made fibre producing establishments)	412	433.4
	Silk creping	412	433.4
	Silk throwing	412	433.4
4340/1	Spinning of flax, hemp and ramie		
	Dressed (line) flax manufacturing	412	434.1
	Flax carding	412	434.1
	Flax deseeding	412	434.1
	Flax dressing	412	434.1
	Flax hackling	412	434.1
	Flax preparing	412	434.1
	Flax roughing	412	434.1
	Flax sorting	412	434.1
	Flax spinning	412	434.3
	Hemp carding	412	434.1
	Hemp dressing	412	434.1
	Hemp sorting	412	434.1
	Hemp spinning	412	434.3
	Hemp thread manufacturing	412	434.4
	Line yarn of flax manufacturing	412	434.3
	Linen thread manufacturing	412	434.4
	Spinning, flax system	412	434.3
	Tow, flax, manufacturing	412	434.1
4340/2	Weaving of flax, hemp and ramie		
	Awning cloth weaving	413	434.5
	Canvas weaving	413	434.5
	Cloth, linen and union, manufacturing	413	434.5
	Flax woven cloth manufacturing	413	434.5
	Hemp weaving	413	434.5
	Linen buckram weaving	413	434.5
	Linen weaving	413	434.5
	Sailcloth weaving	413	434.5
	Scrim weaving (from flax, hemp, ramie and man-made fibre processed on the flax system)	413	434.5
	Sheeting weaving (from flax and man-made fibre processed on the flax system)	413	434.5
	Shirting weaving (from flax and man-made fibre processed on the flax system)	413	434.5
	Sunn hemp manufacturing	412	434.5
	Union cloth (cotton/linen) manufacturing	413	434.5
	Weaving (linen and union)	413	434.5
4350/1	Spinning of jute etc.		
	Jute sorting	415	435.3
	Jute spinning	415	435.3
	Jute thread manufacturing	415	435.3
	Jute winding	415	435.3
	Jute yarn manufacturing	415	435.3
	Tow, jute manufacturing	415	435.3
4350/2	Weaving of jute, etc.		
	Bagging cloth manufacturing	415	435.5
	Carpet, jute, manufacturing	415	438.1
	Cloth, jute, manufacturing	415	435.5
	Floor rug, jute, manufacturing	415	438.1
	Hessian manufacturing	415	435.5
	Mat, jute, manufacturing	415	438.1
	Sacking, jute, manufacturing	415	435.5
	Weaving, jute	415	435.5
4350/3	Production of fibrillated yarn and polypropylene fabric		
	Polypropylene woven cloth manufacturing	415	435.5
	Yarn, fibrillated, manufacturing	415	435.3
4363/1	Hosiery, including tights and panti-hose		
	Bedsock manufacturing	417	436.1
	Blank (hosiery) manufacturing	417	436.1
	Children's hose manufacturing	417	436.1
	Children's sock manufacturing	417	436.1
	Fancy hosiery manufacturing	417	436.1
	Men's sock manufacturing	417	436.1
	Panti-hose manufacturing	417	436.1
	Sock and stocking (knitted) manufacturing	417	436.1
	Stockinette goods manufacturing	417	436.1
	Stocking manufacturing	417	436.1
	Tights manufacturing	417	436.1
	Women's sock manufacturing	417	436.1
	Women's stocking manufacturing	417	436.1
4363/2	Weft knitted garments and other goods of weft knitted fabric		
	Balaclava helmet manufacturing	417	436.2
	Beret (knitted) manufacturing	417	436.2
	Bootees, knitted, manufacturing	417	436.2
	Cardigan, knitted, manufacturing	417	436.2
	Children's outerwear, knitted, manufacturing	417	436.2
	Children's underwear, knitted, manufacturing	417	436.2

SIC 1980	Activity	SIC 1968	NACE
	Dress and jacket ensemble, knitted, manufacturing	417	436.2
	Dress, women's knitted, manufacturing	417	436.2
	Glove, knitted, manufacturing	417	436.2
	Infants' swimwear, knitted manufacturing	417	436.2
	Infants' underclothing, knitted, manufacturing	417	436.2
	Jumper knitting	417	436.2
	Knitted bonnet manufacturing	417	436.2
	Knitted glove manufacturing	417	436.2
	Knitted scarf manufacturing	417	436.2
	Knitted shawl manufacturing	417	436.2
	Knitted swimsuit manufacturing	417	436.2
	Knitted underwear (excluding making up from purchased material) manufacturing	417	436.2
	Knitwear manufacturing	417	436.2
	Men's outerwear, knitted, manufacturing	417	436.2
	Men's swimwear, knitted, manufacturing	417	436.2
	Men's underwear (knitted) manufacturing	417	436.2
	Mittens and mitts, knitted, manufacturing	417	436.2
	Nightwear, knitted, manufacturing	417	436.2
	Outerwear, knitted, manufacturing	417	436.2
	Pullover, knitted, manufacturing	417	436.2
	Shirt, knitted, manufacturing	417	436.2
	Skirt, knitted, manufacturing	417	436.2
	Suit women's and girls', knitted, manufacturing	417	436.2
	Swimwear, knitted, manufacturing	417	436.2
	Tie, knitted, manufacturing	417	436.2
	Twin set, knitted, manufacturing	417	436.2
	Underclothing, knitted (children's), manufacturing	417	436.2
	Underwear, knitted, manufacturing	417	436.2
	Vest, knitted, manufacturing	417	436.2
	Women's and girls' nightwear, knitted, manufacturing	417	436.2
	Women's outerwear, knitted, manufacturing	417	436.2
	Women's underwear, knitted, manufacturing	417	436.2
4363/3	Weft knitted fabrics		
	Crocheted fabric manufacturing	417	436.2
	Fabric, crocheted, manufacturing	417	436.2
	Fabric, netted, manufacturing	417	436.2
	Fabric, pile, knitted, manufacturing	417	436.2
	Fabric, sliver knitted, manufacturing	417	436.2
	Locknit fabric manufacturing	417	436.2
	Netted fabric manufacturing	417	436.2
	Pile fabric, knitted, manufacturing	417	436.2
	Sliver knitted fabric manufacturing	417	436.2
	Weft knitted fabric manufacturing	417	436.2
4364	Warp knitted goods		
	Elastic or elastomeric fabric more than 30cm wide, knitted or netted, manufacturing	417	439.4
	Fabric, elastic and elastomeric, manufacturing	417	439.4
	Knitted or netted elastic over 30cm wide manufacturing	417	439.4
	Net curtaining fabric (knitted or crocheted) manufacturing	417	436.2
	Warp knitted fabric manufacturing	417	436.2
	Warp knitting	417	436.2
	Window furnishing fabric (knitted) manufacturing	417	436.2
4370/1	Foam backing and fabric to fabric bonding		
	Bonding (fabric to fabric)	423	437.4
	Foam backed fabric, finishing	423	437.4
	Foam backing (single textile material)	423	437.4
	Foam backing (textile material sandwich)	423	437.4
	Laminating textile material	423	437.4
4370/2	Other finishing processes		
	Binding and mending (textile)	423	437.4
	Bleach works	423	437.1
	Block printing (textile)	423	437.3
	Calendering (textile)	423	437.4
	Calico printing	423	437.3
	Chintz glazing	423	437.4
	Cloth (piece goods) printing	423	437.3
	Cloth beetling	423	437.4
	Cloth crease resisting treatment	423	437.4
	Cloth degreasing	423	437.4
	Cloth dressing	423	437.4
	Cloth dyeing	423	437.2
	Cloth embossing	423	437.4
	Cloth ending and mending	423	437.4
	Cloth finishing	423	437.4
	Cloth fireproofing	423	437.4
	Cloth mercerising	423	437.4
	Cloth proofing	423	437.4
	Cloth rotproofing	423	437.4
	Cloth shrinking	423	437.4
	Cloth waterproofing	423	437.4
	Commission mending (textile)	423	437.4
	Cotton cord and velveteen finishing	423	437.4
	Cotton fabric, bleaching, dyeing or otherwise finishing	423	437
	Cotton waste, bleaching, dyeing or otherwise finishing	423	437
	Cotton yarn gassing	423	437.4
	Cotton yarn polishing	423	437.4
	Cotton yarn printing	423	437.3
	Cotton, raw, bleaching, dyeing or otherwise finishing	423	437
	Dyework	423	437.2
	Ending and mending (textile)	423	437.4
	Fabric, woven, bleaching, dyeing or otherwise finishing	423	437
	Flannel ending	423	437.4
	Flannel filling	423	437.4
	Flannel finishing	423	437.4
	Flannel preparing	423	437.4
	Flannel scouring	423	437.4
	Flannel shrinking	423	437.4
	Flannelette raising, finishing	423	437.4
	Flax yarn, bleaching, dyeing or otherwise finishing	423	437
	Fulling mill	423	437.4
	Hair dyeing (textile)	423	437.2
	Hand block printing (textile)	423	437.3
	Hose, bleaching, dyeing or otherwise finishing	423	437
	Hosiery finishing	423	437.4
	Hosiery printing	423	437.2
	Hosiery scouring	423	437.4
	Hosiery shrinking	423	437.4
	Hosiery trimming	423	437.4
	Jute calendering	423	437.4
	Jute fabrics, bleaching, dyeing or otherwise finishing	423	437
	Knitted goods finishing	423	437.4

SIC 1980	Activity	SIC 1968	NACE	SIC 1980	Activity	SIC 1968	NACE
	Knitted goods printing	423	437.3		Carpet, pile, weaving	419	438.1
	Knitted goods scouring	423	437.4		Rug weaving (not travelling rug)	419	438.1
	Knitted goods shrinking	423	437.4		Wilton carpet manufacturing	419	438.1
	Knitted goods trimming	423	437.4	4384/2	Tufted, etc. carpets		
	Lace bleaching, dyeing, and dressing (on commission)	423	437		Carpet, tufted, manufacturing	419	438.1
	Lapping (textile)	423	437.4		Rug tufting	419	438.1
	Linen bleaching	423	437.1	4385/1	Needled and bonded carpets, carpeting and rugs		
	Linen dyeing	423	437.2		Carpeting, needleloom, manufacturing	429/2	438.1
	Linen printing	423	437.3		Needlefelt (carpet underlay) manufacturing	429/2	438.1
	Machine printing (textile)	423	437.3		Needleloom carpet manufacturing	429/2	438.1
	Man-made fibre fabric bleaching, dyeing, printing or otherwise finishing	423	437		Needleloom felt (carpet underlay) manufacturing	429/2	438.1
	Man-made fibre yarn finishing (bleaching, dyeing etc.)	423	437		Rag rug manufacturing	419	438.1
	Muslin clipping	423	437.4	4385/2	Hard fibre rugs, mats and matting		
	Muslin dressing	423	437.4		Coir mat and matting manufacturing	429/2	438.1
	Muslin ending	423	437.4		Mat and matting, coconut fibre, manufacturing	429/2	438.1
	Muslin finishing	423	437.4		Rug, coir, manufacturing	429/2	438.1
	Muslin gassing	423	437.4		Sisal mat and matting manufacturing	419	438.1
	Muslin mending	423	437.4	4395	Lace		
	Piece goods dyeing	423	437.2		Bedspread, lace, manufacturing	418	439.5
	Pile fabric bleaching and finishing	423	437		Embroidery lace manufacturing	418	439.5
	Plaiting (textile)	423	437.4		Furnishing lace manufacturing	418	439.5
	Rag bleaching	423	437.1		Hair net (lace) manufacturing	418	439.5
	Rag dyeing	423	437.2		Lace manufacturing	418	439.5
	Raw silk dyeing	423	437.2		Lace bleaching (not on commission)	418	439.5
	Roller printing (textile)	423	437.3		Lace clipping	418	439.5
	Screen printing (textile)	423	437.3		Lace curtain manufacturing	418	439.5
	Silk bleaching	423	437.1		Lace designing	418	439.5
	Silk dyeing	423	437.2		Lace drawing	418	439.5
	Silk finishing and weighting	423	437.4		Lace dressing	418	439.5
	Silk printing	423	437.3		Lace dyeing (not on commission)	418	439.5
	Slub dyeing	423	437.2		Lace edging manufacturing	418	439.5
	Smallware bleaching	423	437.1		Lace embroidery manufacturing	418	439.5
	Smallware dyeing	423	437.2		Lace ending	418	439.5
	Tape bleaching	423	437.1		Lace flouncing manufacturing	418	439.5
	Textile bleaching	423	437.1		Lace mending	418	439.5
	Textile dyeing	423	437.2		Lace net manufacturing	418	439.5
	Textile embossing	423	437.4		Lace scalloping	418	439.5
	Textile lacquering	423	437.4		Lace trimming manufacturing	418	439.5
	Tracing cloth manufacture (textile finishing)	423	437.4		Leavers lace manufacturing	418	439.5
	Velvet cutting or shearing	423	437.4		Napery lace manufacturing	418	439.5
	Velvet dyeing	423	437.2		Net, lace (plain and spotted), manufacturing	418	439.5
	Velveteen cutting or shearing	423	437.4		Nottingham lace manufacturing	418	439.5
	Velveteen dyeing	423	437.2		Raschel lace manufacturing	418	439.5
	Warp knitted fabric, dyeing and finishing	423	437		Scarf, lace, manufacturing	418	439.5
	Waste, textile, dyeing	423	437.2		Schiffli embroidery manufacturing	418	439.5
	Weft knitted fabric, dyeing and finishing	423	437		Swiss embroidery manufacturing	418	439.5
	Wool printing	423	437.3		Tablecloth, lace, manufacturing	418	439.5
	Wool, cop, hank, warp etc., bleaching	423	437.1		Veiling (not silk) manufacturing	418	439.5
	Wool, loose, dyeing	423	437.2	4396	Rope, twine and net		
	Woollen and worsted fabric bleaching, dyeing or otherwise finishing	423	437		Agricultural twine manufacturing	416	439.6
	Yarn finishing	423	437.4		Baler twine manufacturing	416	439.6
	Yarn gassing	423	437.4		Binder twine manufacturing	416	439.6
	Yarn mercerising	423	437.4		Cable (textile materials) manufacturing	416	439.6
	Yarn polishing	423	437.4		Cargo sling manufacturing	416	439.6
	Yarn storing	423	437.4		Combination rope manufacturing	416	439.6
	Yarn, bleaching, dyeing or otherwise finishing	423	437		Cordage (textile material) manufacturing	416	439.6
4384/1	Woven carpets and rugs				Cotton rope manufacturing	416	439.6
	Axminster carpet manufacturing	419	438.1		Fibre core for wire rope manufacturing	416	439.6
	Brussels carpet manufacturing	419	438.1		Fishing line manufacturing	416	439.6
	Carpet mat (pile) weaving	419	438.1		Fishing net manufacturing	416	439.7
	Carpet weaving	419	438.1				

SIC 1980	Activity	SIC 1968	NACE
	Fishing net mending	416	439.7
	Garden and horticultural net manufacturing	416	439.7
	Hammock manufacturing	416	439.7
	Hemp rope, cord or line manufacturing	416	439.6
	Horticultural net (textile) manufacturing	416	439.7
	Jute rope, cord or line manufacturing	416	439.6
	Line yarn of hard fibre manufacturing	416	439.6
	Man-made fibre rope, cord or line manufacturing	416	439.6
	Manila rope, cord or line manufacturing	416	439.6
	Reaper twine manufacturing	416	439.6
	Rope (textile materials) manufacturing	416	439.6
	Rope sling manufacturing	416	439.6
	Rope walk	416	439.6
	Sash line manufacturing	416	439.6
	Sheep net manufacturing	416	439.7
	Sisal rope, cord or line manufacturing	416	439.6
	Sports net manufacturing	416	439.7
	String manufacturing	416	439.6
	String bag manufacturing	416	439.7
	Tow yarn of hard fibres manufacturing	416	439.6
	Towing rope manufacturing	416	439.6
	Twine manufacturing	416	439.6
	Window cord manufacturing	416	439.6
4398/1	Elastics and elastomerics, narrow fabrics		
	Elastic braid manufacturing	421/1	439.4
	Elastic cord manufacturing	421/1	439.4
	Elastic fabric (not more than 30 cm wide) manufacturing	421/1	439.4
	Elastomeric braid manufacturing	421/1	439.4
	Elastomeric cord manufacturing	421/1	439.4
	Elastomeric fabric (not more than 30 cm wide) manufacturing	421/1	439.4
4398/2	Other narrow fabrics and solid woven machinery belting		
	Banding (woven) manufacturing	421/2	439.3
	Bias binding manufacturing	421/3	439.3
	Binding (woven) manufacturing	421/3	439.3
	Boot lace, braided, manufacturing	421/3	439.3
	Braid (textile material) manufacturing	421/3	439.3
	Carding of trimmings	421/3	439.3
	Coach lace and trimming manufacturing	421/3	439.3
	Coffin frilling manufacturing	421/3	439.3
	Conveyor belting, woven, manufacturing	421/2	439.3
	Corset lace manufacturing	421/3	439.3
	Curtain loop manufacturing	421/3	439.3
	Dress binding manufacturing	421/3	439.3
	Dressing gown cord and girdle manufacturing	421/3	439.3
	Frilling manufacturing	421/3	439.3
	Fringe (textile material) manufacturing	421/3	439.3
	Galloon ribbon manufacturing	421/3	439.3
	Gimp manufacturing	421/3	439.3
	Haberdashery (narrow fabrics) manufacturing	421/3	439.3
	Hat band manufacturing	421/3	439.3
	Label, woven, manufacturing	421/3	439.7
	Lace (boot and shoe) manufacturing	421/3	439.3
	Ladder tape (textile material) manufacturing	421/3	439.3
	Narrow fabric (not elastic or elastomeric) manufacturing	422/1	439.3
	Non-elastic braid manufacturing	421/3	439.3
	Petersham ribbon manufacturing	421/3	439.3
	Printed label (textile material) manufacturing	421/3	439.7
	Pyjama cord manufacturing	421/3	439.3
	Ribbon (textile) manufacturing	421/3	439.3
	Shoe lace, braided, manufacturing	421/3	439.3
	Shoe trimming (textile material) manufacturing	421/3	439.3
	Smallware, textile, manufacturing	421/3	439.3
	Tape, non-elastic and non-elastomeric, (textile material) manufacturing	421/3	439.3
	Tassel (textile material) manufacturing	421/3	439.3
	Textile smallware (narrow fabric) manufacturing	421/3	439.3
	Trimming, woven, manufacturing	421/3	439.3
	Twist cord (fabric) manufacturing	421/3	439.3
	Umbrella trimming (textile material) manufacturing	421/3	439.3
	Upholsterers' trimming (textile material) manufacturing	421/3	439.3
	Webbing weaving	421/3	439.3
	Webbing, non-elastic and non-elastomeric, manufacturing	421/3	439.3
	Wick (lamp, stove or candle) manufacturing	421/3	439.7
	Woven machinery belting manufacturing	421/2	439.7
4399/1	Felt		
	Baize manufacturing	414/5	439.1
	Billiard table cloth manufacturing	414/5	439.1
	Bonded fibre fabric manufacturing	429/2	439.2
	Felt (woven) manufacturing	414	439.1
	Felt, pressed, (not paper or roofing) manufacturing	414/6	439.1
	Needlefelt (other than carpet underlay) manufacturing	429/2	439.1
	Needleloom felt (other than carpet underlay) manufacturing	429/2	439.1
	Non-woven (bonded fibre) fabric manufacturing	429/2	439.2
	Wool felt, pressed, manufacturing	414/6	439.1
4399/2	Other miscellaneous textiles not elsewhere specified		
	Down, vegetable, manufacturing	429/2	439.7
	Fabric, tufted, (other than household textile) manufacturing	429/2	439.7
	Hair dressing (for upholsterers)	429/2	439.7
	Horsehair curling	429/2	439.7
	Horsehair dressing	429/2	439.7
	Horsehair hackling	429/2	439.7
	Horsehair sorting	429/2	439.7
	Horsehair teasing	429/2	439.7
	Kapok willowing	429/2	439.7
	Padding (for upholstery) manufacturing	429/2	439.7
	Upholstery hair fibre and filling manufacturing	429/2	439.7
4410/1	Tanning and dressing of leather		
	Box and willow calf leather manufacturing	431/1	441.3
	Buckskin manufacturing	431/1	441.3
	Cattle hide leather manufacturing	431/1	441.3
	Chrome tanning	431/1	441.1

SIC 1980	Activity	SIC 1968	NACE
	Clothing leather manufacturing	431/1	441.3
	Combing leather manufacturing	431/1	441.3
	Dressing leather	431/1	441.1
	Footwear leather preparation	431/1	441.3
	Gill leather manufacturing	431/1	441.3
	Glace kid manufacturing	431/1	441.3
	Glove leather preparation	431/1	441.3
	Goldbeaters' skin or bung manufacturing	431/1	441.3
	Harness and saddlery leather preparation	431/1	441.3
	Hat and cap leather preparation	431/1	441.3
	Hide curing	431/1	441.1
	Hide degreasing	431/1	441.1
	Hide dressing	431/1	441.1
	Hide pickling	431/1	441.1
	Hide trimming	431/1	441.1
	Hydraulic leather manufacturing	431/1	441.3
	Leather dyeing	431/1	441.3
	Leather enamelling	431/1	441.3
	Leather gilding	432	441.3
	Leather proofing	431/1	441.3
	Leather tanning	431/1	441.1
	Leather, chamois, manufacturing	431/1	441.3
	Lining leather preparation	431/1	441.3
	Mechanical leather preparation	431/1	441.3
	Parchment leather manufacturing	431/1	441.3
	Patent leather manufacturing	431/1	441.3
	Reptile leather manufacturing	431/1	441.3
	Sheep skin preparation	431/2	456.1
	Sheepskin rug manufacturing	431/2	456.3
	Skin curing	431/1	441.1
	Skin dressing	433	441.1
	Skin drying	431/1	441.1
	Skin dyeing	431/1	441.3
	Skin pickling	431/1	441.1
	Skin rug manufacturing	431/2	456.3
	Skin sorting	431/1	441.1
	Sole leather preparation	431/1	441.3
	Tannery	431/1	441.1
	Upholstery leather preparation	431/1	441.3
	Upper leather manufacturing	431/1	441.3
	Vellum manufacturing	431/1	441.3
4410/2	Fellmongery		
	De-woolling	431/2	431.1
	Fellmongery	431/2	431.1
	Pelt (fellmongery) manufacturing	431	431.1
	Sheep and lambskin pulling	431/2	431.1
	Wool (fellmongery) manufacturing	431	431.1
4420/1	Travel goods, saddlery and other consumer goods		
	Army accoutrement, leather, manufacturing	432	442.1
	Art leather work manufacturing	432	442.1
	Attache case (leather or leather substitute) manufacturing	432	442.1
	Bag (leather or leather substitute) manufacturing	432	442.1
	Belt (leather or leather substitute) manufacturing	432	442.1
	Billfold (leather) manufacturing	432	442.1
	Braces, leather, manufacturing	432	442.1
	Bridle cutting	432	442.1
	Brown saddlery manufacturing	432	442.1
	Case for cutlery, instruments, etc., (leather) manufacturing	432	442.1
	Container for typewriter, radio, etc., (leather) manufacturing	432	442.1
	Cycle bag (leather) manufacturing	432	442.1
	Dog lead, leather, manufacturing	432	442.1
	Dressing case (leather) or leather substitute) manufacturing	432	442.1
	Fancy leather goods manufacturing	432	442.1
	Gun case (leather) manufacturing	432	442.1
	Hand luggage (leather) manufacturing	432	442.1
	Handbag (leather or leather substitute) manufacturing	432	442.1
	Harness front and rosette (leather) manufacturing	432	442.1
	Hat box (leather or leather substitute) manufacturing	432	442.1
	Horse collar (leather) manufacturing	432	442.1
	Key tag and case (leather) manufacturing	432	442.1
	Ladies' handbag (leather) manufacturing	432	442.1
	Leather goods (not industrial) manufacturing	432	442.1
	Leather lace manufacturing	431/1	442.1
	Leather trimmings manufacturing	432	442.1
	Luggage (leather or leather substitute) manufacturing	432	442.1
	Manicure case (leather) manufacturing	432	442.1
	Novelty goods (leather) manufacturing	432	442.1
	Pochette (leather) manufacturing	432	442.1
	Pocket book (leather) manufacturing	432	442.1
	Pouch (leather or leather substitute) manufacturing	432	442.1
	Purse (leather or leather substitute) manufacturing	432	442.1
	Radio case (leather) manufacturing	432	442.1
	Saddle, horse, manufacturing	432	442.1
	Sample case (leather) manufacturing	432	442.1
	Satchel (leather) manufacturing	432	442.1
	Spectacle case (leather) manufacturing	432	442.1
	Strap (leather) manufacturing	432	442.1
	Suitcase (leather or leather substitute) manufacturing	432	442.1
	Toilet case, fitted, (leather) manufacturing	432	442.1
	Toolbag (leather) manufacturing	432	442.1
	Travel goods (leather or leather substitute) manufacturing	432	442.1
	Trunk (leather) manufacturing	432	442.1
	Trunk handle (leather) manufacturing	432	442.1
	Typewriter case (leather) manufacturing	432	442.1
	Wallet (leather or leather substitute) manufacturing	432	442.1
	Watchstrap (leather or leather substitute) manufacturing	432	442.1
4420/2	Leather goods for industrial use		
	Buff and mop (leather) manufacturing	432	442.3
	Buffalo pickers (leather) manufacturing	431/1	442.3
	Check strap (leather) manufacturing	431/1	442.3
	Conveyor band (leather) manufacturing	431/1	442.3
	Driving belt (leather) manufacturing	431/1	442.3
	Elevator band (leather) manufacturing	431/1	442.3
	Gas meter diaphragm (leather) manufacturing	431/1	442.3
	Industrial leather manufacturing	431/1	442.3
	Leather for roller covering manufacturing	431/1	442.3

SIC 1980	Activity	SIC 1968	NACE
	Leather mill band and strap manufacturing	431/1	442.3
	Leather picker manufacturing	431/1	442.3
	Leather tuft manufacturing	432	442.3
	Machinery accessories (leather) manufacturing	431/1	442.3
	Machinery belting (leather) manufacturing	431/1	442.3
	Picking band (leather) manufacturing	431/1	442.3
	Pump leather manufacturing	432	442.3
	Roller skin (cut), leather, manufacturing	431/1	442.3
	Skip (leather) manufacturing	431/1	442.3
	Strop (leather) manufacturing	432	442.3
	Washer (leather) manufacturing	432	442.3
4510	Footwear		
	Ballet shoe manufacturing	450	451.3
	Beach footwear manufacturing	450	451.3
	Boot manufacturing	450	451.1
	Boot and shoe pattern making and designing	450	451.1
	Boot closing	450	451.1
	Boot stiffener manufacturing	450	451.4
	Boot upper manufacturing	450	451.4
	Bootee, rubber protective, manufacturing	450	481.2
	Clog manufacturing	450	465.4
	Cut sole (footwear) manufacturing	450	451.4
	Footwear manufacturing	450	451
	Gaiter, leather, manufacturing	450	451.4
	Heel, leather, manufacturing	450	451.4
	House shoe manufacturing	450	451.2
	Insole, leather, manufacturing	450	451.4
	Leather fillings manufacturing	450	451.4
	Leather spat manufacturing	450	451.4
	Legging, leather, manufacturing	450	451.4
	Overboot manufacturing	450	451.3
	Overshoe, rubber, manufacturing	450	481.2
	Plastics protective footwear manufacturing	450	483
	Rubber galosh manufacturing	450	481.2
	Rubber protective footwear manufacturing	450	481.2
	Safety boot manufacturing	450	451.3
	Sandal manufacturing	450	451.3
	Shoe (footwear) manufacturing	450	451.1
	Slipper manufacturing	450	451.2
	Slipper sole manufacturing	450	451.4
	Sock, leather, manufacturing	450	451.4
	Sports footwear manufacturing	450	451.3
	Surgical boot manufacturing	450	452
	Toe puff manufacturing	450	451.4
	Wellington boot manufacturing	450	481.2
4531	Weatherproof outerwear		
	Anorak manufacturing	441	453
	Climbing clothing, weatherproof, manufacturing	441	453
	Clothing, recreational, (weatherproofed) manufacturing	441	453
	Industrial clothing, weather protective, manufacturing	441	453
	Infants' weatherproof outerwear manufacturing	441	453
	Jacket, weatherproof, manufacturing	441	453
	Mackintosh manufacturing	441	453
	Oilskin manufacturing	441	453
	Outerwear, plastics, manufacturing	441	453
	Plastic raincoat manufacturing	441	453
	Protective clothing, industrial, manufacturing	441	453
	Raincoat, men's and boys', manufacturing	441	453
	Raincoat, women's and girls', manufacturing	441	453
	Rainproof garment manufacturing	441	453
	Recreational clothing (weatherproofed) manufacturing	441	453
	Sailing clothing, weatherproof, manufacturing	441	453
	Skiing clothing, weatherproof, manufacturing	441	453
	Waterproof garment manufacturing	441	453
	Weatherproof outerwear manufacturing	441	453
4532	Men's and boys' tailored outerwear		
	Battledress, men's, manufacturing	442	453
	Boys' blazer (not retail bespoke) manufacturing	442	453
	Boys' jacket (not retail bespoke) manufacturing	442	453
	Boys' outerwear, tailored, (not retail bespoke) manufacturing	442	453
	Boys' overcoat (not retail bespoke) manufacturing	442	453
	Boys' shorts manufacturing	442	453
	Boys' suit (not retail bespoke) manufacturing	442	453
	Boys' trousers, tailored, (not retail bespoke) manufacturing	442	453
	Boys' waistcoat, tailored, (not retail bespoke) manufacturing	442	453
	Breeches (not retail bespoke) manufacturing	442	453
	Cassock manufacturing	442	453
	Clerical vestment (not retail bespoke) manufacturing	442	453
	Cloak, men's and boys', manufacturing	442	453
	Coat (men's and boys', not retail bespoke) manufacturing	442	453
	Gown (academic, legal and ecclesiastical) manufacturing	442	453
	Kilt (tailored, not retail bespoke) manufacturing	442	453
	Leather garment (men's) manufacturing	442	453
	Livery (not retail bespoke) manufacturing	442	453
	Male nurses' uniform manufacturing	442	453
	Men's blazer (not retail bespoke) manufacturing	442	453
	Men's jacket (not retail bespoke) manufacturing	442	453
	Men's outerwear, tailored, (not retail bespoke) manufacturing	442	453
	Men's overcoat (not retail bespoke) manufacturing	442	453
	Men's shorts, tailored, manufacturing	442	453
	Men's suit (not retail bespoke) manufacturing	442	453
	Men's waistcoat (not retail bespoke) manufacturing	442	453
	Military clothing (not retail bespoke) manufacturing	442	453
	Robe (academic, legal and ecclesiastical) manufacturing	442	453
	Sportswear (men's and boys' tailored; not retail bespoke) manufacturing	442	453
	Surplice manufacturing	442	453

SIC 1980	Activity	SIC 1968	NACE
	Trousers, men's, (not retail bespoke) (tailored) manufacturing	442	453
	Uniform (by men's tailors; not retail bespoke) manufacturing	442	453
4533	Women's and girls' tailored outerwear		
	Battledress, women's, manufacturing	443	453
	Blazer, women's and girls', tailored, (not retail bespoke) manufacturing	443	453
	Cloak, women's and girls', manufacturing	443	453
	Coat, women's and girls' tailored, (not retail bespoke) manufacturing	443	453
	Costume (not retail bespoke) manufacturing	443	453
	Jacket, women's and girls', tailored, (not retail bespoke) manufacturing	443	453
	Leather garments (women's and girls') manufacturing	443	453
	Outerwear, tailored, (women's and girls') (not retail bespoke) manufacturing	443	453
	Overcoat, women's and girls', (not retail bespoke) manufacturing	443	453
	Skirt, tailored, (not retail bespoke) manufacturing	443	453
	Sportswear, women's and girls', tailored, (not retail bespoke) manufacturing	443	453
	Suit, women's and girls'; tailored (not retail bespoke) manufacturing	443	453
	Trouser suit, women's and girls', tailored, (not retail bespoke) manufacturing	443	453
	Trousers, women's and girls', tailored, (not retail bespoke) manufacturing	443	453
	Uniform, women's and girls', (not retail bespoke) manufacturing	443	453
	Women's clothing, tailored, (not retail bespoke) manufacturing	443	453
4534	Work clothing and men's and boys' jeans		
	Apron, industrial, manufacturing	444/1	453
	Boiler suit manufacturing	444/1	453
	Boys' overall manufacturing	444/1	453
	Chefs' clothing manufacturing	444/1	453
	Clothing, industrial, manufacturing	444/1	453
	Dungarees manufacturing	444/1	453
	Girls' overall manufacturing	444/1	453
	Jeans, boys', manufacturing	444/1	453
	Jeans, men's, manufacturing	444/1	453
	Men's apron manufacturing	441/1	453
	Men's overall manufacturing	441/1	453
	Shirt, industrial, manufacturing	444/2	453
	Trouser, work, manufacturing	444/1	453
	Women's industrial overall manufacturing	444/1	453
4535	Men's and boys' shirts, underwear and nightwear		
	Athletic clothing manufacturing	444/2	453
	Collar (men's and boys') manufacturing	444/2	453
	Cuff (men's and boys') manufacturing	444/2	453
	Dressing gown (men's and boys') manufacturing	444/2	453

SIC 1980	Activity	SIC 1968	NACE
	Nightwear (men's and boys') manufacturing	444/2	453
	Pants (men's underwear) manufacturing	444/2	453
	Pyjama (men's and boys') manufacturing	444/2	453
	Shirt (men's and boys') manufacturing	444/2	453
	Shirt front manufacturing	444/2	453
	Shirt neckband manufacturing	444/2	453
	Tracksuit manufacturing	444/1	453
	Underwear (men's and boys') manufacturing	444/2	453
	Vest (men's and boys') manufacturing	444/2	453
4536/1	Light outerwear		
	Apron, domestic, manufacturing	445/1	453
	Beachwear (women's and girls') manufacturing	445/1	453
	Blouse manufacturing	445/1	453
	Clothing, disposable, manufacturing	445/1	453
	Costume, lightweight, (dressmade) manufacturing	445/1	453
	Divided skirt, lightweight, (dressmade) manufacturing	445/1	453
	Dress designing	445/1	453
	Dressing gown (women's and girls') manufacturing	445/1	453
	Dressmaking (not retail bespoke)	445/1	453
	Gown (not retail bespoke) manufacturing	445/1	453
	Housecoat manufacturing	445/1	453
	Jacket, women's lightweight, manufacturing	445/1	453
	Jeans (women's and girls') manufacturing	444/1	453
	Light outerwear (women's and girls') manufacturing	445/1	453
	Nun's clothing manufacturing	445/1	453
	Overall, domestic, manufacturing	445/1	453
	Pinafore manufacturing	445/1	453
	Pinarette manufacturing	445/1	453
	Shirt (women's and girls') manufacturing	445/1	453
	Skirt (women's and girls' dressmade) manufacturing	445/1	453
	Sportswear (women's and girls') manufacturing	445/1	453
	Suit (women's and girls'; dressmade) manufacturing	445/1	453
4536/2	Lingerie		
	Brief (women's) manufacturing	445/2	453
	Knickers manufacturing	445/2	453
	Lingerie manufacturing	445/2	453
	Nightdress manufacturing	445/2	453
	Nightwear (women's and girls') manufacturing	445/2	453
	Pantie manufacturing	445/2	453
	Petticoat manufacturing	445/2	453
	Pyjama (women's and girls') manufacturing	445/2	453
	Slip manufacturing	445/2	453
	Underskirt manufacturing	445/2	453
	Underwear (women's and girls') manufacturing	445/2	453
	Vest (women's and girls') manufacturing	445/2	453
4536/3	Infants' wear		
	Baby clothing manufacturing	445/3	453
	Baby linen manufacturing	445/3	453

SIC 1980	Activity	SIC 1968	NACE
	Children's dress manufacturing	445/1	453
	Infants' underclothing manufacturing	445/3	453
	Nightwear, infants', manufacturing	445/3	453
	Outerwear, infants', manufacturing	445/3	453
	Underclothing (children's) manufacturing	445/3	453
4537/1	Felt hats, caps and millinery		
	Capeline, felt, manufacturing	446/1	453
	Felt hat (men's) manufacturing	446/1	453
	Felt hat bleaching and dyeing	446/1	453
	Felt hat body making	446/1	453
	Felt hat finishing	446/1	453
	Hat, felt, manufacturing	446/1	453
	Hat, women's and girls', (felt) manufacturing	446/1	453
	Millinery of felt	446/1	453
	Wool felt and fur felt hood and capeline manufacturing	446/1	453
4537/2	Hats and caps of other materials		
	Beret (not knitted) manufacturing	446/2	453
	Buckram shape manufacturing	446/2	453
	Cap peak manufacturing	446/2	453
	Cloth cap manufacturing	446/2	453
	Fur fabric hat manufacturing	446/2	453
	Hat (cloth) manufacturing	446/2	453
	Hat lining manufacturing	446/2	453
	Hat pad manufacturing	446/2	453
	Hat shape manufacturing	446/2	453
	Hat, men's and boy's, (not felt or fur) manufacturing	446/2	453
	Industrial headgear, protective, (not plastics) manufacturing	446/2	453
	Protective headgear (not plastics) manufacturing	446/2	453
	Riding cap manufacturing	446/2	453
	Silk hat manufacturing	446/2	453
	Straw hat manufacturing	446/2	453
	Straw hat blocking	446/2	453
	Tropical helmet manufacturing	446/2	453
	Uniform hat and cap manufacturing	446/2	453
	Uniform helmet manufacturing	446/2	453
4538	Gloves		
	Abestos glove manufacturing	449/2	244
	Children's glove manufacturing	449/2	453
	Cloth glove manufacturing	449/2	453
	Fabric dress glove manufacturing	449/2	453
	Gauntlet manufacturing	449/2	442.2
	Glove (other than knitted) manufacturing	449/2	453
	Glove, cloth, manufacturing	449/2	453
	Glove, fur, manufacturing	449/2	456.3
	Glove, industrial (not rubber), manufacturing	449/2	453
	Glove, leather (not sports), manufacturing	449/2	442.2
	Household glove (textile) manufacturing	449/2	453
	Men's glove manufacturing	449/2	453
	Mitten and Mitt (not knitted) manufacturing	449/2	453
	Women's glove manufacturing	449/2	453
4539/1	Swimwear and foundation garments		
	Brassiere manufacturing	449/1	453
	Corselet manufacturing	449/1	453
	Corset manufacturing	449/1	453
	Corset belt manufacturing	449/1	453
	Foundation garment manufacturing	449/1	453
	Surgical corset manufacturing	449/1	453
	Suspender manufacturing	449/4	453
	Suspender belt manufacturing	449/1	453
	Swimwear manufacturing	449/1	453
4539/2	Umbrellas		
	Parasol manufacturing	449/3	453
	Sunshade manufacturing	449/3	453
	Umbrella manufacturing	449/3	453
4539/3	Miscellaneous dress industries		
	Artificial flower (textile) manufacturing	449/4	453
	Belt, dress (not leather or leather substitute), manufacturing	449/4	453
	Braces (not leather or leather substitute) manufacturing	449/4	453
	Clothing pad manufacturing	449/4	453
	Costume, theatrical, manufacturing	449/4	453
	Cravat manufacturing	449/4	453
	Dress shield manufacturing	449/4	453
	Fan, ladies', manufacturing	449/4	453
	Feather ornament manufacturing	449/4	453
	Garter manufacturing	449/4	453
	Hair pad making	449/4	453
	Handkerchief (of textile material) manufacturing	422/1	453
	Handkerchief folding	422/1	453
	Handkerchief hemming	422/1	453
	Headsquare manufacturing	449/4	453
	Legging and gaiter (cloth) manufacturing	449/4	453
	Necktie manufacturing	449/4	453
	Neckwear (ladies) manufacturing	449/4	453
	Scarf (not lace or knitted) manufacturing	449/4	453
	Silk tie manufacturing	449/4	453
	Sporran manufacturing	449/4	453
	Tailors' pad manufacturing	449/4	453
	Wig manufacturing	449/4	453
4555	Soft furnishings		
	Bolster manufacturing	473	455.2
	Curtain, made-up, manufacturing	473	455.3
	Cushion cover manufacturing	422/1	455.1
	Cushion manufacturing	473	455.2
	Loose cover (furniture) manufacturing	473	455.3
	Pillow manufacturing	473	455.2
	Stretch cover (furniture) manufacturing	473	455.3
4556	Canvas goods, sacks and other made-up textiles		
	Awning manufacturing	422/2	455.4
	Bag, canvas, manufacturing	422/2	455.4
	Banner (making up only) manufacturing	422/1	455.4
	Blinds, canvas, manufacturing	422/2	455.4
	Brattice cloth manufacturing	422/2	455.4
	Bucket, canvas, manufacturing	422/2	455.4
	Bunting (making up only) manufacturing	422/1	455.4
	Canvas goods manufacturing	422/2	455.4
	Canvas shute manufacturing	422/2	455.4
	Canvas tube (for ventilating purposes) manufacturing	422/2	455.4
	Cart cover (canvas) manufacturing	422/2	455.4
	Coal sack manufacturing	422/2	455.4
	Cover, water proofed, (canvas) manufacturing	422/2	455.4
	Flag (making up only) manufacturing	422/1	455.4
	Flexible ventilating ducting (textile) manufacturing	422/2	455.4

SIC 1980	Activity	SIC 1968	NACE
	Haversack manufacturing	422/2	455.4
	Jute sack manufacturing	422/2	439.7
	Made-up filter cloth manufacturing	422/2	455.4
	Marquee manufacturing	422/2	455.4
	Noil sack and bag manufacturing	422/2	439.7
	Perambulator awning manufacturing	422/1	455.4
	Rick cloth and cover manufacturing	422/2	455.4
	Sack, canvas, manufacturing	422/2	455.4
	Sack, woven, manufacturing	422/2	455.4
	Sail manufacturing	422/2	455.4
	Sailcloth, made up goods, manufacturing	422/2	455.4
	Tarpaulin manufacturing	422/2	455.4
	Tarpaulin repairing	422/2	455.4
	Tent manufacturing	422/2	455.4
	Wagon cover manufacturing	422/2	455.4
	Web equipment making-up	422/2	455.4
4557	**Household textiles**		
	Art needlework manufacturing	422/1	455.1
	Bath mat manufacturing	422/1	455.1
	Bath towel manufacturing	422/1	455.1
	Bed linen manufacturing	422/1	455.1
	Bedspread manufacturing	422/1	455.2
	Blanket making up (outside weaving or knitting establishment)	422/1	455.2
	Bolster case manufacturing	422/1	455.1
	Cleaning cloth (not of bonded fibre fabric) manufacturing	422/1	455.1
	Cot blanket (outside weaving or knitting establishment) manufacturing	422/1	455.2
	Cot quilt manufacturing	422/1	455.2
	Cotton patch quilt manufacturing	422/1	455.2
	Cotton, silk, etc., embroidering (except lace and apparel)	422/1	455.1
	Counterpane manufacturing	422/1	455.2
	Doily, textile, manufacturing	422/1	455.1
	Duchess set manufacturing	422/1	455.1
	Dust sheet manufacturing	422/1	455.1
	Duster (cleaning cloth; not of bonded fibre fabric) manufacturing	422/1	455.1
	Duvet manufacturing	422/1	455.2
	Embroidering on made-up textile goods	422/1	455.1
	Hand towel manufacturing	422/1	455.1
	Household textile manufacturing	422/1	455.1
	Lavatory seat cover manufacturing	422/1	455.1
	Machine hemming	422/1	455.1
	Machine quilting	422/1	455.2
	Machine tucking	422/1	455.1
	Nursery square manufacturing	422/1	455.1
	Pedestal mat manufacturing	422/1	455.1
	Pillow case manufacturing	422/1	455.1
	Pincushion manufacturing	422/1	455.2
	Polishing cloth and pad (unprepared; not bonded fibre fabric) manufacturing	422/1	455.1
	Pram blanket (outside knitting or weaving establishment) manufacturing	422/1	455.2
	Quilt fringing manufacturing	422/1	455.2
	Quilt, filled, manufacturing	422/1	455.2
	Roller towel manufacturing	422/1	455.1
	Sheet hemming (textile)	422/1	455.1
	Shroud and cerement manufacturing	422/1	455.1
	Sleeping bag manufacturing	422/1	455.2
	Table linen manufacturing	422/1	455.1
	Table mat (textile) manufacturing	422/1	455.1
	Table runner (not lace) manufacturing	422/1	455.1
	Tea towel manufacturing	422/1	455.1
	Textile, household, manufacturing	422/1	455.1
	Towel manufacturing	422/1	455.1
	Travelling rug making-up outside weaving establishment	422/1	455.2
	Tufting blankets	422/1	455.2
	Tufting household textiles	422/1	455.1
4560	**Fur goods**		
	Apparel, fur, manufacturing	433	456.3
	Cape, fur, manufacturing	433	456.3
	Coat, fur, manufacturing	433	456.3
	Cravat, fur, manufacturing	433	456.3
	Dyed lamb (including beaver lamb) manufacturing	433	456.1
	Fur dressing	433	456.1
	Fur dyeing manufacturing	433	456.1
	Fur mat and rug manufacturing	433	456.3
	Hat, fur, manufacturing	433	456.3
	Hatters' fur manufacturing	433	456.2
	Lambskin clothing manufacturing	433	456.3
	Manufacturing furrier	433	456
	Moleskin finishing	433	456.1
	Muff, fur, manufacturing	433	456.3
	Rabbit fur garment manufacturing	433	456.3
	Rabbit skin sorting	433	456.1
	Sheepskin clothing manufacturing	433	456.3
	Stole, fur, manufacturing	433	456.3
	Trimmings, fur, manufacturing	433	456.1
4610/1	**Sawn wood**		
	Bent timber manufacturing	471/1	461.1
	Boxboard manufacturing	471/1	461.1
	Fencing pole manufacturing	471/1	461.1
	Fencing, sawn, manufacturing	471/1	461.1
	Fuelwood manufacturing	471/1	461.1
	Log sawing	471/1	461.1
	Mining timber, sawn, manufacturing	471/1	461.1
	Picket, wood, manufacturing	471/1	461.1
	Piling, wood, manufacturing	471/1	461.1
	Pit prop, wood, manufacturing	471/1	461.1
	Pole, wood, manufacturing	471/1	461.1
	Post, wood, manufacturing	471/1	461.1
	Pulpwood manufacturing	471/1	461.1
	Roundwood manufacturing	471/1	461.1
	Sawlog manufacturing	471/1	461.1
	Sawmilling	471/1	461.1
	Sleeper, wood, manufacturing	471/1	461.1
	Splitwood manufacturing	471/1	461.1
	Stake, wood, manufacturing	471/1	461.1
	Telegraph pole manufacturing	471/1	461.1
	Veneer log sawing	471/1	461.1
	Wagon timber, sawn, manufacturing	471/1	461.1
	Wood sawing	471/1	461.1
4610/2	**Planed wood**		
	Bargeboard manufacturing	471/1	461.2
	Beaded wood manufacturing	471/1	461.2
	Chamfered wood manufacturing	471/1	461.2
	Flooring, wood, (not parquet flooring) manufacturing	471/1	461.2
	Grooved wood manufacturing	471/1	461.2
	Plank manufacturing	471/1	461.2
	Rebated wood manufacturing	471/1	461.2
	Skirting board (unmoulded) wood, manufacturing	471/1	461.2
	Tongued wood manufacturing	471/1	461.2
	V-jointed wood manufacturing	471/1	461.2
	Weather board manufacturing	471/1	461.2
	Wood grooving	471/1	461.2
	Wood planing	471/1	461.2

SIC 1980	Activity	SIC 1968	NACE
4620/1	Semi-finished wood products		
	Battenboard manufacturing	471/1	462.1
	Blockboard manufacturing	471/1	462.1
	Building board (made from wood waste) manufacturing	471/1	462.2
	Cellular wood panel manufacturing	471/1	462.1
	Chipboard, agglomerated with non-mineral binding substances, manufacturing	471/1	462.2
	Fibre building board manufacturing	471/1	462.2
	Hardboard manufacturing	471/1	462.2
	Improved wood manufacturing	471/1	462.3
	Inlaid wood manufacturing	471/1	462.1
	Laminated wood product manufacturing	471/1	462.1
	Laminboard manufacturing	471/1	462.1
	Particleboard, agglomerated with non-mineral binding substances, manufacturing	471/1	462.2
	Plywood manufacturing	471/1	462.1
	Veneer manufacturing	471/1	462.1
	Veneer sheet manufacturing	471/1	462.1
	Wood chipboard, agglomerated with non-mineral binding substances, manufacturing	471/1	462.2
	Wood marquetry manufacturing	471/1	462.1
	Wood veneer manufacturing	471/1	462.1
4620/2	Preservation and treatment of wood		
	Immersion treatment of wood	471/1	462.4
	Pressure treatment of wood	471/1	462.4
	Vacuum treatment of wood	471/1	462.4
	Wood creosoting	471/1	462.4
	Wood impregnation	471/1	462.4
	Wood preservation	471/1	462.4
	Wood spraying	471/1	462.4
	Wood treatment	471/1	462.4
	Wood varnishing	471/1	462.4
4630	Builders' carpentry and joinery		
	Banister rail, wooden, manufacturing	471/2	463.1
	Blind (not shop blind), wooden, manufacturing	471/2	463.2
	Bridge, wooden, manufacturing	471/2	463.1
	Builders' carpentry and joinery manufacturing	471/2	463.2
	Builders' woodwork (window frames, etc.) manufacturing	471/2	463.2
	Display stand manufacturing	474	463.1
	Door frame, wooden, manufacturing	471/2	463.2
	Door, wooden, manufacturing	471/2	463.2
	Exhibition stand manufacturing	474	463.1
	Fence, wooden (assembled), manufacturing	479/3	463.2
	Garage, wooden, manufacturing	471/2	463.1
	Garden frame, wooden, manufacturing	471/2	463.1
	Gate, wooden, manufacturing	479/3	463.2
	Greenhouse, wooden, manufacturing	471/2	463.1
	Hardwood flooring strip manufacturing	471/1	463.3
	Hut, wooden, manufacturing	471/2	463.1
	Parquet flooring manufacturing	471/1	463.3
	Portable wooden building manufacturing	471/2	463.1
	Poultry house, wooden, manufacturing	471/2	463.1
	Prefabricated wooden building manufacturing	471/2	463.1
	Roof, timber (prefabricated), manufacturing	471/2	463.1
	Shed, wooden, manufacturing	471/2	463.1
	Shuttering, wooden, manufacturing	471/2	463.2
	Silo, wooden, manufacturing	471/2	463.1
	Staircase, wooden, manufacturing	471/2	463.2
	Timber industrialised building component manufacturing	471/2	463
	Tower, wooden, manufacturing	471/2	463.1
	Trellis work, wooden, manufacturing	471/2	463.2
	Truss rafter manufacturing	471/2	463.1
	Window frame, wooden, manufacturing	471/2	463.2
	Wood paving block manufacturing	471/1	463.3
4640/1	Wooden boxes, packing cases, crates, pallets and the like		
	Box pallet manufacturing	479/3	464.1
	Box, wooden, manufacturing	475/2	464.1
	Chest, wooden, manufacturing	475/2	464.1
	Cigar box, wooden, manufacturing	475/2	464.1
	Collapsible box, wooden, manufacturing	475/2	464.1
	Container, wooden, manufacturing	475	464
	Crate, wooden, manufacturing	475/2	464.1
	Drum, wooden, manufacturing	475/2	464.1
	Egg box, wooden, manufacturing	475/2	464.1
	Fish box, wooden, manufacturing	475/2	464.1
	Packing case, wooden, manufacturing	475/2	464.1
	Pallet, wooden, manufacturing	479/3	464.1
	Stillage, wooden, manufacturing	479/3	464.1
	Suitcase, wooden, manufacturing	475/2	464.1
	Tea chest, wooden, manufacturing	475/2	464.1
	Travelling trunk, wooden, manufacturing	475/2	464.1
	Wirebound box, wooden, manufacturing	475/2	464.1
4640/2	Cooperage		
	Barrel, wooden, manufacturing	475/1	464.2
	Bucket, wooden, manufacturing	475/1	464.2
	Bung, wooden, manufacturing	475/1	464.2
	Cask head, wooden, manufacturing	475/1	464.2
	Cask, wooden, manufacturing	475/1	464.2
	Churn, wooden, manufacturing	475/1	464.2
	Cock, wooden, manufacturing	475/1	464.2
	Cooper's product manufacturing	475/1	464.2
	Coopers' products reconditioning	475/1	464.2
	Coopers' wood manufacturing	475/1	464.2
	Hoop, wooden, manufacturing	475/1	464.2
	Hoopwood manufacturing	475/1	464.2
	Keg, wooden, manufacturing	475/1	464.2
	Stave, wooden, manufacturing	475/1	464.2
	Tub, wooden, manufacturing	475/1	464.2
	Tun, wooden, manufacturing	475/1	464.2
	Vat, wooden, manufacturing	475/1	464.2
4650	Other wooden articles (except furniture)		
	Bead, wooden, manufacturing	479/3	465.1
	Beading, wooden, manufacturing	471/1	465.1
	Beehive, wooden, manufacturing	479/3	465.1
	Bobbin (not textile accessory), wooden, manufacturing	479/3	465.1
	Boot tree, wooden, manufacturing	479/2	465.1
	Breadboard manufacturing	479/3	465.1
	Broom handle, wooden, manufacturing	479/3	465.1
	Brush back, wooden, manufacturing	479/3	465.1
	Brush head, wooden, manufacturing	479/3	465.1
	Brush top, wooden, manufacturing	479/3	465.1
	Brush wood-ware manufacturing	479/3	465.1
	Button and button mould, wooden, manufacturing	479/3	465.1

SIC 1980	Activity	SIC 1968	NACE
	Carpenter (not mainly engaged on building site)	479/3	not classified
	Clothes horse, wooden, manufacturing	479/3	465.1
	Clothes peg, wooden, manufacturing	479/3	465.1
	Coat hanger, wooden, manufacturing	479/3	465.1
	Deck chair, wooden, manufacturing	479/3	467.3
	Dish, wooden, manufacturing	479/3	465.1
	Domestic woodware manufacturing	479/3	465.1
	Dowel pin manufacturing	471/1	465.1
	Foundry moulding pattern, wooden, manufacturing	479/3	465.1
	Fruit bowl, wooden, manufacturing	479/3	465.1
	Grid, wooden, manufacturing	479/3	465.1
	Gunstock, wooden, manufacturing	479/3	465.1
	Handcart, wooden, manufacturing	479/3	465.1
	Handicraft article, wood, manufacturing	479/3	465.1
	Handle, wooden, manufacturing	479/3	465.1
	Household utensil, wooden, manufacturing	479/3	465.1
	Hurdle, wooden, manufacturing	479/3	465.1
	Ladder, wooden, manufacturing	479/3	465.1
	Last, wooden, manufacturing	479/3	465.1
	Loom, wooden, manufacturing	479/3	465.1
	Machine part, wooden, manufacturing	479/3	465.1
	Mirror frame, wooden, manufacturing	479/3	465.1
	Moulded skirting board, wooden, manufacturing	471/1	465.1
	Moulding pattern, wood, manufacturing	479/3	465.1
	Moulding, wooden, manufacturing	471/1	465.1
	Picture frame, wooden, manufacturing	479/3	465.1
	Pulley, wooden, manufacturing	349/3	465.1
	Rake, wooden, manufacturing	479/3	465.1
	Reel, wooden, manufacturing	479/3	465.1
	Roller, wooden (mangle and wringer), manufacturing	479/3	465.1
	Rolling pin, wooden, manufacturing	479/3	465.1
	Shoe part, wooden, manufacturing	479/2	465.1
	Shoe, wooden, manufacturing	450	465.4
	Shoetree, wooden, manufacturing	479/3	465.1
	Slat (for manufacture of pencil) manufacturing	479/3	465.1
	Spill, wooden, manufacturing	479/3	465.1
	Spinning wheel, wooden, manufacturing	479/3	465.1
	Spoon, wooden, manufacturing	479/3	465.1
	Step ladder, wooden, manufacturing	479/3	465.1
	Steps, wooden, manufacturing	479/3	465.1
	Tent pole, wooden, manufacturing	479/3	465.1
	Tool handle, wooden, manufacturing	479/3	465.1
	Tool, wooden, manufacturing	479/3	465.1
	Tray, wooden, manufacturing	479/3	465.1
	Turned wood product manufacturing	479/3	465.1
	Vehicle, wooden, manufacturing	479/3	465.1
	Walking stick, wooden, manufacturing	449/3	465.1
	Wine rack, wooden, manufacturing	479/3	465.1
	Wire and cable drum, wooden, manufacturing	479/3	465.1
	Wood carving	479/3	465.1
	Wood chip manufacturing	479/3	465.1
	Wood flour manufacturing	479/3	465.2
	Wood shavings manufacturing	479/3	465.1
	Wood wool manufacturing	479/3	465.3
4663	Brushes and brooms		
	Artists' brush manufacturing	493	466.3
	Besom manufacturing	479/3	466.3
	Birch broom manufacturing	479/3	466.3
	Bristle dressing for brushes	493	466.3
	Broom manufacturing	493	466.3
	Brush manufacturing	493	466.3
	Brush (not electrical), part of machine, manufacturing	493	466.3
	Clothes brush manufacturing	493	466.3
	Cosmetic brush manufacturing	493	466.3
	Distemper brush manufacturing	493	466.3
	Feather duster manufacturing	493	466.3
	Fibre dressing for brushes	493	466.3
	Flue brush manufacturing	493	466.3
	Hair brush manufacturing	493	466.3
	Hair dressing for brushes	493	466.3
	Hearth brush manufacturing	493	466.3
	Household broom and brush manufacturing	493	466.3
	Household mop manufacturing	493	466.3
	Industrial broom and mop manufacturing	493	466.3
	Industrial brush manufacturing	493	466.3
	Laundry brush manufacturing	493	466.3
	Mop manufacturing	493	466.3
	Nail brush manufacturing	493	466.3
	Painters' brush manufacturing	493	466.3
	Painting roller manufacturing	493	466.3
	Paste brush manufacturing	493	466.3
	Pastry brush manufacturing	493	466.3
	Plastics brush (complete) manufacturing	493	466.3
	Polishing mop manufacturing	493	466.3
	Scrubbing brush manufacturing	493	466.3
	Shaving brush manufacturing	493	466.3
	Shoe brush manufacturing	493	466.3
	Toilet brush manufacturing	493	466.3
	Tooth brush (not electric) manufacturing	493	466.3
	Whitewash brush manufacturing	493	466.3
	Wire brush manufacturing	493	466.3
4664/1	Cork and cork articles		
	Agglomerated cork manufacturing	479/1	466.1
	Buoyancy apparatus, cork, manufacturing	479/1	466.1
	Composition cork manufacturing	479/1	466.1
	Cork insulating material manufacturing	479/1	466.1
	Cork product manufacturing	479/1	466.1
	Fender, cork, manufacturing	479/1	466.1
	Life-jacket, cork, manufacturing	479/1	466.1
	Lifebelt, cork, manufacturing	479/1	466.1
	Lifebuoy, cork, manufacturing	479/1	466.1
	Mat, cork, manufacturing	479/1	466.1
	Sheet, cork, manufacturing	479/1	466.1
	Slab, cork, manufacturing	479/1	466.1
	Stopper inset, cork, manufacturing	479/1	466.1
	Stopper, cork, manufacturing	479/1	466.1
	Tile, cork, manufacturing	479/1	466.1
	Tip, cork, manufacturing	479/1	466.1
4664/2	Basketware, wickerwork and other articles of plaiting materials		
	Bamboo preparation	475/1	466.2
	Basket manufacturing	475/1	466.2
	Basketware manufacturing	475/1	466.2
	Cane preparation	475/1	466.2
	Cane splitting and weaving	475/1	466
	Cane working	475/1	466

SIC 1980	Activity	SIC 1968	NACE
	Chair seating, cane or wicker, manufacturing	475/1	466.2
	Hamper manufacturing	475/1	466.2
	Loofah article manufacturing	499/2	466.2
	Matting, cane, manufacturing	475/1	466.2
	Osier article manufacturing	475/1	466.2
	Osier preparation	475/1	466.2
	Plaiting material preparation	475/1	466.2
	Punnet manufacturing	475/1	466.2
	Raffia goods manufacturing	475/1	466.2
	Reed article manufacturing	475/1	466.2
	Reed preparation manufacturing	475/1	466.2
	Rush matting manufacturing	475/1	466.2
	Straw article manufacturing	475/1	466.2
	Straw envelope for bottle manufacturing	475/1	466.2
	Trug manufacturing	475/1	466.2
	Wicker basket manufacturing	475/1	466.2
	Wickerwork manufacturing	475/1	466.2
4671/1	**Upholstered furniture**		
	Armchair (upholstered) manufacturing	472	467.4
	Bed-settee manufacturing	472	467.4
	Bench seat (upholstered) manufacturing	472	467.4
	Chair (upholstered) manufacturing	472	467.4
	Chaise-longue manufacturing	472	467.4
	Cinema seat (upholstered) manufacturing	472	467.4
	Convertible (furniture) manufacturing	472	467.4
	Couch manufacturing	472	467.4
	Day-bed manufacturing	472	467.4
	Dining chair (upholstered) manufacturing	472	467.4
	Kitchen seating (upholstered) manufacturing	472	467.4
	Metal framed upholstery manufacturing	472	316.6
	Office furniture (upholstered) manufacturing	472	467.4
	Ottoman manufacturing	472	467.4
	Outdoor furniture (upholstered) manufacturing	472	467.4
	Plastic shell upholstery manufacturing	472	483
	Pouffe manufacturing	472	467.4
	Settee manufacturing	472	467.4
	Sofa manufacturing	472	467.4
	Studio couch manufacturing	472	467.4
	Theatre seat (upholstered) manufacturing	472	467.4
	Unit seating (upholstered), domestic, manufacturing	472	467.4
	Upholstery manufacturing	472	467.4
4671/2	**Other wooden domestic furniture**		
	Armchair (non-upholstered) manufacturing	472	467.3
	Bamboo furniture manufacturing	472	467.7
	Basket chair manufacturing	472	467.7
	Basket furniture manufacturing	472	467.7
	Bedroom furniture (other than beds and mattresses) manufacturing	472	467.1
	Bench seat (non-upholstered) manufacturing	472	467.3
	Bentwood furniture manufacturing	472	467.3
	Bookcase manufacturing	472	467.1
	Built-in furniture manufacturing	472	463.2
	Camp furniture (wooden) manufacturing	472	467
	Cane chair manufacturing	472	467.7
	Cane furniture manufacturing	472	467.7
	Chair (non-upholstered) manufacturing	472	467.3
	Chair frame, wooden, manufacturing	472	467.3
	Chest of drawers manufacturing	472	467.1
	Cocktail cabinet manufacturing	472	467.1
	Coffee table manufacturing	472	467.1
	Cupboard manufacturing	472	467.1
	Dining chair (non-upholstered) manufacturing	472	467.3
	Dining table manufacturing	472	467.1
	Display cabinet (domestic) manufacturing	472	467.1
	Dressing table manufacturing	472	467.1
	Fire screen manufacturing	472	467.5
	Furniture kit manufacturing	472	467.1
	Garden furniture manufacturing	472	467.3
	Hall stand manufacturing	472	467.1
	Kitchen cabinet manufacturing	472	467.1
	Kitchen furniture manufacturing	472	467.1
	Living room furniture manufacturing	472	467.1
	Nursery furniture manufacturing	472	467.1
	Outdoor furniture (non-upholstered) manufacturing	472	467.3
	Room divide system manufacturing	472	467.1
	Rustic furniture manufacturing	479/3	467.3
	Seating (non-upholstered) manufacturing	472	467.3
	Sideboard manufacturing	472	467.1
	Storage cabinet (domestic) manufacturing	472	467.1
	Table, domestic, manufacturing	472	467.1
	Unit furniture (non-upholstered) manufacturing	472	467.1
	Wall unit manufacturing	472	467.1
	Wardrobe manufacturing	472	467.1
	Wicker furniture manufacturing	472	467.7
	Woven fibre furniture manufacturing	472	467.7
4671/3	**Non-domestic wooden furniture**		
	Church furniture manufacturing	472	467.5
	Cinema furniture manufacturing	472	467
	Coatstand (not domestic) manufacturing	472	467.5
	Desk, wooden, manufacturing	472	467.2
	Drawing-office furniture, wooden, manufacturing	472	467.2
	Easel manufacturing	472	467.2
	Filing cabinet, wooden, manufacturing	472	467.2
	Hotel furniture manufacturing	472	467
	Laboratory furniture, wooden, manufacturing	472	467.5
	Lectern manufacturing	472	467.5
	Library furniture manufacturing	472	467.5
	Locker, wooden, manufacturing	472	467.5
	Museum furniture manufacturing	472	467.5
	Office furniture, wooden, manufacturing	472	467.2
	Pew manufacturing	472	467.5
	Public house furniture manufacturing	472	467.5
	Pulpit manufacturing	472	467.5
	Restaurant furniture manufacturing	472	467.5
	School furniture manufacturing	472	467.2
	Seating, office or school (non-upholstered) manufacturing	472	467
	Ships' furniture manufacturing	472	467.5
	Shop furniture manufacturing	472	467.5
	Table, office or school, manufacturing	472	467.2
4671/4	**Wooden cabinet work and components for furniture**		
	Cabinet case, wood, manufacturing	472	467.5
	Cabinet-making	472	467.5

SIC 1980	Activity	SIC 1968	NACE
	Clock case, wooden, manufacturing	352	467.5
	Coffin manufacturing	479/3	467.6
	Coffin board manufacturing	479/3	467.6
	Component for furniture, wooden, manufacturing	472	467.5
	Cutlery case, wooden, manufacturing	499/2	467.5
	Drawing instrument case, wooden, manufacturing	499/2	467.5
	Frame for mattress support, wooden, manufacturing	472	467.5
	Gramophone cabinet manufacturing	472	467.5
	Ice box (wooden) manufacturing	472	467.5
	Ice chest (wooden) manufacturing	472	467.5
	Instrument case (wooden) manufacturing	499/2	467.5
	Insulated cabinet, wooden, manufacturing	472	467.5
	Musical instrument case, wooden, manufacturing	499/2	467.5
	Parts of furniture, wooden, manufacturing	472	467.5
	Radio cabinet, wooden, manufacturing	472	467.5
	Record player cabinet, wooden, manufacturing	472	467.5
	Tape recorder cabinet, wooden, manufacturing	472	467.5
	Television cabinet, wooden, manufacturing	472	467.5
	Violin etc. case (wooden) manufacturing	499/2	467.5
4671/5	Beds and mattresses		
	Bed manufacturing	472	467.1
	Bedstead, wooden, manufacturing	472	467.1
	Box spring mattress manufacturing	473	467.8
	Bunk bed manufacturing	472	467.1
	Cot manufacturing	472	467.1
	Cot mattress manufacturing	473	467.8
	Divan bed manufacturing	473	467.1
	Folding bed manufacturing	472	467.1
	Interior sprung mattress manufacturing	473	467.8
	Mattress base manufacturing	473	467.8
	Mattress, fully finished, manufacturing	473	467.8
	Plastics foam mattress manufacturing	473	467.8
	Sponge mattress manufacturing	473	467.8
	Upholstered base for mattress manufacturing	472	467.8
4672	Shop and office fitting		
	Bank fittings and furnishings manufacturing	474	467.5
	Bar fittings and furnishings manufacturing	474	467.5
	Counter (shop) manufacturing	474	467.5
	Fixture (shop), for display and storage of goods, manufacturing	474	467.5
	Hotel fittings and furnishings manufacturing	474	467.5
	Laboratory fittings and furnishings manufacturing	474	467.5
	Library fittings and furnishings manufacturing	474	467.5
	Museum fittings and furnishings manufacturing	474	467.5
	Office fittings and furnishings manufacturing	474	467.5
	Partition, wooden, manufacturing	474	463.2
	Public house fittings and furnishings manufacturing	474	467.5
	Racking, wooden, manufacturing	474	467.5
	Restaurant fittings and furnishings manufacturing	474	467.5
	Revolving door manufacturing	474	463.2
	Roller blind, wooden, manufacturing	474	463.2
	Screen, wooden, manufacturing	474	467.5
	Shelving, wooden, manufacturing	474	467.5
	Shop fittings and furnishings manufacturing	474	467.5
	Shop front (other than aluminium) manufacturing	474	463.2
	Shop fronts and entrances, aluminium, manufacturing	399/2	314.1
	Show case, wooden, manufacturing	474	467.5
	Shutter, wooden, manufacturing	474	463.2
	Sign, wooden, manufacturing	474	467.5
	Signwriting	474	463.2
4710/1	Pulp		
	Chemical woodpulp manufacturing	481	471.1
	Dissolving chemical wood-pulp manufacturing	481	471.1
	Mechanical woodpulp manufacturing	481	471.1
	Pulping recycled paper	481	471.1
	Recycled fibre pulp manufacturing	481	471.1
	Semi-chemical woodpulp manufacturing	481	471.1
	Sulphate and soda woodpulp manufacturing	481	471.1
	Sulphite woodpulp manufacturing	481	471.1
	Synthetic fibre woodpulp manufacturing	481	471.1
	Vegetable fibre pulp manufacturing	481	471.1
	Wood-pulp manufacturing	481	471.1
4710/2	Newsprint		
	Newsprint manufacturing	481	471.3
4710/3	Other writing and printing papers		
	Banknote paper manufacturing	481	471.3
	Base paper (for printing and writing paper) manufacturing	481	471.3
	Bible paper manufacturing	481	471.3
	Bristol board manufacturing	481	471.3
	Carbonising base paper manufacturing	481	471.3
	Drawing paper manufacturing	481	471.3
	Hand made paper manufacturing	481	471.3
	Magazine paper manufacturing	481	471.3
	Photographic base paper manufacturing	481	471.3
	Printing paper manufacturing	481	471.3
	Punched card and punched paper tape stock manufacturing	481	471.3
	Security paper manufacturing	481	471.3
	Stencil basepaper manufacturing	481	471.3
	Tracing paper manufacturing	481	471.3
	Wallpaper base manufacturing	481	471.3
	Writing paper manufacturing	481	471.3
4710/4	Wrapping and packaging papers		
	Case-making materials manufacturing	481	471.3
	Fluting paper manufacturing	481	471.3
	Glassine paper manufacturing	481	471.3
	Greaseproof paper manufacturing	481	471.3
	Kraft wrapping and packaging paper manufacturing	481	471.3
	Paper for corrugated cardboard (of vegetable fibres) manufacturing	481	471.3
	Parchment and imitation parchment paper manufacturing	481	471.3
	Sack kraft paper manufacturing	481	471.3
	Strawpaper manufacturing	481	471.2

SIC 1980	Activity	SIC 1968	NACE
	Sulphite wrapping paper manufacturing	481	471.3
	Wrapping and packaging paper (including coated) manufacturing	481	471.3
4710/5	Household, toilet papers and tissues		
	Cellulose wadding manufacturing	481	471.3
	Household paper (uncut) manufacturing	481	471.3
	Hygienic paper (uncut) manufacturing	481	471.3
	Tissue paper (uncut) manufacturing	481	471.3
	Toilet paper (uncut) manufacturing	481	471.3
4710/6	Industrial and special purpose papers		
	Abrasive base paper manufacturing	481	471.3
	Blotting paper manufacturing	481	471.3
	Cigarette paper (uncut, in rolls) manufacturing	481	471.3
	Electrical paper manufacturing	481	471.3
	Fancy paper manufacturing	481	472.7
	Filter paper manufacturing	481	471.3
	Industrial paper manufacturing	481	471.3
	Multilayer paper obtained by compression manufacturing	481	471.3
	Paper (not sensitized) manufacturing	481	471.3
	Paper yarn manufacturing	481	471.3
	Saturated and impregnated base paper manufacturing	481	472.6
	Special purpose paper manufacturing	481	471.3
	Waterproof paper manufacturing	481	471.3
4710/7	Packaging boards including corrugated		
	Cardboard manufacturing	481	471.3
	Corrugated paper board manufacturing	481	471.3
	Folding boxboard manufacturing	481	471.3
	Grey board manufacuring	481	471.3
	Strawboard manufacturing	481	471.2
4710/8	Building board including bituminised		
	Building board, bituminised, manufacturing	481	472.5
	Building board, paper, manufacturing	481	472.5
4710/9	Other boards		
	Boot and shoe board manufacturing	481	471.3
	Feltboard (including felt paper) manufacturing	481	471.3
	Flong paperboard manufacturing	481	471.3
	Mill board manufacturing	481	471.3
	Pressboard manufacturing	481	471.3
	Presspahn manufacturing	481	471.3
4721	Wall coverings		
	Fabric wallcoverings manufacturing	484/1	472.1
	Lincrusta manufacturing	484/1	472.1
	Paper and board articles for interior decoration manufacturing	484/1	472.1
	Paper staining	484/1	472.1
	Vinyl wallpaper manufacturing	484/1	472.1
	Wallpaper and lining paper manufacturing	484/1	472.1
4722	Household and personal hygiene products of paper		
	Baby napkins (disposable), paper or cellulose wadding, manufacturing	not classified	472.2
	Handkerchief, paper, manufacturing	484/2	472.2
	Kitchen cloth, paper, manufacturing	484/2	472.2
	Kitchen towel, paper, manufacturing	484/2	472.2
	Paper lace manufacturing	484/2	472.2
	Sanitary towel, paper, manufacturing	279/6	472.2
	Serviette manufacturing	484/2	472.2
	Tablecloth, paper, manufacturing	484/2	472.2
	Toilet paper (cut to size) manufacturing	484/2	472.2
	Towel, paper, manufacturing	484/2	472.2
	Underwear, paper, manufacturing	445/2	472.2
4723/1	Notepaper		
	Boxed stationery manufacturing	483	472.3
	Envelope manufacturing	483	472.3
	Label, paper, manufacturing	483	472.8
	Label, paper, gummed, manufacturing	483	472.8
	Notepad manufacturing	483	472.3
	Postcard (plain) manufacturing	483	472.3
	Printers cards manufacturing	483	472.3
	Writing paper pad manufacturing	483	472.3
4723/2	Binders, etc.		
	Account book manufacturing	483	472.3
	Card cutting for index cards	483	472.3
	Continuous stationery manufacturing	483	472.3
	Index card manufacturing	483	472.3
	Letter card manufacturing	483	472.3
	Letter file manufacturing	483	472.3
	Loose leaf binder and refill manufacturing	483	472.3
	Machine ruling	483	472.3
	Manuscript book manufacturing	483	472.3
	Office systems (of paper and board) manufacturing	483	472.3
	Paper ruling	483	472.3
	School stationery manufacturing	483	472.3
	Tabulating machine card manufacturing	483	472.3
4724/1	Sacks and bags		
	Multi-wall paper sack manufacturing	482/2	472.4
	Paper bag manufacturing	482/2	472.4
	Paper sack manufacturing	482/2	472.4
	Printed paper bag manufacturing	482/2	472.4
4724/2	Other packaging products of paper and pulp		
	Beaker, paper, manufacturing	484/2	472.4
	Box, paper, manufacturing	482/1	472.4
	Cylinder, hardened paper, manufacturing	482/1	472.4
	Egg tray, paper manufacturing	482/1	472.4
	Flexible packaging, paper, manufacturing	482/2	472.4
	Plate, paper, manufacturing	484/2	472.4
	Pot, paper, manufacturing	482/1	472.4
	Wrapping paper, cut, packed, ready to use in sheets or rolls, manufacturing	482/2	472.4
4725/1	Fibre board packing cases		
	Fibre board packing case manufacturing	482/1	472.4
4725/2	Rigid boxes		
	Rigid box, board, manufacturing	482/1	472.4
	Rigid box, corrugated board, manufacturing	482/1	472.4
4725/3	Cartons, etc.		
	Cardboard container and canister manufacturing	482/1	472.4
	Carton, board, manufacturing	482/1	472.4

SIC 1980	Activity	SIC 1968	NACE
	Cylinder, board, manufacturing	482/1	472.4
	Folding box, board, manufacturing	482/1	472.4
	Packing material, board, manufacturing	482/1	472.4
4728	Other paper and board products		
	Artificial flowers and fruit, paper, manufacturing	484/2	472.8
	Bed linen (disposable), paper or cellulose wadding, manufacturing	484/2	472.8
	Blind, paper, manufacturing	484/2	472.8
	Bobbin, paper, manufacturing	484/2	472.8
	Bon-bon (paper) manufacturing	484/2	472.8
	Cake board manufacturing	484/2	472.8
	Cap, paper, manufacturing	484/2	472.8
	Carbon paper stencil (e.g. for spirit duplicator) manufacturing	484/2	472.8
	Cardboard tube (not packaging) manufacturing	484/2	472.8
	Christmas cracker manufacturing	484/2	472.8
	Christmas decorations, paper, manufacturing	484/2	472.8
	Cigarette paper, in booklets, manufacturing	484/2	472.8
	Cigarette tube manufacturing	484/2	472.8
	Confetti, paper, manufacturing	484/2	472.8
	Cop tube manufacturing	484/2	472.8
	Disc, cardboard, manufacturing	484/2	472.8
	Doilies, paper, manufacturing	484/2	472.8
	Duplicating paper, cut to size, manufacturing	481	472.8
	Gummed paper manufacturing	484/2	472.6
	Mount cutting	484/2	472.8
	Mounting paper on linen	484/2	472.8
	Paper converting (unspecified)	484/2	472.8
	Paper creping	484/2	472.8
	Paper embossing	484/2	472.8
	Paper hat manufacturing	484/2	472.8
	Paper pattern manufacturing	484/2	472.8
	Paper perforating	484/2	472.8
	Paper shavings manufacturing	484/2	472.8
	Paper transfer (e.g. for embroidery) manufacturing	484/2	473.2
	Paper, cut to size (not packaging products), manufacturing	481	472.8
	Papier mache works	484/2	472.8
	Pattern card manufacturing	484/2	472.8
	Photograph mount manufacturing	484/2	472.8
	Picture frame mount manufacturing	484/2	472.8
	Pleated paper manufacturing	484/2	472.8
	Spools, paper, manufacturing	484/2	472.8
	Stamp hinge manufacturing	484/2	472.8
	Ticket cutting and punching	484/2	472.8
	Tube, paper, manufacturing	484/2	472.8
	Twine, paper, manufacturing	484/2	472.8
	Vulcanized fibre manufacturing	484/2	472.8
	Wood pulp vessel manufacturing	484/2	472.8
4751/1	Publishers of newspapers		
	Newspaper publisher	485	474.4
4751/2	Printer-publishers of newspapers		
	Newspaper printer-publisher	485	473.1
4751/3	Printers of newspapers		
	Newspaper printer	485	473.1
4752/1	Publishers of periodicals		
	Amusement guide, periodical, publishing	486	474.4
	Magazine publishing	486	474.4
	Periodical publishing	486	474.4
	Review publishing	486	474.4
	Trade journal publishing	486	474.4
4752/2	Printer-publishers of periodicals		
	Amusement guide, periodical, printing-publishing	486	473.1
	Magazine printing-publishing	486	473.1
	Periodical printing-publishing	486	473.1
	Review printing-publishing	486	473.1
	Trade journal printing-publishing	486	473.1
4752/3	Printers of periodicals		
	Amusement guide, periodical, printing	486	473.1
	Magazine printing	486	473.1
	Periodical printing	486	473.1
	Review printing	486	473.1
	Trade journal printing	486	473.1
4753/1	Publishers of books		
	Book publishing	489	474.1
	Brochure publishing	489	474.1
	Pamphlet publishing	489	474.1
4753/2	Printer-publishers of books		
	Book printing-publishing	489	473.2
	Brochure printing-publishing	489	473.2
	Pamphlet printing-publishing	489	473.2
4753/3	Printers of books		
	Book printing	489	473.2
	Brochure printing	489	473.2
	Pamphlet printing	489	473.2
4754/1	Other publishers		
	Law publishing	489	474.5
	Letterpress publishing	489	474.1
	Music publisher	489	474.3
	Publishers, other than of newspapers and periodicals	489	474
	Religious tract publishing	489	474.1
4754/2	Other printer-publishers		
	Architectural drawing printing and publishing	489	473 and 474
	Art printing and publishing	489	473 and 474
	Engineering drawing printing and publishing manufacturing	489	473 and 474
	Geographical printing and publishing	489	473 and 474
	Her Majesty's Stationery Office	489	473 and 474
	Map and plan printing, publishing and colouring	489	473 and 474
4754/3	Security printing		
	Banknote printing	489	473.2
	Cheque book printing	489	473.2
	National Insurance Stamp printing	489	473.2
	Passport printing	489	473.2
	Postage stamp printing	489	473.2

SIC 1980	Activity	SIC 1968	NACE
	Security printing	489	473.2
	Stamp embossed paper manufacturing	489	473.2
	Ticket printing	489	473.2
	Title document printing	489	473.2
4754/4	Other printing		
	Album printing	489	473.2
	Almanac printing	489	473.2
	Calendar printing	489	473.2
	Chart printing	489	473.2
	Christmas card printing	489	473.2
	Decal printing	489	473.2
	Diary printing	489	473.2
	Directory printing	489	473.2
	Fashion printing	489	473.2
	General printing	489	473.2
	Greeting card manufacturing	489	473.2
	Map manufacturing	489	473.2
	Picture postcard manufacturing	489	473.2
	Plan printing	489	473.2
	Playing card manufacturing	489	473.2
	Poster printing	489	473.2
	Printed matter for accounting and technical use manufacturing	489	473.2
	Printing screen manufacturing	489	473.4
	Sheet music printing	489	473.2
	Showcard manufacturing	489	473.2
	Timetable printing	489	473.2
	Transfer printing	489	473.2
	Window ticket manufacturing	489	473.2
4754/5	Ancillary printing services		
	Aerographing	489	473.4
	Book repairing	489	473.3
	Bookbinding	489	473.3
	Braille copying	489	473.2
	Braille printing	489	473.2
	Calico printers' engraving	489	473.4
	Card embossing	489	473.3
	Ceramic transfer (litho) engraving	489	473.4
	Collotype printing	489	473.2
	Copper plate printing	489	473.2
	Die sinking (stationery)	489	473.4
	Die stamping (stationery)	489	473.4
	Electrotyping	489	473.4
	Engraving	489	473.4
	Etching	489	473.4
	Gilding (printing service)	489	473.3
	Gold blocking	489	473.3
	Gold stamping	489	473.3
	Heraldic chasing and seal engraving	489	473.4
	Heraldic engraving manufacturing	489	473.4
	Job printing	489	473.4
	Lithographic draughtsman	489	473.4
	Lithographic printing	489	473.2
	Lithography	489	473.4
	Metal etching	489	473.4
	Music plate engraving	489	473.4
	Phonetic printing	489	473.2
	Photo-engraving	489	473.4
	Photogravure printing	489	473.2
	Photo-lithography	489	473.4
	Postage stamp perforating	489	473.4
	Poster aerographing	489	473.4
	Poster writing	489	473.2
	Print colouring	489	473.4
	Printers' designing	489	473.4
	Printing (undefined)	489	473.2
	Printing plate engraving	489	473.4
	Printing roller engraving	489	473.4
	Process block making	489	473.4
	Process engraving	489	473.4
	Process plate engraving	489	473.4
	Publisher's case making	489	473.4
	Rag book making	489	473.4
	Relief stamping	489	473.4
	Sheet metal printing	489	473.4
	Stereotype manufacturing	489	473.4
	Ticket writing	489	473.4
	Tillot and seal making	489	473.4
	Tin printing	489	473.4
4811	Rubber tyres and inner tubes		
	Aircraft tyre manufacturing	491/1	481.1
	Car and van tyre manufacturing	491/1	481.1
	Commercial vehicle tyre manufacturing	491/1	481.1
	Cycle tyre manufacturing	491/1	481.1
	Industrial tyre manufacturing	491/1	481.1
	Inner tube for tyre manufacturing	491/1	481.1
	Motor cycle and moped tyre manufacturing	491/1	481.1
	Puncture repair outfit manufacturing	491/1	481.1
	Rubber tyre manufacturing	491/1	481.1
	Scooter tyre manufacturing	491/1	481.1
	Solid rubber tyre manufacturing	491/1	481.1
	Tractor tyre manufacturing	491/1	481.1
	Tyre manufacturing	491/1	481.1
	Tyre repair materials and kit manufacturing	491/1	481.2
4812/1	Rubber or plastic hose and tubing		
	Armoured hose (rubber or plastics) manufacturing	491/2	481.2
	Delivery hose (rubber or plastics) manufacturing	491/2	481.2
	Garden hose (rubber or plastics) manufacturing	491/2	481.2
	Hydraulic hose (rubber or plastics) manufacturing	491/2	481.2
	Plastics hose manufacturing	491/2	483
	Plastics tubing manufacturing	491/2	483
	Reinforced hose (rubber or plastics) manufacturing	491/2	481.2
	Rubber hose manufacturing	491/2	481.2
	Rubber tubing manufacturing	491/2	481.2
	Suction and discharge hose (rubber or plastics) manufacturing	491/2	481.2
4812/2	Rubber or plastics belting		
	Balata belting manufacturing	491/2	481.2
	Belting (rubber or plastics) manufacturing	491/2	481.2
	Conveyor belting (rubber or plastics) manufacturing	491/2	481.2
	Domestic appliance belting (rubber or plastics) manufacturing	491/2	481.2
	Elevator belting (rubber or plastics) manufacturing	491/2	481.2
	Industrial belting (rubber or plastics) manufacturing	491/2	481.2
	Motor vehicle fan belt manufacturing	491/2	481.2
	Motor vehicle timing belt manufacturing	491/2	481.2
	Plastics belting manufacturing	491/2	483
	Rubber belting manufacturing	491/2	481.2
	Transmission belting (rubber or plastics) manufacturing	491/2	481.2
4812/3	Rubber products not elsewhere specified, including reclaimed rubber		
	Balata goods (not belting) manufacturing	491/2	481.2

SIC 1980	Activity	SIC 1968	NACE
	Ball, uncovered rubber, manufacturing	491/2	481.2
	Balloon, rubber, (excluding pilot and sounding balloons) manufacturing	491/2	481.2
	Band, rubber, manufacturing	491/2	481.2
	Bathing cap, rubber, manufacturing	491/2	481.2
	Bellows, rubber, manufacturing	491/2	481.2
	Bucket, rubberised fabric, manufacturing	491/2	481.2
	Carpet underlay, rubber, manufacturing	491/2	481.2
	Cellular rubber product manufacturing	491/2	481.2
	Cushioning for upholstery, rubber, manufacturing	491/2	481.2
	Dinghy, rubber, manufacturing	491/2	481.2
	Diving suit, rubber or plastics, manufacturing	491/2	481.2
	Ebonite, vulcanite or hard rubber goods manufacturing	491/2	481.2
	Eraser, rubber, manufacturing	491/2	481.2
	Expansion joint, rubber, manufacturing	491/2	481.2
	Felting, rubber, manufacturing	491/2	481.2
	Flooring, rubber, manufacturing	491/2	481.2
	Fluid seal, rubber, manufacturing	491/2	481.2
	Foam rubber manufacturing	491/2	481.2
	Folding boat, rubber, manufacturing	491/2	481.2
	Football bladder, rubber, manufacturing	491/2	481.2
	Golf ball core manufacturing	491/2	481.2
	Groundsheet, rubber, manufacturing	491/2	481.2
	Gutta-percha goods manufacturing	491/2	481.2
	Heel and sole, rubber, manufacturing	491/2	481.2
	Hot water bottle, rubber, manufacturing	491/2	481.2
	Inflatable cushion, rubber, manufacturing	491/2	481.2
	Inflatable dinghy, rubber, manufacturing	491/2	481.2
	Inflatable liferaft, rubber, manufacturing	491/2	481.2
	Inflatable mattress, rubber, manufacturing	491/2	481.2
	Insulating material, rubber, manufacturing	491/2	481.2
	Latex foam manufacturing	491/2	481.2
	Leisure craft, rubber, manufacturing	491/2	481.2
	Lifebelt, rubber, manufacturing	491/2	481.2
	Lifebuoy, rubber, manufacturing	491/2	481.2
	Lifejacket, rubber, manufacturing	491/2	481.2
	Mat, rubber, manufacturing	491/2	481.2
	Medical rubber dressing manufacturing	279/6	481.2
	Medical rubber goods (not dressings) manufacturing	491/2	481.2
	Moulded rubber bottoms for footwear	491/2	481.2
	Mouldings for upholstery, rubber, manufacturing	491/2	481.2
	Piece goods, unsupported rubber sheeting, manufacturing	491/2	481.2
	Playball, rubber, manufacturing	491/2	481.2
	Printers' blanket, rubber, manufacturing	491/2	481.2
	Ring and washer, rubber, manufacturing	491/2	481.2
	Roller cover (rubber) manufacturing	491/2	481.2
	Rubber compound manufacturing	491/2	481.2
	Rubber doll manufacturing	491/2	481.2
	Rubber reclamation	491/2	481.2
	Rubber sponge manufacturing	491/2	481.2
	Rubber thread, uncovered, manufacturing	491/2	481.2
	Rubber tiling manufacturing	491/2	481.2
	Rubber toy manufacturing	491/2	481.2
	Rubberised hair manufacturing	491/2	481.2
	Rubberised textile fabric manufacturing	491/2	481.2
	Surgical rubber goods manufacturing	491/2	481.2
	Tennis ball core manufacturing	491/2	481.2
	Toy balloon, rubber, manufacturing	491/2	481.2
	Underwater swimming suit, rubber or plastics, manufacturing	491/2	481.2
	Unstitched rubber glove and gauntlet manufacturing	491/2	481.2
	Waterwings, rubber, manufacturing	491/2	481.2
4820	Retreading and specialist repairing of rubber tyres		
	Repairing tyre and inner tube (by specialists)	491/1	482
	Retreading tyres	491/1	482
4831	Plastic coated textile fabric		
	Leathercloth manufacturing	492	438.3
	Nitro-cellulose coated textile fabric manufacturing	492	438.3
	Polyurethane coated textile fabric manufacturing	492	438.3
	Polyvinyl chloride leathercloth manufacturing	492	438.3
	Textile fabric coated with plastic material manufacturing	492	438.3
4832	Plastics semi-manufactures		
	Carpet underlay (plastics) manufacturing	496	483
	Decorative polyvinyl chloride film and sheet, unsupported, manufacturing	492	483
	Flexible plastics foam manufacturing	496	483
	Laminated thermosetting plastics sheet manufacturing	276/1	483
	Photographic film, unsensitized, manufacturing	276/1	483
	Polyethylene film manufacturing	276/1	483
	Polyethylene sheet manufacturing	276/1	483
	Polypropylene film manufacturing	276/1	483
	Polypropylene sheet manufacturing	276/1	483
	Polyvinyl chloride film manufacturing	276/1	483
	Polyvinyl chloride sheet manufacturing	276/1	483
	Profile shapes of plastics materials (rods, tubes etc.) manufacturing	276/1	483
	Rigid plastics foam manufacturing	496	483
4833	Plastics floorcoverings		
	Asphalt tile, thermoplastic, manufacturing	492	438.2
	Felt base floorcovering, printed, manufacturing	492	438.2
	Linoleum manufacturing	492	438.2
	Plastics floorcovering manufacturing	492	483
	Plastics matting, woven, manufacturing	429/2	438.2
	Vinyl asbestos tile manufacturing	492	438.2
	Vinyl floorcovering, homogeneous and printed, manufacturing	492	438.2
	Vinyl floorcovering, supported, manufacturing	492	438.2
4834	Plastics building products		
	Architrave (plastics) manufacturing	496	483
	Bath (plastics) manufacturing	496	483

SIC 1980	Activity	SIC 1968	NACE
	Building products (plastics) manufacturing	496	483
	Ceiling tile (plastics) manufacturing	496	483
	Cistern (plastics) manufacturing	496	483
	Cistern float (plastics) manufacturing	496	483
	Coving (plastics) manufacturing	496	483
	Dome light (plastics) manufacturing	496	483
	Door (plastics) manufacturing	496	483
	Door frame (plastics) manufacturing	496	483
	Door furniture of plastics (handles, hinges, knobs, etc.), for buildings, manufacturing	496	483
	Ducting (plastics) manufacturing	496	483
	Fencing (plastics) manufacturing	496	483
	Gutter and fittings (plastics) manufacturing	496	483
	Insulating (heat and sound) sheet, tiles, blocks and granules of plastics, manufacturing	496	483
	Intermediate bulk container (other than drum), plastics, manufacturing	496	483
	Pipes and fittings (plastics) manufacturing	496	483
	Roof light (plastics) manufacturing	496	483
	Sanitary ware (plastics) manufacturing	496	483
	Sheeting of plastics for roofs and cladding, manufacturing	496	483
	Shiplap cladding (plastics) manufacturing	496	483
	Sink (plastics) manufacturing	496	483
	Skirting board (plastics) manufacturing	496	483
	Storage tank (plastics) manufacturing	496	483
	Tank, open and closed, (plastics) manufacturing	496	483
	Tap and valve (plastics) manufacturing	496	483
	Tile, other than floor tile, (plastics) manufacturing	496	483
	Wash basin (plastics) manufacturing	496	483
	Water stop and bar (plastics) manufacturing	496	483
	WC seat and cover unit (plastics) manufacturing	496	483
	Weatherboarding (plastics) manufacturing	496	483
	Window frame (plastics) manufacturing	496	483
4835	Plastics packaging products		
	Bag (plastics) for packaging purposes manufacturing	496	483
	Bag of transparent regenerated cellulose film manufacturing	482/2	483
	Barrel (plastics) manufacturing	496	483
	Bin liners (plastics) manufacturing	496	483
	Bottle (plastics) manufacturing	496	483
	Bottle crate (plastics) manufacturing	496	483
	Box (plastics) manufacturing	496	483
	Canister (plastics) manufacturing	496	483
	Cap and closure (plastics) manufacturing	496	483
	Cap for bottle (plastics) manufacturing	496	483
	Closure (plastics) manufacturing	496	483
	Drum (container; plastics) manufacturing	496	483
	Jam pot cover (plastics) manufacturing	496	483
	Jar (plastics) manufacturing	496	483
	Jerry can (plastics) manufacturing	496	483
	Keg (plastics) manufacturing	496	483
	Laminate (wholly of plastics and/or transparent regenerated cellulose film) manufacturing	482	483
	Laminate, plastics, (packaging product) manufacturing	496	483
	Laminated plastics film manufacturing	496	483
	Packaging product (plastics) manufacturing	496	483
	Polyethylene liner, non-woven, manufacturing	496	483
	Polyethylene sack, non-woven, manufacturing	496	483
	Polypropylene reel, printed, manufacturing	496	483
	Pot (not flower pot) (plastics) manufacturing	496	483
	Sachet (plastics) manufacturing	496	483
	Transit container (plastics), closed, manufacturing	496	483
	Tub (plastics) manufacturing	496	483
	Tube (container; plastics) manufacturing	496	483
4836	Plastics products not elsewhere specified		
	Advertising material (plastics) manufacturing	496	483
	Air bed, inflatable, (plastics) manufacturing	496	483
	Aircraft parts and accessories (plastics) manufacturing	496	483
	Artificial flower (plastics) manufacturing	496	483
	Awnings (plastics) manufacturing	496	483
	Baby bath (plastics) manufacturing	496	483
	Basket (plastics) manufacturing	496	483
	Bin (plastics) manufacturing	496	483
	Blinds (plastics) manufacturing	496	483
	Bowl (plastics) manufacturing	496	483
	Bucket (plastics) manufacturing	496	483
	Buoy (plastics) manufacturing	496	483
	Button and button mould (plastics) manufacturing	499/2	483
	Cabinet component (plastics) manufacturing	496	483
	Cabinet, plastics, manufacturing	496	483
	Chain (plastics) manufacturing	496	483
	Colander (plastics) manufacturing	496	483
	Components, accessories and parts (at plastics processing establishments) manufacturing	496	483
	Cup (plastics) manufacturing	496	483
	Curtain hook, ring and runner (plastics) manufacturing	496	483
	Curtain rail and roller and fittings (plastics) manufacturing	496	483
	Cutlery (plastics) manufacturing	496	483
	Dish (plastics) manufacturing	496	483
	Doily (plastics) manufacturing	496	483
	Domestic hollow-ware (plastics) manufacturing	496	483
	Dustbin (plastics) manufacturing	496	483
	Dustpan (plastics) manufacturing	496	483
	Egg cup (plastics) manufacturing	496	483
	Flower pot and tub (plastics) manufacturing	496	483
	Footwear parts and accessories (plastics) manufacturing	496	483
	Fork (plastics) manufacturing	496	483
	Funnel (plastics) manufacturing	496	483

SIC 1980	Activity	SIC 1968	NACE
	Furniture, complete or parts, (plastics) manufacturing	496	483
	Glove, unstitched, (plastics) manufacturing	449/2	483
	Haberdashery (plastics) manufacturing	496	483
	Hair comb (plastics) manufacturing	496	483
	Hair curler (plastics) manufacturing	496	483
	Handle for furniture (plastics) manufacturing	496	483
	Hollow-ware (plastics) manufacturing	496	483
	Inflatable plastics product (excluding playball) manufacturing	496	483
	Kitchen-ware (plastics) manufacturing	496	483
	Knife (plastics) manufacturing	496	483
	Knitting needle (plastics) manufacturing	496	483
	Knob for furniture (plastics) manufacturing	496	483
	Label (plastics), not self-adhesive, manufacturing	496	483
	Lampshades, reflectors, covers and diffusers, (plastics) manufacturing	496	483
	Mesh bag (plastics) manufacturing	496	483
	Model for window display (plastics) manufacturing	496	483
	Motor vehicle accessories, fittings and parts, (plastics) manufacturing	496	483
	Nameplate (plastics) manufacturing	496	483
	Netting (plastics), not woven or knotted, manufacturing	496	483
	Notice plate (plastics) manufacturing	496	483
	Novelty (plastics) manufacturing	496	483
	Ornament (plastics) manufacturing	496	483
	Pallet (plastics) manufacturing	496	483
	Pedal bin (plastics) manufacturing	496	483
	Pelmet (plastics) manufacturing	496	483
	Plate (plastics) manufacturing	496	483
	Powder compact (plastics) manufacturing	496	483
	Resin bonded glass fibre moulding (excluding those for motor vehicles) manufacturing	496	483
	Road sign (plastics) manufacturing	496	483
	Ruler (plastics) manufacturing	496	483
	Safety helmet (plastics) manufacturing	446/2	483
	Screw (plastics) manufacturing	496	483
	Seed tray (plastics) manufacturing	496	483
	Shopping bag (plastics) manufacturing	496	483
	Sign (plastics) manufacturing	496	483
	Slide (zip) fastener (plastics) manufacturing	496	483
	Spoon (plastics) manufacturing	496	483
	Storage container, domestic, (plastics) manufacturing	496	483
	Tableware (plastics) manufacturing	496	483
	Tailor's dummy (plastics) manufacturing	496	483
	Tray (plastics) manufacturing	496	483
	Vase (plastics) manufacturing	496	483
	Water butt (plastics) manufacturing	496	483
	Watering can (plastics) manufacturing	496	483
	Window blind and accessories (plastics) manufacturing	496	483
	Wire and cable covering and sleeve (plastics) manufacturing	496	483
	Zip (slide) fasteners (plastics) manufacturing	496	483
4910/1	Jewellery and goldsmiths' and silversmiths' wares of precious metals		
	Cutlery, gold plated, manufacturing	392	491.1
	Cutlery, precious metal, manufacturing	392	491.2
	Findings and stampings, precious metal, for jewellery manufacturing	396	491.1
	Gold and silver braid manufacturing	396	491.2
	Gold and silver embroidery manufacturing	396	491.1
	Gold and silver mounting manufacturing	396	491.2
	Gold laceman	396	491.2
	Gold leaf manufacturing	396	491.2
	Goldsmiths' work	396	491.2
	Jewellery engraving (not in distributive trades)	396	491.1
	Jewellery polishing	396	491.1
	Jewellery, gold or silver plated, manufacturing	396	491.1
	Jewellery, precious metal, manufacturing	396	491.1
	Ornament, gold or silver plated, manufacturing	396	491.1
	Ornament, precious metal, manufacturing	396	491.1
	Platinum jewellery manufacturing	396	491.1
	Silver burnishing	396	491.1
	Silversmiths' work	396	491.2
	Tableware, gold plated, manufacturing	392	491.2
	Tableware, precious metal, manufacturing	392	491.2
4910/2	Worked precious and semi-precious stones and pearls		
	Diamond cutting	396	491.4
	Jet ornament and jewellery manufacturing	396	491.5
	Pearl drilling	396	491.5
	Pearl stringing	396	491.5
	Precious stone cutting	396	491.5
	Precious stone jewellery manufacturing	396	491.5
	Semi-precious stone jewellery manufacturing	396	491.5
	Watchmakers' jewels manufacturing	396	491.5
4910/3	Fancy jewellery and pewterware		
	Bag, chain, manufacturing	396	491.3
	Britannia metalware manufacturing	396	491.3
	Buhl cutting	396	491.3
	Ceramic jewellery manufacturing	499/2	491.3
	Costume jewellery manufacturing	499/2	491.3
	Fashion jewellery manufacturing	499/2	491.3
	Findings and stampings, base metal, for jewellery manufacturing	396	491.3
	Gilt manufacturing	396	491.3
	Imitation pearl manufacturing	499/2	491.5
	Jewellery, gilded and silvered, manufacturing	396	491.3
	Pewter ware manufacturing	396	491.3
4910/4	Struck coins and medals		
	Coin striking	396	491.6
	Medal making	396	491.6
	Royal Mint	396	491.6
4920/1	Keyboard instruments		
	Harpsichord manufacturing	499/1	492.1
	Organ rebuilding and repairing (in factory)	499/1	492.1

SIC 1980	Activity	SIC 1968	NACE
	Organ tuning	499/1	984
	Piano manufacturing	499/1	492.1
	Piano repairing (in factory)	499/1	492.1
	Pipe organ manufacturing	499/1	492.1
4920/2	**Other musical instruments**		
	Accordion manufacturing	499/1	492.2
	Bagpipe and bagpipe reed manufacturing	499/1	492.2
	Cello manufacturing	499/1	492.2
	Concertina manufacturing	499/1	492.2
	Double bass manufacturing	499/1	492.2
	Drum (musical instrument) manufacturing	499/1	492.2
	Electronic musical instrument manufacturing	499/1	492.2
	Guitar manufacturing	499/1	492.2
	Mouth organ manufacturing	499/1	492.2
	Musical box manufacturing	499/1	492.2
	Percussion instrument manufacturing	499/1	492.2
	Recorder (plastic or wood) manufacturing	499/1	492.2
	Reed (for musical instrument) manufacturing	499/1	492.2
	Repair and reconditioning of musical instruments (other than keyboard: in factory)	499/1	492.2
	Tuning fork manufacturing	499/1	492.2
	Viola manufacturing	499/1	492.2
	Violin manufacturing	499/1	492.2
	Wind instrument manufacturing	499/1	492.2
	Woodwind instrument manufacturing	499/1	492.2
4930	**Photographic and cinematographic processing laboratories**		
	Cinematographic film colouring, developing, printing or repairing	881/1	493
	Photograph copying	899/2	493.2
	Photograph developing	899/2	493.2
	Photograph enlarging	899/2	493.2
	Photograph finishing	899/2	493.2
	Photograph printing	899/2	493.2
	Printing of sound tracks	881/1	493.1
4941	**Toys and games**		
	Bagatelle board manufacturing	494/1	494.1
	Bicycle, children's, manufacturing	494/1	494.1
	Board game manufacturing	494/1	494.1
	Boxed game manufacturing	494/1	494.1
	Cardboard toy manufacturing	494/1	494.1
	Carnival article manufacturing	494/1	494.1
	Chess set manufacturing	494/1	494.1
	Conjuring apparatus manufacturing	494/1	494.1
	Construction model manufacturing	494/1	494.1
	Constructional toy manufacturing	494/1	494.1
	Doll (not rubber) manufacturing	494/1	494.1
	Dolls' clothes manufacturing	494/1	494.1
	Dolls' cots manufacturing	494/1	494.1
	Dolls' houses manufacturing	494/1	494.1
	Dolls' prams manufacturing	494/1	494.1
	Draughts set manufacturing	494/1	494.1
	Electric toy train manufacturing	494/1	494.1
	Electric toy-car circuit manufacturing	494/1	494.1
	Electronic toys and games (not linked with television set) manufacturing	494/1	not classified
	Indoor game manufacturing	494/1	494.1
	Jig-saw puzzle manufacturing	494/1	494.1
	Mechanical toy manufacturing	494/1	494.1
	Metal toy manufacturing	494/1	494.1
	Model kit manufacturing	494/1	494.1
	Modelling material manufacturing	494/1	256.7
	Paper toy and game manufacturing	494/1	494.1
	Pedal toy car manufacturing	494/1	494.1
	Plastics game manufacturing	494/1	494.1
	Plastics toy manufacturing	494/1	494.1
	Plush toy on wheels manufacturing	494/1	494.1
	Puppet (not of rubber) manufacturing	494/1	494.1
	Push cart, toy, manufacturing	494/1	494.1
	Scooter, children's, manufacturing	494/1	494.1
	Soft toy (not of rubber) manufacturing	494/1	494.1
	Stuffed toy manufacturing	494/1	494.1
	Table game manufacturing	494/1	494.1
	Technical toy manufacturing	494/1	494.1
	Toy (not rubber) manufacturing	494/1	494.1
	Toy animal manufacturing	494/1	494.1
	Toy furniture manufacturing	494/1	494.1
	Toy gun (not operated by compressed air) manufacturing	494/1	494.1
	Toy musical instrument manufacturing	494/1	494.1
	Toy perambulator and pushchair manufacturing	494/1	494.1
	Toy wheelbarrow manufacturing	494/1	494.1
	Tricycle, children's, manufacturing	494/1	494.1
	Wooden toy and game manufacturing	494/1	494.1
4942	**Sports goods**		
	Archery equipment manufacturing	494/3	494.2
	Athletic equipment manufacturing	494/3	494.2
	Badminton shuttlecock manufacturing	494/3	494.2
	Bagatelle table, manufacturing	472	494.2
	Ball, finished, for all sports manufacturing	494/3	494.2
	Billiard ball manufacturing	494/3	494.2
	Billiard cue manufacturing	494/3	494.2
	Billiard table manufacturing	472	494.2
	Bowls and bowls equipment manufacturing	494/3	494.2
	Boxing glove manufacturing	494/3	442.2
	Climbing frame manufacturing	494/3	494.2
	Cricket ball and equipment manufacturing	494/3	494.2
	Dart manufacturing	494/3	494.2
	Dartboard manufacturing	494/3	494.2
	Fabric sports bag manufacturing	494/3	442
	Fish hook manufacturing	399/8	316.9
	Fishing tackle manufacturing	494/3	494.2
	Fly dressing	494/3	494.2
	Football case, leather, manufacturing	494/3	494.2
	Golf ball (finished) manufacturing	494/3	494.2
	Golf club manufacturing	494/3	494.2
	Gymnasium equipment and appliance manufacturing	494/3	494.2
	Hockey stick manufacturing	494/3	494.2
	Leather sports bag manufacturing	494/3	442.1
	Mountain climbing equipment manufacturing	494/3	494.2
	Plastics sports equipment manufacturing	494/3	494.2
	Playground and nursery equipment manufacturing	494/3	494.2
	Racket and racket frame manufacturing	494/3	494.2
	Rock climbing equipment manufacturing	494/3	494.2
	Skate, ice, manufacturing	494/3	494.2
	Skate, roller, manufacturing	494/3	494.2
	Skateboard manufacturing	494/3	494.2
	Skiing equipment manufacturing	494/3	494.2

SIC 1980	Activity	SIC 1968	NACE
	Sports glove (specialist) manufacturing	494/3	442.2
	Sports goods carrier manufacturing	494/3	442.1
	Squash racket manufacturing	494/3	494.2
	Swing (playground equipment) manufacturing	494/3	494.2
	Table tennis ball manufacturing	494/3	494.2
	Table tennis equipment manufacturing	494/3	494.2
	Tennis ball (finished) manufacturing	494/3	494.2
	Tennis racket manufacturing	494/3	494.2
	Water sports equipment manufacturing	494/3	494.2
4954/1	**Pens and pencils**		
	Ballpoint pen (and refill) manufacturing	495/1	495.1
	Cartridge refill for fountain pen manufacturing	495/1	495.1
	Chalk (drawing and writing) manufacturing	495/1	259.3
	Crayon manufacturing	495/1	259.3
	Felt-tipped pen manufacturing	495/1	495.1
	Fibre tipped pen manufacturing	495/1	495.1
	Fountain pen manufacturing	495/1	495.1
	Fountain pen nib manufacturing	495/1	495.1
	Pastel manufacturing	495/1	259.3
	Pen (writing or drawing) manufacturing	495/1	495.1
	Pen nib manufacturing	495/1	495.1
	Pencil manufacturing	495/1	259.3
	Pencil lead manufacturing	495/1	259.3
	Penholder manufacturing	495/1	495.1
	Propelling pencil manufacturing	495/1	495.1
	Roller pen (and refill) manufacturing	495/1	495.1
	Stylographic pen manufacturing	495	495.1
4954/2	**Inks and duplicating materials**		
	Carbon paper manufacturing	495/2	259.3
	Carbon ribbon manufacturing	495/2	259.3
	Carbonless copy paper manufacturing	495/2	259.3
	Drawing ink manufacturing	495/2	259.3
	Duplicating ink manufacturing	495/2	259.3
	Indian ink manufacturing	495/2	259.3
	Ink for impregnating ink pads manufacturing	495/2	259.3
	Marking ink manufacturing	495/2	259.3
	Ribbon, inked, manufacturing	495/2	259.3
	Stencil, duplicating, manufacturing	495/2	259.3
	Typewriter ribbon manufacturing	495/2	259.3
	Writing ink manufacturing	495/2	259.3
4954/3	**Stationers' goods not elsewhere specified**		
	Date stamp and accessories manufacturing	495/2	495.2
	Ink pad manufacturing	495/2	495.2
	Office accessory manufacturing	495/2	495
	Pencil sharpener manufacturing	495/2	495
	Rubber stamp manufacturing	495/2	495.2
	Seal (for use with sealing wax) manufacturing	495/2	495.2
	Staple (office) manufacturing	394	316.9
	Stapling machine (office) manufacturing	495/2	495
4959	**Other manufactures not elsewhere specified**		
	Alabaster bowl cutting	499/2	495.3
	Amber turning	499/2	495.3
	Architectural model manufacturing	499/2	495.3
	Artists' sundries manufacturing	499/2	495.3
	Bladder dressing	499/2	495.3
	Blinds (other than wood, canvas or plastics) manufacturing	499/2	495.3
	Boiler covering (not asbestos or slag wool) manufacturing	499/2	495.3
	Boiler packing (not asbestos or slag wool) manufacturing	499/2	495.3
	Bone working	499/2	495.3
	Briar pipe manufacture and repair	499/2	495.3
	Brush case (not leather or plastics) manufacturing	499/2	495.3
	Button carding	499/2	495.3
	Button covering	499/2	495.3
	Canvas stretcher manufacturing	499/2	495.3
	Catgut manufacturing	499/2	495.3
	Cigar holder manufacturing	499/2	495.3
	Cigarette holder manufacturing	499/2	495.3
	Cigarette lighter manufacturing	399/12	495.3
	Cinema screen manufacturing	499/2	495.3
	Comb (horn and tortoise-shell) manufacturing	499/2	495.3
	Cutlery case (not leather or plastics) manufacturing	499/2	495.3
	Cutlery handle (horn, ivory, tortoise-shell, etc.) manufacturing	499/2	495.3
	Devotional article manufacturing	499/2	495.3
	Feather curling	499/2	495.3
	Feather purifying	499/2	495.3
	Feather sorting	499/2	495.3
	Geographical model (wax, plaster) manufacturing	499/2	495.3
	Gut (for musical instruments and sports goods) manufacturing	499/2	495.3
	Gut scraping and spinning	499/2	495.3
	Hair preparation (for wig making)	449/4	495.3
	Horn and tortoise-shell working	499/2	495.3
	Horn pressing	499/2	495.3
	Ivory working	499/2	495.3
	Jewel case (not wood or metal) manufacturing	499/2	495.3
	Knitting needle (not plastics) manufacturing	499/2	495.3
	Lampshade (not glass or plastics) manufacturing	499/2	495.3
	Lifebelt (not cork or rubber) manufacturing	499/2	495.3
	Lifejacket (not cork or rubber) manufacturing	499/2	495.3
	Musical instrument case (not wooden) manufacturing	499/2	495.3
	Natural sponge preparation	499/2	495.3
	Pipe case (not leather or plastics) manufacturing	499/2	495.3
	Pipe, smoker's, manufacturing	499/2	495.3
	Plaster cast manufacturing	499/2	495.3
	Plaster model manufacturing	499/2	495.3
	Powder puff manufacturing	499/2	495.3
	Smokers' requisite manufacturing	499/2	495.3
	Spectacle case (not leather or plastics) manufacturing	499/2	495.3
	Sponge bleaching	499/2	495.3
	Sponge dressing	499/2	495.3
	Sponge trimming	499/2	495.3
	Surgical instrument case (not leather or plastics) manufacturing	499/2	495.3
	Tailors' dummy (not plastics) manufacturing	499/2	495.3
	Taxidermy	499/2	495.3
	Tobacco pouch manufacturing	499/2	495.3
	Toothpick manufacturing	499/2	495.3

SIC 1980	Activity	SIC 1968	NACE
	Violin case (not wooden) manufacturing	499/2	495.3
	Wax model manufacturing	499/2	495.3
	Whalebone cutting and splitting	499/2	495.3
5000	General construction and demolition work		
	Builder and contractor	500	500.1
	Construction plant hire with operatives	500	500
	Demolition contracting	500	500.2
	Government department (building and civil engineering works division)	500	500.1
	Housing association (building work)	500	500.1
	Local authority or new town direct labour department	500	500.1
	Scottish Special Housing Association (building work)	500	500.1
5010	Construction and repair of buildings		
	Brick furnace construction	500	501.3
	Brick kiln construction	500	501.3
	Bricklaying	500	501
	Building maintenance and restoration	500	501.5
	Carpentry (structural)	500	501.7
	Chimney construction	500	501.3
	Claddings (external)	500	501
	Concrete work (building)	500	501
	Dampproofing of buildings	500	501.4
	Fence contractor (not on agricultural sites)	500	501.7
	Grouting contractor (building)	500	501
	Mason (building)	500	501.7
	Piling (building)	500	501.7
	Roofing contractor	500	501.2
	Scaffolding hiring and erecting	500	501.6
	Steelwork erection (building)	500	501.7
	Stone walling	500	501.7
	Stonemasonry (building)	500	501.7
	Stonework cleaning and renovation	500	501.5
	Structural steelwork erection (building)	500	501.7
	Waterproofing buildings	500	501.4
5020	Civil engineering		
	Aerial mast (self supporting) erection	500	502.7
	Airport runway construction	500	502.5
	Artesian well contractor	500	502.6
	Asphalting contractor (civil engineering)	500	502.5
	Boring (civil engineering)	500	502.3
	Bridge building	500	502.3
	Cable laying	500	502.7
	Car park construction	500	502
	Civil engineering contractor	500	502.1
	Constructional engineering	500	502.1
	Dam construction	500	502.4
	Dredging contractor	500	502.4
	Earthmoving contractor	500	502.2
	Ferro-concrete bar bending and fixing contractor	500	502.7
	Formwork (civil engineering)	500	502.7
	Grouting contractor (civil engineering)	500	502
	Harbour construction	500	502.4
	Hydraulic construction	500	502.4
	Irrigation system construction	500	502.6
	Land drainage contractor	500	502.6
	Mine sinking	500	502.3
	Oil production platform, fixed concrete or composite steel/concrete, construction of	500	502.7
	Overhead line construction	500	502.7
	Paving contractor	500	502.5
	Piling contractor (civil engineering)	500	502.7
	Public works contractor	500	502.1
	Pylon erection	500	502.7
	Railway construction	500	502.5
	Reinforced concrete engineer (civil engineering)	500	502.1
	Reservoir construction	500	502.6
	Retort setting	500	501.3
	Sewerage construction	500	502.6
	Shaft drilling (civil engineering)	500	502.3
	Sports and recreation grounds, laying out of	500	502.7
	Steelwork erection (civil engineering)	500	502.7
	Structural steelwork erection (civil engineering)	500	502.7
	Tar spraying contractor (civil engineering)	500	502.5
	Transmission line construction	500	502.7
	Tunnelling contractor	500	502.3
	Well sinking (except gas or oil)	500	502.3
5030	Installation of fixtures and fittings		
	Acoustical engineering	500	503.4
	Aerial erection (domestic)	500	503.6
	Air conditioning plant installation	500	503.3
	Cavity wall insulation	500	503.4
	Electric sign erection and maintenance	500	503.5
	Electrical contractor (construction)	500	503.5
	Electrical wiring (buildings)	500	503.5
	Heating and ventilation apparatus installation	500	503.3
	Heating engineering (buildings)	500	503.3
	Hot water engineer	500	503.2
	Insulating contractor (buildings)	500	503.4
	Lightning conductor installation	500	503.6
	Plumbing contractor	500	503.2
	Roof insulation contractor	500	503.4
	Sanitary engineering for buildings	500	503.2
	Steeplejacking	500	503.6
	Telephone line installation (not by post office corporation)	500	503.6
	Thermal insulation contractor	500	503.4
5040	Building completion work		
	Carpentry (not structural)	500	504.3
	Claddings (internal)	500	504.5
	Decorating (buildings)	500	504.4
	Double glazing installation	500	504.4
	Flooring contractor	500	504.5
	Glazing contractor	500	504.4
	Metal window fixing	500	504.6
	Painting contractor	500	504.4
	Paperhanging	500	504.4
	Parquet floor laying (not by manufacturer)	500	504.3
	Plastering contractor	500	504.2
	Suspended ceiling installation	500	504.1
	Terrazzo work (building)	500	504.5
	Tiling contractor (floors and walls)	500	504.5
6110	Wholesale distribution of agricultural raw materials, live animals, textile raw materials and semi-manufactures		
	Compound feeding stuffs, dealing in	831/3	611.2
	Corn chandler	831/3	611.3
	Corn merchant	831/3	611.1
	Corn, dealing in	831/3	611.2
	Cotton, dealing in	832/4	611.6

SIC 1980	Activity	SIC 1968	NACE
	Fatstock Marketing Corporation	810/2	611.5
	Feathers, dealing in	832/8	611
	Fertilizer, dealing in	831/3	611.3
	Flax, dealing in	832/4	611.6
	Flock, dealing in	832/4	611.6
	Flower salesman, wholesale	812/4	611.4
	Flowers, wholesale dealing in	812/4	611.4
	Fodder, dealing in	831/3	611.2
	Forage, dealing in	831/3	611.2
	Grain, dealing in	831/3	611.1
	Guano, dealing in	831/3	611.3
	Hair, dealing in	832/8	611.6
	Hay, dealing in	831/3	611.2
	Hemp, dealing in	832/4	611
	Hides and skins, dealing in	832/3	611.7
	Horse breaking	831/4	611.5
	Horse training (not race horse)	831/4	979
	Horsedealer	831/4	611.5
	Horsehair, dealing in	832/8	611
	Horses, dealing in	831/4	611.5
	Insecticides, dealing in	831/3	611
	Leather seller, wholesale	832/3	611.8
	Livestock, dealing in	831/4	611.5
	Manure, dealing in	831/3	611.3
	Merchant converter	812/2	616
	Moss litter, dealing in	831/3	611
	Mungo, dealing in	832/4	611.6
	Noil, dealing in	832/4	611.6
	Oil cake, dealing in	831/3	611.2
	Peat, dealing in	831/1	611.3
	Pig, dealing	831/4	611.5
	Pig, jobbing	831/4	611.5
	Poultry (live) dealing	831/4	611
	Poultry spice, dealing in	831/3	611.2
	Provender, dealing in	831/3	611.2
	Pulse, dealing in	831/3	611.2
	Seed merchant	831/3	611.2
	Sheep dealing	831/4	611.5
	Shoddy, dealing in	832/4	611.6
	Silk, dealing in	832/4	611.6
	Straw, dealing in	831/3	611.2
	Tops, dealing in	832/4	611.6
	Wool, dealing in	832/4	611.6
	Woollen flock, dealing in	832/4	611.6
6120	Wholesale distribution of fuels, ores, metals and industrial materials		
	Coal depot, wholesale	831/1	612.3
	Coal merchant, wholesale	831/1	612.3
	Coal, wholesale dealing in	831/1	612.3
	Coke merchant, wholesale	831/1	612.3
	Coke, wholesale dealing in	831/1	612.3
	Copper, dealing in	832/1	612.6
	Cotton size, dealing in	832/8	612
	Culm, dealing in	831/1	612.3
	Dealing in industrial materials (general or undefined)	832/9	612
	Dyes, dealing in	832/8	612.7
	Essential oils merchant	832/8	612.7
	Explosives, dealing in	832/8	612
	Fluorspar, dealing in	832/8	612.5
	Fuel oil, distribution (bulk)	811	612.2
	Galvanised sheets, dealing in	832/1	612.6
	Gas oil, dealing in	831/1	612.2
	Grease, dealing in	832/8	612.7
	Gums, dealing in	832/8	612.7
	Herring oil, dealing in	832/8	612.7
	Indigo, dealing in	832/8	612.7
	Industrial chemicals and dyes, dealing in	832/8	612.7
	Industrial materials (general or undefined), dealing in	832/9	612
	Iron yard	832/7	612.4
	Iron, dealing in	832/1	612.4
	Lead, dealing in	832/1	612.6
	Limestone, dealing in	832/8	612.4
	Lubricants, wholesale distribution of	811	612.2
	Metal stockholder	832/1	612
	Motor spirit, wholesale distribution of	811	612.2
	National Coal Board, marketing department	831/1	612.3
	Nitrate of soda importer	832/8	612.7
	Oil merchant, wholesale	831/1	612.2
	Oil seeds, dealing in	832/8	612.7
	Ore, dealing in	832/1	612.5
	Palm oil, dealing in	832/8	612.7
	Paraffin, dealing in, not retail	831/1	612.2
	Patent fuel, wholesale dealing in	831/1	612.3
	Petroleum products, wholesale distribution of	811	612.2
	Resin, dealing in	832/8	612.7
	Rubber, dealing in	832/8	612.7
	Salt merchant	832/8	612.7
	Sawdust, dealing in	832/8	612.7
	Spelter, dealing in	832/1	612.6
	Starch, dealing in	832/8	612.7
	Steel stockholder	832/1	612.4
	Steel, dealing in	832/1	612.4
	Stones, dealing in	832/8	612.5
	Tallow, dealing in	832/8	612.7
	Tinplate, dealing in	832/1	612.6
	Whale oil, dealing in	832/8	612.7
	Woodpulp and paper making materials, dealing in	832/8	612.7
	Zinc, dealing in	832/1	612.6
6130	Wholesale distribution of timber and building materials		
	Cement marketing company	831/2	613.2
	Clay, dealing in	832/8	612
	Drainpipes, dealing in	831/2	613.3
	Flag (flagstone) merchant	831/2	613.2
	Ganister, dealing in	832/8	613
	Glass merchant (flat glass)	831/2	613.4
	Granite, dealing in	832/8	613
	Hardwood, dealing in	832/2	613.1
	Marble, dealing in	832/8	613.2
	Pit props, dealing in	832/2	613.1
	Plaster, dealing in	831/2	613.2
	Plasterboard, dealing in	831/2	613.2
	Plumbers' merchant	831/2	613.3
	Plywood, dealing in	832/2	613.1
	Pre-cast concrete products, dealing in	831/2	613.2
	Sand and gravel merchant	831/2	612.5
	Sanitary ware, dealing in	831/2	613.3
	Slate slabs, dealing in	832/8	612.5
	Slate, dealing in	831/2	613.2
	Sleepers, wholesale, dealing in	832/2	613.1
	Tiles, dealing in	831/2	613.2
	Timber importer	832/2	613.1
	Timber merchant	832/2	613.1
	Timber yard	832/2	613.1
	Wall board, dealing in	831/2	613.2
	Wood, dealing in	832/2	613.1
6148	Wholesale distribution of motor vehicles and parts and accessories therefore		
	Motor accessories, wholesale dealing in	894	614.7
	Motor cycle importer	894	614.7
	Motor vehicle importer	894	614.7

SIC 1980	Activity	SIC 1968	NACE
6149	Wholesale distribution of machinery, industrial equipment and transport equipment other than motor vehicles		
	Contractors' plant (not hiring), dealing in	832/5	614
	Electrical appliances, accessories and fittings (industrial), wholesale dealing in	812/4	614
	Engineers' plant and stores, dealing in	832/5	614
	Farm dairy machinery, dealing in	832/6	614.6
	Garage tools, dealing in	832/5	614.5
	Horticultural machinery, dealing in	832/6	614.6
	Jigs and gauges, dealing in	832/5	614
	Machine tools, dealing in	832/5	614.1
	Machinery stockist	832/5	614
	Machinery, dealing in	832/5	614
	Office machinery, dealing in	832/5	614.4
	Public address equipment, wholesale dealing in	812/4	614
	Pumping plant, dealing in	832/5	614.5
	Tractors, agricultural, repairing	832/5	614.6
	Tractors, dealing in	832/5	614.6
	Wheeled tractors, dealing in	832/6	614.6
	Yachts, wholesale dealing in	812/4	614.7
6150	Wholesale distribution of household goods, hardware and ironmongery		
	Audio separates, wholesale dealing in	812/4	615.3
	Cork, dealing in	832/8	615.6
	Cutlery, wholesale dealing in	812/4	615.2
	Domestic ironmongery, wholesale dealing in	812/4	615.2
	Domestic machinery, wholesale dealing in	812/4	615.2
	Earthenware, wholesale dealing in	812/4	615.4
	Furniture, wholesale dealing in	812/4	615.1
	Gardening tools, wholesale dealing in	812/4	615.2
	Glassware, wholesale dealing in	812/4	615.4
	Gramophone records, wholesale dealing in	812/4	615.3
	Ironmonger, wholesale	812/4	615.2
	Musical instruments, wholesale dealing in	812/4	615.3
	Office furniture, wholesale dealing in	812/4	615.1
	Paint and varnish, wholesale dealing in	832/8	615.5
	Radio and television, wholesale dealing in	812/4	615.3
	Record players, wholesale dealing in	812/4	615.3
	School furniture, wholesale dealing in	812/4	615.1
	Sheffield warehouse	812/4	615.2
6160	Wholesale distribution of textiles, clothing, footwear and leather goods		
	Carpets, wholesale dealing in	812/4	616.9
	Cloth merchant, wholesale	812/2	616
	Clothing, wholesale dealing in	812/2	616
	Draper, wholesale	812/2	616.1
	Fur merchant, wholesale	832/3	616.6
	Furrier, wholesale	812/2	616.6
	Haberdashery, wholesale dealing in	812/2	616.5
	Hand knitting yarn, wholesale dealing in	812/2	616.5
	Hand mending yarns, wholesale dealing in	812/2	616.5
	Handbags, wholesale dealing in	812/4	616.8
	Hat materials, wholesale dealing in	812/2	616
	Hessian, wholesale dealing in	812/2	616
	Hosiery, wholesale dealing in	812/2	616

SIC 1980	Activity	SIC 1968	NACE
	Household textiles, wholesale dealing in	812/2	616.9
	Leather goods, wholesale dealing in	812/4	616.8
	Linen and linen goods, wholesale dealing in	812/2	616.9
	Linoleum, wholesale dealing in	812/4	616.9
	Manchester warehouse	812/2	616
	Mantle warehouse, wholesale	812/2	616
	Millinery importer	812/2	616.3
	Millinery, wholesale dealing in	812/2	616.3
	Oil cloth, wholesale dealing in	812/4	616.9
	Outfitter, wholesale	812/2	616.1
	Piece goods, wholesale dealing in	812/2	616
	Rugs, wholesale dealing in	812/4	616.9
	Sacks and bags, new, wholesale dealing in	812/4	616
	Saddlery and leather goods, wholesale dealing in	812/4	616.8
	Shoes, wholesale dealing in	812/2	616.7
	Straw and felt hat warehouse	812/2	616.3
	Tailors' trimmings, wholesale dealing in	812/2	616.5
	Tarpaulins, wholesale dealing in	812/4	616
	Textile converter	812/2	616
	Threads, wholesale dealing in	812/2	616.5
	Upholsterers' trimmings, wholesale dealing in	812/2	616
	Wholesale dealer in cloth	812/2	616.4
	Wool merchant, wholesale	832/4	616
	Woollens, wholesale dealing in	812/2	616.6
6170	Wholesale distribution of food, drink and tobacco		
	Cash and carry wholesaler, predominantly food	810/1	617
	Cheese, wholesale dealing in	810/1	617.4
	Chocolate and sugar confectionery, wholesaler dealing in	810/1	617.7
	Cider merchant, wholesale	810/1	617.5
	Cigar importer, wholesale	812/1	617.6
	Cigar merchant, wholesale	812/1	617.6
	Cigarette importer, wholesale	812/1	617.6
	Cigarette merchant, wholesale	812/1	617.6
	Coffee, wholesale dealing in	810/1	617.8
	Cream, wholesale dealing in	810/2	617.4
	Dried fish, wholesale dealing in	810/2	617.9
	Dried fruit, wholesale dealing in	810/1	617.2
	Edible oils and hard fats, dealing in	832/8	617.4
	Eels, wholesale dealing in	810/2	617.9
	Egg dealer, wholesale	810/1	617.4
	Egg marketing board	810/1	617.4
	Egg packing station, wholesale	810/1	617.4
	Fish salesman, wholesale	810/2	617.9
	Fish, wholesale dealing in	810/2	617.9
	Fishmonger, wholesale	810/2	617.9
	Flour confectionery, wholesale dealing in	810/1	617.9
	Flour, wholesale dealing in	810/1	617.9
	Fruit salesman, wholesale	810/2	617.2
	Fruit, wholesale dealing in	810/2	617.2
	Fruiterer, wholesale	810/2	617.2
	Game, wholesale dealing in	810/2	617.3
	Grocer, wholesale	810/1	617.1
	Herrings, wholesale dealing in	810/2	617.9
	Honey, wholesale dealing in	810/1	617
	Hops, wholesale dealing in	810/2	617.9
	Ice cream, wholesale dealing in	810/1	617.7
	Lard, wholesale dealing in	810/1	617.4
	Liqueur dealer, wholesale	810/1	617.5
	Margarine, wholesale dealing in	810/1	617.4
	Market porterage (fruit and vegetable)	810/2	617.2

SIC 1980	Activity	SIC 1968	NACE
	Market porterage (meat or fish)	810/2	617
	Meat for domestic animals, wholesale dealing in	810/2	617.3
	Meat porter	810/2	617.3
	Meat salesman, wholesale	810/2	617.3
	Milk Marketing Board (milk depots)	810/2	617.4
	Milk, wholesale dealing in	810/2	617.4
	Mushrooms, wholesale dealing in	810/2	617.2
	Nuts, wholesale dealing in	810/2	617.2
	Offal salesman, wholesale	810/2	617.3
	Oysters, wholesale dealing in	810/2	617.9
	Pork butcher, wholesale	810/2	617.3
	Potato Marketing Board	810/2	617.2
	Potato salesman, wholesale	810/2	617.2
	Potatoes, wholesale dealing in	810/2	617.2
	Poultry, wholesale dealing in	810/2	617.3
	Provision dealer, wholesale	810/1	617.1
	Quick frozen food, wholesale dealing in	810/1	617.1
	Sausage skins, dealing in	832/8	617
	Shellfish, wholesale dealing in	810/2	617.9
	Shrimps, wholesale dealing in	810/2	617.9
	Soft drinks dealer, wholesale	810/1	617.5
	Spices, wholesale dealing in	810/1	617.8
	Sugar, wholesale dealing in	810/1	617.7
	Tea, wholesale dealing in	810/1	617.8
	Tobacco merchant, wholesale	812/1	617.6
	Tobacconist, wholesale	812/1	617.6
	Tobacconists' sundriesman, wholesale	812/1	617.6
	Vegetables, wholesale dealing in	810/2	617.2
	Wet fish, wholesale dealing in	810/2	617.9
	Wine and spirit merchant, wholesale	810/1	617.5
	Wine importer, wholesale	810/1	617.5
	Yeast, wholesale dealing in	810/2	617.9
6180	Wholesale distribution of pharmaceutical, medical and other chemists' goods		
	Druggists' sundries, wholesale dealing in	812/4	618.1
	Druggists' sundriesman, wholesale	812/4	618.1
	Drugs, wholesale dealing in	812/4	618.1
	Hairdressers' sundriesman	812/4	618
	Patent medicines, wholesale dealing in	812/4	618.1
	Perfumer, wholesale (not manufacturing)	812/4	618.3
	Pharmaceutical chemist, wholesale	812/4	618.1
	Soap, wholesale dealing in	812/4	618.4
	Sponge importer	812/4	618.1
	Surgical and dental instruments and appliances, wholesale dealing in	812/4	618.2
	Toilet preparations, wholesale dealing in	812/4	618.3
6190	Other wholesale distribution including general wholesalers		
	Cycles, wholesale dealing in	812/4	619.6
	Educational supplies (not furniture), wholesale dealing in	812/3	619
	Fancy goods, wholesale dealing in	812/4	619.6
	Imitation pearls, wholesale dealing in	812/4	619.4
	Jeweller, wholesale	812/4	619.4
	Jewellers' materials, wholesale dealing in	812/4	619.4
	Newsagent, wholesale	812/3	619.2
	Optical goods, wholesale dealing in	812/4	619.3
	Paper bags, wholesale dealing in	812/3	619.1
	Paper boards, wholesale dealing in	812/3	619.1
	Paper merchant, wholesale	812/3	619.1
	Perambulators, wholesale dealing in	812/4	619.6
	Photographic goods, wholesale dealing in	812/4	619.3
	Precious stones, wholesale dealing in	812/4	619.4
	Rope, new, wholesale dealing in	812/4	619.6
	Scientific instruments and glassware, wholesale dealing in	812/4	619
	Sports goods, wholesale dealing in	812/4	619.5
	Stationer, wholesale	812/3	619.1
	Stationers' sundries, wholesale dealing in	812/3	619.1
	Toys, wholesale dealing in	812/4	619.5
	Twine, wholesale dealing in	812/4	619.6
	Watch and clock movements, wholesale dealing in	812/4	619.4
	Watches and clocks, wholesale dealing in	812/4	619.4
	Wholesale merchant (predominantly non-food, general or undefined)	812/5	619.7
6210	Dealing in scrap metals		
	Boiler breaking, for scrap	832/7	621
	Metal broker (scrap metal)	832/7	621
	Motor car breaking, for scrap	832/7	621
	Old iron merchant	832/7	621
	Scrap iron dealer	832/7	621
	Scrap metal breaking, collecting, compressing, sorting etc. (by dealers)	832/7	621
	Scrap metal, dealing in	832/7	621
6220	Dealing in other scrap materials, or general dealers		
	Bottle sorting and washing	832/7	622
	Cotton rags, dealing in (including shaking, breaking and opening)	832/7	622
	Cotton waste, dealing in	832/7	622
	Engine cleaning waste, dealing in	832/7	622
	Fat and bone collector (own account)	832/7	622
	Hotel contracting (waste collecting)	832/7	622
	Marine store waste dealer	832/7	622
	Rag merchant	832/7	622
	Rags and bones, dealing in	832/7	622
	Rags, dealing in	832/7	622
	Scrap leather, dealing in	832/7	622
	Scrap merchant (general dealer)	832/7	622
	Textile waste, dealing in	832/7	622
	Wash and fat contracting (waste collecting)	832/7	622
	Waste paper sorting and dealing in	832/7	622
	Waste rubber, dealing in	832/7	622
	Waste string, dealing in	832/7	622
	Woollen rag blending or sorting	832/7	622
6300	Commission agents		
	Clay agent	832/8	632
	Coal agent	831/1	632
	Coal factor	831/1	632
	Confirming house, export (general or undefined)	812/5	619.7
	Corn Exchange	831/3	631
	Corn factor	831/3	631
	Cotton broker	832/3	631
	Diamond broker	812/4	638
	Fish factor	810/2	637
	Fruit and vegetable commission agent	810/2	637
	Fur broker	832/3	638
	Fur commission merchant	832/3	638
	Furniture agent or broker	812/4	635
	Grain broker	831/3	631
	Hide and skin broker	832/3	631
	Iron agent	832/1	632

SIC 1980	Activity	SIC 1968	NACE
	Machine broker	832/5	634
	Machinery agent	832/5	634
	Metal broker (not scrap metal)	832/1	632
	Mineral broker	832/1	632
	Provision Exchange	810/1	617.1
	Purchasing agent, export, general or undefined	812/5	639
	Soft goods agent	812/2	636
	Spice broker	810/1	617.8
	Tea Exchange	810/1	617.8
	Timber broker	832/2	633
	Tobacco broker	812/1	617.6
	Wood agent	832/2	633
	Wool broker	832/4	631
	Wool Exchange	812/4	616
	Yarn agent	832/4	631
6410	Food retailing		
	Bread, retailing in	820/2	641.7
	Cooked meat shop	820/1	641.4
	Dairy (grocer's shop) retail	820/1	641.3
	Dairyman (not farmer) retail	820/1	641.3
	Delicatessen shop	820/1	641.1
	Eels, retail dealing in	820/2	641.5
	Fish stall	820/2	641.5
	Fish, retail dealing in	820/2	641.5
	Fishmonger (retail)	820/2	641.5
	Flour confectionery, retail dealing in	820/2	641.8
	Food (general), retail dealing in	820/1	641.1
	Fruit seller (street)	820/2	641.2
	Fruit stall keeper	820/2	641.2
	Fruit, retail dealing in	820/2	641.2
	Fruiterer, retail	820/2	641.2
	Game, retail dealing in	820/2	641.6
	Greengrocer, retail	820/2	641.2
	Grocer, retail	820/1	641/642
	Grocery stall, retail	820/1	641/642
	Health foods, retail dealing in	820/1	642.3
	Herb seller (food)	821/4	642.3
	Herbalist (food)	821/4	642.3
	Hypermarket (selling mainly foodstuffs)	820/1	641.1
	Ice cream van	820/1	641.9
	Ice cream, (take away) retailer	820/1	641.9
	Meat, retail dealing in	820/2	641.4
	Milk roundsman (not farmer) retail	820/2	641.3
	Milkman (not farmer) retail	820/2	641.3
	Nuts (edible), retail dealing in	820/2	642.3
	Pastry, retail dealing in	820/1	641.8
	Pork butcher	820/1	641.4
	Potatoes, retail dealing in	820/2	641.2
	Poultry, retail dealing in	820/2	641.6
	Provisions, retail dealing in	820/1	641.1
	Shellfish, retail dealing in	820/2	641.5
	Soft drinks, retail dealing in	820/1	642.1
	Supermarket, retail (selling mainly foodstuffs)	820/1	641.1
	Superstore (selling mainly foodstuffs)	820/1	641.1
	Tea and coffee grocer, retail	820/1	642.3
	Tripe dealer, retail	820/1	641.4
	Vegetables, retail dealing in	820/2	641.2
	Vegetarian foods, retail dealing in	820/1	642.3
	Village general store (selling mainly foodstuffs)	820/1	642.3
6420	Confectioners, tobacconists and newsagents and off-licences		
	Beer, retail dealing in	820/2	642.1
	Chocolate and sweets, retail dealing in	821/1	641.9
	Cigarettes, retail dealing in	821/1	642.2
	Cigars, retail dealing in	821/1	642.2
	Cinema kiosk	821/1	641/642
	Confectioner and newsagent	821/1	641.1
	Confectioner and tobacconist	821/1	641/642
	Confectioner, tobacconist and newsagent	821/1	641.1
	Confectionery, sugar, retail dealing in	821/1	641.9
	Off-licence (not public house)	820/2	642.1
	Smokers' requisites, retail dealing in	821/1	642.2
	Sugar confectionary, retail dealing in	821/1	641.9
	Sweets, retail dealing in	821/1	641.9
	Tobacco, retail dealing in	821/1	642.2
	Tobacconist and newsagent, retail	821/1	642.3
	Tobacconist, retail	821/1	642.2
	Wine and spirits, retail dealing in	820/2	642.1
6430	Dispensing and other chemists		
	Chemist, retail	821/4	644
	Cosmetics, retail dealing in	821/4	644.2
	Dispensing chemist	821/4	643
	Drug store	821/4	644
	Druggist, retail	821/4	643
	Drugs, retail dealing in	821/4	643
	Medical appliances, retail dealing in	821/4	644.1
	Medicines, retail dealing in	821/4	643
	Orthopaedic appliances, retail dealing in	821/4	644.1
	Perfume, retail dealing in	821/4	644.2
	Pharmaceutical chemist, retail	821/4	643
	Pharmacy, retail	821/4	643
	Surgical appliances, retail dealing in	821/4	644.1
	Toilet goods, retail dealing in	821/4	644.2
6450	Retail distribution of clothing		
	Bespoke tailor, retail	821/2	645
	Children's wear, retail dealing in	821/2	645.6
	Clothier and outfitter, retail	821/2	645
	Corsetiere, retail	821/2	645.7
	Draper, retail	821/2	645.6
	Dress material, retail dealing in	821/2	645.6
	Dressmaker, retail	821/2	645
	Fabrics, clothing, retail dealing in	821/2	645.6
	Furrier, retail	821/2	645.9
	Glover, retail	821/2	645
	Haberdasher, retail	821/2	645.8
	Hand knitting yarns, retail dealing in	821/2	645.8
	Hats, retail dealing in	821/2	645.7
	Hatter, retail	821/2	645.7
	Hosiery, retail dealing in	821/2	645
	Juvenile outfitter, retail	821/2	645
	Ladies' outfitter, retail	821/2	645
	Men's outfitter, retail	821/2	645
	Mens' wear, retail dealing in	821/2	645
	Millinery, retail dealing in	821/2	645.7
	Misfit clothing, retail dealing in	821/2	645
	Outfitter, retail clothing	821/2	645.1
	Piece goods, retail dealing in	821/2	645.6
	Small-wares dealer, retail	821/2	645
	Tailor, retail	821/2	645
	Umbrellas, retail dealing in	821/2	645.7
	Womens' outfitter, retail	821/2	645
	Womens' wear, retail dealing in	821/2	645
	Woollen draper, retail	821/2	645.6
6460	Retail distribution of footwear and leather goods		
	Boots and shoes, retail dealing in	821/2	646.1
	Handbags, retail dealing in	821/4	646.2
	Leather goods, retail dealing in	821/4	646.2

SIC 1980	Activity	SIC 1968	NACE
	Saddlery, retail dealing in	821/4	646.2
	Shoes, retail dealing in	821/2	646.1
	Travel goods, retail dealing in	821/4	646.2
	Wallets, retail dealing in	821/4	646.2
6470	**Retail distribution of furnishing fabrics and household textiles**		
	Bed linen, retail dealing in	821/2	647.6
	Bedding, retail dealing in	821/2	647.1
	Carpet tiles, retail dealing in	821/3	647.1
	Carpets, retail dealing in	821/2	647.1
	Curtain material, retail dealing in	821/2	647
	Curtains (made up), retail dealing in	821/2	647
	Household textiles, retail dealing in	821/2	647
	Rugs, retail dealing in	821/2	647
	Soft furnishings, retail dealing in	821/2	647
	Table linen, retail dealing in	821/2	647
6480	**Retail distribution of household goods, hardware and ironmongery**		
	Art dealer (retail)	821/3	649.6
	Audio equipment, retail dealing in	821/3	648.8
	Beds, retail dealing in	821/3	648.2
	China, retail dealing in	821/3	648.7
	Coins, retail dealing in	821/3	649.6
	Copper goods, retail dealing in	821/3	648/649
	Curios, retail dealing in	821/3	649.6
	Cutlery, retail dealing in	821/3	648.6
	Do-it-yourself materials, retail dealing in	821/3	648.1
	Domestic electrical appliances, retail dealing in	821/3	648.4
	Earthenware, retail dealing in	821/3	648.7
	Electrical appliances, accessories and fittings, retail dealing in	821/3	648.4
	Fancy goods: retail dealing in	821/4	649.5
	Fine art, retail dealing in	821/3	649.6
	Floor coverings (not carpets), retail dealing in	821/3	649.1
	Floor tiles (not carpet), retail dealing in	821/3	649.1
	Furniture, domestic, retail dealing in	821/3	648.2
	Gardening tools, retail dealing in	821/3	648.6
	Gas appliances, retail dealing in	821/3	648.1
	Gift shop	821/4	649.5
	Glassware, retail dealing in	821/3	648.7
	Gramophone records, retail dealing in	821/3	648.8
	Hardware, retail dealing in	821/3	648.6
	Hi-fi equipment, retail dealing in	821/3	648.8
	House furnisher, retail	821/3	648.2
	Household stores	821/3	648.1
	Ironmonger, retail	821/3	648.6
	Knitting machines, retail dealing in	821/3	649.3
	Lampshades, retail dealing in	821/3	648.5
	Lighting, retail dealing in	821/3	648.5
	Lino tiles, retail dealing in	821/3	649.1
	Medals, retail dealing in	821/3	649.6
	Music shop, retail	821/3	649.4
	Musical instruments, retail dealing in	821/3	649.4
	Numismatist, retail	821/3	649.6
	Oriental goods, retail dealing in	821/3	649.6
	Packaging products for food (aluminium foil, plastic foil, bags etc.), retail dealing in	821/3	648.3
	Paint and varnish, retail dealing in	821/3	644.3
	Philatelist, retail	821/4	653.4
	Pianofortes, retail dealing in	821/3	649.4
	Picture framing	821/3	675
	Pictures, retail dealing in	821/3	649.6
	Pottery, retail dealing in	821/3	648.7
	Prints, retail dealing in	821/3	649.6
	Radio sets and equipment, retail dealing in	821/3	648.8
	Record players, retail dealing in	821/3	648.8
	Records and tapes, retail dealing in	821/3	648.8
	Religious goods, retail dealing in	821/4	649.6
	Sewing machines, retail dealing in	821/3	649.3
	Sheet music, retail dealing in	821/3	649.4
	Stamp dealer, retail	821/4	653.4
	Tape recorders, retail dealing in	821/3	648.8
	Television sets and equipment, retail dealing in	821/3	648.8
	Tiles, wall or floor, ceramic, retail dealing in	821/3	649.2
	Tools (not machine tools), retail dealing in	821/3	648.6
	Video recorders, retail dealing in	821/3	648.8
	Wallpaper, retail dealing in	821/3	649.1
	Works of art, retail dealing in	821/3	649.6
6510	**Retail distribution of motor vehicles and parts**		
	Battery (car), retail dealing in	894	651.1
	Caravan, retail dealing in	894	651.1
	Motor accessories, retail dealing in	894	651.1
	Motor cycle agent, retail	894	651.2
	Motor vehicles, retail dealing in	894	651.1
	Tyre dealer (retail)	894	651
6520	**Filling stations (motor fuel and lubricants)**		
	Filling station (motor fuel and lubricants)	894	652
	Petrol filling station	894	652
6530	**Retail distribution of books, stationery and office supplies**		
	Bookseller, retail	821/4	653.1
	Calculating machines, office, retail dealing in	821/4	653.3
	Chart seller	821/4	653.1
	Furniture, office, retail dealing in	821/4	653.3
	Map seller	821/4	653.1
	Newsvendor	821/1	653.1
	Office equipment, retail dealing in	821/4	653.3
	Picture postcards, retail dealing in	821/4	653
	Railway bookstall	821/1	653.1
	Second-hand bookseller, retail	821/4	653.1
	Stationer, retail	821/4	653.2
	Typewriters, retail dealing in	821/4	653.3
6540	**Other specialised retail distribution (non-food)**		
	Coal and coke, retailing	831/1	654.9
	Coal order office, retail	831/1	654.9
	Cycle accessories dealer, retail	821/4	651.1
	Cycle agent, retail	821/4	651.2
	Dispensing optician	821/4	654.1
	Firewood, retail dealing in	821/4	654.9
	Fishing tackle, retail dealing in	821/4	654.4
	Florist, retail	821/4	654.6
	Flowers, retail dealing in	821/4	654.6
	Games apparatus, retail dealing in	821/4	654.4
	Garden centre, retail	821/4	654.6
	Garden seeds and plants, retail dealing in	821/4	654.6
	Handicrafts shop	821/4	655.2
	Jeweller, retail	821/4	654.2
	Oil merchant, retail	821/3	654.9
	Optical goods, retail dealing in	821/4	654.1
	Optician, dispensing	821/4	654.1
	Paraffin, retail dealing in	821/3	654.9
	Perambulators, retail dealing in	821/4	655.2

SIC 1980	Activity	SIC 1968	NACE
	Pet food, retail dealing in	821/4	654.8
	Pet shop	821/4	654.7
	Photographic goods, retail dealing in	821/4	654.1
	Scientific goods, retail dealing in	821/4	655.2
	Second-hand clothing, retail dealing in	821/2	655.1
	Second-hand furniture, retail dealing in	821/3	655.1
	Second-hand goods, general, retail dealing in	821/4	655.1
	Silverware, retail dealing in	821/4	654.2
	Sports goods, retail dealing in	821/4	654.4
	Sports outfitter, retail	821/4	654.4
	Toys, retail dealing in	821/4	654.3
	Watches and clocks, retail dealing in	821/4	654.2
6560	Mixed retail businesses		
	Credit trader (general) retail	821/5	656
	Department store	821/5	656
	Mail order house (general) retail	821/5	656
	Mixed businesses retailing both food and non-food goods	821/5	656
6611/1	Licensed eating places		
	Buffet, licensed	885	661
	Cafe, licensed	885	661
	Chop house, licensed	885	661
	Civic restaurant, licensed	885	661
	Function room, licensed	885	661
	Luncheon bar, licensed	885	661
	Oyster bar, room (licensed)	885	661
	Railway dining car or buffet	885	661
	Restaurant, licensed	885	661
	Steak houses, licensed	885	661
6611/2	Unlicensed eating places		
	Cafe, unlicensed	885	661
	Cafeteria, unlicensed	885	661
	Coffee bar, room, saloon or stall	885	661
	Dining room (unlicensed)	885	661
	Ice cream parlour	885	661
	Milk bar	885	661
	Mobile tea bar	885	661
	Refreshment room (unlicensed)	885	661
	Restaurant, unlicensed	885	661
	Snack bar	885	661
	Supper bar or room (unlicensed)	885	661
	Tea bar, mobile	885	661
	Tea garden	885	661
	Tea room or shop	885	661
	Temperance buffet	885	661
6612	Take-away food shops		
	Baked chestnut man	885	661
	Eel pie shop	885	661
	Fish and chip shop	885	661
	Fried fish shop	885	661
	Hot dog vendor	885	661
	Jellied eel stall or shop	885	661
	Meat pie shop	885	661
	Pea and pie vendor	885	661
	Sandwich bar	885	661
	Take-away food shop	885	661
6620	Public houses and bars		
	Beer garden	886	662
	Licensed bar	886	662
	Licensed victualler (public house)	886	662
	Public house	886	662
	Tavern	886	662
6630	Night clubs and licensed clubs		
	Luncheon club	887	664
	NAAFI: club	887	664
	Night club	887	663
	Refreshment club	887	663
	Social Club	887	664
	Working men's club	887	664
6640/1	Catering contractors		
	Catering contractor	888	664
	Industrial canteen (run by catering contractor)	888	664
	NAAFI: canteen	888	664
	NAAFI: headquarters	888	664
	Pleasure steamer caterer	888	664
	Refreshment contracting	888	664
	School canteen (run by catering contractor)	888	664
	Staff canteen (run by catering contractor)	888	664
6640/2	Other canteens and messes		
	House of Commons Refreshment Department	887	664
	School canteen	872	664
	University canteen	872/3	664
6650/1	Licensed hotels, etc.		
	Guest house, licensed	884	665.3
	Hotel, licensed	884	665
	Inn	886	662
	Motel, licensed	884	665
	Private hotel, licensed	884	665.1
6650/2	Unlicensed hotels, etc.		
	Boarding house	884	665.3
	Guest house, unlicensed	884	665.3
	Hotel, unlicensed	884	665
	Private hotel, unlicensed	884	665.1
	Temperance hotel	884	665
6670/1	Camping and caravan sites		
	Camping site operator	884	667.2
	Caravan site (holiday) operator	884	667.2
6670/2	Holiday camps		
	Holiday camp	884	667.3
6670/3	Other tourist or short-stay accommodation not elsewhere specified		
	Apartment letting (holiday)	884	667.5
	Convalescent home (without medical care)	874/1	667.4
	Holiday home (not charitable)	884	667.3
	Hotel, self catering	884	665.2
	Hydro	884	667.4
	Lodging house, private	884	665.3
	Pension (accommodation)	884	665.3
	Youth hostel	884	667.1
6710	Repair and servicing of motor vehicles		
	Motor car repairing	894	671
	Motor repair depot	894	671
	Motor vehicle depot, Hendon (Department of Transport)	894	671
	Motor vehicle painting and body repairing	894	671
	Motor vehicle repairing	894	671
	Omnibus repair depot (if separately identifiable)	894	671
	REME workshop (civilian personnel)	894	671
	Servicing, motor vehicles	894	671

SIC 1980	Activity	SIC 1968	NACE
6720	**Repair of footwear and leather goods**		
	Handbag repairer	821/4	672
	Shoe repairing	895	672
6730/1	**Repair of electrical household goods**		
	Domestic electrical appliance repairer	821/3	673
	Radio and television repairer	821/3	673
6730/2	**Repair of watches, clocks and jewellery**		
	Jewellery repairer	821/4	674
	Watch and clock repairer	821/4	674
6730/3	**Goods not elsewhere specified, general repairing**		
	Cycle repairer	821/4	671
	Furniture repairer	821/3	675
	Toy repairer	821/4	675
	Umbrella repairer	821/2	675
	Upholstery repairer	821/3	675
7100	**Railways**		
	British Railways Board	701	710
	Motive power depot (British Rail or Northern Ireland Railways)	701	710
	Northern Ireland Railways	701	710
	Railway (other than passenger transport executive)	701	710
	Railway running shed	701	710
	Railway, independent	701	710
7210/1	**Urban railways**		
	Greater Glasgow Passenger Transport Executive (railways)	701	721.1
	London Transport Executive (railways)	701	721.1
	Passenger Transport Executive (railways)	701	721.1
	Railway (Passenger Transport Executive)	701	721.1
7210/2	**Bus, motor coach and tramway services**		
	Airline coach service	702/1	721.2
	Bus service	702/1	721.2
	Express coach service	702/1	721.2
	Factory bus service	702/1	721.2
	London Transport Executive (road services and headquarters)	702/1	721.2
	Motor coach service	702/1	721.2
	Motor coach, private hire	702/2	722
	Municipal bus service	702/1	721.2
	National Bus Company (scheduled service subsidiary)	702/1	721.2
	Omnibus service	702/1	721.2
	Passenger Transport Executive (road services and headquarters)	702/1	721.2
	Public service vehicle operator	702/1	721.2
	School bus service	702/1	721.2
	Tramway service	702/1	721.2
	Ulsterbus	702/1	721.2
7220	**Other road passenger transport**		
	Cab hire	702/2	722
	Chauffeur	702/2	722
	Private hire car with driver	702/2	722
	Taxi-cab service	702/2	722
7230	**Road haulage**		
	Car delivery service (by independent contractors)	703	723
	Car delivery service (by motor manufacturers)	704	723
	Carrier (for general hire or reward)	703	723.2
	Cartage contractor	703	723.2
	Commercial vehicle hire with driver	703	723.2
	Furniture removal	703	723.1
	Haulage contractor (road)	703	723.2
	Motor vehicle collection	709/1	723.2
	Parcels delivery service (not Post Office)	703	723.2
	Removal contractor	703	723.1
	Road haulage contracting for general hire or reward	703	723.2
	Security transport of valuables and money	703	723.2
	Transport department (if a separate 'establishment' ancillary to the main activity of a business)	704	723.2
7260/1	**Pipeline transport**		
	Pipeline operator	709	724
7260/2	**Other transport by land**		
	Funicular railway	709	725
	Lift operating company	702/1	725
	Lift operator	709/3	725
	Rack railway	709	725
7260/3	**Inland water transport**		
	Barge lessee or owner	706	730
	Canal carrier	706	730
	Ferry (river or estuary)	706	730
	Ferry boat proprietor (inland waterway service)	706	730
	Inland water transport	706	730
	Keel owner	706	730
	Lake steamer service	706	730
	River ferry	706	730
	Tug lessee or owner (inland waterways service)	706	730
	Tugboat (for inland waterway) service	706	730
7400/1	**Deep sea routes**		
	Shipping service (deep sea route)	705/2	741
7400/2	**Short sea routes**		
	Ferry (sea) (between UK and international ports)	705	742
	Hovercraft operator (between UK and international ports)	705	742
	Sea ferry (between UK and international ports)	705	742
	Shipping service (short sea route between UK and international ports)	705/1	742
	Tug-boat (for sea barge or servicing off shore well)	705	742
7400/3	**Domestic and coastal routes**		
	Coasting service (sea transport)	705	742
	Ferry (domestic or coastal route)	705	742
	Hovercraft operator (domestic or coastal route)	705	742
	Sea ferry (domestic or coastal route)	705	742
	Shipping service (domestic or coastal route)	705	742
	Tug-boat (for sea barge on domestic coastal route)	705	742
	Tug-boat (for servicing off-shore installation)	705	742
7400/4	**Shore bases**		
	Shore base (sea transport)	705	742

SIC 1980	Activity	SIC 1968	NACE
7500	Air transport		
	Air charter service	707	750
	Air terminal operated by airline	707	750
	Air transport	707	750
	Air-taxi service	707	750
	Airline	707	750
7610/1	Supporting services to land transport		
	Bus station (not managed directly by public service vehicle operator)	709/1	761
	Car park	709/1	761
	Commercial vehicle park	709/1	761
	Garage (parking)	709/1	761
	Lessee of tolls	709/1	761
	Motoring organisations (road patrols)	709/1	761
	Motorists' organisation (road patrol)	709/1	761
	Motorway maintenance unit	709	761
	Toll bridge, road or tunnel	709/1	761
7610/2	Supporting services to inland water transport		
	British Waterways Board	706	762
	Canal	706	762
	Floating bridge company	706	762
	Navigation	706	762
	Tyne Improvement Commissioners	706	762
7630	Supporting services to sea transport		
	British Transport Docks Board	706	763
	Cargo superintendent	706	763
	Dock authority	706	763
	Harbour authority	706	763
	Landing stage	706	762
	Lighter lessee or owner	706	763
	Lighthouse authority	706	763
	Lightship	706	763
	Marine cargo lighterage	706	763
	Marine cargo superintendent	706	763
	Marine salvage	706	763
	National Dock Labour Board	706	763
	National Ports Council	706	763
	Northern Lighthouses, Commissioners of	706	763
	Pier Operator (not amusement)	706	763
	Pier owner or authority (not amusement)	706	763
	Pilotage	705/3	763
	Port authority	706	763
	Port of London Authority	706	763
	Salvage, marine, company	706	763
	Stevedoring	706	763
	Trinity House	706	763
	Tug owner or lessee for in-port service or salvage	706	763
	Wharfinger	706	763
	Wreck raising	706	763
7640	Supporting services to air transport		
	Aerodrome	707	764
	Air traffic control centre	707	764
	Airport	707	764
	British Airports Authority	707	764
	Civil Aviation Authority	707	764
	Communication centre (civil air)	707	764
7700/1	Travel agents		
	Courier	709/1	771
	Excursion agency	709/1	771
	Motorists' organisation (touring department)	709/1	771
	Passage agent	709/1	771
	Passenger agent (not transport authority)	709/1	771
	Ticket agency (travel)	709/1	771
	Tour operator	709/1	771
	Travel agent	709/1	771
7700/2	Freight brokers and other agents facilitating freight transport		
	Air freight agent or broker	709/1	772
	Customs agent	865	772
	Export packer	709/1	772
	Forwarding agents	709/1	772
	Freight broker	709/1	772
	Freight contractor	709/1	772
	Goods agent (not transport authority)	709/1	772
	Licensed messenger or porter	709/3	772
	Maritime agent	709/1	772
	Messenger (own account)	709/3	772
	Messenger service	709/3	772
	Outside porter	709/3	772
	Packer and shipper	709/1	772
	Packing service	709/1	772
	Packing, textile	709/1	772
	Porter (own account)	709/3	772
	Porterage service	709/3	772
	Railway agent (not transport authority)	709/1	772
	Railway wagon agent	709/1	772
	Shipping agent or broker	709/1	772
7700/3	Storage and warehousing		
	Bonded store, vault or warehouse	709/2	773
	Cold store	709/2	773
	Cotton warehouse	709/2	773
	Film bonded warehouse	709/2	773
	Furniture repository	709/2	773
	Grain warehouse	709/2	773
	Granary	709/2	773
	Repository	709/2	773
	Safe deposit company	709/2	773
	Storage	709/2	773
	Tea warehouse	709/2	773
	Warehouse	709/2	773
	Wool warehouse	709/2	773
7901	Postal services		
	Post Office Corporation (postal and agency services)	708	790
	Post Office Purchasing and Supplies Department	708	790
	Postal Headquarters	708	790
	Postal sorting office	708	790
	Regional Headquarters, Post Office	708	790
7902	Telecommunications		
	British Telecom	708	790
	British Telecom Telecommunications Satellite Relay Station	708	790
	Cable service	708	790
	Hull Telephone Service	708	790
	Radio Station, British Telecom	708	790
	Telecommunications Headquarters, British Telecom	708	790
	Telegram service	708	790
	Telegraph Manager's Office	708	790
	Telephone exchange	708	790
	Telephone Manager's Office	708	790
	Telephone service	708	790
	Telex service	708	790

SIC 1980	Activity	SIC 1968	NACE
8140/1	Central banking authorities		
	Bank of England	861	811
8140/2	Banks and discount houses		
	Accepting house (recognised by the Bank of England under The Banking Act 1979)	861	831
	Access Card	861	812
	Bank (recognised by the Bank of England under The Banking Act 1979)	861	812
	Barclaycard Department	861	812
	Discount broker (licensed under The Banking Act 1979)	861	not classified
	Discount house (licensed under The Banking Act 1979)	861	not classified
	Finance House (licensed under The Banking Act 1979)	861	812
	Foreign exchange dealer (authorised by Bank of England)	862	831
	Hire purchase company (licensed under The Banking Act 1979)	862	812
	National Girobank	861	812
8140/3	Savings banks		
	Central Trustee Savings Bank	861	812
	Department for National Savings (Savings bank and Savings Certificate Offices)	861	812
	Municipal Savings Bank	861	812
	National Savings Bank	861	812
	Savings bank	861	812
	Savings Certificate Office	861	812
	Trustee Savings Bank	861	812
8150/1	Institutions specialising in the granting of credit		
	Agricultural Mortgage Corporation	862	813.1
	Bank (not recognised by the Bank of England under The Banking Act 1979)	861	813.1
	Building society	862	813.1
	Check issuing company	862	812
	Check trader	862	813.1
	Commonwealth Development Finance Co. Ltd.	862	813.1
	Consumer credit granting company (not licensed under The Banking Act 1979)	862	813.1
	Credit card issuer (not requiring payment in full at the end of each credit period)	862	813.1
	Credit unions	not classified	not classified
	Export finance company (not licensed under The Banking Act 1979)	862	813.1
	Factoring company (buying book debts)	862	831.1
	Finance Corporation for Industry	862	813.1
	Finance House (not licensed under The Banking Act 1979)	862	813.1
	Hire purchase company (not licensed under The Banking Act 1979)	862	813.1
	Housing Corporation	862	813.1
	Industrial and Commercial Finance Corporation	862	813.1
	Industrial banker (not licensed under The Banking Act 1979)	862	813.1
	Loan and discount company (not licensed under The Banking Act 1979)	862	813.1
	Loan company	862	813.1
	Money lender	862	813.1
	National Film Finance Corporation	862	813.1
	National Research Development Corporation	862	813
	Northern Ireland Finance Corporation	862	813.1
	Pawnbroker	821/4	813.1
	Scottish Agricultural Securities Corporation Ltd.	862	813.1
	Ship Mortgage Finance Co. Ltd.	862	813.1
8150/2	Institutions specialising in investment in securities		
	Bank holding company	862	813.2
	Department for National Savings (Bonds and Stocks Office)	861	813.2
	Development capital company	862	813.2
	Financial holding company	862	813.2
	Investment company	862	813.2
	Investment trust	862	813.2
	National Enterprise Board	862	813.2
	Nominee company	862	813.2
	Public Trustee Office	862	813.2
	Trustee	862	813.2
	Unit trust	862	813.2
8200/1	Composite insurance institutions		
	Friendly society (not collecting society)	860	821
	Insurance company (composite)	860	821
	Salvation Army Insurance Department	860	821
	Underwriter (insurance)	860	821
8200/2	Institutions specialising in ordinary long-term (including life) insurance		
	Autonomous pension fund	860	822
	Collecting society	860	822
	Industrial assurance company	860	822
	Insurance company (long-term)	860	822
	Life assurance	860	822
	Pension fund (autonomous)	860	822
	Provident fund	860	822
	Superannuation fund (autonomous)	860	822
	Underwriter (life)	860	822
8200/3	Institutions specialising in insurance other than long-term		
	Accident insurance	860	823
	Benevolent fund	860	823
	Boiler insurance	860	823
	Export Credit Guarantee Department	860	823
	Fire insurance	860	823
	Friendly society	860	823
	General insurance company	860	823
	Hospital contribution scheme	860	823
	Hospital Saving Association	860	823
	House insurance	860	823
	Industrial insurance	860	823
	Livestock insurance	860	823
	Lloyd's underwriter	860	823
	Marine insurance	860	823
	Member of Lloyd's	860	823
	Motor car insurance	860	823
	Plate glass insurance	860	823
	Re-insurance company	860	823
	Underwriter (fire, accident, health, marine etc.)	860	823
	Underwriter (Lloyd's)	860	823

SIC 1980	Activity	SIC 1968	NACE
8310	Activities auxiliary to banking and finance		
	Bankers' clearing house	861	812
	Bill broker (other than discount house)	862	831
	Bullion broker	862	831
	Bullion dealer	862	831
	Bureau de Change	862	831
	Clearing house (banking)	861	812
	Company promoter	862	831
	Company registration agent	862	831
	Council of The Stock Exchange	862	831
	Credit card issuer (requiring full payment at end of credit period)	862	831
	Dealer in securities	862	831
	Deposit broker	862	831
	Discount broker	861	831
	Exchange broker	862	831
	Financial agency	862	831
	Investment broker	862	831
	Issuing house	862	831
	Jobber	862	831
	Money changer	862	831
	Mortgage agent	862	831
	Mortgage broker	862	831
	Outside broker	862	831
	Paying agent	862	831
	Share dealer	862	831
	Stock broker	862	831
	Stock exchange	862	831
	Stock jobber	862	831
	Underwriter (stock and share issues)	862	831
8320	Activities auxiliary to insurance		
	Actuary (own account)	879/2	832
	Average adjuster	860	832
	Corporation of Lloyds	860	832
	Insurance agent (not employed by insurance company)	860	832
	Insurance broker (not employed by insurance company)	860	832
	Loss adjuster	860	832
	Property unit trust (acting for insurance companies)	862	813.2
	Salvage corps (in London, Liverpool and Glasgow)	860	832
8340	House and estate agents		
	Estate agent	863	834
	Flat agency	863	834
	House agent	863	834
	House auctioneer	863	834
	Land agent	863	834
	Land auctioneer	863	834
	Land valuer or surveyor	863	834
	Property management (as agents for owners)	863	834
	Rent collecting	863	834
	Surveyor and valuer (real estate)	863	834
	Valuer (real estate)	863	834
8350	Legal services		
	Advocate	873	835
	Attorney	873	835
	Barrister (own account)	873	835
	Law agent	873	835
	Law writing	873	835
	Lawyer (own account)	873	835
	Parliamentary agent	873	835
	Patent agent	879/2	835
	Process server (own account)	873	835
	Public notary	873	835
	Q.C.	873	835
	Queen's Counsel	873	835
	Scrivenery	873	835
	Sheriff's officer	873	835
	Solicitor (own account)	873	835
	Writer to the Signet	873	835
8360	Accountants, auditors, tax experts		
	Accountancy services	871	836
	Accountant (own account)	871	836
	Audit clerk (own account)	871	836
	Auditor (own account)	871	836
	Book-keeping service	871	836
	Cost accountant (own account)	871	836
	Financial advisor (own account)	871	836
	Investment advisor (not arranging transactions directly)	865	836
	Tax consultant	865	836
8370/1	Architects, surveyors and consulting engineers		
	Architect (private practice)	879/1	837
	Architectural draughtsman (private practice)	879/1	837
	Consultant civil or structural engineer	879/1	837
	Engineer (civil or structural), consultant	879/1	837/1
	Land surveyor (not valuer)	879/1	837
	Quantity surveyor (private practice)	879/1	837
	Surveyor (other than valuer)	879/1	837
8370/2	Technical services		
	Aerial survey	879/1	837
	Analytical chemist (private practice)	879/2	837
	Assay Office	879/2	837
	Bacteriologist (non-medical)	879/2	837
	Chemist (own account)	879/2	837
	Design office	879	837
	Draughtsman (private practice)	879/1	837
	Engineer (other than civil or structural) consultant	879/1	837
	Engineers' draughtsman (private practice)	879/1	837
	Fuel technologist (private practice)	879/2	837
	Geologist (consultant)	879/2	837
	Industrial design service	879/5	837
	Inventor (so described)	879/2	837
	Laboratory	879	837
	Lloyd's Register of Shipping	860	832
	Marine cargo surveyor	879/1	837
	Marine surveyor	879/1	837
	Metallurgist (private practice)	879/2	837
	Mineral surveyor	879/1	837
	Naval architect (private practice)	879/1	837
	Oil logging company	879/2	837
	Palaeontologist (consultant)	879/2	837
	Petroleum geologist (private practice)	879/2	837
	Physicist (own account)	879/2	837
	Research chemist (private practice)	879/2	837
	Scientist, consultant	879/2	837
	Ship surveyor (private practice)	879/1	837
	Testing or analysing laboratory	879/2	837
8380	Advertising		
	Advertising agency	864	838
	Advertising contractor (outdoor)	864	838
	Advertising film production	864	838
	Bill distributor (advertising)	864	838
	Bill posting agency	864	838
	Commercial artist (private practice)	879/5	838
	Copywriter, freelance	865	838

SIC 1980	Activity	SIC 1968	NACE
	Photographer, commercial	899/2	838
	Window dressing, freelance	865	838
8394	Computer services		
	Computer bureau	865	839.2
	Computer consultancy	865	839.2
	Software house	865	839.2
	Time hire (computer)	865	839.2
8395/1	Management consultants		
	Business consultant	865	839.1
	Management consultant (own account)	865	839.1
8395/2	Market research and public relations consultants		
	Exhibition contracting and organising	865	839.3
	Market research agency	864	839.1
	Market research consultant	864	839.1
	Market research organisation	864	839.1
	Public relations consultant (not advertising agency)	865	839.1
	Publicity consultant	865	839.1
	Trades exhibition or fair	864	839.1
8395/3	Document copying, duplicating and tabulating services		
	Circular addressing	865	839.3
	Document copying service	865	839.2
	Duplicating service	865	839.2
	Envelope addressing service	865	839.3
	Tabulating service	865	839.2
8395/4	Miscellaneous business services		
	Agricultural valuer	865	839.3
	Appraiser and valuer (not insurance or real estate)	865	839.3
	Arbitrator	865	839.3
	Auctioneer (not house auctioneer)	865	839.3
	Business agency	865	839.3
	Business transfer agent	865	839.3
	Chartered secretaries, firm acting as	865	839.3
	Code compiling	899/7	839.3
	Company secretaries (specialist undertakings acting as)	865	839.3
	Debt collector	865	839.3
	Domestic agency	865	839.3
	Drapers' valuer	865	839
	Economist (own account)	879/2	836
	Employment agency (not government)	865	839.3
	Enquiry agency	899/7	839.3
	Financial and credit reporting	865	839.3
	Information bureau	899/7	839.3
	Inquiry agency	899/7	839.3
	Journalist, free-lance	879/5	839.3
	Literary agency	865	839.3
	Luncheon voucher company	865	839.3
	News agency	865	839.3
	Partnership agent	865	839.3
	Patent broker	865	839.3
	Picture agency	865	839.3
	Press cutting agency	865	839.3
	Private detective	899/7	839.3
	Public record searching	865	839.3
	Publicans' broker	865	839.3
	Registry office for servants	865	839.3
	Secretary (own account)	865	839.3
	Security service (not government)	865	839.3
	Shorthand writing	865	839.3
	Statistician (own account)	865	839.3
	Stock market reporting service	865	839.3

SIC 1980	Activity	SIC 1968	NACE
	Stocktaking	865	839.3
	Sworn broker	865	839.3
	Sworn timber measurer	865	839.3
	Sworn weigher	865	839.3
	Telegraphic code expert	865	839.3
	Telephone answering service	865	839.3
	Telephone sterilizing	899/7	839.3
	Timber measurer	865	839.3
	Trading stamp company	865	839.3
	Translation service	865	839.3
	Typing service	865	839.3
	Valuer (any trade except real estate)	865	839.3
8396/1	Head offices of enterprises operating abroad		
	Head office of company operating abroad	866/1	not classified
8396/2	Central offices of enterprises with mixed activities		
	Head office of holding company	866/2	not classified
8410	Hiring out agricultural and horticultural equipment		
	Agricultural machinery hire (without staff)	832/6	841
	Horticultural machinery hire (without staff)	832/6	841
	Tractor, agricultural, hire (without driver)	832/6	841
8420	Hiring out construction machinery and equipment		
	Civil engineering machinery hire (without staff)	500	842
	Construction equipment hire (without staff)	500	842
	Hazard warning lamp hire	500	842
	Ladder hire	500	842
	Plant hire for construction (without staff)	500	842
	Portable road sign hire (for construction)	500	842
	Scaffolding hire (without staff)	500	842
	Tools, for construction, hire (without staff)	500	842
8430	Hiring out office machinery and furniture		
	Automatic data processing equipment hire	832/10	843
	Cash register hire	832/10	843
	Computer hire	832/10	843
	Office equipment hire	832/10	843
	Office furniture hire	832/10	847
	Ticket machine hire	832/10	843
	Typewriters, leasing of	832/10	843
8460/1	Television and radio hire		
	Radio (domestic) hire	821/3	846.2
	Television (domestic) hire	821/3	846.2
8460/2	Hiring other consumer goods		
	Camera hire	832/10	847
	Clothes hire	821/2	846.1
	Crockery hire	821/3	846.1
	Garden tool hire	821/3	846.1

SIC 1980	Activity	SIC 1968	NACE
	Hiring cutler (lets out cutlery for dinners, etc.)	899/7	846.2
	Household goods hire	821/3	846.1
	Musical instrument hire	821/3	846.2
	Photographic equipment hire	832/10	847
	Piano hire	821/3	846.2
8480/1	Self-drive car hire		
	Car hire, self drive	702/2	844
	Contract car hire	702/2	844
	Self-drive car hire	702/2	844
8480/2	Light commercial vehicle hire		
	Light commercial vehicle hire (without driver)	703	845
	Van hire, self drive	703	845
8480/3	Hiring other commercial vehicles		
	Commercial vehicle (medium and heavy types) hire (without driver)	703	845
	Commercial vehicle contract hire (medium and heavy types) without driver	703	845
	Road trailer hire	703	845
8480/4	Hiring other transport equipment		
	Aircraft hire (without crew)	707	845
	Barrow hiring	709/3	845
	Bicycle hire	709/3	845
	Boat hire (without crew) (not linked with recreational service)	706	845
	Freight container hire	703	845
	Hand cart hire	709/3	845
	Motor cycle hire	702/2	845
	Perambulator hiring and letting	821/4	845
	Railway vehicle hire	832/10	845
	Ship hire (without crew)	706	845
	Wheelbarrow hiring	709/3	845
8490	Hiring out other movables		
	Amusement machine hire (not gaming machine)	812/4	847
	Burglar alarm hire	832/10	847
	Exhibition stand hire	865	847
	Fire alarm hire	832/10	847
	Fuel bunkers, leasing of	832/10	847
	Hiring goods (miscellaneous or unspecified)	not classified	847
	Industrial floor cleaning equipment, leasing of	832/10	847
	Industrial plant and equipment hire	832/10	847
	Juke boxes, leasing of	812/4	847
	Leasing of industrial machinery	832/10	847
	Packaging machinery, leasing of	832/10	847
	Telephone hire (other than by public telephone undertakings)	832/10	847
	Tool (for mechanics or engineers) hire	832/10	847
8500	Owning and dealing in real estate		
	Agricultural land letting	863	850
	Caravan site owner (not for holidays)	863	850
	Commission for the New Towns	863	850
	Estate company, owning and managing	863	850
	Factory letting	863	850
	Flat letting	863	850
	Freeholder of leasehold property	863	850
	Garage (lock-up) letting	863	850
	Garden city company	863	850
	Ground landlord	863	850
	House letting	863	850
	Housing association	863	850
	Industrial estate owner	863	850
	Land and building company	863	833
	Land investment company	863	850
	Landlord (of real estate)	863	850
	Local authority housing department	863	850
	Maisonettes letting	863	850
	Mansions letting	863	850
	New Town Corporation Housing Department	863	850
	Offices letting	863	850
	Property company	863	850
	Property developer	863	850
	Property investment company	863	833
	Real estate owner	863	850
	Residential chambers letting	863	850
	Scottish Special Housing Association (Housing Management Department)	863	850
	Service flat letting	863	850
	Shop letting	863	850
9111	National government service not elsewhere specified		
	Area Health Authority	874/2	911
	Arts Council	901/6	911
	British Council	899/4	968
	Buckingham Palace	901/6	911
	Coastguard	901/6	911
	College of Arms, HM	901/6	911
	Commision for Racial Equality	901/6	911
	Community dental service (administration)	874/2	911
	Community medical service (administration)	874/2	911
	Companies Registration Office	901/6	911
	Controller of Stamps, Office of	901/6	911
	Crafts Advisory Committee	901/6	911
	Deeds, Registry of (Northern Ireland)	901/6	911
	Deemster, Isle of Man, Office of	901/6	911
	Dental Estimates Board	874/4	911
	Department for National Savings	901/6	911
	Development Commission	901/6	911
	District community physician	874/2	911
	Employment Office	901/6	911
	Employment Rehabilitation Centre	901/6	911
	Employment Services Department of the Manpower Services Commission	901/6	911
	Equal Opportunities Commission	901/6	911
	Family Practitioner Committee	874/3	911
	General Register and Record Office of Shipping and Seamen	901/6	911
	Government departments (except HMSO and ECGD)	901/6	911
	Hampton Court Gardens and Park	901/6	911
	Hampton Court Palace	901/6	911
	Health and Safety Executive	901/6	911
	Health Board (Scotland)	874/3	911
	Holyrood Palace	901/6	911
	House of Commons	901/6	911
	House of Lords	901/6	911
	Houses of Parliament	901/6	911
	Hyde Park	901/6	911
	Industrial Training Board (not training centre)	865	911
	Job Centre (government)	901/6	911

SIC 1980	Activity	SIC 1968	NACE
	Kensington Gardens	901/6	911
	Kensington Palace	901/6	911
	Law Officer's Department	901/6	911
	Manpower Services Commission	901/6	911
	Member of Parliament	901/6	911
	National Economic Development Office	901/6	911
	National Health Prescription Pricing Authority	874/3	911
	National Health Service Administration	901/6	911
	National Health Welsh Pricing Committee	901/6	911
	Office of Manpower Economics	901/6	911
	Official Receiver in Bankruptcy, Office of	901/6	911
	Parliamentary Commissioner for Administration, Office of the	901/6	911
	Port health authority	906/3	911
	Probate Registry (principal or district)	901/6	911
	Property Services Agency	901/6	911
	Public Record Office	901/6	911
	Public Works Loan Board	901/6	911
	Regent's Park and Primrose Hill	901/6	911
	Regional health authority	874/2	911
	Register Of Friendly Societies	901/6	911
	Richmond Park	901/6	911
	Royal Commission	901/6	911
	Royal Households	901/6	911
	Royal Observatory (civilian staff)	901/5	911
	Royal Observatory, Edinburgh	901/6	911
	Royal Palaces	901/6	911
	Royal Park	901/6	911
	St. James's Palace	901/6	911
	St. James's Park	901/6	911
	Training Services Department (not Skillcentre) of the Manpower Services Commission	901/6	911
	University Grants Committee	901/6	911
	Windsor Castle	901/6	911
	Windsor Great Park	901/6	911
9112	Local government service not elsewhere specified		
	Borough council	906/3	911
	Burgh council	906/3	911
	Careers office (local education authority)	906/3	911
	City corporation	906/3	911
	City council	906/3	911
	City of London, Corporation of	906/3	911
	Common conservators	906/3	911
	Council of Isles of Scilly	906/3	911
	County council	906/3	911
	District council	906/3	911
	Education authority (administration only)	872/4	911
	Education committee	872/4	911
	Greater London Council	906/3	911
	Local authority	906/3	911
	Local education authority (administration only)	872/4	911
	London borough council	906/3	911
	Metropolitan county council	906/3	911
	Metropolitan district, borough or city council	906/3	911
	Parish council or meeting	906/3	911
	Registrar of Births, Deaths or Marriages	906/3	911
	Salt Compensation Board	906/3	911
	School medical officer	874/2	911
9120	Justice		
	Appeal Committee of the House of Lords	901/6	912
	Appeal, Court of	901/6	912
	Attendance centre	901/6	912
	Borstal	872/5	912
	Community home (for child offenders)	872/5	912
	Coroner's court	906/3	912
	County court	901/6	912
	Court of Protection	901/6	912
	Court of the Lord Lyon	901/6	912
	Crown court	901/6	912
	Detention centre	901/6	912
	Judge	901/6	912
	Judicial Committee of the Privy Council	901/6	912
	Justice of the Peace	901/6	912
	Justiciary, High Court of (Scotland)	901/6	912
	Juvenile court	901/6	912
	Magistrate's court	906/3	912
	Master	901/6	912
	Official Solicitor	901/6	912
	Pensions Appeal Tribunal	901/6	912
	Prison (not naval or military)	901/6	912
	Registrar	901/6	912
	Registrar's Office (Courts of Justice)	901/6	912
	Remand centre	901/6	912
	Sheriff court	901/6	912
	Stipendiary magistrate	901/6	912
	Supreme Court	901/6	912
	Training school (Northern Ireland)	872/5	912
	Tribunal	901/6	912
9130	Police		
	Civil defence	906/1	913
	Criminal Investigation Department	906/1	913
	Joint police authority	906/1	913
	Metropolitan Police Commissioner's Office	906/1	913
	Office of the Receiver for the Metropolitan Police District	906/1	911
	Police authority	906/1	913
	Police force	906/1	913
	Policeman	906/1	913
	Regional Crime Squad	906/1	913
	School crossing patrol	709/1	913
	Scotland Yard	906/1	913
	Standing joint committee (police)	906/1	913
	Traffic warden	906/1	913
9140	Fire services		
	Fire authority	906/2	914
	Fire brigade	906/2	914
9150	National defence		
	Ammunition depot (Ministry of Defence)	901/5	915
	Army	901/2	915
	Army establishment (civilian personnel)	901/5	915
	Army establishment (service personnel)	901/2	915
	Central Ordnance Depot	901/5	915
	College, military	901/5	915
	District Command of armed forces	901/5	915
	Hospital, military	901/5	915
	Pay and Record Office of armed forces	901/5	915
	Port, military	901/5	915
	Princess Mary's RAFNS	901/4	915
	Queen Alexandra's RANC	901/4	915
	Queen Alexandra's RNNS	901/4	915

SIC 1980	Activity	SIC 1968	NACE
	Royal Air Force	901/3	915
	Royal Air Force establishment (civilian personnel)	901/5	915
	Royal Air Force establishment (service personnel)	901/5	915
	Royal Air Force stores unit	901/5	915
	Royal Marines	901/1	915
	Royal Naval armament depot	901/5	915
	Royal Navy	901/1	915
	Royal Navy establishment (civilian personnel)	901/5	915
	Royal Navy establishment (service personnel)	901/1	915
	School, military	901/5	915
	Submarine base (Military of Defence)	901/5	915
	Vehicle depot (Ministry of Defence)	901/5	915
	WRAC.	901/2	915
	WRAF.	901/3	915
	WRNS.	901/1	915
9190	Social security		
	DHSS, local social security office	901/6	919
	Department of Employment unemployment benefit office	901/6	919
	Social security office, local	901/6	919
	Unemployment benefit office	901/6	919
9211	Refuse disposal, street cleaning, fumigation etc.		
	Cleansing department, local authority	906/3	921
	Disinfection service	899/7	921
	Dustman	906/3	921
	Fumigation service (not specially for agriculture)	899/7	921
	Local authority cleansing department	906/3	921
	Pest destruction service (not specially for agriculture)	899/7	921
	Rat catcher (not specially for agriculture)	899/7	921
	Refuse disposal plant or tip (local authority or municipally owned)	906/3	921
	Refuse disposal service (not specially for agriculture)	899/7	921
	Refuse disposal tip operator	906/3	921
	Street cleaning	906/3	921
	Toxic waste treatment service	899/7	921
	Vermin destroying (not agricultural)	899/7	921
	Wood worm preventive treatment service	899/7	921
	Woodrot preventive treatment service	899/7	921
9212	Sewage disposal		
	Land drainage	906/3	921
	Sewage farm (owned by public authority)	906/3	921
	Sewage works	906/3	921
	Sewerage system maintenance and operation	906/3	921
9230	Cleaning services		
	Boiler cleaning and scaling	899/7	923
	Chimney sweeping	899/7	923
	Cleaning service, factory office or shop	899/7	923
	Contract cleaning service	899/7	923
	Factory cleaning contractor	899/7	923
	Office cleaning contractor	865	923
	Ship fumigating and scrubbing	899/7	923
	Telephone cleaning and sterilising service	899/7	923
	Window cleaning	899/7	923

SIC 1980	Activity	SIC 1968	NACE
9310	Higher education		
	College of education	872/3	931
	Correspondence college (if specialising in higher education courses)	872/3	931
	Council for National Academic Awards	872/3	931
	Cranfield Institute of Technology	872/3	931
	Dental college or school	872/3	931
	London Graduate School of Business Studies	872/3	931
	Manchester School of Business Studies	872/3	931
	Medical school	872/3	931
	Music, college of	872/3	931
	Open University	872/3	931
	Polytechnic (the 30 designated in England and Wales)	872/3	931
	Post graduate college	872/3	931
	Royal College of Art	872/3	931
	Scottish Central Institution	872/3	931
	Teacher training college	872/3	931
	Theological college (if specialising in higher education course)	872/3	931
	Ulster College	872/3	931
	Universities' Central Council on Admissions	872/3	931
	University	872/3	931
	University college	872/3	931
	University medical or dental school	872/3	931
9320	School education (nursery, primary and secondary)		
	Church school	872	932
	Comprehensive school	872/1	932
	Convent school	872	932
	Direct grant school	872/2	932
	First school	872/1	932
	Girls Public Day School Trust	872/4	932
	Grammar school	872	932
	Hospital school	872/1	932
	Independent school (non-local authority)	872/2	932
	Infant school	872/1	932
	Joint Matriculation Board and Examining Body	872/4	932
	Junior school	872/1	932
	Kindergarten	872/2	934
	Middle school	872/1	932
	Nursery school	872	934
	Orphanage school	872/2	932
	Preparatory school	872/2	934
	Primary school	872/1	932
	Private school	872/2	932
	Public school	872/2	932
	Royal Masonic Institution for Boys	872/2	932
	Royal Masonic Institution for Girls	872/2	932
	School examination board (local authority)	872/4	932
	School examination board (non-local authority)	872/4	932
	School for the mentally handicapped (local authority)	872	932
	School for the mentally handicapped (non-local authority)	872	932
	School for the physically handicapped (local authority)	872	932
	School for the physically handicapped (non-local authority)	872	932
	Secondary modern school (local authority)	872/1	932
	Secondary school (local authority)	872/1	932
	Sixth form college	872/1	932
	Special school	872	932

SIC 1980	Activity	SIC 1968	NACE
9330	Education not elsewhere specified, and vocational training		
	Adult education centre	872/3	933
	Adult education residential college	872/3	933
	Agricultural college	872/3	933
	Apprentice school	872/5	933
	Arts and crafts, School of	872/3	933
	Ballet school	872/3	933
	Business Education Council	872/4	933
	City and Guilds of London Institute	872/4	933
	Civil Service College	872/5	933
	College of art	872/3	933
	College of music	872/3	933
	Commercial school	872/3	933
	Continuation school	872/3	933
	Correspondence college (not leading to degree level qualifications)	872/5	935
	Council for Accreditation of Correspondence Colleges	872/5	935
	Day continuation school	872/3	933
	Evening Institute	872/3	933
	Farm institute	872/3	933
	Flying school (for airline pilots)	709/1	933
	Further education college	872/3	933
	Further education establishment	872/3	933
	Joint Committee for National Diplomas and Certificates	872/4	933
	Management training establishment	872/5	933
	Music teacher (own account)	872/5	935
	National Institute for Adult Education	872/4	933
	Nautical school	872/3	933
	Royal Academy of Dramatic Art	872/3	933
	School of languages	872/3	933
	School of speech and drama	872/3	933
	Secretarial college	872/5	933
	Seminary	872/3	933
	Skillcentre	872/5	933
	Teacher (own account, not recreational activities)	872/5	935
	Teacher (undefined)	872/1	933
	Technical college	872/3	933
	Training centre of Industrial Training Board	872/5	933
	University extra-mural department (if separately identifiable)	872/3	931
	Workers' Educational Association	872/4	933
	Works school (if separately identifiable)	872/3	933
9360	Driving and flying schools		
	Flying school (not for airline pilots)	709/1	936
	School of motoring	709/1	936
9400	Research and development		
	Agricultural Research Council	876	940
	Atomic Energy Research Establishment	876	940
	Building research establishment	876	940
	Cancer Research Fund	874/1	940
	Educational research	872/4	940
	Government research establishment	876	940
	Hydraulic research station	876	940
	Medical Research Council	874/1	940
	Medical research establishment (not attached to hospital)	874	940
	National Coal Board: coal research establishments	876	940
	National Foundation for Educational Research	872/4	940
	National Institute for Economic and Social Research	876	940
	National Physical Laboratory	876	940
	Natural Environment Research Council	876	940
	Research and development consultants	876	940
	Research association	876	940
	Research charity	876	940
	Research institution	876	940
	Research laboratory	876	940
	Science Research Council	876	940
	Social Science Research Council	876	940
9510	Hospitals, nursing homes, etc.		
	Accident and emergency service (hospital)	874/1	951
	Anaesthetist	874/1	951
	Broadmoor Hospital	874/1	951
	Children's hospital	874/1	951
	Chronic sick hospital	874/1	951
	Convalescent home (providing medical care)	874/1	951
	Dental hospital	874/1	954
	Ear, nose and throat hospital	874/1	951
	Ear, nose and throat specialist (hospital)	874/1	951
	Eye hospital	874/1	951
	Eye specialist (hospital)	874/1	951
	General hospital	874/1	951
	General hospital psychiatric unit	874/1	951
	General medical consultant (hospital)	874/1	951
	Genito-urinary specialist (hospital)	874/1	951
	Geriatric hospital	874/1	951
	Geriatrician (hospital)	874/1	951
	Gynaecologist (hospital)	874/1	951
	Haematologist (hospital)	874/1	951
	Hospital	874/1	951
	Infectious disease hospital	874/1	951
	Infectious disease specialist (hospital)	874/1	951
	Infirmary	874/1	951
	Isolation hospital	874/1	951
	London Clinic	874/1	951
	Maternity hospital	874/1	951
	Medical consultant (hospital)	874/1	951
	Mental handicap hospital	874/1	951
	Mental health specialist (hospital)	874/1	951
	Mental hospital	874/1	951
	Morbid anatomy specialist (hospital)	874/1	951
	Moss Side Hospital	874/1	951
	Nuffield Hospital Trust	874/1	951
	Nursing home	874/1	951
	Opthalmic hospital	874/1	951
	Orthopaedic hospital	874/1	951
	Park Lane Hospital	874/1	951
	Pre-convalescent hospital	874/1	951
	Private hospital	874/1	951
	Radiologist (hospital service)	874/1	951
	Radiotherapist (hospital service)	874/1	951
	Rampton Hospital	874/1	951
	Rehabilitation hospital	874/1	951
	Sanatorium	874/1	951
	Smallpox hospital	874/1	951
	Social medicine specialist (hospital)	874/1	951
	Special hospital	874/1	951
	Surgeon (hospital)	874/1	951
	Tuberculosis sanatorium or hospital	874/1	951
	Urologist (hospital)	874/1	951
9520	Other medical care institutions		
	Ambulance service	874/2	952
	Artificial kidney unit	874/1	952
	Artificial limb and appliance centre	874/1	952
	Blood Transfusion Service	874/1	952
	Chiropodist (National Health Service)	874/5	952

SIC 1980	Activity	SIC 1968	NACE
	Community medical service (clinics)	874/2	952
	Community psychiatric nurse (National Health Service)	874/2	952
	District nurse	874/2	952
	Family Planning Association (clinics)	874/2	952
	Foot clinic	874/2	952
	Health centre	874/2	952
	Health visitor	874/2	952
	Home nurse (National Health Service)	874/2	952
	Mass radiography service	874/1	952
	Maternity and child welfare services	874/2	952
	Maternity clinic	874/2	952
	Midwife (National Health Service)	874/2	952
	Opthalmic clinic	874/2	952
	Pathological laboratory	874/1	952
	Physiotherapy clinic	874/2	952
	Psychiatric clinic	874/1	952
	Psychiatric day hospital	874/1	952
	Public health laboratory	874/1	952
	School health service	874/2	952
	School medical clinic	874/2	952
	Scottish Ambulance Service	874/2	952
	St. Andrew's Ambulance Brigade	874/5	952
	St. John's Ambulance Brigade	874/5	952
9530	Medical practices		
	Doctor (unspecified)	874/3	953
	Ear, nose and throat specialist (private practice)	874/1	953
	Eye specialist (private practice)	874/1	953
	General medical consultant (private practice)	874/1	953
	General medical practitioner	874/3	953
	Genito-urinary specialist (private practice)	874/1	953
	Gynaecologist (private practice)	874/1	953
	Homeopath (registered medical practitioner)	874/3	953
	Infectious disease specialist (private practice)	874/1	953
	Medical consultant (private practice)	874/1	953
	Mental health specialist (private practice)	874/1	953
	Morbid anatomy specialist (private practice)	874/1	953
	Osteopath (registered medical practitioner)	874/3	953
	Physician and surgeon	874/3	953
	Receptionist, doctor's surgery	874/3	953
	Social medicine specialist (private practice)	874/1	953
	Specialist (not employed full-time by a hospital)	874/1	953
	Surgeon (private practice)	874/1	953
	Surgery, doctor's	874/3	953
	Urologist (private practice)	874/1	953
9540	Dental practices		
	Community dental service (clinics)	874/2	954
	Dental clinic	874/2	954
	Dental practitioner	874/4	954
	Dental surgeon (not employed full-time by a hospital)	874/4	954
	Dentist	874/4	954
	Receptionist, dentist's	874/4	954
9550	Agency and private midwives, nurses, etc.		
	Chiropodist (private)	874/5	955
	Foot clinic (private)	874/5	955
	Homeopath (not registered medical practitioner)	874/5	955
	Homeopath (private)	874/5	955
	Midwife (private)	874/5	955
	Neuropath	874/5	955
	Nurse (private)	874/5	955
	Nursing agency employing nurses	874/5	955
	Nursing co-operative	874/5	955
	Occupational therapist (private)	874/5	955
	Osteopath (not registered medical practitioner)	874/5	955
	Physiotherapist (private)	874/5	955
	Radiographer (private)	874/5	955
9560/1	Practices and hospitals run by veterinary surgeons		
	Animal hospital (run by veterinary surgeon)	879/4	956
	Veterinary surgeon	879/4	956
	Veterinary surgery	879/4	956
9560/2	Other animal hospitals under the supervision of registered veterinarians		
	Animal hospital (RSPCA or PDSA)	879/4	956
	Animal hospital (supervised or run by registered veterinarian)	879/4	956
	Registered veterinarian	879/4	956
	Veterinarian, registered	879/4	956
9611/1	Social work		
	Benevolent fund	899/3	961
	Blue Cross	899/3	961
	Charitable service	899/3	961
	Creche	874/2	961
	Day centres for the elderly, the physically or mentally handicapped or the mentally ill	874/2	961
	Day nursery	874/2	961
	Family Planning Association (not clinics)	899/3	961
	Family Welfare Association	899/3	961
	Home help service	899/3	961
	Jewish Board of Guardians	899/3	961
	National Society for the Prevention of Cruelty to Children	899/3	961
	Nursery, day	874/2	961
	Occupation and training centres for the mentally disordered	874/2	961
	Oxfam	899/3	961
	People's Dispensary for Sick Animals (not animal-care units)	899/3	961
	Police Court Mission	899/3	961
	Probation and After-Care Service	899/3	961
	Red Cross Society	874/5	961
	Royal Masonic Benevolent Institution	899/3	961
	Royal National Lifeboat Institution	899/3	968
	Royal Society for the Prevention of Cruelty to Animals (not animal hospitals or homes)	899/3	961
	Shelter (the charity)	899/3	961
	Social services department (not units providing accommodation)	899/3	961
	Social welfare society	899/3	961
	Social worker	899/3	961
	St. Bride's Institute	899/3	961
	Temperance association	899/3	961
	Welfare service	899/3	961
	Women's Royal Voluntary Service	899/3	961
9611/2	Social and residential homes		
	Children's home	899/3	962
	Crippleage	899/3	962
	DHSS reception centre	899/3	962
	Discharged prisoners' hostel	899/3	962

SIC 1980	Activity	SIC 1968	NACE
	Home for epileptics	899/3	962
	Home for handicapped children	899/3	962
	Home for the blind	899/3	962
	Home for the disabled	899/3	962
	Home for the elderly	899/3	962
	Home for the mentally handicapped	899/3	962
	Home for the mentally ill	899/3	962
	Homeless, temporary accommodation for	899/3	962
	Hostel (nurses', students', ex-prisoners', Salvation Army, YMCA, YWCA)	884	962
	Hostel for the homeless	899/3	962
	Lodging house (local authority)	899/3	962
	Nurses' home	884	962
	Old persons' home (local authority or charity)	899/3	962
	Orphanage	899/3	962
	Re-establishment centre (DHSS)	899/3	962
	Reception centre (DHSS)	899/3	962
	Refugee camp	899/3	962
	Salvation Army Hostel	884	962
	Salvation Army Shelter	899/3	962
	Social settlement (Toynbee Hall, etc.)	899/3	962
	Students' hostel or hall of residence	884	962
	YMCA hostel	884	962
	YWCA hostel	884	962
9631/1	**Professional and scientific organisations**		
	Association of Corporate and Certified Accountants	879/3	963
	British Association for the Advancement of Science	879/3	963
	British Computer Society	879/3	963
	British Dental Association	879/3	963
	British Medical Association	879/3	963
	Central Midwives Board	879/3	963
	Chartered Institute of Secretaries	879/3	963
	City Guild (Goldsmiths' Company, Stationers' Company, etc.)	879/3	963
	Faculty of Actuaries	879/3	963
	General Council of the Bar	879/3	963
	General Medical Council	879/3	963
	General Nursing Council	879/3	963
	Guild, City	879/3	963
	Inns of Court	879/3	963
	Institute of Actuaries	879/3	963
	Institute of British Water Colour Painters	879/3	963
	Institute of Chartered Accountants	879/3	963
	Institute of Chartered Accountants of Scotland	879/3	963
	Institute of Civil Engineers	879/3	963
	Institute of Cost and Management Accountants	879/3	963
	Institute of Hygiene	879/3	963
	Institute of Incorporated Photographers	879/3	963
	Institute of Mechanical Engineers	879/3	963
	Institute of Metals	879/3	963
	Law Society	879/3	963
	National Maritime Board	879/3	963
	Nursing Society	879/3	963
	Pharmaceutical Society	879/3	963
	Queen's Institute of District Nursing	879/3	963
	Royal Academy of Arts	879/3	963
	Royal Aeronautical Society	879/3	963
	Royal Agricultural Society of England	899/6	963
	Royal College of Midwives	879/3	963
	Royal College of Nursing	879/3	963
	Royal College of Physicians	879/3	963
	Royal College of Surgeons	879/3	963
	Royal Colonial Institute	879/3	963
	Royal Geographical Society	879/3	963
	Royal Institute of Chartered Surveyors	879/3	963
	Royal Institute of Public Health	879/3	963
	Royal Society	879/3	963
	Royal Society for the Promotion of Health	879/3	963
	Royal Society of Medicine	879/3	963
	Royal Statistical Society	879/3	963
	Royal United Services Institution	879/3	963
	Scientific organisation	879/3	963
	Society of Apothecaries	879/3	963
	Society of Arts	879/3	963
	Teachers' Registration Council	879/3	963
9631/2	**Business organisations**		
	Advisory, Conciliation and Arbitration Service	901/6	911
	Chamber of agriculture	899/6	963
	Chamber of commerce	899/6	963
	Confederation of British Industry	899/6	964
	Copyright Protection Society	899/6	963
	Educational association	872/4	963
	Employers' association or federation	899/6	964
	Joint organisation of employers and trade unions	899/6	964
	Performing Right Society	899/6	963
	Property owners' association	899/6	963
	Trade association	899/6	963
	Trade protection society	899/6	963
9631/3	**Trade unions**		
	Employers' representatives	899/6	965
	Trade union	899/6	965
	Trades Union Congress	899/6	965
	Union, trade	899/6	965
	Whitley Council (Staff Side)	899/6	965
9660	**Religious organisations and similar associations**		
	Army Scripture Readers Association	875	966
	Baptist Church	875	966
	Bible Society	875	966
	Board of Schecheta	875	966
	British Humanist Association	899/3	966
	British Jews Society	875	966
	Calvinistic Methodist Church	875	966
	Catholic Apostolic Church	875	966
	Church	875	966
	Church Army	875	966
	Church Commission	875	966
	Church in Wales	875	966
	Church Missionary Society	875	966
	Church of Christ Scientist	875	966
	Church of England	875	966
	Church of Ireland	875	966
	Church of Scotland	875	966
	City Mission	875	966
	Convent (not school or orphanage)	875	966
	Crusaders' Union	875	966
	Episcopal Church in Scotland	875	966
	Established Church	875	966
	Evangelist society	875	966
	Freemasons	899/3	966
	Inter-varsity Fellowship of Evangelical Unions	875	966
	Jewish Synagogue	875	966
	Lord's Day Observance Society	875	966
	Methodist Church	875	966
	Missionary society	875	966
	Monastery	875	966

SIC 1980	Activity	SIC 1968	NACE
	Mosque	875	966
	National Sunday League	875	966
	National Sunday School Union	875	966
	Presbyterian Church	875	966
	Presbyterian Church of Wales	875	966
	Roman Catholic Church	875	966
	Salvation Army (not hostels, Emigration Department or Missing Persons Office)	875	966
	Society of Friends	875	966
	Spiritualist Church	875	966
	Student Christian Movement	875	966
	Synagogue	875	966
	Temple (for worship)	875	966
	Theosophical Society	875	966
	Unitarian Church	875	966
	United Reform Church	875	966
	United Society for Christian Literature	875	966
	Wesleyan Reform Union	875	966
9690/1	Tourist offices		
	British Tourist Authority	901/6	967
	Holiday information centre	899/7	967
	Information bureau for tourists	899/7	967
	Tourist board or information service	899/7	967
9690/2	Other community services		
	Automobile Association	899/7	968
	Band of Hope Union	899/3	966
	Bishopsgate Institute	899/3	968
	Boy Scouts	899/3	968
	Boys' Brigade	899/3	968
	Boys' club	899/3	968
	British Legion (other than social club)	899/3	968
	British Safety Council	899/4	968
	Church Lads' Brigade	899/3	968
	Civic Trust	899/4	968
	Communist Party	899/4	968
	Community centre	899/4	968
	Conservative and Unionist party	899/4	968
	Conservative association	899/4	968
	Consumers' Association	899/7	968
	Cripplegate Institute	899/3	968
	Fabian Society	899/4	968
	Girl Guides Association	899/3	968
	Girls' Brigade	899/3	968
	Girls' club	899/3	968
	Girls' Friendly Society	899/3	968
	Independent Labour Party	899/4	968
	Labour Party	899/4	968
	Legal Aid Society	899/3	968
	Liberal association	899/4	968
	Liberal Party	899/4	968
	Motorists' organisation (not road patrol or touring service)	899/7	968
	National Council for Civil Liberties	899/4	968
	National Union of Students (not trading activities)	899/4	968
	Plaid Cymru	899/4	968
	Political organisation	899/4	968
	Rotary Club	899/3	968
	Round Table	899/3	968
	Royal Automobile Club	899/7	968
	Royal Scottish Automobile Club	899/7	968
	Royal Society for the Prevention of Accidents	899/4	968
	Scottish National Party	899/4	968
	Scout Association	899/3	968
	Sea Scouts Association	899/3	968
	Social Reform Society	899/3	968
	Student Union	887	968
	Unionist association	899/4	968
	United Nations Association	899/4	968
	YMCA (not hostel)	899/3	968
	YWCA (not hostel)	899/3	968
	Youth centre	899/3	968
	Youth club	899/3	968
	Zionist organisation	899/4	968
9711/1	Film production		
	Film sound track dubbing and synchronisation	881/1	971
	Film studios	881/1	971
	Motion picture production	881/1	971
9711/2	Film distribution		
	Film broker	881/1	972
	Film distribution	881/1	972
	Film hiring agency	881/1	972
	Film library	881/1	972
	Film renting	881/1	972
9711/3	Cinemas		
	Cinema club	881/1	973
	Cinema, public	881/1	973
9741/1	Radio and television services		
	British Broadcasting Corporation	881/2	974
	Broadcasting station, radio or television	881/2	974
	Independent Broadcasting Authority	881/2	974
	Radio relay service	881/2	974
	Radio studio	881/2	974
	Television relay service	881/2	974
	Television service	881/2	974
	Television studio	881/2	974
9741/2	Theatres, concert halls, etc.		
	Concert hall	881/2	975
	Impresario	881/2	975
	Music hall	881/2	975
	Opera house	881/2	975
	Recording studio	881/2	975
	Theatre	881/2	975
9760	Authors, music composers and other own account artists not elsewhere specified		
	Actor (own account)	881/2	976
	Art expert	879/5	976
	Artist	879/5	976
	Author	879/5	976
	Ballet company	881/2	976
	Band (orchestra)	881/2	976
	Calico printers' designer	879/5	976
	Cartoonist	879/5	976
	Commercial artist (own account)	879/5	976
	Concert party	881/2	976
	Conjuror	881/2	976
	Copper plate engraver (artist)	879/5	976
	Costume designing	879/5	976
	Dance band	881/2	976
	Designing (artist)	879/5	976
	Designing for calico printing	879/5	976
	Designing for textile or wallpaper printing	879/5	976
	Engraver (artist)	879/5	976
	Etcher (artist)	879/5	976
	Explorer	879/5	976
	Fashion artist	879/5	976
	Fashion: designing	879/5	976
	Fine art expert	879/5	976

SIC 1980	Activity	SIC 1968	NACE
	Heraldic painting	879/5	976
	Illuminating (illustrating)	879/5	976
	Jewellery designing	879/5	976
	Librettist	879/5	976
	Lithographic artist (own account)	879/5	976
	Lyric author	879/5	976
	Marionette show	881/2	976
	Music composer	879/5	976
	Music copyist and transcriber (own account)	881/2	976
	Musician (own account)	881/2	976
	Opera company	881/2	976
	Orchestra	881/2	976
	Organist (own account)	881/2	976
	Painter (artist)	879/5	976
	Picture restoring	879/5	976
	Playwright	879/5	976
	Poet	879/5	976
	Pop group	881/2	976
	Public speaker	879/5	976
	Repertory company	881/2	976
	Revue company	881/2	976
	Scenario writer	879/5	976
	Scenic artist	879/5	976
	Sculptor	879/5	976
	Singer (own account)	881/2	976
	Song writer	879/5	976
	Street musician or singer	899/7	976
	Touring company (theatre)	881/2	976
	Variety artiste (own account)	881/2	976
	Ventriloquist	881/2	976
	Wood engraver (artist)	879/5	976
9770	Libraries, museums, art galleries etc.		
	Art gallery (not dealer)	899/4	977
	Bethnal Green Museum	899/4	977
	British Museum	899/4	977
	Bushey Park	901/6	977
	Imperial War Museum	899/4	977
	Kew Gardens	899/4	977
	Library (run by local authority)	906/3	977
	Library for general public	821/4	977
	London Museum	899/4	977
	Menagerie	882	977
	Museum	899/4	977
	National Galleries (Scotland)	899/4	977
	National Gallery	899/4	977
	National Library	899/4	977
	National Library for the Blind	899/3	977
	National Library of Wales	899/4	977
	National Library, Scotland	899/4	977
	National Maritime Museum	899/4	977
	National Portrait Gallery	899/4	977
	Reading room (library)	899/4	977
	Royal Botanic Gardens	899/4	977
	Royal Scottish Museum, Edinburgh	899/4	977
	Science Museum	899/4	977
	Tate Gallery	899/4	977
	Victoria and Albert Museum	899/4	977
	Wallace Collection	899/4	977
	Zoological Gardens	882	977
9791/1	Sporting facilities and professional sports players		
	Animal training (racehorses or greyhounds)	882	978
	Athletic club	882	978
	Badminton Club	882	978
	Bathing pool proprietor	882	978
	Billiard room or saloon	882	978
	Billiards and snooker club	882	978
	Boat hiring (for pleasure)	882	978
	Bowling alley	882	978
	Bowls club	882	978
	Boxing	882	978
	Boxing promoter	882	978
	Coursing	882	978
	Cricket	882	978
	Cricket club	882	978
	Croquet club	882	978
	Cycle club	882	978
	Dirt track	882	978
	Dog: breeding (greyhound for racing)		978
	Dog: racing	882	978
	Drag hounds	882	978
	Flying club	882	978
	Football Association	882	978
	Football club and ground	882	978
	Glider club	882	978
	Golf club	882	978
	Golf course or links	882	978
	Greyhound security police	882	978
	Greyhound track	882	978
	Greyhound training	882	978
	Groundsman	882	978
	Gymnasium	882	978
	Hockey club	882	978
	Horse training (race horse)	882	978
	Hunt kennels	882	978
	Hunt stables	882	978
	Hunting	882	978
	Ice hockey	882	978
	Jockey	882	978
	Jockey Club	882	978
	Kennel master	882	978
	MCC	882	978
	National Greyhound Racing Club	882	978
	National Hunt Committee	882	978
	Newmarket Heath	882	978
	Physical culture expert	882	978
	Pony club	882	978
	Race horse trainer	882	978
	Racecourse (not betting)	882	978
	Racquet club	882	978
	Riding school	882	978
	Riding stables	882	978
	Rifle butts	882	978
	Rink (ice skating)	882	978
	Rink (roller skating)	882	978
	Rowing club	882	978
	Rugby League	882	978
	Rugby Union	882	978
	Ski instructor (own account)	882	978
	Skittle alley	882	978
	Speedway racing	882	978
	Sports club	882	978
	Squash club	882	978
	Swimming bath	882	978
	Swimming club	882	978
	Tennis club	882	978
	Tennis court	882	978
	Trainer, racehorse or greyhound	882	978
	Training stables	882	978
	Trotting club	882	978
	Wrestling	882	978
	Yacht club	882	978
9791/2	Betting and gambling		
	Amusement arcade	883	979
	Betting shop	883	979
	Bingo hall	883	979
	Bookmaker	883	979
	Casino	883	979

SIC 1980	Activity	SIC 1968	NACE
	Football pools	883	979
	Gambling	883	979
	Gaming Board for Great Britain	883	979
	Gaming club	883	979
	Horse Race Betting Levy Board	883	979
	Horserace Totalisator Board	883	979
	Lottery	883	979
	Racing pool	883	979
	Racing tipster	883	979
	Tic-tac man	883	979
	Totalisator	883	979
	Turf accountant	883	979
	Turf commission agency	883	979
9791/3	Other recreational services		
	Amusement catering	882	979
	Amusement park	882	979
	Animal training (for circuses etc.)	882	979
	Band agency	881/2	979
	Beach hut proprietor	882	979
	Bridge instructor	882	979
	Chess instructor	882	979
	Circus	881/2	979
	Coconut shy	882	979
	Common (local authority or municipally owned)	906/3	979
	Dance hall	882	979 and 663
	Dancing (ballroom) academy	882	979
	Dancing master	882	979
	Dog trainer (not greyhounds)	882	979
	Fortune telling (fairground)	882	979
	Fun fair	882	979
	Hobby instructor (own account)	882	979
	Park (local authority or municipally owned)	906/3	979
	Pleasure ground	882	979
	Pleasure pier	882	979
	Psychometry	882	979
	Public park	882	979
	Punch and Judy show	881/2	979
	Shooting gallery	882	979
	Switchback	882	979
	Theatre ticket agency	881/2	979
	Theatrical agency	881/2	979
	Theatrical costumier (hiring)	821/2	979
	Travelling show	881/2	979
	Variety agency	881/2	979
	Waxworks	882	979
9811	Laundries		
	Clean towel company	892	981
	Industrial clothing hire	892	981
	Launderette	892	981
	Laundry	892	981
	Laundry receiving office	892	981
	Linen hire (associated with laundry service)	892	981
	Towel hire	892	981
	Towel supply company	892	981
9812	Dry cleaning and allied services		
	Alteration or repair of clothing (specialists)	893	981
	Carpet cleaning	893	981
	Curtain cleaning (not lace dressing)	893	981
	Dry cleaner	893	981
	Dyer and cleaner	893	981
	Glove cleaning	893	981
	Hat renovating	893	981

SIC 1980	Activity	SIC 1968	NACE
	Invisible mending	893	981
	Job dyeing	893	981
	Lace cleaning and mending (not net mending)	893	981
	Pressing and valeting	893	981
	Shirt and collar pressing	892	981
	Valet service	893	981
9820	Hairdressing and beauty parlours		
	Barber	889	982
	Bath, public sauna or turkish etc.	899/7	982
	Beauty parlour	889	982
	Beauty specialist	889	982
	Coiffeur	889	982
	Electrolysis specialist	889	982
	Hairdresser	889	982
	Manicurist	889	982
	Public baths	899/7	982
	Russian baths	899/7	982
	Sauna baths	899/7	982
	Trichologist	889	982
	Turkish baths	899/7	982
9890/1	Photographic studios		
	Photograph colouring	899/2	983
	Photograph mounting	899/2	983
	Photographer	899/2	983
	Photographic studio	899/2	983
	Portrait photography	899/2	983
	Street photographer	899/2	983
	Wedding photograph service	899/2	983
9890/2	Other personal services		
	Animal home	899/7	01
	Animal pound	899/7	01
	Artists' model	899/7	984
	Astrologer	882	984
	Bait digging	899/7	984
	Bootblack	899/7	984
	Breed society	899/6	963
	Cats' home	899/7	01
	Cemetery	899/1	922
	Clairvoyant	882	984
	Cloakroom (not railway etc.)	899/7	984
	Computer dating agency	899/7	984
	Cremation board	906/3	911
	Crematorium	899/1	984
	Dogs' home	899/7	01
	Educational agency	899/7	984
	Educational agency	899/7	984
	Emigration agency (not of foreign government, etc.)	899/7	984
	Enquiry agent	899/7	984
	Escort agency	899/7	984
	Fashion agent	899/7	984
	Fortune telling (not fairground)	882	984
	Funeral direction	899/1	984
	Funeral furnishing	899/1	984
	Genealogist	879/5	984
	Graphologist	899/7	984
	Guide	899/7	984
	Historical research	899/7	984
	Horse breeding society	899/6	963
	Horse clipping	899/7	984
	Interpreter (own account)	899/7	984
	Jobbing waiter	899/7	984
	Kennels	899/7	01
	Knifegrinder, travelling	899/7	984
	Laying out the dead	899/7	984
	Marriage bureaux	899/7	984
	Master of ceremonies	899/7	984
	Musical instrument tuning	899/7	984

SIC 1980	Activity	SIC 1968	NACE
	Naturalisation agent	899/7	984
	Palmist	882	984
	Pavement artist	899/7	984
	Poodle clipping	899/7	984
	Private detective	899/7	984
	Salvation Army Emigration Department	899/7	984
	Scholastic agent	899/7	984
	School agent	899/7	984
	Shire Horse Association	899/6	963
	Tattooist	899/7	984
	Toast-master (own account)	899/7	984
	Town crier (own account)	899/7	968
	Undertaking	899/1	984
9900	Domestic services		
	Charwoman (private service)	891/2	990
	Daily maid	891/2	990
	Domestic servant	891/1	990
	Governess (resident)	891/1	990
	Jobbing gardener	891/2	990
	Private domestic service (non-resident)	891/2	990
	Private domestic service (resident)	891/1	990
	Private gardener	891/2	990
	Private tutor (resident)	891/1	990
	Secretary (private household)	865	990

SIC 1980	Activity	SIC 1968	NACE
0000	Diplomatic representation, international organisations, allied armed forces		
	Chargé d'affaires	899/5	000
	Commonwealth armed forces	899/5	000
	Commonwealth government service	899/5	000
	Commonwealth Institute	899/5	000
	Commonwealth Secretariat	899/5	000
	Commonwealth War Graves Commission	899/5	000
	Consular office	899/5	000
	Crown Agents for overseas governments and administrations	899/5	000
	Embassy	899/5	000
	European Communities representatives and information office	899/5	000
	Foreign armed forces	899/5	000
	Foreign embassy	899/5	000
	Foreign government service	899/5	000
	International Labour Office	899/5	000
	International organisation (e.g. United Nations, International Labour Office)	899/5	000
	Legation	899/5	000
	Office of High Commissioner	899/5	000
	United Nations and affiliated organisations (not United Nations Association)	899/5	000

PART 2

ALPHABETICAL INDEX

A-AIR

Activity	SIC 1980	1968	NACE
A			
Abattoir	4121	810/2	412.1
Abrasive products, manufacturing			
base paper	4710/6	481	471.3
bonded disc, wheel and segment	2460	469/1	246.1
cloth	2460	469/1	246.3
grains, aluminium oxide	2460	469/1	246
grains, artificial	2460	469/1	246
grains, artificial corundum	2460	469/1	246
grains, boron carbide	2460	469/1	246
grains, silicon carbide	2460	469/1	246.1
paper	2460	469/1	246.3
polishes	2460	469/1	256.7
soap	2581	275	258.1
Abrasives, manufacturing			
agglomerated	2460	469/1	246.1
bonded	2460	469/1	246.1
coated	2460	469/1	246
garnet	2460	469/1	246
organic bonded	2460	469/1	246.1
ABS polymers, manufacturing	2514	276/1	251
Absorptiometer, manufacturing	3710	354/2	371
Absorption drum, glass, manufacturing	2479/5	463/1	247.4
Academic, legal and ecclesiastical			
gown, manufacturing	4532	442	453
robe, manufacturing	4532	442	453
Acaricide, manufacturing	2568	279/4	256.8
Accelerometer, manufacturing	3710	354/2	371.2
Accepting house (recognised by the Bank of England under the Banking Act 1979)	8140/2	861	831
Access credit card	8140/2	861	812
Accident			
and emergency service (hospital)	9510	874/1	951
insurance	8200/3	860	823
Accordion, manufacturing	4920/2	499/1	492.2
Account book, manufacturing	4723/2	483	472.3
Accountancy services	8360	871	836
Accountant (own account)	8360	871	836
Accounting machine, manufacturing	3301	338	330
Accumulator, manufacturing			
and cell case, glass	2479/5	463/1	247.4
battery	3432/2	369/3	343.2
for hydraulic equipment	3283/2	333/4	328.3
Acetone, manufacturing	2512	271/2	251
Acetylene, manufacturing	2567	271/2	256.1
Acid, manufacturing			
dye	2516	277	251
fatty	2563	275	256.3
inorganic	2511	271/1	251
Acids, organic, and their esters and halogenated, nitrosated and sulphonated derivatives, manufacturing	2512	271/2	251
Acoustical engineering	5030	500	503.4
Acrylic, manufacturing			
adhesives	2562	279/2	256.2
paints	2551	274	255
resins	2514	276/1	251
Acrylonitrile, manufacturing	2512	271/2	251
Acrylonitrile-butadiene-styrene (ABS) polymers, manufacturing	2514	276/1	251
Activated and unactivated charcoal (other than wood charcoal) manufacturing	2511	271/1	251
Activated earths, manufacturing	2567	271/1	256.7
Active gauge, manufacturing	3710	390	371.5
Actor (own account)	9760	881/2	976
Actuary (own account)	8320	879/2	832
Actuator, manufacturing			
electric	3442	354/2	344
for hydraulic equipment	3283/2	333/4	328.3
Acyclic (fatty) alcohols, manufacturing	2563	275	256.3
Address plate embossing machine, manufacturing	3301	338	330
Addressing machine, manufacturing	3301	338	330
Adhesive products, manufacturing			
coating	2562	279/2	256.2
formulated	2562	279/2	256.2
labels of cellulose or plastic	2569	491/2	259.3
paste	2562	279/2	256.2
plaster and bandage (surgical)	2570	279/6	257
repair material	2569	not classified	
tape	2569	491/2	259.3
Adult education			
centre	9330	872/3	933
residential college	9330	872/3	933
Advertising			
agency	8380	864	838
contractor (outdoor)	8380	864	838
film production	8380	864	838
light, manufacturing	3470/2	369/4	347.2
material, plastics, manufacturing	4836	496	483
Advisory, Conciliation and Arbitration Service	9631/2	901/6	911
Advocate	8350	873	835
Adze, manufacturing	3161/1	391	316.1
Aerated water, manufacturing	4283/1	232	428.2
Aerating powder, manufacturing	4239/5	229/2	423.6
Aeration plant (effluent treatment) manufacturing	3245/3	341/2	324.1
Aerial			
(non-domestic) manufacturing	3443	367/2	344
domestic, manufacturing	3453	364/3	345.1
erection (domestic)	5030	500	503.6
mast (self supporting) erection	5020	500	502.7
ropeway and cableway, manufacturing	3255/1	337/1	325.5
survey	8370/2	879/1	837
Aero-engine			
all types, manufacturing or repairing	3640	383/2	364
parts and sub-assemblies, manufacturing or repairing	3640	383/2	364
Aerodrome	7640	707	764
Aerographing	4754/5	489	473.4
Aerosol can, metal, manufacturing	3164	395	316.4
Aerospace equipment, manufacturing and repairing	3640	383	364
After-shave lotion, manufacturing	2582	273	258.2
Agglomerated			
abrasives, manufacturing	2460	469/1	246.1
cork, manufacturing	4664/1	479/1	466.1
Agricultural			
building steelwork, manufacturing	3204/1	341/4	314.1
ceramic ware, manufacturing	2489/4	462/3	248.9
college	9330	872/3	933
contracting	0100/3	001/2	01
knife, manufacturing	3161/1	392	316.1
land letting	8500	863	850
lime processing, manufacturing	2420	469/1	242.2
machinery engine, manufacturing	3281/1	334/1	328.1
machinery hire (without staff)	8410	832/6	841
Mortgage Corporation	8150/1	862	813.1
Research Council	9400	876	940
tractor, manufacturing	3212	380	321.2
trailer (motor drawn) manufacturing	3522	381	352
twine, manufacturing	4396	416	439.6
valuer	8395/4	865	839.3
Air			
bed, inflatable, plastics, manufacturing	4836	496	483
charter service	7500	707	750
cleansing plant (not for air conditioning equipment) manufacturing	3245/3	341/2	328.4
compressor, manufacturing	3283/1	333/3	328.3

Activity	SIC 1980	NACE 1968	
conditioning equipment for aircraft, manufacturing	3640	383/4	364
conditioning package, manufacturing	3284/4	339/4	328.4
conditioning plant, installation	5030	500	503.3
cushion vehicle, manufacturing or repairing	3640	383/3	364
filter, manufacturing	3284/4	339/4	328.4
freight agent or broker	7700/2	709/1	772
gun, manufacturing	3290/1	342	328.9
pistol, manufacturing	3290/1	342	328.9
rifle, manufacturing	3290/1	342	328.9
terminal operated by airline	7500	707	750
Traffic control centre	7640	707	764
transport	7500	707	750
Air-taxi service	7500	707	750
Airborne electronic equipment, manufacturing	3443	367/2	344
Aircraft			
bomb, manufacturing	3290/2	342	328.9
brake (not brake lining) manufacturing or repairing	3640	383/4	364
complete, manufacturing or repairing	3640	383/1	364
galley, manufacturing	3640	383/4	364
hire (without crew)	8480/4	707	845
manufacturing or repairing	3640	383/1	364
parts and accessories, plastics, manufacturing	4836	496	483
parts and sub-assemblies, not electrical, manufacturing or repairing	3640	383/4	364
propeller, manufacturing or repairing	3640	383/4	364
seat, manufacturing	3640	383/4	364
tyre, manufacturing	4811	491/1	481.1
Airfield control and approach aid (electronic) manufacturing	3443	367/2	344
Airframe			
manufacturing or repairing	3640	383/1	364
parts and sub-assemblies, not electrical, manufacturing or repairing	3640	383/4	364
Airline	7500	707	750
Airline coach service	7210/2	702/1	721.2
Airport	7640	707	764
Airport runway construction	5020	500	502.5
Airscrew, manufacturing	3640	383/4	364
Airship, manufacturing	3640	383/1	364
Alabaster			
bowl cutting	4959	499/2	495.3
mine	2310/5	109/4	231.2
Alarm clock, manufacturing	3740	352	374
Alarms, burglar, fire and security, manufacturing	3433	367/1	343.1
Album printing	4754/4	489	473.2
Alcohols, synthetic, manufacturing	2512	271/2	251
Aldehyde, manufacturing	2512	271/2	251
Ale brewing	4270/1	231	427/1
Alginates, manufacturing	2514	276/1	251
Alizarine dye, manufacturing	2516	277	251
Alkali, manufacturing	2511	271/1	251
Alkyd			
paint, manufacturing	2551	274	255
resins, manufacturing	2514	276/1	251
Allotment farming	0100/2	001/3	01
Almanac printing	4754/4	489	473.2
Almond grinding	4239/9	229/2	414.6
Alpaca			
and mohair spinning	4310/2	414/2	431.3
weaving	4310/3	414/3	431.5
Alteration or repair of clothing (specialists)	9812	893	981
Alternating current generator, manufacturing	3420/1	361/1	342
Alternator, manufacturing			
for vehicle	3434	369/1	343.1
not for vehicle	3420/1	361/1	342
Altimeter, manufacturing	3710	354/2	371.3
Alum mine	2396	109/4	239.4
Alumina brick, manufacturing	2481	461/1	248.1
Aluminium processing and products, manufacturing			
angle	2245/2	321	224.1
bar	2245/2	321	224.1
billet	2245/2	321	224.1
blank	2245/2	321	224.1
cable sheathing	2245/2	321	224.3
cable, uninsulated	2245/2	321	224.3
can and box	3164/1	395	316.4
castings	3112	321	311.2
circle	2245/2	321	312.2
collapsible tube (packaging)	3164/1	321	316.4
compounds (excluding bauxite and abrasives)	2511	271/1	251
conductor steel reinforced cable	2245/2	394	224.3
continuous cast rod	2245/2	321	224.3
corrugated plate, sheet or strip	2245/2	321	224.3
deoxidiser	2245/2	321	224.1
die casting	3112	321	311.2
disc	2245/2	321	312.2
domestic utensil	3167	399.6	316.7
drawn product	2245/2	321	224.3
extruded section	2245/2	321	224.3
extruded tube	2245/2	321	224.3
extrusion	2245/2	321	224.3
extrusion ingot	2245/1	321	224.1
flake	2245/2	321	224.3
foil containers	3164/4	395	316.4
foil laminate	3164/4	321	316.4
foil packaging goods	3164/4	395	316.4
foil stock	2245/2	321	224.3
forging bar	2245/2	321	224.3
foundry alloy	2245/1	321	224.1
foundry ingot	2245/1	321	224.1
hardener	2245/1	321	224.1
hollow section	2245/2	321	224.3
notched bar	2245/1	321	224.1
oxide abrasive grain	2460	469/1	246
paint	2551	274	255
paste	2245/2	321	224.3
pipe	2245/2	321	224.3
pipe fittings	2245/2	321	224.3
plate	2245/2	321	224.3
powder	2245/2	321	224.3
refining	2245/1	321	224.1
remelt ingot	2245/1	321	224.1
rod	2245/2	321	224.3
rolled product	2245/2	321	224.3
rolling ingot and slab	2245/1	321	224.1
saucepan	3167	399/6	316.7
section	2245/2	321	224.3
sheet	2245/2	321	224.3
shop fronts and entrances	4672	399/2	314.1
slug	2245/2	321	224.3
smelting	2245/1	321	224.1
solid section	2245/2	321	224.3
strands for cable	2245/2	321	224.3
strip	2245/2	321	224.3
structure (for building)	3204/1	341/4	314.1
structure (for civil engineering)	3204/2	341/4	314.1
tube fittings	2245/2	321	224.3
tubular containers	3164/1	395	316.4
unwrought	2245/1	321	224.1
wire	2245/2	394	224.3
wire strands	2245/2	394	224.3
wirebar	2245/1	321	224.1
Aluminous cement, manufacturing	2420	464	242.1
Alums, manufacturing	2511	271/1	251

AMB-ARM

Activity	SIC 1980	1968	NACE
Amber, turning	4959	499/2	495.3
Ambulance			
manufacturing	3510/2	381	351
service	9520	874/2	952
Amines, manufacturing	2512	271/2	251
Aminoplastic resins, manufacturing	2514	276/1	251
Ammeter, manufacturing	3442	354/2	344
Ammonia, manufacturing	2511	271/1	251
Ammoniacal liquor (from coke ovens) manufacturing	1200	261/1	120
Ammonium			
compounds, manufacturing (excluding ammonium nitrate, sulphate and phosphate)	2511	271/1	251
nitrate (explosives) manufacturing	2565	279/3	256.5
nitrate (not for explosives) manufacturing	2513	278	251
phosphate, manufacturing	2513	278	251
sulphate (from coke ovens) manufacturing	1200	261/1	120.2
sulphate, manufacturing	2513	278	251
Ammunition			
depot (Ministry of Defence)	9150	901/5	915
manufacturing	3290/2	342	328.9
Amorce, manufacturing	2565	279/3	256.5
Amplifier, manufacturing			
audio separate	3454/1	365/2	345.1
for broadcasting studio	3443	367/2	344
Amplifying valve, manufacturing	3453/1	364/1	345.1
Ampoule, glass (hygienic and pharmaceutical) manufacturing	2478	463/2	247.7
Amusement			
(automatic slot) machine, manufacturing	3286/1	339/9	328.9
arcade	9791/2	883	979
catering	9791/3	882	979
guide, periodical, printing	4752/3	486	473.1
guide, periodical, printing—publishing	4752/2	486	473.1
guide, periodical, publishing	4752/1	486	474.4
machine hire (not gaming machines)	8490	812/4	847
park	9791/3	882	979
Anaerobic adhesive, manufacturing	2562	279/2	256.2
Anaesthetic equipment, manufacturing	3720/1	353/1	372.2
Anaesthetics, manufacturing	2570	272	257
Anaesthetist	9510	874/1	951
Analgesics, manufacturing	2570	272	257
Analogue computer, manufacturing	3302	366	330
Analytical chemist (private practice)	8370/2	879/2	837
Anchor, manufacturing	3169/4	399/12	316.9
Angle, manufacturing			
aluminium	2245/2	321	224.1
steel, cold formed	2235	311/2	223.3
Angora rabbit breeding	0100/1	001/1	01
Anhydrite			
mine or quarry	2310/5	109/4	231.6
plaster, manufacturing	2420	469/2	242.3
Aniline dye, manufacturing	2516	277	251
Animal			
feed supplement, manufacturing	4222/2	272	422
grease, manufacturing	4126/1	221	412.4
hair preparation	4310/1	414/1	431.2
home	9890/2	899/7	01
hospital (RSPCA, PDSA)	9560/2	879/4	956
hospital (run by veterinary surgeon)	9560/1	879/4	956
hospital (supervised or run by registered veterinarian)	9560/2	879/4	956
oil, manufacturing	4126/1	221	411.4
pound	9890/2	899/7	01
rearing for production of serum	0100/1	001/1	01
training (for circuses, etc.)	9791/3	882	979
training (racehorses or greyhounds)	9791/1	882	978
toy, manufacturing	4941	494/1	494.1
Annealing lehr, manufacturing	3275/5	339/9	328.6
Anodising	3138	399/11	313.5
Anorak, manufacturing	4531	441	453
Anthracene, manufacturing	2512	271/2	251
Anti-corrosive paint, manufacturing	2551	274	255
Anti-freeze mixtures, excluding pure ethylene glycol, manufacturing	2567	271/3	256.7
Anti-icing equipment and systems for aircraft, manufacturing	3640	383/4	364
Anti-infectives, manufacturing	2570	272	257
Anti-knock compounds, manufacturing	2567	271/3	256.7
Anti-perspirant, manufacturing	2582	273	258.2
Anti-roll bar (motor vehicle) manufacturing	3530	381	353
Anti-rust preparations, manufacturing	2567	271/3	256.7
Anti-sprouting compound, manufacturing	2568	279/4	256.8
Antibiotics, manufacturing	2570	272	257
Antifriction metal, manufacturing	2247/1	323	224.2
Antimony, manufacturing	2247/1	323	224.1
Antique glass, manufacturing	2471/1	463/1	247.1
Antiques, retail distribution	6480	821/3	648
Antiseptics, manufacturing	2570	272	257
Apartment letting (holiday)	6670/3	884	667.5
Aperitif, spirit based, manufacturing	4240/2	239/1	424.3
Apparatus for testing physical and mechanical properties of materials, manufacturing	3710	354/2	371.2
Apparel			
cloth (woven from yarns spun on the cotton system) manufacturing	4322	413	432.5
fur, manufacturing	4560	433	456.3
Appeal			
Committee of the House of Lords	9120	901/6	912
Court of	9120	901/6	912
Apple			
pomace and pectin, manufacturing	4261/2	239/2	426
wine making	4261/3	239/2	426
Appraiser and valuer (not insurance or real estate)	8395/4	865	839.3
Apprentice school	9330	872/5	933
Apron, manufacturing			
domestic	4536/1	445/1	453
industrial	4534	444/1	453
Aquarium heater (electric) manufacturing	3460	368	346
Arable farming	0100/1	001/1	01
Arbitrator	8395/4	865	839.3
Arc lamp, manufacturing	3470/2	369/5	347.2
Archery equipment, manufacturing	4942	494/3	494.2
Archimedian screw pump, manufacturing	3287	333/1	328.3
Architect (private practice)	8370/1	879/1	837
Architectural			
draughtsman (private practice)	8370/1	879/1	837
drawing, printing and publishing	4754/2	489	473 and 474
glass, manufacturing	2479/5	463/1	247.4
model, manufacturing	4959	499/2	495.3
Architrave, plastics, manufacturing	4834	496	483
Area Health Authority	9111	874/2	911
Arm-rest (motor vehicle) manufacturing	3530	381	353
Armature repairing and rewiring	3420/3	361/3	342
Armchair, manufacturing			
non-upholstered	4671/2	472	467.3
upholstered	4671/1	472	467.4
Armed forces, Pay and Records Office	9150	901/5	915
Armoured			
car, manufacturing	3510/2	381	351
hose, rubber or plastics, manufacturing	4812/1	491/2	481.2

Activity	SIC 1980	1968	NACE
Army	9150	901/2	915
accoutrement, leather, manufacturing	4420/1	432	442.1
establishment (civilian personnel)	9150	901/5	915
establishment (service personnel)	9150	901/2	915
Scripture Readers Association	9660	875	966
Aromatic hydrocarbons, manufacturing	2512	271/2	251
Arrowroot, manufacturing	4180	229/2	418.4
Arsenic, manufacturing	2247/1	323	224.1
Art			
college, of	9330	872/3	933
dealer, retail	6480	821/3	649.6
expert	9760	879/5	976
gallery, not dealer	9770	899/4	977
leather work, manufacturing	4420/1	432	442.1
metal work, manufacturing	3169/4	399/12	319
needlework, manufacturing	4557	422/1	455.1
pottery, manufacturing	2489/3	462/3	248
printing and publishing	4754/2	489	473 and 474
tile, earthenware, glazed, manufacturing	2489/1	462/2	248.3
Artesian well contractor	5020	500	502.6
Artificial			
corundum abrasive grain, manufacturing	2460	469/1	246
eye, manufacturing	3720/3	353/1	372.4
flower, plastics, manufacturing	4836	496	483
flower, textile, manufacturing	4539/3	449/4	453
flowers and fruit, paper, manufacturing	4728	484/2	472.8
horizon, manufacturing	3710	354/2	371.3
kidney, unit	9520	874/1	952
limb and appliance centre	9520	874/1	952
limb, manufacturing	3720/3	353/1	372.4
manure, manufacturing	2513	278	251
Artillery			
ammunition, manufacturing	3290/2	342	328.9
manufacturing	3290/1	342	328.9
Artist	9760	879/5	976
Artists'			
brush, manufacturing	4663	493	466.3
colours, manufacturing	2551	274	255
model	9890/2	899/7	984
sundries, manufacturing	4959	499/2	495.3
Arts			
and crafts, school of	9330	872/3	933
Council	9111	901/6	911
Asbestos processing and products, manufacturing			
board	2440	429/1	244
boiler packing	2440	429/1	244
brake lining	2440	429/1	244
building board	2437	469/2	243.1
carded fibre	2440	429/1	244
carding	2440	429/1	244
cement building board	2437	469/2	243.1
cement pipe	2437	469/2	243.1
cement products	2437	469/2	243.1
cloth	2440	429/1	244
clutch lining	2440	429/1	244
engine packing	2440	429/1	244
felting	2440	429/1	244
gasket	2440	429/1	244
glove	4538	449/2	244
insulation	2440	429/1	244
mixing	2440	429/1	244
moulding	2440	429/1	244
packing (woven)	2440	429/1	244
sheet and sheeting (woven)	2440	429/1	244
sock	2440	429/1	244
spinning	2440	429/1	244
tape	2440	429/1	244
tile (woven)	2440	429/1	244
weaving	2440	429/1	244
Aseptic hospital furniture, manufacturing	3720/1	353/1	372
Asphalt			
laying plant, manufacturing	3254/2	336	325.4
manufacturing	2450/1	469/2	245.1
processing plant, manufacturing	3254/2	336	325.4
tile, thermoplastic, manufacturing	4833	492	438.2
Asphalting contractor (civil engineering)	5020	500	502.5
Assay Office	8370/2	879/2	837
Association of Corporate and Certified Accountants	9631/1	879/3	963
Astrologer	9890/2	882	984
Athletic			
clothing, manufacturing	4535	444/2	453
club	9791/1	882	978
equipment, manufacturing	4942	494/3	494.2
footwear, manufacturing	4510	450	451.3
Atomic Energy Research Establishment	9400	876	940
Attache case, leather or leather substitute, manufacturing	4420/1	432	442.1
Attendance centre	9120	901/6	912
Attorney	8350	873	835
Auctioneer (not house auctioneer)	8395/4	865	839.3
Audio			
equipment, retail dealing in	6480	821/3	648.8
separate, manufacturing	3454/1	365/2	345.1
separates, wholesale dealing in	6150	812/4	615.3
tape recording, manufacturing	3452	365/1	345.2
Audit clerk (own account)	8360	871	836
Auditor (own account)	8360	871	836
Auger and auger bit, manufacturing	3161/2	391	316.1
Author	9760	879/5	976
Auto-correlator (optical) manufacturing	3732	354/1	373
Auto-cycle, manufacturing	3633	382	363.1
Autoclave, manufacturing	3720/1	353	372.2
Automatic			
data processing equipment, hire	8430	832/10	843
data processing equipment (computer) manufacturing	3302	366	330
gun, manufacturing	3290/1	342	328.9
process control valve, manufacturing	3288	333/2	328.8
stop motion (textile machinery) manufacturing	3230/2	335	323.1
Automobile Association	9690/2	899/7	968
Autonomous pension fund	8200/2	860	822
Auxiliary power unit for aircraft, manufacturing	3640	383/2	364
Average adjuster	8320	860	832
Aviation			
spirit, manufacturing	1401	262	140.1
turbine fuel, manufacturing	1401	262	140.1
Awning			
cloth weaving	4340/2	413	434.5
manufacturing	4556	422/2	455.4
plastics, manufacturing	4836	496	483
Axe, manufacturing	3161/1	391	316.1
Axial			
compressor, manufacturing	3283/1	333/3	328.3
flow pump, manufacturing	3287	333	328.3
Axle, manufacturing			
motor cycle	3633	382	363.2
motor vehicle	3530	381	353
steel (railway and tramway)	3120	311/2	312
Axminster carpet, manufacturing	4384/1	419	438.1
Azoic dye, manufacturing	2516	277	251

B-BAR

Activity	SIC 1980	NACE 1968	
B			
Baby			
bath, plastics, manufacturing	4836	496	483
carriage, manufacturing	3650/1	494/2	365.1
clothing, manufacturing	4536/3	445/3	453
food, milk based, manufacturing	4130/3	215/2	413.2
food, other than milk based, manufacturing	4239/4	229/2	423.5
linen, manufacturing	4536/3	445/3	453
napkins (disposable), paper or cellulose wadding, manufacturing	4722	not classified	472.2
Backing and curling, machinery (carpet making) manufacturing	3230/2	335	323.1
Backward wave oscillator, manufacturing	3453/1	364/1	345.1
Bacon			
curing	4122/1	214/2	412.2
smoking	4122/1	214/2	412.2
Bacteria bed tile, manufacturing	2489/4	461/2	248
Bacteriologist	8370/2	879/2	837
Badminton			
club	9791/1	882	978
shuttlecock, manufacturing	4942	494/3	494.2
Bag			
canvas, manufacturing	4556	422/2	455.4
chain, manufacturing	4910/3	396	491.3
clasp, manufacturing	3169/2	399/8	316.9
cycle, leather, manufacturing	4420/1	432	442.1
frame, manufacturing	3169/2	399/8	316.9
leather or leather substitute, manufacturing	4420/1	432	442.1
of transparent regenerated cellulose film, manufacturing	4835	482/2	483
plastics, for packaging purposes, manufacturing	4835	496	483
shopping, plastics, manufacturing	4836	496	483
Bagatelle			
board, manufacturing	4941	494/1	494.1
table, manufacturing	4942	472	494.2
Bagging cloth, manufacturing	4350/2	415	435.5
Bagpipe and bagpipe reed, manufacturing	4920/2	499/1	492.2
Bait			
digging	9890/2	899/7	984
production	0100/3	001/2	01
Baize, manufacturing	4399/1	414/5	439.1
Baked chestnut man	6612	885	661
Baker, retail distribution	6410	820/2	641
Bakers' yeast (from distillery) production	4240/1	239/1	424.1
Bakery	4196	212	419.1
Bakery machinery and oven, manufacturing	3244/1	339/7	324.1
Baking			
bread and flour, confectionery	4196	212	419.1
dish, pan and tin, manufacturing	3167	399/6	316.7
powder, manufacturing	4239/5	229/2	423.6
Balaclava helmet, manufacturing	4363/2	417	436.2
Balata belting, manufacturing	4812/2	491/2	481.2
Balata goods (not belting) manufacturing	4812/3	491/2	481.2
Bale			
handler (agricultural machinery) manufacturing	3211/2	331	321
tie, steel, manufacturing	2234	394	223.4
Baler, machine, hay and straw, manufacturing	3211/2	331	321.1
Baler twine, manufacturing	4396	416	439.6
Baling press (not agricultural) manufacturing	3244/2	339/8	324.2

Activity	SIC 1980	NACE 1968	
Ball			
bearing, manufacturing	3262	349/1	326.2
clay mine or opencast working	2310/6	103	231.7
core, rubber	4812/3	491/2	481.2
finished, for all sports, manufacturing	4942	494/3	494.2
glass, manufacturing	2479/3	463/1	247.4
uncovered rubber, manufacturing	4812/3	491/2	481.2
valve, manufacturing	3288	333/2	328.8
Ballet			
company	9760	881/2	976
school	9330	872/3	933
shoe manufacturing	4510	450	451.3
Balloon, manufacturing			
not toy	3640	383/4	364
rubber (excluding pilot and sounding balloons)	4812/3	491/2	481.2
toy, rubber	4812/3	491/2	481.2
Ballotini, glass, manufacturing	2479/5	463/1	247.4
Ballpoint pen and refill, manufacturing	4954/1	495/1	495.1
Bamboo			
furniture, manufacturing	4671/2	472	467.2
preparation	4664/2	475/1	466.2
Band			
agency	9791/3	881/2	979
of Hope Union	9690/2	899/3	966
orchestra	9760	881/2	976
rubber, manufacturing	4812/3	491/2	481.2
Bandage			
cloth, weaving	4322	413	432.5
surgical, manufacturing	2570	279/6	257
Banding (woven) manufacturing	4398/2	421/2	439.3
Bandsaw blade (for all materials) manufacturing	3222/1	390	322.2
Banister rail, wooden, manufacturing	4630	471/2	463.1
Bank			
(not recognised by the Bank of England under the Banking Act 1979)	8150/1	861	813.1
(recognised by the Bank of England under the Banking Act 1979)	8140/2	861	812
fittings and furnishings, manufacturing	4672	474	467.5
holding company	8150/2	862	813.2
note counting machine, manufacturing	3301	338	330
Bank of England	8140/1	861	811
Bankers clearing house	8310	861	812
Banknote			
paper, manufacturing	4710/3	481	471.3
printing	4754/3	489	473.2
Banner (making up only) manufacturing	4556	422/1	455.4
Baptist Church	9660	875	966
Bar	6620	886	662
Bar manufacturing			
aluminium	2245/2	321	224.1
copper	2246/2	322	224.2
fittings and furnishings	4672	474	467.5
glass	2479/3	463/1	247.4
steel (semi-finished)	2210	311/2	221.1
Barbed wire, steel, manufacturing	2234	394	223.4
Barber	9820	889	982
Barclaycard Department	8140/2	861	812
Barge			
lessee or owner	7260/3	706	730
river and sea going, manufacturing	3610/1	370/1	361
Bargeboard, manufacturing	4610/2	471/1	461.2
Barley			
(blocked, flaked, puffed or pearl) processing	4160	211/2	416.2
malting	4270/2	231	427.2
meal production	4160	211/2	416.1
milling	4160	211/2	416.1

Activity	SIC 1980	1968	NACE
Barometer, manufacturing	3710	354/2	371.2
Barrel, manufacturing			
metal	3164/2	399/7	316.4
plastics	4835	496	483
wooden	4640/2	475/1	464.2
Barrister (own account)	8350	873	835
Barrow hiring	8480/4	709/3	845
Barytes mine	2396	109/4	239.4
Basalt mine	2310/2	102/1	231.2
Base			
exchange plant (water treatment) manufacturing	3245/3	341/2	324.1
paper (for printing and writing paper) manufacturing	4710/3	481	471.3
Basement light, glass, manufacturing	2479/5	463/1	247.4
Basic dye, manufacturing	2516	277	251
Basic slag (ground) manufacturing	2513	278	251
Basic slag (uncrushed)	2210	313	221.1
Basin, metal, manufacturing	3169/4	399/12	316.7
Basket, manufacturing			
chair	4671/2	472	467.7
furniture	4671/2	472	467.7
of material other than plastic	4664/2	475/1	466.2
plastics	4836	496	483
Basketware, manufacturing	4664/2	475/1	466.2
Bat, ceramic, manufacturing	2489/4	462/3	248.9
Bath			
cast iron bath, manufacturing	3111	313/4	311.1
chair, manufacturing	3650/1	494/2	365.2
mat, manufacturing	4557	422/1	455.1
of metal other than cast iron, manufacturing	3169/4	399/12	316.7
plastic, manufacturing	4834	496	483
preparations, manufacturing	2582	273	258.2
public sauna or turkish etc.	9820	899/7	982
towel, manufacturing	4557	422/1	455.1
Bathing			
cap, rubber, manufacturing	4812/3	491/2	481.2
pool proprietor	9791/1	882	978
Battenboard, manufacturing	4620/1	471/1	462.1
Battery			
for motor vehicle, retail dealing in	6510	894	651.1
charger, manufacturing	3435	361	343.1
dry, non-rechargeable, manufacturing	3432/1	369/2	343.2
making machine, manufacturing	3286/3	339/9	328.9
powered, electric commercial vehicle, manufacturing	3510/2	381	351
primary, manufacturing	3432/1	369/2	343.2
secondary, manufacturing	3432/2	369/3	343.2
Battledress, manufacturing			
men's	4532	442	453
women's	4533	443	453
Bauxite brick, manufacturing	2481	461/1	248.1
Bayonet, manufacturing	3162/1	392	316.8
Beach			
footwear, manufacturing	4510	450	451.3
hut proprietor	9791/3	882	979
Beachwear (women's and girls') manufacturing	4536/1	445/1	453
Beacon (for shipping) manufacturing	3610	370/1	361.1
Bead, manufacturing			
glass	2479/5	463/1	247.4
wooden	4650	479/3	465.1
Beaded wood, manufacturing	4610/2	471/1	461.2
Beading, wooden, manufacturing	4650	471/1	465.1
Beaker, paper, manufacturing	4724/2	484/2	472.4
Beam, rolled steel, manufacturing	2210	311/2	221.1
Beaming machinery (textiles) manufacturing	3230/2	335	323.1
Bean			
grinding	4160	211/2	416.2
milling	4160	211/2	416.2
splitting	4160	211/2	416.2
Beauty			
parlour	9820	889	982
specialist	9820	889	982
Bed, manufacturing	4671/5	472	467.1
Bed head, metal, manufacturing	3166/1	399/1	316.6
Bed linen, manufacturing	4557	422/1	455.1
Bed linen (disposable) paper or cellulose wadding, manufacturing	4728	484/2	472.8
Bed linen, retail dealing in	6470	821/2	647.6
Bed-settee, manufacturing	4671/1	472	467.4
Bedding, retail dealing in	6470	821/2	647.1
Bedfolder, manufacturing	3650/1	494/2	365.1
Bedford cord weaving			
not worsted	4322	413	432.5
worsted	4310/3	414/3	431.5
Bedroom furniture (other than beds and mattresses) manufacturing	4671/2	472	467.1
Beds, retail dealing in	6480	821/3	648.2
Bedsock, manufacturing	4363/1	417	436.1
Bedspread, manufacturing			
lace	4395	418	439.5
other than lace	4557	422/2	455.2
Bedstead, manufacturing			
metal	3166/1	399/1	316.6
wooden	4671/5	472	467.1
Bee keeping	0100/1	001/1	01
Beef			
extract manufacturing	4122/3	214/2	412.2
paste manufacturing	4122/3	214/2	412.2
pickling	4122/3	214/2	412.2
Beehive, wooden, manufacturing	4650	479/3	465.1
Beer			
brewing	4270/1	231	427.1
garden	6620	886	662
non-alcoholic, manufacturing	4283/1	232	428.2
retail dealing in	6420	820/2	642.1
Beet			
pulp, manufacturing	4200	216	420.1
sugar, manufacturing	4200	216	420.1
Bell			
electronic (other than telephone type) manufacturing	3433	369/5	343.1
founding	3112	399/12	311.2
(pedal cycle) manufacturing	3634	382	363.2
(telephone type) manufacturing	3441	363	344
Belleville washer, manufacturing	3137/2	399/4	313.2
Bellows, rubber, manufacturing	4812/3	491/2	481.2
Belt, manufacturing			
car, safety	3530	381	353
dress, not leather or leather substitute	4539/3	449/4	453
leather or leather substitute	4420/1	432	442.1
Belting			
duck weaving	4322	413	432.5
rubber or plastics, manufacturing	4812/2	491/2	481.2
Bench			
seat, non-upholstered, manufacturing	4671/2	472	467.3
seat, upholstered, manufacturing	4671/1	472	467.4
vice, manufacturing	3161/2	391	316.1
Bending machine, metal forming, manufacturing	3221/2	332/2	322.1
Benevolent society (charitable organization)	9611/1	899/3	961
Benevolent society (insurance fund)	8200/3	860	823
Benniseed			
crushing	4116/2	221	411.3
oil refining	4116/3	221	411.4
Bent timber, manufacturing	4610/1	471/1	461.1
Bentwood furniture, manufacturing	4671/2	472	467.3
Benzene, manufacturing	2512	271/2	251

BEN-BLU

Activity	SIC 1980	1968	NACE
Benzole, manufacturing			
crude, from coke ovens	1200	261/1	120
crude, from gas works	1620	601	162.1
industrial	1401	262	140.1
Beret, manufacturing			
knitted	4363/2	417	436.2
not knitted	4537/2	446/2	453
Beryllium, manufacturing	2247/1	323	224.1
Besom, manufacturing	4663	479/3	466.3
Bespoke tailor, retail	6450	821/2	645
Bethnal Green Museum	9770	899/4	977
Betting	9791/2	883	979
shop	9791/2	883	979
Beverage processing machinery, manufacturing	3244/1	339/7	324.1
Bias binding, manufacturing	4398/2	421/3	439.3
Bible			
paper, manufacturing	4710/3	481	471.3
Society	9660	875	966
Bicycle			
chain, manufacturing	3261/1	349/2	326.1
childrens', manufacturing	4941	494/1	494.1
hire	8480/4	709/3	845
pedal type and parts thereof, manufacturing	3634	382	363
Bidet, ceramic, fireclay, etc, manufacturing	2489/2	462/2	248.5
Bifurcated rivet, manufacturing	3137/1	393	316.9
Bile processing (by knackers)	4126/3	214/2	412.5
Bill			
broker (other than discount house)	8310	862	831
distributor (advertising)	8380	864	838
posting agency	8380	864	838
Billet manufacturing			
aluminium	2245/1	321	224.1
copper	2246/1	322	224.1
steel	2210	311/2	221.1
Billfold, leather, manufacturing	4420/1	432	442.1
Billiard			
and snooker club	9791/1	882	978
ball, manufacturing	4942	494/3	494.2
cue, manufacturing	4942	494/3	494.2
room or saloon	9791/1	882	978
table, manufacturing	4942	472	494.2
table cloth, manufacturing	4399/1	414/5	439.1
Bin			
liners, plastic, manufacturing	4835	496	483
metal, manufacturing	3163	399/7	316.4
plastic, manufacturing	4836	496	483
Binder twine, manufacturing	4396	416	439.6
Binding			
and mending (textile)	4370/2	423	437.4
machine, manufacturing	3301	338	330
woven, manufacturing	4398/2	421/3	439.3
Bingo hall	9791/2	883	979
Binocular, manufacturing	3732	354/1	373.2
Birch broom, manufacturing	4663	479/3	466.3
Bird food, manufacturing	4222/1	219	422
Biscuit			
making	4197	213	419.5
making machinery, manufacturing	3244/1	339/7	324.1
tile, manufacturing	2489/1	462/2	248.3
Bishopsgate Institute	9690/2	899/4	968
Bismuth, manufacturing	2247/1	323	224.1
Bit stock, drill, manufacturing	3222/1	390	322.2
Bitumen, manufacturing	1401	262	140.1
Bituminous			
and flax felts, for roofing or damp proof courses, manufacturing	2450/4	469/2	245
paint, manufacturing	2551	274	255
sealants, manufacturing	2562	279/2	256.2
Black			
beer brewing	4283/1	232	428
powder, manufacturing	2565	279/3	256.5
pudding making	4122/3	214/2	412.2
Blackplate			
can, manufacturing	3164/1	395	316.4
manufacturing	2210	311/2	221.2
Blackstone quarry	2310/2	102/1	231.2
Bladder			
dressing	4959	499/2	495.3
processing	4126/2	214/2	412.5
Blancmange powder, manufacturing	4239/5	229/2	423.6
Blank			
aluminium, manufacturing	2245/2	321	224.1
for corrective spectacle lenses, manufacturing	2479/5	463/1	247.4
hosiery, manufacturing	4363/1	417	436.1
Blanket			
cot (outside weaving or knitting establishment) manufacturing	4557	422/1	455.2
electric, manufacturing	3460	368	346
making up (outside weaving or knitting establishment)	4557	422/1	455.2
woollen, manufacturing	4310/3	414/5	431.5
Blast furnace			
gas, manufacturing	2210	311/2	221.1
manufacturing	3245/2	341/2	328.6
Blasting powder, manufacturing	2565	279/3	256.5
Blazer, manufacturing			
boys' (not retail bespoke)	4532	442	453
men's (not retail bespoke)	4532	442	453
women's and girls', tailored (not retail bespoke)	4533	443	453
Bleach works	4370/2	423	437.1
Bleaching			
dyeing or otherwise finishing yarn	4370/2	423	437
machinery (textile) manufacturing	3230/3	335	323.1
Blending of mineral oil	1402	263	140.2
Blinds			
canvas, manufacturing	4556	422/2	455.4
(not shop blind) wooden, manufacturing	4630	471/2	463.2
other than wood, canvas or plastics, manufacturing	4959	499/2	495.3
paper, manufacturing	4728	484/2	472.8
plastics, manufacturing	4836	496	483.1
Blister copper, manufacturing	2246/1	322	224.1
Block			
boiler, manufacturing	2481	461/1	248.1
concrete, manufacturing	2437	469/2	243.2
flooring, clay, manufacturing	2410	461/2	241
for industrial engine, manufacturing	3281/1	334/1	328.1
graphite, manufacturing	2481	461/1	248.1
printing (textile)	4370/2	423	437.3
Blockboard, manufacturing	4620/1	471/1	462.1
Blocking machine, manufacturing	3276	339/2	327.2
Blood			
pudding, manufacturing	4122/3	214/2	412.2
transfusion service	9520	874/1	952
Bloom, manufacturing			
copper	2246/1	322	224.1
steel	2210	311/2	221.1
Blotting paper, manufacturing	4710/6	481	471.3
Blouse, manufacturing	4536/1	445/1	453
Blow			
lamp, manufacturing	3161/2	391	316.1
moulding machine, manufacturing	3275/2	339/9	324.3
Blown glass, manufacturing	2471/1	463/1	247.1
Blowroom machinery (textiles) manufacturing	3230/1	335	323.1
Blue			
brick, manufacturing	2410	461/2	241

BOA-BOW

Activity	SIC 1980	1968	NACE
Cross	9611/1	899/3	961
lias lime kiln	2420	469/2	242.2
pennant stone quarry	2310/2	102/1	231.2
Board			
asbestos, manufacturing	2440	429/1	244
game, manufacturing	4941	494/1	494.1
glass fibre, manufacturing	2479/4	463/1	247.5
(except chipboard) making machinery, manufacturing	3275/4	339/9	327.2
of Schecheta	9660	875	966
Boarding house	6650/2	884	665.3
Boat			
building or repairing, pleasure boats and yachts (less than 100 gross tons)	3610/2	370/1	361.3
hire (without crew, not linked with recreational service)	8480/4	706	845
hire for pleasure	9791/1	882	978
kit, for assembly, manufacturing	3610/2	370/1	361.3
Bobbin, manufacturing			
(not textile accessory) wooden	4650	479/3	465.1
(textile machine accessory)	3230/4	335	323.1
cotton	4321/1	412	432
paper	4728	484/2	472.8
Body building, motor vehicle	3521	381	352
Boiled sugar confectionery, manufacturing	4214/2	217/2	421.2
Boiler			
block, manufacturing	2481	461/1	248.1
breaking, for scrap	6210	832/7	621
central heating, manufacturing	3284/2	339/4	311.1 and 315.1
cleaning and scaling	9230	899/7	923
covering, not asbestos or slag wool, manufacturing	4959	499/2	495.3
drum, manufacturing	3205/1	341/1	315.1
house plant, manufacturing	3205/1	341/1	315.1
insurance	8200/3	860	823
marine engineering, manufacturing	3289/1	370/2	315.1
oil (domestic type) manufacturing	3165	399/12	311.1
packing (not asbestos or slag wool) manufacturing	4959	499/2	495.3
packing, asbestos, manufacturing	2440	429/1	244
solid fuel (domestic type) manufacturing	3165	399/12	311.1
suit, manufacturing	4534	444/1	453
Boilers and associated equipment and parts (not marine or central heating) manufacturing	3205/1	341/1	315.1
Bolster			
case, manufacturing	4557	422/1	455.1
manufacturing	4555	473	455.2
Bolt			
cropper, manufacturing	3161/2	391	316.1
end, manufacturing	3137/1	393	313.1
manufacturing	3137/1	393	313.1
Bomb fuse, manufacturing	3290/2	342	328.9
Bon-bon, paper, manufacturing	4728	484/2	472.8
Bonded			
fabric (main fabric woven) manufacturing	4310/3	414	431.5
fibre fabric, manufacturing	4399/1	429/2	439.2
store, vault or warehouse	7700/3	709/2	773
Bonding			
clays, foundry, manufacturing	2567	271/3	256.7
fabric to fabric	4370/1	423	437.4
Bone			
boiling (by knackers)	4126/3	221	412.4
crushing (by knackers)	4126/3	221	412.4
degreasing (by knackers)	4126/3	221	412.4
flour (from knackers) manufacturing	4126/3	221	412.5
glue, manufacturing	2562	279/2	256.2
meal (from knackers) manufacturing	4126/3	221	412.5
oil, manufacturing	4126/1	221	411.4
raw (from knackers) production	4126/3	899/7	412.5
scraping (by knackers)	4126/3	221	412.4
sorting (by knackers)	4126/3	221	412.4
working	4959	499/2	495.3
Book			
cloth weaving	4322	413	432.5
printing	4753/3	489	473.2
printing-publishing	4753/2	489	473.2
publishing	4753/1	489	474.1
repairing	4754/5	489	473.3
Bookbinding	4754/5	489	473.3
Bookbinding machine, manufacturing	3276	339/2	327.2
Bookcase, manufacturing	4671/2	472	467.1
Bookcase, metal, manufacturing	3166/1	399/1	316.6
Bookkeeping machine, manufacturing	3301	338	330
Bookkeeping service	8360	871	836
Bookmaker	9791/2	883	979
Bookseller, retail	6530	821/4	653.1
Boot			
and shoe board, manufacturing	4710/9	481	471.3
and shoe pattern making and designing	4510	450	451.1
and shoe tip and protector (malleable casting) manufacturing	3111	313/4	311.1
closing	4510	450	451.1
lace, braided, manufacturing	4398/2	421/3	439.3
last, iron, manufacturing	3111	313/3	311.1
manufacturing	4510	450	451.1
stiffener, manufacturing	4510	450	451.4
tree, wooden, manufacturing	4650	479/2	465.1
upper, manufacturing	4510	450	451.4
wellington, manufacturing	4510	450	481.2
Bootblack	9890/2	899/7	984
Bootee, rubber protective, manufacturing	4510	450	481.2
Bootees knitted, manufacturing	4363/2	417	436.2
Boots and shoes, retail dealing in	6460	821/2	646.1
Borer (mining machinery) manufacturing	3251	339/1	325.1
Boring			
civil engineering	5020	500	502.3
machine (metal cutting) manufacturing	3221/1	332/1	322.1
Boron carbide abrasive grain, manufacturing	2460	469/1	246
Borough council	9112	906/3	911
Borstal institute	9120	872/5	912
Botany spinning	4310/2	414/5	431.3
Bottle			
cleaning and or drying machinery, manufacturing	3244/2	339/8	324.2
crate, plastics, manufacturing	4835	496	483
glass, manufacturing	2478	463/2	247.2
plastics, manufacturing	4835	496	483
sorting and washing	6220	832/7	622
stopper, glass, manufacturing	2478	463/2	247.2
top, metal, manufacturing	3164/3	399/10	316.4
Bottling			
machinery, manufacturing	3244/2	339/8	324.2
of fruit and vegetables	4147/4	218/3	414
Bovine hides and skins production (from knackers)	4126/3	899/7	412.1
Bow thruster, manufacturing	3289/1	370	361
Bowl, manufacturing			
glass	2479/1	463/1	247
plastics	4836	496	483
Bowling alley	9791/1	882	978
Bowls			
and bowls equipment, manufacturing	4942	494/3	494.2

BOX-BRI

Activity	SIC 1980	1968	NACE
club	9791/1	882	978
Box			
and willow calf leather, manufacturing	4410/1	431/1	441.3
furnace, manufacturing	3245/2	341/2	328.6
irons, manufacture of iron castings for	3111	313/4	311.1
pallet, manufacturing	4640/1	479/3	464.1
paper, manufacturing	4724/2	482/1	472.4
plastics, manufacturing	4835	496	483
spring mattress, manufacturing	4671/5	473	467.8
wooden, manufacturing	4640/1	475/2	464.1
Boxboard			
folding, manufacturing	4710/7	481	471.3
manufacturing	4610/1	471/1	461.1
Boxed			
game, manufacturing	4941	494/1	494.1
stationery, manufacturing	4723/1	483	472.3
Boxing			
as a sport	9791/1	882	978
glove, manufacturing	4942	494/3	442.2
promoter	9791/1	882	978
Boy scouts	9690/2	899/3	968
Boys'			
blazer (not retail bespoke), manufacturing	4532	442	453
Brigade	9690/2	899/3	968
club	9690/2	899/3	968
jacket (not retail bespoke) manufacturing	4532	442	453
jeans, manufacturing	4534	444/1	453
outerwear, tailored, (not retail bespoke manufacturing	4532	442	453
overall, manufacturing	4534	444/1	453
overcoat (not retail bespoke) manufacturing	4532	442	453
shorts, manufacturing	4532	442	453
suit (not retail bespoke) manufacturing	4532	442	453
trousers, tailored, (not retail bespoke) manufacturing	4532	442	453
waistcoat, tailored, (not retail bespoke) manufacturing	4532	442	453
Braces, manufacturing			
leather	4420/1	432	442.1
not leather or leather substitute	4539/3	449/4	453
Bracket, base metal, manufacturing	3169/3	399/12	316.3
Braid, manufacturing			
elastic	4398/1	421/1	439.4
elastomeric	4398/1	421/1	439.4
textile material	4398/2	421/3	439.3
Braille			
copying	4754/5	489	473.2
printing	4754/5	489	473.2
Brake			
and parts (not brake lining) (motor vehicle) manufacturing	3530	381	353
lining, asbestos, manufacturing	2440	429/1	244
Braking system, locomotive, manufacturing	3620/1	349/3	362.1
Bran production	4160	211/1	416.1
Brass			
bar, manufacturing	2246/2	322	224.2
billet, manufacturing	2246/1	322	224.2
casting, ornamental	3112	399/12	311.2
circle, manufacturing	2246/2	322	312.2
disc, manufacturing	2246/2	322	312.2
foil, manufacturing	2246/2	322	224.2
ingot, manufacturing	2246/1	322	224.2
pipe and pipe fittings, manufacturing	2246/2	322	224.2
powder, manufacturing	2246/2	322	224.2
rod, manufacturing	2246/2	322	224.2

Activity	SIC 1980	1968	NACE
section, manufacturing	2246/2	322	224.2
sheet, manufacturing	2246/2	322	224.2
slab, manufacturing	2246/1	322	224.2
strip, manufacturing	2246/2	322	224.2
tube, manufacturing	2246/2	322	224.2
unwrought, manufacturing	2246/1	322	224.2
Brassiere, manufacturing	4539/1	449/1	453
Brattice cloth, manufacturing	4556	422/2	455.4
Brawn, manufacturing	4122/3	214/2	412.2
Brazing			
equipment, electric, manufacturing	3435	368	343.1
equipment, gas, manufacturing	3289/3	332/3	328.7
lamp, manufacturing	3161/2	391	316.1
Bread			
baking (including rolls)	4196	212	419.1
retailing in	6410	820/2	641.7
Breadboard, manufacturing	4650	479/3	465.1
Breakdown lorry, manufacturing	3510/2	381	351
Breakfast cereal, manufacturing			
cooked	4239/8	211/2	423.8
uncooked	4160	211/2	416.2
Breeches (not retail bespoke) manufacturing	4532	442	453
Breed society	9890/2	899/6	963
Breeze block, manufacturing	2437	469/2	243.2
Brewing			
machinery and plant, manufacturing	3244/1	339/7	324.1
preparations (excluding yeast) manufacturing	2567	271/3	256.8
Briar pipe, manufacture and repair	4959	499/2	495.3
Brick			
alumina, manufacturing	2481	461/1	248.1
bauxite, manufacturing	2481	461/1	248.1
blue, manufacturing	2410	461/2	241
building, unglazed, manufacturing	2410	461/2	241
chrome, manufacturing	2481	461/1	248.1
chromite, manufacturing	2481	461/1	248.1
clay, manufacturing	2410	461/2	241
concrete, manufacturing	2437	469/2	243.2
dolomite, manufacturing	2481	461/1	248.1
engineering, manufacturing	2410	461/2	241
furnace construction	5010	500	501.3
ganister, manufacturing	2481	461/1	248.1
glass, manufacturing	2479/5	463/1	247.4
high alumina, manufacturing	2481	461/1	248.1
kiln construction	5010	500	501.3
magnesite, manufacturing	2481	461/1	248.1
magnesite-chrome, manufacturing	2481	461/1	248.1
quarry floor, manufacturing	2410	461/2	241
refractory, insulating, manufacturing	2481	461/1	248.1
refractory, manufacturing	2481	461/1	248.1
sand lime, manufacturing	2437	469/2	243.4
silica, manufacturing	2481	461/1	248.1
siliceous, manufacturing	2481	461/1	248.1
sillimanite, manufacturing	2481	461/1	248.1
Bricklaying	5010	500	501
Brickmaking machine, manufacturing	3275/5	339/9	325.3
Bridge			
building	5020	500	502.3
instructor	9791/3	882	979
steelwork, manufacturing	3204/2	341/4	314.1
wooden, manufacturing	4630	471/2	463.1
Bridgelayer (tracked-military) manufacturing	3290/3	342	328.9
Bridle cutting	4420/1	432	442.1
Brief (women's) manufacturing	4536/2	445/2	453
Bright steel bar, manufacturing	2235	311/2	223.2
Brine pit	2330	109/3	233.2
Briquette, solid fuel, manufacturing	1115	261/2	111.2
Bristle dressing for brushes	4663	493	466.3
Bristles (from knackers) production	4126/3	899/7	412.5
Bristol board, manufacturing	4710/3	481	471.3

Activity	SIC 1980	1968	NACE
Britannia			
metal, founding	3112	323	311.2
metal, manufacturing	2247/1	323	224.2
metalware, manufacturing	4910/3	396	491.3
British			
Airports Authority	7640	707	764
Association for the Advancement of Science	9631/1	879/3	963
Broadcasting Corporation	9741/1	881/2	974
Computer Society	9631/1	871/3	963
Council	9111	899/4	968
Dental Association	9631	879/3	963
Humanist Association	9660	899/3	966
Jews Society	9660	875	966
Legion (other than social club)	9690/2	899/3	968
Medical Association	9631/1	879/3	963
Museum	9770	899/4	977
Railways Board	7100	701	710
Safety Council	9690/2	899/4	968
Sugar Corporation	4200	216	420.1
Telecom	7902	708	790
Tourist Authority	9690/1	901/6	967
Transport Docks Board	7630	706	763
Waterways Board	7610/2	706	762
wine, manufacturing	4261/1	239/2	425.1
Broach (for metal-working machine tools) manufacturing	3222/1	390	322.2
Broaching machine (metal-cutting) manufacturing	3221/1	332/1	322.1
Broadcaster (agricultural machinery) manufacturing	3211/1	331	321.1
Broadcasting station, radio or television	9741/1	881/2	974
Broadmoor Hospital	9510	874/1	951
Brocade weaving	4322	413	432.5
Brochure			
printing	4753/3	489	473.2
printing-publishing	4753/2	489	473.2
publishing	4753/1	489	474.1
Bromine and bromides, manufacturing	2511	271/1	251
Bronze			
founding (general)	3112	322	311.2
founding (ornamental)	3112	399/12	311.2
unwrought, manufacturing	2246/1	322	224.2
Broom			
handle, wooden, manufacturing	4650	479/3	465.1
manufacturing	4663	493	466.3
Broth			
canned, containing meat or vegetables or both, manufacturing	4239/6	218/3	423.7
powdered, containing meat or vegetables or both, manufacturing	4239/6	218/3	423.7
Brown saddlery, manufacturing	4420/1	432	442.1
Brown stone pottery, manufacturing	2489/3	462/3	248.6
Brush			
(not electrical), part of machine, manufacturing	4663	493	466.3
back, wooden, manufacturing	4650	479/3	465.1
carbon, manufacturing	3435	469/2	343.1
case, not leather or plastics, manufacturing	4959	499/2	495.3
dental, manufacturing	3720/2	493	372.3
head, wooden, manufacturing	4650	479/3	465.1
manufacturing	4663	493	466.3
top, wooden, manufacturing	4650	479/3	465.1
wood-ware, manufacturing	4650	479/3	465.1
Brushless shaving cream, manufacturing	2581	275	258.1
Brussels carpet, manufacturing	4384	419	438.1
Bucket			
canvas, manufacturing	4556	422/2	455.4
construction machinery, manufacturing	3254/1	336	325.4
metal, manufacturing	3167	399/6	316.7
plastics, manufacturing	4836	496	483
rubberised fabric, manufacturing	4812/3	491/2	481.2
wheel reclaimer, manufacturing	3255/1	337/1	325.5
wooden, manufacturing	4640/2	475/1	464.2
Buckingham Palace	9111	901/6	911
Buckle, metal, manufacturing	3169/1	399/8	316.9
Buckram shape, manufacturing	4537/2	446/2	453
Buckskin, manufacturing	4410/1	431/1	441.3
Buff and mop, leather, manufacturing	4420/2	432	442.3
Buffalo pickers, leather, manufacturing	4420/2	431/1	442.3
Buffet licensed	6611/1	885	661
Buhl cutting	4910/3	396	491.3
Builder and contractor	5000	500	500.1
Builder's knife, manufacturing	3161/2	391	316.1
Builders'			
carpentry and joinery, manufacturing	4630	471/2	463.2
hoist, manufacturing	3255/4	337/4	325.5
woodwork (window frames, etc) manufacturing	4630	471/2	463.2
Building			
board, asbestos, manufacturing	2437	469/2	243.1
board, asbestos cement, manufacturing	2437	469/2	243.1
board, bituminised, manufacturing	4710/8	481	472.5
board, fibre, manufacturing	4620/1	471/1	462.2
board, made from wood paste, manufacturing	4620/1	471/1	462.2
board, paper, manufacturing	4710/8	481	472.5
brick, clay, manufacturing	2410	461/2	241
brick, unglazed, manufacturing	2410	461/2	241
component, industrialised, timber, manufacturing	4630	471/2	463
contractor	5000	500	500.1
maintenance and restoration	5010	500	501.5
plaster, manufacturing	2420	469/2	242.3
products, plastics, manufacturing	4834	496	483
Research Establishment	9400	876	940
society	8150/1	862	813.1
stone, decorated, manufacturing	2450/3	469/2	245
Built-in furniture, manufacturing	4671/2	472	463.2
Bulb			
for vacuum flask inner, manufacturing	2479/5	463/1	247.2
glass, manufacturing	2479/2	463/1	247.4
growing	0100/2	001/3	01
Bulk carrier (cargo ship) manufacturing	3610/1	370/1	361.1
Bullion			
broker	8310	862	831
dealer	8310	862	831
gold and silver, manufacturing	2247/2	396	224.1
Bung, wooden, manufacturing	4640/2	475/1	464.2
Bunk bed, manufacturing	4671/5	472	467.1
Bunk bed, metal, manufacturing	3166/1	399/1	316.6
Bunker, of heavy steel plate, manufacturing	3205/3	341/5	314.1
Bunting			
cotton weaving	4322	413	432.5
making up only, manufacturing	4556	422/1	455.4
woollen	4310/3	414/5	431.5
Buoy, manufacturing			
not plastics	3610/1	370/1	361.2
plastics	4836	496	483
Buoyancy apparatus, cork, manufacturing	4664/1	479/1	466.1
Bureau de Change	8310	862	831
Burette, glass, manufacturing	2479/3	463/1	247.7
Burgh council	9112	906/3	911
Burglar alarm			
and system, manufacturing	3433	367/1	343.1

BUR-CAN

Activity	SIC 1980	1968	NACE
hire	8490	832/10	847
Burner, manufacturing			
gas	3284/5	399/9	328.6
oil fuel	3284/5	349/3	328.6
Burning oil, manufacturing	1401	262	140.1
Bus			
bar, manufacturing	3420/3	361/2	342
body, manufacturing	3521	381	352
manufacturing	3510/2	381	351
service	7210/2	702/1	721.2
station (not managed directly by public service vehicle operator)	7610/1	709/1	761
Bush (for bearing) manufacturing	3261/2	349/1	326.1
Bushy Park	9770	901/6	977
Business			
agency	8395/4	865	839.3
consultant	8395/1	865	839.1
Education Council	9330	872/4	933
transfer agent	8395/4	865	839.3
Butadiene, manufacturing	2512	271/2	251
Butane			
extraction (from natural gas)	1300	104	132
manufacturing	1401	262	140.1
Butchers shop	6410	820/2	641.4
Butter			
blending	4130/2	215/2	413.1
dish, metal, manufacturing	3167	392	316.7
knife, manufacturing	3162/1	392	316.2
manufacturing	4130/2	215/2	413.1
milk, manufacturing	4130/2	215/2	413.1
oil, manufacturing	4130/2	215/2	413.1
Butterfat, manufacturing	4130/2	215/2	413.1
Butterfly valve, manufacturing	3288	333/2	328.8
Butterscotch, manufacturing	4214/2	217/2	421.2
Button			
and button mould, plastics, manufacturing	4836	496	483
carding	4959	499/2	495.3
covering	4959	499/2	495.3
glass, manufacturing	2479/5	463/1	247.4
metal, manufacturing	3169/2	399/8	316.9

C

Activity	SIC 1980	1968	NACE
Cab hire	7220	702/2	722
Cabinet			
case, wood, manufacturing	4671/4	472	467.5
component, plastics, manufacturing	4836	496	483
for non-domestic electronic apparatus, manufacturing	3444	364/3	344
making	4671/4	472	467.5
metal, manufacturing	3166/1	399/12	316.6
plastics	4836	496	483
Cable			
accessory, manufacturing	3410	362	341
aluminium conductor, steel reinforced, manufacturing	2245/2	394	224.3
cloth, manufacturing	2569	491/2	438.3
conduit, clay, manufacturing	2410	461/2	241
drum, metal, manufacturing	3164/5	399/7	316.4
insulated, electrical, manufacturing	3410	362	341
jointing material, manufacturing	3410	362	341
laying	5020	500	502.7
making machine, manufacturing	3286/3	339/9	328.9
service	7902	708	790
sheathing, aluminium, manufacturing	2245/2	321	224.3
ship, manufacturing	3610/1	370/1	361.1
telecommunication, manufacturing	3410	362	341
textile material, manufacturing	4396	416	439.6
uninsulated, of aluminium, manufacturing	2245/2	321	224.3
wire, steel, manufacturing	2234	394	223.4
Cableway			
excavator, manufacturing	3255/1	337/1	325.5
manufacturing	3255/1	337/1	325.5
Cadmium			
copper, unwrought, manufacturing	2246/1	322	224.2
manufacturing	2247/1	323	224.1
Cafe			
licensed	6611/1	885	661
unlicensed	6611/2	885	661
Cafeteria, unlicensed	6611/2	885	661
Cage plant (mining) manufacturing	3251	339/1	325.1
Caisson, manufacturing	3610/1	370/1	361.2
Cake			
board, manufacturing	4728	484/2	472.8
making	4196	212	419.3
mixture, manufacturing	4239/5	229/2	423.6
Calcareous cement, manufacturing	2420	464	242.1
Calcium			
and calcium compounds, manufacturing	2511	271/1	251
carbide, manufacturing	2511	271/1	251
Calculating machine			
manufacturing	3301	338	330
office, retail dealing in	6530	821/4	653.3
Calculator, electronic, manufacturing	3301	338	330
Calender			
for rubber or plastics working, manufacturing	3275/2	339/9	324.3
printing	4754/4	489	473.2
Calendering			
machinery (textile) manufacturing	3230/3	335	323.1
textile	4370/2	423	437.4
Calico			
printers' designer	9760	879/5	976
printers' engraving	4754/5	489	473.4
printing	4370/2	423	437.3
weaving	4322	413	432.5
Calorifier, manufacturing	3284/2	339/4	328.4
Calves' foot jelly, manufacturing	4122/3	214/2	412.2
Calvinistic Methodist Church	9660	875	966
Cambric weaving	4322	413	432.5
Camel hair			
spinning	4310/2	414/2	431.3
weaving	4310/3	414/3	431.5
Camera			
hire	8460/2	832/10	847
(still and cine) manufacturing	3733	351	373.3
television, manufacturing	3443	367/2	344
Camp furniture, wooden, manufacturing	4671/2	472	467
Camping site operator	6670/1	884	667.2
Camshaft (motor vehicle engine) manufacturing	3530	381	353
Camshaft (not for motor vehicle, etc. engine) manufacturing	3261/3	349/3	326.1
Can			
aerosol, metal, manufacturing	3164/1	395	316.4
and box, aluminium, manufacturing	3164/1	395	316.4
metal, manufacturing	3164/1	395	316.4
Canal			
carrier	7260/3	706	730
cruiser, manufacturing	3610/2	370/1	361.3
operating	7610/2	706	762
Cancer Research Fund	9400	874/1	940
Candelabra, base metal, manufacturing	3167	392	316.7
Candied peel, manufacturing	4147/3	218/1	421.2
Candle, manufacturing	2599	275	259.4
Cane			
chair, manufacturing	4671/2	472	467.7

Activity	SIC 1980	1968	NACE
furniture, manufacturing	4671/2	472	467.7
preparation	4664/2	475/1	466.2
splitting and weaving	4664/2	475/1	466
working	4664/2	475/1	466
Canister, plastics, manufacturing	4835	496	483
Canned			
broth, containing meat or vegetables or both, manufacturing	4239/6	218/3	423.7
pudding, including rice pudding, manufacturing	4239/5	229/2	not classified
soup, containing meat or vegetables or both, manufacturing	4239/6	218/3	423.7
Canning			
machinery, manufacturing	3244/2	339/8	324.2
of fish	4150/2	214/2	415.2
of fruit and vegetables	4147/4	218/3	414.6
Canoe, manufacturing	3610/2	370/1	361.3
Canvas			
bag, manufacturing	4556	422/2	455.4
bucket, manufacturing	4556	422/2	455.4
goods, manufacturing	4556	422/2	455.4
sack, manufacturing	4556	422/2	455.4
shute, manufacturing	4556	422/2	455.4
stretcher, manufacturing	4959	499/2	495.3
tube (for ventilation) manufacturing	4556	422/2	455.4
weaving	4340/2	413	434.5
Cap			
and closure, plastics, manufacturing	4835	496	483
for bottle, plastics, manufacturing	4835	496	483
for petrol, oil or radiator (motor vehicle) manufacturing	3530	381	353
paper, manufacturing	4728	484/2	472.8
peak, manufacturing	4537/2	446/2	453
Capacitor			
for electronic apparatus, manufacturing	3444	364/3	344
for power factor improvement, manufacturing	3420/1	361/1	342
Cape, fur, manufacturing	4560	433	456.3
Capeline, felt, manufacturing	4537/1	446/1	453
Capstan, manufacturing	3255/4	337/4	325.5
Capsule			
medicinal, manufacturing	2570	272	257
metal, manufacturing	3164/3	399/10	316.4
Capsuling machinery, manufacturing	3244/2	339/8	324.2
Car			
and van tyre, manufacturing	4811	491/1	481.1
battery, manufacturing	3432/2	369/3	343.2
body, manufacturing	3521	381	352
clock, manufacturing	3740	352	374
delivery service (by independent contractors)	7230	703	723
delivery service (by motor manufacturers)	7230	704	723
hire, self drive	8480/1	702/2	844
KD set (at least 50 per cent of value of complete vehicle) manufacturing	3510/1	381	351
(3 or 4 wheeled) manufacturing	3510/1	381	351
park	7610/1	709/1	761
park construction	5020	500	502
polish, manufacturing	2599	279/1	259.2
Caramel			
not sweets, manufacturing	4200	216	420.3
sweets, manufacturing	4214/2	217/2	421.2
Caravan			
chassis, manufacturing	3522	381	352
manufacturing	3523	381	352
retail dealing in	6510	894	651.1
site (holiday) operator	6670/1	884	667.2
site owner (not for holidays)	8500	863	850

Activity	SIC 1980	1968	NACE
Carbine, military, manufacturing	3290/1	342	328.9
Carbon			
black, manufacturing	2511	271/1	251
brush, manufacturing	3435	469/2	343.1
decolouring or other activating (except wood charcoal) manufacturing	2511	271/1	251
dioxide, manufacturing	2567	271/1	256.1
disulphide, manufacturing	2511	271/1	251
manufacturing	2511	271/1	251
paper, manufacturing	4954/2	495/2	259.3
paper stencil, manufacturing (e.g. for spirit duplicator)	4728	484/2	472.8
product (not carbon paper or electrical carbon) manufacturing	2450/4	469/2	245.5
ribbon, manufacturing	4954/2	495/2	259.3
Carbonated soft drink, manufacturing	4283/1	232	428.2
Carbonising base paper, manufacturing	4710/3	481	471.3
Carbonisation, coal, manufacturing	1200	261/1	120
Carbonless copy paper, manufacturing	4954/2	495/2	259.3
Carboy, glass, manufacturing	2478	463/2	247.2
Carburettor			
(for industrial engine) manufacturing	3281/1	334/1	328.1
and parts (motor vehicle) manufacturing	3530	381	353
Card			
cutting for index cards	4723/2	483	472.3
embossing	4754/5	489	473.3
tape reader (for textile machinery) manufacturing	3230/2	335	323.1
Cardboard			
box making machine, manufacturing	3276	339/2	327.2
container and canister, manufacturing	4725/3	482/1	472.4
manufacturing	4710/7	481	471.3
toy, manufacturing	4941	494/1	494.1
tube (not packed) manufacturing	4728	484/2	472.8
Carded			
fibre, asbestos, manufacturing	2440	429/1	244
sliver (textiles industry) preparation	4310/1	414/1	431.2
Cardigan, knitted, manufacturing	4363/2	417	436.2
Carding			
machinery, manufacturing	3230/1	335	323.1
of trimmings	4398/2	421/3	439.3
Careers office (local education authority)	9112	906/3	911
Cargo			
ship, manufacturing	3610/1	370/1	361.1
sling, manufacturing	4396	416	439.6
superintendent	7630	706	763
Carnival article, manufacturing	4941	494/1	494.1
Carpenter (not mainly engaged on building site)	4650	479/3	not classified
Carpenter's drill, manufacturing	3161/2	391	316.1
Carpentry			
not structural	5040	500	504.3
structural	5010	500	501.7
Carpet			
cleaning	9812	893	981
fittings, metal, manufacturing	3169/3	399/8	316.3
jute, manufacturing	4350/2	415	438.1
making machinery, manufacturing	3230/2	335	323.1
mat, pile, weaving	4384/1	419	438.1
pile yarn (spun on the cotton system) manufacturing	4321/2	412	432.4
pile yarn (spun on the woollen, worsted and semi-worsted systems) manufacturing	4310/2	414	431.3
pile, weaving	4384/1	419	438.1
shampoo appliance (not domestic electric) manufacturing	3286/1	339/9	328.9

CAR-CAT

Activity	SIC 1980	1968	NACE
soap, manufacturing	**2581**	275	258.1
sweeper, manufacturing	**3286/1**	339/9	328.9
tiles, retail dealing in	**6470**	821/3	647.1
tufted, manufacturing	**4384/2**	419	438.1
underlay, plastics, manufacturing	**4832**	496	483
underlay, rubber, manufacturing	**4812/3**	491/2	481.2
weaving	**4384/2**	419	438.1
wilton, manufacturing	**4384/1**	419	438.1
wire, ferrous, manufacturing	**2234**	394	223.4
Carpeting, needleloom, manufacturing	**4385/1**	429/2	438.1
Carpets			
retail dealing in	**6470**	821/2	647.1
wholesale dealing in	**6160**	812/4	616.9
Carrier			
(for general hire or reward)	**7230**	703	723.2
sports goods, manufacturing	**4942**	494/3	442.1
Carry cot, manufacturing	**3650/1**	473	365.1
Cart cover, canvas, manufacturing	**4556**	422/2	455.4
Cartage contractor	**7230**	703	723.2
Carton			
board, manufacturing	**4725/3**	482/1	472.4
making machine, manufacturing	**3276**	339/2	327.2
Cartoning machine, manufacturing	**3244/2**	339/8	324.2
Cartoonist	**9760**	879/5	976
Cartridge			
case, manufacturing	**3290/2**	342	328.9
primer, manufacturing	**3290/2**	342	328.9
refill for fountain pen, manufacturing	**4954/1**	495/1	495.1
Case			
clock and watch, manufacturing	**3740**	352	374
for cutlery, instruments, etc., leather, manufacturing	**4420/1**	432	442.1
for cutlery, not leather or plastics, manufacturing	**4959**	499/2	495.3
jewel, not wood or metal, manufacturing	**4959**	499/2	495.3
opener, manufacturing	**3161/2**	391	316.1
packing machinery, manufacturing	**3244/2**	339/8	324.2
pipe, not leather or plastics, manufacturing	**4959**	499/2	495.3
spectacle, not leather or plastics, manufacturing	**4959**	499/2	495.3
typewriter, leather, manufacturing	**4420/1**	432	442.1
violin, not wooden, manufacturing	**4959**	499/2	495.3
Case-hardening	**3138**	399/11	313.5
Case-making materials, manufacturing	**4710/4**	481	471.3
Casein			
based adhesive, manufacturing	**2562**	279/2	256.2
resins, manufacturing	**2514**	276/1	251
Casement cloth weaving	**4322**	413	432.5
Casement, metal, manufacturing	**3142**	399/2	314.2
Cash			
and carry wholesale, predominantly food	**6170**	810/1	617
and credit card imprinting and embossing machine, manufacturing	**3301**	338	330
box, manufacturing	**3166/2**	399/3	316.6
dispenser, manufacturing	**3301**	338	330
register hire	**8430**	832/10	843
register, manufacturing	**3301**	338	330
Cashmere weaving	**4310/3**	414/3	431.5
Casing (sausage) production	**4126/2**	214/2	412.5
Casino	**9791/2**	883	979
Cask			
head, wooden, manufacturing	**4640/2**	475/1	464.2
metal, manufacturing	**3164/2**	399/7	316.4
wooden, manufacturing	**4640/2**	475/1	464.2
Cassock, manufacturing	**4532**	442	453
Cast products, manufacturing			
concrete product	**2437**	469/2	243.2
glass	**2471/1**	463/1	247.1

Activity	SIC 1980	1968	NACE
iron bath	**3111**	313/4	311.1
iron chair for railway track	**3111**	313/3	311.1
iron cistern	**3111**	313/4	311.1
iron cooker	**3111**	313/4	311.1
iron, domestic hot water boiler	**3111**	313/4	311.1
iron fire bar	**3111**	313/3	311.1
iron floor plate	**3111**	313/4	311.1
iron gate	**3111**	313/4	311.1
iron grating	**3111**	313/4	311.1
iron hollow-ware	**3111**	313/4	311.1
iron paving	**3111**	313/4	311.1
iron pipe	**3111**	313/4	311.1
iron radiator	**3111**	313/4	311.1
iron rainwater guttering	**3111**	313/4	311.1
iron rainwater pipe	**3111**	313/4	311.1
iron range	**3111**	313/4	311.1
iron stove	**3111**	313/4	311.1
iron tunnel segment	**3111**	313/3	311.1
stone units, precast concrete	**2437**	469/2	243.2
Castable, refractory, manufacturing	**2481**	461/1	248.1
Casting			
boxes, manufacture of iron castings for	**3111**	313/4	311.1
die, non-ferrous base metal, manufacturing	**3112**	not classified	311.2
ferrous, manufacturing	**3111**	313/3	311.1
gravity, non-ferrous base metal, manufacturing	**3112**	not classified	311.2
grenade, manufacturing	**3111**	313/3	311.1
iron, manufacturing	**3111**	313/3	311.1
malleable, manufacturing	**3111**	313/3	311.1
non-ferrous base metal, manufacturing	**3112**	not classified	311.2
pot, manufacturing	**2481**	461/1	248.1
pressure die, non-ferrous base metal, manufacturing	**3112**	not classified	311.2
sand, non-ferrous base metal, manufacturing	**3112**	not classified	311.2
steel, manufacturing	**3111**	311/2	311.1
Castings machines (for foundries) manufacturing	**3286/2**	339/9	325.2
Castor			
oil processing	**4116/3**	221	411.4
seed crushing	**4116/2**	221	411.3
sugar, manufacturing	**4200**	216	420.2
Cat food, manufacturing	**4222/1**	219	422
Catalyst, industrial, manufacturing	**2567**	271/3	256.7
Catamaran, manufacturing	**3610/2**	370/1	361.3
Catapult (aircraft launching device) manufacturing	**3640**	383/4	364
Catch, door and window, manufacturing	**3169/3**	399/12	316.3
Catering			
contractor	**6640/1**	888	664
cooking appliance, commercial, non-electric, manufacturing	**3165**	399/12	316.5
equipment, manufacturing	**3435**	368	343.1
Catgut, manufacturing	**4959**	499/2	495.3
Catheter, manufacturing	**3720/1**	353	372.2
Cathode ray tube, manufacturing	**3453/1**	364/1	345.1
Catholic Apostle Church	**9660**	875	966
Cats home	**9890/2**	899/7	01
Catseye reflector, manufacturing	**2479/5**	463/1	247.4
Catsup, manufacturing	**4239/6**	218/3	423.7
Cattle			
dip, manufacturing	**2568**	279/4	256.8
farming	**0100/1**	001/1	01

Activity	SIC 1980	1968	NACE
hide leather, manufacturing	4410/1	431/1	441.3
Cautery and light unit, manufacturing	3443	367/2	344
Cavity wall, insulation	5030	500	503.4
Ceiling			
rose, manufacturing	3420/3	369/5	342
tile, manufacturing	4843	496	483
Celestite pit	2396	109/4	239.4
Cello, manufacturing	4920/2	499/1	492.2
Cellular			
rubber product, manufacturing	4812/3	491/2	481.2
wood panel, manufacturing	4620/1	471/1	462.1
Cellulose products, manufacturing			
acetate	2514	271/2	251
adhesive tape	2569	491/2	259.3
based adhesive	2562	279/2	256.2
ester and ether ester	2514	271/2	251
nitrate	2514	279/3	251
paint	2551	274	255
varnish	2551	274	255
wadding	4710/5	481	471.3
Cement			
block making machine, manufacturing	3275/5	339/9	325.3
dolomite, manufacturing	2481	461/1	248.1
fireclay, manufacturing	2481	461/1	248.1
high alumina, manufacturing	2481	461/1	248.1
manufacturing	2420	464	242.1
marketing company	6310	831/2	613.2
portland, manufacturing	2420	464	242.1
processing kiln, manufacturing	3245/2	341/2	328.6
product, manufacturing	2437	469/2	243.2
refractory jointing, manufacturing	2481	461/1	248.1
refractory, manufacturing	2481	461/1	248.1
silica and siliceous, manufacturing	2481	461/1	248.1
Cement-based paint, manufacturing	2437	464	255
Cement-wood product, manufacturing	2437	469/2	243.2
Cemetery	9890/2	899/1	922
Central			
Midwives Board	9631/1	879/3	963
Ordnance Depot	9150	901/5	915
processing unit, computer, manufacturing	3302	366	330
Trustee Savings Bank	8140/3	861	812
Centrifugal			
compressor, manufacturing	3283/1	333/3	328.3
pump, manufacturing	3287	333/1	328.3
Centrifuge (for chemical industry) manufacturing	3245/1	339/9	324.1
Ceramic			
colours, manufacturing	2551	271/3	255
furniture, manufacturing	2489/3	462/3	248.6
glaze, manufacturing	2551	271/3	255
insulating component (electrical) manufacturing	2489/4	462/1	248.8
insulator, manufacturing	2489/4	462/1	248.8
jewellery, manufacturing	4910/3	499/2	491.3
kitchenware, manufacturing	2489/3	462/3	248
making machine, manufacturing	3275/5	339/9	325.3
packaging product, manufacturing	2489/4	462/3	248.9
sanitaryware, manufacturing	2489/2	462/2	248.5
tableware, manufacturing	2489/3	462/3	248
transfer (litho) engraving	4754/5	489	473.4
ware, agricultural, manufacturing	2489/4	462/3	248.9
ware, domestic, manufacturing	2489/3	462/3	248.6
Cereal sausage filler, manufacturing	4197	213	419.5
Chain products, manufacturing			
bag	4910/3	396	491.3
non-precision	3137/3	399/12	313.4
(not articulated transmission)	3137/3	399/12	313.4
plastics	4836	496	483
pulley block	3255/4	337/4	325.5
Chair, manufacturing			
dental	3720/2	353/1	372.3
frame, wooden	4671/2	472	467.3
metal	3166/1	399/1	316.6
non-upholstered	4671/2	472	467.3
seating, cane or wicker	4664/1	475/1	466.2
upholstered	4671/1	472	467.4
Chaise-longue, manufacturing	4671/1	472	467.4
Chalk			
(drawing and writing) manufacturing	4954/1	495/1	259.3
ground, manufacturing	2450/1	469/2	245.1
pit or quarry	2310/3	103	231.3
Chamber of			
agriculture	9631/2	899/6	963
commerce	9631/2	899/6	963
Chamfered wood, manufacturing	4610/2	471/1	461.2
Chamois leather, manufacturing	4410/1	431/1	441.3
Channel impeller pump, manufacturing	3287	333/1	328.3
Charcoal			
activated and unactivated (other than wood charcoal) manufacturing	2511	271/1	251
burning	0200	002	02
Chargé d'affaires	0000	899/5	000
Charitable service	9611/1	899/3	961
Chart			
printing	4754/4	489	473.2
seller	6530	821/4	653.1
Chartered			
Institute of Secretaries	9631/1	879/3	963
secretaries, firm acting as	8395/4	865	839.3
Charwoman (private service)	9900	891/2	990
Chassis			
for caravan, manufacturing	3522	381	352
locomotive, manufacturing	3620/1	384	362.1
motor and parts, manufacturing	3530	381	353
powered invalid carriage, manufacturing	3650	382	365.2
with engine (commercial vehicle) manufacturing	3510/2	381	351
Chauffeur	7220	702/2	722
Check			
issuing company	8150/1	862	812
strap, leather, manufacturing	4420/2	431/1	442.3
trader	8150/1	862	813.1
valve, manufacturing	3288	333/2	328.8
Cheese			
manufacturing	4130/2	215/2	413.1
press, manufacturing	3244/1	339/7	324.1
processed, manufacturing	4130/2	215/2	413.1
wholesale dealing in	6170	810/1	617.4
Chefs' clothing, manufacturing	4534	444/1	453
Chemical			
dresser (seed), for farm use, manufacturing	3211/3	331	321.1
feedstock, manufacturing	1401	262	140.1
industry machinery (other than plant) manufacturing	3245/1	339/9	324.1
process (metal working) machine tool, manufacturing	3221/1	332/4	322.1
woodpulp, manufacturing	4710/1	481	471.1
Chemicals			
photographic, manufacturing	2591	279/7	259.1
specially produced for laboratory use, manufacturing	2567	271/3	256.7
Chemist			
(own account)	8370/2	879/2	837
retail	6430	821/4	644
Chenille, manufacturing	4322	413	432.5
Cheque book printing	4754/3	489	473.2
Cheque-writing and signing machine, manufacturing	3301	338	330

CHE-CIN

Activity	SIC 1980	1968	NACE
Cheroot, manufacturing	4290	240	429
Cherry brandy, production	4240/2	239/1	424.3
Chert quarry	2310/2	102/1	231.2
Chess			
instructor	9791/3	882	979
set, manufacturing	4941	494/1	494.1
Chest			
of drawers, manufacturing	4671/2	472	467.1
wooden, manufacturing	4640/1	475/2	464.1
Chewing gum, manufacturing	4214/2	217/2	421.2
Chicken			
cuts, chilled, production in slaughterhouse	4123/1	214/1	412.3
cuts, fresh, production in slaughterhouse	4123/1	214/1	412.3
cuts, frozen, production in slaughterhouse	4123/1	214/1	412.3
paste, manufacturing	4123/2	214/2	412.3
ready to eat meals, manufacturing	4123/2	214/1	412.3
Chicory root drying, manufacturing	4239/9	229/2	423.2
Chiffon weaving (from yarn spun on the cotton system)	4322	413	432.5
Children's			
bicycle, manufacturing	4941	494/1	494.1
carriage, manufacturing	3650/1	494/2	365.1
dress, manufacturing	4536/3	445/1	453
glove, manufacturing	4538	449/2	453
home	9611/2	899/3	962
hose, manufacturing	4363/1	417	436.1
hospital	9510	874/1	951
outerwear, knitted, manufacturing	4363/2	417	436.2
scooter, manufacturing	4941	494/1	494.1
sock, manufacturing	4363/1	417	436.1
tricycle, manufacturing	4941	494/1	494.1
underclothing, manufacturing	4536/3	445/3	453
underwear, knitted, manufacturing	4363/2	417	436.2
wear, retail dealing in	6450	821/2	645.6
Chimney			
construction	5010	500	501.3
liner, clay, manufacturing	2410	461/2	241
pot, clay, manufacturing	2410	461/2	241
steel, manufacturing	3205/3	341/5	314.1
sweeping	9230	899/7	923
China			
clay pit	2310/6	103	231.7
clay, ground, manufacturing	2450/1	469/2	245.1
retail dealing in	6480	821/3	648.7
stone mine	2310/6	103	231.7
Chintz			
glazing	4370/2	423	437.4
weaving (from yarn spun on the cotton system)	4322	413	432.5
Chipboard			
agglomerated with non-mineral binding substances, manufacturing	4620/1	471/1	462.2
press, manufacturing	3275/1	339/9	327.1
Chiropodist			
NHS	9520	874/5	952
private	9550	874/5	955
Chisel manufacturing			
cold	3161/2	391	316.1
wood	3161/2	391	316.1
Chlorate explosives, manufacturing	2565	279/3	256.5
Chlorinated rubber based paint, manufacturing	2551	274	255
Chlorination plant (water treatment) manufacturing	3245/3	341/2	324.1
Chlorine and chlorides, manufacturing	2511	271/1	251
Chocolate			
and cocoa making machinery, manufacturing	3244/1	339/7	324.1
and sugar confectionery, wholesale dealing in	6170	810/1	617.7
and sweets, retail dealing in	6420	821/1	641.9
confectionery, manufacturing	4214/1	217/1	421.1
couverture, manufacturing	4214/1	217/1	421.1
manufacturing	4214/1	217/1	421.1
Choke and coil (for power) manufacturing	3420/1	361/1	342
Chop house, licensed	6611/1	885	661
Chopped roving and strand, glass fibre, manufacturing	2479/4	463/1	247.5
Christmas			
card printing	4754/4	489	473.2
cracker, manufacturing	4728	484/2	472.8
decorations, paper, manufacturing	4728	484/2	472.8
Chrome			
brick, manufacturing	2481	461/1	248.1
tanning	4410/1	431/1	441.1
Chrome-magnesite shape, manufacturing	2481	461/1	248.1
Chromite brick, manufacturing	2481	461/1	248.1
Chromium			
compounds (excluding prepared pigments) manufacturing	2511	271/1	251
manufacturing	2247/1	323	224.1
pigment, manufacturing	2516	277	251
Chronic sick hospital	9510	874/1	951
Chronometer, manufacturing	3740	352	374
Church	9660	875	966
Church			
Army	9660	875	966
Commission	9660	875	966
furniture, manufacturing	4671/3	472	467.5
in Wales	9660	875	966
Lads' Brigade	9690/2	899/3	968
Missionary Society	9660	875	966
of Christ Scientists	9660	875	966
of England	9660	875	966
of Ireland	9660	875	966
of Scotland	9660	875	966
school	9320	872	932
Churn, manufacturing			
metal	3164/2	399/7	316.4
wooden	4640/2	475/1	464.2
Chutney, pickle, manufacturing	4147/2	218/3	414.3
Cider			
alcoholic, manufacturing	4261/2	239/2	426
apple growing	0100/2	001/3	01
making machinery, manufacturing	3244/1	339/7	324.1
merchant, wholesale	6170	810/1	617.5
non-alcoholic, manufacturing	4283/1	232	428.2
Cigar			
box, wooden, manufacturing	4640/1	475/2	464.1
holder, manufacturing	4959	499/2	495.3
importer, wholesale	6170	812/1	617.6
making machinery, manufacturing	3244/3	339/9	324.1
manufacturing	4290	240	429
merchant, wholesale	6170	812/1	617.6
Cigarette			
holder, manufacturing	4959	499/2	495.3
importer, wholesale	6170	812/1	617.6
lighter, manufacturing	4959	399/12	495.3
making machinery, manufacturing	3244/3	339/9	324.1
manufacturing	4290	240	429
merchant, wholesale	6170	812/1	617.6
paper (uncut, in rolls) manufacturing	4710/6	481	471.3
paper, in booklets, manufacturing	4728	484/2	472.8
retail dealing in	6420	821/1	642.2
tube, manufacturing	4728	484/2	472.8
Cigarillo, manufacturing	4290	240	429
Cigars, retail dealing in	6420	821/1	642.2
Cine camera, manufacturing	3733	351	373.3

Activity	SIC 1980	1968	NACE
Cinema			
club	9711/3	881/1	973
furniture, manufacturing	4671/3	472	467
kiosk	6420	821/1	641/642
projector, manufacturing	3733	351	373.3
public	9711/3	881/1	973
screen, manufacturing	4959	499/2	495.3
seat (upholstered) manufacturing	4671/1	472	467.4
Cinematographic			
equipment, manufacturing	3733	351	373.3
film, sensitized, manufacturing	2591	279/7	259.1
film colouring, developing, printing or repairing	4930	881/1	493.1
Circle, aluminium, manufacturing	2245/2	321	312.2
Circuit			
breaker (power) manufacturing	3420/2	361/2	342
breaker, moulded case, manufacturing	3420/2	361/3	342
protection device, electronic, manufacturing	3444	364/3	344
Circular			
addressing	8395/3	865	839.3
saw (for all materials) manufacturing	3222/1	390	322.2
Circulator pump, manufacturing	3287	333/1	328.3
Circus	9791/3	881/2	979
Cistern			
cast iron, manufacturing	3111	313/4	311.1
float, plastics, manufacturing	4834	496	483
metal (not cast iron) manufacturing	3163	399/7	316.4
plastics, manufacturing	4834	496	483
Citric acid, manufacturing	2512	271/2	251
City			
and Guilds of London Institute	9330	872/4	933
Corporation	9112	906/3	911
Council	9112	906/3	911
Guild (Goldsmiths' Company, Stationers' Company, etc.)	9631/1	879/3	963
Mission	9660	875	966
of London, Corporation of	9112	906/3	911
Civic			
restaurant, licensed	6611/1	885	661
trust	9690/2	899/4	968
Civil			
Aviation Authority	7640	707	764
defence	9130	906/1	913
engineering contractor	5020	500	502.1
engineering machinery hire (without staff)	8420	500	842
Service College	9330	872/5	933
Cladding			
shiplap, plastics, manufacturing	4834	496	483
wall panels, precast concrete, manufacturing	2437	469/2	243.2
Claddings			
external	5010	500	501
internal	5040	500	504.5
Clairvoyant	9890/2	882	984
Clamp, manufacturing	3161/2	391	316.1
Clarification plant (water treatment) manufacturing	3245/3	341/2	324.1
Clay			
agent	6300	832/8	632
brick, manufacturing	2410	461/2	241
building brick, manufacturing	2410	461/2	241
chimney liner, manufacturing	2410	461/2	241
chimney pot, manufacturing	2410	461/2	241
dealing in	6130	832/8	612
drainpipes and fittings, manufacturing	2410	461/2	241
flag, manufacturing	2410	461/2	241
floor quarry and tile unglazed, manufacturing	2410	461/2	241
flooring block, manufacturing	2410	461/2	241
foundry, bonding, manufacturing	2567	271/3	256.7
hollow partition, manufacturing	2410	461/2	241
pit	2310/6	103	231.7
Clean towel company	9811	892	981
Cleaning			
cloth (not of bonded fibre fabric) manufacturing	4557	422/1	455.1
powder (other than detergents and scouring powder) manufacturing	2599	279/1	259.2
preparation, industrial, manufacturing	2567	271/3	256.7
service, factory office or shop	9230	899/7	923
Cleansing department, local authority	9211	906/3	921
Clear gum (confectionery) manufacturing	4214/2	217/2	421.2
Clearing			
agents (photographic) manufacturing	2591	279/7	259.1
house (banking)	8310	861	812
Cleat (for pleasure boat) manufacturing	3610/2	370/1	361.3
Clerical vestment (not retail bespoke) manufacturing	4532	442	453
Climbing			
clothing, weatherproof, manufacturing	4531	441	453
frame, manufacturing	4942	494/3	494.2
Cloak, manufacturing			
men's and boys'	4532	442	453
women's and girls'	4533	443	453
Cloakroom (not railway etc.)	9890/2	899/7	984
Clock			
and watchglass, manufacturing	2479/5	463/1	247.4
case, wooden, manufacturing	4671/4	352	467.5
electric, manufacturing	3740	352	374
manufacturing	3740	352	374
Clog, manufacturing	4510	450	465.4
Closed die forging	3120	399/5	312.1
Closed circuit television equipment, manufacturing	3443	367/2	344
Closing machinery, manufacturing	3244/2	339/8	324.2
Closure, manufacturing			
metal	3164/3	399/10	316.4
plastics	4835	496	483
Cloth			
beetling	4370/2	423	437.4
cap, manufacturing	4537/2	446/2	453
cleaning (not of bonded fibre fabric) manufacturing	4557	422/1	455.1
cotton and similar man-made fibre, manufacturing	4322	413	432.5
crease resisting treatment	4370/2	423	437.4
degreasing	4370/2	423	437.4
dressing	4370/2	423	437.4
dyeing	4370/2	423	437.2
embossing	4370/2	423	437.4
ending and mending	4370/2	423	437.4
finishing	4370/2	423	437.4
fireproofing	4370/2	423	437.4
glove, manufacturing	4538	449/2	453
hat, manufacturing	4537/2	446/2	453
jute, manufacturing	4350	415	435.5
leggings and gaiter, manufacturing	4539/3	449/4	453
linen and union, manufacturing	4340/2	415	434.5
mercerising	4370/2	423	437.4
merchant, wholesale	6160	812/2	616
piece goods, printing	4370/2	423	437.3
proofing	4370/2	423	437.4
rotproofing	4370/2	423	437.4
sensitized, manufacturing	2591	279/7	259.1
shrinking	4370/2	423	437.4
tracing, woven	4322	413	432.5
waterproofing	4370/2	423	437.4

CLO-COK

Activity	SIC 1980	1968	NACE
Clothes			
airer, electric, manufacturing	3460	368	346
brush, manufacturing	4663	493	466.3
dolls', manufacturing	4941	494/1	494.1
hire	8460/2	821/2	846.1
hook, manufacturing	3169/3	399/12	316.3
horse, wooden, manufacturing	4650	479/3	465.1
peg, plastics, manufacturing	4836	496	483
peg, wooden, manufacturing	4650	479/3	465.1
Clothier and outfitter, retail	6450	821/2	645
Clothing			
disposable, manufacturing	4536/1	445/1	453
industrial, manufacturing	4534	444/1	453
leather, manufacturing	4410/1	431/1	441.3
pad, manufacturing	4539/3	449/4	453
paper, manufacturing	4722	not classified	472.2
recreational, weatherproofed, manufacturing	4531	441	453
wholesale dealing in	6160	812/2	616
Clotted cream manufacturing	4130/1	215/2	413.1
Clutch			
and parts, manufacturing (motor vehicle)	3530	381	353
lining, asbestos, manufacturing	2440	429/1	244
not for motor vehicle, etc., manufacturing	3261/3	349/3	326.1
Co-polymers, plastics, manufacturing	2514	276/1	251
Coach			
body, manufacturing	3521	381	352
lace and trimming, manufacturing	4398/2	421/3	439.3
motor, manufacturing	3510/2	381	351
screw, manufacturing	3137/1	393	313.1
Coal			
agent	6300	831/1	632
and coke, retailing	6540	831/1	654.9
bunker, metal, manufacturing	3163	399/7	316.4
carbonization	1200	261/1	120
contractor, opencast	1114	500	111.1
cutter, manufacturing	3251	339/1	325.1
depot, wholesale	6120	831/1	612.3
factor	6300	831/1	632
merchant, wholesale	6120	831/1	612.3
mine (deep or drift)	1113	101	111.1
mining (not opencast)	1113	101	111.1
order office, retail	6540	831/1	654.9
plough, manufacturing	3251	339/1	325.1
preparation	1113	101	111.1
preparation plant, manufacturing	3251	339/1	325.1
recovery (from old dumps etc.)	1114	500	111.1
sack, manufacturing	4556	422/2	455.4
site, opencast	1114	500	111.1
tar (crude, from coke ovens) manufacturing	1200	261/1	120
tar (crude, from gas works) manufacturing	1620	601	162.1
tar (crude) from manufactured fuel plants, manufacturing	1115	261/2	111.2
tar naphtha, manufacturing	2512	271/2	251
tar, refined, manufacturing	2567	271/2	256.7
washing	1113	101	111.1
wholesale dealing in	6120	831/1	612.3
Coastguard	9111	901/6	911
Coasting service (sea transport)	7400/3	705	742
Coat			
fur, manufacturing	4560	433	456.3
hanger, plastics, manufacturing	4836	496	483
hanger, wooden, manufacturing	4650	479/3	465.1
men's and boys', not retail bespoke, manufacturing	4532	442	453
stand, metal, manufacturing	3166/1	399/1	316.6
women's and girls' tailored, not retail bespoke, manufacturing	4533	443	453
Coated			
abrasives, manufacturing	2460	469/1	246
roadstone, manufacturing	2450/1	469/2	245
tarmacadam, manufacturing	2450/1	102	245
Coating			
adhesive, manufacturing	2562	279/2	256.2
machine (bookbinding or paper working) manufacturing	3276	339/2	327.2
machinery (textile) manufacturing	3230/3	335	323.1
woollen, manufacturing	4310/3	414/5	431.5
worsted, weaving	4310/1	414/3	431.5
Coatstand (not domestic) manufacturing	4671/3	472	467.5
Cobalt, manufacturing	2247/1	323	224.1
Cock, manufacturing			
(industrial type)	3288	333/2	328.8
wooden	4640/2	475/1	464.2
Cockle gathering	0300/1	003/1	03
Cocktail cabinet, manufacturing	4671/2	472	467.1
Cocoa			
bean roasting and dressing	4214/1	217/1	421.1
butter, manufacturing	4214/1	217/1	421.1
powder (drinking chocolate, etc.) manufacturing	4214/1	217/1	421.1
Coconut			
fibre mat and matting, manufacturing	4385/3	429/2	438.1
flaked (including dessicated but not sugared) manufacturing	4239/9	229/2	414.6
oil refining	4116/3	221	411.4
shy	9791/3	882	979
Cod liver oil, refining	4116/3	221	411.4
Code, compiling	8395/4	899/7	839.3
Coffee			
bag, manufacturing	4239/1	229/2	423.1
bar, room, saloon or stall	6611/2	885	661
blending	4239/1	229/2	423.1
chicory essence and extract, manufacturing	4239/1	229/2	423.2
essence and extract, manufacturing	4239/1	229/2	423.1
grinding and roasting (not retail)	4239/1	229/2	423.1
percolator, electric, manufacturing	3460	368	346
processing machinery, manufacturing	3244/1	339/7	324.1
table, manufacturing	4671/2	472	467.1
wholesale dealing in	6170	810/1	617.8
Coffer dam, manufacturing	3610/1	370/1	361.2
Coffin			
board, manufacturing	4671/4	479/3	467.6
cloth, manufacturing	4310/3	414/5	431.5
frilling, manufacturing	4398/2	421/3	439.3
manufacturing	4671/4	479/3	467.6
Coiffeur	9820	889	982
Coil, manufacturing			
copper	2246/2	322	224.2
ignition	3434	369/1	343.1
spring (not motor vehicle suspension)	3137/2	399/4	313.2
wide, hot-rolled (other than coil classed as a finished product)	2210	311/2	221.1
Coin			
sorting and coin counting machine, manufacturing	3301	338	330
striking	4910/4	396	491.6
Coins, retail dealing in	6480	821/3	649.6
Coir mat and matting, manufacturing	4385/2	429/2	438.1
Coke			
breeze, hard, manufacturing	1200	261/1	120
foundry, manufacturing	1200	261/1	120.2
hard, manufacturing	1200	261/1	120
merchant wholesale	6120	831/1	612.3
metallurgical, manufacturing	1200	261/1	120.2
oven gas, manufacturing	1200	261/1	120

Activity	SIC 1980	1968	NACE
petroleum, manufacturing	**1401**	262	140.1
wholesale dealing in	**6120**	831/1	612.3
Cola oil refining	**4116/3**	221	411.4
Colander			
metal, manufacturing	**3167**	399/6	316.7
plastics, manufacturing	**4836**	496	483
Cold			
cathode valve, manufacturing	**3453/1**	364/1	345.1
pressing (of base metals)	**3120**	399/12	312.2
stamping (of base metals)	**3120**	399/12	312.2
storage equipment, manufacturing	**3284/1**	339/3	328.5
store	**7700/3**	709/2	773
Collapsible			
boat (not inflatable dinghy) manufacturing	**3610/2**	370/1	361.3
box, wooden, manufacturing	**4640/1**	475/2	464.1
tube, metal, (for packaging) manufacturing	**3164/1**	395	316.4
Collar			
(men's and boys') manufacturing	**4535**	444/2	453
stud, manufacturing	**3169/2**	399/8	316.9
Collating machine (bookbinders) manufacturing	**3276**	339/2	327.2
Collecting society (insurance)	**8200/2**	860	822
College			
of Arms, HM	**9111**	901/6	911
of art	**9330**	872/3	933
of education	**9310**	872/3	931
of music	**9330**	872/3	933
military	**9150**	901/5	915
technical	**9330**	872/3	933
Colliery	**1113**	101	111.1
Collotype printing	**4754/5**	489	473.2
Colognes, manufacturing	**2582**	273	258.2
Colour			
filter (unmounted) manufacturing	**3731**	354/1	373.1
lake, manufacturing	**2516**	277	251
Coloured glass, manufacturing	**2471/2**	463/1	247.6
Colours, manufacturing			
artists	**2551**	274	255
ceramic	**2551**	271/3	255
for food and cosmetics	**2516**	271/3	251
in dry, liquid or paste form	**2516**	277	251
Column			
(fabricated structural steelwork) manufacturing	**3204/2**	341/4	314.1
(process plant) manufacturing	**3205/2**	341/5	324.1
Comb, manufacturing			
horn and tortoise-shell	**4959**	499/2	495.3
textile machinery accessory	**3230/4**	335	323.1
Combers' shoddy (woollen industry) manufacturing	**4310/1**	414/4	439.7
Combination rope, manufacturing	**4396**	416	439.6
Combine			
harvester engine, manufacturing	**3281/1**	334/1	328.1
harvester, manufacturing	**3211/2**	331	321.1
Combing			
leather, manufacturing	**4410/1**	431/1	441.3
machinery (textiles) manufacturing	**3230/1**	335	323.1
Commercial			
artist (own account)	**9760**	879/5	976
artist (private practice)	**8380**	879/5	838
building steelwork, manufacturing	**3204/1**	341/4	314.1
catering cooking appliance, non-electric, manufacturing	**3165**	399/12	316.5
school	**9330**	872/3	933
vehicle body, manufacturing	**3521**	381	352
vehicle contract hire (medium and heavy types) without driver	**8480/3**	703	845
vehicle hire with driver	**7230**	703	723.2
vehicle KD set (at least 50 per cent of value of complete vehicle) manufacturing	**3510/2**	381	351
vehicle park	**7610/1**	709/1	761
vehicle tyre, manufacturing	**4811**	491/1	481.1
Comminution plant (effluent treatment) manufacturing	**3245/3**	341/2	324.1
Commission			
for Racial Equality	**9111**	901/6	911
combing and slubbing (wool)	**4310/1**	414/1	431.2
for the New Towns	**8500**	863	850
mending (textile)	**4370/2**	423	437.4
Common			
conservators	**9112**	906/3	911
local authority or municipally owned	**9791/3**	906/3	979
Commonwealth			
armed forces	**0000**	899/5	000
Development Finance Co., Ltd	**8150/1**	862	813.1
government service	**0000**	899/5	000
Institute	**0000**	899/5	000
Secretariat	**0000**	899/5	000
War Graves Commission	**0000**	899/5	000
Communication centre (civil air)	**7640**	707	764
Communist Party	**9690/2**	899/4	968
Community			
centre	**9690/2**	899/4	968
dental service (administration)	**9111**	874/2	911
dental service (clinics)	**9540**	874/2	954
home (for child offenders)	**9120**	872/5	912
medical service (administration)	**9111**	874/2	911
medical service (clinics)	**9520**	874/2	952
psychiatric nurse (NHS)	**9520**	874/2	952
Companies Registration Office	**9111**	901/6	911
Company			
promoter	**8310**	862	831
registration agent	**8310**	862	831
secretaries (specialist undertakings, acting as)	**8395/4**	865	839.3
Compass			
drawing, manufacturing	**3710**	354/2	371.4
magnetic, manufacturing	**3710**	367/2	371.3
Component for furniture, wooden, manufacturing	**4671/4**	472	467.5
Components, accessories and parts (at plastics processing establishments) manufacturing	**4836**	496	483
Composing room equipment, manufacturing	**3276**	339/2	327.2
Composition, manufacturing			
asbestos	**2440**	429/1	244
cork	**4664/1**	479/1	466.1
Compound			
animal feed, manufacturing	**4221**	219	422
cooking fat, manufacturing	**4115**	229/1	411.5
feeding stuffs, dealing in	**6110**	831/3	611.2
fertilizer, manufacturing	**2513**	278	251
flavour (blended flavour concentrates) manufacturing	**2564**	271/3	256.4
Comprehensive school	**9320**	872/1	932
Compressed air, production and distribution	**1630**	not classified	163
Compressibility testing equipment, manufacturing	**3710**	354/2	371.2
Compression ignition engine (for industrial use) manufacturing	**3281/1**	334/1	328.1
Compression ignition engine (for motor vehicle) manufacturing	**3510/3**	381	351
Compressor			
engine, manufacturing	**3281/1**	334/1	328.1

COM-COO

Activity	SIC 1980	1968	NACE
for refrigerator, manufacturing	3284/1	339/3	328.5
Computer			
bureau	8394	865	839.2
consultancy	8394	865	839.2
dating agency	9890/2	899/7	984
electronic, manufacturing	3302	366	330
hire	8430	832/10	843
peripheral equipment, manufacturing	3302	366	330
store, manufacturing	3302	366	330
system, manufacturing	3302	366	330
Concert			
hall	9741/2	881/2	975
party	9760	881/2	976
Concertina, manufacturing	4920/2	499/1	492.2
Concrete			
block, manufacturing	2437	469/2	243.2
block making machine, manufacturing	3275/5	339/9	325.3
brick, manufacturing	2437	469/2	243.2
dry-mix, manufacturing	2437	469/2	243.2
mixer, manufacturing	3254/2	336	325.4
pipe, manufacturing	2437	469/2	243.2
placing machinery, manufacturing	3254/2	336	325.4
products, precast, manufacturing	2437	469/2	243.2
products, pre-stressed, manufacturing	2437	469/2	243.2
products, reinforced, manufacturing	2437	469/2	243.2
ready-mixed, manufacturing	2436	469/2	243.6
terrazzo floor and wall tile, manufacturing	2437	469/2	243.2
tube, manufacturing	2437	469/2	243.2
work, building	5010	500	501
Condensation, polycondensation and polyaddition products, plastics materials, manufacturing	2514	276/1	251
Condensed milk, manufacturing	4130/3	215/2	413.2
Condenser, manufacturing			
air or water cooled for air conditioning equipment	3284/4	339/4	328.4
for refrigerator	3284/1	339/3	328.5
steam	3205/2	341/5	315.1
vapour—not steam	3205/2	341/5	324.1
Condensing unit (for refrigerator) manufacturing	3284/1	339/3	328.5
Condiment set, metal, manufacturing	3167	392	316.7
Conduit, steel, manufacturing	2220	312	222
Confectioner			
and newsagent	6420	821/1	641.1
and tobacconist	6420	821/1	641/642
tobacconist and newsagent	6420	821/1	641.1
Confectioner's novelty, manufacturing	4214/2	217/2	421.2
Confectionery			
chocolate and sugar, manufacturing	4214	217	421
(medicated) manufacturing	2570	272	257
machinery, manufacturing	3244/1	339/7	324.1
sugar, retail dealing in	6420	821/1	641.9
Confederation of British Industry	9631/2	899/6	964
Confetti, paper, manufacturing	4728	484/2	472.8
Confirming house, export (general or undefined)	6300	812/5	619.7
Conjuring apparatus, manufacturing	4941	494/1	494.1
Conjuror	9760	881/2	976
Conservative			
and Unionist Party	9690/2	899/4	968
association	9690/2	899/4	968
Construction			
equipment engine, manufacturing	3281/1	334/1	328.1
equipment hire (without staff)	8420	500	842
model, manufacturing	4941	494/1	494.1
plant hire with operatives	5000	500	500
Constructional			
engineering	5020	500	502.1
toy, manufacturing	4941	494/1	494.1
Consular office	0000	899/5	000
Consultant civil or structural engineer	8370/1	879/1	837
Consumer credit granting company (not licensed under the Banking Act 1979)	8150/1	862	813.1
Consumers' Association	9690/2	899/7	968
Contact lens, manufacturing	3731	353/2	373.1
Container			
foil, manufacturing	3164/4	395	316.4
for typewriter, radio etc., leather, manufacturing	4420/1	432	442.1
glass, manufacturing	2478	463/2	247
glass, manufactured from tubing, (hygienic and pharmaceutical) manufacturing	2478	463/2	247.7
handling crane, manufacturing	3255/2	337/2	325.5
ship, manufacturing	3610/1	370/1	361.1
transit, plastics, closed, manufacturing	4835	496	483
tubular glass, manufacturing	2478	463/2	247.7
wooden, manufacturing	4640/1	475	464
Continuation school	9330	872/3	933
Continuous			
cast rod, aluminium, manufacturing	2245/2	321	224.3
cast rod, copper, manufacturing	2246/1	322	224.1
cast rod, other base non-ferrous metal, manufacturing	2247/1	323	224.1
filament yarn (man-made fibres) manufacturing	2600	411	260
miner, manufacturing	3251	339/1	325.1
stationery, manufacturing	4723/2	483	472.3
Contract			
car hire	8480/1	702/2	844
cleaning service	9230	899/7	923
Contractors' plant (not hiring), dealing in	6149	832/5	614
Control unit, computer, manufacturing	3302	366	330
Controller of Stamps, Office of	9111	901/6	911
Convalescent			
home (providing medical care)	9510	874/1	951
home (without medical care)	6670/3	874/1	667.4
Convent			
not school or orphanage	9660	875	966
school	9320	872	932
Conversions to ships	3610/1	370/1	361.1
Converter, for computers, manufacturing	3302	366	330
Convertible, furniture, manufacturing	4671	472	467.4
Converting machinery, electrical, manufacturing	3420/3	361/3	342
Conveying plant (hydraulic and pneumatic) manufacturing	3255/1	337/1	325.5
Conveyor			
agricultural, manufacturing	3211/3	331	321.1
and feeder (not for agriculture or mining) manufacturing	3255/1	337/1	325.5
band, leather, manufacturing	4420/2	431/1	442.3
belting, rubber or plastics, manufacturing	4812/2	491/2	481.2
belting, woven, manufacturing	4398/2	421/2	439.3
underground (mining) manufacturing	3251	339/1	325.1
Cooked			
and preserved meat, manufacturing	4122/3	214/2	412.2
meat shop	6410	820/1	641.4
polony, manufacturing	4122/3	214/2	412.2
Cooker, manufacturing			
cast iron	3111	313/4	311.1
electric	3460	368	346
gas	3165	399/9	316.5
oil	3165	399/12	316.5
solid-fuel	3165	399/12	316.5
Cooking			
appliance, commercial catering, non-electric, manufacturing	3165	399/12	316.5

Activity	SIC 1980	1968	NACE
equipment, electric (commercial catering) manufacturing	3435	368	343.1
foil, manufacturing	3164/4	321	316.4
Cooling tower (for air conditioning) manufacturing	3284/4	339/4	328.4
Cooper's product, manufacturing	4640/2	475/1	464.2
Coopers'			
products, reconditioning	4640/2	475/1	464.2
wood, manufacturing	4640/2	475/1	464.2
Cop tube, manufacturing	4728	484/2	472.8
Copper			
bar, manufacturing	2246/2	322	224.2
billet, manufacturing	2246/2	322	224.2
bloom, manufacturing	2246/1	322	224.1
circle, manufacturing	2246/2	322	312.2
coil, manufacturing	2246/2	322	224.2
disc, manufacturing	2246/2	322	312.2
drawn products, manufacturing	2246/2	322	224.2
dealing in	6120	832/1	612.6
extruded products, manufacturing	2246/2	322	224.2
flake, manufacturing	2246/2	322	224.2
foil, manufacturing	2246/2	322	224.2
goods, retail dealing in	6480	821/3	648/649
ingot, manufacturing	2246/1	322	224.1
matte, manufacturing	2246/1	322	224.2
or copper alloy die casting, manufacturing	3112	322	311.2
ore and concentrate extractions and preparations	2100	109/2	212
pipe, manufacturing	2246	322	224.2
pipe blank, manufacturing	2246/2	322	224.2
pipe fittings, manufacturing	2246/2	322	224.2
plate engraver (artist)	9760	879/5	976
plate, printing	4754/5	489	473.2
powder, manufacturing	2246/2	322	224.2
primary, manufacturing	2246/1	322	224.1
refining	2246/1	322	224.1
rod, manufacturing	2246/2	322	224.2
rolled products, manufacturing	2246/2	322	224.2
secondary, manufacturing	2246/1	322	224.1
section, manufacturing	2246/2	322	224.2
semi-manufactures, manufacturing	2246/2	322	224.2
sheet, manufacturing	2246/2	322	224.2
slab, manufacturing	2246/1	322	224.1
smelting	2246/1	322	224.1
stranded wire (uninsulated) manufacturing	2246/2	394	224.2
strip, manufacturing	2246/2	322	224.2
tube, manufacturing	2246/2	322	224.2
tube blank, manufacturing	2246/2	322	224.2
tube fittings, manufacturing	2246/2	322	224.2
tube shell, manufacturing	2246/2	322	224.2
unwrought, manufacturing	2246/1	322	224.1
wire product, uninsulated, manufacturing	2246/2	394	224.2
wire rod, manufacturing	2246/2	322	224.2
wire, uninsulated	2246/2	394	224.2
Copra, coconut, crushing	4116/2	221	411.3
Copying			
equipment, document, manufacturing	3733	351	373.3
machine, xerographic, manufacturing	3733	351	373.3
Copyright Protection Society	9631/2	899/6	963
Copywriter, freelance	8380	865	838
Cord, manufacturing			
elastic	4398/1	421/1	439.4
elastomeric	4398/1	421/1	439.4
Cordage (textile material) manufacturing	4396	416	439.6
Cordial (non-alcoholic) manufacturing	4283/1	232	428.2
Cordite, manufacturing	2565	279/3	256.5
Corduroy weaving (from yarn spun on the cotton system)	4322	413	432.5
Core spun yarn (cotton system) manufacturing	4321/1	412	432.3
Cork			
agglomerated, manufacturing	4664/1	479/1	466.1
buoyancy apparatus, manufacturing	4664/1	479/1	466.1
fender, manufacturing	4664/1	479/1	466.1
insulating material, manufacturing	4664/1	479/1	466.1
life-jacket, manufacturing	4664/1	479/1	466.1
lifebelt, manufacturing	4664/1	479/1	466.1
lifebuoy, manufacturing	4664/1	479/1	466.1
mat, manufacturing	4664/1	479/1	466.1
product, manufacturing	4664/1	479/1	466.1
stopper, manufacturing	4664/1	479/1	466.1
stopper inset, manufacturing	4664/1	479/1	466.1
tile, manufacturing	4664/1	479/1	466.1
tip, manufacturing	4664/1	479/1	466.1
wholesale, dealing in	6150	832/8	615.6
Corn			
chandler	6110	831/3	611.3
exchange	6300	831/3	631
factor	6300	831/3	631
merchant	6110	831/3	611.1
wholesale, dealing in	6110	831/3	611.2
Cornflake, manufacturing	4239/8	211/2	423.8
Cornflour, manufacturing	4239/5	229/2	423.6
Coroner's court	9120	906/3	912
Corporation of Lloyds	8320	860	832
Correlator (optical) manufacturing	3732	354/1	373
Correspondence college			
if specialising in higher education courses	9310	872/3	931
not leading to degree level qualifications	9330	872/5	935
Corrugated			
iron, manufacturing	2235	311/2	223.3
paperboard, manufacturing	4710/7	481	471.3
plate, sheet or strip, aluminium, manufacturing	2245/2	321	224.3
Corselet, manufacturing	4539/1	449/1	453
Corset			
belt, manufacturing	4539/1	449/1	453
cloth weaving (from yarn spun on the cotton system)	4322	413	432.5
lace, manufacturing	4398/2	421/3	439.3
manufacturing	4539/1	449/1	453
Corsetiere, retail dealing in	6450	821/2	645.7
Cosmetic			
brush, manufacturing	4663	493	466.3
manufacturing	2582	273	258.2
Cosmetics, retail dealing in	6430	821/4	644.2
Cost accountant (own account)	8360	871	836
Costume			
designing	9760	879/5	976
jewellery	4910/3	499/2	491.3
lightweight, (dressmade) manufacturing	4536/1	445/1	453
not retail bespoke, manufacturing	4533	443	453
theatrical, manufacturing	4539/3	449/4	453
Cot			
blanket (outside weaving or knitting establishment) manufacturing	4557	422/1	455.2
manufacturing	4671/5	472	467.1
mattress, manufacturing	4671/5	473	467.8
quilt, manufacturing	4557	422/1	455.2
Cots			
(textile machinery accessory) manufacturing	3230/4	335	323;1
dolls', manufacturing	4941	494/1	494.1
Cotter			
manufacturing	3137/1	393	313.1
pin, manufacturing	3137/1	393	313.1

COT-CRI

Activity	SIC 1980	1968	NACE
Cotton			
and man-made fibre cloth, manufacturing	4322	413	432.5
broker	6300	832/4	631
bunting, weaving	4322	413	432.5
carding	4321/1	412	432.3
combing	4321/1	412	432.3
cord and velveteen, finishing	4370/2	423	437.4
dealing in	6110	832/4	611.6
doubling	4321/2	412	432.4
drawing	4321/1	412	432.3
fabric, bleaching, dyeing or otherwise finishing	4370/2	423	437
felt, weaving	4322	413	432.5
fishing net yarn, manufacturing	4321/2	412	432.4
flag, weaving	4322	413	432.5
flock, manufacturing	4322	413	432.5
gaberdine, weaving	4322	413	432.5
lap, sliver, ravings and other intermediate bobbin, manufacturing	4321/1	412	432
opening	4321/1	412	432.3
patch quilt, manufacturing	4557	422/1	455.2
rags, dealing in (including shaking, breaking and opening)	6220	832/7	622
raw, bleaching, dyeing or otherwise finishing	4370/2	423	437
reeling	4321/2	412	432.4
rope, manufacturing	4396	416	439.6
seed crushing (including delinting or cleaning)	4116/2	221	411.3
seed oil, refining	4116/3	221	411.4
silk, etc. embroidery (except lace and apparel)	4557	422/1	455.1
size, dealing in	6120	832/8	612
sorting	4321/1	412	432.3
spinning	4321/1	412	432.3
thread mill	4321/2	412	432.4
warehouse	7700/3	709/2	773
warp, manufacturing	4321/1	412	432.3
waste, bleaching, dyeing or otherwise finishing	4370/2	423	437
waste, dealing in	6220	832/7	622
waste, spinning	4321/1	412	432.3
weaving	4322	413	432.5
wool and tissues, manufacturing	2570	279/6	257
yarn, doubling	4321/2	412	432.4
yarn, gassing	4370/2	423	437.4
yarn, manufacturing	4321/1	412	432.3
yarn, polishing	4370/2	423	437.4
yarn, printing	4370/2	423	437.3
yarn, twisting	4321/2	412	432.4
yarn, warping	4321/2	412	432.4
yarn, winding	4321/2	412	432.4
Couch, manufacturing	4671/1	472	467.4
Council			
for Accreditation of Correspondence Colleges	9330	872/5	935
for National Academic Awards	9310	872/3	931
of Isles of Scilly	9112	906/3	911
of the Stock Exchange	8310	862	831
Counter (shop) manufacturing	4672	474	467.5
Counterpane, manufacturing	4557	422/1	455.2
Counting			
and dating machine, manufacturing	3301	338	330
instrument, e.g. counter (non-electric) manufacturing	3710	338	330
County			
council	9112	906/3	911
court	9120	901/6	912
Coupling for articulated motor vehicle, manufacturing	3530	381	353
Courier	7700/1	709/1	771
Coursing	9791/1	882	978
Court of			
Appeal	9120	901/6	912
Protection	9120	901/6	912
the Lord Lyon	9120	901/6	912
Cover, water proofed, canvas, manufacturing	4556	422/2	455.4
Coving, plastics, manufacturing	4834	496	483
Crabbing machinery (textile) manufacturing	3230/3	335	323.1
Cracker (process plant) manufacturing	3205/2	341/5	324.1
Crafts Advisory Committee	9111	901/6	911
Cramp, manufacturing	3161/2	391	316.1
Crane			
floating, manufacturing	3610/1	370/1	361.2
hook, manufacturing	3169/4	399/12	316.9
lorry, manufacturing	3510/2	381	351
manufacturing	3255/2	337/2	325.5
Cranfield Institute of Technology	9310	872/3	931
Crank wheel (pedal cycle) manufacturing	3634	382	363.2
Crankshaft, manufacturing			
motor vehicle engine	3530	381	353
not for motor vehicle etc. engine	3261/3	349/3	326.1
Crate			
bottle, plastics, manufacturing	4835	496	483
wooden, manufacturing	4640/1	475/2	464.1
Crating and de-crating machinery, manufacturing	3244/2	339/8	324.2
Cravat			
fur, manufacturing	4560	433	456.3
manufacturing	4539/3	449/4	453
Crawler			
loader, manufacturing	3254/1	336	325.4
tractor, manufacturing	3254/1	336	325.4
Crayon, manufacturing	4954/1	495/1	259.3
Cream			
cheese, manufacturing	4130/2	215/2	413.1
manufacturing	4130/1	215/2	413.1
separator, industrial, manufacturing	3244/1	339/7	324.1
soda, manufacturing	4283/1	232	428.2
sterilized, manufacturing	4130/1	215/2	413.1
wholesale dealing in	6170	810/2	617.6
Creamery (not farm or retail shop)	4130/1	215/2	413.1
Creasing machine (bookbinding) manufacturing	3276	339/2	327.2
Creche	9611/1	874/2	961
Credit			
card issuer (not requiring payment in full at the end of each credit period)	8150/1	862	813.1
card issuer (requiring payment in full at the end of each credit period)	8310	862	831
trader (general) retail	6560	821/5	656
unions	8150/1	not classified	not classified
Cremation board	9890/2	906/3	911
Crematorium	9890/2	899/1	984
Creosote, manufacturing	2512	271/2	251
Crepe, woven, manufacturing	4322	413	432.5
Cresylic			
acid, manufacturing	2512	271/2	251
resins, manufacturing	2514	276/1	251
Cretonne, weaving	4322	413	432.5
Cricket			
ball and equipment, manufacturing	4942	494/3	494.2
club	9791/1	882	978
Criminal Investigation Department	9130	906/3	913
Crippleage	9611/2	899/3	962
Cripplegate Institute	9690/2	899/3	968
Crispbread, making	4197	213	419

Activity	SIC 1980	1968	NACE
Crocheted fabric, manufacturing	4363/3	417	436.2
Crockery, hire	8460/2	821/3	846.1
Crop			
and grass drying plant operation by contractor	0100/3	001/2	01
spraying by contractor	0100/3	001/2	01
Cropping machinery (textile) manufacturing	3230/3	335	323.1
Croquet club	9791/1	882	978
Cross-linking adhesive, manufacturing	2562	279/2	256.2
Crown			
Agents for Overseas Governments and Administration	0000	899/5	000
cork, manufacturing	3164/3	399/10	316.4
court	9120	901/6	912
Crucible, manufacturing			
fireclay or graphite	2481	461/1	248.1
plumbago	2481	461/1	248.1
Crude			
benzole (from coke ovens) manufacturing	1200	261/1	120
coal tar (from coke ovens) manufacturing	1200	261/1	120
coal tar (from manufactured fuel plants) manufacturing	1115	261/2	111.2
oil exploration	1300	104	134
oil extraction	1300	104	131
oil refining	1401	262	140.1
steel, manufacturing	2210	311/2	221.1
Crumpet, making	4196	212	419.1
Crusaders' Union	9660	875	966
Crushed pigment colours, manufacturing	2516	277	251
Crusher, food or drink machinery, manufacturing	3244/1	339/7	324.1
Crushing			
machine (mining) manufacturing	3251	339/1	325.1
plant (not for mines) manufacturing	3254/2	336	325.3
Crustaceans, freezing of	4150/1	214/1	415.1
Crystallised fruit, manufacturing	4147/3	218/1	421.2
Crystalliser (for chemical industry) manufacturing	3245/1	339/9	324.1
Cue, billiard, manufacturing	4942	494/3	494.2
Cuff			
link, manufacturing	3169/2	399/8	316.9
men's and boys', manufacturing	4535	444/2	453
Culinary glassware, manufacturing	2479/1	463/1	247
Culm, dealing in	6120	831/1	612.3
Cultivator			
manufacturing	3211/1	331	321.1
tine, manufacturing	3211/1	331	321.1
Cumene, manufacturing	2512	271/2	251
Cup			
and saucer, china or porcelain, manufacturing	2489/3	462/3	248.7
plastics, manufacturing	4836	496	483
Cupboard, manufacturing	4671/2	472	467.1
Cupro-nickel, unwrought, manufacturing	2246/1	322	224.2
Curing machinery (textiles) manufacturing	3230/3	335	323.1
Curios, retail dealing in	6480	821/3	649.6
Curry powder, manufacturing	4239/9	229/2	423.3
Curtain			
cleaning (not lace dressing)	9812	893	981
hook, ring and runner plastics, manufacturing	4836	496	483
loop, manufacturing	4398/2	421/3	439.3
made up, manufacturing	4555	473	455.3
material, retail dealing in	6470	821/2	647
rail and roller and fittings, plastics, manufacturing	4836	496	483
rail and runner, metal, manufacturing	3169/3	399/12	316.3
walling, metal, manufacturing	3142	399/2	314.2
Curtains (made up) retail dealing in	6470	821/2	647
Cushion			
cover, manufacturing	4555	422/1	455.1
manufacturing	4555	473	455.2
Cushioning for upholstery, rubber, manufacturing	4812/3	491/2	481.2
Custard powder, manufacturing	4239/5	229/2	423.6
Customs agent	7700/2	865	772
Cut sole (footwear) manufacturing	4510	450	451.4
Cutlery			
case, not leather, plastics or wooden, manufacturing	4959	499/2	495.3
case, wooden, manufacturing	4671/4	499/2	467.5
domestic, manufacturing	3162/1	392	316.2
gold plated, manufacturing	4910/1	392	491.1
handle, horn, ivory, tortoise-shell etc. manufacturing	4959	499/2	495.3
plastics, manufacturing	4836	496	483
precious metal, manufacturing	4910/1	392	491.2
retail dealing in	6480	821/3	648.6
wholesale dealing in	6150	812/4	615.2
Cutter			
dental, manufacturing	3720/2	353	372.3
for wood, manufacturing	3275/1	339/9	327.1
Cutting			
machine (bookbinding) manufacturing	3276	339/2	327.2
machinery (textiles fabric) manufacturing	3230/3	335	323
machinery (textile fibre) manufacturing	3230/1	335	323.1
machines (for metal) manufacturing	3221	332/1	322.1
oil, manufacturing	1402	263	140.2
or shearing velvet	4370/2	423	437.4
or shearing velveteen	4370/2	423	437.4
torch, manufacturing	3289/3	332/3	328.7
Cyanoacrylate adhesive, manufacturing	2562	279/2	256.2
Cyclamates, manufacturing	2570	272	251
Cycle			
accessories dealer, retail	6540	821/4	651.2
agent, retail	6540	821/4	651.2
and parts, manufacturing	3634	382	363
bag, leather, manufacturing	4420/1	432	442.1
club	9791/1	882	978
dynamo lighting set, manufacturing	3434	369/1	343.1
lamp, manufacturing	3434	369/1	343.1
repairer	6730/3	821/4	671
tyre, manufacturing	4811	491/1	481.1
wholesale dealing in	6190	812/4	619.6
Cyclic hydrocarbons, manufacturing	2512	271/2	251
Cyclohexane, manufacturing	2512	271/2	251
Cyclometer, manufacturing	3634	382	363.2
Cyclotron, manufacturing	3435	367/2	343.1
Cylinder			
board, manufacturing	4725/3	482/1	472.4
direct and indirect, space heating equipment, manufacturing	3284/2	339/4	328.4
for hydraulic equipment, manufacturing	3283/2	333/4	328.3
hardened paper, manufacturing	4724/2	482/1	472.4
head (for industrial engine) manufacturing	3281/1	334/1	328.1
insert, manufacturing	3289/2	349/3	328.9
liner, manufacturing	3289/2	349/3	328.9
pneumatic control equipment, manufacturing	3283/3	333/4	328.3
steel, for compressed or liquefied gas, manufacturing	2220	312	222
Cylindrical roller bearing, manufacturing	3262	349/1	326.2

D-DES

Activity	SIC 1980	1968	NACE
D			
DHSS			
local social security office	9190	901/6	919
reception centre	9611/2	899/3	962
Daily maid	9900	891/2	990
Dairy			
concentrate animal feed, manufacturing	4221	219	422
farming	0100/1	001/1	01
grocers shop, retail	6410	820/1	641.3
machinery and plant (not agricultural) manufacturing	3244/1	339/7	324.1
Dairyman (not farmer) retail	6410	820/2	641.3
Dam construction	5020	500	502.4
Damask			
(not woollen or worsted) weaving	4322	413	432.5
woollen, manufacturing	4310/3	414/5	431.5
worsted, weaving	4310/3	414/3	431.5
Damproofing of buildings	5010	500	501.4
Dance			
band	9760	881/2	976
hall	9791/3	882	979 and 663
Dancing			
(ballroom) academy	9791/3	882	979
master	9791/3	882	979
Dandelion coffee, manufacturing	4239/1	229/2	423.2
Darkroom equipment, manufacturing	3733	351	373.3
Dart, manufacturing	4942	494/3	494.2
Dartboard, manufacturing	4942	494/3	494.2
Dashboard instrument (electric) manufacturing	3434	369/1	343.1
Data			
processing equipment, electronic (other than electronic calculator) manufacturing	3302	366	330
processing equipment (non-electronic) manufacturing	3301	338	330
transmission link (line) manufacturing	3441	363	344
Date stamp and accessories, manufacturing	4954/3	495/2	495.2
Day			
centres for the elderly, the physically or mentally handicapped or the mentally ill	9611/1	874/2	961
continuation school	9330	872/3	933
nursery	9611/1	874/2	961
Day-bed, manufacturing	4671/1	472	467.4
De-aeration plant (water treatment) manufacturing	3245/3	341/2	324.1
De-icing equipment for aircraft, manufacturing	3640	383/4	364
De-sizing machinery (textile) manufacturing	3230/3	335	323.1
De-woolling	4410/2	431/2	431.1
Dealer in securities	8310	862	831
Dealing in industrial materials (general or undefined)	6120	832/9	612
Debt collector	8395/4	865	839.3
Decaffeinated coffee, manufacturing	4239/1	229/2	423.1
Decal printing	4754/4	489	473.2
Decatising machinery (textile) manufacturing	3230/3	335	323.1
Deck			
chair, wooden, manufacturing	4650	479/3	467.3
oil platform, manufacturing	3204/2	314/4	314.1
Decking, ships', manufacturing	3610/1	370/1	361.1
Decompression chamber, manufacturing	3289/1	349/3	371.1
Decorating (buildings)	5040	500	504.4

Activity	SIC 1980	1968	NACE
Decorative			
polyvinyl chloride film and sheet unsupported, manufacturing	4832	492	483
tile, earthenware, glazed, manufacturing	2489/1	462/2	248.3
Decorators' size, manufacturing	2562	279/2	256.2
Deed box, manufacturing	3166/2	399/3	316.6
Deeds, Registry of (Northern Ireland)	9111	901/6	911
Deemster, Isle of Man, Office of	9111	901/6	911
Deep freeze unit (domestic) manufacturing	3460	368	346
Defrosting and demisting equipment (for vehicles) manufacturing	3434	369/1	343.1
Dehydrating			
fruit for human consumption	4147/4	218/3	414.6
of vegetables for human consumption	4147/4	218/3	414.6
potatoes for animal feeding	4222/2	219	422
Delay lines and networks, manufacturing	3444	364/3	344
Delicatessen shop	6410	820/1	641.1
Delivery			
hose, rubber or plastic, manufacturing	4812/1	491/2	481.2
pump, manufacturing	3287	333/1	328.3
Delta metal, unwrought, manufacturing	2246/1	322	224.2
Demolition contracting	5000	500	500.2
Denim weaving	4322	413	432.5
Density measuring equipment, optical, manufacturing	3732	354/1	373.2
Dental			
cement, manufacturing	2570	353/1	257
chair, manufacturing	3720/2	353/1	372.3
cleansing preparation, manufacturing	2582	273	258.2
clinic	9540	874/2	954
college or school	9310	872/3	931
Estimates Board	9111	874/4	911
filling, manufacturing	2570	353/1	257
hospital	9510	874/1	954
instrument, manufacturing	3720/2	353/1	372.3
laboratory instrument and equipment, manufacturing	3720/2	353	372.3
mirror, manufacturing	3720/2	353/1	372.3
practitioner	9540	874/4	954
surgeon (not employed full-time by a hospital)	9540	874/4	954
surgical instrument and equipment, manufacturing	3720/2	353	372.3
Dentist	9540	874/4	954
Denture, manufacturing	3720/3	353	372.4
Deodorant (personal) manufacturing	2582	273	258.2
Deoxidiser, aluminium, manufacturing	2245/2	321	224.1
Department			
for National Savings	9111	901/6	911
for National Savings (Bonds and Stocks Office)	8150/2	861	813.2
for National Savings (Savings bank and Savings Certificate Offices)	8140/3	861	812
of Employment unemployment benefit office	9190	901/6	919
store	6560	821/5	656
Depilatory, manufacturing	2582	273	258.2
Deposit broker	8310	862	831
Derv, manufacturing	1401	262	140.1
Desalination plant (water treatment) manufacturing	3245/3	341/2	324.1
Desiccants (chemical) manufacturing	2567	271/3	256.7
Desiccator, glass, manufacturing	2479/3	463/1	247.7
Design office	8370/2	879	837
Designing			
artist	9760	879/5	976
for calico printing	9760	879/5	976
for textiles or wallpaper printing	9760	879/5	976

Activity	SIC 1980	1968	NACE
Desk			
metal, manufacturing	3166/1	399/1	316.6
tray, metal, manufacturing	3166/1	399/1	316.6
wooden, manufacturing	4671/3	472	467.2
Desserts, with a milk base, manufacturing	4130/3	229/2	413.2
Detention centre	9120	901/6	912
Detergent			
soapless, (formulated) manufacturing	2581	275	258.1
synthetic, manufacturing	2581	275	258.1
Detonating fuse, manufacturing	2565	279/3	256.5
Detonator, manufacturing	2565	279/3	256.5
Developer (photographic) manufacturing	2591	279/7	259.1
Development			
capital company	8150/2	862	813.2
Commission	9111	901/6	911
Devotional article, manufacturing	4959	499/2	495.3
Dextrin			
based adhesive, manufacturing	2562	279/2	256.2
manufacturing	4180	229/2	418.2
Dextrose, manufacturing	4180	229/2	418.2
Diabetic food, manufacturing	4239/4	229/2	423.5
Dial			
for electronic apparatus, manufacturing	3444	364/3	344
telephone, manufacturing	3441	363	344
Dialysis plant (water treatment) manufacturing	3245/3	341/2	324.1
Diamond			
broker	6300	812/4	638
cutting	4910/2	396	491.4
impregnated disc and wheel, manufacturing	2460	469/1	246.2
tipped tool, manufacturing	3222/1	390	322.2
Diaphragm			
pump, manufacturing	3287	333/1	328.3
valve, manufacturing	3288	333/2	328.8
Diary printing	4754/4	489	473.2
Diathermy apparatus, manufacturing	3443	367/2	344
Diatomite bed	2396	109/4	239.4
Dictating machine and accessory, manufacturing	3454/1	365/2	345.1
Die			
casting, aluminium, manufacturing	3112	321	311.2
casting, copper or copper alloy, manufacturing	3112	322	311.2
casting, non-ferrous base metal, manufacturing	3112	not classified	311.2
(for machine tools) manufacturing	3222/1	390	322.2
forging, ferrous metals	3120	399/5	312.1
pellet, manufacturing	3222/1	390	322.2
(press tool) manufacturing	3222/2	390	322.2
sinking, stationery	4754/5	489	473.4
stamping, stationery	4754/5	489	473.4
Die-casting machine (for foundries) manufacturing	3286/2	339/9	325.2
Dielectric heating equipment (electric) manufacturing	3435	367/2	343.1
Diesel			
electric locomotive, manufacturing	3620/1	384	362.1
engine (for industrial use) manufacturing	3281/1	334/1	328.1
locomotive, manufacturing	3620/1	384	362.1
oil, manufacturing	1401	262	140.1
Dietary food (pharmaceutical) manufacturing	2570	272	423.5
Dietetic			
food, excluding milk based, manufacturing	4239/4	229/2	423.5
food, with a milk base, manufacturing	4130/3	215/2	413.2
Differential unit (motor vehicle) manufacturing	3530	381	353
Digger (elevator and shaker) manufacturing	3211/2	331	321
Digital computer, manufacturing	3302	366	330
Dinghy, rubber, manufacturing	4812/3	491/2	481.2
Dining			
chair, non-upholstered, manufacturing	4671/2	472	467.3
chair, upholstered, manufacturing	4671/1	472	467.4
room, unlicensed	6611/2	885	661
table, manufacturing	4671/2	472	467.1
Dinting machine (mining) manufacturing	3251	339/1	325.1
Diode, manufacturing	3453/1	364/1	345.1
Direct			
arc furnace, manufacturing	3245/2	341/2	343.1
dye, manufacturing	2516	277	251
grant school	9320	872/2	932
Directly reduced iron, manufacturing	2210	313/2	221.1
Directory, printing	4754/4	489	473.2
Dirt track (Speedway)	9791/1	882	978
Disc			
abrasive, bonded, manufacturing	2460	469/1	246.1
aluminium, manufacturing	2245/2	321	312.2
cardboard, manufacturing	4728	484/2	472.8
copper, manufacturing	2246/2	322	312.2
diamond impregnated, manufacturing	2460	469/1	246.2
harrow, manufacturing	3211/1	331	321.1
Discharge lamp, manufacturing	3470/1	369/4	347.1
Discharged prisoners' hostel	9611/2	899/3	962
Discount			
broker	8310	861	831
broker (licensed under the banking act 1979)	8140/2	861	not classified
house (licensed under the banking act 1979)	8140/2	861	not classified
Dish manufacturing			
plastics	4836	496	483
wooden	4650	479/3	465.1
Dishwasher (domestic) manufacturing	3460	368	346
Dishwashing machine (commercial catering type) manufacturing	3286/1	339/9	324.1
Disinfectant, manufacturing	2570	279/4	257
Disinfection, service	9211	899/7	921
Dispensing			
chemist	6430	821/4	643
optician	6540	821/4	654.1
optician, wholesale	3731	354/1	373.1
Disperse dye, manufacturing	2516	277	251
Dispersions of synthetic resin, manufacturing	2514	276/1	251
Display			
cabinet (domestic) manufacturing	4671/2	472	467.1
cabinet, refrigerated, manufacturing	3284/1	339/3	328.5
stand, manufacturing	4630	474	463.1
Disposable clothing, manufacturing	4536/1	445/1	453
Dissecting instruments, manufacturing	3720/1	353	372.2
Dissolving chemical wood-pulp, manufacturing	4710/1	481	471.1
Distemper			
brush, manufacturing	4663	493	466.3
manufacturing	2551	274	255
Distillery draff production	4240/1	239	424
Distilling machinery (for potable spirits) manufacturing	3244/1	339/7	324.1
District			
command of armed forces	9150	901/5	915

DIV-DRA

Activity	SIC 1980	1968	NACE
community physician	**9112**	874/2	911
council	**9112**	874/2	911
heating plant	**1630**	602	163
nurse	**9520**	874/2	952
Divan bed, manufacturing	**4671/5**	473	467.1
Divided skirt, lightweight, (dressmade) manufacturing	**4536/1**	445/1	453
Diving			
equipment (breathing apparatus only) manufacturing	**3710**	349/3	371.7
equipment (excluding breathing apparatus) manufacturing	**3289/1**	349/3	371.7
suit, rubber or plastics, manufacturing	**4812/3**	491/2	481.2
Do-it-yourself materials, retail dealing in	**6480**	821/3	648.1
Dobby (textile machinery) manufacturing	**3230/2**	335	323.1
Dock			
authority	**7630**	706	763
floating, manufacturing	**3610/1**	370/1	361.2
gates, steel, manufacturing	**3204/2**	341/4	314.1
leveller, manufacturing	**3255/4**	337/4	325.5
steelwork, manufacturing	**3204/2**	341/4	314.1
Dockside crane, manufacturing	**3255/2**	337/2	325.5
Doctor (unspecified)	**9530**	874/3	953
Document			
copying equipment, manufacturing	**3733**	351	373.3
copying service	**8395/3**	865	839.2
handling machine, manufacturing	**3301**	338	330
shredder, manufacturing	**3301**	338	330
Dog			
biscuit, manufacturing	**4222/1**	219	422
breeding (greyhound for racing)	**9791/1**	882	978
food, manufacturing	**4222/1**	219	422
lead, leather, manufacturing	**4420/1**	432	442.1
soap, manufacturing	**2581**	275	258.1
racing	**9791/1**	882	978
trainer (not greyhounds)	**9791/3**	882	979
Dogs' home	**9890/2**	899/7	01
Doily			
paper, manufacturing	**4728**	484/2	472.8
plastics, manufacturing	**4836**	496	483
textiles, manufacturing	**4557**	422/1	455.1
Doll			
not rubber, manufacturing	**4941**	494/1	494.1
rubber, manufacturing	**4812/3**	491/2	481.2
Dolls'			
clothes, manufacturing	**4941**	494/1	494.1
cots, manufacturing	**4941**	494/1	494.1
houses, manufacturing	**4941**	494/1	494.1
prams, manufacturing	**4941**	494/1	494.1
Dolomite			
brick, manufacturing	**2481**	461/1	248.1
cement, manufacturing	**2481**	461/1	248.1
ground, manufacturing	**2450/1**	469/2	245.1
mine or quarry	**2310/2**	102/1	239.3
Dome light, plastics, manufacturing	**4834**	496	483
Domestic			
aerial, manufacturing	**3453/2**	364/3	345.1
agency	**8395/4**	865	839.3
appliance belting, rubber or plastics, manufacturing	**4812/2**	491/2	481.2
apron, manufacturing	**4536/1**	445/1	453
building steelwork, manufacturing	**3204**	341/4	314.1
ceramic ware, manufacturing	**2489/4**	462/3	248.6
cooking appliance, non-electric, manufacturing	**3165**	399/12	316.5
cutlery, manufacturing	**3162/1**	392	316.2
electrical appliance, manufacturing	**3460**	368	346
electrical appliance, repairing	**6730/1**	368	673
electrical appliances, retail dealing in	**6480**	821/3	648.4

Activity	SIC 1980	1968	NACE
glassware, manufacturing	**2479/1**	463/1	247
heating appliance, non-electric, manufacturing	**3165**	399/12	316.5
hollow-ware, metal, manufacturing	**3167**	399/6	316.7
hollow-ware, plastics, manufacturing	**4836**	496	483
ironmongery, wholesale dealing in	**6150**	812/4	615.2
machinery, wholesale dealing in	**6150**	812/4	615.2
overall, manufacturing	**4536/1**	445/1	453
servant	**9900**	891/1	990
tap and stopcock, manufacturing	**3169/4**	399/12	328.8
woodware, manufacturing	**4650**	479/3	465.1
Door			
fittings, metal, manufacturing	**3169/3**	399/12	316.3
frame, metal, manufacturing	**3142**	399/2	314.2
frame, plastics, manufacturing	**4834**	496	483
frame, wooden, manufacturing	**4630**	471/2	463.2
furniture of plastics (handles, hinges, knobs etc.) for buildings, manufacturing	**4834**	496	483
metal (other than safe door) manufacturing	**3142**	399/2	314.2
motor vehicle, manufacturing	**3530**	381	353
plastics, manufacturing	**4834**	496	483
revolving, manufacturing	**4672**	474	463.2
wooden, manufacturing	**4630**	471/2	463.2
Dosing			
and proportioning pump, manufacturing	**3287**	333/1	328.3
plant (water treatment) manufacturing	**3245/3**	341/2	324.1
Double			
bass, manufacturing	**4920/2**	499/1	492.2
cream, manufacturing	**4130/1**	215/2	413.1
glazing, installation	**5040**	500	504.4
Doubled glass fibre yarn, manufacturing	**4321/2**	412	432.4
Doubling machinery (textile) manufacturing	**3230/1**	335	323.1
Dough making machinery, manufacturing	**3244/1**	339/7	324.1
Dowel pin, manufacturing	**4650**	471/1	465.1
Down, vegetable, manufacturing	**4399/2**	429/2	439.7
Downproof cloth weaving	**4322**	413	432.5
Dozer blade, manufacturing	**3254/1**	336	325.4
Drag			
hounds	**9791/1**	882	978
scraper, manufacturing	**3255/1**	337/1	325.4
Dragline excavator, manufacturing	**3254/1**	336	325.4
Draglines, walking, manufacturing	**3254/1**	336	325.4
Drainpipes			
and fittings, clay, manufacturing	**2410**	461/2	241
dealing in	**6130**	831/2	613.3
metal, manufacturing	**3169/4**	399/12	316.7
plastics, manufacturing	**4834**	496	483
Draper			
retail	**6450**	821/2	645.6
wholesale	**6160**	812/2	616.1
Drapers' valuer	**8395/4**	865	839
Draughts set, manufacturing	**4941**	494/1	494.1
Draughtsman (private practice)	**8370/2**	879/1	837
Draw			
bench (metal forming) manufacturing	**3221/2**	332/2	322.1
knife, manufacturing	**3161/2**	392	316.1
Drawer			
metal, manufacturing	**3166/1**	399/1	316.6
wooden, manufacturing	**4671/3**	472	467.2
Drawing			
ink, manufacturing	**4954/2**	495/2	259.3
instrument, manufacturing	**3710**	354/2	371.4
instrument case, wooden, manufacturing	**4671/4**	499/2	467.5

Activity	SIC 1980	1968	NACE
machine (metal forming) manufacturing	3221	332/2	322.1
machinery (textiles) manufacturing	3230/1	335	323.1
paper, manufacturing	4710/3	481	471.3
pin, manufacturing	3169/2	399/8	316.9
Drawing-office furniture, wooden, manufacturing	4671/3	472	467.2
Drawn			
product, aluminium, manufacturing	2245/2	321	224.3
product, copper, manufacturing	2246/2	322	224.2
sheet glass, manufacturing	2471/1	463/1	247.1
steel, cold, other than steel wire, manufacturing	2235	311/2	223.1
Dredger, manufacturing	3610	370/1	361
Dredging contractor	5020	500	502.4
Dress			
and jacket ensemble, knitted, manufacturing	4363/2	417	436.2
binding	4398/2	421/3	439.3
designing	4536/1	445/1	453
fabric, woven (not wool) manufacturing	4322	413	432.5
glove, fabric, manufacturing	4538	449/2	453
goods, woollen, manufacturing	4310/3	414/5	431.5
goods, worsted, weaving	4310/3	414/3	431.5
material, retail dealing in	6450	821/2	645.6
shield, manufacturing	4539/1	449/4	453
shop	6450	821/2	645
women's knitted, manufacturing	4363/2	417	436.2
Dressed, (line) flax, manufacturing	4340/1	412	434.1
Dressing			
case, leather or leather substitute, manufacturing	4420/1	432	442.1
gown (men's and boys') manufacturing	4535	444/2	453
gown (women's and girls') manufacturing	4536/1	445/1	453
gown cord and girdle, manufacturing	4398/2	421/3	439.3
leather	4410/1	431/1	441.1
surgical, manufacturing	2570	279/6	257
table, manufacturing	4671/2	472	467.1
Dressings			
medicated, manufacturing	2570	279/6	257
sheep and cattle, manufacturing	2570	279/4	257
Dressmaker, retail	6450	821/2	645
Dressmaking (not retail bespoke)	4536/1	445/1	453
Dried			
egg, manufacturing	4239/9	229/2	423.8
fish, wholesale dealing in	6170	810/2	617.9
fruit (except field dried) manufacturing	4147/4	218/3	414.6
fruit, cleaning	4147/4	218/3	414.6
fruit, wholesale dealing in	6170	810/1	617.2
herbs (except field dried) manufacturing	4239/9	218/3	423.3
milk, manufacturing	4130/3	215/2	413.2
vegetables (except field dried) manufacturing	4147/4	218/3	414.6
Drill			
agricultural, manufacturing	3211/1	331	321.1
chuck, manufacturing	3222/3	390	322.2
dental, manufacturing	3720/2	353/1	372.3
powered, portable, manufacturing	3285/2	339/6	343.1
weaving (from yarn spun on the cotton system)	4322	413	432.5
Drilling			
contractor for off-shore oil or gas well	1300	104	502.3
machine (metal cutting) manufacturing	3221/1	332/1	322.1
rig, off-shore (floating) manufacturing	3610/1	370/1	361.1
ship, manufacturing	3610/1	370/1	361.1
Drink processing (including combined processing and packaging or bottling machinery) manufacturing	3244/1	339/7	324.1
Drinking			
chocolate, manufacturing	4214/1	217/1	421.1
glass, manufacturing	2479/1	463/1	247
Dripping, manufacturing	4126/1	221	412.4
Drive shaft (motor vehicle) manufacturing	3530	381	353
Driving belt, leather, manufacturing	4420/2	431/1	442.3
Drop			
forging, ferrous metals	3120	399/5	312.1
stamping, base non-ferrous metals	3120	321, 322 and 323	312.2
stamping, ferrous metals	3120	399/5	312.2
Drug			
manufacturing	2570	272	257
store	6430	821/4	644
Druggist, retail	6430	821/4	643
Druggists'			
sundries, wholesale dealing in	6180	812/4	618.1
sundriesman, wholesale	6180	812/4	618.1
Drugs			
retail dealing in	6430	821/4	643
wholesale dealing in	6180	812/4	618.1
Drum			
container, plastics, manufacturing	4835	496	483
metal, manufacturing	3164/2	399/7	316.4
musical instrument, manufacturing	4920/2	499/1	492.2
wooden, manufacturing	4640/1	475/2	464.1
Dry			
battery (non-rechargeable) manufacturing	3432/1	369/2	343.2
cleaner	9812	893	981
cleaning machinery, manufacturing	3275/6	339/9	327.3
Drying machine, manufacturing			
for chemical industry	3245/1	339/9	328.4
for laundry or dry cleaner	3275/6	339/9	327.3
for textiles	3230/3	335	323.1
Duchess set, manufacturing	4557	422/1	455.1
Duck			
(fresh, chilled, or frozen) slaughtering and dressing	4123/1	214/1	412.3
weaving	4322	413	432.5
Duct, of heavy steel plate, manufacturing	3205/3	341/5	315.2
Ducting, plastics, manufacturing	4834	496	483
Dump truck, manufacturing	3254/1	336	325.4
Dumper, manufacturing	3254/1	336	325.4
Dungarees, manufacturing	4534	444/1	453
Duplicating			
ink, manufacturing	4954/2	495/2	259.3
machine, manufacturing (excluding copiers)	3301	338	330
paper, cut to size, manufacturing	4728	481	472.8
service	8395/3	865	839.2
Dust			
collector (air conditioning equipment) manufacturing	3284/4	339/4	328.4
sheet, manufacturing	4557	422/1	455.1
Dustbin, manufacturing			
metal	3163	399/6	316.4
plastics	4836	496	483
Duster (cleaning cloth; not of bonded fibre fabric) manufacturing	4557	422/1	455.1
Dustman	9211	906/3	921
Dustpan, metal, manufacturing	3167	399/6	316.7
Dustpan, plastics, manufacturing	4836	496	483
Duvet, manufacturing	4557	422/1	455.2

DYE-ELE

Activity	SIC 1980	1968	NACE
Dye			
cycle controller (textile machinery) manufacturing	3230/3	335	323.1
manufacturing	2516	277	251
shoe, manufacturing	2599	279/1	259.2
Dyed lamb (including beaver lamb) manufacturing	4560	433	456.1
Dyeing			
machinery (textiles) manufacturing	3230/3	335	323.1
velvet	4370/2	423	437.2
velveteen	4370/2	423	437.2
Dyeline copying machine, manufacturing	3733	351	373.3
Dyer and cleaner	9812	893	981
Dyes			
(for food, drink and cosmetics) manufacturing	2516	271/3	251
dealing in	6120	832/8	612.7
modified for dyeing acrylic fibres, manufacturing	2516	277	251
Dyesprings (textile machinery accessory) manufacturing	3230/4	335	323.1
Dyework	4370/2	423	437.2
Dynamite, manufacturing	2565	279/3	256.5
Dynamo, manufacturing			
for vehicles	3434	369/1	343.1
lighting set, cycle	3434	369/1	343.1
not for vehicles	3420/1	361/1	342

E

Activity	SIC 1980	1968	NACE
Ear nose and throat			
hospital	9510	874/1	951
specialist (hospital)	9510	874/1	951
specialist (private practice)	9530	874/1	953
Earphone, manufacturing	3453/2	364/3	345.1
Earth			
boring machine, manufacturing	3254/3	336	325.4
colours extraction	2396	103	239.4
leveller, manufacturing	3254/1	336	325.4
mover (construction equipment) manufacturing	3254/1	336	325.4
Earthenware			
domestic, manufacturing	2489/3	462/3	248.6
retail dealing in	6480	821/3	648.7
tile, glazed, manufacturing	2489/1	462/2	248.3
wholesale dealing in	6150	812/4	615.4
Earthmoving contractor	5020	500	502.2
Earths, activated, manufacturing	2567	271/1	256.7
Easel, manufacturing	4671/3	472	467.2
Ebonite, vulcanite or hard rubber goods, manufacturing	4812/3	491/2	481.2
Economic boiler, manufacturing	3205/1	341/1	315.1
Economist (own account)	8395/4	879/2	836
Edible			
offals (processed) production	4126/2	214/2	412.5
oil, manufacturing	4116/3	221	411.4
oil and fat processing machinery, manufacturing	3244/1	339/7	324.1
oils and hard fats, dealing in	6170	832/8	617.4
tallow production	4126/1	221	412.4
Education			
authority (administration only)	9112	872/4	911
committee	9112	872/4	911
Educational			
agency	9890/2	899/7	984
association	9631/2	872/4	963
research	9400	872/4	940
supplies (not furniture) wholesale dealing in	6190	812/3	619
Eel pie shop	6612	885	661
Eels, retail dealing in	6410	820/2	614.5
Eels, wholesale dealing in	6170	810/2	617.9
Effluent treatment plant, manufacturing	3245/3	341/2	324.1
Egg			
box, paper, manufacturing	4724/2	482/1	472.4
box, plastics, manufacturing	4835	496	483
box, wooden, manufacturing	4640/1	475/2	464.1
cup, plastics, manufacturing	4836	496	483
dealer wholesale	6170	810/1	617.4
drying	4239/9	229/2	423.8
hatchery	0100/1	001/1	01
Marketing Board	6170	810/1	617.4
packing station, wholesale	6170	810/1	617.4
pickling	4239/9	229/2	423.8
substitute, manufacturing	4239/9	229/2	423.8
tray, paper, manufacturing	4724/2	482/1	472.4
Ejector			
pump, manufacturing	3287	333/1	328.3
seat for aircraft, manufacturing	3640	383/4	364
Elastic			
and elastomeric fabric, knitted or netted, manufacturing	4364	417	439.4
band, manufacturing	4812/3	491/2	481.2
braid, manufacturing	4398/1	421/1	439.4
cord, manufacturing	4398/1	421/1	439.4
fabric (not more than 30 cm wide) manufacturing	4398/1	421/1	439.4
or elastomeric fabric not more than 30 cm wide, knitted or netted, manufacturing	4364	417	439.4
Elasticity testing equipment, manufacturing	3710	354/2	371.2
Elastomeric			
braid, manufacturing	4398/1	421/1	439.4
cord, manufacturing	4398/1	421/1	439.4
fabric (not more than 30 cm wide) manufacturing	4398/1	421/1	439.4
Electric products, manufacturing			
actuator	3442	354/2	344
bell (other than telephone type)	3433	369/5	343.1
bell apparatus (other than telegraphic or telephonic)	3433	367/1	343.1
car	3510/1	381	351
clock	3740	352	374
cooking equipment (commercial catering)	3435	368	343.1
detonator	2565	279/3	256.5
discharge (metal working) machine tool	3221/1	332/4	322.1
domestic, appliances	3460	368	346
fire	3460	368	346
flash lamp case	3470/2	369/5	347.2
furnace	3245/2	341/2	343.1
horn	3434	369/1	343.1
lamp making machine	3275/5	339/9	325.3
light bulb	3470/1	369/4	347.2
light fittings (other than glassware)	3470/2	369/5	347.2
locomotive	3620/1	384	362.1
motor	3420/3	361/1	342
motor starting and controlling gear	3420/2	361/2	342
portable power tool	3285/2	339/6	343.1
process control equipment	3442	354/2	344
recorder	3442	354/2	344
sign erection and maintenance	5030	500	503.5
torch	3470/2	369/5	347.2
toy train	4941	494/1	494.1
toy-car circuit	4941	494/1	494.1
Electricaire unit, manufacturing	3460	368	346
Electrical			
appliance, domestic, manufacturing	3460	368	346

Activity	SIC 1980	1968	NACE
appliances, accessories and fittings (industrial) wholesale dealing in	6149	812/4	614
appliances, accessories and fittings, retail dealing in	6480	821/3	648.4
carbon, manufacturing	3435	469/2	343.1
conduit, steel, manufacturing	2220	312	222
contractor (construction)	5030	500	503.5
equipment (for vehicles and aircraft) manufacturing	3434	369/1	343.1
equipment installation	3480	not classified	348
fittings and furniture, ceramic, manufacturing	2489/4	462/1	248.8
insulator, glass, manufacturing	2479/5	463/1	247.4
paper, manufacturing	4710/6	481	471.3
sheet steel coated and uncoated, manufacturing	2210	311/2	221.1
wiring (buildings)	5030	500	503.5
Electrically powered commercial vehicle, manufacturing	3510/2	381/1	351
Electricity			
Board	1610/1	602	161
Council	1610/1	602	161
meter, manufacturing	3442	354/2	344
production and distribution	1610/1	602	161
showroom	1610/1	602	161
Electro-			
chemical (metal working) machine tool, manufacturing	3221/1	332/4	322.1
medical equipment, manufacturing	3443	367/2	344
medical pacemaker, manufacturing	3443	367/2	344
medical stimulator, manufacturing	3443	367/2	344
plated nickel silver cutlery, manufacturing	3162/1	392	316.2
slag furnace, manufacturing	3245/2	341/2	343.1
Electrochemical apparatus (industrial) manufacturing	3435	341/2	343.1
Electrocoats paint, manufacturing	2551	274	255
Electrode, welding, manufacturing	3435	332/3	223.4
Electrolysis specialist	9820	889	982
Electrolytic			
chemical process plant, manufacturing	3435	341/2	343.1
copper, manufacturing	2246/1	322	224.1
Electron			
microscope, manufacturing	3454/2	364/1	345.1
optical device, manufacturing	3453/1	364/1	345.1
Electronic			
and telecommunications relay, manufacturing	3444	364/3	344
calculator, manufacturing	3301	338	330
circuit protection device, manufacturing	3444	364/3	344
computer, manufacturing	3302	366	330
counter, manufacturing	3442	354/2	344
equipment (miscellaneous unspecified) manufacturing	3454/2	367	345
filter, manufacturing	3444	364/3	344
flight simulator, manufacturing	3443	367/2	344
musical instrument, manufacturing	4920/2	499/1	492.2
plug, manufacturing	3444	364/3	344
process control equipment, manufacturing	3442	354/2	344
testing equipment, manufacturing	3442	354/2	344
timer (not electronic clock or watch) manufacturing	3442	354/2	344
toys and games (not linked with television set) manufacturing	4941	494/1	not classified
tube, manufacturing	3453/1	364/1	345.1
valve, manufacturing	3453/1	364/1	345.1
Electroplating	3138	399/11	313.5
Electroplating equipment, manufacturing	3435	341/2	343.1
Electrostatic			
copying machine, manufacturing	3733	351	373.3
precipitator, manufacturing	3245/3	341/2	343
Electrotyping	4754/5	489	473.4
Elevator			
agricultural, manufacturing	3211/3	331	321.1
band, leather, manufacturing	4420/2	431/1	442.3
belting (rubber or plastics) manufacturing	4812/2	491/2	481.2
manufacturing	3255/1	337/1	325.5
Embassy	0000	899/5	000
Embossing machine, manufacturing			
paper and board working	3276	339/2	327.2
textiles	3230/3	335	323.1
Embrocation, manufacturing	2570	272	257
Embroidering on made up textile goods, manufacturing	4557	422/1	455.1
Embroidery			
cotton, manufacturing	4321/2	412	432.4
lace, manufacturing	4395	418	439.5
Emery			
cloth, manufacturing	2460	469/1	246.3
paper, manufacturing	2460	469/1	246.3
wheel, manufacturing	2460	469/1	246.1
Emigration agency (not of foreign government, etc.)	9890/2	899/7	984
Employers'			
association or federation	9631/2	899/6	964
representatives	9631/3	899/6	965
Employment			
agency (not government)	8395/4	865	839.3
office	9111	901/6	911
rehabilitation centre	9111	901/6	911
Services Department of the Manpower Services Commission	9111	901/6	911
Emulsion			
adhesive, manufacturing	2562	279/2	256.2
paint, manufacturing	2551	274	255
Emulsions of synthetic resin, manufacturing	2514	276/1	251
Enamel			
glass, manufacturing	2479/5	463/1	247.4
manufacturing	2551	274	255
Enamelled tile, glaze, manufacturing	2489/1	462/2	248.3
Enamelling metals (including vitreous enamelling)	3138	399/11	313.5
Encaustic tile, manufacturing	2489/1	462/2	248.3
Enclosure and associated mounting component (for non-domestic electronic apparatus) manufacturing	3444	364/3	344
End mill, manufacturing	3222/1	390	322.2
Ending and mending (textiles)	4370/2	423	437.4
Engine			
block, finished (motor vehicle) manufacturing	3530	381	353
cleaning waste, dealing in	6220	832/7	622
components, including bearings (motor vehicle) manufacturing	3530	381	353
industrial, (spark or compression ignition) manufacturing	3281	334/1	328.1
internal combustion (motor vehicle) manufacturing	3510/3	381	351
marine, manufacturing	3281/2	370/2	328.1 and 328.2
motor cycle, internal combustion, manufacturing	3633	382	363.2
packing, asbestos, manufacturing	2440	429/1	244
petrol, (industrial) manufacturing	3281/1	334/1	328.1

ENG-FAB

Activity	SIC 1980	1968	NACE
railway vehicle, manufacturing	3281/1	334/1	328.1
spark ignition (industrial) manufacturing	3281/1	334/1	328.1
Engineer			
(civil or structural) consultant	8370/1	879/1	837.1
(other than civil or structural) consultant	8370/2	879/1	837
Engineering			
brick, manufacturing	2410	461/2	241
contractor responsible for complete process plant	3246	341/3	324
drawing, printing and publishing	4754/2	489	473 and 474
Engineers'			
draughtsman (private practice)	8370/2	879/1	837
plant and stores, dealing in	6149	832/5	614
small tools, manufacturing	3222	390	322
stampings and pressings, base non-ferrous metals, manufacturing	3120	321, 322 and 323	312.2
stampings and pressings, ferrous metals, manufacturing	3120	399/12	312.2
Engraver (artist)	9760	879/5	976
Engraving	4754/5	489	473.4
Enlarger, photographic, manufacturing	3733	351	373.3
Enquiry			
agency (business services)	8395/4	899/7	839.3
agent	9890/2	899/7	984
Envelope			
addressing service	8395/3	865	839.3
glass for light bulbs and electronic valves, manufacturing	2479/2	463/1	247.4
making machine, manufacturing	3276	339/2	327.2
manufacturing	4723/1	483	472.3
Episcopal Church in Scotland	9660	875	966
Episcope, manufacturing	3733	351	373.3
Epoxide			
adhesives, manufacturing	2562	279/2	256.2
resins, manufacturing	2514	276/1	251
Epoxides, manufacturing	2512	271/2	251
Epoxy paint, manufacturing	2551	274	255
Equal Opportunities Commission	9111	901/6	911
Eraser, rubber, manufacturing	4812/3	491/2	481.2
Escalator, manufacturing	3255/3	337/3	325.5
Escape chute for aircraft, manufacturing	3640	383/4	364
Escort agency	9890/2	899/7	984
Essential			
oils and essences (other than turpentine) manufacturing	2564	271/3	256.4
oils merchant	6120	832/8	612.7
Established Church	9660	875	966
Estate			
agent	8340	863	834
car, manufacturing	3510/1	381	351
company, owning and managing	8500	863	850
Esters, but not polyesters, manufacturing	2512	271/2	251
Etcher (artist)	9760	879/5	976
Etching (printing industry)	4754/5	489	473.4
Ethane diol (excluding anti-freeze) mixtures, manufacturing	2512	271/2	251
Ethanol, synthetic, manufacturing	2512	271/2	251
Ethyl alcohol (obtained by fermentation) manufacturing	4240/1	271/2	424.1
Ethylene			
glycol (excluding anti-freeze mixtures) manufacturing	2512	271/2	251
manufacturing	2512	271/2	251
European Communities Representatives and Information Office	0000	899/5	000
Evangelist Society	9660	875	966
Evaporated milk production	4130/3	215/2	413.2
Evaporator			
(refrigeration machinery) manufacturing	3284/1	339/3	328.5
manufacturing	3205/2	341/5	324.1
Evening institute	9330	872/3	933
Excavator, manufacturing	3254/1	336	325.4
Exchange broker	8310	862	831
Excursion agency	7700/1	709/1	771
Exhaust system and component (motor vehicle) manufacturing	3530	381	353
Exhauster, manufacturing	3283/1	333/3	328.3
Exhibition			
centre, steelwork, manufacturing	3204/1	341/4	314.1
contracting and organising	8395/2	865	839.3
stand, hire	8490	865	847
stand, manufacturing	4630	474	463.1
Expanded			
metal, manufacturing	3120	399/12	312.2
vermiculite, manufacturing	2450/4	469/2	245.5
Expansion			
joint, rubber, manufacturing	4812/3	491/2	481.2
meter, manufacturing	3710	354/2	371.2
tank, manufacturing	3163	399/6	316.4
Exploration for gas or oil	1300	104	134
Explorer	9760	879/5	976
Explosives			
manufacturing	2565	279/3	256.5
dealing in	6120	832/8	612
Export			
Credits Guarantee Department	8200/3	860	823
finance company (not licensed under the banking act 1979)	8150/1	862	813.1
packer	7700/2	709/1	772
Exposure meter (electric) manufacturing	3442	351	344
Express coach service	7210/2	702/1	721.2
Extruded			
products, copper, manufacturing	2246/2	322	224.2
section, aluminium, manufacturing	2245/2	321	224.3
tube, aluminium, manufacturing	2245/2	321	224.3
Extruder, for rubber or plastics, manufacturing	3275/2	339/9	324.3
Extruding machinery (textiles) manufacturing	3230/1	335	323.1
Extrusion			
aluminium, manufacturing	2245/2	321	224.3
compounds, plastics, manufacturing	2514	276/1	251
ingot, aluminium, manufacturing	2245/1	321	224.1
Eye			
hospital	9510	874/1	951
specialist (hospital)	9510	874/1	951
specialist (private practice)	9530	874/1	953
Eyelet, manufacturing	3169/2	399/8	316.9

F

Activity	SIC 1980	1968	NACE
Fabian Society	9690/2	899/4	968
Fabric manufacturing			
crocheted	4363/3	417	436.2
dress glove	4538	449/2	453
elastic (not more than 30 cm wide)	4398/1	421/1	439.4
elastic and elastomeric	4364	417	439.4
elastomeric (not more than 30 cm wide)	4398/1	421/1	439.4
narrow (not elastic or elastomeric)	4398/2	422/1	439.3
netted	4363/3	417	436.2

Activity	SIC 1980	1968	NACE
pile, knitted	4363/3	417	436.2
sliver knitted	4363/3	417	436.2
sports bag	4942	494/3	442
tufted (other than household textile)	4399/2	429/2	439.7
wallcoverings	4721	484/1	472.1
weft knitted	4363/3	417	436.2
woven, bleached, dyeing or otherwise finishing	4370/2	423	437
Fabricated structural steelwork (for buildings) manufacturing	3204/1	341/4	314.1
Fabrics, clothing, retail dealing in	6450	821/2	645.6
Face powder or cream, manufacturing	2582	273	258.2
Facsimile transmission apparatus, manufacturing	3441	363	344
Factice, manufacturing	2567	271/3	256.7
Factoring company (buying book debts)	8150/1	862	831.1
Factory			
building steelwork, manufacturing	3204/1	341/4	314.1
bus service	7210/2	702/1	721.2
cleaning contractor	9230	899/7	923
letting	8500	863	850
Faculty of Actuaries	9631/1	879/3	963
Fallers (textiles machinery accessory) manufacturing	3230/4	335	323.1
Family			
Planning Association (clinics)	9520	874/2	952
Planning Association (not clinics)	9611/1	899/3	961
Practitioner Committee	9111	874/3	911
Welfare Association	9611/1	899/3	961
Fan			
belt, motor vehicle, manufacturing	4812/2	491/2	481.2
coil unit (for air conditioning equipment) manufacturing	3284/4	339/4	328.4
electric, domestic, manufacturing	3460	368	346
ladies, manufacturing	4539/3	449/4	453
Fancy			
articles and goods, glass, manufacturing	2479/5	463/1	247.4
goods, retail dealing in	6480	821/4	649.5
goods, wholesale dealing in	6190	812/4	619.6
hosiery, manufacturing	4363/1	417	436.1
leather goods, manufacturing	4420/1	432	442.1
paper, manufacturing	4710/6	481	472.7
pastry, manufacturing	4196	212	419.3
Fans, ventilating, manufacturing	3284/3	339/4	328.4
Farm			
dairy machinery, dealing in	6149	832/6	614.6
institute	9330	872/3	933
Farmer's wife			
(if engaged primarily in farm work) farming and stock rearing	0100/1	001/1	01
(if engaged primarily in farm work) market gardening, fruit, flower and seed growing	0100/2	001/3	01
Farming, undefined	0100/1	001/1	01
Farmyard manure spreader, manufacturing	3211/1	331	321.1
Fashion			
agent	9890/2	899/7	984
artist	9760	879/5	976
designing	9760	879/5	976
jewellery, manufacturing	4910/3	499/2	491.3
printing	4754/4	489	473.2
Fastener, metal, manufacturing	3169/2	399/8	316.9
Fat			
and bone collector (own account)	6220	832/7	622
of marine animals production	4116/1	221	411.1
recovery (from knackers)	4126/1	221	412.4
splitting and distilling	2563	275	256.3
Fatstock Marketing Corporation	6110	810/2	611.5
Fatty			
acid, manufacturing	2563	275	256.3
amines and quaternary ammonium salts, manufacturing	2563	275	256.3
Feather			
curling	4959	499/2	495.3
duster, manufacturing	4663	493	466.3
ornament, manufacturing	4539/3	449/4	453
purifying	4959	499/2	495.3
sorting	4959	499/2	495.3
Feathers, dealing in	6110	832/8	611
Feed water heater (for boilers) manufacturing	3205/1	341/1	315.1
Feedstock, manufacturing			
chemical	1401	262	140.1
petroleum	1401	262	140.1
Fellmongery	4410/2	431/2	431.1
Felt			
base floorcovering, printed, manufacturing	4833	492	438.2
bituminous and flax for roofing etc., manufacturing	2450/4	469/2	245
cotton, weaving	4322	413	432.5
glass fibre, manufacturing	2479/4	463/1	247.5
hat (men's) manufacturing	4537/1	446/1	453
hat bleaching and dyeing	4537/1	446/1	453
hat body, making	4537/1	446/1	453
hat, finishing	4537/1	446/1	453
pressed (not paper or roofing) manufacturing	4399/1	414/6	439.1
woven, manufacturing	4399/1	414	439.1
Felt-tipped pen, manufacturing	4954/1	495/1	495.1
Feltboard, including felt paper, manufacturing	4710/9	481	471.3
Felting, rubber, manufacturing	4812/3	491/2	481.2
Felts, bituminous and flax, for roofing and damproof courses, manufacturing	2450/4	469/2	245
Fence			
contractor (not on agricultural sites)	5010	500	501.7
wooden (assembled) manufacturing	4630	479/3	463.2
Fencing			
by agricultural contractor	0100/3	001/2	01
plastics, manufacturing	4834	496	483
pale, manufacturing	4610/1	471/1	461.1
sawn, manufacturing	4610/1	471/1	461.1
wire, steel, manufacturing	2234	394	223.4
Fender, cork, manufacturing	4664/1	479/1	466.1
Fern collecting, cutting, gathering	0200	002	02
Ferrite part for electronic apparatus, manufacturing	3444	364/3	344
Ferro—			
alloy, manufacturing	2247/1	323	224.2
concrete bar bending and fixing contractor	5020	500	502.7
manganese, high carbon, manufacturing	2210	311/2	211.1
Ferrous castings, manufacturing	3111	313/3	311.1
Ferry			
boat, manufacturing	3610/1	370/1	361
boat proprietor, inland waterway service	7260/3	706	730
domestic or coastal route	7400/3	705	742
river or estuary	7260/3	706	730
sea, between United Kingdom and international ports	7400/2	705	742
Fertilizer			
dealing in	6110	831/3	611.3
distributor or broadcaster, manufacturing	3211/1	331	321.1
manufacturing	2513	278	251
phosphatic, straight, manufacturing	2513	278	251
potassic, straight, manufacturing	2513	278	251

FIB-FIS

Activity	SIC 1980	NACE 1968
Fibre		
board packing case, manufacturing	4725/1 482/1	472.4
building board, manufacturing	4620/1 471/1	462.2
core for wire rope, manufacturing	4396 416	439.6
dressing for brushes	4663 493	466.3
glass body shell (motor vehicle) manufacturing	3521 496	352
tipped pen, manufacturing	4954/1 495/1	495.1
vulcanized, manufacturing	4728 484/2	472.8
Fibrillated yarn, manufacturing	4350/3 415	435.3
Figured glass, manufacturing	2471/1 463/1	247.1
File, hand tool, manufacturing	3161/2 391	316.1
Filing cabinet, manufacturing		
metal	3166/1 399/1	316.9
wooden	4671/3 472	467.2
Filling		
and sealing compounds (painters) manufacturing	2551 274	255
machinery, manufacturing	3244/2 339/8	324.2
station (motor fuel and lubricants)	6520 894	652
Film		
and sheet, polyvinyl chloride, decorative, unsupported, manufacturing	4832 492	483
bonded warehouse	7700/3 709/2	773
broker	9711/2 881/1	972
distribution	9711/2 881/1	972
hiring agency	9711/2 881/1	972
laminated plastics, manufacturing	4835 496	483
library	9711/2 881/1	972
photographic, unsensitized, manufacturing	4832 276/1	483
polyethylene, manufacturing	4832 276/1	483
polypropylene, manufacturing	4832 276/1	483
polyvinyl chloride, manufacturing	4832 276/1	483
reader (for textile machinery) manufacturing	3230/2 335	323.1
renting	9711/2 881/1	972
sound track dubbing and synchronisation	9711/1 881/1	971
studios	9711/1 881/1	971
Filter		
cloth (made up) manufacturing	4556 422/2	455.4
cloth weaving	4322 413	432.5
colour (unmounted) manufacturing	3731 354/1	373.1
electronic, manufacturing	3444 364/3	344
paper, manufacturing	4710/6 481	471.3
pneumatic, control equipment, manufacturing	3283/3 333/4	3283
Filtration		
equipment (for chemical industry) manufacturing	3245/1 339/9	324.1
equipment for hydraulic equipment, manufacturing	3283/2 333/4	328.3
Finance		
Corporation for Industry	8150/1 862	813.1
house (licensed under the Banking Act 1979)	8140/2 861	812
house (not licensed under the Banking Act 1979)	8150/1 862	813.1
Financial		
advisor	8360 871	836
agency	8310 862	831
and credit reporting	8395/4 865	839.3
holding company	8150/2 862	813.2
Findings		
and stampings, base metal, for jewellery, manufacturing	4910/3 396	491.3
and stampings, precious metal, for jewellery, manufacturing	4910/1 396	491.1
Fine		
art expert	9760 879/5	976
art, retail dealing in	6480 821/3	649.6
Fingering wool	4310/2 414/5	431.3
Finings, manufacturing	2567 271/3	256.8
Finishing		
machinery (textiles) manufacturing	3230/3 335	323.1
textiles	4370 423	437
yarn	4370/2 423	437.4
Fire		
alarm and system, manufacturing	3433 367/1	343.1
alarm hire	8490 832/10	874
authority	9140 906/2	914
bar, cast iron, manufacturing	3111 313/3	311.1
brigade	9140 906/2	914
electric, manufacturing	3460 368	346
engine, manufacturing	3510/2 381	351
extinguisher, hand held, manufacturing	3169/4 339/9	328.9
extinguishing apparatus, excluding hand operated chemical extinguishers, manufacturing	3286/1 339/9	328.9
extinguishing chemicals, manufacturing	2567 271/3	256.7
gas, manufacturing	3165 399/9	316.5
insurance	8200/3 860	823
oil, manufacturing	3165 399/12	316.5
refined copper, manufacturing	2246/1 322	224.1
screen, manufacturing	4671/2 472	467.5
tender, manufacturing	3510/2 381	351
Firebrick and shape, manufacturing	2481 461/1	248.1
Fireclay		
cement, manufacturing	2481 461/1	248.1
crucible, manufacturing	2481 461/1	248.1
mine or quarry	2310/6 103	231.7
retort, silica and siliceous, manufacturing	2481 461/1	248.1
sanitaryware, manufacturing	2489/2 462/2	248.5
Firelighter, manufacturing	2565 499/2	256.5
Fireplace		
brick, glazed, manufacturing	2489/1 462/2	248.3
tile, glazed, manufacturing	2489/3 462/2	248.3
Firewood, retail dealing in	6540 821/4	654.9
Firework, manufacturing	2565 279/3	256.5
Firing plant for boilers etc., manufacturing	3205/1 341/1	315.1
First school	9320 872/1	932
Fish		
and chip shop	6612 885	661
box, wooden, manufacturing	4640/1 475/2	464.1
breeding	0300/2 003/2	03
cake (fresh) manufacturing	4150/2 214/2	415.2
cake (frozen) manufacturing	4150/1 214/2	415.1
curing (other than by distributors)	4150/2 214/2	415.2
drying	4150/2 214/2	415.2
factor	6300 810/2	637
farming (including hatcheries)	0300/2 003/2	03
fingers (frozen) manufacturing	4150/1 214/2	415.1
hatchery (freshwater)	0300/2 003/2	03
hatchery (sea)	0300/2 003/1	03
hook, manufacturing	4942 399/8	316.9
liver oil (unrefined) production	4116/1 221	411.1
liver oil refining	4116/2 221	411.4
meal, manufacturing	4222/2 219	422
oil (crude) production	4116/1 221	411.1
paste, manufacturing	4150/2 214/2	415.2
processing (not freezing)	4150/2 214/2	415.2
product quick freezing	4150/1 214/1	415.1
quick freezing	4150/1 214/1	415.1
retail dealing in	6410 820/2	641.5
salesman, wholesale	6170 810/2	617.9
salting	4150/2 214/2	415.2
stall	6410 820/2	641.5
wholesale dealing in	6170 810/2	617.9

FIS-FLO

Activity	SIC 1980	1968	NACE
Fish-eater, manufacturing	3162/1	392	316.2
Fish-plate (railway) steel, manufacturing	2210	311/2	221.1
Fisherman—crofter	0300/1	003/1	03
Fishing			
freshwater	0300/2	003/2	03
inland water	0300/2	003/2	03
line	0300/1	003/1	03
line, manufacturing	4396	416	439.6
net, manufacturing	4396	416	439.7
net mending	4396	416	439.7
rivers	0300/2	003/2	03
sea	0300/1	003/1	03
shellfish	0300/1	003/1	03
tackle, manufacturing	4942	494/3	494.2
tackle, retail dealing in	6540	812/4	654.4
vessel, manufacturing	3610/1	370/1	361
Fishmonger			
retail	6410	820/2	641.5
wholesale	6170	810/2	617.9
Fitted toilet case, leather, manufacturing	4420/1	432	442.1
Fittings for tubes and pipes, steel, manufacturing	2220	312	222
Fixer, photographic, manufacturing	2591	279/7	259.1
Fixture (shop) for display and storage of goods, manufacturing	4672	474	467.5
Fixtures (engineers' small tools) manufacturing	3222/3	390	322.2
Flag			
clay, manufacturing	2410	461/2	241
cotton, weaving	4322	413	432.5
(flagstone) merchant	6130	831/2	613.2
making up only, manufacturing	4556	422/1	455.4
woollen, manufacturing	4310/3	414/5	431.5
Flagstone			
precast concrete, manufacturing	2437	469/2	243.2
quarry	2310/2	102/1	231.2
Flake, manufacturing			
aluminium	2245/2	321	224.3
copper	2246/2	322	224.2
Flaked			
coconut (including desiccated but not sugared) manufacturing	4239/9	229/2	414.6
maize production	4160	211/2	416.2
Flannel			
ending	4370/2	423	437.4
filling	4370/2	423	437.4
finishing	4370/2	423	437.4
manufacturing	4310/3	414/5	431.5
preparing	4370/2	423	437.4
scouring	4370/2	423	437.4
shrinking	4370/2	423	437.4
Flannelette			
raising, finishing	4370/2	423	437.4
weaving	4322	413	432.5
Flash lamp			
battery, manufacturing	3432/1	369/2	343.2
bulb, manufacturing	3470/1	369/4	347.1
case, manufacturing	3470/2	369/5	347.2
Flask, vacuum, manufacturing	2479/5	463/2	247.4
Flat			
agency	8340	863	834
glass, manufacturing	2471/1	463/1	247.1
letting	8500	863	850
steel, hot rolled, manufacturing	2210	311/2	221.1
trailer (motor-drawn) manufacturing	3522	381	352
Flatwork machine (for laundry) manufacturing	3275/6	339/9	327.3
Flax			
carding	4340/1	412	434.1
dealing in	6110	832/4	611.6
deseeding	4340/1	412	434.1
dressing	4340/1	412	434.1
growing	0100/1	001/1	01
hackling	4340/1	412	434.1
preparing	4340/1	412	434.1
roughing	4340/1	412	434.1
sorting	4340/1	412	434.1
spinning	4340/1	412	434.3
tow, manufacturing	4340/1	412	434.1
woven cloth, manufacturing	4340/2	413	434.5
yarn, bleaching, dyeing or otherwise finishing	4370/2	423	437
Fleet tender, manufacturing	3610/1	370/1	361.1
Flexible			
packaging, paper, manufacturing	4724/2	482/2	472.4
plastics foam, manufacturing	4832	496	483
shaft driven tool, manufacturing	3285/2	339/6	not classified
tube, steel, manufacturing	2220	312	222
ventilating ducting (textile) manufacturing	4556	422/2	455.4
Flexographic			
ink, manufacturing	2552	279/5	255
printing machine, manufacturing	3276	339/2	327.2
Flight simulator, electronic, manufacturing	3443	367/2	344
Flint			
bed, pit or quarry	2310/2	102/1	231.2
cloth, manufacturing	2460	469/1	246.3
for lighters, manufacturing	2565	399/12	256.5
grit, manufacturing	2450/1	469/1	245.1
paper, manufacturing	2460	469/1	246.3
Float glass, manufacturing	2471/1	463/1	247.1
Floating			
bridge, operating company	7610/2	706	762
crane, manufacturing	3610/1	370/1	361.2
dock, manufacturing	3610/1	370/1	361.2
drilling rig operation (for petroleum or natural gas exploration or production) manufacturing	1300	104	134
harbour, manufacturing	3610/1	370/1	361.2
Flocculating agents (chemicals) manufacturing	2567	271/3	256.7
Flock			
dealing in	6110	832/4	611.6
glass fibre, manufacturing	2479/4	463/1	247.5
Flong paperboard, manufacturing	4710/9	481	471.3
Floor			
cleanser, manufacturing	2581	275	258.1
coverings (not carpets) retail dealing in	6480	821/3	649.1
polish, manufacturing	2599	279/1	259.2
polisher, electric, manufacturing	3460	368	346
quarry and tile, clay, unglazed, manufacturing	2410	461/2	241
rug, jute, manufacturing	4350/2	415	438.1
seal, manufacturing	2599	279/1	259.2
tiles (not carpet) retail dealing in	6480	821/3	649.1
units, precast concrete, manufacturing	2437	469/2	243.2
Flooring			
block, clay, manufacturing	2410	461/2	241
contractor	5040	500	504.5
parquet, manufacturing	4630	471/1	463.3
rubber, manufacturing	4812/3	491/2	481.2
strip, hardwood, manufacturing	4630	471/1	463.3
systems, metal, manufacturing	3204/2	341/1	314.1
wood (not parquet flooring) manufacturing	4610/2	471/1	461.2
Florist, retail	6540	821/4	654.6

FLO-FOU

Activity	SIC 1980	SIC 1968	NACE
Flotation vessel, of steel, for oil platform, manufacturing	3205/3	341/5	314.1
Flour			
confectionery, manufacturing	4196	212	419.3
confectionery machinery, manufacturing	3244/1	339/7	324.1
confectionery, retail dealing in	6410	820/2	641.8
confectionery, wholesale dealing in	6170	810/1	617.9
milling	4160	211/1	416.1
self raising and patent, manufacturing	4160	211/1	416.1
wholesale dealing in	6170	810/1	617.9
Flow measuring and control instrument (non-electronic) manufacturing	3710	354/2	371.2
Flower			
growing	0100/2	001/3	01
pot and tub, plastics, manufacturing	4836	496	483
pot, clay, manufacturing	2489/4	461/2	248.9
retail dealing in	6540	821/4	654.6
salesman, wholesale	6110	812/4	611.4
wholesale dealing in	6110	812/4	611.4
Flowline assembly (hydraulic equipment) manufacturing	3283/2	333/4	328.3
Flue			
brush, manufacturing	4663	493	466.3
tile, clay, manufacturing	2410	461/2	241
Fluid seal, rubber, manufacturing	4812/3	491/2	481.2
Fluorescent			
brightening agent, manufacturing	2516	277	251
tube, manufacturing	3470/1	369/4	347.1
Fluorimeter, manufacturing	3710	354/2	371.2
Fluorine, hydrofluoric acid and fluorides, manufacturing	2511	271/1	251
Fluorspar			
dealing in	6120	832/8	612.5
mine	2396	109/4	239.4
Fluting paper, manufacturing	4710/4	481	471.3
Flux, manufacturing	2567	271/3	256.7
Fly			
dressing, for angling	4942	494/3	494.2
paper, manufacturing	2568	279/4	256.8
Flying			
club	9791/1	882	978
school (for airline pilots)	9330	709/1	933
school (not for airline pilots)	9360	709/1	936
Flywheel (not for motor vehicle etc. engine) manufacturing,	3261/3	349/3	326.1
Foam			
backed fabric, finishing	4370/1	423	437.4
backing (single textile material)	4370/1	423	437.4
backing (textile material sandwich)	4370/1	423	437.4
flexible plastics, manufacturing	4832	496	483
rigid plastics, manufacturing	4832	496	483
rubber, manufacturing	4812/3	491/2	481.2
Foamed slag, manufacturing	2450/4	469/1	245.5
Fodder, dealing in	6110	831/3	611.2
Foil			
aluminium, (not put up as a packaging product) manufacturing	2245/2	321	224.3
copper, manufacturing	2246/2	322	224.2
decorated, embossed or cut to size, metal, manufacturing	3164/4	321	316.4
packaging goods, metal, manufacturing	3164/4	395	316.4
stock, aluminium, manufacturing	2245/2	321	224.3
Folding			
bed, manufacturing	4671/5	472	467.1
boat, rubber, manufacturing	4812/3	491/2	481.2
box, board, manufacturing	4725/3	482/1	472.4
boxboard, manufacturing	4710/7	481	471.3
machinery for paper and board—not for office use, manufacturing	3276	339/2	327.2
perambulator, manufacturing	3650/1	494/2	365.1
Fondant, manufacturing	4214/2	217/2	421.2
Food (manufacturing	4115–4290)		
freezer, domestic, manufacturing	3460	368	346
freezer (over 12 cu. ft.) manufacturing	3284/1	339/3	328.5
mixer, electric, manufacturing	3460	368	346
general, retail dealing in	6410	820/1	641.1
preservative, manufacturing	2599	271/3	259.4
processing (including combined processing and packaging or bottling machinery) manufacturing	3244/1	339/7	324.1
Foot			
clinic	9520	874/2	952
clinic (private)	9550	874/5	955
support, manufacturing	3720/3	353/1	372.4
Football			
Association	9791/1	882	978
bladder, rubber, manufacturing	4812/3	491/2	481.2
case, leather or plastics, manufacturing	4942	494/3	494.2
club and ground	9791/1	882	978
pools	9791/1	883	979
Footwear			
beach, manufacturing	4510	450	451.3
leather, preparation	4410/1	431/1	441.3
making machine, manufacturing	3275/3	339/9	327.4
manufacturing	4510	450	451
parts and accessories, plastics, manufacturing	4836	496	483
repairing machine, manufacturing	3275/3	339/9	327.4
Forage			
dealing in	6110	831/3	611.2
harvester, manufacturing	3211/2	331	321.1
Forcemeat, manufacturing	4239/9	229/2	423.3
Foreign			
armed forces	0000	899/5	000
embassy	0000	899/5	000
exchange dealer (authorised by the Bank of England)	8140/2	862	831
government service	0000	899/5	000
Forestry	0200	002	02
Forestry Commission	0200	002	02
Forging	3120	not classified	312.1
Forging bar, aluminium, manufacturing	2245/2	321	224.3
Forging furnace, manufacturing	3245/2	341/2	328.6
Forging machine (metal-forming) manufacturing	3221/2	332/2	322.1
Fork			
cutlery, manufacturing	3162/1	392	316.2
garden, manufacturing	3161/1	391	316.1
lift truck, engine, manufacturing	3281/1	334/1	328.1
lift truck, manufacturing	3255/5	337/5	325.5
plastics, manufacturing	4836	496	483
Formaldehyde, manufacturing	2512	271/2	251
Forming machine, manufacturing			
for rubber or plastics	3275/2	339	327.1
high energy rate,	3221/2	332/2	322.1
multi-head, glass working	3275/5	339/9	325.3
Formulated pesticide, manufacturing	2568	279/4	256.8
Formwork (civil engineering)	5020	500	502.7
Fortune telling			
fairground	9791/3	882	979
not fairground	9890/2	882	984
Forwarding agents	7700/2	709/1	772
Foundation garment, manufacturing	4539/1	449/1	453
Founding, non-ferrous base metal	3112	not classified	311.2

Activity	SIC 1980	1968	NACE
Foundry			
alloy, aluminium, manufacturing	2245/1	321	224.1
bonding clays, manufacturing	2567	271/3	256.7
coke, manufacturing	1200	261/1	120.2
core binder, manufacturing	2567	271/3	256.7
facing, manufacturing	2567	279/1	256.7
ingot, aluminium, manufacturing	2245/1	321	224.1
moulding pattern, wooden, manufacturing	4650	479/3	465.1
preparation, manufacturing	2567	279/1	256.7
Fountain			
pen, manufacturing	4954/1	495/1	495.1
pen nib, manufacturing	4954/1	495/1	495.1
Fourdrinier, manufacturing	3275/4	339/9	327.2
Frame			
climbing, manufacturing	4942	494/3	494.2
for mattress support, wooden, manufacturing	4671/4	472	467.5
motor cycle, manufacturing	3633	382	363.2
motor tricycle, manufacturing	3633	382	363.2
pedal cycle, manufacturing	3634	382	363.2
pedal tricycle, manufacturing	3634	382	363.2
Franking machine, manufacturing	3301	338	330
Free wheel (pedal cycle) manufacturing	3634	382	363.2
Free-lance journalist	8395/4	879/5	839.3
Freeholder of leasehold property	8500	863	850
Freemasons	9660	899/3	966
Freestone mine or quarry	2310/2	102/1	231.2
Freezer			
domestic, manufacturing	3460	368	346
over 12 cu. ft., manufacturing	3284/1	339/3	328.5
Freight			
broker	7700/2	709/1	772
container, manufacturing	3522	381	315.2
container, hire	8480/4	703	845
contractor	7700/2	709/1	772
French			
chalk, manufacturing	2450/1	469/2	245.1
polish, manufacturing	2551	274	255
Frequency			
converter (not power) manufacturing	3442	354/2	344
meter, manufacturing	3442	354/2	344
Fried fish shop	6612	885	661
Friendly			
society	8200/3	860	823
society (not collecting society)	8200/1	860	821
Frieze cloth, manufacturing	4310/2	414/5	431.5
Frilling, manufacturing	4398/2	421/3	439.3
Fringe (textile materials) manufacturing	4398/2	421/3	439.3
Frozen meal based on meat, manufacturing	4122/2	214/1	412.2
Fruit			
and vegetables commission agent	6300	810/2	637
bowl, wooden, manufacturing	4650	479/3	465.1
cake baking	4196	212	419.3
cordial, manufacturing	4283/1	232	428.2
dropping compound, manufacturing	2568	279/4	256.8
growing (all)	0100/2	001/3	01
jelly (preserve) manufacturing	4147/3	218/1	414.6
juice, manufacturing	4283/2	232	414.4
juice preparation machinery, manufacturing	3244/1	339/7	324.1
loaf baking	4196	212	419
picking and sorting machinery, manufacturing	3211/2	331	321.1
pickling	4147/2	218/3	414.3
pie making	4196	212	419.3
pudding (canned) manufacturing	4239/5	229/2	not classified
pulp, manufacturing	4147/3	218/1	414.5
quick freezing	4147/1	218/2	414.1
retail dealing in	6410	820/2	641.2
salesman, wholesale	6170	810/2	617.2
seller (street)	6410	820/2	641.2
setting compound, manufacturing	2568	279/4	256.8
squash, manufacturing	4283/1	232	428.2
stall keeper	6410	820/2	641.2
syrup, manufacturing	4283/1	232	428.1
wholesale dealing in	6170	810/2	617.2
wine, manufacturing	4261/3	239/2	426
Fruiterer			
retail	6410	820/2	641.2
wholesale	6170	810/2	617.2
Frying pan, manufacturing	3167	399/6	316.7
Fuel			
additive, manufacturing	2567	271/3	256.7
bunker, metal, manufacturing	3163	399/7	316.4
bunkers, leasing of	8490	832/10	847
economiser for boilers, manufacturing	3205/1	341/1	315.1
handling equipment for boilers, manufacturing	3205/1	341/1	315.1
injection equipment (for industrial engine) manufacturing	3281/1	334/1	328.1
oil, manufacturing	1401	262	140.1
oil, distribution (bulk)	6120	811	612.2
other than oil or gas, burner, manufacturing	3284/5	399/9	328.6
pump (for industrial engine) manufacturing	3281/1	334/1	328.1
pump for aero-engine, manufacturing	3640	383/2	364
tank (motor vehicle) manufacturing	3530	381	353
technologist (private practice)	8370/2	879/2	837
Fuelwood, manufacturing	4610/1	471/1	461.1
Fuller's earth pit	2310/6	103	231.7
Fulling mill (textile finishing)	4370/2	423	437.4
Fumigating block, manufacturing	2568	279/4	256.8
Fumigation service (not specially for agriculture)	9211	899/7	921
Fun fair	9791/3	882	979
Function room, licensed	6611/1	885	661
Funeral			
direction	9890/2	899/1	984
furnishing	9890/2	899/1	984
Funerary stonework, manufacturing	2450/3	469/2	245.4
Fungicide, manufacturing	2568	279/4	256.8
Funicular railway	7260/2	709	725
Funnel, plastics, manufacturing	4836	496	483
Fur			
apparel, manufacturing	4560	433	456.3
broker	6300	832/3	638
cape, manufacturing	4560	433	456.3
coat, manufacturing	4560	433	456.3
commission merchant	6300	832/3	638
cravat, manufacturing	4560	433	456.3
dressing	4560	433	456.1
dyeing, manufacturing	4560	433	456.1
fabric hat, manufacturing	4537/2	446/2	453
farming	0100/1	001/1	01
hat, manufacturing	4560	433	456.3
mat and rug, manufacturing	4560	433	456.3
merchant, wholesale	6160	832/3	616.6
muff, manufacturing	4560	433	456.3
trimmings, manufacturing	4560	433	456.1
Furnace			
block and pot, manufacturing	2481	461/1	248.1
for strip processing line, manufacturing	3245/2	341/2	328.6
Furnishing			
fabric, window (knitted) manufacturing	4364	417	436.2
fabric, woollen, manufacturing	4310/3	414/5	431.5

FUR-GAS

Activity	SIC 1980	SIC 1968	NACE
fabric, worsted, weaving	4310/3	414/3	431.5
fabric, woven (not wool or worsted) manufacturing	4322	413	432.5
lace, manufacturing	4395	418	439.5
Furniture			
agent or broker	6300	812/4	635
bamboo, manufacturing	4671/2	472	467.7
basket, manufacturing	4671/2	472	467.7
ceramic, manufacturing	2489/3	462/3	248.6
complete or parts, plastics, manufacturing	4836	496	483
component, wooden, manufacturing	4671/4	472	467.5
domestic, retail dealing in	6480	821/3	648.2
fittings, metal, manufacturing	3169/3	399/12	316.3
kit, manufacturing	4671/2	472	467.1
metal, not upholstered, manufacturing	3166/1	399/1	316.6
office, retail dealing in	6530	821/4	653.3
parts, wooden, manufacturing	4671/4	472	467.5
polish, manufacturing	2599	279/1	259.2
removal	7230	703	723.1
repairer	6730/3	821/3	675
repository	7700/3	709/2	773
toy, manufacturing	4941	494/1	494.1
upholstered, manufacturing	4671/1	472	467.4
wholesale dealing in	6150	812/4	615.1
wooden, domestic, not upholstered, manufacturing	4671/2	472	467.1
Furrier			
retail	6450	821/2	645.9
wholesale	6160	812/2	616.6
Further education			
college	9330	872/3	933
establishment	9330	872/3	933
Furze collecting, cutting, gathering	0200	002	02
Fuse			
and fusegear, power, manufacturing	3420/2	316/2	342
bomb, manufacturing	3290/2	342	328.9
box, domestic type, manufacturing	3420/3	369/5	342
domestic type, manufacturing	3420/3	369/5	342
for explosives, manufacturing	2565	279/3	256.5
for shells and bombs, manufacturing	3290/2	342	328.9
wire, manufacfuring	3420/3	369/5	342
Fusel oil, manufacturing	4240/1	239	424
Fustian, weaving	4322	413	432.5

G

Activity	SIC 1980	SIC 1968	NACE
Gaberdine, cotton, weaving	4322	413	432.5
Gaiter, leather, manufacturing	4510	450	451.4
Galloon ribbon, manufacturing	4398/2	421/3	439.3
Galosh, rubber, manufacturing	4510	450	481.2
Galvanised			
sheet, steel, manufacturing	2210	311/2	221.2
sheets, dealing in	6120	832/1	612.6
tank, manufacturing	3163	399/7	316.4
Galvanising	3138	399/11	313.5
Galvanometer, manufacturing	3442	354/2	344
Gambling	9791/2	883	979
Game			
bird, farming	0100/1	001/1	01
bird, fresh, frozen or chilled, dressing or preparation	4123/1	214/1	412.3
retail dealing in	6410	820/2	641.6
wholesale dealing in	6170	810/2	617.3
Games apparatus, retail dealing in	6540	821/4	654.4
Gaming			
(automatic slot) machine, manufacturing	3286/1	339/9	328.9
Board for Great Britain	9791/2	883	979
club	9791/2	883	979
Ganister			
brick, manufacturing	2481	461/1	248.1
dealing in	6130	832/8	613
extraction	2396	109/4	239.4
Garage			
asbestos cement and concrete, manufacturing	2437	469/2	243.2
equipment and plant, manufacturing	3286/1	339/9	328.9
lock-up, letting	8500	863	850
parking	7610/1	709/1	761
tools, dealing in	6149	832/5	614.5
wooden, manufacturing	4630	471/2	463.1
Garden			
and horticultural net, manufacturing	4396	416	439.7
centre, retail	6540	821/4	654.6
city company	8500	863	850
fork, manufacturing	3161/1	391	316.1
frame, metal, manufacturing	3142	399/12	314.2
frame, wooden, manufacturing	4630	471/2	463.1
furniture, manufacturing	4671/2	472	467.3
hose, rubber or plastics, manufacturing	4812/1	491/2	481.2
seeds and plants, retail dealing in	6540	821/4	654.6
shears, manufacturing	3161/1	391	316.1
spade, manufacturing	3161/1	391	316.1
tool hire	8460/2	821/3	846.1
trowel, manufacturing	3161/1	391	316.1
Gardening tools			
retail dealing in	6480	821/3	648.6
wholesale dealing in	6150	812/4	615.2
Garment, rainproof, manufacturing	4531	441	453
Garnet abrasives, manufacturing	2460	469/1	246
Garter, manufacturing	4539/3	449/4	453
Gas			
appliances, retail dealing in	6480	821/3	648.1
blast furnace, manufacturing	2210	311/2	221.1
burner, manufacturing	3284/5	399/9	328.6
chromatograph, manufacturing	3710	354/2	371.2
cleansing plant, manufacturing	3245/3	341/2	328.4
coke, manufacturing	1620	601	162.1
coke oven, manufacturing	1200	261/1	120
compressor, manufacturing	3283/1	333/3	328.3
cooker, manufacturing	3165	399/9	316.5
Corporation	1620	601	162
discharge lamp, manufacturing	3470/1	369/4	347.1
fire, manufacturing	3165	399/9	316.5
fired domestic cooking and heating appliance, manufacturing	3165	399/9	316.5
lighter, electric, manufacturing	3460	368	346
mantle ring and rod, manufacturing	2481	461/1	248.1
meter, manufacturing	3710	354/2	371.1
meter diaphragm, leather, manufacturing	4420/2	431/1	442.3
natural, production well	1300	104	132
off-shore pipeline laying	1300	104	502.7
oil, manufacturing	1401	262	140.1
oil, dealing in	6120	831/1	612.2
petroleum, manufacturing	1401	262	140.1
pipe, steel, manufacturing	2220	312	222
rare, manufacturing	2567	271/1	256.1
retort and kiln lining, manufacturing	2481	461/1	248.1
showroom	1620	601	162
stove, manufacturing	3165	399/9	316.5
tail, manufacturing	1401	262	140.1
turbine (industrial engine) manufacturing	3281/3	334/1	328.2
turbine (marine) manufacturing	3281/2	370/2	328.1 and 328.2
works	1620	601	162.1

Activity	SIC 1980	1968	NACE
Gasket			
asbestos, manufacturing	2440	429/1	244
manufacturing	3289/2	349/3	328.9
Gassing yarn	4370/2	423	437.4
Gate			
metal, manufacturing	3142	399/12	314.2
valve, manufacturing	3288	333/2	328.8
wooden, manufacturing	4630	479/3	463.2
Gathering machine (paper working) manufacturing	3276	339/2	327.2
Gauge			
active, manufacturing	3710	390	371.5
glass, manufacturing	2479/5	463/1	247.4
pressure, manufacturing	3710	354/2	371.2
static, manufacturing	3710	390	371.5
vernier, manufacturing	3710	390	371.5
Gauntlet, manufacturing	4538	449/2	442.2
Gauze			
surgical, manufacturing	2570	279/6	257
weaving	4322	413	432.5
Gear			
box (not for motor vehicle, etc.) manufacturing	3261/3	349/3	326.1
box, manual or automatic (motor vehicle) manufacturing	3530	381	353
box, motor cycle, manufacturing	3633	382	363.2
cutting (not for motor vehicle, etc.)	3261/3	349/3	326.1
making or finishing (metal cutting) machine, manufacturing	3221/1	332/1	322.1
pedal cycle, manufacturing	3634	382	363.2
Geared motor unit, manufacturing	3261/3	361/3	326.1
Gelatine, manufacturing	2562	279/2	256.2
Gelignite, manufacturing	2565	279/3	256.5
Genealogist	9890/2	879/5	984
General			
Council of the Bar	9631/1	879/3	963
hospital	9510	874/1	951
hospital psychiatric unit	9510	874/1	951
insurance company	8200/3	860	823
medical consultant (hospital)	9510	874/1	951
medical consultant (private practice)	9530	874/1	953
Medical Council	9631/1	879/3	963
medical practitioner	9530	874/3	953
Nursing Council	9631/1	879/3	963
printing	4754/4	489	473.2
Register and Record Office of Shipping and Seamen	9111	901/6	911
wiring cable, manufacturing	3410	362	341
Generating			
Board	1610/1	602	161
station (other than public supply)	1610/2	602	161
station (public supply)	1610/1	602	161
Generator			
alternating current, manufacturing	3420/1	361/1	342
direct current, manufacturing	3420/1	361/1	342
engine, manufacturing	3281/1	334/1	328.1
set, manufacturing	3420/1	361/1	342
Genito-urinary specialist			
hospital	9510	874/1	951
private practice	9530	874/1	953
Geographical			
model, wax, plaster, manufacturing	4959	499/2	495.3
printing and publishing	4754/2	489	473 and 474
Geological surveying for petroleum or natural gas (not geological consultancy)	1300	104	134
Geologist (consultant)	8370/2	879/2	837
Geophysical instrument, manufacturing	3710	354/2	371.3
Geriatric hospital	9510	874/1	951
Geriatrician (hospital)	9510	874/1	951
German silver, unwrought, manufacturing	2246/1	322	224.2
Germanium, manufacturing	2247/1	323	224.1
Gherkin pickling	4147/2	218/3	414.3
Gift shop	6480	821/4	649.5
Gilding			
metals	3138	399/11	313.5
printing service	4754/5	489	473.3
Gill leather, manufacturing	4410/1	431/1	441.3
Gilt, manufacturing	4910/3	396	491.3
Gimp, manufacturing	4398/2	421/3	439.3
Gin distilling and rectifying	4240/2	239/1	424.2
Gingelly			
oil, refining	4116/3	221	411.4
seed, crushing	4116/2	221	411.3
Ginger beer, manufacturing	4283/1	232	428.2
Gingham weaving	4322	413	432.5
Girder, steel, manufacturing	2210	311/2	221.1
Girl Guides Association	9690/2	899/3	968
Girls Public Day School Trust	9320	872/4	932
Girls'			
Brigade	9690/2	899/3	968
club	9690/2	899/3	968
Friendly Society	9690/2	899/3	968
overall, manufacturing	4534	444/1	453
Glacé kid, manufacturing	4410/1	431/1	441.3
Glass			
ampoule (hygienic and pharmaceutical) manufacturing	2478	463/2	247.7
ball, bar, rod and tube for processing, manufacturing	2479/3	463/1	247.4
bead, manufacturing	2479/5	463/1	247.4
bottle, manufacturing	2478	463/2	247.2
bottle stopper, manufacturing	2478	463/2	247.2
brick, manufacturing	2479/5	463/1	247.4
button, manufacturing	2479/5	463/1	247.4
carboy, manufacturing	2478	463/2	247.2
container made from tubing, (hygienic and pharmaceutical) manufacturing	2478	463/2	247.7
container, manufacturing	2478	463/2	247
cutter, manufacturing	3161/2	391	316.1
fibre felt, manufacturing	2479/4	463/1	247.5
fibre flock, manufacturing	2479/4	463/1	247.5
fibre mat, manufacturing	2479/4	463/1	247.5
fibre mattress, manufacturing	2479/4	463/1	247.5
fibre moulding, resin bonded, (excluding those for motor vehicles) manufacturing	4836	496	483
fibre spinning and doubling	4321/2	412	432.4
fibre thermal and sound insulating material, manufacturing	2479/4	463/1	247.5
fibre tissue, manufacturing	2479/4	463/1	247.5
fibre yarn, manufacturing	4321/2	412	432.4
fibre yarn, doubled, manufacturing	4321/2	412	432.4
fibre, woven fabric, manufacturing	4322	413	432.5
in the mass, manufacturing	2479/5	463/1	247
jar, manufacturing	2478	463/2	247.2
making machinery, manufacturing	3275/5	339/9	325.3
merchant (flat glass)	6130	831/2	613.4
mirror suitable for motor vehicle (not further assembled) manufacturing	2471/2	463/1	247.6
ovenware, manufacturing	2479/1	463/1	247
paper, manufacturing	2460	469/1	246.3
parts of electric lamps and electronic valves, manufacturing	2479/2	463/1	247.4
pot, manufacturing	2478	463/2	247.2
powder, manufacturing	2479/5	463/1	247.4
stopper, manufacturing	2478	463/2	247.2
syphon, manufacturing	2478	463/2	247.7
tableware, manufacturing	2479/1	463/1	247
tile, manufacturing	2479/5	463/1	247.4

GLA-GRE

Activity	SIC 1980	1968	NACE
tubing, manufacturing	2479/3	463/1	247.4
wool, manufacturing	2479/4	463/1	247.5
working machine, manufacturing	3275/5	339/9	325.3
Glasshouse			
crop growing	0100/2	001/3	01
metal framed, manufacturing	3204/1	341/4	314.1
Glassine, paper manufacturing	4710/4	481	471.3
Glassware			
domestic, manufacturing	2479/1	463/1	247
heat resisting, for cooking purposes, manufacturing	2479/1	463/1	247
retail dealing in	6480	821/3	648.7
wholesale dealing in	6150	812/4	615.4
Glazed			
fireplace brick, manufacturing	2489/1	462/2	248.3
tile, manufacturing	2489/1	462/2	248.3
Glazing			
bar, manufacturing	3142	399/2	314.2
contractor	5040	500	504.4
Glider			
club	9791/1	882	978
manufacturing	3640	383/1	364
Globe			
glass, manufacturing	2479/2	463/1	247.4
valve, manufacturing	3288	333/2	328.8
Glove			
(other than knitted) manufacturing	4538	449/2	453
and gauntlet, unstitched, rubber, manufacturing	4812/3	491/2	481.2
cleaning	9812	893	981
cloth, manufacturing	4538	449/2	453
fur, manufacturing	4538	449/2	456.3
industrial, not rubber, manufacturing	4538	449/2	453
knitted, manufacturing	4363/2	417	436.2
leather (not sports) manufacturing	4538	449/2	442.2
leather, preparation	4410/1	431/1	441.3
sports (specialists) manufacturing	4942	494/3	442.2
unstitched, plastics manufacturing	4836	449/2	483
Glover, retail	6450	821/2	645
Glucose, manufacturing	4180	229/2	418.3
Glue, manufacturing	2562	279/2	256.2
Glueing machinery (bookbinders, etc.) manufacturing	3276	339/2	327.2
Glycerol, manufacturing	2563	275	256.3
Goggles, manufacturing	3731	353/2	373.1
Gold			
and silver braid, manufacturing	4910/1	396	491.2
and silver bullion, manufacturing	2247/2	396	224.1
and silver embroidery, manufacturing	4910/1	396	491.1
and silver mounting, manufacturing	4910/1	396	491.2
blocking	4754/5	489	473.3
laceman	4910/1	396	491.2
leaf, manufacturing	4910/1	396	491.2
manufacturing	2247/2	396	224.1
stamping	4754/5	489	473.3
Goldbeaters' skin or bung, manufacturing	4410/1	431/1	441.3
Goldsmiths' work	4910/1	396	491.2
Golf			
ball (finished) manufacturing	4942	494/3	494.2
ball core, manufacturing	4812/3	491/2	481.2
club, manufacturing	4942	494/3	494.2
course or links	9791/1	882	978
Goliath type crane, manufacturing	3255/2	337/2	325.5
Goods			
agent (not transport authority)	7700/2	709/1	772
wagon (railway) manufacturing	3620/2	385	362.2
Goose, fresh, chilled or frozen, slaughtering and dressing	4123/1	214/1	412.3
Gouge, wood frame, manufacturing	3161/2	391	316.1
Governess, resident	9900	891/1	990
Government			
department (building and civil engineering works division)	5000	500	500.1
departments (except HMSO and ECGD)	9111	901/6	911
research establishment	9400	876	940
Gown, manufacturing			
academic, legal and ecclesiastical	4532	442	453
not retail bespoke	4536/1	445/1	453
Grab, manufacturing	3254/1	336	325.4
Grader, manufacturing	3254/1	336	325.4
Graduated glassware, manufacturing	2479/3	463/1	247.4
Grain			
auger, manufacturing	3211/3	331	321.1
broker	6300	831/3	631
dealing in	6110	831/3	611.1
drier, manufacturing	3211/2	331	321.1
processing machinery and plant, manufacturing	3244/1	341/2	324.1
warehouse	7700/3	709/2	773
Grains, abrasive, artificial, manufacturing	2460	469/1	246
Grammar school	9320	872	932
Gramophone			
accessory, manufacturing	3453/2	365/2	345.1
cabinet, manufacturing	4671/4	472	467.5
manufacturing	3454/1	365/2	345.1
record (including blanks for cutting) manufacturing	3452	365/1	345.2
records, retail dealing in	6480	821/3	648.8
records, wholesale dealing in	6150	812/4	615.3
Granary	7700/3	709/2	773
Granite			
dealing in	6130	832/8	613
quarry	2310/2	102/1	231.2
working	2450/3	469/2	245.3
Granulator (for chemical industry) manufacturing	3245/1	339/9	324.1
Graphite			
block, manufacturing	2481	461/1	248.1
crucible, manufacturing	2481	461/1	248.1
mine	2396	109/4	239.4
product (other than block and crucible) manufacturing	2450/4	469/2	245.5
retort, manufacturing	2481	461/1	248.1
Graphologist	9890/2	899/7	984
Grapnel, manufacturing	3169/4	399/12	316.9
Grate, cast iron, manufacturing	3111	313/4	311.1
Grating			
(mounted) manufacturing	3733	354	373.3
(unmounted, optical) manufacturing	3731	354	373.1
cast iron, manufacturing	3111	313/4	311.1
Gravel pit	2310/4	103	231.4
Gravity casting non-ferrous base metal, manufacturing	3112	not classified	311.2
Gravure			
ink, manufacturing	2552	279/5	255
printing machine, manufacturing	3276	339/2	327.2
Gravy			
manufacturing	4239/9	229/2	423.3
salt (not at salt mine or brine pit) manufacturing	4239/9	229/2	423.3
Grazing	0100/1	001/1	01
Grease			
(at refineries) manufacturing	1401	262	140.1
dealing in	6120	832/8	612.7
Greaseproof paper, manufacturing	4710/4	481	471.3
Greater			
Glasgow Passenger Transport Executive (railways)	7210/1	701	721.1

Activity	SIC 1980	1968	NACE
London Council	9112	906/3	911
Greengrocer, retail	6410	820/2	641.2
Greenhouse			
metal framed, manufacturing	3204/1	341/4	314.1
wooden, manufacturing	4630	471/2	463.1
Greeting card, manufacturing	4754/4	489	473.2
Grenade			
casting, manufacturing	3111	313/3	311.1
manufacturing	3290/2	342	328.9
Grey board, manufacturing	4710/7	481	471.3
Greyhound			
security police	9791/1	882	978
track	9791/1	882	978
training	9791/1	882	978
Grid, wooden, manufacturing	4650	479/3	465.1
Grille, metal, (not cast) manufacturing	3142	399/12	314.2
Grinding			
machine, for glass etc., manufacturing	3275/5	339/9	325.3
machine, metal-cutting, manufacturing	3221/1	332/1	322.1
metal finishing	3138	399/11	313.5
mill, agricultural, manufacturing	3211/3	331	321.1
paste, manufacturing	2460	469/1	256.7
tool (powered), portable, manufacturing	3285/2	339/6	not classified
Grindstones of bonded abrasives, manufacturing	2460	469/1	246.1
Grist, milling	4160	211/1	416.2
Grit extraction plant (effluent treatment) manufacturing	3245/3	341/2	324.1
Gritting machine, manufacturing	3254/2	336	325.4
Grocer			
retail	6410	820/1	641/642
wholesale	6170	810/1	617.1
Grocery stall, retail	6410	820/1	641/642
Grooved wood, manufacturing	4610/2	471/1	461.2
Ground			
effect vehicle, manufacturing	3640	383/3	364
equipment for spacecraft (excluding electronic or telemetric equipment) manufacturing	3640	383/1	364
landlord	8500	863	850
pepper, manufacturing	4239/9	229/2	423.3
spice, manufacturing	4239/9	229/2	423.3
station (for relay satellite communication) manufacturing	3443	363	344
Groundnut			
crushing	4116/2	221	411.3
oil refining	4116/3	221	411.4
Groundsheet, rubber, manufacturing	4812/3	491/2	481.2
Groundsman	9791/1	882	978
Grouting			
contractor (building)	5010	500	501
contractor (civil engineering)	5020	500	502
Guano, dealing in	6110	831/3	611.3
Guest house			
licensed	6650/1	884	665.3
unlicensed	6650/2	884	665.3
Guide	9890/2	899/7	984
Guided weapon			
airborne delivery system, manufacturing	3640	383/1	364
launching gear or launch control post, manufacturing	3640	383/1	364
manufacturing	3640	383/1	364
warhead, manufacturing	3290/2	342	328.9
Guild, City	9631/1	879/3	963
Guitar, manufacturing	4920/2	499/1	492.2
Gully, concrete, manufacturing	2437	469/2	243.2
Gum, manufacturing	2562	279/2	256.2
Gummed			
paper, manufacturing	4728	484/2	472.6
paper label, manufacturing	4723/1	483	472.8
Gums, dealing in	6120	832/8	612.7
Gun			
air, manufacturing	3290/1	342	328.9
carriage, mounting or platform, manufacturing	3290/1	342	328.9
case, leather, manufacturing	4420/1	432	442.1
manufacturing	3290/1	342	328.9
metal, unwrought, manufacturing	2246/1	322	224.2
toy, (not operated by compressed air) manufacturing	4941	494/1	494.1
Guncotton, manufacturing	2565	279/3	256.5
Gunnery control instrument			
manufacturing	3710	354/2	371.2
optical, manufacturing	3732	354	373.2
Gunpowder, manufacturing	2565	279/3	256.5
Gunstock, wooden, manufacturing	4650	479/3	465.1
Gut			
(for musical instruments and sports goods) manufacturing	4959	499/2	495.3
scraping and spinning	4959	499/2	495.3
Gutter-percha goods, manufacturing	4812/3	491/2	481.2
Gutter and fittings, plastics, manufacturing	4834	496	483
Gymnasium	9791/1	882	978
Gymnasium equipment and appliance, manufacturing	4942	494/3	494.2
Gynaecologist			
hospital	9510	874/1	951
private practice	9530	874/1	953
Gypsum			
mine or quarry	2310/5	109/4	231.6
plaster, manufacturing	2420	469/2	242.3
plaster products, manufacturing	2437	469/2	243.3
Gyroscope, manufacturing	3710	367/2	371

H

Activity	SIC 1980	1968	NACE
HM Stationery Office	4754/2	489	473/474
Haberdasher, retail	6450	821/2	645.8
Haberdashery			
(narrow fabrics) manufacturing	4398/2	421/3	439.3
plastics, manufacturing	4836	496	483
wholesale dealing in	6160	812/2	616.5
Hacksaw blade			
for hand tool, manufacturing	3161/2	391	316.1
for machines and for all materials, manufacturing	3222/1	390	322.2
Haematite quarry	2100	109/1	211
Haematologist (hospital)	9510	874/1	951
Haggis making	4122/3	214/2	412.2
Hair			
animal by-product from knackers, production	4126/3	899/7	412.5
brush, manufacturing	4663	493	466.3
clipper, electric, manufacturing	3460	368	346
comb, plastics, manufacturing	4836	496	483
curler, plastics, manufacturing	4836	496	483
dealing in	6110	832/8	611.6
dressing (for upholstery)	4399/2	429/2	439.7
dressing for brushes	4663	493	466.3
dryer, electric, manufacturing	3460	368	346
dyeing (textile)	4370/2	423	437.2
grip and pin, metal, manufacturing	3169/2	399/8	316.9

HAI-HEA

Activity	SIC 1980	1968	NACE
net, lace, manufacturing	**4395**	418	439.5
pad making	**4539/3**	449/4	453
preparation, for wig making	**4959**	449/4	495.3
preparations, manufacturing	**2582**	273	258.2
Haircord weaving	**4322**	413	432.5
Hairdresser	**9820**	889	982
Hairdressers' sundriesman	**6180**	812/4	618
Half shaft, manufacturing	**3530**	381	353
Hall stand, manufacturing	**4671/2**	472	467.1
Halogen and halides (inorganic) manufacturing	**2511**	271/1	251
Halogenated derivatives of hydrocarbon, manufacturing	**2512**	271/2	251
Ham			
boiling	**4122/1**	214/2	412.2
cooking or preparing in bulk	**4122/1**	214/2	412.2
curing	**4122/1**	214/2	412.2
smoking	**4122/1**	214/2	412.2
Hammer			
forging, steel	**3120**	311/2	312.1
manufacturing	**3161/2**	391	316.1
powered, portable, manufacturing	**3285/2**	339/6	not classified
Hammock, manufacturing	**4396**	416	439.7
Hamper, manufacturing	**4664/2**	475/1	466.2
Hampton			
Court Gardens and Park	**9111**	901/6	911
Court Palace	**9111**	901/6	911
Hand			
block printing (textiles)	**4370/2**	423	437.3
cart, hire	**8480/4**	709/3	845
cream, manufacturing	**2582**	273	258.2
knitting yarn, retail dealing in	**6450**	821/2	645.8
knitting yarn, wholesale dealing in	**6160**	812/2	616.5
luggage, leather, manufacturing	**4420/1**	432	442.1
made paper, manufacturing	**4710/3**	481	471.3
mending yarns, wholesale dealing in	**6160**	812/2	616.5
pump, manufacturing	**3287**	333/1	328.3
tools, manufacturing	**3161**	391 and 392	316.1
towel, manufacturing	**4557**	422/1	455.1
truck, metal, manufacturing	**3169/4**	399/12	316.9
Handbag			
leather or leather substitute, manufacturing	**4420/1**	432	442.1
repairer	**6720**	821/4	672
Handbags			
retail dealing in	**6460**	821/4	646.2
wholesale dealing in	**6160**	812/4	616.8
Handcart manufacturing			
not wooden	**3650/2**	399/12	365.2
wooden	**4650**	479/3	465.1
Handicraft article, wood, manufacturing	**4650**	479/3	465.1
Handicrafts shop	**6540**	821/4	655.2
Handkerchief			
of textile material, manufacturing	**4539/3**	422/1	453
folding	**4539/3**	422/1	453
hemming	**4539/3**	422/1	453
paper, manufacturing	**4722**	484/2	472.2
Handle			
cutlery, horn, ivory, tortoise-shell etc., manufacturing	**4959**	499/2	495.3
for furniture, plastics, manufacturing	**4836**	496	483
wooden, manufacturing	**4650**	479/3	465.1
Handlebar, manufacturing			
motor cycle	**3633**	382	363.2
pedal cycle	**3634**	382	363.2
Handling plant (hydraulic and pneumatic) manufacturing	**3255/1**	337/1	325.5
Handsaw, manufacturing	**3161/2**	391	316.1
Harbour			
authority	**7630**	706	763
construction	**5020**	500	502.4
floating, manufacturing	**3610/1**	370/1	361.2
steelwork, manufacturing	**3204/2**	341/4	314.1
Hard			
coke, manufacturing	**1200**	261/1	120
coke breeze, manufacturing	**1200**	261/1	120
metal tipped tool, manufacturing	**3222/1**	390	322.2
soap, manufacturing	**2581**	275	258.1
Hardboard, manufacturing	**4620/1**	471/1	462.2
Hardener, aluminium, manufacturing	**2245/1**	321	224.1
Hardness testing instrument, manufacturing	**3710**	354/2	371.2
Hardware, retail dealing in	**6480**	821/3	648.6
Hardwood			
dealing in	**6130**	832/2	613.1
flooring strip, manufacturing	**4630**	471/1	463.3
Harness			
and saddlery leather preparation	**4410/1**	431/1	441.3
front and rosette, leather, manufacturing	**4420/1**	432	442.1
Harpsichord, manufacturing	**4920/1**	499/1	492.1
Harrow, manufacturing	**3211/1**	331	321.1
Hat			
and cap leather preparation	**4410/1**	431/1	441.3
band, manufacturing	**4398/2**	421/3	439.3
box, leather or leather substitute, manufacturing	**4420/1**	432	442.1
cloth, maufacturing	**4537/2**	446/2	453
felt, manufacturing	**4537/1**	446/1	453
fur fabric, manufacturing	**4537/2**	446/2	453
fur, manufacturing	**4560**	433	456.3
lining, manufacturing	**4537/2**	446/2	453
materials, wholesale dealing in	**6160**	812/2	616
men's and boys', not felt or fur, manufacturing	**4537/2**	446/2	453
pad, manufacturing	**4537/2**	446/2	453
renovating	**9812**	893	981
shape, manufacturing	**4537/2**	446/2	453
women's and girls' felt, manufacturing	**4537/1**	446/1	453
Hatch cover (mechanically operated), manufacturing	**3289/1**	370	361
Hatchet, manufacturing	**3161/1**	391	316.1
Hats, retail dealing in	**6450**	821/2	645.7
Hatter, retail	**6450**	821/2	645.7
Hatters' fur, manufacturing	**4560**	433	456.2
Haulage contractor (road)	**7230**	703	723.2
Hauling engine, stationery, (mining) manufacturing	**3251**	339/1	325.1
Haversack, manufacturing	**4556**	422/2	455.4
Hay			
dealing in	**6110**	831/3	611.2
making equipment, manufacturing	**3211/2**	331	321.1
Hazard warning lamp hire	**8420**	500	842
Head			
office of company operating abroad	**8396/1**	866/1	not classified
office of holding company	**8396/2**	866/2	not classified
Heading machine (mining) manufacturing	**3251**	339/1	325.1
Headset (not telecommunication type) manufacturing	**3453/2**	364/3	345.1
Headsquare, manufacturing	**4539/3**	449/4	453
Healds (textile machinery accessory) manufacturing	**3230/4**	335	323.1

Activity	SIC 1980	1968	NACE
Health			
and Safety Executive	9111	901/6	911
Board (Scotland)	9111	874/3	911
centre	9520	874/2	952
foods, retail dealing in	6410	820/1	642.3
visitor	9520	874/2	952
Hearing aid (electronic) manufacturing	3443	367/2	344
Hearth			
brush, manufacturing	4663	493	466.3
tile, clay, unglazed, manufacturing	2410	461/2	241
Heat			
emitter (space-heating equipment) manufacturing	3284/2	339/4	328.4
exchanger, manufacturing	3205/2	341/5	324.1
resisting glassware for cooking purposes, manufacturing	2479/1	463/1	247
sensitive adhesive tape, manufacturing	2569	496	259.3
treatment furnace, manufacturing	3245/2	341/2	328.6
treatment of fruit and vegetables	4147/4	218/3	414.6
treatment of milk	4130/1	215/1	413.1
treatment salts, manufacturing	2567	271/3	256.7
Heat-setting machinery (textile) manufacturing	3230/3	335	323.1
Heater (motor vehicle) manufacturing	3530	381	353
Heath collecting, cutting, gathering	0200	002	02
Heating			
and ventilation apparatus, installation	5030	500	503.3
engineering (buildings)	5030	500	503.3
melting equipment, electric (high frequency induction or dielectric) manufacturing	3435	341/2	343.1
Heavy			
forging	3120	311/2	312.1
section, steel, 80 mm and over, manufacturing	2210	311/2	221.1
wire, manufacturing	3137/2	394	313.1
Hedge trimmer, powered, portable, manufacturing	3285/2	339/6	not classified
Hedgecutter (agricultural type) manufacturing	3211/3	331	321.1
Heel			
and sole, rubber, manufacturing	4812/3	491/2	481.2
leather, manufacturing	4510	450	451.4
Helical rotor pump, manufacturing	3287	333/1	328.3
Helicopter, manufacturing	3640	383/1	364
Helmet			
safety, plastics, manufacturing	4836	446/2	483
tropical, manufacturing	4537/2	446/2	453
uniform, manufacturing	4537/2	446/2	453
Hemp			
carding	4340/1	412	434.1
dealing in	6110	832/4	611
dressing	4340/1	412	434.1
rope, cord or line, manufacturing	4396	416	439.6
sorting	4340/1	412	434.1
spinning	4340/1	412	434.3
thread, manufacturing	4340/1	412	434.4
weaving	4340/2	413	434.5
Heraldic			
chasing and seal engraving	4754/5	489	473.4
engraving, manufacturing	4754/5	489	473.4
painting	9760	879/5	976
Herb			
growing	0100/2	001/3	01
seller (food)	6410	821/4	642.3
tea, manufacturing	4239/9	229/2	423.1
Herbalist (food)	6410	821/4	642.3
Herbicide, manufacturing	2568	279/4	256.8
Herring			
oil refining	4116/3	221	411.4
oil, dealing in	6120	832/8	612.7
Herrings, wholesale dealing in	6170	810/2	617.9
Hessian			
manufacturing	4350/2	415	435.5
wholesale dealing in	6160	812/4	616
Heterocyclic compounds, manufacturing	2512	271/2	251
Hi-fi equipment			
manufacturing	3454/1	365/2	345.1
retail dealing in	6480	821/3	648.8
Hide			
and skin broker	6300	832/3	631
curing	4410/1	431/1	441.1
degreasing	4410/1	431/1	441.1
dressing	4410/1	431/1	441.1
pickling	4410/1	431/1	441.1
trimming	4410/1	431/1	441.1
Hides			
and skins from animals (from abattoirs) production	4121	810/2	412.1
and skins from animals (from knackers) production	4126/3	899/7	412.1
and skins, dealing in	6110	832/3	611.7
High			
alumina brick, manufacturing	2481	461/1	248.1
alumina cement, manufacturing	2481	461/1	248.1
energy rate forming machine, manufacturing	3221/2	332/2	322.1
Hinge, manufacturing	3169/3	399/12	316.3
Hire			
purchase company (licensed under the Banking Act 1979)	8140/2	862	812
purchase company (not licensed under the Banking Act 1979)	8150/1	862	813.1
Hiring			
cutler (lets out cutlery for dinners, etc.)	8460/2	899/7	846.2
goods (miscellaneous or unspecified)	8490	not classified	847
Historical research	9890/2	899/7	984
Hobby instructor, own account	9791/3	882	979
Hockey			
club	9791/1	882	978
stick manufacturing	4942	494/3	494.2
Hoe, manufacturing	3161/1	391	316.1
Hoist, manufacturing			
electric, wire, rope or chain	3255/4	337/4	325.5
hand operated, pulley and sheave block	3255/4	337/4	325.5
hydraulic, mechanical and pneumatic, other than builders' hand operated and electric types	3255/1	337/4	325.5
Holder, cigar, manufacturing	4959	499/2	495.3
Holding company head office	8396/2	866/2	not classified
Holiday			
camp	6670/2	884	667.3
home (not charitable)	6670/3	884	667.3
information centre	9690/1	899/7	967
Hollow			
partition, clay, manufacturing	2410	461/2	241
section, aluminium, manufacturing	2245/2	321	224.3
Hollow-ware			
cast iron, manufacturing	3111	313/4	311.1
plastics, manufacturing	4836	496	483
refractory, manufacturing	2481	461/1	248.1
Holyrood Palace	9111	901/6	911
Home			
for epileptics	9611/2	899/3	962

HOM-HOU

Activity	SIC 1980	1968	NACE
for handicapped children	9611/2	899/3	962
for the blind	9611/2	899/3	962
for the disabled	9611/2	899/3	962
for the elderly	9611/2	899/3	962
for the mentally handicapped	9611/2	899/3	962
for the mentally ill	9611/2	899/3	962
help service	9611/1	899/3	961
nurse (National Health Service)	9520	874/2	952
Homeless, temporary accommodation for	9611/2	899/3	962
Homeopath			
not registered medical practitioner	9550	874/5	955
private	9550	874/5	955
registered medical practitioner	9530	874/3	953
Homogenized			
fruit and vegetables, manufacturing	4147/3	218/3	414.5
milk production	4130/1	215/1	413.1
Hones, bonded, manufacturing	2460	469/1	246.1
Honey			
processing and packing	4239/9	218/1	423.8
wholesale dealing in	6170	810/1	617
Honing machine (metal cutting) manufacturing	3221/1	332/1	322.1
Hook and eye, manufacturing	3169/2	399/8	316.9
Hoop, manufacturing			
steel, cold rolled	2235	311/2	223.2
steel, hot rolled	2210	311/2	221.1
wooden	4640/2	475/1	464.2
Hoopwood, manufacturing	4640/2	475/1	464.2
Hooves (from knackers) production	4126/3	899/7	412.1
Hop			
bitters, manufacturing	4283/1	232	428.2
extract, manufacturing	4239/9	218/3	423.3
growing	0100/1	001/3	01
wholesale dealing in	6170	810/2	617.9
Hormone, manufacturing			
not plant hormone	2570	272	251
plant	2568	279/4	256.8
Horn			
and tortoise-shell working	4959	499/2	495.3
electric, manufacturing	3434	369/1	343.1
pressing	4959	499/2	495.3
Horse			
breaking	6110	831/4	611.5
breeding	0100/1	001/1	01
Breeding Society	9890/2	899/6	963
clipping	9890/2	899/7	984
collar, leather, manufacturing	4420/1	432	442.1
Race Betting Levy Board	9791/2	883	979
training (not race horse)	6110	831/4	979
training (race horse)	9791/1	882	978
Horse-drawn			
trailer, not wooden, manufacturing	3650/2	399/12	365.2
truck, not wooden, manufacturing	3650/2	399/12	365.2
Horsedealer	6110	831/4	611.5
Horsehair			
curling	4399/2	429/2	439.7
dealing in	6110	832/8	611
dressing	4399/2	429/2	439.7
hackling	4399/2	429/2	439.7
sorting	4399/2	429/2	439.7
teasing	4399/2	429/2	439.7
Horserace Totalisator Board	9791/2	883	979
Horses, dealing in	6110	831/4	611.5
Horticultural			
knife, manufacturing	3161/1	391	316.1
machinery hire (without staff)	8410	832/6	841
machinery, dealing in	6149	832/6	614.6
net (textiles) manufacturing	4396	416	439.7
Horticulture	0100/2	001/3	01

Activity	SIC 1980	1968	NACE
Hose			
bleaching, dyeing or otherwise finishing	4370/2	423	437
rubber or plastics, manufacturing	4812/1	491/2	481.2 and 483
Hosiery			
blank, manufacturing	4363/1	417	436.1
finishing	4370/2	423	437.4
knitting machinery, manufacturing	3230/2	335	323.1
printing	4370/2	423	437.2
retail dealing in	6450	821/2	645
scouring	4370/2	423	437.4
shrinking	4370/2	423	437.4
trimming	4370/2	423	437.4
wholesale dealing in	6160	812/2	616
Hospital	9510	874/1	951
Hospital			
building, steelwork, manufacturing	3204/1	341/4	314.1
contribution scheme	8200/3	860	823
military	9150	901/5	915
saving association	8200/3	860	823
school	9320	872/1	932
Hostel			
(nurses', students', ex-prisoners', Salvation Army, YMCA, YWCA)	9611/2	884	962
for the homeless	9611/2	899/3	962
Hot			
dip coating (metal finishing)	3138	399/11	313.5
dog vendor	6612	885	661
melt adhesive, manufacturing	2562	279/2	256.2
pressing, ferrous metals, manufacturing	3120	399/5	312.2
stamping, ferrous metals	3120	399/5	312.2
water bottle, rubber, manufacturing	4812/3	491/2	481.2
water engineer	5030	500	503.2
water production and distribution	1630	602	163
Hotel			
contracting (waste collecting)	6220	832/7	622
fittings and furnishings, manufacturing	4672	474	467.5
furniture, manufacturing	4671/3	472	467
licensed	6650/1	884	665
self catering	6670/3	884	665.2
unlicensed	6650/2	884	665
House			
agent	8340	863	834
auctioneer	8340	863	834
building and repairing	5010	500	501
furnisher, retail	6480	821/3	648.2
insurance	8200/3	860	823
letting	8500	863	850
of Commons	9111	901/6	911
of Commons Refreshment Department	6640/2	887	664
of Lords	9111	901/6	911
shoe, manufacturing	4510	450	451.2
Houseboat, manufacturing	3610/2	370/1	361.3
Housecoat, manufacturing	4536/1	445/1	453
Household			
broom and brush, manufacturing	4663	493	466.3
deodoriser, manufacturing	2599	279/4	258.2
glove (textile) manufacturing	4538	449/2	453
goods hire	8460/2	821/3	846.1
mop, manufacturing	4663	493	466.3
paper (uncut) manufacturing	4710/5	481	471.3
stores	6480	821/3	648.1
textile, manufacturing	4557	422/1	455.1
textiles, retail dealing in	6470	821/2	647
textiles, wholesale dealing in	6160	812/2	616.9
utensil, metal	3167	399/6	316.7

Activity	SIC 1980	1968	NACE
utensil, plastics, manufacturing	4836	496	483
utensil, wooden, manufacturing	4650	479/3	465.1
Houses			
dolls', manufacturing	4941	494/1	494.1
of Parliament	9111	901/6	911
Housing			
association	8500	863	850
association (building work)	5000	500	500.1
Corporation	8150/1	862	813.1
Hovercraft			
manufacturing	3640	383/3	364
operator, between United Kingdom and international ports	7400/2	705	742
operator, domestic or coastal route	7400/3	705	742
Howitzer, manufacturing	3290/1	342	328.9
Hull Telephone Service	7902	708	790
Humidifier, manufacturing	3284/4	339/4	328.4
Hunt			
kennels	9791/1	882	978
stables	9791/1	882	978
Hunting, sport	9791/1	882	978
Hunting, commercial	0100/1	001/2	01
Hurdle, wooden, manufacturing	4650	479/3	465.1
Hut, manufacturing			
metal	3142	341/4	314.1
wooden	4630	471/2	463.1
Hybrid computer, manufacturing	3302	366	330
Hyde Park	9111	901/6	911
Hydrated lime, manufacturing	2420	469/2	242.2
Hydraulic			
and pneumatic conveying plant, manufacturing	3255/1	337/1	325.5
and pneumatic handling plant, manufacturing	3255/1	337/1	325.5
construction	5020	500	502.4
equipment (aircraft) manufacturing	3640	383/4	364
hose, rubber or plastics, manufacturing	4812/1	491/2	481.2
leather, manufacturing	4410/1	431/1	441.3
lime, manufacturing	2420	469/2	242.2
oil (outside refineries) formulation	1402	263	140.2
power production and distribution	1630	603/2	163
press (metal forming) manufacturing	3221/2	332/2	322.1
research station	9400	876	940
Hydro	6670/3	884	667.4
Hydro-electric power station			
not for public supply	1610/2	602	161.6
public supply	1610/1	602	161.2
Hydro-electricity board	1610/1	602	161
Hydro-pneumatic device, manufacturing	3283/3	333/4	328.3
Hydrocarbons			
not fuels, manufacturing	2512	271/2	251
sulphonated, nitrated or nitrosated derivatives, manufacturing	2512	271/2	251
Hydrochloric acid, manufacturing	2511	271/1	251
Hydrofoil, manufacturing	3610/1	370/1	361
Hydrogen			
manufacturing	2567	271/1	256.1
peroxide, manufacturing	2511	271/1	251
Hydrographic instrument and apparatus, manufacturing	3710	354/2	371.3
Hydrological instrument, manufacturing	3710	354/2	371.3
Hydrostatic transmission, manufacturing	3283/2	333/4	328.3
Hydrosulphite, manufacturing	2511	271/3	251
Hygienic			
glassware (other than container) manufacturing	2479/3	463/1	247.7
paper, uncut, manufacturing	4710/5	481	471.3
Hypermarket (selling mainly foodstuffs)	6410	820/1	641.1
Hypodermic syringe and equipment, manufacturing	3720/1	353/1	372.2

Activity	SIC 1980	1968	NACE
I			
Ice			
box, wooden, manufacturing	4671/4	472	467.5
chest, wooden, manufacturing	4671/4	472	467.5
cream (all flavours) manufacturing	4213	215/3	421.3
cream conservator, manufacturing	3284/1	339/3	328.5
cream parlour	6611/2	885	661
cream powder, manufacturing	4213	229/2	421.3
cream, take away, retailer	6410	820/1	641.9
cream van	6410	820/1	641.9
cream, wholesale dealing in	6170	810/1	617.7
hockey	9791/1	882	978
manufacturing	4239/9	229/2	423.4
skates, manufacturing	4942	494/3	494.2
Ices, water, manufacturing	4213	215/3	421.3
Icing sugar, manufacturing	4200	216	420.2
Igneous rock quarry	2310/2	102/1	231.2
Ignition			
coil, manufacturing	3434	369/1	343.1
equipment (other than coils or magnetos) manufacturing	3434	369/1	343.1
Illuminating			
glassware, manufacturing	2479/2	463/1	247.4
(illustrating)	9760	879/5	976
Imitation			
fur, man-made fibre, manufacturing	4322	413	432.5
fur, woollen, manufacturing	4310/3	414/5	431.5
pearl, manufacturing	4910/3	499/2	491.5
pearls, wholesale dealing in	6190	812/4	619.4
Immersion			
heater, electric, manufacturing	3460	368	346
treatment of wood	4620/2	471/1	462.4
Imperial War Museum	9770	899/4	977
Impregnated cleaning and polishing cloth, manufacturing	2599	279/1	259.2
Impresario	9741/2	881/2	975
Improved wood, manufacturing	4620/1	471/1	462.3
Incandescent mantle, manufacturing	2565	499/2	256.5
Incendiary composition, manufacturing	2565	279/3	256.5
Incinerator, manufacturing	3245/3	341/2	328.6
Independent			
Broadcasting Authority	9741/1	881/2	974
Labour Party	9690/2	899/4	968
school (non-local authority)	9320	872/2	932
suspension unit, manufacturing	3530	381	353
Index card, manufacturing	4723/2	483	472.3
Indian ink, manufacturing	4954/2	495/2	259.3
Indicating measuring instrument (electric) for vehicles and aircraft, manufacturing	3434	369/1	344
Indicator panel, manufacturing	3433	367/1	343.1
Indigo, dealing in	6120	832/8	612.7
Indoor game, manufacturing	4941	494/1	494.1
Induction			
furnace, manufacturing	3245/2	341/2	343.1
unit (air conditioning equipment) manufacturing	3284/4	339/4	328.4
Inductor (electronic) manufacturing	3444	364/3	344
Industrial			
air heater (for boilers) manufacturing	3205/1	341/1	328.4
and Commercial Finance Corporation	8150/1	862	813.1
apron, manufacturing	4534	444/1	453
assurance company	8200/2	860	822
banker (not licensed under the Banking Act 1979)	8150/1	862	813.1
belting, rubber or plastics, manufacturing	4812/2	491/2	481.2
benzole, manufacturing	1401	262	140.1
broom and mop, manufacturing	4663	493	466.3
brush, manufacturing	4663	493	466.3
canteen (run by catering contractor)	6640/1	888	664

Activity	SIC 1980	1968	NACE
catalyst, manufacturing	2567	271/3	256.7
ceramic product, non-refractory, manufacturing	2489/4	462/3	248.9
chemicals and dyes, dealing in	6120	832/8	612.7
cleaning preparation, manufacturing	2567	271/3	256.7
clothing, hire	9811	892	981
clothing, manufacturing	4534	444/1	453
clothing, weather protective, manufacturing	4531	441	453
design service	8370/2	879/5	837
engine (spark or compression ignition) manufacturing	3281/1	334/1	328.1
estate owner	8500	863	850
floor cleaning equipment, leasing of	8490	832/10	847
glassware (not container) manufacturing	2479/5	463/1	247.4
glove, not rubber, manufacturing	4538	449/2	453
headgear, protective, not plastics, manufacturing	4537/2	446/2	453
insurance	8200/3	860	823
knife, manufacturing	3161/2	392	316.1
leather, manufacturing	4420/2	431/1	442.3
materials (general or undefined) dealing in	6120	832/9	612
mixing equipment (for chemical industry) manufacturing	3245/1	339/9	324.1
nucleonic apparatus, manufacturing	3443	367/2	344
overall, men's, manufacturing	4534	444/1	453
overall, women's, manufacturing	4534	444/1	453
paper, manufacturing	4710/6	481	471.3
plant and equipment hire	8490	832/10	847
shirt, manufacturing	4534	444/2	453
soap, manufacturing	2581	275	258.1
spirit, manufacturing	1401	262	140.1
timer, manufacturing	3740	352	374
tractor, manufacturing	3255/5	337/5	325.5
Training Board (not training centre)	9111	865	911
transformer, manufacturing	3420/1	361/1	342
trucks, special purpose, manufacturing	3255/5	337/5	325.5
tyre, manufacturing	4811	491/1	481.1
Infant			
food (milk based) manufacturing	4130/3	215/2	413.2
food (other than milk based) manufacturing	4239/4	229/2	423.5
school	9320	872/1	932
Infants'			
outerwear, manufacturing	4536/3	445/3	453
swimwear, knitted, manufacturing	4363/2	417	436.2
underclothing, manufacturing	4536/3	445/3	453
underclothing, knitted, manufacturing	4363/2	417	436.2
weatherproof outerwear, manufacturing	4531	441	453
Infectious disease			
hospital	9510	874/1	951
specialist (hospital)	9510	874/1	951
specialist (private practice)	9530	874/1	953
Infirmary	9510	874/1	951
Inflatable			
air bed, plastics, manufacturing	4836	496	483
cushion, rubber, manufacturing	4812/3	491/2	481.2
dinghy, rubber, manufacturing	4812/3	491/2	481.2
liferaft, rubber, manufacturing	4812/3	491/2	481.2
mattress, rubber, manufacturing	4812/3	491/2	481.2
plastics product (excluding playball) manufacturing	4836	496	483
Inflator, tyre, (cycle type) manufacturing	3634	382	363.2
Information bureau	8395/4	899/7	839.3
Information bureau for tourists	9690/1	899/7	967
Ingot			
copper, manufacturing	2246/1	322	224.1
mould and bottom, manufacturing	3111	313/4	311.1
steel, manufacturing	2210	311/2	221.1
Injection moulding machinery, manufacturing	3275/2	339/9	324.3
Ink			
flexographic, manufacturing	2552	279/5	255
for impregnating ink pads, manufacturing	4954/2	495/2	259.3
gravure, manufacturing	2552	279/5	255
letterpress, manufacturing	2552	279/5	255
lithographic, manufacturing	2552	279/5	255
news, manufacturing	2552	279/5	255
pad, manufacturing	4954/3	495/2	495.2
printing, manufacturing	2552	279/5	255
screen process, manufacturing	2552	279/5	255
writing, manufacturing	4954/2	495/2	259.3
Inlaid wood, manufacturing	4620/1	471/1	462.1
Inland water transport	7260/3	706	730
Inn	6650/1	886	662
Inner tube for tyre, manufacturing	4811	491/1	481.1
Inns of Court	9631/1	879/3	963
Inorganic acid, manufacturing	2511	271/1	251
Inquiry agency	8395/4	899/7	839.3
Insecticide, manufacturing	2568	279/4	256.8
Insecticides, dealing in	6110	831/3	611
Insole, leather, manufacturing	4510	450	451.4
Installation of electrical equipment	3480	not classified	348
Instant coffee, manufacturing	4239/1	229/2	423.1
Instep support, manufacturing	3720/3	353/1	372.4
Institute of			
Actuaries	9631/1	879/3	963
British Water Colour Painters	9631/1	879/3	963
Chartered Accountants	9631/1	879/3	963
Chartered Accountants of Scotland	9631/1	879/3	963
Civil Engineers	9631/1	879/3	963
Cost and Management Accountants	9631/1	879/3	963
Hygiene	9631/1	879/3	963
Incorporated Photographers	9631/1	879/3	963
Mechanical Engineers	9631/1	879/3	963
Metals	9631/1	879/3	963
Instrument			
case, surgical, not leather, plastics, wood, manufacturing	4959	499/2	495.3
case, wooden, manufacturing	4671/4	499/2	467.5
electric, manufacturing	3442	354/2	344
for educational or exhibition purposes, manufacturing	3710	354/2	371.6
for testing physical and mechanical properties of materials, manufacturing	3710	354/2	371.2
panel clock, manufacturing	3740	352	374
Insulated			
cabinet, wooden, manufacturing	4671/4	472	467.5
electrical cable, manufacturing	3410	362	341
wire, manufacturing	3410	362	341
Insulating			
component, ceramic (electrical) manufacturing	2489/4	462/1	248.8
contractor (buildings)	5030	500	503.4
fitting, other than ceramic (for vehicles and aircraft) manufacturing	3434	369/1	343.1
(heat and sound) sheet, tiles, blocks and granules of plastics, manufacturing	4834	496	483
material, cork, manufacturing	4664/1	479/1	466.1
material, glass fibre, manufacturing	2479/4	463/1	247.5
material, rubber, manufacturing	4812/3	491/2	481.2
oil (at refineries) manufacturing	1401	262	140.1
oil (outside refineries) formulation	1402	263	140.2
tape, cloth, manufacturing	2569	491/2	438.3

Activity	SIC 1980	1968	NACE
Insulation, asbestos, manufacturing	2440	429/1	244
Insulator, ceramic, manufacturing	2489/4	462/1	248.8
Insurance			
agent (not employed by insurance company)	8320	860	832
broker (not employed by insurance company)	8320	860	832
company (composite)	8200/1	860	821
company (long-term)	8200/2	860	822
Integrated circuit			
manufacturing	3453/1	364/2	345.1
monolithic, hybrid and passive, manufacturing	3453/1	364/2	345.1
Intensifier			
hydraulic equipment, manufacturing	3283/2	333/4	328.3
photographic, manufacturing	2591	279/7	259.1
pneumatic control equipment, manufacturing	3283/3	333/4	328.3
Inter-varsity Fellowship of Evangelical Unions	9660	875	966
Interior sprung mattress, manufacturing	4671/5	473	467.8
Interlining weaving (from yarn spun on the cotton system)	4322	413	432.5
Intermediate bulk container (other than drum), plastics, manufacturing	4834	496	483
Internal combustion engine, manufacturing			
motor cycle	3633	382	363.2
motor vehicle	3510/3	381	351
tractor	3212	380	321.2
International			
Labour Office	0000	899/5	000
organisation (e.g. United Nations, International Labour Office)	0000	899/5	000
Interpreter (own account)	9890/2	899/7	984
Invalid			
car (body shell) manufacturing	3650/2	382	365.2
carriage (electrically propelled) manufacturing	3650/2	382	365
carriage (power operated) and parts, manufacturing	3650/2	382	365.2
carriage, manually propelled, manufacturing	3650/1	494/2	365.2
food (milk based) manufacturing	4130/3	215/2	413.2
food (other than milk based) manufacturing	4239/4	229/2	423.5
Inventor (so described)	8370/2	879/2	837
Invert sugar, manufacturing	4200	216	420.3
Investment			
adviser (not arranging transactions directly)	8360	865	836
broker	8310	862	831
casting equipment, manufacturing	3286/2	339/9	325.2
company	8150/2	862	813.2
trust	8150/2	862	813.2
Invisible mending	9812	893	981
Invoicing machine, manufacturing	3301	338	330
Iodine and iodides, manufacturing	2511	271/1	251
Ion exchange plant (water treatment) manufacturing	3245/3	341/2	324.1
Iridium, manufacturing	2247/2	323	224.1
Iron			
agent	6300	832/1	632
casting, manufacturing	3111	313/3	311.1
compounds, manufacturing	2511	271/1	251
dealing in	6120	832/1	612.4
directly reduced, manufacturing	2210	313/2	221.1
electric, manufacturing	3460	368	346
foundry	3111	313	311.1
ore calcining	2100	109/1	211.2
ore crushing	2100	109/1	211.2
ore mine or quarry	2100	109/1	211
ore preparation	2100	109/1	211.2
ore sintering	2100	109/1	211.2
ore washing	2100	109/1	211.2
oxide, synthetic, manufacturing	2511	277	251
pig, manufacturing	2210	313	221.1
pyrites extraction, not for iron production	2396	109/4	239.1
refined, manufacturing	2210	313/2	221.1
wire, manufacturing	2234	394	223.4
wrought, manufacturing	2210	311/1	221.1
yard	6120	832/7	612.4
Ironing machine, manufacturing			
electric, domestic	3460	368	346
non domestic	3275/6	339/9	327.3
Ironmonger			
retail	6480	821/3	648.6
wholesale	6150	812/4	615.2
Irrigation system, construction	5020	500	502.6
Isinglass, manufacturing	4239/9	229/2	423.8
Isolation hospital	9510	874/1	951
Issuing house	8310	862	831
Ivory working	4959	499/2	495.3

J

Activity	SIC 1980	1968	NACE
Jacket			
boys' (not retail bespoke) manufacturing	4532	442	453
leg of steel plate, for oil platform, manufacturing	3205/3	341/5	314.1
men's (not retail bespoke) manufacturing	4532	442	453
weatherproof, manufacturing	4531	441	453
women's and girls' tailored (not retail bespoke) manufacturing	4533	443	453
women's lightweight, manufacturing	4536/1	445/1	453
Jacks (other than for motor vehicles) manufacturing	3255/4	337/4	325.5
Jacquard			
(textile machinery) manufacturing	3230/2	335	323.1
machinery, carpet making, manufacturing	3230/2	335	323.1
Jam			
manufacturing	4147/3	218/1	414.6
pot cover, plastics, manufacturing	4835	496	483
Japanning, metal finishing	3138	399/11	313.5
Jar			
glass, manufacturing	2478	463/2	247.2
plastics, manufacturing	4835	496	483
Jeans			
boys', manufacturing	4534	444/1	453
cloth weaving	4322	413	432.5
men's, manufacturing	4534	444/1	453
women's and girls', manufacturing	4536/1	444/1	453
Jellied eel stall or shop	6612	885	661
Jelly, manufacturing			
powder	4147/3	218/1	423.6
table	4147/3	218/1	423.6
Jerry can, plastics, manufacturing	4835	496	483
Jet			
engine, manufacturing or repairing	3640	383/2	364
mine	2396	109/4	239.4
ornament and jewellery, manufacturing	4910/2	396	491.5
pump, manufacturing	3287	333/1	328.3
ware, pottery, manufacturing	2498/3	462/3	248.6
Jetty steelwork, manufacturing	3204/2	341/4	314.1
Jewel case, not wood or metal, manufacturing	4959	499/2	495.3

JEW-KNI

Activity	SIC 1980	NACE 1968	
Jeweller			
retail	6540	821/4	654.2
wholesale	6190	812/4	619.4
Jeweller's rouge, manufacturing	2460	469/1	246
Jewellers' materials, wholesale dealing in	6190	812/4	619.4
Jewellery			
designing	9760	879/5	976
engraving (not in distributive trades)	4910/1	396	491.1
gilded and silvered, manufacturing	4910/3	396	491.3
gold or silver plated, manufacturing	4910/1	396	491.1
polishing	4910/1	396	491.1
precious metal, manufacturing	4910/1	396	491.1
repairer	6730/2	821/4	674
Jewish			
Board of Guardians	9611/1	899/3	961
synagogue	9660	875	966
Jig, manufacturing	3222/3	390	322.2
Jig-saw puzzle, manufacturing	4941	494/1	494.1
Jigs and gauges, dealing in	6149	832/5	614
Job			
centre (government)	9111	901/6	911.1
dyeing	9812	893	981
printing	4754/5	489	473.4
Jobber	8310	862	831
Jobbing			
gardener	9900	891/2	990
waiter	9890/2	899/7	984
Jockey	9791/1	882	978
Jockey Club	9791/1	882	978
Joint			
Committee for National Diplomas and Certificates	9330	872/4	933
Matriculation Board and Examining Body	9320	872/4	932
organisation of employers and trade unions	9631/2	899/6	964
police authority	9130	906/1	913
Jointing (precision component) manufacturing	3289/2	349/3	328.9
Joints, asbestos, manufacturing	2440	429/1	244
Joist, steel, manufacturing	2210	311/2	221.1
Journalist, free-lance	8395/4	879/5	839.3
Judge	9120	901/6	912
Judicial Committee of the Privy Council	9120	901/6	912
Jujube, manufacturing	4214/2	217/2	421.2
Juke boxes, leasing of	8490	812/4	847
Jumper, knitting	4363/2	417	436.2
Junction box			
manufacturing	3420/3	369/5	342
steel, manufacturing	2220	312	222
Junior school	9320	872/1	932
Junket powder, manufacturing	4239/5	229/2	423.6
Justice of the Peace	9120	901/6	912
Justiciary, High Court of (Scotland)	9120	901/6	912
Jute			
calendering	4370/2	423	437.4
carpet, manufacturing	4350/2	415	438.1
cloth, manufacturing	4350/2	415	435.5
fabrics, bleaching, dyeing or otherwise finishing	4370/2	423	437
rope, cord or line, manufacturing	4396	416	439.6
sack, manufacturing	4556	422/2	439.7
sacking, manufacturing	4350/2	415	435.5
sorting	4350/1	415	435.3
spinning	4350/1	415	435.3
thread, manufacturing	4350/1	415	435.3
tow, manufacturing	4350/1	415	435.3
weaving	4350/2	415	435.5
winding	4350/1	415	435.3
yarn, manufacturing	4350/1	415	435.3
Juvenile			
court	9120	901/6	912
outfitter, retail	6450	821/2	645

K

Activity	SIC 1980	NACE 1968	
Kapok			
seed crushing	4116/2	221	411.3
seed oil refining	4116/3	221	411.4
willowing	4399/2	429/2	439.7
KD set manufacturing			
car (at least 50 per cent of value of complete vehicle)	3510/1	381	351
commercial vehicle (at least 50 per cent of value of complete vehicle)	3510/2	381	351
for car and commercial vehicle (value less than 50 per cent of complete vehicle)	3530	381	353
Keel owner	7260/3	706	730
Keene's cement, manufacturing	2420	469/2	242.3
Keg			
metal, manufacturing	3164/2	399/7	316.4
plastics, manufacturing	4835	496	483
wooden, manufacturing	4640/2	475/1	464.2
Kelp collecting, cutting and gathering uncultivated	0300/1	002	03
Kennel master	9791/1	882	978
Kennels	9890/2	899/7	01
Kensington			
Gardens	9111	901/6	911
Palace	9111	901/6	911
Kerb and edging, pre-cast concrete, manufacturing	2437	469/2	243.2
Kerbstone (not concrete) manufacturing	2450/3	469/2	245.3
Kernel crushing	4116/2	221	411.3
Kerosene, manufacturing	1401	262	140.1
Ketchup, manufacturing	4239/6	218/3	423.7
Ketones, manufacturing	2512	271/2	251
Kettle			
electric, manufacturing	3460	368	346
non-electric, manufacturing	3167	399/6	316.7
Kew Gardens	9770	899/4	977
Key			
blank, manufacturing	3169/1	399/3	316.3
manufacturing	3169/1	399/3	316.3
tag and case, leather, manufacturing	4420/1	432	442.1
Kiln			
furniture, manufacturing	2489/4	462/3	248.9
lining, manufacturing	2481	461/1	248.1
Kilt (tailored, not retail bespoke), manufacturing	4532	442	453
Kindergarten	9320	872/2	934
Kipper, manufacturing	4150/2	214/2	415.2
Kit, model, manufacturing	4941	494/1	494.1
Kitchen			
cabinet, manufacturing	4671/2	472	467.1
cloth, paper, manufacturing	4722	484/2	472.2
foil, metal, manufacturing	3164/4	321	316.4
furniture, manufacturing	4671/2	472	467.1
knife, manufacturing	3162/1	392	316.2
seating (upholstered) manufacturing	4671/1	472	467.4
towel, paper, manufacturing	4722	484/2	472.2
Kitchenware, manufacturing			
ceramic	2489/3	462/3	248
glass	2479/1	463/1	247
plastics	4836	496	483
Kite (not toy) manufacturing	3640	383/4	364
Klystron, manufacturing	3453/1	364/1	345.1
Knickers, manufacturing	4536/2	445/2	453

Activity	SIC 1980	1968	NACE
Knife, manufacturing			
cutlery	3162/1	392	316.2
horticultural	3161/1	391	316.1
industrial	3161/2	392	316.1
plastics	4836	496	483
tradesmen's	3161/2	392	316.1
with folding blade	3162/1	392	316.2
Knifegrinder, travelling	9890/2	899/7	984
Knitted			
bonnet, manufacturing	4363/2	417	436.2
bootees, manufacturing	4363/2	417	436.2
cardigan, manufacturing	4363/2	417	436.2
dress and jacket ensemble, manufacturing	4363/2	417	436.2
fabric, weft, manufacturing	4363/3	417	436.2
glove, manufacturing	4363/2	417	436.2
goods finishing	4370/2	423	437.4
goods printing	4370/2	423	437.3
goods scouring	4370/2	423	437.4
goods shrinking	4370/2	423	437.4
goods trimming	4370/2	423	437.4
or netted elastic over 30cm wide, manufacturing	4364	417	439.4
scarf, manufacturing	4363/2	417	436.2
shawl, manufacturing	4363/2	417	436.2
swimsuit, manufacturing	4363/2	417	436.2
tie, manufacturing	4363/2	417	436.2
twin set, manufacturing	4363/2	417	436.2
underwear, manufacturing	4363/2	417	436.2
underwear (excluding making up from purchased material) manufacturing	4363/2	417	436.2
vest, manufacturing	4363/2	417	436.2
Knitting			
machine, manufacturing	3230/2	335	323.1
machines, retail dealing in	6480	821/3	649.3
needle, metal, manufacturing	3169/2	399/8	316.9
needle, not plastics or metal, manufacturing	4959	499/2	495.3
needle, plastics, manufacturing	4836	496	483
wool, manufacturing	4310/2	414/5	431.3
worsted yarn, manufacturing	4310/2	414/2	431.3
yarns of cotton, manufacturing	4321/2	412	432.4
yarns of man-made fibres, manufacturing	4321/2	412	432.4
yarns of wool, manufacturing	4310/2	414/5	431.3
Knitwear, manufacturing	4363/2	417	436.2
Knives for machines, manufacturing	3222/1	392	322.2
Knob			
for electronic apparatus, manufacturing	3444	364/3	344
for furniture, plastics, manufacturing	4836	496	483
Kraft wrapping and packaging paper, manufacturing	4710/4	481	471.3

L

Activity	SIC 1980	1968	NACE
Label, manufacturing			
paper	4723/1	483	472.8
paper, gummed	4723/1	483	472.8
plastics, not self adhesive	4836	496	483
woven	4398/2	421/3	439.7
Labelling			
machine (for office use) manufacturing	3301	338	330
machinery (not for office use) manufacturing	3244/2	339/8	324.2
Laboratory	8370/2	879	837
Laboratory			
ceramic product, non-refractory, manufacturing	2489/4	462/3	248.9
fittings and furnishings, manufacturing	4672	474	467.5
furnace, manufacturing	3245/2	341/2	328.6
furniture, wooden, manufacturing	4671/3	472	467.5
glassware (not container) manufacturing	2479/3	463/1	247.4
Labour Party	9690/2	899/4	968
Lace			
(boot and shoe) manufacturing	4398/2	421/3	439.3
bedspread, manufacturing	4395	418	439.5
bleaching (not on commission)	4395	418	439.5
bleaching, dyeing, and dressing (on commission)	4370/2	423	437
cleaning and mending (not net mending)	9812	893	981
clipping	4395	418	439.5
curtain, manufacturing	4395	418	439.5
designing	4395	418	439.5
drawing	4395	418	439.5
dressing	4395	418	439.5
dyeing (not on commission)	4395	418	439.5
edging, manufacturing	4395	418	439.5
embroidery, manufacturing	4395	418	439.5
ending	4395	418	439.5
flouncing, manufacturing	4395	418	439.5
manufacturing	4395	418	439.5
mending	4395	418	439.5
net, manufacturing	4395	418	439.5
scalloping	4395	418	439.5
scarf, manufacturing	4395	418	439.5
tablecloth, manufacturing	4395	418	439.5
trimming, manufacturing	4395	418	439.5
Lacquer, manufacturing	2551	274	255
Lacquering (metal finishing)	3138	399/11	313.5
Lactones, manufacturing	2512	271/2	251
Lactose, manufacturing	4130/3	215/2	413.1
Ladder			
hire	8420	500	842
metal, manufacturing	3169/4	399/12	316.9
tape (textile material) manufacturing	4398/2	421/3	439.3
wooden, manufacturing	4650	479/3	465.1
Ladies'			
handbag, leather, manufacturing	4420/1	432	442.1
outfitter, retail	6450	821/2	645
Ladle, manufacturing	3162/1	392	316.2
Lager brewing	4270/1	231	427.1
Lagging rope, asbestos, manufacturing	2440	429/1	244
Lake			
pigment, manufacturing	2516	277	251
steamer service	7260/3	706	730
Lambskin clothing, manufacturing	4560	433	456.3
Laminate, manufacturing			
plastics, packaging product	4835	496	483
wholly of plastics and/or transparent regenerated cellulose film	4835	482	483
Laminated			
glass, manufacturing	2471/2	463/1	247.6
plastics film, manufacturing	4835	496	483
thermosetting plastics sheet, manufacturing	4832	276/1	483
wood products, manufacturing	4620/1	471/1	462.1
Laminates, metal foil with other materials, manufacturing	3164/4	321	316.4
Laminating			
machine (for office use) manufacturing	3301	338	330
machinery (paper working) manufacturing	3276	339/2	327.2
textile material	4370/1	423	437.4
Laminboard, manufacturing	4620/1	471/1	462.1
Lamp			
chimney, glass, manufacturing	2479/2	463/1	247.4

LAM-LEA

Activity	SIC 1980	1968	NACE
cycle, manufacturing	3434	369/1	343.1
glass, manufacturing	2479/2	463/1	247.4
holder, electric, manufacturing	3420/3	369/5	342
Lampshade			
not glass or plastics, manufacturing	4959	499/2	495.3
reflectors, covers and diffusers, plastics, manufacturing	4836	496	483
Lampshades, retail dealing in	6480	821/3	648.5
Land			
agent	8340	863	834
auctioneer	8340	863	834
clearing equipment machinery, manufacturing	3254/1	336	325.4
drainage	9212	906/3	921
drainage contractor	5020	500	502.6
investment company	8500	863	850
surveyor (not valuer)	8370/1	879/1	837
valuer or surveyor	8340/1	863	834
Landing			
stage, operation	7630	706	762
stage (floating) manufacturing	3610/1	370/1	361.2
Landlord (of real estate)	8500	863	850
Landscape gardening	0100/3	001/3	01
Lanolin recovery (from knackers)	4126/1	221	412.4
Lapping			
machine, metal cutting, manufacturing	3221/1	332/1	322.1
textile	4370/2	423	437.4
Lard			
(from knackers) manufacturing	4126/1	221	412.4
oil, manufacturing	4126/1	221	412.4
refining	4126/1	214/2	412.4
wholesale dealing in	6170	810/1	617.4
Laser			
(excluding laser system) manufacturing	3732	367/2	373
cutting or welding (metal working) machine tool, manufacturing	3221/1	332/4	322.1
Last, wooden, manufacturing	4650	479/3	465.1
Latch, manufacturing	3169/1	399/3	316.3
Latex foam, manufacturing	4812/3	491/2	481.2
Lathe			
chuck, manufacturing	3222/3	390	322.2
metal-cutting, manufacturing	3221/1	332/1	322.1
tool, manufacturing	3222/1	390	322.2
Launch vehicle for spacecraft, manufacturing	3640	383/1	364
Launderette	9811	892	981
Laundry	9811	892	981
Laundry			
blue, manufacturing	2516	229/2	259.4
brush, manufacturing	4663	493	466.3
machinery, manufacturing	3275/6	339/9	327.3
receiving office	9811	892	981
starch, manufacturing	4180	229/2	418.4
Lavatory seat cover, manufacturing	4557	422/1	455.1
Laver gathering (cultivated)	0300/2	002	03
Law			
agent	8350	873	835
Officer's Department	9111	901/6	911
publishing	4754/1	489	474.5
Society	9631/1	879/3	963
writing	8350	873	835
Lawn			
mower, manufacturing	3286/1	339/9	321.1
mower engine, manufacturing	3281/1	334/1	328.1
sand, manufacturing	2513	278	256.8
Lawyer (own account)	8350	873	835
Laying out of the dead	9890/2	899/7	984
Lead			
compounds, manufacturing	2511	271/1	251
crystal tableware, manufacturing	2479/1	463/1	247

Activity	SIC 1980	1968	NACE
dealing in	6120	832/1	612.6
manufacturing	2247/1	323	224.1
mining	2100	109/2	212.1
ore and concentrate extraction and preparation	2100	109/2	212
paint, manufacturing	2551	274	255
Leaded light, manufacturing	2471/2	463/1	247.6
Leasing of industrial, machinery	8490	832/10	847
Leather			
army accoutrement, manufacturing	4420/1	432	442.1
braces, manufacturing	4420/1	432	442.1
buff and mop, manufacturing	4420/2	432	442.3
buffalo pickers, manufacturing	4420/2	431/1	442.3
chamois, manufacturing	4410/1	431/1	441.3
check strap, manufacturing	4420/2	431/1	442.3
conveyor band, manufacturing	4420/2	431/1	442.3
dog lead, manufacturing	4420/1	432	442.1
dressing	4410/1	431/1	441.1
driving belt, manufacturing	4420/2	431/1	442.3
dyeing	4410/1	431/1	441.3
elevator band, manufacturing	4420/2	431/1	442.3
enamelling	4410/1	431/1	441.3
fillings, manufacturing	4510	450	451.4
football case, manufacturing	4942	494/3	494.2
for roller covering, manufacturing	4420/2	431/1	442.3
gaiter, manufacturing	4510	450	451.4
garment (men's) manufacturing	4532	442	453
garments (women's and girls') manufacturing	4533	443	453
gas meter diaphragm, manufacturing	4420/2	431/1	442.3
gilding	4410/1	432	441.3
glove (not sports) manufacturing	4538	449/2	442.2
goods (not industrial) manufacturing	4420/1	432	442.1
goods, retail dealing in	6460	821/4	646.2
goods, wholesale dealing in	6160	812/4	616.8
heel, manufacturing	4510	450	451.4
insole, manufacturing	4510	450	451.4
lace, manufacturing	4420/1	431/1	442.1
legging, manufacturing	4510	450	451.4
machinery belting, manufacturing	4420/2	431/1	442.3
mill band and strap, manufacturing	4420/2	431/1	442.3
or leather substitute dressing case, manufacturing	4420/1	432	442.1
or leather substitute handbag, manufacturing	4420/1	432	442.1
or leather substitute hat box, manufacturing	4420/1	432	442.1
or leather substitute pouch, manufacturing	4420/1	432	442.1
or leather substitute purse, manufacturing	4420/1	432	442.1
or leather substitute wallet, manufacturing	4420/1	432	442.1
or leather substitute watchstrap, manufacturing	4420/1	432	442.1
picker, manufacturing	4420/2	431/1	442.3
proofing	4410/1	431/1	441.3
seller, wholesale	6110	832/3	611.8
skip, manufacturing	4420/2	431/1	442.3
sock, manufacturing	4510	450	451.4
sole preparation	4410/1	431/1	441.3
spat, manufacturing	4510	450	451.4
sports bag, manufacturing	4942	494/3	442.1
tanning	4410/1	431/1	441.1
trimmings, manufacturing	4420/1	432	442.1
trunk handle, manufacturing	4420/1	432	442.1
tuft, manufacturing	4420/2	432	442.3
upper, manufacturing	4410/1	431/1	441.3
washer, manufacturing	4420/2	432	442.3
working machine, manufacturing	3275/3	339/9	327.4
Leathercloth, manufacturing	4831	492	438.3
Leavers lace, manufacturing	4395	418	439.5

Activity	SIC 1980	1968	NACE
Lectern, manufacturing	4671/3	472	467.5
Legal Aid Society	9690/2	899/3	968
Legation	0000	899/5	000
Legging			
and gaiter (cloth) manufacturing	4539/3	449/4	453
leather, manufacturing	4510	450	451.4
Leisure craft, rubber, manufacturing	4812/3	491/2	481.2
Lemonade powder, manufacturing	4283/1	232	428.2
Leno fabric weaving	4322	413	432.5
Lens, manufacturing			
contact	3731	353/2	373.1
of coloured glass for rail and road signals (not optically worked)	2479/2	463/1	247.4
mounted	3733	354	373.3
pressed or moulded, unworked (not of coloured glass for traffic signals)	2479/5	463/1	247.4
unmounted	3731	354/1	373.1
Lentil splitting, grinding or milling	4160	211/2	416.2
Lessee of tolls	7610/1	709/1	761
Letter			
card, manufacturing	4723/2	483	472.3
file, manufacturing	4723/2	483	472.3
Letter-opening machine, manufacturing	3301	338	330
Letterpress			
ink, manufacturing	2552	279/5	255
printing machine, manufacturing	3276	339/2	327.2
publishing	4754/1	489	474.1
Level measuring and control instrument, manufacturing	3710	354/2	371.2
Liberal			
association	9690/2	899/4	968
Party	9690/2	899/4	968
Library			
fittings and furnishings, manufacturing	4672	474	467.5
for general public	9770	821/4	977
furniture, manufacturing	4671/3	472	467.5
run by local authority	9770	906/3	977
Librettist	9760	879/5	976
Licensed			
bar	6620	886	662
messenger or porter	7700/2	709/3	772
victualler (public house)	6620	886	662
Life assurance	8200/2	860	822
Life-jacket, cork, manufacturing	4664/1	479/1	466.1
Lifebelt, manufacturing			
cork	4664/1	479/1	466.1
not cork or rubber	4959	499/2	495.3
rubber	4812/3	491/2	481.2
Lifeboat, manufacturing	3610/1	370/1	361.1
Lifebuoy, manufacturing			
cork	4664/1	479/1	466.1
rubber	4812/3	491/2	481.2
Lifejacket, manufacturing			
cork	4664/1	479/1	466.1
not cork or rubber	4959	499/2	495.3
rubber	4812/3	491/2	481.2
Liferaft, not rubber inflatable, manufacturing	3610/1	370/1	361.1
Lift			
manufacturing	3255/3	337/3	325.5
operating company	7260/2	702/1	725
operator	7260/2	709/3	725
Light			
commercial vehicle, hire (without driver)	8480/2	703	845
meter (electric) manufacturing	3442	351	344
outerwear (women's and girls') manufacturing	4536/1	445/1	453
Lighter			
cigarette, manufacturing	4959	399/12	495.3
lessee or owner	7630	706	763

Activity	SIC 1980	1968	NACE
(ship) manufacturing	3610/1	370/1	361.2
Lighthouse authority	7630	706	763
Lighting			
equipment (for vehicles) manufacturing	3434	369/1	343.1
fitting, electric (other than glassware) manufacturing	3470/2	369/5	347.2
retail dealing in	6480	821/3	648.5
Lightning conductor installation	5030	500	503.6
Lightship, operation	7630	706	763
Lightship, manufacturing	3610/1	370/1	361.1
Lime			
(ammonium nitrate) manufacturing	2513	278	251
hydrated, manufacturing	2420	469/2	242.2
hydraulic, manufacturing	2420	469/2	242.2
processing, agricultural, manufacturing	2420	469/2	242.2
processing kiln, manufacturing	3245/2	341/2	328.6
Limestone			
dealing in	6120	832/8	612.4
ground, manufacturing	2450/1	469/2	245.1
mine or quarry	2310/2	102/1	231.2
working	2450/3	469/2	245.3
Linch pin, manufacturing	3137/1	393	313.1
Lincrusta, manufacturing	4721	484/1	472.1
Line			
apparatus (carrier, duplex and repeater) manufacturing	3441	363	344
yarn of flax, manufacturing	4340/1	412	434.3
yarn of hard fibre, manufacturing	4396	416	439.6
Linen			
and linen goods, wholeale dealing in	6160	812/2	616.9
and union cloth, manufacturing	4340/2	413	434.5
bleaching	4370/2	423	437.1
buckram weaving	4340/2	413	434.5
dyeing	4370/2	423	437.2
hire (associated with laundry service)	9811	892	981
printing	4370/2	423	437.2
thread, manufacturing	4340/1	412	434.4
weaving	4340/2	413	434.5
Liner			
chimney, clay, manufacturing	2410	461/2	241
polyethylene, non woven, manufacturing	4835	496	483
(ship) manufacturing	3610/1	370/1	361.1
Lingerie, manufacturing	4536/2	445/2	453
Lining			
hat, manufacturing	4537/2	446/2	453
leather preparation	4410/1	431/1	441.3
Lino tiles, retail dealing in	6480	821/3	649.1
Linoleum			
manufacturing	4833	492	438.2
wholesale dealing in	6160	812/4	616.9
Linseed			
crushing	4116/2	221	411.3
oil refining	4116/3	221	411.4
Lint (surgical) manufacturing	2570	279/6	257
Lipstick, manufacturing	2582	273	258.2
Liqueur			
dealer, wholesale	6170	810/1	617.5
manufacturing	4240/2	239/1	424.3
Liquid			
coffee, manufacturing	4239/1	229/2	423.1
soap, manufacturing	2581	275	258.1
steel (primary) manufacturing	2210	311/2	221.1
sugar, manufacturing	4200	216	420
supply meter, manufacturing	3710	354/2	371.1
Liquorice, manufacturing	4214/2	217/2	421.2
Listing machine, manufacturing	3301	338	330
Literary agency	8395/4	865	839.3
Litho stone working	2450/3	469/2	245.3

LIT-MAG

Activity	SIC 1980	1968	NACE
Lithographic			
artist (own account)	9760	879/5	976
draughtsman	4754/5	489	473.4
ink, manufacturing	2552	279/5	255
printing	4754/5	489	473.2
Lithography	4754/5	489	473.4
Litter, moss, manufacturing	2450/4	499/2	495.3
Live storage rack, manufacturing	3255/1	337/1	325.5
Livery (not retail bespoke) manufacturing	4532	442	453
Livestock			
dealing in	6110	831/4	611.5
insurance	8200/3	860	823
Living room furniture, manufacturing	4671/2	472	467.1
Lloyd's			
Register of Shipping	8370/2	860	832
underwriter	8200/3	860	823
Loader (mining) manufacturing	3251	339/1	325.1
Loading shovel, manufacturing	3254/1	336	325.4
Loan			
and discount company (not licensed under the Banking Act 1979)	8150/1	862	813.1
company	8150/1	862	813.1
Lobe, pump, manufacturing	3287	333/1	328.3
Local			
authority	9112	906/3	911
authority cleansing department	9211	906/3	921
authority housing department	8500	863	850
authority or new town direct labour department	5000	500	500.1
education authority (administration only)	9112	872/4	911
Lock			
manufacturing	3169/1	399/4	316.3
motor vehicle, manufacturing	3530	381	316.3
washer, manufacturing	3137/2	399/4	313.2
Locker, manufacturing			
metal	3166/1	399/1	316.6
wooden	4671/3	472	467.5
Locknit fabric, manufacturing	4363/3	417	436.2
Locomotive			
body, manufacturing	3620/1	384	362.1
bogie, manufacturing	3620/1	384	362.1
braking system, manufacturing	3620/1	349/3	362.1
chassis, manufacturing	3620/1	384	362.1
diesel, manufacturing	3620/1	384	362.1
engine, manufacturing	3281/1	334/1	328.1
manufacturing	3620/1	384	362.1
parts and accessories, manufacturing	3620/1	384	362.1
Lodging House			
local authority	9611/2	899/3	962
private	6670/3	884	665.3
Log sawing	4610/1	471/1	461.1
London			
borough council	9112	906/3	911
Clinic	9510	874/1	951
Graduate School of Business Studies	9310	872/3	931
Museum	9770	899/4	977
Transport Executive (railways)	7210/1	701	721.1
Transport Executive (road services and headquarters)	7210/2	702/1	721.2
Loofah article manufacturing	4664/2	499/2	466.2
Loom			
manufacturing	3230/2	335	323.1
winder, manufacturing	3230/2	335	323.1
wooden, manufacturing	4650	479/3	465.1
Loose			
cover (furniture) manufacturing	4555	473	455.3
glassfibre, manufacturing	2479/4	463/1	247.5
leaf binder and refill, manufacturing	4723/2	483	472.3
Lord's Day Observance Society	9660	875	966

Activity	SIC 1980	1968	NACE
Lorry			
cab, manufacturing	3521	381	352
loader, manufacturing	3255/4	337/4	325.5
manufacturing	3510/2	381	351
Loss adjuster	8320	860	832
Lottery	9791/2	883	979
Loudspeaker, manufacturing	3453/2	364/3	345.1
Low			
alcohol drink (not exceeding 2 degrees of proof) brewing	4283/1	232	428.2
loader (trailer) manufacturing	3522	381	352
temperature carbonization solid fuel (not ovoids or briquettes) manufacturing	1200/4	261/2	120.3
Lozenge, manufacturing			
medicated	2570	272	257
not medicated	4214/2	217/2	421.2
Lubricants, wholesale distribution of	6120	811	612.2
Lubricating			
grease (outside refineries) formulation	1402	263	140.2
oil (at refineries) manufacturing	1401	262	140.1
oil (outside refineries) formulation	1402	263	140.2
oil additive, manufacturing	2567	271/3	256.7
pump (not for internal combustion engine) manufacturing	3287	333/1	328.3
Lubricator, manufacturing	3289/2	349/3	328.9
Luggage			
leather or leather substitute, manufacturing	4420/1	432	442.1
van, railway, manufacturing	3620/2	385	362.2
Luncheon			
bar, licensed	6611/1	885	661
club	6630	887	664
voucher company	8395/4	865	839.3
Lyric author	9760	879/5	976

M

Activity	SIC 1980	1968	NACE
MCC	9791/1	882	978
Macaroni, manufacturing	4239/7	229/2	417
Machine			
broker	6300	832/5	634
gun, manufacturing	3290/1	342	328.9
hemming	4557	422/1	455.1
part, wooden, manufacturing	4650	479/3	465.1
printing (textiles)	4370/2	423	437.3
quilting	4557	422/1	455.2
ruling	4723/2	483	472.3
tool, manufacturing	3222/1	390	322.2
tools, dealing in	6149	832/5	614.1
tucking	4557	422/1	455.1
Machinery			
accessories, leather, manufacturing	4420/2	431/1	442.3
agent	6300	832/5	634
belting, leather, manufacturing	4420/2	431/1	442.3
belting, woven, manufacturing	4398/2	421/2	439.7
dealing in	6149	832/5	614
stockist	6149	832/5	614
Machining centre (metal-working) manufacturing	3221/1	332/1	322.1
Mackintosh, manufacturing	4531	441	453
Made-up			
curtain, manufacturing	4555	473	455.3
filter cloth, manufacturing	4556	422/2	455.4
Magazine			
paper, manufacturing	4710/3	481	471.3
printing	4752/3	486	473.1
printing—publishing	4752/2	486	473.1
publishing	4752/1	486	474.4
Magistrate's court	9120	906/3	912

Activity	SIC 1980	1968	NACE
Magnesite			
brick, manufacturing	2481	461/1	248.1
brick and moulding, manufacturing	2481	461/1	248.1
Magnesite-chrome			
brick, manufacturing	2481	461/1	248.1
shape, manufacturing	2481	461/1	248.1
Magnesium			
compounds, manufacturing	2511	271/1	251
manufacturing	2247/1	323	224.1
Magnetic			
compass, manufacturing	3710	367/2	371
recording head, manufacturing	3453/2	364/3	345.1
tape, unrecorded, manufacturing	2599	364/3	259.4
Magneto, manufacturing	3434	369/1	343.1
Magnetron, manufacturing	3453/1	364/1	345.1
Magnolia metal, manufacturing	2247/1	323	224.2
Mail			
handling machine, manufacturing	3301	338	330
order house (general) retail	6560	821/5	656
Mains (power distribution) cable (insulated) manufacturing	3410	362	341
Maisonettes letting	8500	863	850
Maize			
flaked, production	4160	211/2	416.2
flour and meal production	4160	211/2	416.1
starch, manufacturing	4180	229/2	418.1
Make-up preparation, manufacturing	2582	273	258.2
Male nurses' uniform, manufacturing	4532	442	453
Malleable casting, manufacturing	3111	313/3	311.1
Malt			
and malt products	4270/2	231	427.2
extract, manufacturing	4239/4	229/2	423.5
Malted milk production	4130/3	215/2	413.1
Man-made			
fibre, not glass fibre, manufacturing	2600	411	260
fibre bulking (carried out in man-made fibre producing establishments)	2600	411	260
fibre bulking (other than in man-made fibre producing establishments)	4336	412	433.4
fibre crimping (carried out in man-made fibre producing establishments)	2600	411	260
fibre crimping (other than in man-made fibre producing establishments)	4336	412	433.4
fibre fabric bleaching, dyeing, printing or otherwise finishing	4370/2	423	437
fibre rope, cord or line, manufacturing	4396	416	439.6
fibre spinning on the cotton system	4321/1	412	432.3
fibre spinning on the woollen, worsted and semi-worsted systems	4310/2	414	431.3
fibre texturing (carried out in man-made fibre producing establishments)	2600	411	260
fibre texturing (other than in man-made fibre producing establishments)	4336	412	433.4
fibre twisting (carried out in man-made fibre producing establishments)	2600	411	260
fibre twisting on the cotton system	4321/2	412	432.4
fibre twisting on the woollen, worsted and semi-worsted systems	4310/2	414	431.4
fibre warping (carried out in man-made fibre producing establishments)	2600	411	260
fibre warping on the cotton system	4321/2	412	432.4
fibre warping on the woollen, worsted and semi-worsted systems	4310/2	414	431.3
fibre weaving (from yarns spun on the cotton system)	4322	413	432.5
fibre weaving of fabrics from yarns spun on the woollen, worsted and semi-worsted systems	4310/3	414/5	431.5
fibre winding (carried out in man-made fibre producing establishments)	2600	411	260
fibre winding on the cotton system	4321/2	412	432.4
fibre winding on the woollen, worsted or semi-worsted systems	4310/2	414	431.4
fibre yarn finishing (bleaching, dyeing etc.)	4370/2	423	437
tow, manufacturing	2600	411	260
Management			
consultant (own account)	8395/1	865	839.1
training establishment	9330	872/5	933
Manchester			
School of Business Studies	9310	872/3	931
warehouse	6160	812/2	616
Manganese			
bronze, unwrought, manufacturing	2246/1	322	224.2
manufacturing	2247/1	323	224.1
oxide, manufacturing	2511	271/1	251
Manicure			
case, leather, manufacturing	4420/1	432	442.1
preparations, manufacturing	2582	273	258.2
Manicurist	9820	889	982
Manifold (for industrial engine) manufacturing	3281/1	334/1	328.1
Manila rope, cord or line, manufacturing	4396	416	439.6
Manpower Services Commission	9111	901/6	911
Mansions letting	8500	863	850
Mantle warehouse, wholesale	6160	812/2	616
Manually propelled			
invalid carriage, manufacturing	3650/1	494/2	365.2
truck, not wooden, manufacturing	3650/2	399/12	365.2
Manufacturing furrier	4560	433	456
Manure			
dealing in	6110	831/3	611.3
spreader, manufacturing	3211/1	331	321.1
Manuscript book, manufacturing	4723/2	483	472.3
Map			
and plan printing, publishing and colouring	4754/2	489	473 and 474
manufacturing	4754/4	489	473.2
seller	6530	821/4	653.1
Marble			
dealing in	6130	832/8	613.2
glass, manufacturing	2479/3	463/1	247.4
masonry working	2450/3	469/2	245.4
quarry	2310/2	102/1	231.2
Margarine			
manufacturing	4115	229/1	411.5
wholesale dealing in	6170	810/1	617.4
Marine			
animal crude oils and fats production	4116/1	221	411.1
cargo lighterage	7630	706	763
cargo superintendent	7630	706	763
cargo surveyor	8370/2	879/1	837
diesel oil, manufacturing	1401	262	140.1
engine, manufacturing	3281/2	370/2	328.1 and 328.2
insurance	8200/3	860	823

MAR-MEN

Activity	SIC 1980	SIC 1968	NACE
non-propulsion engine, manufacturing	3281/2	370/2	328.1 and 328.2
paint, manufacturing	2551	274	255
propulsion engine, manufacturing	3281/2	370/2	328.1 and 328.2
salvage	7630	706	763
store waste dealer	6220	832/7	622
surveyor	8370/2	879/1	837
Marionette show	9760	881/2	976
Maritime agent	7700/2	709/1	772
Market			
gardening	0100/2	001/3	01
porterage, fruit and vegetables	6170	810/2	617.2
porterage, meat or fish	6170	810/2	617
research agency	8395/2	864	839.1
research consultant	8395/2	864	839.1
research organisation	8395/2	864	839.1
Marking ink, manufacturing	4954/2	495/2	259.3
Marl pit	2310/6	103	231.5
Marmalade, manufacturing	4147/3	218/1	414.6
Marquee, manufacturing	4556	422/2	455.4
Marquetry, wood, manufacturing	4620/1	471/1	462.1
Marriage bureaux	9890/2	899/7	984
Marshmallow, manufacturing	4214/2	217/2	421.2
Marzipan sweets, manufacturing	4214/2	217/2	421.2
Mask and respirator (not medical) manufacturing	3710	349/3	371.7
Mason (building)	5010	500	501.7
Mass radiography service	9520	874/1	952
Mast and spar (for pleasure boat) manufacturing	3610/2	370/1	361.3
Master			
alloys of copper, manufacturing	2246/1	322	224.2
of ceremonies	9890/2	899/7	984
Mat			
and matting, coconut fibre, manufacturing	4385/2	429/2	438.1
bath, manufacturing	4557	422/1	455.1
cork, manufacturing	4664/1	479/1	466.1
glass fibre, manufacturing	2479/4	463/1	247.5
jute, manufacturing	4350/2	415	438.1
rubber, manufacturing	4812/3	491/2	481.2
woven, manufacturing	4384/1	419	438.1
Match, manufacturing	2565	279/3	256.5
Matchet, manufacturing	3161/1	391	316.1
Maternity			
and child welfare services	9520	874/2	952
clinic	9520	874/2	952
hospital	9510	874/1	951
Mathematical instrument and machine, manufacturing	3710	354/2	371.4
Matrice, manufacturing	3276	339/2	327.2
Matting, manufacturing			
cane	4664/2	475/1	466.2
plastic woven	4833	429/2	438.2
rush	4664/2	475/1	466.2
Mattock, manufacturing	3161/1	391	316.1
Mattress			
base, manufacturing	4671/5	473	467.8
fully finished, manufacturing	4671/5	473	467.8
glass fibre, manufacturing	2479/4	463/1	247.5
interior sprung, manufacturing	4671/5	473	467.8
plastics foam, manufacturing	4671/5	473	467.8
sponge, manufacturing	4671/5	473	467.8
support, metal, manufacturing	3166/1	399/1	316.6
Matzos making	4197	213	419.1
Mayonnaise, manufacturing	4239/6	218/3	423.7
Measuring			
instrument, indicating (electric) for vehicles and aircraft, manufacturing	3434	369/1	344
rule, manufacturing	3710	391	371
tape, manufacturing	3710	391	371.5
Meat			
and bone meal (from knackers)	4126/3	221	412.5
canning	4122/3	214/2	412.2
chilling or freezing for human consumption	4121	214/2	412.1
for domestic animals, wholesale dealing in	6170	810/2	617.3
meal (ground meat) manufacturing	4126/3	221	412.5
pie (fresh or canned) manufacturing	4122/3	214/2	412.2
pie shop	6612	885	661
pies and puddings (frozen) manufacturing	4122/2	214/1	412.2
porter	6170	810/2	617.3
processing, machinery, manufacturing	3244/1	339/7	324.1
retail dealing in	6410	820/2	641.4
salesman, wholesale	6170	810/2	617.3
Mechanical			
leather preparation	4410/1	431/1	441.3
power transmission plant, manufacturing	3261/3	349/2	326.1
press (metal forming) manufacturing	3221/2	332/2	322.1
toy, manufacturing	4941	494/1	494.1
woodpulp, manufacturing	4710/1	481	471.1
Medal making	4910	396	491.6
Medals, retail dealing in	6480	821/3	649.6
Medical			
appliances, retail dealing in	6430	821/4	644.1
consultant (hospital)	9510	874/1	951
consultant (private practice)	9530	874/1	953
instrument (non-optical) manufacturing	3720/1	353	372
nucleonic apparatus, manufacturing	3443	367/2	344
Research Council	9400	874/1	940
research establishment (not attached to hospital)	9400	874	940
rubber dressing, manufacturing	4812/3	279/6	481.2
rubber goods (not dressings) manufacturing	4812/3	491/2	481.2
school	9310	872/3	931
Medicated dressings, manufacturing	2570	279/6	257
Medicinal			
feed additives (veterinary) manufacturing	2570	272	257
paraffin, manufacturing	1401	262	140.1
Medicine, manufacturing	2570	272	257
Medicines, retail dealing in	6430	821/4	643
Melamine			
manufacturing	2512	271/2	251
resin, manufacturing	2514	276/1	251
Melting furnace, manufacturing	3245/2	341/2	328.6
Member of			
Lloyd's	8200/3	860	823
Parliament	9111	901/6	911
Memory store, computer, manufacturing	3302	366	330
Men's			
and boys' hat, not felt or fur, manufacturing	4537/2	446/2	453
and boys' raincoat, manufacturing	4531	441	453
and boys' shirt, manufacturing	4535	444/2	453
and boys' underwear, manufacturing	4535	444/2	453
and boys' vest, manufacturing	4535	444/2	453
apron, manufacturing	4534	441/1	453
battledress, manufacturing	4532	442	453

Activity	SIC 1980	1968	NACE
blazer (not retail bespoke), manufacturing	4532	442	453
felt hat, manufacturing	4537/1	446/1	453
glove, manufacturing	4538	449/2	453
jacket (not retail bespoke) manufacturing	4532	442	453
jeans, manufacturing	4534	444/1	453
outerwear, knitted, manufacturing	4363/2	417	436.2
outerwear, tailored, (not retail bespoke) manufacturing	4532	442	453
outfitter, retail	6450	821/2	645
overall, manufacturing	4534	441/1	453
overcoat (not retail bespoke) manufacturing	4532	442	453
shorts, tailored, manufacturing	4532	442	453
sock, manufacturing	4363/1	417	436.1
suit (not retail bespoke) manufacturing	4532	442	453
swimwear, knitted, manufacturing	4363/2	417	436.2
trousers (not retail bespoke) (tailored) manufacturing	4532	442	453
underwear (knitted) manufacturing	4363/2	417	436.2
waistcoat (not retail bespoke) manufacturing	4532	442	453
Menagerie	9770	882	977
Mens' wear, retail dealing in	6450	821/2	645
Mental			
handicapped hospital	9510	874/1	951
health specialist (hospital)	9510	874/1	951
health specialist (private practice)	9530	874/1	953
hospital	9510	874/1	951
Mentally			
handicapped, home for the	9611/2	899/3	962
handicapped, school for the (non-local authority)	9320	872	932
ill, home for the	9611/2	899/3	962
Mercerising			
machinery (textile) manufacturing	3230/3	335	323.1
yarn	4370/2	423	437.4
Merchant converter	6110	812/2	616
Mercury vapour lamp, manufacturing	3470/1	369/4	347.1
Merino yarn, spinning	4310/2	414/2	431.3
Mesh bag, plastics, manufacturing	4836	496	483
Messenger			
(own account)	7700/2	709/3	772
service	7700/2	709/3	772
Metal			
badge, manufacturing	3169/2	399/8	316.9
bin, manufacturing	3163	399/7	316.4
broker, not scrap metal	6300	832/1	632
broker, scrap metal	6210	832/7	621
can, manufacturing	3164/1	395	316.4
casement, manufacturing	3142	399/2	314.2
curtain walling, manufacturing	3142	399/2	314.2
cutting machine (numerically controlled) manufacturing	3221/1	332/1	322.1
cutting machine tool, manufacturing	3221/1	332/1	322.1
door (other than safe door) manufacturing	3142	399/2	314.2
door frame, manufacturing	3142	399/2	314.2
drum, reconditioning	3164/2	399/7	316.4
etching	4754/5	489	473.4
furniture, not upholstered, manufacturing	3166/1	399/1	316.6
framed upholstery, manufacturing	4671/1	472	316.6
garden frame, manufacturing	3142	399/12	314.2
gate, manufacturing	3142	399/12	314.2
greenhouse, manufacturing	3204/1	341/4	314.1
grille (not cast) manufacturing	3142	399/12	314.2
hut, manufacturing	3142	341/4	314.1
pallet, manufacturing	3164/5	399/12	316.4
partitioning, manufacturing	3142	399/2	314.2
polish, manufacturing	2599	279/1	259.2
pre-treatment paint, manufacturing	2551	274	255
railing, manufacturing	3142	399/12	314.1
shed, manufacturing	3142	341/4	314.1
skylight, manufacturing	3142	399/2	314.2
spraying	3138	399/11	313.5
spraying machine, manufacturing	3286/3	339/9	328.7
stockholder	6120	832/1	612
toy, manufacturing	4941	494/1	494.1
treatment chemical, manufacturing	2567	271/3	256.7
window fixing	5040	500	504.6
window frame, manufacturing	3142	399/2	314.2
Metallic			
closure, manufacturing	3164/3	399/10	316.4
compounds, inorganic, manufacturing	2511	271/1	251
paint, manufacturing	2551	274	255
Metallurgical coke, manufacturing	1200	261/1	120.2
Metallurgist (private practice)	8370/2	879/2	837
Meteorological			
instrument, manufacturing	3710	354/2	371.3
instrument (optical) manufacturing	3732	354/1	373.2
Meter			
electricity, manufacturing	3442	354/2	344
liquid supply, manufacturing	3710	354/2	371.1
other than electricity and parking meter, manufacturing	3710	354/2	371.1
parking, manufacturing	3740	354/2	374
petrol pump, manufacturing	3710	354/2	371.1
water, manufacturing	3710	354/2	371.1
Metering pump, manufacturing	3287	333/1	328.3
Methane extraction (from natural gas)	1300	104	132
Methanol, manufacturing	2512	271/2	251
Methodist Church	9660	875	966
Methylated spirits, manufacturing	4240/1	271/2	424.1
Metronome (electronic or mechanical) manufacturing	3740	352	374
Metropolitan			
county council	9112	906/3	911
district, borough or city council	9112	906/3	911
Police Commissioner's Office	9130	906/1	913
Mica			
goods, manufacturing	2450/4	469/2	245.5
mine	2396	109/4	239.4
slab and sheet processing	2450/4	469/2	245.5
Microcircuit, manufacturing	3453/1	364/2	345.1
Microfilm equipment, manufacturing	3733	351	373.3
Micrometer, manufacturing	3710	390	371.5
Microphone, manufacturing	3453/2	364/3	345.1
Microscope, manufacturing	3732	354/1	373.2
Microwave			
component (not tube) manufacturing	3444	364/3	344
tube, manufacturing	3453/1	364/1	345.1
Middle school	9320	872/1	932
Midwife			
National Health Service	9520	874/2	952
private	9550	874/5	955
Military			
carbine, manufacturing	3290/1	342	328.9
clothing (not retail bespoke) manufacturing	4532	442	453
rifle, manufacturing	3290/1	342	328.9
Milk			
bar	6611/2	885	661
chocolate, manufacturing	4214/1	217/1	421.1
churn, metal, manufacturing	3164/2	399/7	316.4
cocoa, manufacturing	4214/1	217/1	421.1
homogenizing	4130/1	215/1	413.1
Marketing Board (milk depots)	6170	810/2	617.4

MIL-MOR

Activity	SIC 1980	1968	NACE
Marketing Board cattle breeding centres	0100/1	001/1	01
pan, manufacturing	3167	399/6	316.7
pasteurization plant, manufacturing	3244/1	339/7	324.1
powder, manufacturing	4130/3	215/2	413.2
products factory, butter and cheese	4130/2	215/2	413.1
roundsman (not farmer), retail	6410	820/2	641.3
shake base, manufacturing	4283/1	232	428.2
sterilizing	4130/1	215/1	413.1
ultra heat treatment	4130/1	215/1	413.1
wholesale dealing in	6170	810/2	617.4
Milking machine, manufacturing	3211/3	331	321.1
Milkman (not farmer), retail	6410	820/2	641.3
Mill board, manufacturing	4710/9	481	471.3
Mill board, asbestos, manufacturing	2440	429/1	244
Miller (undefined)	4160	211/1	416.1
Millinery			
importer	6160	812/2	616.3
of felt	4537/1	446/1	453
retail dealing in	6450	821/2	645.7
wholesale dealing in	6160	812/2	616.3
Milling			
(food processing) machine, manufacturing	3244/1	339/7	324.1
cutter, manufacturing	3222/1	390	322.2
machine (metal working) manufacturing	3221/1	332/1	322.1
machinery (textile) manufacturing	3230/3	335	323.1
Millstone and grindstone cutting	2450/3	469/2	245.3
Millstones of bonded abrasives, manufacturing	2460	469/1	246.1
Mincemeat, manufacturing	4147/3	218/1	414.6
Mine			
case and component, manufacturing	3290/2	342	328.9
salt	2330	109/3	233.2
sinking	5020	500	502.3
Mineral			
and pharmaceutical nutritional ingredients for food and feedingstuff, manufacturing	2570	272	not classified
broker	6300	832/1	632
colours, manufacturing	2516	277	251
cutter, manufacturing	3251	339/1	325.1
dressing plant, manufacturing	3251	339/1	325.1
insulation product, manufacturing	2450/4	469/2	245.5
oil blending	1402	263	140.2
oil extraction	1300	104	131
surveyor	8370/2	879/1	837
water bottling	4283/1	232	428.1
wool, manufacturing	2450/4	469/2	245.5
Miners'			
lamp, manufacturing	3470/2	369/5	347.2
rescue station	1113	101	111.1
Miniature circuit breaker, manufacturing	3420/3	369/5	342
Mining			
machinery, manufacturing	3257	339/1	325.1
of non-ferrous metal ores	2100	109/2	212.1
timber, sawn, manufacturing	4610/1	471/1	461.1
tool (bit) manufacturing	3222/1	390	325.1
tool (powered), portable, manufacturing	3285/2	339/6	325.1
Mint sauce, manufacturing	4239/6	229/2	423.7
Mirror			
dental, manufacturing	3720/2	353/1	372.3
frame, wooden, manufacturing	4650	479/3	465.1
glass, manufacturing	2471/1	463/1	247.1
interior and wing (motor vehicle) manufacturing	3530	381	247.6
Misfit clothing, retail dealing in	6450	821/2	645

Activity	SIC 1980	1968	NACE
Missile (guided weapon) manufacturing	3640	383/1	364
Missionary society	9660	875	966
Mitre, manufacturing	3710	391	371.5
Mitten and mitts (not knitted) manufacturing	4538	449/2	453
Mittens and mitts (knitted), manufacturing	4363/2	417	436.2
Mixed businesses retailing both food and non-food goods	6560	821/5	656
Mixing machine, rubber or plastics working, manufacturing	3275/2	339/9	324.3
Mobile			
bank (not self propelled) manufacturing	3523	381	352
canteen (not self propelled) manufacturing	3523	381	352
crane, manufacturing	3255/2	337/2	325.5
library (not trailer) manufacturing	3510/2	381	351
tea bar	6611/2	885	661
X-ray unit (not trailer) manufacturing	3510	381	351
Model			
for window display, plastics, manufacturing	4836	496	483
geographical, wax, plaster, manufacturing	4959	499/2	495.3
kit, manufacturing	4941	494/1	494.1
of ship, (made by shipbuilders) manufacturing	3610/1	370/1	361.1
plaster, manufacturing	4959	499/2	495.3
wax, manufacturing	4959	499/2	495.3
Modelling material, manufacturing	4941	494/1	256.7
Models for educational or exhibition purposes, manufacturing	3710	354/2	371.6
Module			
(oil platform) manufacturing	3204/2	341/4	314.1
tubular (for oil rig) manufacturing	3205/3	341/5	314.1
Mohair			
spinning	4310/2	414/2	431.3
weaving	4310/3	414/3	431.5
Molassed feeding stuff (containing more than 30 per cent molasses) manufacturing	4221	219	422
Molasses, manufacturing	4200	216	420.1
Mole catching by contractors	0100/3	001/1	01
Moleskin finishing	4560	433	456.1
Molybdenum, manufacturing	2247/1	323	224.1
Monastery	9660	875	966
Money			
changer	8310	862	831
lender	8150/1	862	813.1
Monitoring equipment, radio and television, manufacturing	3443	367/2	344
Monocle, manufacturing	3731	353/2	373.1
Monocular, manufacturing	3732	354/1	373.2
Monopod tower, of steel plate, manufacturing	3205/3	341/5	314.2
Monumental stonework, manufacturing	2450/3	469/2	245.4
Mop, manufacturing	4663	493	466.3
Moped, manufacturing	3633	382	363.1
Moquette			
not woollen, weaving	4322	413	432.5
woollen, manufacturing	4310/3	414/5	431.5
Morbid anatomy specialist			
hospital	9510	874/1	951
private practice	9530	874/1	953
Mordant dye, manufacturing	2516	277	251
Mortar			
bomb, manufacturing	3290/2	342	328.9
manufacturing	2420	469/2	242.2
(ordnance) manufacturing	3290/1	342	328.9

MOR-MUS

Activity	SIC 1980	1968	NACE
Mortars, wet, ready mixed, manufacturing	2436	469/2	243.6
Mortgage			
agent	8310	862	831
broker	8310	862	831
Mosaic			
cube, manufacturing	2450/3	469/2	245.4
cube (glass) manufacturing	2479/5	463/1	247.4
tile, glazed, manufacturing	2489/1	462/2	248.3
Mosque	9660	875	966
Moss			
collecting, cutting, gathering	0200	002	02
litter, manufacturing	2450/4	499/2	495.3
litter, dealing in	6110	831/3	611
Side Hospital	9510	874/1	951
Motel, licensed	6650/1	884	665
Motion picture production	9711/1	881/1	971
Motive power depot (British Rail or Northern Ireland Railways)	7100	701	710
Motor			
accessories, retail dealing in	6510	894	651.1
accessories, wholesale dealing in	6148	894	614.7
car breaking, for scrap	6210	832/7	621
car, insurance	8200/3	860	823
car, passenger, manufacturing	3510/1	381	351
car repairing	6710	894	671
chassis and parts, manufacturing	3530	381	353
coach, manufacturing	3510/2	381	351
coach service	7210/2	702/1	721.2
coach, private hire	7210/2	702/2	722
cycle, manufacturing	3633	382	363.1
cycle agent, retail	6510	894	651.2
cycle and moped tyre, manufacturing	4811	491/1	481.1
cycle axle, manufacturing	3633	382	363.2
cycle frame, manufacturing	3633	382	363.2
cycle hire	8480/4	702/2	845
cycle importer	6148	894	614.7
cycle parts and accessories, manufacturing	3633	382	363.2
for hydraulic equipment, manufacturing	3283/2	333/4	328.3
(pneumatic) manufacturing	3283/3	333/4	328.3
repair depot	6710	894	671
scooter, manufacturing	3633	382	363.1
spirit, manufacturing	1401	262	140.1
spirit, wholesale distribution of	6120	811	612.2
tricycle and parts, manufacturing	3633	382	363
tricycle frame, manufacturing	3633	382	363.2
vehicle accessories, fittings and parts, plastics, manufacturing	4836	496	483
vehicle body building	3521	381	352
vehicle collection	7230	709/1	723.2
vehicle, commercial, manufacturing	3510/2	381	351
vehicle depot, Hendon (Department of the Environment)	6710	894	671
vehicle engine, manufacturing	3510/3	381	351
vehicle fan belt, manufacturing	4812/2	491/2	481.2
vehicle importer	6148	894	614.7
vehicle jack, manufacturing	3255/4	337/4	325.5
vehicle lift, manufacturing	3255/4	337/4	325.5
vehicle painting and body repairing	6710	894	671
vehicle reconditioning	3510/2	381	351
vehicle repairing	6710	894	671
vehicle seat, manufacturing	3530	381	316.6
vehicle timing belt, manufacturing	4812/2	491/2	481.2
vehicles servicing	6710	894	671
vehicles, retail dealing in	6510	894	651.1
Motoring organisations (road patrols)	7610/1	709/1	761
Motorised caravan, manufacturing	3523	381	351
Motorists'			
organisation (not road patrol or touring service)	9690/2	899/7	968
organisation (road patrol)	7610/1	709/1	761
organisation (touring department)	7700/1	709/1	771
Motorway maintenance unit	7610/1	709	761
Mould			
(engineers' small tools) manufacturing	3222/2	390	322.2
(for foundry) manufacturing	3286/2	339/9	325.2
preparation plant, manufacturing	3286/2	339/9	325.2
silica, manufacturing	2481	461/1	248.1
Mouldable, refractory, manufacturing	2481	461/1	248.1
Moulded			
case circuit breaker, manufacturing	3420/3	361/3	342
glassware, manufacturing	2479/5	463/1	247.4
rubber bottoms for footwear, manufacturing	4812/3	491/2	481.2
skirting board, wooden, manufacturing	4650	471/1	465.1
Moulding			
box, manufacturing	3289/2	349/3	322.2
compounds, plastics, manufacturing	2514	276/1	251
machine, manufacturing	3286/2	339/9	325.2
machine, for wood, etc., manufacturing	3275/1	339/9	327.1
machine, rubber or plastics working, manufacturing	3275/2	339/9	327.1
magnesite, manufacturing	2481	461/1	248.1
pattern, wood, manufacturing	4650	479/3	465.1
wooden, manufacturing	4650	471/1	465.1
Mouldings for upholstery, rubber, manufacturing	4812/3	491/2	481.2
Mount, of paper, cutting	4728	484/2	472.8
Mountain climbing equipment, manufacturing	4942	494/3	494.2
Mountant, manufacturing	2562	279/2	256.2
Mounting paper on linen	4728	484/2	472.8
Mouth organ, manufacturing	4920/2	499/1	492.2
Movement (clock and watch) manufacturing	3740	352	374
Mower, agricultural, manufacturing	3211/2	331	321.1
Mowers for lawns, parks and sportsgrounds, manufacturing	3286/1	339/9	321.1
Muff, fur, manufacturing	4560	433	456.3
Muffle (refractory product) manufacturing	2481	461/1	248.1
Multi-wall paper sack, manufacturing	4724/1	482/2	472.4
Multicellular glass block, manufacturing	2479/5	463/1	247.4
Multilayer paper obtained by compression, manufacturing	4710/6	481	471.3
Multiple insulating glass, manufacturing	2471/2	463/1	247.6
Mungo, dealing in	6110	832/4	611.6
Municipal			
bus service	7210/2	702/1	721.2
savings bank	8140/3	861	812
Museum	9770	899/4	977
Museum			
fittings and furnishings, manufacturing	4672	474	467.5
furniture, manufacturing	4671/3	472	467.5
Mushroom growing (cultivated)	0100/2	001/3	01
Mushrooms, wholesale dealing in	6170	810/2	617.2
Music			
college of	9310	872/3	931
composer	9760	879/5	976
copyist and transcriber (own account)	9760	881/2	976
hall	9741/2	881/2	975

MUS-NEE

Activity	SIC 1980	SIC 1968	NACE
plate engraving	4754/5	489	473.4
publisher	4754/1	489	474.3
shop, retail	6480	821/3	649.4
teacher, (own account)	9330	872/5	935
Musical			
box, manufacturing	4920/2	499/1	492.2
instrument case, not wooden, manufacturing	4959	499/2	495.3
instrument case, wooden, manufacturing	4671/4	499/2	467.5
instrument hire	8460/2	821/3	846.2
instruments, manufacturing	4920	499/1	492
instrument tuning	9890/2	899/7	984
instrument, toy, manufacturing	4941	494/1	494.1
instruments, retail dealing in	6480	821/3	649.4
instruments, wholesale dealing in	6150	812/4	615.3
Musician (own account)	9760	881/2	976
Muslin			
clipping	4370/2	423	437.4
dressing	4370/2	423	437.4
ending	4370/2	423	437.4
finishing	4370/2	423	437.4
gassing	4370/2	423	437.4
mending	4370/2	423	437.4
weaving	4322	413	432.5
Mussel gathering	0300/1	003/1	03
Mustard			
manufacturing	4239/9	229/2	423.3
processing machine, manufacturing	3244/1	339/7	324.1
seed crushing	4116/2	211	411.3
Myograph manufacturing	3720/1	353	372

N

Activity	SIC 1980	SIC 1968	NACE
NAAFI			
canteen	6640/1	888	664
club	6630	887	664
headquarters	6640/1	888	664
Nail			
brush, manufacturing	4663	493	466.3
not wire, manufacturing	3137/1	393	316.9
preparation, cosmetics, manufacturing	2582	273	258.2
steel wire, manufacturing	2234	394	223.4
Nameplate, plastics, manufacturing	4836	496	483
Napery lace, manufacturing	4395	418	439.5
Naptha (LDF) manufacturing	1401	262	140.1
Napthalene, manufacturing	2512	271/2	251
Narrow fabric (not elastic or elastomeric) manufacturing	4398/2	422/1	439.3
National			
Bus Company (scheduled service subsidiary)	7210/2	702/1	721.2
Coal Board, central workshop	1113	101	111.1
Coal Board, coal research establishments	9400	876	940
Coal Board, coal stocking	1113	101	111.1
Coal Board, colliery road transport	1113	101	111.1
Coal Board, dirt disposal	1113	101	111.1
Coal Board, engineering establishment	1113	101	111.1
Coal Board, internal railway	1113	101	111.1
Coal Board, marketing department	6120	831/1	612.3
Coal Board, mining research establishment	1113	876	940
Coal Board, opencast executive	1114	500	111.1
Coal Board, plant pool	1113	101	111.1
Coal Board, pumping station	1113	101	111.1
Council for Civil Liberties	9690/2	899/4	968
Dock Labour Board	7630	706	763
Economic Development Office	9111	901/6	911
Enterprise Board	8150/2	862	813.2
Film Finance Corporation	8150/1	862	813.1
Foundation for Educational Research	9400	872/4	940
Galleries (Scotland)	9770	899/4	977
Gallery	9770	899/4	977
Girobank	8140/2	861	812
Greyhound Racing Club	9791/1	882	978
Health Prescription Pricing Authority	9111	874/3	911
Health Service Administration	9111	901/6	911
Health Welsh Pricing Committee	9111	901/6	911
Hunt Committee	9791/1	882	978
Institute for Adult Education	9330	872/4	933
Institute for Economic and Social Research	9400	876	940
Insurance stamp printing	4754/3	489	473.2
Library	9770	899/4	977
Library for the Blind	9770	899/3	977
Library of Wales	9770	899/4	977
Library, Scotland	9770	899/4	977
Maritime Board	9631/1	879/3	963
Maritime Museum	9770	899/4	977
Physical Laboratory	9400	876	940
Portrait Gallery	9770	899/4	977
Ports Council	7630	706	763
Research Development Corporation	8150/1	862	813
Savings Bank	8140/3	861	812
Society for the Prevention of Cruelty to Children	9611/1	899/3	961
Sunday League	9660	875	966
Sunday School Union	9660	875	966
Union of Students (not trading activities)	9690/2	899/4	968
Water Council	1700	603/1	170
Natural			
Environment Research Council	9400	876	940
gas booster/compression site	1620	601	162.2
gas condensates separation	1300	104	132
gas distribution	1620	601	162.2
gas exploration	1300	104	134
gas production well	1300	104	132
gas storage	1620	601	162.2
material used in flavours or perfumes, manufacturing	2564	271/3	256.4
sponge preparation	4959	499/2	495.3
Naturalisation agent	9890/2	899/7	984
Nautical			
instrument (not electronic) manufacturing	3710	354/2	371.3
instrument (optical) manufacturing	3732	354/2	373.2
school	9330	879/1	933
Naval			
architect (private practice)	8370/2	879/1	837
brass, unwrought, manufacturing	2246/1	322	224.2
dockyard (shipbuilding and repairing)	3610/1	370/1	361.1
ships (of all types) manufacturing	3610/1	370/1	361.1
Navigation	7610/2	706	762
Navigational aid, electronic, manufacturing	3443	367/2	344
Neatsfoot oil, manufacturing	4116/3	221	411.4
Necktie, manufacturing	4539/3	449/4	453
Neckware (ladies) manufacturing	4539/3	449/4	453
Needle			
knitting, not plastics or metal, manufacturing	4959	499/2	495.3
knitting, plastics, manufacturing	4836	496	483
metal, manufacturing	3169/2	399/8	316.9
roller bearings, manufacturing	3262	349/1	326.2
Needlefelt			
carpet underlay, manufacturing	4385/1	429/2	438.1

Activity	SIC 1980	1968	NACE
other than carpet underlay, manufacturing	4399/1	429/2	439.1
Needleloom			
carpet, manufacturing	4385/1	429/2	438.1
carpeting, manufacturing	4385/1	429/2	438.1
felt (carpet underlay) manufacturing	4385/1	429/2	438.1
felt (other than carpet underlay) manufacturing	4399/1	429/2	439.1
Nematocide, manufacturing	2568	279/4	256.8
Neon tube, manufacturing	3470/1	369/4	347.1
Net			
curtaining fabric (knitted or crocheted) manufacturing	4364	417	436.2
fishing, manufacturing	4396	416	439.7
garden, manufacturing	4396	416	439.7
lace (plain and spotted) manufacturing	4395	418	439.5
sports, manufacturing	4396	416	439.7
Netted fabric, manufacturing	4363/3	417	436.2
Netting			
plastics, not woven or knotted, manufacturing	4836	496	483
wire steel, manufacturing	2234	394	223.4
Neuropath	9550	874/5	955
New Town Corporation Housing Department	8500	863	850
Newmarket Heath	9791/1	882	978
News			
agency	8395/4	865	839.3
ink, manufacturing	2552	279/5	255
Newsagent, wholesale	6190	812/3	619.2
Newspaper			
printer	4751/3	485	473.1
printer-publisher	4751/2	485	473.1
publisher	4751/1	485	474.4
Newsprint, manufacturing	4710/2	481	471.3
Newsvendor	6530	821/1	653.1
Nickel			
manufacturing	2247/1	323	224.1
silver, manufacturing	2246/1	322	224.2
Nicotine preparation, manufacturing	2568	279/4	256.8
Night			
club	6630	887	663
safe, manufacturing	3166/2	399/3	316.6
Nightdress, manufacturing	4536/2	445/2	453
Nightlight, manufacturing	2599	275	259.4
Nightwear, manufacturing			
infants'	4536/3	445/3	453
knitted	4363/2	417	436.2
men's and boys'	4535	444/2	453
women's and girls'	4536/2	445/2	453
Nippers, hand tool, manufacturing	3161/2	391	316.1
Nitrate of soda importer	6120	832/8	612.7
Nitric acid and nitrates, manufacturing	2511	271/1	251
Nitro-cellulose coated textiles fabric, manufacturing	4831	492	438.3
Nitro-glycerine, manufacturing	2565	279/3	256.5
Nitrogen			
manufacturing	2567	271/1	256.7
resin type paint, manufacturing	2551	274	255
Nitrogenous straight fertilizer, manufacturing	2513	278	251
Noil			
dealing in	6110	832/4	611.6
sack and bag, manufacturing	4556	422/2	439.7
Noils (woollen industry) manufacturing	4310/1	414/1	431.2
Nominee company	8150/2	862	813.2
Non-alcoholic			
beer, manufacturing	4283/1	232	428.2
cider, manufacturing	4283/1	232	428.2
wine, manufacturing	4283/1	232	428.2
Non-compound animal feed and cattle feeding stuffs (excluding output of grain offals and oilseed cakes and meals) manufacturing	4222/2	219	422
Non-elastic			
and non elastomeric tape (textile material) manufacturing	4398/2	421/3	439.3
and elastomeric webbing, manufacturing	4398/2	421/3	439.3
braid, manufacturing	4398/2	421/3	439.3
Non-ferrous metal ore			
mining of	2100	109/2	212.1
quarrying of	2100	109/2	212.1
Non-precision chain, manufacturing	3137/3	399/12	313.4
Non-propulsion engine, marine, manufacturing	3281/2	370/2	328.1 and 328.2
Non-woven (bonded fibre) fabric, manufacturing	4399/1	429/2	439.2
Noodle, manufacturing	4239/7	229/2	417
Northern			
Ireland Finance Corporation	8150/1	862	813.1
Ireland Railways	7100	701	710
Lighthouses, Commissioners of	7630	706	763
Notched bar, aluminium, manufacturing	2245/1	321	224.1
Notepad, manufacturing	4723/1	483	472.3
Notice plate, plastics, manufacturing	4836	496	483
Nottingham lace, manufacturing	4395	418	439.5
Nougat, manufacturing	4214/2	217/2	421.2
Novelty			
goods, leather, manufacturing	4420/1	432	442.1
plastics, manufacturing	4836	496	483
Nozzle for gas turbine aero-engine, manufacturing	3640	383/2	364
Nuclear			
fired boiler (not marine) manufacturing	3205/1	341/1	315.1
fuel, manufacturing	1520	271/3	152
fuel plant, manufacturing	3205/2	341/2	324.1
power station (public supply)	1610/1	602	161.3
Nucleonic			
apparatus, industrial, manufacturing	3443	367/2	344
apparatus, medical, manufacturing	3443	367/2	344
instrument, manufacturing	3442	354/2	344
Nuffield Hospital Trust	9510	874/1	951
Numerical control and indication equipment for machine tools, manufacturing	3442	354/2	344
Numerically controlled			
metal cutting machine, manufacturing	3221/2	332/2	322.1
metal forming machine, manufacturing	3221/1	332/1	322.1
Numismatist, retail	6480	821/3	649.6
Nun's clothing, manufacturing	4536/1	445/1	453
Nurse			
hospital	9510	874/1	951
private	9550	874/5	955
Nursery			
and playground equipment, manufacturing	4942	494/3	494.2
day	9611/1	874/2	961
furniture, manufacturing	4671/2	472	467.1
school	9320	872	934
square, manufacturing	4557	422/1	455.1
Nurseryman	0100/2	001/3	01
Nurses' home	9611/2	884	962
Nursing			
agency employing nurses	9550	874/5	955
co-operative	9550	874/5	955
home	9510	874/1	951

NUT-OPT

Activity	SIC 1980	1968	NACE
society	9631/1	879/3	963
Nut			
and bean confectionery, manufacturing	4214/2	217/2	421.2
and bolt, manufacturing	3137/1	393	313.1
food, manufacturing	4239/9	229/2	414.6
shelling, grinding and preparing	4239/9	229/2	414.6
Nuts			
edible, retail dealing in	6410	820/2	642.3
wholesale dealing in	6170	810/2	617.2

O

Activity	SIC 1980	1968	NACE
Oat			
cake, manufacturing	4197	213	419
flour and meal, manufacturing	4160	211/2	416.1
grinding, rolling, crushing or flaking	4160	211/2	416.2
Occupation and training centres for the mentally disordered	9611/1	874/2	961
Occupational therapist (private)	9550	874/5	955
Ochre pit	2396	103	239.4
Ochres (pigments) manufacturing	2516	277	251
Off-licence (not public house)	6420	820/2	642.1
Off-shore			
drilling rig (floating) manufacturing	3610/1	370/1	361.1
pipeline installation (from oil or gas well)	1300	104	502.7
pipeline operating (natural gas)	1300	104	132
pipeline operating (oil)	1300	104	131
support vessel, manufacturing	3610/1	370/1	361.1
Offal			
(edible) preparation (i.e. removal, freezing, packing, etc)	4121	810/2	412.1
salesman, wholesale	6170	810/2	617.3
Office			
accessory, manufacturing	4954/3	495/2	495
cleaning contractor	9230	865	923
equipment hire	8430	832/10	843
equipment, retail dealing in	6530	821/4	653.3
fittings and furnishings, manufacturing	4672	474	467.5
furniture (upholstered) manufacturing	4671/1	472	467.4
furniture hire	8430	832/10	847
furniture, metal, manufacturing	3166/1	399/1	316.6
furniture, retail dealing in	6530	821/4	653.3
furniture, wholesale dealing in	6150	812/4	615.1
furniture, wooden, manufacturing	4671/3	472	467.2
machinery, dealing in	6149	832/5	614.4
machinery, manufacturing	3301	338	330
of High Commissioner	0000	899/5	000
of Manpower Economics	9111	901/6	911
of the Receiver for the Metropolitan Police District	9130	906/1	911
systems (of paper and board) manufacturing	4723/2	483	472.3
Offices letting	8500	863	850
Official			
Receiver in Bankruptcy, Office of	9111	901/6	911
Solicitor	9120	901/6	912
Offset litho printing machine, manufacturing	3276	339/2	327.2
Ohmmeter, manufacturing	3442	354/2	344
Oil			
additive, manufacturing	2567	271/3	256.7
based sealants, manufacturing	2562	279/2	256.2
burning, manufacturing	1401	262	140.1
cake, dealing in	6110	831/3	611.2
cooker, manufacturing	3165	399/12	316.5
diesel, manufacturing	1401	262	140.1
filter (motor vehicle) manufacturing	3530	381	353
fire, manufacturing	3165	399/12	316.5
fired domestic heating and cooking appliance, manufacturing	3165	399/12	316.5
fuel burner, manufacturing	3284/5	349/3	328.6
fuel, manufacturing	1401	262	140.1
gas, manufacturing	1401	262	140.1
logging company	8370/2	879/2	837
merchant, retail	6540	821/3	654.9
merchant, wholesale	6120	831/1	612.2
off-shore pipeline, laying	1300	104	502.7
pipeline terminal, operating (for petroleum)	1300	104	131
platform fabrication, of steel plate, manufacturing	3205/3	341/5	314.1
platform, operation	1300	104	131
platform (structural) sections, manufacturing	3204/2	341/4	314.1
production platform, fixed concrete or composite steel/concrete, construction of	5020	500	502.7
production well or platform, operating	1300	104	131
refining industry machinery (other than plant) manufacturing	3245/1	339/9	324.1
seal, manufacturing	3289/2	349/3	328.9
seed cake and meal, manufacturing	4116/2	221	411.3
seed, crushing	4116/2	221	411.3
seeds, dealing in	6120	832/8	612.7
shale mine	1300	104	133
shale retorting	1300	104	133
stabilisation plant, operating	1300	104	131
storage tank, domestic, manufacturing	3163	399/7	316.4
stove, manufacturing	3165	399/12	316.5
transformer (at refineries) manufacturing	1401	262	140.1
vapourizing, manufacturing	1401	262	140.1
Oilcloth, wholesale dealing in	6160	812/4	616.9
Oilskin, manufacturing	4531	441	453
Oilstones, bonded, manufacturing	2460	469/1	246.1
Ointment, manufacturing	2570	272	257
Old iron merchant	6210	832/7	621
Old persons' home (local authority or charity)	9611/2	899/3	962
Oleic acid, manufacturing	2563	275	256.3
Oleine, manufacturing	2563	275	256.3
Oleo resinous paint, manufacturing	2551	274	255
Oleo-stearine, manufacturing	4126/1	221	412.4
Olive			
oil refining	4116/3	221	411.4
preserving in salt or brine	4147/2	218/3	414.3
Omelette pan, manufacturing	3167	399/6	316.7
Omnibus			
repair depot (if separately identifiable)	6710	894	671
service	7210/2	702/1	721.2
Open University	9310	872/3	931
Opencast coal			
contractor	1114	500	111.1
disposal point	1114	500	111.1
site	1114	500	111.1
Opera			
company	9760	881/2	976
house	9741/2	881/2	975
Opthalmic			
clinic	9520	874/2	952
hospital	9510	874/1	951
instrument, manufacturing	3720/1	354	372.1
Optical			
bleaching agent, manufacturing	2516	277	251
density measuring equipment, manufacturing	3732	354/1	373.2
element (mounted) manufacturing	3733	351	373.3

Activity	SIC 1980	1968	NACE
element (unmounted) manufacturing	3731	354/1	373.1
glass, manufacturing	2479/5	463/1	247.4
goods, retail dealing in	6540	821/4	654.1
goods, wholesale dealing in	6190	812/4	619.3
instrument and appliance (other than photographic goods and analytical instruments) manufacturing	3732	354/1	373.2
meteorological instrument, manufacturing	3732	354/1	373.2
projector (meteorological) manufacturing	3732	354	373.2
surveying instrument, manufacturing	3732	354/1	373.2
Optician, dispensing	6540	821/4	654.1
Opticians, dispensing, wholesale	3731	354/1	373.1
Optometer, manufacturing	3720/1	353	372.1
Orchestra	9670	881/2	976
Ore, dealing in	6120	832/1	612.5
Organ			
rebuilding and repairing (in factory)	4920/1	499/1	492.1
tuning	4920/1	499/1	984
Organdie weaving	4322	413	432.5
Organic bonded abrasives, manufacturing	2460	469/1	246.1
Organist (own account)	9760	881/2	976
Oriental goods, retail dealing in	6480	821/3	649.6
Ornament			
glass, manufacturing	2479/1	463/1	247.4
gold or silver plated, manufacturing	4910/1	396	491.1
plastics, manufacturing	4836	496	483
precious metal, manufacturing	4910/1	396	491.1
Ornamental			
brass, casting	3112	399/12	311.2
ceramic ware, manufacturing	2489/3	462/3	248
tile, earthenware, glazed, manufacturing	2489/1	462/2	248.3
tree and shrub, growing	0100/2	001/3	01
Orphanage	9611/2	899/3	962
Orphanage school	9320	872/2	932
Orthopaedic			
appliance, not footwear, manufacturing	3720/3	353/1	372.4
appliances, retail dealing in	6430	821/4	644.1
hospital	9510	874/1	951
Oscilloscope, manufacturing	3442	354/2	344
Osier			
article, manufacturing	4664/2	475/1	466.2
growing	0100/1	001/1	01
preparation	4664/2	475/1	466.2
Osteopath			
not registered medical practitioner	9550	874/5	955
registered medical practitioner	9530	874/3	953
Ottoman, manufacturing	4671/1	472	467.4
Outdoor furniture, manufacturing			
metal	3166/1	399/1	316.6
non-upholstered	4671/2	472	467.3
upholstered	4671/1	472	467.4
Outerwear, manufacturing			
boys', tailored (not retail bespoke)	4532	442	453
children's knitted	4363/2	417	436.2
infants'	4536/3	445/3	453
knitted	4363/2	417	436.2
knitted, women's	4363/2	417	436.2
men's, tailored (not retail bespoke)	4532	442	453
plastics	4531	441	453
tailored (women's and girls') (not retail bespoke)	4533	443	453
weatherproof, manufacturing	4531	441	453
Outfitter			
retail clothing	6450	821/2	645.1
wholesale	6160	812/2	616.1
Outside			
broker	8310	862	831
porter	7700/2	709/3	772
Oven (food processing) machine, manufacturing	3244/1	339/7	324.1
Ovenware, glass, manufacturing	2479/1	463/1	247
Overall, manufacturing			
boys'	4534	444/1	453
domestic	4536/1	445/1	453
girls'	4534	444/1	453
men's	4534	441/1	453
Overboot, manufacturing	4510	450	451.3
Overcoat, manufacturing			
boys' (not retail bespoke)	4532	442	453
men's (not retail bespoke)	4532	442	453
women's and girls' (not retail bespoke)	4533	443	453
Overcoating, manufacturing	4310/3	414/5	431.5
Overhauling of electrical machinery	3420/3	361/3	342
Overhead			
line construction	5020	500	502.7
line fitting, manufacturing	3410	362	341
runway, manufacturing	3255/1	337/1	325.5
Overshoe, rubber, manufacturing	4510	450	481.2
Ovoid, solid fuel, manufacturing	1115	261/2	111.2
Oxfam	9611/1	899/3	961
Oxygen			
breathing equipment (medical) manufacturing	3720/1	353	372.2
compounds of non-metals (excluding carbon dioxide) manufacturing	2511	271/1	251
manufacturing	2567	271/1	256.1
Oyster			
bar, room (licensed)	6611/1	885	661
fishery	0300/1	003/1	03
Oysters, wholesale dealing in	6170	810/2	617.9

P

Activity	SIC 1980	1968	NACE
Pacemaker, electro-medical, manufacturing	3443	367/2	344
Packaging			
machinery, leasing of	8490	832/10	847
machinery, manufacturing	3244/2	339/8	324.2
product, plastics, manufacturing	4835	496	483
product, ceramic	2489/4	462/3	248.9
products for food (aluminium foil, plastic foil, bags, etc) retail dealing in	6480	821/3	648.3
Packer and shipper	7700/2	709/1	772
Packing			
asbestos (woven) manufacturing	2440	429/1	244
boiler, not asbestos or slag wool, manufacturing	4959	499/2	495.3
case, wooden, manufacturing	4640/1	475/2	464.1
machinery, manufacturing	3244/2	339/8	324.2
material, board, manufacturing	4725/3	482/1	472.4
service	7700/2	709/1	772
textiles	7700/2	709/1	772
Pad, hat, manufacturing	4537/2	446/2	453
Padding (for upholstery) manufacturing	4399/2	429/2	439.7
Padlock, manufacturing	3169/1	399/3	316.3
Paint			
and varnish, manufacturing	2551	274	255
and varnish, retail dealing in	6480	821/3	644.3
and varnish, wholesale dealing in	6150	832/8	615.5
cement-based, manufacturing	2437	464	255
not cement based, manufacturing	2551	274	255
spraying machine, manufacturing	3286/3	339/9	328.3
Painter (artist)	9760	879/5	976

PAI-PAS

Activity	SIC 1980	1968	NACE
Painters' brush, manufacturing	**4663**	493	466.3
Painting			
contractor	**5040**	500	504.4
roller, manufacturing	**4663**	493	466.3
Palaeontologist (consultant)	**8370/2**	879/2	837
Palladium, manufacturing	**2247/2**	323	224.1
Pallet			
hoist, manufacturing	**3255/1**	337/1	325.5
metal, manufacturing	**3164/5**	399/12	316.4
plastics, manufacturing	**4836**	496	483
truck, manufacturing	**3255/5**	337/5	325.5
wooden, manufacturing	**4640/1**	479/3	464.1
Palletizer, manufacturing	**3255/1**	337/1	325.5
Palm			
kernel crushing	**4116/2**	221	411.3
kernel oil refining	**4116/3**	221	411.4
oil, dealing in	**6120**	832/8	612.7
oil, refining	**4116/3**	221	411.4
Palmist	**9890/2**	882	984
Pamphlet			
printing	**4753/3**	489	473.2
printing-publishing	**4753/2**	489	473.2
publishing	**4753/1**	489	474.1
Pancake making	**4196**	212	419.3
Panel			
asbestos, manufacturing	**2440**	429/1	244
for motor vehicle bodywork, fibreglass, metal, manufacturing	**3530**	381	353
Panti-hose, manufacturing	**4363/1**	417	436.1
Pantie, manufacturing	**4536/2**	445/2	453
Pants (men's underwear) manufacturing	**4535**	444/2	453
Paper			
and board articles for interior decoration, manufacturing	**4721**	484/1	472.1
asbestos, manufacturing	**2440**	429/1	244
bag, manufacturing	**4724/1**	482/2	472.4
bag making, machinery, manufacturing	**3276**	339/2	327.2
bags, wholesale dealing in	**6190**	812/3	619.1
beaker, manufacturing	**4724/2**	484/2	472.4
blind, manufacturing	**4728**	484/2	472.8
boards, wholesale dealing in	**6190**	812/3	619.1
bobbin, manufacturing	**4728**	484/2	472.8
box, manufacturing	**4724/2**	482/1	472.4
clip, manufacturing	**3169/2**	399/8	316.9
converting (unspecified)	**4728**	484/2	472.8
creping	**4728**	484/2	472.8
cut to size (not packaging products) manufacturing	**4728**	481	472.8
egg tray, manufacturing	**4724/2**	482/1	472.4
embossing	**4728**	484/2	472.8
fastener, manufacturing	**3169/2**	399/8	316.9
for corrugated cardboard, of vegetable fibres, manufacturing	**4710/4**	481	471.3
handerchief, manufacturing	**4722**	484/2	472.2
hat, manufacturing	**4728**	484/2	472.8
kitchen towel, manufacturing	**4722**	484/2	472.2
label, manufacturing	**4723/1**	483	472.8
lace, manufacturing	**4722**	484/2	472.2
making machinery, manufacturing	**3275/4**	339/9	327.2
merchant, wholesale	**6190**	812/3	619.1
not sensitized, manufacturing	**4710/6**	481	471.3
pattern, manufacturing	**4728**	484/2	472.8
perforating	**4728**	484/2	472.8
plate, manufacturing	**4724/2**	484/2	472.4
pot, manufacturing	**4724/2**	482/1	472.4
ruling	**4723/2**	483	472.3
sack, manufacturing	**4724/1**	482/2	472.4
sensitized, manufacturing	**2591**	279/7	259.1
shavings, manufacturing	**4728**	484/2	472.8
staining	**4721**	484/1	472.1
towel, manufacturing	**4722**	484/2	472.2
toy and game, manufacturing	**4941**	494/1	494.1
transfer (e.g. for embroidery) manufacturing	**4728**	484/2	473.2
underwear, manufacturing	**4722**	445/2	472.2
yarn, manufacturing	**4710/6**	481	471.3
Paperhanging	**5040**	500	504.4
Papier mache works	**4728**	484/2	472.8
Parachute, manufacturing	**3640**	383/4	364
Paraffin			
dealing in, not retail	**6120**	831/1	612.2
manufacturing	**1401**	262	140.1
medicinal, manufacturing	**1401**	262	140.1
retail dealing in	**6540**	821/3	654.9
wax, manufacturing	**1401**	262	140.1
Parallel slide valve, manufacturing	**3288**	333/2	328.8
Parasol, manufacturing	**4539/2**	449/3	453
Parcels delivery service (not Post Office)	**7230**	703	723.2
Parchment			
and imitation parchment paper, manufacturing	**4710/4**	481	471.3
leather, manufacturing	**4410/1**	431/1	441.3
Parish council or meeting	**9112**	906/3	911
Park			
Lane Hospital	**9510**	874/1	951
local authority or municipally owned	**9791/3**	906/3	979
Parking meter, manufacturing	**3740**	354/2	374
Parliamentary			
agent	**8350**	873	835
Commissioner for Administration, Office of the	**9111**	901/6	911
Parquet			
floor laying (not by manufacturer)	**5040**	500	504.3
flooring, manufacturing	**4630**	471/1	463.3
Particle accelerator, manufacturing	**3435**	367/2	343.1
Particleboard, agglomerated with non-mineral binding substances, manufacturing	**4620/1**	471/1	462.2
Partition			
hollow, clay, manufacturing	**2410**	461/2	241
wooden, manufacturing	**4672**	474	463.2
Partitioning, metal, manufacturing	**3142**	399/2	314.2
Partnership agent	**8395/4**	865	839.3
Parts			
of furniture, wooden, manufacturing	**4671/4**	472	467.5
of industrial engine, manufacturing	**3281/1**	334/1	328.1
of motor vehicle (not electric) manufacturing	**3530**	381	353
Passage agent	**7700/1**	709/1	771
Passenger			
agent (not Transport Authority)	**7700/1**	709/1	771
carriage, railway, manufacturing	**3620/2**	385	362.2
conveyor, manufacturing	**3255/3**	337/3	325.5
Transport Executive (road services and headquarters)	**7210/2**	702/1	721.2
Transport Executive; railways	**7210/1**	701	721.1
Passenger-cargo liner, manufacturing	**3610/1**	370/1	361.1
Passport printing	**4754/3**	489	473.2
Paste			
adhesive, manufacturing	**2562**	279/2	256.2
aluminium, manufacturing	**2245/2**	321	224.3
asbestos, manufacturing	**2440**	429/1	244
brush, manufacturing	**4663**	493	466.3
Pastel, manufacturing	**4954/1**	495/1	259.3
Pastille, manufacturing	**4214/2**	217/2	421.2
Pastry			
brush, manufacturing	**4663**	493	466.3
retail dealing in	**6410**	820/1	641.8
including buns, making	**4196**	212	419
roller (food preparation machinery) manufacturing	**3244/1**	339/7	324.1

Activity	SIC 1980	1968	NACE
Patent			
agent	8350	879/2	835
broker	8395/4	865	839.3
fuel, solid, manufacturing	1115	261/2	111.2
fuel, solid, wholesale dealing in	6120	831/1	612.3
leather, manufacturing	4410/1	431/1	441.3
medicines, wholesale dealing in	6180	812/4	618.1
Pathological laboratory	9520	874/1	952
Pattern			
card, manufacturing	4728	484/2	472.8
casting, ferrous, manufacturing	3111	313/3	311.1
Pavement			
artist	9890/2	899/7	984
light, manufacturing	2479/5	463/1	247.4
Paving			
block, wood, manufacturing	4630	471/1	463.3
cast iron, manufacturing	3111	313/4	311.1
contractor	5020	500	502.5
slab, manufacturing	2450/3	469/2	245.3
stone, manufacturing	2450/3	469/2	245.3
tile, clay, unglazed, manufacturing	2410	461/2	241
Pawnbroker	8150/1	821/4	813.1
Pay and Record Office of armed forces	9150	901/5	915
Paying agent	8310	862	831
Pea			
and pie vendor	6612	885	661
splitting, milling or grinding	4160	211/2	416.2
Peanut butter, manufacturing	4239/9	229/2	423.7
Pearl			
drilling	4910/2	396	491.5
stringing	4910/2	396	491.5
Peat			
cutting and digging	2396	109/4	239.5
dealing in	6110	831/1	611.3
product (e.g. briquette, pot or for chemical use) manufacturing	2450/4	469/2	245.5
Pebble dredging	2310/4	103	231.4
Pedal			
bin, metal, manufacturing	3163	399/6	316.4
bin, plastics, manufacturing	4836	496	483
cycle frame, manufacturing	3634	382	363.2
cycle parts and accessories, manufacturing	3634	382	363.2
for pedal cycle, manufacturing	3634	382	363.2
toy car, manufacturing	4941	494/1	494.1
tricycle frame, manufacturing	3634	382	363.2
Pedestal mat, manufacturing	4557	422/1	455.1
Pelmet, plastics, manufacturing	4836	496	483
Pelt (fellmongery) manufacture	4410/2	431	431.1
Pen			
fountain, manufacturing	4954/1	495/1	495.1
nib, manufacturing	4954/1	495/1	495.1
writing or drawing, manufacturing	4954/1	495/1	495.1
Pencil			
lead, manufacturing	4954/1	495/1	259.3
manufacturing	4954/1	495/1	259.3
propelling, manufacturing	4954/1	495/1	495.1
sharpener, manufacturing	4954/3	495/2	495
Penetrating oil, manufacturing	1402	263	140.2
Penholder, manufacturing	4954/1	495/1	495.1
Pension			
accommodation	6670/3	883	665.3
fund (autonomous)	8200/2	860	822
Pensions appeal tribunal	9120	901/6	912
Penstock			
steel, manufacturing	3205/3	341/5	315.2
valve, manufacturing	3288	333/2	328.8
People's Dispensary for Sick Animals (not animal-care units)	9611/1	899/3	961
Pepper			
ground, manufacturing	4239/9	229/2	423.3
substitute, manufacturing	4239/9	229/2	423.3
Perambulator			
and pushchair, toy, manufacturing	4941	494/1	494.1
awning, manufacturing	4556	422/1	455.4
hiring and letting	8480/4	821/4	845
manufacturing	3650/1	494/2	365.1
Perambulators, dealing in			
retail	6540	821/4	655.2
wholesale	6190	812/4	619.6
Perchlorate explosives, manufacturing	2565	279/3	256.5
Percolator			
electric, manufacturing	3460	368	346
non-electric, manufacturing	3167	399/6	316.7
Percussion			
cap, manufacturing	2565	279/3	256.5
instrument, manufacturing	4920/2	499/1	492.2
Perforated metal, manufacturing	3120	399/12	312.2
Performing Right Society	9631/2	899/6	963
Perfume			
compounds (blended perfume concentrates) manufacturing	2564	271/3	256.4
manufacturing	2582	273	258.2
retail dealing in	6430	821/4	644.2
Perfumer, wholesale (not manufacturing)	6180	812/4	618.3
Perfumery and flavour chemicals, synthetic, manufacturing	2564	271/3	251
Periodical			
printing	4752/3	486	473.1
printing-publishing	4752/2	486	473.1
publishing	4752/1	486	474.4
Peripheral equipment (including card punches and verifiers) for computer uses, manufacturing	3302	366	330
Periwinkle gathering	0300/1	003/1	03
Permanent caravan (residential) manufacturing	3523	381	352
Peroxides, inorganic, manufacturing	2511	271/1	251
Perry, manufacturing	4261/2	239/2	426
Personnel carrier (tracked armoured fighting vehicle) manufacturing	3290/3	342	328.9
Pest destruction service (not specially for agriculture)	9211	899/7	921
Pesticide chemical, manufacturing			
inorganic (excluding formulated preparations)	2511	271/1	251
organic (excluding formulated preparations)	2512	271/2	251
Pet			
food, including canned, manufacturing	4222/1	219	422
food, retail dealing in	6540	821/4	654.8
shop	6540	821/4	654.8
Petersham ribbon, manufacturing	4398/2	421/3	439.3
Petro-chemical industry machinery (other than plant) manufacturing	3245/1	339/9	324.1
Petrol			
engine (industrial) manufacturing	3281/1	334/1	328.1
filling station	6520	894	652
manufacturing	1401	262	140.1
pump meter, manufacturing	3710	354/2	371.1
station pump, manufacturing	3287	333/1	328.3
Petroleum			
coke, manufacturing	1401	262	140.1
drilling equipment, manufacturing	3254/3	336	325.1
exploration	1300	104	134
feedstock, manufacturing	1401	262	140.1
gas, manufacturing	1401	262	140.1
geologist (private practice)	8370/2	879/2	837
grease (at refineries) manufacturing	1401	262	140.1
grease (outside refineries) formulation	1402	263	140.2
jelly (outside refineries) formulation	1402	263	140.2

PET-PIL

Activity	SIC 1980	1968	NACE
jelly, crude, (at refineries) manufacturing	1401	262	140.1
product (at oil refineries) manufacturing	1401	262	140.1
products, wholesale distribution of	6120	811	612.2
refining	1401	262	140.1
Petticoat, manufacturing	4536/2	445/2	453
Pew, manufacturing	4671/3	472	467.5
Pewter			
manufacturing	2247/1	323	224.2
ware, manufacturing	4910/3	396	491.3
Pharmaceutical			
chemicals, manufacturing	2570	272	251
chemist, retail	6430	821/4	643
chemist, wholesale	6180	812/4	618.1
glassware (other than container) manufacturing	2479/3	463/1	247.4
preparations, manufacturing	2570	272	257
Society	9631/1	879/3	963
Pharmaceuticals, veterinary, manufacturing	2570	272	257
Pharmacy, retail	6430	821/4	643
Phenol, manufacturing	2512	271/2	251
Phenolic resins, manufacturing	2514	276/1	251
Philatelist, retail	6480	821/4	653.4
Phonetic printing	4754/5	489	473.2
Phosphatic straight fertiliser, manufacturing	2513	278	251
Phosphorus compounds (excluding phosphatic fertiliser) manufacturing	2511	271/1	251
Photo			
engraving	4754/5	489	473.4
semi-conductor device, manufacturing	3453/1	364/1	345.1
Photo-diode, manufacturing	3453/1	364/1	345.1
Photo-electric			
cell, manufacturing	3453/1	364/1	345.1
exposure meter, manufacturing	3442	351	344
Photo-lithography	4754/5	489	473.4
Photoengraving machine, manufacturing	3276	339/2	327.2
Photoflash bulb, manufacturing	3470/1	369/4	347.1
Photogrammetric equipment, manufacturing	3732	354	373.2
Photograph			
colouring	9890/1	899/2	983
copying	4930	899/2	493.2
developing	4930	899/2	493.2
enlarging	4930	899/2	493.2
finishing	4930	899/2	493.2
mount, manufacturing	4728	484/2	472.8
mounting	9890/1	899/2	983
printing	4930	899/2	493.2
Photographer	9890/1	899/2	983
Photographer, commercial	8380	899/2	838
Photographic			
base paper, manufacturing	4710/3	481	471.3
chemicals, manufacturing	2591	279/7	259.1
enlarger, manufacturing	3733	351	373.3
equipment, hire	8460/2	832/10	847
film (sensitized) manufacturing	2591	279/7	259.1
film, unsensitized, manufacturing	4832	276/1	483
goods, retail dealing in	6540	821/4	654.1
goods, wholesale dealing in	6190	812/4	619.3
instrument, manufacturing	3733	351	373.3
plate (sensitized) manufacturing	2591	279/7	259.1
studio	9890/1	899/2	983
Photogravure			
machine, manufacturing	3276	339/2	327.2
printing	4754/5	489	473.2
Photolitho machine, manufacturing	3276	339/2	327.2
Phthalic anhydride, manufacturing	2512	271/2	251
Physical			
culture expert	9791/1	882	978
process (metal working) machine tool, manufacturing	3221/1	332/4	322.1
Physician and surgeon	9530	874/3	953
Physicist (own account)	8370/2	879/2	837
Physico-chemical process welding machine (metal working) manufacturing	3221/1	332/4	322.1
Physiotherapist (private)	9550	874/5	955
Physiotherapy clinic	9550	874/5	955
Piano			
hire	8460/2	821/3	846.2
manufacturing	4920/1	499/1	492.1
repairing (in factory)	4920/1	499/1	492.1
wire, manufacturing	2234	394	223.4
Pianofortes, retail dealing in	6480	821/3	649.4
Piccalilli, production	4147/2	218/3	414.3
Pick, manufacturing	3161/1	391	316.1
Pick-up			
arm and cartridge, for record player, manufacturing	3453/2	364/3	345.1
baler, manufacturing	3211/2	331	321.1
Picket, wood, manufacturing	4610/1	471/1	461.1
Picking band, leather, manufacturing	4420/2	431/1	442.3
Pickle (including beetroot and onion) manufacturing	4147/2	218/3	414.3
Pickling			
of fruit	4147/2	218/3	414.3
of vegetables	4147/2	218/3	414.3
preparations for metal treatment, manufacturing	2567	271/3	256.7
Picture			
agency	8395/4	865	839.3
frame mount, manufacturing	4728	484/2	472.8
frame, wooden, manufacturing	4650	479/3	465.1
framing	6480	821/3	675
postcard, manufacturing	4754/4	489	473.2
postcard, retail dealing in	6530	821/4	653
restoring	9760	879/5	976
transmitter, manufacturing	3441	363	344
Pictures, retail dealing in	6480	821/3	649.6
Pie			
meat, fresh or canned, manufacturing	4122/3	214/2	412.2
other than meat, manufacturing	4196	212	419.3
Piece goods			
dyeing	4370/2	423	437.2
retail dealing in	6450	821/2	645.6
unsupported rubber sheeting, manufacturing	4812/3	491/2	481.2
wholesale dealing in	6160	812/2	616
Pier			
operator (not amusement)	7630	706	763
owner or authority (not amusement)	7630	706	763
Piercing of base metal	3120	399/12	312.2
Piezo-electric crystal, manufacturing	3453/1	364/1	345.1
Pig			
dealing	6110	831/4	611.5
farming	0100/1	001/1	01
iron, manufacturing	2210	313	221.1
jobbing	6110	831/4	611.5
Pigment, synthetic organic, manufacturing	2516	277	251
Pikelet making	4196	212	419.3
Pile			
carpet, weaving	4384/1	419	438.1
driving equipment, manufacturing	3254/3	336	325.4
fabric, bleaching and finishing	4370/2	423	437
fabric, knitted, manufacturing	4363/3	417	436.2
Pilfer-proof cap, metal, manufacturing	3164/3	399/10	316.4
Piling			
building	5010	500	501.7
contractor (civil engineering)	5020	500	502.7
tubular welded, manufacturing	3205/3	341/5	315.2

Activity	SIC 1980	1968	NACE
wood, manufacturing	4610/1	471/1	461.1
Pillar, ceramic, manufacturing	2489/4	462/3	248.9
Pillion seat (for motor cycle) manufacturing	3633	382	363.2
Pillow			
case, manufacturing	4557	422/1	455.1
manufacturing	4555	473	455.2
Pills, medicinal, manufacturing	2570	272	257
Pilotage	7630	705/3	763
Pin, manufacturing	3169/2	399/8	316.9
Pinafore, manufacturing	4536/1	445/1	453
Pinarette, manufacturing	4536/1	445/1	453
Pincers, manufacturing	3161/2	391	316.1
Pincushion, manufacturing	4557	422/1	455.2
Pinking shears, manufacturing	3162/1	392	316.2
Pipe			
aluminium, manufacturing	2245/2	321	224.3
asbestos cement, manufacturing	2437	469/2	243.1
blank, copper, manufacturing	2246/2	322	224.2
case, not leather or plastics, manufacturing	4959	499/2	495.3
cast iron, manufacturing	3111	313/4	311.1
concrete, manufacturing	2437	469/2	243.2
copper, manufacturing	2246/2	322	224.2
covering section, asbestos, manufacturing	2440	429/1	244
cutter, manufacturing	3161/2	390	316.1
fabricated steel, manufacturing	3205/3	341/5	315.2
fittings, aluminium, manufacturing	2245/2	321	224.3
fittings, copper, manufacturing	2246/2	322	224.2
fittings, steel, manufacturing	2220	312	222
organ, manufacturing	4920/1	499/1	492.1
smoker's, manufacturing	4959	499/2	495.3
steel, manufacturing	2220	312	222
Pipeclay pit	2310/6	103	231.7
Pipeline operator	7260/1	709	724
Pipes and fittings			
pitch-fibre, manufacturing	2437	469/2	243.1
plastics, manufacturing	4834	496	483
Pipette, glass, manufacturing	2479/3	463/1	247.7
Pique weaving	4322	413	432.5
Pirns (textile machinery accessory) manufacturing	3230/4	335	323.1
Pistol, manufacturing	3290/1	342	328.9
Piston			
manufacturing	3289/2	349/3	328.9
ring, manufacturing	3289/2	349/3	328.9
Pit			
bottom machinery, manufacturing	3251	339/1	325.1
brine	2330	109/3	233.2
hydraulic, roof support, manufacturing	3251	339/1	314.3
prop, wood, manufacturing	4610/1	471/1	461.1
props, dealing in	6130	832/2	613.2
Pitch, manufacturing	2512	271/2	251
Pitch-fibre pipes and fittings, manufacturing	2437	469/2	243.1
Plaid Cymru	9690/2	899/4	968
Plain bearing, manufacturing	3261/2	349/1	326.1
Plaiting			
machinery (textile) manufacturing	3230/3	335	323.1
material, preparation	4664/2	475/1	466.2
textile	4370/2	423	437.4
Plan			
chest, metal, manufacturing	3166/1	399/1	316.6
printing	4754/4	489	473.2
Plane, manufacturing	3161/2	391	316.1
Planer tool, manufacturing	3222/1	390	322.2
Planing machine, manufacturing			
for wood (not portable power)	3275/1	339/9	327.1
metal-cutting	3221/1	332/1	322.1
Plank, manufacturing	4610/2	471/1	461.2
Plant			
hire for construction (without staff)	8420	500	842
hormone, manufacturing	2568	279/4	256.8
support, fabricated steelwork, manufacturing	3204/2	341/4	314.1
Planter, agricultural machinery, manufacturing	3211/1	331	321.1
Plaster			
anhydrite, manufacturing	2420	469/2	242.3
building, manufacturing	2420	469/2	242.3
cast, manufacturing	4959	499/2	495.3
dealing in	6130	831/2	613.2
gypsum, manufacturing	2420	469/2	242.3
model, manufacturing	4959	499/2	495.3
of Paris, manufacturing	2420	469/2	242.3
sticking (surgical) manufacturing	2570	279/6	257
tile, manufacturing	2437	469/2	243.3
Plasterboard			
dealing in	6130	831/2	613.2
manufacturing	2437	469/2	243.3
Plastering contractor	5040	500	504.2
Plastic			
body shell (motor vehicle) manufacturing	3521	496	352
raincoat, manufacturing	4531	441	453
shell upholstery, manufacturing	4671/1	472	483
Plastics			
belting, manufacturing	4812/2	491/2	483
brush (complete) manufacturing	4663	493	466.3
floorcovering, manufacturing	4833	492	483
foam mattress, manufacturing	4671/5	473	467.8
game, manufacturing	4941	494/1	494.1
hose, manufacturing	4812/1	491/2	483
laminate (packing product) manufacturing	4835	496	483
matting, woven, manufacturing	4833	429/2	438.2
outerwear, manufacturing	4531	441	453
protective footwear, manufacturing	4510	450	483
sports equipment, manufacturing	4942	494/3	494.2
toy, manufacturing	4941	494/1	494.1
tubing, manufacturing	4812/1	491/2	483
working machinery, manufacturing	3275/2	339/9	324.3
Plate			
aluminium, manufacturing	2245/2	321	224.3
domestic, ceramic, manufacturing	2489/3	462/3	248
glass, manufacturing	2471/1	463/1	247.1
glass, insurance	8200/3	860	823
plastics, manufacturing	4836	496	483
polish, manufacturing	2599	279/1	259.2
paper, manufacturing	4724/2	484/2	472.4
steel, manufacturing	2210	311/2	221.1
Plate-warmer (electric) manufacturing	3460	368	346
Platform			
drilling rig, manufacturing	3610/1	370/1	361.1
trailer (motor-drawn) manufacturing	3522	381	352
Plating (metal finishing)	3138	399/11	313.5
Platinum			
group metals, manufacturing	2247/2	396	224.1
jewellery, manufacturing	4910/1	396	491.1
manufacturing	2247/2	396	224.1
Playball, rubber, manufacturing	4812/3	491/2	481.2
Playground and nursery equipment, manufacturing	4942	494/3	494.2
Playing card, manufacturing	4754/4	489	473.2
Playwright	9760	879/5	976
Pleasure			
ground	9791/3	882	979
pier	9791/3	882	979
steamer caterer	6640/1	888	664
Pleated paper, manufacturing	4728	484/2	472.8
Pliers, manufacturing	3161/2	391	316.1

Activity	SIC 1980	1968	NACE
Plough			
disc, manufacturing	3211/1	331	321.1
manufacturing	3211/1	331	321.1
Plug, manufacturing			
electric	3420/3	369/5	342
electronic	3444	364/3	344
valve	3288	333/2	328.8
Plumbago crucible, manufacturing	2481	461/1	248.1
Plumbers' merchant	6130	831/2	613.3
Plumbing			
and pipe fittings, metal, not cast, manufacturing	3169/4	399/12	316.9
contractor	5030	500	503.2
Plush			
silk, manufacturing	4322	413	433.5
toy on wheels, manufacturing	4941	494/1	494.1
wool, manufacturing	4310/3	414/5	431.5
worsted, weaving	4310/3	414/3	431.5
Plutonium, processing	1520	271/3	152
Plywood			
dealing in	6130	832/2	613.1
manufacturing	4620/1	471/1	462.1
press, manufacturing	3275/1	339/9	327.1
Pneumatic			
and hydraulic conveying plant, manufacturing	3255/1	337/1	325.5
and hydraulic handling plant, manufacturing	3255/1	337/1	325.5
equipment and systems for aircraft, manufacturing	3640	383/4	364
portable power tool, manufacturing	3285/2	339/6	328.3
press (metal forming) manufacturing	3221/2	332/2	322.1
Pochette, leather, manufacturing	4420/1	432	442.1
Pocket			
book, leather, manufacturing	4420/1	432	442.1
knife, manufacturing	3162/1	392	316.2
timer, manufacturing	3740	352	374
watch; manufacturing	3740	352	374
Pocketing weaving	4322	413	432.5
Poet	9760	879/5	976
Point of sale unit, manufacturing	3301	338	330
Points and crossings for railway track, manufacturing	3289/3	311/2	314.4
Pole, wood, manufacturing	4610/1	471/1	461.1
Police			
authority	9130	906/1	913
court mission	9611/1	899/3	961
force	9130	906/1	913
Policeman	9130	906/1	913
Polish			
french, manufacturing	2551	274	255
manufacturing	2599	279/1	259.2
Polishes, abrasives, manufacturing	2460	469/1	256.7
Polishing			
(metal finishing)	3138	399/11	313.5
cloth and pad (unprepared: not bonded fibre fabric) manufacturing	4557	422/1	455.1
machine (for glass) manufacturing	3275/5	339/9	325.3
mop, manufacturing	4663	493	466.3
paste and powder, manufacturing	2599	279/1	259.2
stones of bonded abrasives, manufacturing	2460	469/1	246.1
yarn	4370/2	423	437.4
Political organisations	9690/2	899/4	968
Pollution control plant, atmospheric, manufacturing	3245/3	341/2	328.4
Polyamide			
compounds, manufacturing	2514	276/1	251
man-made fibre, manufacturing	2600	411	260
Polyester			
adhesive, manufacturing	2562	279/2	256.2
man-made fibre, manufacturing	2600	411	260
paint, manufacturing	2551	274	255
Polyesters, manufacturing	2514	276/1	251
Polyethylene			
film, manufacturing	4832	276/1	483
liner, non-woven, manufacturing	4835	496	483
manufacturing	2514	276/1	251
sack, non-woven, manufacturing	4835	496	483
sheet, manufacturing	4832	276/1	483
Polypropylene			
film, manufacturing	4832	276/1	483
manufacturing	2514	276/1	251
reel, printed, manufacturing	4835	496	483
sheet, manufacturing	4832	276/1	483
woven cloth, manufacturing	4350/3	415	435.5
Polystyrene, manufacturing	2514	276/1	251
Polytechnic (the 30 designated in England and Wales)	9310	872/3	931
Polytetrafluoroethylene (PTFE) manufacturing	2514	276/1	251
Polyurethane			
adhesive	2562	279/2	256.2
coated textile fabric, manufacturing	4831	492	438.3
paint, manufacturing	2551	274	255
Polyvinyl			
acetate, manufacturing	2514	276/1	251
acetate (and co-polymer) adhesive, manufacturing	2562	279/2	256.2
chloride film, manufacturing	4832	276/1	483
chloride leathercloth, manufacturing	4831	492	438.3
chloride, manufacturing	2514	276/1	251
chloride sheet, manufacturing	4832	276/1	483
Pomfret (Pontefract) cake, manufacturing	4214/2	217/2	421.2
Pontoon, manufacturing	3610/1	370/1	361.2
Pony club	9791/1	882	978
Poodle clipping	9890/2	899/7	984
Pop group	9760	881/2	976
Poplin weaving	4322	413	432.5
Pork			
butcher	6410	820/1	641.4
butcher, wholesale	6170	810/2	617.3
pie, manufacturing	4122/3	214/2	412.2
salted or pickled, manufacturing	4122/1	214/2	412.2
Porosimeter, manufacturing	3710	354/2	371
Port			
authority	7630	706	763
health authority	9111	906/3	911
military	9150	901/5	915
of London Authority	7630	706	763
Portable			
building metalwork, manufacturing	3204/1	341/4	314.1
lamp (electric) manufacturing	3470/2	369/4	347.2
power tool, manufacturing	3285/2	339/6	not classified
road sign hire (for construction)	8420	500	842
wooden building, manufacturing	4630	471/2	463.1
Porter			
brewing	4270/1	231	427.1
own account	7700/2	709/3	772
Porterage service	7700/2	709/3	772
Portland cement, manufacturing	2420	464	242.1
Portrait photography	9890/1	899/2	983
Positioner (pneumatic control equipment) manufacturing	3283/3	333/4	328.3
Positive displacement pump (reciprocating) manufacturing	3287	333/1	328.3
Post			
graduate college	9310	872/3	931
Office Corporation (postal and agency services)	7901	708	790

Activity	SIC 1980	1968	NACE
Office Purchasing and Supplies Department	**7901**	708	790
pre-cast concrete, manufacturing	**2437**	469/2	243.2
van, railway, manufacturing	**3620/2**	385	362.2
wood, manufacturing	**4610/1**	471/1	461.1
Postage stamp			
perforating	**4754/5**	489	473.4
printing	**4754/3**	489	473.2
Postal			
Headquarters	**7901**	708	790
sorting office	**7901**	708	790
Postcard (plain) manufacturing	**4723/1**	483	472.3
Poster			
aerographing	**4754/5**	489	473.4
printing	**4754/5**	489	473.2
writing	**4754/5**	489	473.2
Pot			
chimney, clay, manufacturing	**2410**	461/2	241
flower, clay, manufacturing	**2489/4**	461/2	248.9
flower, plastics, manufacturing	**4836**	496	483
glass, manufacturing	**2478**	463/2	247.2
paper, manufacturing	**4724/2**	482/1	472.4
plastics (not flower pot) manufacturing	**4835**	496	483
Potash mine	**2396**	109/4	232
Potassic straight fertilizer, manufacturing	**2513**	278	251
Potassium compounds, manufacturing	**2511**	271/1	251
Potato			
crisp, manufacturing	**4239/3**	218/3	423.8
flour, manufacturing	**4147/4**	218/3	423.8
growing	**0100/1**	001/1	01
harvester and sorter, manufacturing	**3211/2**	331	321.1
Marketing Board	**6170**	810/2	617.2
puff, manufacturing	**4239/3**	218/3	423.8
salesman, wholesale	**6170**	810/2	617.2
starch, manufacturing	**4180**	229/2	418.4
stick, manufacturing	**4239/3**	218/3	423.8
straw, manufacturing	**4239/3**	218/3	423.8
Potatoes, dealing in			
retail	**6410**	820/2	641.2
wholesale	**6170**	810/2	617.2
Potentiometric recorder, manufacturing	**3442**	354/2	344
Potted			
meat, manufacturing	**4122/3**	214/2	412.2
shrimp, manufacturing	**4150/2**	214/2	415.2
Potters' clay mine or quarry	**2310/6**	103	231.7
Pottery			
domestic, manufacturing	**2489/3**	462/3	248.6
making machinery, manufacturing	**3275/5**	339/9	325.3
retail dealing in	**6480**	821/3	648.7
wholesale dealing in	**6150**	812/4	615.4
Pouch, leather or leather substitute, manufacturing	**4420/1**	432	442.1
Pouffe, manufacturing	**4671/1**	472	467.4
Poult, weaving	**4322**	413	432.5
Poultry			
canning	**4123/2**	214/2	412.3
dressing	**4123/1**	214/2	412.3
farming	**0100/1**	001/1	01
grit, manufacturing	**4222/2**	219	422
house, wooden, manufacturing	**4630**	471/1	463.1
(live) dealing in	**6110**	831/4	611
potting	**4123/2**	214/2	412.3
retail dealing in	**6410**	820/2	641.6
spice, dealing in	**6110**	831/3	611.2
wholesale dealing in	**6170**	810/2	611.3
Powder			
aluminium, manufacturing	**2245/2**	321	224.3
compact, plastics, manufacturing	**4836**	496	483
copper, manufacturing	**2246/2**	322	224.2
glass, manufacturing	**2479/5**	463/1	247.4
puff, manufacturing	**4959**	499/2	495.3
Powdered			
broth, containing meat or vegetables or both, manufacturing	**4239/6**	218/3	423.7
soup, containing meat or vegetables or both, manufacturing	**4239/6**	218/3	423.7
sugar, manufacturing	**4200**	216	420
Power			
boats (of all types) manufacturing	**3610/2**	370/1	361.3
control for aircraft, manufacturing	**3640**	383/4	364
station (not for public supply)	**1610/2**	602	161
station (public supply)	**1610/1**	602	161
station structural steelwork, manufacturing	**3204/1**	341.4	314.1
supply unit for electronic applications, manufacturing	**3442**	354/2	344
tool, electric, portable, manufacturing	**3285/2**	339/6	343.1
Powered			
barrow, manufacturing	**3254/1**	336	325.4
hammer, portable, manufacturing	**3285/2**	339/6	not classified
invalid carriage chassis, manufacturing	**3650/2**	382	365.2
roof support (mining) manufacturing	**3251**	339/1	314.3
Pram blanket (outside knitting or weaving establishment) manufacturing	**4557**	422/1	455.2
Prams, dolls', manufacturing	**4941**	494/1	494.1
Pre-cast concrete products			
dealing in	**6130**	831/2	613.2
manufacturing	**2437**	469/2	243.2
Pre-convalescent hospital	**9510**	874/1	951
Pre-recorded tape, manufacturing	**3452**	365/1	345.2
Pre-shave lotion, manufacturing	**2582**	273	258.2
Pre-stressed concrete products, manufacturing	**2437**	469/2	243.2
Precious			
stone cutting	**4910/2**	396	491.5
stone jewellery, manufacturing	**4910/2**	396	491.5
stones, wholesale dealing in	**6190**	812/4	619.4
Precision			
balance, manufacturing	**3710**	354/2	371.6
chain, manufacturing	**3261/1**	349/2	326.1
drawing instrument and machine, manufacturing	**3710**	354/2	371.4
screw, manufacturing	**3137/1**	393	313.1
Prefabricated			
building metalwork, manufacturing	**3204/1**	341/4	314.1
buildings and components, concrete, manufacturing	**2437**	469/2	243.2
wooden building, manufacturing	**4630**	471/2	463.1
Premier-jus, manufacturing	**4126/1**	221	412.4
Preparatory school	**9320**	872/2	934
Presbyterian Church	**9660**	875	966
Preserved			
cream, manufacturing	**4130/3**	215/2	413.2
meat, manufacturing	**4122/3**	214/2	412.2
Press			
cloth, manufacturing	**4310/3**	414/5	431.5
cutting agency	**8395/4**	865	839.3
for food and drink manufacture, manufacturing	**3244/1**	339/7	324.1
hydraulic (metal forming) manufacturing	**3221/2**	332/2	322.1
mechanical (metal forming) manufacturing	**3221/2**	332/2	322.1
metal forming, manufacturing	**3221/2**	332/2	322.1
pneumatic (metal forming) manufacturing	**3221**	332/2	322.1
stud, manufacturing	**3169/2**	399/8	316.9
tool, manufacturing	**3222/2**	390	322.2
Pressboard, manufacturing	**4710/9**	481	471.3

PRE-PRO

Activity	SIC 1980	1968	NACE
Pressed			
felt, not paper or roofing, manufacturing	4399/1	414/6	439.1
wool felt, manufacturing	4399/1	414/6	439.1
Presses, rubber or plastics working, machinery, manufacturing	3275/2	339/9	327.1
Pressing			
and valeting	9812	893	981
of base metal	3120	399/12	312.2
Presspahn, manufacturing	4710/9	481	471.3
Pressure			
cooker, manufacturing	3167	399/6	316.7
die-casting non-ferrous base metal, manufacturing	3112	not classified	311.2
forming machine, for rubber or plastics, manufacturing	3275/2	339/9	327.1
gauge, manufacturing	3710	354/2	371.2
measuring and control instrument, manufacturing	3710	354/2	371.2
pipe, pre-stressed concrete, manufacturing	2437	469/2	243.2
sensitive adhesive tape, manufacturing	2569	491/2	259.3
switch, manufacturing	3710	354/2	371.2
treatment of wood	4620/2	471/1	462.4
Primary			
battery, manufacturing	3432/1	369/2	343.2
copper, manufacturing	2246/1	322	224.1
school	9320	872/1	932
Primer			
for cartridge, manufacturing	3290/2	342	328.9
paint, manufacturing	2551	274	255
Princess Mary's RAFNS	9150	901/4	915
Print cloth, weaving	4322	413	432.5
Print colouring	4754/5	489	473.4
Printed			
circuit, manufacturing	3444	364/3	344
felt base floorcovering, manufacturing	4833	492	438.2
label (textile material) manufacturing	4398/2	421/3	439.7
matter for accounting and technical use, manufacturing	4754/4	489	473.2
paper bag, manufacturing	4724/1	482/2	472.4
vinyl floorcovering, manufacturing	4833	492	438.2
Printer, computer, manufacturing	3302	366	330
Printers cards, manufacturing	4723/1	483	472.3
Printers'			
blanket, rubber, manufacturing	4812/3	491/2	481.2
designing	4754/5	489	473.4
varnish, manufacturing	2552	279/5	255
weaving	4322	413	432.5
Printing			
ink, manufacturing	2552	279/5	255
machine or press, manufacturing	3276	339/2	327.2
machinery (textile) manufacturing	3230/3	335	323.1
of sound tracks	4930	881/1	493.1
paper, manufacturing	4710/3	481	471.3
plate engraving	4754/5	489	473.4
roller engraving	4754/5	489	473.4
screen, manufacturing	4754/4	489	473.4
undefined	4754/5	489	473.2
Prints, retail dealing in	6480	821/3	649.6
Prism, manufacturing			
mounted	3733	354/1	373.3
pressed or moulded, unworked	2479/5	463/1	247.4
unmounted	3731	354/1	373.1
Prison (not naval or military)	9120	901/6	912
Private			
detective	8395/4 and 9890/2	899/7	839.3 and 984

Activity	SIC 1980	1968	NACE
domestic service (non-resident)	9900	891/2	990
domestic service (resident)	9900	891/1	990
gardener	9900	891/2	990
hire car with driver	7220	702/2	722
hospital	9510	874/1	951
hotel, licensed	6650/1	884	665.1
hotel, unlicensed	6650/2	884	665.1
lodging house	6670/3	884	665.3
school	9320	872/2	932
tutor (resident)	9900	891/1	990
Probate registry (principal or district)	9111	901/6	911
Probation and After-Care Service	9611/1	899/3	961
Process			
block making	4754/5	489	473.4
control equipment, electric, manufacturing	3442	354/2	344
control equipment, electronic, manufacturing	3442	354/2	344
engineering contractor	3246	341/3	324
engraving	4754/5	489	473.4
heater, manufacturing	3205/1	341/2	324.1
oil refining	1401	262	140.1
pipework, manufacturing	3205/3	341/5	315.2
plate, engraving	4754/5	489	473.4
pressure sphere, manufacturing	3205/2	341/5	315.2
pressure vessel, manufacturing	3205/2	341/5	315.2
server (own account)	8350	873	835
Processed			
cheese, manufacturing	4130/2	215/2	413.1
fibre, asbestos, manufacturing	2440	429/1	244
Profile shapes of plastics materials (rods, tubes, etc.) manufacturing	4832	276/1	483
Programmer (textile machinery) manufacturing	3230/3	335	323.1
Projector			
lamp, manufacturing	3470/1	369/4	347.1
photographic or cinematographic, manufacturing	3733	351	373.3
Prop, ceramic, manufacturing	2489/4	462/3	248.9
Propane			
extraction (from natural gas)	1300	104	132
manufacturing	1401	262	140.1
Propellent powder, manufacturing	2565	279/3	256.5
Propeller			
aircraft, manufacturing	3640	383/4	364
marine—built-up or machined casting, manufacturing	3289/1	370	361
shaft, motor vehicle, manufacturing	3530	381	353
Propelling pencil, manufacturing	4954/1	495/1	495.1
Property			
company	8500	863	850
developer	8500	863	850
investment company	8500	863	833
management (as agents for owners)	8340	863	834
owners' association	9631/2	899/6	963
Services Agency	9111	901/6	911
unit trust (acting for insurance companies)	8320	862	813.2
Propulsion engine, marine, manufacturing	3281/2	370/2	328.1 and 328.2
Propylene			
manufacturing	2512	271/2	251
oxide, manufacturing	2512	271/2	251
Protective			
clothing, industrial, manufacturing	4531	441	453
headgear, not plastics, manufacturing	4537/2	446/2	453
helmet, plastics, manufacturing	4836	496	483
industrial headgear, not plastics, manufacturing	4537/2	446/2	453

Activity	SIC 1980	1968	NACE
Protein			
concentrates, animal food, manufacturing	4221	219	422
synthetic, for animal feed, manufacturing	4222/2	219	422
Proton microscope, manufacturing	3454/2	364/1	345.1
Provender, dealing in	6110	831/3	611.2
Provident fund	8200/2	860	822
Provision			
dealer, wholesale	6170	810/1	617.1
exchange	6300	810/1	617.1
Provisions, retail dealing in	6410	820/1	641.1
Pruning			
knife, manufacturing	3162/1	391	316.2
shears, manufacturing	3161/1	391	316.1
Psychiatric			
clinic	9520	874/1	952
day hospital	9520	874/1	952
unit (general hospital)	9510	874/1	951
Psychometry	9791/3	882	979
PTFE (polytetrafluoraethylene) manufacturing	2514	276/1	251
Public			
address equipment, wholesale dealing in	6149	812/4	614
address system, manufacturing	3454/1	365/2	345.1
baths	9820	899/7	982
broadcasting equipment, manufacturing	3443	365/2	344
health laboratory	9520	874/1	952
house	6620	886	662
house fittings and furnishings, manufacturing	4672	474	467.5
house furniture, manufacturing	4671/3	472	467.5
notary	8350	873	835
park	9791/3	882	979
Record Office	9111	901/6	911
record searching	8395/4	865	839.3
relations consultant (not advertising agency)	8395/2	865	839.1
school	9320	872/2	932
service vehicle, operator	7210/2	702/1	721.2
speaker	9760	879/5	976
Trustee Office	8150/2	862	813.2
works contractor	5020	500	502.1
Works Loan Board	9111	901/6	911
Publicans' broker	8395/4	865	839.3
Publicity consultant	8395/2	865	839.1
Publisher's case making	4754/5	489	473.4
Publishers, other than newspapers and periodicals	4754/1	489	474
Pudding mixture, manufacturing	4239/5	229/2	423.6
Puffed			
rice, manufacturing	4239/8	211/2	423.8
wheat, manufacturing	4239/8	211/2	423.8
Pulley			
block, manufacturing	3255/4	337/4	325.5
manufacturing	3261/3	349/3	326.1
wheel, manufacturing	3261/3	349/3	326.1
wooden, manufacturing	4650	349/3	465.1
Pullover, knitted, manufacturing	4363/2	417	436.2
Pulp making machine, manufacturing	3275/4	399/9	327.2
Pulping recycled paper	4710/1	481	471.1
Pulpit, manufacturing	4671/3	472	467.5
Pulpwood, manufacturing	4610/1	471/1	461.1
Pulse, dealing in	6110	831/3	611.2
Pulverising			
machinery (for chemical industry) manufacturing	3245/1	339/9	324.1
plant (not for mines) manufacturing	3254/2	336	325.3
Pumice stones, bonded, manufacturing	2460	469/1	246.1

Activity	SIC 1980	1968	NACE
Pump			
and parts, non electric for oil, gas, petrol, or water (motor vehicle) manufacturing	3530	381	353
for hydraulic equipment, manufacturing	3283/2	333/4	328.3
leather, manufacturing	4420/2	432	442.3
not hydraulic or for internal combustion engine, manufacturing	3287	333/1	328.3
tyre, (cycle type) manufacturing	3634	382	363.2
Pumping plant, dealing in	6149	832/5	614.5
Punch and Judy Show	9791/3	881/2	979
Punched			
card and punched paper tape stock, manufacturing	4710/3	481	471.3
card machine (other than for computer use) manufacturing	3301	338	330
Punching machine (metal forming) manufacturng	3221/2	332/2	322.1
Puncture repair outfit, manufacturing	4811	491/1	481.1
Punnet, manufacturing	4664/2	475/1	466.2
Punt, manufacturing	3610/2	370/1	361.3
Puppet, not of rubber, manufacturing	4941	494/1	494.1
Purchasing agent, export, general or undefined	6300	812/5	639
Purse, leather or leather substitute, manufacturing	4420/1	432	442.1
Push			
cart, toy, manufacturing	4941	494/1	494.1
chair, manufacturing	3650/1	494/2	365.1
Putty, manufacturing	2551	274	255
Pyjama, manufacturing			
cord	4398/2	421/3	439.3
men's and boys'	4535	444/2	453
women's and girls'	4536/2	445/2	453
Pylon			
erection	5020	500	502.7
pre-cast concrete, manufacturing	2437	469/2	243.2
Pyridine base, manufacturing	2512	271/2	251
Pyrometer (non electronic) manufacturing	3710	354/2	371
Pyrotechnics, manufacturing	2565	279/3	256.5

Q

Activity	SIC 1980	1968	NACE
Quantity surveyor (private practice)	8370/1	879/1	837
Quarry			
floor brick, manufacturing	2410	461/2	241
tile, clay, manufacturing	2410	461/2	241
Quarrying of non-ferrous metal ore	2100	109/2	212.1
Quartz			
crystal, manufacturing	3453/1	364/1	345.1
quarry	2396	109/4	239.4
Quarternary ammonium salts fatty amines, manufacturing	2563	275	256.3
Queen Alexandra's			
RANC	9150	901/4	915
RNNS	9150	901/4	915
Queen's			
Counsel	8350	873	835
Institute of District Nursing	9631/1	879/3	963
Quick			
freezing of fruit and vegetables	4147/1	218/2	414.1
frozen foods, wholesale dealing in	6170	810/1	617.1
Quicklime, manufacturing	2420	469/2	242.2
Quilt			
cot, manufacturing	4557	422/1	455.2
filled, manufacturing	4557	422/1	455.2
fringing, manufacturing	4557	422/1	455.2
weaving	4322	413	432.5

R-RAP

Activity	SIC 1980	1968	NACE
R			
REME workshop (civilian personnel)	6710	894	671
Rabbit			
destroying and trapping on agricultural land	0100/3	001/2	01
fur garment, manufacturing	4560	433	456.3
skin sorting	4560	433	456.1
Race horse trainer	9791/1	882	978
Racecourse (not betting)	9791/1	882	978
Racing			
pool	9791/2	883	979
tipster	9791/2	883	979
Rack			
and mounting for electronic apparatus, manufacturing	3444	364/3	344
railway	7260/2	709	725
Racket and racket frame, manufacturing	4942	494/3	494.2
Racking, manufacturing			
metal	3166/1	399/1	316.6
wooden	4672	474	467.5
Racquet club	9791/1	882	978
Radar equipment, manufacturing	3443	367/2	344
Radial flowpump, manufacturing	3287	333/1	328.3
Radiant			
for gas and electric fire, manufacturing	2481	461/1	248.1
panel (space-heating equipment)	3284/2	339/4	328.4
Radiation measuring and detection equipment, manufacturing	3442	354/2	344
Radiator			
cast iron, manufacturing	3111	313/4	311.1
electric, manufacturing	3460	368	346
grill, manufacturing	3530	381	353
motor vehicle, manufacturing	3530	381	353
space-heating equipment, manufacturing	3284/2	339/4	328.4
Radio			
and television monitoring equipment, manufacturing	3443	367/2	344
and television repairer	6730/1	821/3	673
and television transmitter, manufacturing	3443	367/2	344
and television, wholesale dealing in	6150	812/4	615.3
cabinet, wooden, manufacturing	4671/4	472	467.5
case, leather, manufacturing	4420/1	432	442.1
communications equipment, manufacturing	3443	367/2	344
domestic, hire	8460/1	821/3	846.2
receiving set, manufacturing	3454/1	365/2	345.1
relay service	9741/1	881/2	974
sets and equipment, retail dealing in	6480	821/3	648.8
station, British Telecom	7902	708	790
studio	9741/1	881/2	974
transmitter, manufacturing	3443	367/2	344
Radio-active isotopes (other than uranium, thorium or plutonium) manufacturing	2511	271/3	251
Radiogram, manufacturing	3454/1	365/2	345.1
Radiographer (private)	9550	874/5	955
Radiologist (hospital service)	9510	874/1	951
Radiotherapist (hospital service)	9510	874/1	951
Radium, manufacturing	2247/1	323	224.1
Raffia goods, manufacturing	4664/2	475/1	466.2
Rag			
bleaching	4370/2	423	437.1
book making	4754/5	489	473.2
dyeing	4370/2	423	437.2
merchant	6220	832/7	622
rug, manufacturing	4385/1	419	438.1
Rags			
and bones, dealing in	6220	832/7	622
dealing in	6220	832/7	622
Ragstone quarry	2310/2	102/1	231.2
Rail (railway) steel, manufacturing	2210	311/2	221.1
Railing, metal, manufacturing	3142	399/12	314.1
Railway			
(other than Passenger Transport Executive)	7100	701	710
(Passenger Transport Executive)	7210/1	701	721.1
agent (not transport authority)	7700/2	709/1	772
and tramway rolling stock, manufacturing	3620/2	385	362.2
bookstall	6530	821/1	653.1
car, self-propelled, manufacturing	3620/2	385	362.2
coach, manufacturing	3620/2	385	362.2
construction	5020	500	502.5
dining car or buffet	6611/1	885	661
goods wagon, manufacturing	3620/2	385	362.2
independent	7100	701	710
locomotive, manufacturing	3620/1	384	362.1
locomotive, repairing	3620/3	384	362.3
luggage van, manufacturing	3620/2	385	362.2
passenger carriage, manufacturing	3620/2	385	362.2
post van, manufacturing	3620/2	385	362.2
refrigerated wagon, manufacturing	3620/2	385	362.2
rolling stock repairing	3620/3	385	362.3
running shed	7100	701	710
signalling equipment (electric) manufacturing	3433	384	343.1
signalling equipment (mechanical) manufacturing	3289/3	384	328.9
sleeper, pre-cast concrete, manufacturing	2437	469/2	243.2
tanker wagon, manufacturing	3620/2	385	362.2
test wagon, manufacturing	3620/2	385	362.2
track equipment (mechanical) manufacturing	3289/3	384	314.4
vehicle engine, manufacturing	3281/1	334/1	328.1
vehicle hire	8480/4	832/10	845
wagon, manufacturing	3620/2	385	362.2
wagon agent	7700/2	709/1	772
wagon axle box and axle lubricator, manufacturing	3620/2	385	362.2
wagon, special purpose, manufacturing	3620/2	385	362.2
workshop wagon, manufacturing	3620/2	385	362.2
Raincoat, manufacturing			
men's and boys'	4531	441	453
women's and girls'	4531	441	453
Rainproof garment, manufacturing	4531	441	453
Rainwater			
gutter, cast iron, manufacturing	3111	313/4	311.1
pipe, cast iron, manufacturing	3111	313/4	311.1
pipes and gutters, plastics, manufacturing	4834	496	483
Raising machinery (textile) manufacturing	3230/3	335	323.1
Rake			
garden, manufacturing	3161/1	391	316.1
wooden, manufacturing	4650	479/3	465.1
Ramming material, refractory, manufacturing	2481	461/1	248.1
Rampton Hospital	9510	874/1	951
Ranching	0100/1	001/1	01
Range, cast iron, manufacturing	3111	313/4	311.1
Range-finder (optical) manufacturing	3732	354/1	373.2
Ranging drum shearer (mining) manufacturing	3251	339/1	325.1
Rape			
oil, refining	4116/3	221	411.4
seed, crushing	4116/2	221	411.3

Activity	SIC 1980	1968	NACE
Rare gas, manufacturing	**2567**	271/1	256.1
Raschel lace, manufacturing	**4395**	418	439.5
Rasp, manufacturing	**3161/2**	391	316.1
Rat			
catcher (not specially for agriculture)	**9211**	899/7	921
destroying and trapping on agricultural land	**0100/3**	001/2	01
Ravioli, manufacturing	**4239/7**	229/2	417
Raw			
cotton, bleaching, dyeing or otherwise finishing	**4370/2**	423	437
silk, dyeing	**4370/2**	423	437.2
Razor			
blade, manufacturing	**3162/2**	392	316.2
electric, manufacturing	**3460**	368	346
not electric, manufacturing	**3162/2**	392	316.2
set, manufacturing	**3162/2**	392	316.2
Re-establishment centre (DHSS)	**9611/2**	899/3	962
Re-heating furnace, manufacturing	**3245/2**	341/2	328.6
Re-insurance company	**8200/3**	860	823
Reaching-in machinery (textile) manufacturing	**3230/2**	335	323.1
Reactor			
column, manufacturing	**3205/2**	341/5	324.1
shunt and limiting, manufacturing	**3420/1**	361/1	342
vessel, manufacturing	**3205/2**	341/5	324.1
Reading room (library)	**9770**	899/4	977
Ready-mixed			
concrete, manufacturing	**2436**	469/2	243.6
wet mortars, manufacturing	**2436**	469/2	243.6
Real estate owner	**8500**	863	850
Reamer, manufacturing	**3222/1**	390	322.2
Reaper twine, manufacturing	**4396**	416	439.6
Rear			
digger, manufacturing	**3254/1**	336	325.4
digger unit, manufacturing	**3254/1**	336	325.4
Rebated wood, manufacturing	**4610/2**	471/1	461.2
Reception centre (DHSS)	**9611/2**	899/3	962
Receptionist			
dentist's	**9540**	874/4	954
doctor's surgery	**9530**	874/3	953
Reciprocating compressor, manufacturing	**3283/1**	333/3	328.3
Reconditioning			
coopers' products	**4640/2**	475/1	464.2
metal drum	**3164/2**	399/7	316.4
Record and tape manufacturing	**3452**	365/1	345.2
player, accessory, manufacturing	**3453/2**	364/3	345.1
player, cabinet, wooden, manufacturing	**4671/4**	472	467.5
player, manufacturing	**3454/1**	365/2	345.1
players, retail dealing in	**6480**	821/3	648.8
players, wholesale dealing in	**6150**	812/4	615.3
playing mechanism, manufacturing	**3453/2**	364/3	345.1
Recorder			
electric, manufacturing	**3442**	354/2	344
plastic or wood, manufacturing	**4920/2**	499/1	492.2
Recording studio	**9741/2**	881/2	975
Records and tapes, retail dealing in	**6480**	821/3	648.8
Recovered wool (mungo and shoddy) manufacturing	**4310/1**	414/4	439.7
Recovery vehicle (tracked military type) manufacturing	**3290/3**	342	328.9
Recreational clothing (weatherproofed) manufacturing	**4531**	441	453
Rectangular hollow section, steel, manufacturing	**2220**	312	222
Rectifier			
electric (for power) manufacturing	**3420/3**	361/3	342
plant, manufacturing	**3420/3**	361/3	342
selenium, manufacturing	**3444**	364/3	344
solid state, (not power) manufacturing	**3453/1**	364/1	345.1
Rectifying valve and tube, manufacturing	**3453/1**	364/1	345.1
Recycled fibre pulp, manufacturing	**4710/1**	481	471.1
Red			
Cross Society	**9611/1**	874/5	961
metal, unwrought, manufacturing	**2246/1**	322	224.2
Reducer (photographic) manufacturing	**3733**	351	373.3
Reducing valve, manufacturing	**3288**	333/2	328.8
Reduction gear (marine) manufacturing	**3289/1**	370	326.1
Reed			
(for musical instrument) manufacturing	**4920/2**	499/1	492.2
(textile machinery accessory) manufacturing	**3230/4**	335	323.1
article, manufacturing	**4664/2**	475/1	466.2
collecting, cutting, gathering	**0200**	002	02
preparation	**4664/2**	475/1	466.2
Reel			
polypropylene, printed, manufacturing	**4835**	496	483
wooden, manufacturing	**4650**	479/3	465.1
Reeling machinery (textiles) manufacturing	**3230/2**	335	323.1
Refined			
coal tar, manufacturing	**2567**	271/2	256.7
iron, manufacturing	**2210**	313/2	221.1
Refinery gas, manufacturing	**1401**	262	140.1
Refitting			
pleasure craft	**3610/2**	370/1	361.3
ship	**3610/1**	370/1	361
Reformer, manufacturing	**3205/2**	341/5	324.1
Refractory			
brick, manufacturing	**2481**	461/1	248.1
brick, insulating, manufacturing	**2481**	461/1	248.1
castable, manufacturing	**2481**	461/1	248.1
cement, manufacturing	**2481**	461/1	248.1
goods, manufacturing	**2481**	461/1	248.1
hollow-ware, manufacturing	**2481**	461/1	248.1
jointing cement, manufacturing	**2481**	461/1	248.1
mouldable, manufacturing	**2481**	461/1	248.1
ramming material, manufacturing	**2481**	461/1	248.1
Refreshment			
club	**6630**	887	663
contracting	**6640/1**	888	664
room (unlicensed)	**6611/2**	885	661
Refrigerated			
lorry, manufacturing	**3510/2**	381	351
wagon, railway, manufacturing	**3620/2**	385	362.2
Refrigerator			
(electric and non-electric) domestic, manufacturing	**3460**	368	346
commercial, manufacturing	**3284/1**	339/3	328.5
Refugee camp	**9611/2**	899/3	962
Refuse			
disposal plant, manufacturing	**3245/3**	341/2	324.1
disposal plant or tip (local authority or municipally owned)	**9211**	906/3	921
disposal service (not specially for agriculture)	**9211**	899/7	921
disposal tip operator	**9211**	906/3	921
disposal vehicle, manufacturing	**3510/2**	381	351
Regent's Park and Primrose Hill	**9111**	901/6	911
Regional			
Crime Squad	**9130**	906/1	913
Headquarters, Post Office	**7901**	708	790
health authority	**9111**	874/2	911
Register of Friendly Societies	**9111**	901/6	911
Registered veterinarian	**9560/2**	879/4	956
Registrar	**9120**	901/6	912
Registrar of Births, Deaths or Marriages	**9112**	906/3	911
Registrar's Office (Courts of Justice)	**9120**	901/6	912

REG-ROA

Activity	SIC 1980	1968	NACE
Registration plate (motor vehicle) manufacturing	3530	381	353
Registry office for servants	8395/4	865	839.3
Rehabilitation hospital	9510	874/1	951
Reinforced			
concrete engineer (civil engineering)	5020	500	502.1
concrete products, manufacturing	2437	469/2	243.2
hose, rubber or plastics, manufacturing	4812/1	491/2	481.2
Reinforcing fabrication of steel wire for concrete, manufacturing	2234	394	223.4
Relay			
electronic and telecommunication, manufacturing	3444	364/3	344
link apparatus, manufacturing	3443	367/2	344
satellite, manufacturing	3443	367/2	344
Relief			
stamping	4754/5	489	473.4
valve, manufacturing	3288	333/2	328.8
Religious			
goods, retail dealing in	6480	821/4	649.6
tract, publishing	4754/1	489	474.1
Relish, manufacturing	4239/6	218/3	423.7
Remand centre	9120	901/6	912
Remelt ingot, aluminium, manufacturing	2245/1	321	224.1
Removal contractor	7230	703	723.1
Rennet (not artificial) manufacturing	4126/3	229/2	412.5
Rent collecting	8340	863	834
Repair and reconditioning of musical instruments (other than keyboard: in factory)	4920/2	499/1	492.2
Repair of			
electrical household goods	6730/1	821/3	673
footwear and leather goods	6720	895	672
motor vehicles	6710	894	671
watches and clocks	6730/2	821/4	674
Repairing			
pleasure craft	3610/2	370/1	361.3
ships	3610/1	370/1	361
tyre and inner tube (by specialists)	4820	491/1	482
Repertory company	9760	881/2	976
Repository	7700/3	709/2	773
Reptile leather, manufacturing	4410/1	431/1	441.3
Research			
and development consultants	9400	876	940
association	9400	876	940
charity	9400	876	940
chemist (private practice)	8370/2	879/2	837
institution	9400	876	940
laboratory	9400	876	940
vessel, manufacturing	3610/1	370/1	361.1
Reservoir			
construction	5020	500	502.6
(hydraulic) manufacturing	3283/2	333/4	328.3
(pneumatic) manufacturing	3283/3	333/4	328.3
Residential chambers letting	8500	863	850
Resin			
adhesive, synthetic, manufacturing	2562	279/2	256.2
bonded glass fibre moulding (excluding those for motor vehicles) manufacturing	4836	496	483
dealing in	6120	832/8	612.7
Resins			
for paint, manufacturing	2514	276/1	251
synthetic, manufacturing	2514	276/1	251
Resistor, manufacturing	3444	364/3	344
Resorcinal formaldehyde adhesive, manufacturing	2562	279/2	256.2
Respirator and mask, medical, manufacturing	3720/1	353/1	372.2
Restaurant			
fittings and furnishings, manufacturing	4672	474	467.5
furniture, manufacturing	4671/3	472	467.5
licensed	6611/1	885	661
unlicensed	6611/2	885	661
Resuscitation equipment, manufacturing	3720/1	353/1	372.2
Retort			
fireclay, silica and siliceous, manufacturing	2481	461/1	248.1
graphite, manufacturing	2481	461/1	248.1
setting	5020	500	501.3
Retreading tyres	4820	491/1	482
Review			
printing	4752/3	486	473.1
printing-publishing	4752/2	486	473.1
publishing	4752/1	486	474.4
Revolver, manufacturing	3290/1	342	328.9
Revolving door, manufacturing	4672	474	463.2
Revue company	9760	881/2	976
Rhodium, manufacturing	2247/2	396	224.1
Ribbon			
inked, manufacturing	4954/2	495/2	259.3
textile, manufacturing	4398/2	421/3	439.3
Rice			
cleaning	4160	211/2	416.2
flaking	4160	211/2	416.2
husking	4160	211/2	416.2
milling	4160	211/2	416.2
pudding, canned, manufacturing	4239/5	229/2	not classified
rolling	4160	211/2	416.2
starch, manufacturing	4180	229/2	418.1
Richmond Park	9111	901/6	911
Rick cloth and cover, manufacturing	4556	422/2	455.4
Riding			
cap, manufacturing	4537/2	446/2	453
school	9791/1	882	978
stables	9791/1	882	978
Rifle butts	9791/1	882	978
Rigging			
for ships, manufacturing	3610/1	370/1	361
machinery (textile) manufacturing	3230/3	335	323.1
Rigid			
box, board, manufacturing	4725/2	482/1	472.4
box, corrugated board, manufacturing	4725/2	482/1	472.4
plastics foam, manufacturing	4832	496	483
Ring			
and washer, rubber, manufacturing	4812/3	491/2	481.2
asbestos, manufacturing	2440	429/1	244
spring, manufacturing	3137/2	399/4	313.2
traveller (textile machinery accessory) manufacturing	3230/4	335	323.1
Rink			
ice skating	9791/1	882	978
roller skating	9791/1	882	978
Ripper, earth moving equipment, manufacturing	3254/1	336	325.4
River			
ferry	7260/3	706	730
management	1700	603	170
Rivet (bifurcated, tubular, etc.) manufacturing	3137/1	393	316.9
Road			
construction of	5020	500	502
haulage contractor for general hire or reward	7230	703	723.2
metal (crushed and processed) manufacturing	2450/1	469/2	245.1
ripper (mining) manufacturing	3251	339/1	325.1

Activity	SIC 1980	1968	NACE
roller, manufacturing	3254/2	336	325.4
sign, plastics, manufacturing	4836	496	483
stone pit or quarry	2310/2	102/1	231.2
tanker (not trailer) manufacturing	3510/2	381	351
tractor trailer, manufacturing	3522	381	352
tractor unit, manufacturing	3510/2	381	351
traffic signalling equipment, manufacturing	3433	367/1	343.1
trailer hire	8480/3	703	845
Roadstone, coated, manufacturing	2450/1	469/2	245
Robe (academic, legal and ecclesiastical) manufacturing	4532	442	453
Rock			
climbing equipment, manufacturing	4942	494/3	494.2
drill (portable) manufacturing	3285/2	339/6	325.1
drilling machinery, manufacturing	3251	339/1	325.1
salt, manufacturing	2330	109/3	233.2
Rocker shovel (mining) manufacturing	3251	339/1	325.1
Rocket			
aerospace, manufacturing	3640	383/2	364
motor, manufacturing	3640	383/2	364
signal, manufacturing	2565	279/3	256.5
Rockingham ware, manufacturing	2489/3	462/3	248.6
Rod			
aluminium, manufacturing	2245/2	321	224.3
copper, manufacturing	2246/2	322	224.2
glass, manufacturing	2479/1	463/1	247.4
steel, cold drawn, manufacturing	2235	311/2	223.1
steel, hot-rolled, manufacturing	2210	311/2	221.1
Rodent destroying and trapping on agricultural land	0100/3	001/2	01
Rodent destroying (not agricultural)	9211	899/7	921
Rodenticide, manufacturing	2568	279/4	256.8
Rods or wires (for gas welding, soldering or brazing) manufacturing	3289/3	332/3	223.4
Roll			
for rolling mill and rolling mill train (not machines) manufacturing	3111	311/2	311.1
metal, for cable, hose, etc., manufacturing	3164/5	399/7	316.4
mill, for rubber or plastics, manufacturing	3275/2	339/9	324.3
Rolled			
glass, manufacturing	2471/1	463/1	247.1
product, aluminium, manufacturing	2245/2	321	224.3
products, copper, manufacturing	2246/2	322	224.2
steel beam, manufacturing	2210	311/2	221.1
Roller			
(agricultural machinery) manufacturing	3211/1	331	321.1
(textile machinery accessory) manufacturing	3230/4	335	323.1
bearing, manufacturing	3262	349/1	326.2
blind, canvas, manufacturing	4556	422/2	455.4
blind, wooden, manufacturing	4672	474	463.2
cover, rubber, manufacturing	4812/3	491/1	481.2
pen and refill, manufacturing	4954/1	495/1	495.1
printing (textile)	4370/2	423	437.3
skate, manufacturing	4942	494/3	494.2
skin (cut) leather, manufacturing	4420/2	431/1	442.3
towel, manufacturing	4557	422/1	455.1
wooden (mangle and wringer) manufacturing	4650	479/3	465.1
Rolling			
ingot and slab aluminium, manufacturing	2245/1	321	224.1
mill (for metals) manufacturing	3286/2	339/9	325.2
pin, wooden, manufacturing	4650	479/3	465.1
Rolls of iron or steel manufacturing	3289/3	349/3	328.9
Roman Catholic Church	9660	875	966
Roof			
insulation contractor	5030	500	503.4
light, plastics, manufacturing	4834	496	483
support, hydraulic, manufacturing	3251	339/1	314.3
timber, prefabricated, manufacturing	4630	471/2	463.1
truss, metal, manufacturing	3204/1	341/4	314.1
units, precast concrete, manufacturing	2437	469/2	243.2
Roofing			
bitumous and flax felts, manufacturing	2450/4	469/2	245
contractor	5010	500	501.2
tile, clay unglazed, manufacturing	2410	461/2	241
tile, precast concrete, manufacturing	2437	469/2	243.2
Room divide system, manufacturing	4671/2	472	467.1
Root crop harvesting and supporting machinery, manufacturing	3211/2	331	321.1
Rooter (not agricultural) manufacturing	3254/1	336	325.4
Rope			
lagging, asbestos, manufacturing	2440	429/1	244
making machine, manufacturing	3286/3	339/9	328.9
new, wholesale dealing in	6190	812/4	619.6
sling, manufacturing	4396	416	439.6
textile materials, manufacturing	4396	416	439.6
towing, manufacturing	4396	416	439.6
walk	4396	416	439.6
wire, manufacturing	2234	394	223.4
Rosin size, manufacturing	2567	271/2	256.7
Rotary club	9690/2	899/3	968
Rotating compressor, manufacturing	3283/1	333/3	328.3
Rouge, jewellers, manufacturing	2460	469/1	246
Rough terrain industrial trucks, manufacturing	3255/5	337/5	325.5
Round Table	9690/2	899/3	968
Roundwood, manufacturing	4610/1	471/1	461.1
Rowing			
boat, manufacturing	3610/2	370/1	361.3
club	9791/1	882	978
Royal			
Academy of Arts	9631/1	879/3	963
Academy of Dramatic Art	9330	872/3	933
Aeronautical Society	9631/1	879/3	963
Agricultural Society of England	9631/1	899/6	963
Air Force	9150	901/3	915
Air Force establishment (civilian personnel)	9150	901/5	915
Air Force establishment (service personnel)	9150	901/3	915
Air Force stores unit	9150	901/5	915
Automobile Club	9690/2	899/7	968
Botanic Gardens	9770	899/4	977
College of Art	9310	872/3	931
College of Midwives	9631/1	879/3	963
College of Nursing	9631/1	879/3	963
College of Physicians	9631/1	879/3	963
College of Surgeons	9631/1	879/3	963
Colonial Institute	9631/1	879/3	963
Commission	9111	901/6	911
Geographical Society	9631/1	879/3	963
Households	9111	901/6	911
Institute of Charted Surveyors	9631/1	879/3	963
Institute of Public Health	9631/1	879/3	963
Marines	9150	901/1	915
Masonic Benevolent Institution	9611/1	899/3	961
Masonic Institution for Boys	9320	872/2	932
Masonic Institution for Girls	9320	872/2	932
Mint	4910/4	396	491.6
National Lifeboat Institution	9611/1	899/3	968
Naval armament depot	9150	901/5	915
Navy	9150	901/1	915
Navy establishment (civilian personnel)	9150	901/5	915
Navy establishment (service personnel)	9150	901/1	915
Observatory (civilian staff)	9111	901/5	911

Activity	SIC 1980	1968	NACE
Observatory, Edinburgh	9111	901/6	911
Palaces	9111	901/6	911
Park	9111	901/6	911
Scottish Automobile Club	9690/2	899/7	968
Scottish Museum, Edinburgh	9770	899/4	977
Society	9631/1	879/3	963
Society for the Prevention of Accidents	9690/2	899/4	968
Society for the Prevention of Cruelty to Animals (not animal hospitals or homes)	9611/1	899/3	961
Society for the Promotion of Health	9631/1	879/3	963
Society of Medicine	9631/1	879/3	963
Statistical Society	9631/1	879/3	963
United Services Institution	9631/1	879/3	963
Rubber			
ball, uncovered, manufacturing	4812/3	491/2	481.2
balloon (excluding pilot and sounding balloons) manufacturing	4812/3	491/2	481.2
band, manufacturing	4812/3	491/2	481.2
based paint (chlorinated) manufacturing	2551	274	255
bathing cap, manufacturing	4812/3	491/2	481.2
belting, manufacturing	4812/2	491/2	481.2
compound, manufacturing	4812/3	491/2	481.2
dealing in	6120	832/8	612.7
doll, manufacturing	4812/3	491/2	481.2
galosh, manufacturing	4510	450	481.2
hose, manufacturing	4812/1	491/2	481.2
overshoe, manufacturing	4510	450	481.2
processing chemicals, manufacturing	2567	271/3	256.7
protective bootee, manufacturing	4510	450	481.2
protective footwear, manufacturing	4510	450	481.2
reclamation	4812/3	491/2	481.2
sponge, manufacturing	4812/3	491/2	481.2
stamp, manufacturing	4954/2	495/2	495.2
synthetic, manufacturing	2515	276/2	251
thread, uncovered, manufacturing	4812/3	491/2	481.2
tiling, manufacturing	4812/3	491/2	481.2
toy, manufacturing	4812/3	491/2	481.2
tubing, manufacturing	4812/1	491/2	481.2
tyre, manufacturing	4811	491/1	481.1
working, machinery, manufacturing	3275/2	339/9	324.3
Rubber-based adhesive, manufacturing	2562	279/2	481.2
Rubberised			
hair, manufacturing	4812/3	491/2	481.2
textile fabric, manufacturing	4812/3	491/2	481.2
Rubbing stone mine, quarry or pit	2310/2	102/1	231.2
Rug			
coir, manufacturing	4385/2	429/2	438.1
travelling, making-up outside weaving establishments	4557	422/1	455.2
tufting	4384/2	419	438.1
weaving (not travelling rug)	4384/1	419	438.1
Rugby			
League	9791/1	882	978
Union	9791/1	882	978
Rugs			
retail dealing in	6470	821/2	647
wholesale dealing in	6160	812/4	616.9
Rule (measuring) manufacturing	3710	391	371.5
Ruler, plastics, manufacturing	4836	496	483
Ruling machinery (printers') manufacturing	3276	339/2	327.2
Rum distilling	4240/2	239/1	424.2
Running gear (motor vehicle) manufacturing	3530	381	353
Rush matting, manufacturing	4664/2	475/1	466.2
Rusk, making	4197	213	419.4
Russian baths	9820	899/7	982
Rustic furniture, manufacturing	4671/2	479/3	467.3
Rye			
flaking	4160	211/2	416.2
flour and meal, manufacturing	4160	211/2	416.2
milling	4160	211/2	416.1
rolling	4160	211/2	416.2

S

Activity	SIC 1980	1968	NACE
Saccharin			
manufacturing	2570	272	259.4
tablet, manufacturing	2570	272	259.4
Sachet, plastics, manufacturing	4835	481	483
Sack			
canvas, manufacturing	4556	422/2	455.4
kraft paper, manufacturing	4710/4	481	471.3
polyethylene, non-woven, manufacturing	4835	496	483
woven, manufacturing	4556	422/2	455.4
Sacking, jute, manufacturing	4350/2	415	435.5
Sacks and bags, new, wholesale dealing in	6160	812/4	616
Saddle			
horse, manufacturing	4420/1	432	442.1
motor cycle, manufacturing	3633	382	363.2
pedal cycle, manufacturing	3634	382	363
Saddlery			
and leather goods, wholesale dealing in	6160	812/4	616.8
retail dealing in	6460	821/4	646.2
Safe			
deposit company	7700/3	709/2	773
manufacturing	3166/2	399/3	316.6
Safety			
belt or harness for aircraft crew or passengers, manufacturing	3640	383/4	364
belt, car, manufacturing	3530	381	353
boot, manufacturing	4510	450	451.3
frame, tractor, manufacturing	3212	380	321.2
glass, manufacturing	2471/2	463/1	247.6
helmet, plastics, manufacturing	4836	446/2	483
pin, manufacturing	3169/2	399/8	316.9
razor, manufacturing	3162/2	392	316.2
valve, manufacturing	3288	333/2	328.8
Saggar, manufacturing	2489/4	462/3	248.9
Sago grinding	4160	211/2	416.2
Sail, manufacturing	4556	422/2	455.4
Sailcloth			
made up goods, manufacturing	4556	422/2	455.4
weaving	4340/2	413	434.5
Sailing boat, less than 100 gross tons, manufacturing	3610	370/1	361.3
Sailing clothing, weatherproof, manufacturing	4531	441	453
Sailplane, manufacturing	3640	383/1	364
Salad			
cream, manufacturing	4239/6	218/3	423.7
dressing, manufacturing	4239/6	218/3	423.7
Salines, manufacturing	2570	272	257
Salmon			
and trout fishery (hatchery)	0300/2	003/2	03
netting	0300/1	003/1	03
Salt			
Compensation Board	9112	906/3	911
merchant	6120	832/8	612.7
mine	2330	109/3	233.2
preparation (not at salt mine or brine pit)	4239/9	229/2	423.3
rock, manufacturing	2330	109/3	233.2
sea, manufacturing	2330	109/3	233
white, manufacturing	2330	109/3	233
works	2330	109/3	233

Activity	SIC 1980	1968	NACE
Salted or pickled pork, manufacturing	4122/1	214/2	412.2
Salvage			
corps (in London, Liverpool and Glasgow)	8320	860	832
marine, company	7630	706	763
vessel, manufacturing	3610/1	370/1	361.1
Salvation Army (not hostels, emigration department or missing persons office)	9660	875	966
Emigration department	9890/2	899/7	984
hostel	9611/2	884	962
Insurance Department	8200/1	860	821
shelter	9611/2	899/3	962
Samian ware, manufacturing	2489/3	462/3	248.6
Sample case, leather, manufacturing	4420/1	432	442.1
Sanatorium	9510	874/1	951
Sand			
and gravel merchant	6130	831/2	612.5
casting, non-ferrous base metal, manufacturing	3112	not classified	311.2
handling, mixing, treatment or reclamation plant (for foundries) manufacturing	3286/2	339/9	325.2
lawn, manufacturing	2513	278	256.8
lime brick, manufacturing	2437	469/2	243.4
pit	2310/4	103	231.4
Sandal, manufacturing	4510	450	451.3
Sanding			
and polishing machines for wood (not portable) manufacturing	3275/1	339/9	327.1
tool (powered), portable, manufacturing	3285/2	339/6	not classified
Sandpaper, manufacturing	2460	469/1	246.3
Sandstone mine, pit or quarry	2310/2	102/1	231.2
Sandwich			
bar	6612	885	661
cake, baking	4196	212	419.3
spread, manufacturing	4239/6	218/3	423.7
Sanitary			
cleanser, manufacturing	2599	279/1	259.2
engineering for building	5030	500	503.2
towel, paper, manufacturing	4722	279/6	472.2
ware, plastics, manufacturing	4834	496	483
ware and fittings, metal, manufacturing	3169/4	399/12	316.7
ware, dealing in	6130	831/2	613.3
Sanitaryware			
ceramic, manufacturing	2489/2	462/2	248.5
fireclay, manufacturing	2489/2	462/2	248.5
vitreous china, manufacturing	2489/2	462/2	248.5
Sash line, manufacturing	4396	416	439.6
Satchel, leather, manufacturing	4420/1	432	442.1
Sateen weaving	4322	413	432.5
Satellite			
manufacturing	3640	383/1	364
relay, manufacturing	3443	367/2	344
Satin weaving	4322	413	432.5
Saturated and impregnated base paper, manufacturing	4710/6	481	472.6
Sauce, manufacturing	4239/6	218/3	423.7
Saucepan, manufacturing	3167	399/6	316.7
Sauna baths	9820	899/7	982
Sausage			
filler, cereal, manufacturing	4197	213	419.5
manufacturing	4122/3	214/2	412.2
meat making	4122/3	214/2	412.2
roll (frozen) manufacturing	4122/2	214/1	412.2
roll (not frozen) manufacturing	4122/3	214/2	412.2
skins and casings (natural) manufacturing	4126/2	214/2	412.5
skins, dealing in	6170	832/8	617
Savings			
bank	8140/3	861	812
Certificate Office	8140/3	861	812
Saw			
blades for machines (including wood cutting) manufacturing	3222/1	391	322.2
saw, hand tool, manufacturing	3161/2	391	316.1
powered, portable, manufacturing	3285/2	339/6	not classified
Sawdust, dealing in	6120	832/8	612.7
Sawing machine, manufacturing			
for wood	3275/1	339/9	327.1
metal-cutting	3221/1	332/1	322.1
Sawlog, manufacturing	4610/1	471/1	461.1
Sawmilling	4610/1	471/1	461.1
Sawn fencing, manufacturing	4610/1	471/1	461.1
Scaffold			
tie, of ferrous wire, manufacturing	2234	394	223.4
tube, steel, manufacturing	2220	312	222
Scaffolding			
hire (without staff)	8420	500	842
hiring and erecting	5010	500	501.6
manufacturing	3289/3	341/5	314.1
Scales			
domestic, manufacturing	3285/1	339/5	316.7
platform, manufacturing	3285/1	339/5	328.9
postal, manufacturing	3285/1	339/5	328.9
retail, manufacturing	3285/1	339/5	328.9
Scanner (printing machinery) manufacturing	3276	339/2	327.2
Scarf			
lace, manufacturing	4395	418	439.5
not lace or knitted, manufacturing	4539/3	449/4	453
Scenario writer	9760	879/5	976
Scenic artist	9760	879/5	976
Schiffli embroidery, manufacturing	4395	418	439.5
Scholastic agent	9890/2	899/7	984
School			
agent	9890/2	899/7	984
building steelwork, manufacturing	3204/1	341/4	314.1
bus service	7210/2	702/1	721.2
canteen	6640/2	872	664
canteen (run by catering contractor)	6640/1	888	664
crossing patrol	9130	709/1	913
examination board (local authority)	9320	872/4	932
examination board (non-local authority)	9320	872/4	932
for the mentally handicapped (local authority)	9320	872	932
for the mentally handicapped (non-local authority)	9320	872	932
for the physically handicapped (local authority)	9320	872	932
for the physically handicapped (non-local authority)	9320	872	932
furniture, manufacturing	4671/3	472	467.2
furniture, wholesale dealing in	6150	812/4	615.1
health service	9520	874/2	952
independent (non-local authority)	9320	877/2	932
medical clinic	9520	874/2	952
medical officer	9112	874/2	911
military	9150	901/5	915
of Arts and Crafts	9330	872/3	933
of languages	9330	872/3	933
of motoring	9360	709/1	936
of speech and drama	9330	872/3	933
stationery, manufacturing	4723/2	483	472.3
Science			
Museum	9770	899/4	977
Research Council	9400	876	940

Activity	SIC 1980	NACE 1968	
Scientific			
goods, retail dealing in	6540	821/4	655.2
instruments and glassware, wholesale dealing in	6190	812/4	619
laboratory instrument (non-electrical or non-optical) manufacturing	3710	354/2	371.6
model for educational and exhibition purposes, manufacturing	3710	354/2	371.6
organisation	9631/1	879/3	963
Scientist, consultant	8370/2	879/2	837
Scissor lift, manufacturing	3255/4	337/4	325.5
Scissors, manufacturing	3162/1	392	316.2
Scone baking	4196	212	419.3
Scooter			
children's, manufacturing	4941	494/1	494.1
tyre, manufacturing	4811	491/1	481.1
Scotland Yard	9130	906/1	913
Scottish			
Agricultural Securities Corporation Ltd	8150/1	862	813.1
Ambulance Service	9520	874/2	952
Central Institution	9310	872	931
National Party	9690/2	899/4	968
Special Housing Association (building work)	5000	500	500.1
Special Housing Association (Housing Management Department)	8500	863	850
Scourer, of metal, manufacturing	3167	399/12	316.7
Scouring			
machinery (textile) manufacturing	3230/3	335	323.1
powder, manufacturing	2581	275	258.1
Scout Association	9690/2	899/3	968
Scrap			
iron dealer	6210	832/7	621
leather, dealing in	6220	832/7	622
merchant (general dealer)	6220	832/7	622
metal breaking, collecting, compressing sorting etc. (by dealers)	6210	832/7	621
metal, dealing in	6210	832/7	621
Scraper			
(earth moving equipment) manufacturing	3254/1	336	325.4
manufacturing	3161/2	391	316.1
Screen			
printing (textile)	4370/2	423	437.3
process ink, manufacturing	2552	279/5	255
wooden, manufacturing	4672	474	467.5
Screening plant, manufacturing			
effluent treatment	3245/3	336	324.1
not for mines	3254/2	336	325.3
Screw			
cap, metal, manufacturing	3164/3	399/10	316.4
compressor, manufacturing	3283/1	333/3	328.3
metal, all types, manufacturing	3137/1	393	313.1
plastics, manufacturing	4836	496	483
pump, manufacturing	3287	333/1	328.3
Screwdriver, manufacturing	3161/2	391	316.1
Screwing machine (metal-cutting) manufacturing	3221/1	332/1	322.1
Scrim weaving (from flax, hemp, ramie and man-made fibre processed on the flax system)	4340/2	413	434.5
Scrivenery	8350	873	835
Scrubber (air conditioning equipment) manufacturing	3284/4	339/4	328.4
Scrubbing brush, manufacturing	4663	493	466.3
Sculptor	9760	879/5	976
Scythe, manufacturing	3161/1	391	316.1
Sea			
ferry between United Kingdom and international ports	7400/2	705	742
ferry domestic or coastal routes	7400/3	705	742
salt, manufacturing	2330	109/3	233
Scouts Association	9690/2	899/3	968
Sea-going luxury yacht (of 100 gross tons or more) manufacturing	3610/1	370/1	361.3
Seal (for use with sealing wax) manufacturing	4954/3	495.2	495.2
Sealants			
bituminous, manufacturing	2562	279/2	256.2
manufacturing	2562	279/2	255
oil based, manufacturing	2562	279/2	256.2
Sealing			
and filling compounds (painters) manufacturing	2551	274	255
machinery, manufacturing	3244/2	339/8	324.2
Seamless tube, steel, manufacturing	2220	312	222
Searchlight, manufacturing	3470/2	369/5	347.2
Seasoning, manufacturing	4239/2	229/2	432.3
Seat			
for aircraft, manufacturing	3640	383/4	316.6
motor vehicle, manufacturing	3530	381	316.6
Seating			
metal (not for road vehicles or aircraft) manufacturing	3166/1	399/1	316.6
non-upholstered, manufacturing	4671/2	472	467.3
office or school (non-upholstered) manufacturing	4671/3	472	467
upholstered, manufacturing	4671/1	472	467.4
Seaweed collecting, cutting and gathering (uncultivated)	0300/1	002	03
Secateurs, manufacturing	3161/1	391	316.1
Second-hand			
bookseller, retail	6530	821/4	653.1
clothing, retail dealing in	6540	821/2	655.1
furniture, retail dealing in	6540	821/3	655.1
goods, general, retail dealing in	6540	821/4	655.1
Secondary			
battery, manufacturing	3432/2	369/3	343.2
copper, manufacturing	2246/1	322	224.1
modern school (local authority)	9320	872/1	932
school (local authority)	9320	872/1	932
Secretarial college	9330	872/5	933
Secretary			
own account	8395/4	865	839.3
private household	9900	865	990
Section			
aluminium, manufacturing	2245/2	321	224.3
copper, manufacturing	2246/2	322	224.2
heavy steel, 80 mm and over, manufacturing	2210	311/2	221.1
steel, manufacturing	2210	311/2	221.1
steel, cold formed, manufacturing	2235	399/12	223.3
Sectional coldroom, manufacturing	3284/1	339/3	328.5
Securities, dealing in	8310	862	831
Security			
alarms and systems, manufacturing	3433	367/1	343.1
paper, manufacturing	4710/3	481	471.3
printing	4754/3	489	473.2
service (not government)	8395/4	865	839.3
transport of valuables and money	7230	703	723.2
Sedimentation plant (effluent treatment) manufacturing	3245/3	341/2	324.1
Seed			
and nut, crushing	4116/2	221	411.3
cleaner or pre-cleaner (agricultural machinery) manufacturing	3211/3	331	321.1
dressing, manufacturing	2568	279/4	256.8
growing (not farming)	0100/2	001/3	01
merchant	6110	831/3	611.2
tray, plastics, manufacturing	4836	496	483
Segment, bonded abrasives, manufacturing	2460	469/1	246.1
Seismic surveying for petroleum	1300	104	134

Activity	SIC 1980	1968	NACE
Selenium rectifier, manufacturing	3444	364/3	344
Self-drive car, hire	8480/1	702/2	844
Self-propelled railway car, manufacturing	3620/2	385	362.2
Self-raising and patent flour, manufacturing	4160	211/1	416.1
Semi-chemical woodpulp, manufacturing	4710/1	481	471.1
Semi-conductor			
control equipment, manufacturing	3442	354/2	344
not power, manufacturing	3453/1	364/1	345.1
Semi-manufactures, copper, manufacturing	2246/2	322	224.2
Semi-precious			
stone jewellery, manufacturing	4910/2	396	491.5
stones, extraction	2396	109/4	239.4
Semi-trailer, manufacturing	3522	381	352
Semi-worsted yarn, spinning	4310/2	414/2	431.3
Seminary	9330	872/3	933
Semolina, milling	4160	211/1	416.1
Sensitized			
cloth, manufacturing	2591	279/7	259.1
paper, manufacturing	2591	279/7	259.1
photographic film, manufacturing	2591	279/7	259.1
Sensor for electric process control equipment, manufacturing	3442	354/2	344
Separation terminal operation, natural gas	1300	104	132
Sera, manufacturing	2570	272	257
Service			
cabinet, refrigerated, manufacturing	3284/1	339/3	328.5
flat letting	8500	863	850
Servicing, motor vehicles	6710	894	671
Serviette, manufacturing	4722	484/2	472.2
Serving dish, base metal, manufacturing	3167	392	316.7
Sesame			
oil, refining	4116/3	221	411.4
seed, crushing	4116/2	221	411.3
Sett quarry	2310/2	102/1	231.2
Settee, manufacturing	4671/1	472	467.4
Settlement plant (water treatment) manufacturing	3245/3	341/2	324.1
Sewage			
farm (owned by public authority)	9212	906/3	921
treatment plant, manufacturing	3245/3	341/2	324.1
works	9212	906/3	921
Sewerage			
construction of	5020	500	502.6
system maintenance and operation	9212	906/3	921
Sewing			
and embroidery yarn, cotton, manufacturing	4321/2	412	432.4
machine, manufacturing	3286/1	339/9	323.2
machinery (bookbinding) manufacturing	3276	339/2	327.2
machines, retail dealing in	6480	821/3	649.3
needle, manufacturing	3169/2	399/8	316.9
thread, cotton, manufacturing	4321/2	412	432.4
Sextant, manufacturing	3732	354/1	373.2
Shackle, manufacturing	3169/4	399/12	316.9
Shade, glass, manufacturing	2479/4	463/1	247.4
Shaft drilling (civil engineering)	5020	500	502.3
Shale oil, refining	1401	262	140.1
Shampoo, manufacturing	2582	275	258.1
Shandy, manufacturing	4283/1	232	428.2
Shape			
chrome-magnesite, manufacturing	2481	461/1	248.1
hat, manufacturing	4537/2	446/2	453
magnesite chrome, manufacturing	2481	461/1	248.1
steel, cold drawn, manufacturing	2235	311/2	223.1
Shaping machine (metal cutting) manufacturing	3221/1	332/1	322.1
Share			
dealer	8310	862	831
fisherman	0300/1	003/1	03
Sharpening stones of bonded abrasives, manufacturing	2460	469/1	246.1
Shave hook, manufacturing	3161/2	391	316.1
Shaver, electric, manufacturing	3460	368	346
Shaving			
brush, manufacturing	4663	493	466.3
cream, manufacturing	2581	275	258.1
cream, brushless, manufacturing	2581	275	258.1
soap, manufacturing	2581	275	258.1
Shawl, not knitted, woollen, manufacturing	4310/3	414/5	431.5
Shea			
butter, manufacturing	4116/3	221	411.4
nut crushing	4116/2	221	411.3
Shearing			
machine (metal forming) manufacturing	3221/2	332/2	322.1
machinery (textile) manufacturing	3230/3	335	323.1
Shears			
agricultural and horticultural, manufacturing	3161/1	391	316.1
garden, manufacturing	3161/1	391	316.1
Sheath knife, manufacturing	3162/1	392	316.2
Shed, manufacturing			
metal	3142	341/4	314.1
wooden	4630	471/2	463.1
Sheep			
agisting (grazing)	0100/1	001/1	01
and cattle dressings, manufacturing	2570	279/4	257
and lambskin, pulling	4410/2	431/2	431.1
dealing	6110	831/4	611.5
dip, manufacturing	2568	279/4	256.8
farming	0100/1	001/1	01
net, manufacturing	4396	416	439.7
shears (not power) manufacturing	3161/1	391	316.1
skin, preparation	4410/1	431/2	456.1
Sheepskin			
clothing, manufacturing	4560	433	456.3
rug, manufacturing	4410/1	431/2	456.3
Sheet			
aluminium, manufacturing	2245/2	321	224.3
and sheeting, asbestos (woven) manufacturing	2440	429/1	244
copper, manufacturing	2246/2	322	224.2
cork, manufacturing	4664/1	479/1	466.1
glass fibre, manufacturing	2479/4	276/1	247.5
hemming (textile)	4557	422.1	455.1
laminated thermosetting, manufacturing	4832	276/1	483
metal forming machine, manufacturing	3221/2	332/2	322.1
metal printing	4754/5	489	473.4
metal working, manufacturing	3169/4	399/12	319
music, printing	4754/4	489	473.2
music, retail dealing in	6480	821/3	649.4
polyethylene, manufacturing	4832	276/1	483
polypropylene, manufacturing	4832	276/1	483
polyvinyl chloride, manufacturing	4832	276/1	483
steel (organic coated) manufacturing	2210	311/2	221.2
steel, cold rolled under 3 mm, manufacturing	2210	311/2	221.1
steel, hot rolled, manufacturing	2210	311/2	221.1
steel, electrical, coated and uncoated, manufacturing	2210	311/2	221.1
Sheeting			
non-woven asbestos/rubber, manufacturing	2440	429/1	244

Activity	SIC 1980	1968	NACE
of plastics for roofs and cladding, manufacturing	4834	496	483
weaving (from flax and man-made fibre processed on the flax system)	4340/2	413	434.5
weaving (from yarn spun on the cotton system)	4322	413	432.5
Sheffield warehouse	6150	812/4	615.2
Shell			
boiler (not marine) manufacturing	3205/1	341/1	315.1
case, manufacturing	3290/2	342	328.9
fuse, manufacturing	3290/2	342	328.9
Shellac varnish, manufacturing	2551	274	255
Shellfish			
freezing	4150/1	214/1	415.1
preserving (not freezing)	4150/2	214/2	415.2
retail dealing in	6410	820/2	641.5
wholesale dealing in	6170	810/2	617.9
Shelter (the charity)	9611/1	899/3	961
Shelving, manufacturing			
metal	3166/1	399/1	316.6
wooden	4672	474	467.5
Sheriff court	9120	901/6	912
Sheriff's officer	8350	873	835
Sherry, production	4261/1	239/2	425.1
Shingle dredging	2310/4	103	231.4
Ship			
building	3610/1	370/1	361
cementing	3610/1	370/1	361
conversion	3610/1	370/1	361.1
fumigating and scrubbing	9230	899/7	923
hire (without crew)	8480/4	706	845
Mortgage Finance Co. Ltd.	8150/1	862	813.1
painting	3610/1	370/1	361.4
refitting	3610/1	370/1	361
repairing	3610/1	370/1	361
surveyor (private practice)	8370/2	879/1	837
wiring, manufacturing	3410	362	341
Shipbreaking	3610/3	399/12	361.5
Shiplap cladding, plastics, manufacturing	4834	496	483
Shipping			
agent or broker	7700/2	709/1	772
service, deep sea route	7400/1	705/2	741
service, domestic or coastal route	7400/3	705	742
service, short sea route between United Kingdom and international ports	7400/2	705/1	742
Ships'			
bottom composition, manufacturing	2551	274	255
decking, manufacturing	3610/1	370/1	361.1
furniture, manufacturing	4671/3	472	467.5
mast and spar, manufacturing	3610/1	370/1	361
model (made by shipbuilders) manufacturing	3610/1	370/1	361.1
Shire Horse Association	9890/2	899/6	963
Shirt			
and collar pressing	9812	892	981
front, manufacturing	4535	444/2	453
industrial, manufacturing	4534	444/2	453
men's and boys', manufacturing	4535	444/2	453
neckband, manufacturing	4535	444/2	453
knitted, manufacturing	4363/2	417	436.2
women's and girls', manufacturing	4536/1	444/2	453
Shirting weaving			
from flax and man-made fibre processed on the flax system	4340/2	413	434.5
from yarn spun on the cotton system	4322	413	432.5
Shock absorber (motor vehicle) manufacturing	3530	381	353
Shoddy, dealing in	6110	832/4	611.6
Shoe			
brush, manufacturing	4663	493	466.3
dye, manufacturing	2599	279/1	259.2
footwear, manufacturing	4510	450	451.1
lace, braided, manufacturing	4398/2	421/3	439.3
part, wooden, manufacturing	4650	479/2	465.1
polish, manufacturing	2599	279/1	259.2
repairing	6720	895	672
trimming (textile material) manufacturing	4398/2	421/3	439.3
wooden, manufacturing	4650	450	465.4
Shoes			
retail dealing in	6460	821/2	646.1
wholesale dealing in	6160	812/2	616.7
Shoetree, wooden, manufacturing	4650	479/3	465.1
Shooting gallery	9791/3	882	979
Shop			
fittings and furnishings, manufacturing	4672	474	467.5
fixture, for display and storage of goods, manufacturing	4672	474	467.5
front (other than aluminium) manufacturing	4672	474	463.2
fronts and entrances, aluminium, manufacturing	4672	399/2	314.1
furniture, manufacturing	4671/3	472	467.5
letting	8500	863	850
Shopping bag, plastics, manufacturing	4836	496	483
Shore base, sea transport	7400/4	705	742
Shorthand			
writing	8395/4	865	839.3
writing machine, manufacturing	3301	338	330
Shorts, manufacturing			
boys'	4532	442	453
men's, tailored	4532	442	453
Shovel, manufacturing	3161/1	391	316.1
Show case, wooden, manufacturing	4672	474	467.5
Showcard, manufacturing	4754/4	489	473.2
Shower cabinet, metal, manufacturing	3169/4	399/12	316.7
Shrimp preserving (not freezing)	4150/2	214/2	415.2
Shrimping	0300/1	003/1	03
Shrimps, wholesale dealing in	6170	810/2	617.9
Shrinking machinery (textile) manufacturing	3230/3	335	323.1
Shroud and cerement, manufacturing	4557	422/1	455.1
Shunt and limiting reactor, manufacturing	3420/1	361/1	342
Shutter, wooden, manufacturing	4672	474	463.2
Shuttering, manufacturing			
steel	3204/2	341/4	314.1
wooden	4630	471/2	463.2
Shuttle			
changing mechanism, manufacturing	3230/2	335	323.1
textile machinery accessory, manufacturing	3230/4	335	323.1
Sickle, manufacturing	3161/1	391	316.1
Side loader, manufacturing	3255/5	337/5	325.5
Sideboard, manufacturing	4671/2	472	467.1
Sidecar, motor cycle, manufacturing	3633	382	363.2
Sign			
plastics, manufacturing	4836	496	483
plate, metal, manufacturing	3169/4	399/12	316.9
wooden, manufacturing	4672	474	467.5
Signal			
generator, manufacturing	3442	354/2	344
rocket, manufacturing	2565	279/3	256.5
Signalling			
equipment, railway, electric, manufacturing	3433	384	343.1
equipment, road traffic, manufacturing	3433	367/1	343.1

Activity	SIC 1980	1968	NACE
glassware, manufacturing	2479/2	463/1	247.4
Signwriting	4672	474	463.2
Silage making machine, manufacturing	3211/2	331	321.1
Silencer (motor vehicle) manufacturing	3530	381	353
Silica			
and siliceous cement, manufacturing	2481	461/1	248.1
brick, manufacturing	2481	461/1	248.1
mould, manufacturing	2481	461/1	248.1
stone extraction	2396	109/4	239.4
Siliceous brick, manufacturing	2481	461/1	248.1
Silicon carbide abrasive grain, manufacturing	2460	469/1	246.1
Silicones, manufacturing	2514	276/1	251
Silk			
bleaching	4370/2	423	437.1
creping	4336	412	433.4
dealing in	6110	832/4	611.6
dyeing	4370/2	423	437.2
finishing and weighting	4370/2	423	437.4
hat, manufacturing	4537/2	446/2	453
printing	4370/2	423	437.3
thread, manufacturing	4321/2	412	433.4
throwing	4336	412	433.4
tie, manufacturing	4539/3	449/4	453
twisting	4321/2	412	433.4
veiling, manufacturing	4322	413	433.5
warping	4321/2	412	433.4
waste noil spinning	4321/1	412	433.3
winding	4321/2	412	433.4
woven cloth, manufacturing	4322	413	433.5
yarn, manufacturing	4321/1	412	433.3
Sillimanite brick, manufacturing	2481	461/1	248.1
Silo, manufacturing			
steel	3205/3	341/5	314.1
wooden	4630	471/2	463.1
Siloxanes, manufacturing	2514	276/1	251
Silver			
and gold bullion, manufacturing	2247/2	396	224.1
burnishing	4910/1	396	491.1
manufacturing	2247/2	396	224.1
ore and concentrate extraction and preparation	2100	109/2	212
plated cutlery, manufacturing	3162/1	392	316.2
Silversmiths' work	4910/1	396	491.2
Silverware, retail dealing in	6540	821/4	654.2
Singeing machinery (textile) manufacturing	3230/3	335	323.1
Singer (own account)	9760	881/2	976
Sink, manufacturing			
ceramic, fireclay etc., manufacturing	2489/2	462/2	248.5
metal, other than cast iron	3169/4	399/12	316.7
plastics	4834	496	483
Sinking machine (mining) manufacturing	3251	339/1	325.1
Sintering of metals	3138	399/11	313.3
Sisal			
mat and matting, manufacturing	4385/2	419	438.1
rope, cord or line, manufacturing	4396	416	439.6
Sixth form college	9320	872/1	932
Size			
decorators', manufacturing	2562	279/2	256.2
reduction equipment (for chemical industry) manufacturing	3245/1	339/9	324.1
separation equipment (for chemical industry) manufacturing	3245/1	339/9	324.1
Sizing machinery (textile) manufacturing	3230/3	335	323.1
Skate, manufacturing			
ice	4942	494/3	494.2
roller	4942	494/3	494.2
Skateboard, manufacturing	4942	494/3	494.2
Skeletal trailer (motor drawn) manufacturing	3522	381	352
Ski			
instructor (own account)	9791/1	882	978
wax, manufacturing	2599	279/1	259.4
Skid chain, manufacturing	3137/3	399/12	313.4
Skidded unit, tractor, manufacturing	3212	380	321.2
Skiing			
clothing, weatherproof, manufacturing	4531	441	453
equipment, manufacturing	4942	494/3	494.2
Skillcentre	9330	872/5	933
Skin			
care preparations, manufacturing	2582	273	258.2
curing	4410/1	431/1	441.1
dressing	4410/1	433	441.1
drying	4410/1	431/1	441.1
dyeing	4410/1	431/1	441.3
pickling	4410/1	431/1	441.1
rug, manufacturing	4410/1	431/2	456.3
sorting	4410/1	431/1	441.1
Skip			
leather, manufacturing	4420/2	431/1	442.3
plant (mining) manufacturing	3251	339/1	325.1
Skirt, manufacturing			
knitted	4363/2	417	436.2
tailored (not retail bespoke)	4533	443	453
women's and girls' (dressmade)	4536/1	445/1	453
Skirting board, manufacturing			
plastics	4834	496	483
unmoulded, wood	4610/2	471/1	461.2
Skittle alley	9791/1	882	978
Skylight, metal, manufacturing	3142	399/2	314.2
Slab			
copper, manufacturing	2246/1	322	224.1
cork, manufacturing	4664/1	479/1	466.1
glass fibre, manufacturing	2479/4	463/1	247.5
steel, manufacturing	2210	311/2	221.1
Slaked lime, manufacturing	2420	469/2	242.2
Slat (for manufacture of pencil) manufacturing	4650	479/3	465.1
Slate			
dealing in	6130	831/2	613.2
mine or quarry	2310/1	102/2	231.1
polishing	2450/2	469/2	245.2
slab and sheet cutting and preparation	2450/2	469/2	245.2
slabs, dealing in	6130	832/8	612.5
tile, manufacturing	2450/2	469/2	245.2
working	2450/2	469/2	245.2
Slaughterhouse	4121	810/2	412.1
Slaughterhouse machinery, manufacturing	3244/1	339/7	324.1
Sleeper			
(railway) pre-cast concrete, manufacturing	2437	469/2	243.2
(railway) steel, manufacturing	2210	311/2	221.1
wood, manufacturing	4610	471/1	461.1
Sleepers, wholesale dealing in	6130	832/2	613.1
Sleeping bag, manufacturing	4557	422/1	455.2
Slide			
fastener, metal, manufacturing	3169/2	399/8	316.9
fastener (zip), plastics, manufacturing	4836	496	483
projector, manufacturing	3733	351	373.3
Slip, manufacturing	4536/2	445/2	453
Slipper			
manufacturing	4510	450	451.2
sole, manufacturing	4510	450	451.4
Slitting			
machine (for paper) manufacturing	3276	339/2	327.2
machinery (textile) manufacturing	3230/3	335	323.1
saw, manufacturing	3222/1	390	322.2

Activity	SIC 1980	1968	NACE
Sliver			
can (textile machinery accessory) manufacturing	3230/4	335	323.1
dyeing, wool	4310/1	414/1	431.2
knitted, fabric, manufacturing	4363/3	417	436.2
Slotting machine (metal working) manufacturing	3221/1	332/1	322.1
Slow speed diesel engine, marine, manufacturing	3281/2	370/2	328.1
Slub dyeing	4370/2	423	437.2
Slubbing dyeing, wool	4310/1	414/1	431.2
Sludge vessel, manufacturing	3610/1	370/1	361
Slug, aluminium, manufacturing	2245/2	321	224.3
Sluice gate, steel, manufacturing	3204/2	341/4	314.1
Small holding	0100/1	001/1	01
Smallpox hospital	9510	874/1	951
Smallware			
bleaching	4370/2	423	437.1
dyeing	4370/2	423	437.2
textile, manufacturing	4398/2	421/3	439.3
Smallwares dealer, retail	6450	821/2	645
Smokers' requisites			
manufacturing	4959	499/2	495.3
retail dealing in	6420	821/1	642.2
Snack			
bar	6611/2	885	661
products, puffed or extruded (from farinaceous or proteinaceous material) manufacturing	4239/3	218/3	423.8
Snow			
blower, manufacturing	3254/2	336	325.4
plough, manufacturing	3254/2	336	325.4
Snuff, manufacturing	4290	240	429
Soap			
chips, manufacturing	2581	275	258.1
flakes, manufacturing	2581	275	258.1
making machinery, manufacturing	3245/1	339/9	324.1
manufacturing	2581	275	258.1
powder, manufacturing	2581	275	258.1
wholesale dealing in	6180	812/4	618.4
Social			
club	6630	887	664
medicine specialist (hospital)	9510	874/1	951
medicine specialist (private practice)	9530	874/1	953
Reform Society	9690/2	899/3	968
Science Research Council	9400	876	940
security office, local	9190	901/6	919
services department (not units providing accommodation)	9611/1	899/3	961
settlement (Toynbee Hall, etc.)	9611/2	899/3	962
welfare society	9611/1	899/3	961
worker	9611/1	899/3	961
Society of			
Apothecaries	9631/1	879/3	963
Arts	9631/1	879/3	963
Friends	9660	875	966
Sock			
and stockings (knitted) manufacturing	4363/1	417	436.1
asbestos, manufacturing	2440	429/1	244
leather, manufacturing	4510	450	451.4
Socket			
electric, manufacturing	3420/3	369/5	342
set, manufacturing	3161/2	391	316.1
Soda water, manufacturing	4283/1	232	428.2
Sodium			
and sodium compounds, manufacturing	2511	271/1	251
vapour lamp, manufacturing	3470/1	369/4	347.1
Sofa, manufacturing	4671/1	472	467.4
Soft			
drink machinery, manufacturing	3244/1	339/7	324.1
drink, manufacturing	4283/1	232	428.2
drinks dealer, wholesale	6170	810/1	617.5
drinks, retail dealing in	6410	820/1	642.1
furnishings, retail dealing in	6470	821/2	647
goods agent	6300	812/2	636
toy, not of rubber, manufacturing	4941	494/1	494.1
Software house	8394	865	839.2
Soil fumigant, manufacturing	2568	279/4	256.8
Solder, manufacturing	2247/1	323	224.2
Soldering equipment manufacturing			
electric	3435	391	343.1
gas	3289/3	332/3	328.7
Sole leather preparation	4410/1	431/1	441.3
Solenoid (for electronic apparatus) manufacturing	3444	364/3	344
Soleplate, (railway) steel, manufacturing	2210	311/2	221.1
Solicitor (own account)	8350	873	835
Solid			
fuel stove, manufacturing	3165	399/12	316.5
fuel, low temperature carbonization, (not ovoids or briquettes) manufacturing	1200/4	261/2	120.3
rubber tyre, manufacturing	4811	491/1	481.1
section, aluminium, manufacturing	2245/2	321	224.3
smokeless ovoids and briquettes, preparation of	1115	261/2	111.2
Solid-fuel			
cooker, manufacturing	3165	399/12	316.5
fired domestic heating and cooking appliance, manufacturing	3165	399/12	316.5
Solid-state circuit, manufacturing	3453/1	364/2	345.1
Soluble			
starch, manufacturing	4180	229/2	418.2
tea, manufacturing	4239/2	229/2	423.1
Solvent			
dye, manufacturing	2516	277	251
extraction equipment (for chemical industry) manufacturing	3245/1	339/9	324.1
recovery equipment (for chemical industry) manufacturing	3245/1	339/9	324.1
Song writer	9760	879/5	976
Sound recording and reproducing equipment, manufacturing	3454/1	365/2	345.1
Soup			
canned, containing meat or vegetables or both, manufacturing	4239/6	218/3	423.7
manufacturing	4239/6	218/3	423.7
powdered, containing meat or vegetable or both, manufacturing	4239/6	218/3	423.7
Soya			
bean, crushing	4116/2	221	411.3
bean, grinding	4160	211/2	416.2
bean, milling	4160	211/2	416.2
bean oil, refining	4116/3	221	411.4
flour and meal, manufacturing	4160	211/2	416.2
Space heater, manufacturing			
domestic, electric	3460	368	346
gas	3165	399/9	316.5
oil	3165	399/12	316.5
Spacecraft, manufacturing	3640	383/1	364
Spade, manufacturing	3161/1	391	316.1
Spaghetti			
canning	4239/7	218/3	417
manufacturing	4239/7	229/2	417
Spanner, manufacturing	3161/2	391	316.1
Spark erosion (metal-working) machine, manufacturing	3221/1	332/4	322.1
Spark-ignition engine (industrial) manufacturing	3281/1	334/1	328.1
Sparking plug, manufacturing	3434	369/1	343.1
Spat, leather, manufacturing	4510	450	451.4
Special			
hospital	9510	874/1	951

Activity	SIC 1980	1968	NACE
purpose caravan, manufacturing	3523	381	352
purpose paper, manufacturing	4710/6	481	471.3
purpose railway wagon, manufacturing	3620/2	385	362.2
school	9320	872	932
steelworks crane, manufacturing	3255/2	337/2	325.5
Specialist (not employed full-time by a hospital)	9530	874/1	953
Spectacle			
case, not leather or plastics, manufacturing	4959	499/2	495.3
case, leather, manufacturing	4420/1	432	442.1
frame, manufacturing	3731	353/2	373.1
glass, manufacturing	2479/5	463/1	247.4
lens, manufacturing	3731	353/2	373.1
mounts, manufacturing	3731	353	373.1
Spectacles, manufacturing	3731	353/2	373.1
Spectrofluorimeter, manufacturing	3710	354/2	371.2
Spectrograph, manufacturing	3732	354/2	373.2
Spectrometer, manufacturing	3710	354/2	371.2
Spectrophotometer, manufacturing	3732	354/2	373.2
Speedometer, manufacturing	3710	354/2	371.2
Speedway racing	9791/1	882	978
Spelter, dealing in	6120	832/1	612.6
Spent nuclear fuel re-processing	1520	271/3	152
Sperm oil, refining	4116/3	221	411.4
Spherical roller bearing, manufacturing	3262	349/1	326.2
Spice			
broker	6300	810/1	617.8
ground, manufacturing	4239/9	229/2	423.3
making (in Yorkshire)	4214/2	217/2	421
purifying, manufacturing	4239/9	229/2	423.3
Spices, wholesale dealing in	6170	810/1	617.8
Spiegeleisen, manufacturing	2210	311/2	221.1
Spill, wooden, manufacturing	4650	479/3	465.1
Spin dryer, manufacturing	3460	368	346
Spindle (textile machinery accessory) manufacturing	3230/4	335	323.1
Spinning			
cotton system	4321/1	412	432.3
flax system	4340/1	412	434.3
machinery (textile) manufacturing	3230/1	335	323.1
wheel, wooden, manufacturing	4650	479/3	465.1
woollen, worsted or semi-worsted systems	4310/2	414	431.3
Spirit			
distilling and compounding	4240/2	239/1	424.2
industrial, (from petroleum) manufacturing	1401	262	140.1
level, manufacturing	3710	391	371.5
of turpentine, manufacturing	2567	271/3	256.7
Spiritualist Church	9660	875	966
Splitwood, manufacturing	4610/1	471/1	461.1
Spoke-shave, manufacturing	3161/2	391	316.1
Sponge			
bleaching	4959	499/2	495.3
dressing	4959	499/2	495.3
importer	6180	812/4	618.1
mattress, manufacturing	4671/5	473	467.8
natural, preparation	4959	499/2	495.3
trimming	4959	499/2	495.3
Spool (textile machinery accessory) manufacturing	3230/4	335	323.1
Spooling machinery (carpet making) manufacturing	3230/2	335	323.1
Spools, paper, manufacturing	4728	484/2	472.8
Spoon			
plastics, manufacturing	4836	496	483
manufacturing	3162/1	392	316.2
wooden, manufacturing	4650	479/3	465.1
Sporran, manufacturing	4539/3	449/4	453

Activity	SIC 1980	1968	NACE
Sporting			
carbine, manufacturing	3290/1	342	328.9
gun, manufacturing	3290/1	342	328.9
rifle, manufacturing	3290/1	342	328.9
Sports			
and recreation grounds, laying out of	5020	500	502.7
bag, fabric, manufacturing	4942	494/3	442
bag, leather, manufacturing	4942	494/3	442.1
club	9791/1	882	978
equipment, plastics, manufacturing	4942	494/3	494.2
footwear, manufacturing	4510	450	451.3
glove (specialist) manufacturing	4942	494/3	442.2
goods carrier, manufacturing	4942	494/3	442.1
goods, retail dealing in	6540	821/4	654.4
goods, wholesale dealing in	6190	812/4	619.5
net, manufacturing	4396	416	439.7
outfitter, retail	6540	821/4	654.4
Sportswear			
men's and boys' tailored (not retail bespoke) manufacturing	4532	442	453
women's and girls', manufacturing	4536/1	445/1	453
women's and girls', tailored (not retail bespoke) manufacturing	4533	443	453
Spotlight, manufacturing	3470/2	369/5	347.2
Spotting table, manufacturing	3275/6	339/9	327.3
Spraying			
lorry, manufacturing	3510/2	381	351
machine (agricultural) manufacturing	3211/3	331	321.1
paint, machine, manufacturing	3286/3	339/9	328.3
Spring			
balance, manufacturing	3285/1	339/5	328.9
presswork, manufacturing	3137/2	399/4	313.2
suspension (motor vehicle) manufacturing	3530	381	313.2
upholstery, steel, manufacturing	2234	399/4	223.4
washer, manufacturing	3137/2	399/4	313.2
wire mattress, manufacturing	3166/1	399/1	316.6
Springs, upholsterers', manufacturing	2234	399/4	223.4
Sprinkler (for fire extinguishing) manufacturing	3286/1	339/9	328.9
Sprocket chain, manufacturing	3261/1	349/2	326.1
Squash			
club	9791/1	882	978
drink, manufacturing	4283/1	232	428.2
racket, manufacturing	4942	494/3	494.2
St. Andrew's Ambulance Brigade	9520	874/5	952
St. Bride's Institute	9611/1	899/3	961
St. James's Palace	9111	901/6	911
St. James's Park	9111	901/6	911
St. John's Ambulance Brigade	9520	874/5	952
Stabilisers and extenders for PVC processing, manufacturing	2567	271/3	256.7
Stabilising valve, manufacturing	3453/1	364/1	345.1
Stabilizer (ship's) manufacturing	3289/1	370	361
Stacking machine, manufacturing	3255/1	337/1	325.5
Staff canteen (run by catering contractor)	6640/1	888	664
Stage lighting, manufacturing	3470/2	369/5	347.2
Stain, manufacturing	2551	274	255
Stained glass, manufacturing	2471/2	463/1	247.6
Stair rod			
metal, manufacturing	3169/3	399/12	316.3
wooden, manufacturing	4650	479/3	465.1
Staircase, wooden, manufacturing	4630	471/2	463.2
Stake, wood, manufacturing	4610/1	471/1	461.1
Stamp			
dealer, retail	6480	821/4	653.4
embossed paper, manufacturing	4754/3	489	473.2
hinge, manufacturing	4728	484/2	472.8
Stamping of base metal	3120	399/12	312.2
Standing joint committee (police)	9130	906/1	913

STA-STI

Activity	SIC 1980	1968	NACE
Staple			
fibre (acetate, synthetic or viscose) production	2600	411	260
man-made fibre, manufacturing	2600	411	260
not wire, manufacturing	3137/1	394	316.9
office, manufacturing	4954/3	394	316.9
Stapling machine (office) manufacturing	4954/3	495/2	495
Starch			
based adhesive, manufacturing	2562	279/2	256.2
dealing in	6120	832/8	612.7
manufacturing	4180	229/2	418
Starter motor (for vehicle) manufacturing	3434	369/1	343.1
Static gauge, manufacturing	3710	390	371.5
Station wagon, manufacturing	3510/1	381	351
Stationer			
retail	6530	821/4	653.2
wholesale	6190	812/3	619.1
Stationers' sundries, wholesale dealing in	6190	812/3	619.1
Statistician (own account)	8395/4	865	839.3
Stave, wooden, manufacturing	4640/2	475/1	464.2
Steak house, licensed	6611/1	885	661
Steam			
engine, manufacturing	3281/3	334/2	328.2
production and distribution	1630	602	163
turbine (not marine or for electricity generation) manufacturing	3281/3	334/2	328.2
turbine, marine, manufacturing	3281/2	370/2	328.2
Steaming machinery (textile) manufacturing	3230/3	335	323.1
Stearic acid, manufacturing	2563	275	256.3
Stearine, manufacturing	2563	275	256.3
Steel			
angle, cold formed, manufacturing	2235	311/2	223.3
axle (railway and tramway) manufacturing	3120	311/2	312
bail tie, manufacturing	2234	394	223.4
billet, manufacturing	2210	311/2	221.1
bloom, manufacturing	2210	311/2	221.1
bright bar, manufacturing	2235	311/2	223.2
casting, manufacturing	3111	311/2	311.1
cold drawn, other than steel wire, manufacturing	2235	311/2	223.1
cold forming of	2235	399/12	223.3
cold rolling of	2235	311/2	223.2
conduit, manufacturing	2220	312	222
crude, manufacturing	2210	311/2	221.1
cylinder for compressed or liquified gas, manufacturing	2220	312	222
dealing in	6120	832/1	612.4
fish plate (railway) manufacturing	2210	311/2	221.1
girder, manufacturing	2210	311/2	221.1
hoop, cold-rolled, manufacturing	2235	311/2	223.2
hoop, hot-rolled, manufacturing	2210	311/2	221.1
ingot, manufacturing	2210	311/2	221.1
joist, manufacturing	2210	311/2	221.1
junction box, manufacturing	2220	312	222
liquid, (primary) manufacturing	2210	311/2	221.1
moulders' composition, manufacturing	2481	461/1	248.1
pipe fittings, manufacturing	2220	312	222
pipe, manufacturing	2220	312	222
plate, manufacturing	2210	311/2	221.1
rectangular hollow section, manufacturing	2220	312	222
reinforcement for concrete, manufacturing	2234	394	223.4
rod, cold drawn, manufacturing	2235	311/2	223.1
rod, hot drawn, manufacturing	2210	311/2	221.1
scaffold tube, manufacturing	2220	312	222
seamless tube, manufacturing	2220	312	222
section, cold formed, manufacturing	2235	399/12	223.3
section, manufacturing	2210	311/2	221.1
shape, cold drawn, manufacturing	2235	311/2	223.1
sheet, cold-rolled under 3 mm, manufacturing	2210	311/2	221.1
sheet, galvanised, manufacturing	2210	311/2	221.2
sheet, hot-rolled manufacturing	2210	311/2	221.1
sheet (organic coated) manufacturing	2210	311/2	221.2
slab, manufacturing	2210	311/2	221.1
sleeper (railway) manufacturing	2210	311/2	221.1
soleplate (railway) manufacturing	2210	311/2	221.1
stockholder	6120	832/1	612.4
strip, cold-rolled, manufacturing	2235	311/2	223.2
strip for tinplate, manufacturing	2210	311/2	221.1
strip, hot-rolled, manufacturing	2210	311/2	221.1
tube fittings, manufacturing	2220	312	222
tube, manufacturing	2220	312	222
tube round, manufacturing	2210	311/2	221.1
tube square, manufacturing	2210	311/2	221.1
tube strip, hot-rolled, manufacturing	2210	311/2	221.1
tube, welded, manufacturing	2220	312	222
tube, wrought, manufacturing	2220	312	222
upholstery spring, manufacturing	2234	399/4	223.4
wire cable, manufacturing	2234	394	223.4
wire fabric, manufacturing	2234	394	223.4
wire nail, manufacturing	2234	394	223.4
wire netting, manufacturing	2234	394	223.4
wire rod, manufacturing	2210	311/2	221.1
wool, for domestic use, manufacturing	3167	399/12	316.7
Steelmaking furnace, manufacturing	3245/2	341/2	328.6
Steelwork			
erection (building)	5010	500	501.7
erection (civil engineering)	5020	500	502.7
for buildings, manufacturing	3204/1	341/4	314.1
for glass roofs, manufacturing	3204/1	341/4	314.1
Steeplejacking	5030	500	503.6
Steering			
column and gear (powered invalid carriage) manufacturing	3650/2	382	365.2
equipment components (motor vehicle) manufacturing	3530	381	353
gear (marine) manufacturing	3289/1	370	361
Stemmed drinking vessel, glass, manufacturing	2479/1	463/1	247
Stencil			
basepaper, manufacturing	4710/3	481	471.3
duplicating, manufacturing	4954/2	495/2	259.3
Stentering machinery (textile) manufacturing	3230/3	335	323.1
Step ladder, wooden, manufacturing	4650	479/3	465.1
Steps, manufacturing			
metal	3169/4	399/12	316.9
wooden	4650	479/3	465.1
Stereo system, manufacturing	3454/1	365/2	345.1
Stereotype, manufacturing	4754/5	489	473.4
Sterilisation (for food and drink) equipment, manufacturing	3244/1	339/7	324.1
Sterilised			
bone flour (not for fertilizers) manufacturing	4126/3	221	412.5
cream-manufacturing	4130/1	215/2	413.1
Sterilising equipment (medical) manufacturing	3720/1	353/1	372.2
Sterio metal, manufacturing	2247/1	323	224.2
Stern gear, manufacturing	3289/1	370	361
Stevedoring	7630	706	763
Stewpan, manufacturing	3167	399/6	316.7
Stick, hockey, manufacturing	4942	494/3	494.2
Sticking plaster (surgical) manufacturing	2570	279/6	257

Activity	SIC 1980	1968	NACE
Stillage			
metal, manufacturing	3164/5	399/12	316.4
truck, manufacturing	3255/5	337/5	325.5
wooden, manufacturing	4640/1	479/3	464.1
Stilt, ceramic, manufacturing	2489/4	462/3	248.9
Stimulator, electro-medical, manufacturing	3443	367/2	344
Stipendiary magistrate	9120	901/6	912
Stitching machine (bookbinding) manufacturing	3276	339/2	327.2
Stock			
broker	8310	862	831
exchange	8310	862	831
Exchange, Council of the	8310	862	831
jobber	8310	862	831
Market Reporting Service	8395/4	865	839.3
preparation plant, paper or board, manufacturing	3275/4	339/9	327.2
Stockbreeding and farming	0100/1	001/1	01
Stockinette goods, manufacturing	4363/3	417	436.1
Stocking, manufacturing	4363/3	417	436.1
Stocktaking	8395/4	865	839.3
Stole, fur, manufacturing	4560	433	456.3
Stone			
chippings, manufacturing	2450/1	469/2	245.1
dust, manufacturing	2450/1	469/2	245.1
pit or quarry	2310	102/1	231.2
walling	5010	500	501.7
working	2450/3	469/2	245.3
Stonemasonry (building)	5010	500	501.7
Stones			
dealing in	6120	832/8	612.5
sharpening, of bonded abrasives, manufacturing	2460	469/1	246.1
Stoneware, domestic, manufacturing	2489/3	462/3	248.6
Stonework cleaning and renovation	5010	500	501.5
Stop watch, manufacturing	3740	352	374
Stopcock, domestic, manufacturing	3169/4	399/12	328.8
Stopper			
cork, manufacturing	4664/1	479/1	466.1
glass, manufacturing	2478	463/2	247.2
inset, cork, manufacturing	4664/1	479/1	466.1
metal, manufacturing	3164/3	399/10	316.4
Storage	7700/3	709/2	773
Storage			
cabinet, domestic, manufacturing	4671/2	472	467.1
container, domestic, plastics, manufacturing	4836	496	483
heater, manufacturing	3460	368	346
tank, of heavy steel plate, manufacturing	3205/3	341/5	315.2
tank, plastics, manufacturing	4834	496	483
Store, computer, manufacturing	3302	366	330
Storing yarn	4370/2	423	437.4
Stout, brewing	4270/1	231	427.1
Stove			
cast iron, manufacturing	3111	313/4	311.1
gas, manufacturing	3165	399/9	316.5
oil, manufacturing	3165	399/12	316.5
painting	3138	399/11	313.5
solid fuel, manufacturing	3165	399/12	316.5
Stowing machine (mining) manufacturing	3251	339/1	325.1
Straddle carrier, manufacturing	3255/5	337/5	325.5
Strained			
fruit, manufacturing	4147/3	218/3	414.5
vegetables, manufacturing	4147/3	218/3	414.6
Stranded wire, copper (uninsulated) manufacturing	2246/2	394	224.2
Strands for cable, aluminium, manufacturing	2245/2	321	224.3
Strap			
leather, manufacturing	4420/1	432	442.1
paste for transmission belts, manufacturing	1402	263	140.2
Straw			
and felt hat warehouse	6160	812/2	616.3
article, manufacturing	4664.2	475/1	466.2
dealing in	6110	831/3	611.2
envelope for bottle, manufacturing	4664/2	475/1	466.2
hat, blocking	4537/2	446/2	453
hat, manufacturing	4537/2	446/2	453
Strawboard, manufacturing	4710/7	481	471.2
Strawpaper, manufacturing	4710/4	481	471.2
Street			
cleaning	9211	906/3	921
musician or singer	9760	899/7	976
photographer	9890/1	899/2	983
sweeping lorry, manufacturing	3510/2	381	351
Stretch cover (furniture) manufacturing	4555	473	455.3
String			
bag, manufacturing	4396	416	439.7
manufacturing	4396	416	439.6
Strip			
aluminium, manufacturing	2245/2	321	224.3
copper, manufacturing	2246/2	322	224.2
processing line furnace, manufacturing	3245/2	341/2	328.6
steel, cold-rolled, manufacturing	2235	311/2	223.2
steel, hot-rolled, manufacturing	2210	311/2	221.1
Stroboscope, manufacturing	3710	354/2	371
Strong			
box, manufacturing	3166/2	399/3	316.6
room, manufacturing	3166/2	399/3	316.6
Strongroom door, manufacturing	3166/2	399/3	316.6
Strop, leather, manufacturing	4420/2	432	442.3
Structural			
steelwork erection (building)	5010	500	501.7
steelwork erection (civil engineering)	5020	500	502.7
steelwork (for buildings) manufacturing	3204/1	341/4	314.1
wall panels, pre-cast concrete, manufacturing	2437	469/2	243.2
Stud			
farming	0100/1	001/1	01
link chain, manufacturing	3137/3	399/12	313.4
Student			
Christian Movement	9660	875	966
union	9690/2	887	968
Students' hostel or hall of residence	9611/2	884	962
Studio couch, manufacturing	4671/1	472	467.4
Stuffed toy, manufacturing	4941	494/1	494.1
Stuffing, manufacturing	4239/9	229/2	423.3
Stylographic pen, manufacturing	4954/1	495	495.1
Stylus for record player, manufacturing	3453/2	364/3	345.1
Styrene, manufacturing	2512	271/2	251
Submarine			
base (Ministry of Defence)	9150	901/5	915
cable, manufacturing	3410	362	341
manufacturing	3610/1	370/1	361.1
Submersible motor pump, manufacturing	3287	333/1	328.3
Subscriber apparatus (telephone) manufacturing	3441	363	344
Suction and discharge hose, rubber or plastics, manufacturing	4812/1	491/2	481.2
Suet, manufacturing	4126/1	221	412.4
Sugar			
beet, growing	0100/1	001/1	01
beet harvester, manufacturing	3211/2	331	321.1
beet, manufacturing	4200	216	420.1
confectionery, retail dealing in	6420	821/1	641.9

Activity	SIC 1980	1968	NACE
confectionery making machinery, manufacturing	3244/1	339/7	324.1
confectionery, manufacturing	4214/2	217/2	421.2
making and refining machinery, manufacturing	3244/1	339/7	324.1
manufacturing	4200	216	420
milling	4200	216	420
refining	4200	216	420.2
wholesale dealing in	6170	810/1	617.7
Suit			
boys' (not retail bespoke) manufacturing	4532	442	453
mens' (not retail bespoke) manufacturing	4532	442	453
women's and girls', dressmade, manufacturing	4536/1	445/1	453
women's and girls', knitted, manufacturing	4363/2	417	436.2
women's and girls' tailored (not retail bespoke) manufacturing	4533	443	453
Suitcase			
fittings, metal, manufacturing	3169/3	399/12	316.3
leather or leather substitute, manufacturing	4420/1	432	442.1
wooden, manufacturing	4640/1	475/2	464.1
Suiting			
woollen, manufacturing	4310/3	414/5	431.5
worsted, weaving	4310/3	414/3	431.5
Sulphate			
and soda woodpulp, manufacturing	4710/1	481	471.1
of ammonia (from coke ovens) manufacturing	1200	261/1	120.2
of ammonia (from gas works) manufacturing	1620	601	162.1
Sulphite			
woodpulp, manufacturing	4710/1	481	471.1
wrapping paper, manufacturing	4710/4	481	471.3
Sulphonamides, manufacturing	2570	272	251
Sulphur			
dye, manufacturing	2516	277	251
manufacturing	2511	271/1	251
Sulphuric acid, manufacturing	2511	271/1	251
Sun car, manufacturing	3650/1	494/2	365.1
Sunflower			
oil, refining	4116/3	221	411.4
seed, crushing	4116/2	221	411.3
Sunglass blank, manufacturing	2479/5	463/1	247.4
Sunglasses, manufacturing	3731	353	373.1
Sunn hemp, manufacturing	4340/2	412	434.5
Sunshade, manufacturing	4539/2	449/3	453
Superannuation fund (autonomous)	8200/2	860	822
Supermarket, retail (selling mainly foodstuffs)	6410	820/1	641.1
Superphosphate, manufacturing	2513	278	251
Superstore (selling mainly foodstuffs)	6410	820/1	641.1
Supper bar or room (unlicensed)	6611/2	885	661
Supported vinyl, floorcovering, manufacturing	4833	492	438.2
Supreme Court	9120	901/6	912
Surface active chemical (excluding finished detergent and scouring powder) manufacturing	2567	271/3	256.7
Surge damper (hydraulic equipment) manufacturing	3283/2	333/4	328.3
Surgeon			
hospital	9510	874/1	951
private practice	9530	874/1	953
Surgery, doctor's	9530	874/3	953
Surgical			
and dental instruments and appliances, wholesale dealing in	6180	812/4	618.2
appliances, retail dealing in	6430	821/4	644.1
boot, manufacturing	4510	450	452
corset, manufacturing	4539/1	449/1	453
dressing, manufacturing	2570	279/6	257
gauze, manufacturing	2570	279/6	257
hosiery, manufacturing	3720/3	353/1	372.4
instrument, manufacturing	3720/1	353/1	372.2
instrument case (not leather or plastics) manufacturing	4959	499/2	495.3
lint, manufacturing	2570	279/6	257
rubber goods, manufacturing	4812/3	491/2	481.2
truss, manufacturing	3720/3	353/1	372.4
wadding, manufacturing	2570	279/6	257
Surplice, manufacturing	4532	442	453
Surveying instrument (optical) manufacturing	3732	354/1	373.2
Surveyor			
and valuer (real estate)	8340	863	834
other than valuer	8370/1	879/1	837
Suspended ceiling, installation	5040	500	504.1
Suspender			
belt, manufacturing	4539/1	449/1	453
manufacturing	4539/1	449/4	453
Suspension			
railway, manufacturing	3255/1	337/1	325.5
spring (motor vehicle) manufacturing	3530	381	313.2
Suture, surgical, manufacturing	2570	279/6	257
Swaging machine (metal forming) manufacturing	3221/2	332/2	322.1
Sweetened skimmed whey, production	4130/3	215/2	413.2
Sweets			
retail dealing in	6420	821/1	641.9
sugar confectionery, manufacturing	4214/2	217/2	421.2
Swimming			
bath	9791/1	882	978
club	9791/1	882	978
Swimwear			
infants', knitted, manufacturing	4363/2	417	436.2
knitted, manufacturing	4363.2	417	436.2
manufacturing	4539/1	449/1	453
Swing, playground equipment, manufacturing	4942	494/3	494.2
Swiss embroidery, manufacturing	4395	418	439.5
Switch			
electric, manufacturing	3420/3	369/5	342
for electronic apparatus, manufacturing	3444	364/3	344
Switchback	9791/3	882	979
Switchboard, telecommunication, manufacturing	3441	363	344
Switchgear (power) manufacturing	3420/2	361/2	342
Switching equipment (telegraph and telex) manufacturing	3441	363	344
Sword, manufacturing	3162/1	392	316.8
Sworn			
broker	8395/4	865	839.3
timber measurer	8395/4	865	839.3
weigher	8395/4	865	839.3
Synagogue	9660	875	966
Synthetic products, manufacturing			
detergent	2581	275	258.1
dyestuffs	2516	277	251
fibre	2600	411	260
fibre woodpulp	4710/1	481	471.1
organic pigment	2516	277	251
protein, for animal feed	4222/2	219	422
resin adhesive	2562	279/2	256.2
resin adhesive, unformulated	2514	276/1	251
resins	2514	276/1	251
rubber	2515	276/2	251
Syphon, glass, manufacturing	2478	463/2	247.7
Syrup (sugar) manufacturing	4200	216	420.3

Activity	SIC 1980	1968	NACE
T			
TNT (trinitrotoluene) manufacturing	2565	279/3	256.5
Table			
domestic, manufacturing	4671/2	472	467.1
game, manufacturing	4941	494/1	494.1
jelly, manufacturing	4147/3	218/1	423.6
linen, manufacturing	4557	422/1	455.1
linen, retail dealing in	6470	821/2	647
mat (textile) manufacturing	4557	422/1	455.1
metal, manufacturing	3166/1	399/1	316.6
office or school, manufacturing	4671/3	472	467.2
runner, not lace, manufacturing	4557	422/1	455.1
tennis ball, manufacturing	4942	494/3	494.2
tennis equipment, manufacturing	4942	494/3	494.2
water, manufacturing	4283/1	232	428.1
Tablecloth, manufacturing			
lace	4395	418	439.5
paper	4722	484/2	472.2
Tablet, saccharin, manufacturing	2570	272	259.4
Tableting and pelleting press (for chemical industry) manufacturing	3245/1	339/9	324.1
Tableware			
base metal, manufacturing	3167	392	316.7
ceramic, manufacturing	2489/3	462/3	248
glass, manufacturing	2479/1	463/1	247
gold plated, manufacturing	4910/1	392	491.2
plastics, manufacturing	4836	496	483
precious metal, manufacturing	4910/1	392	491.2
Tabulating			
machine card, manufacturing	4723/2	483	472.3
machine, manufacturing	3301	338	330
service	8395/3	865	839.2
Tachometer, manufacturing	3710	354/2	371.2
Tack, (not wire) manufacturing	3137/1	393	316.9
Taffeta			
not woollen, weaving	4322	413	432.5
woollen, manufacturing	4310/3	414/5	431.5
Tail gas, manufacturing	1401	262	140.1
Tailboard lift, manufacturing	3255/4	337/4	325.5
Tailor, retail	6450	821/2	645
Tailored outerwear			
men's and boys' (not retail bespoke) manufacturing	4532	442	453
women's and girls (not retail bespoke) manufacturing	4533	443	453
Tailors'			
dummy, not plastics, manufacturing	4959	499/2	495.3
dummy, plastics, manufacturing	4836	496	483
pad, manufacturing	4539/3	449/4	453
shears, manufacturing	3162/1	392	316.2
trimmings, wholesale dealing in	6160	812/2	616.5
Take-away food shop	6612	885	661
Talc mine or quarry	2396	109/4	239.4
Talcum powder, manufacturing	2582	273	258.2
Tallow, dealing in	6120	832/8	612.7
Tandem, manufacturing	3634	382	363.1
Tank			
(armoured fighting vehicle, tracked) manufacturing	3290/3	342	328.9
expansion, manufacturing	3163	399/6	316.4
galvanised, manufacturing	3163	399/7	316.4
glass, manufacturing	2479/3	463/1	247
open and closed, plastics, manufacturing	4834	496	483
storage, domestic, manufacturing	3163	399/7	316.4
storage, plastics, manufacturing	4834	496	483
Tanker			
(ship) manufacturing	3610/1	370/1	361.1
trailer (motor drawn) manufacturing	3522	381	352
wagon (railway) manufacturing	3620/2	385	362.2
Tannery	4410/1	431/1	441.1
Tanning			
agents, synthetic, manufacturing	2567	271/3	256.6
and dyeing extracts, vegetable manufacturing	2516	277	251
leather	4410/1	431/1	441.1
Tantalum, manufacturing	2247/1	323	224.1
Tap			
and valve, plastics, manufacturing	4834	496	483
domestic, manufacturing	3169/4	399/12	328.8
Tape			
asbestos, manufacturing	2440	429/1	244
bleaching	4370/2	423	437.1
deck (not for computer) manufacturing	3453/2	364/3	345.1
measuring, manufacturing	3710	391	371.5
non-elastic and non-elastomeric (textile material) manufacturing	4398/2	421/3	439.3
player and recorder (audio and visual) manufacturing	3454/1	365/2	345.1
reader, computer, manufacturing	3302	366	330
recorder cabinet, wooden, manufacturing	4671/4	472	467.5
recorders, retail dealing in	6480	821/3	648.8
unrecorded, magnetic, manufacturing	2599	364.3	259.4
varnished (insulating) manufacturing	2569	491	438.3
Tapered roller bearing, manufacturing	3262	349/1	326.2
Tapestry			
(not woollen or worsted) manufacturing	4322	413	432.5
woollen, manufacturing	4310/3	414/5	431.5
Tapioca, grinding	4160	211/2	416.2
Tar			
acids, manufacturing	2512	271/2	251
laying plant, manufacturing	3254/2	336	325.4
macadam laying plant, manufacturing	3254/2	336	325.4
macadam processing plant, manufacturing	3254/2	336	325.4
processing plant, manufacturing	3254/2	336	325.4
spraying contractor (civil engineering)	5020	500	502.5
Tarmacadam, coated, manufacturing	2450/1	102	245
Tarpaulin			
manufacturing	4556	422/2	455.4
repairing	4556	422/2	455.4
Tarpaulins, wholesale dealing in	6160	812/4	616
Tassel (textile material) manufacturing	4398/2	421/3	439.3
Tate Gallery	9770	899/4	977
Tattooist	9890/2	899/7	984
Tavern	6620	886	662
Tax consultant	8360	865	836
Taxi, manufacturing	3510/1	381	351
Taxi-cab service	7220	702/2	722
Taxidermy	4959	499/2	495.3
Tea			
and coffee grocer, retail	6410	820/1	642.3
bag, manufacturing	4239/2	229/2	423.1
bar, mobile	6611/2	885	661
blending	4239/2	229/2	423.1
chest, wooden, manufacturing	4640/1	475/2	464.1
exchange	6300	810/1	617.8
extract and essence, manufacturing	4239/2	229/2	423.1
garden	6611/2	885	661
herb, manufacturing	4239/9	229/2	423.1
processing machinery and plant, manufacturing	3244/1	339/7	324.1
room or shop	6611/2	885	661
set, base metal, manufacturing	3167	392	316.7
towel, manufacturing	4557	422/1	455.1

TEA-THA

Activity	SIC 1980	1968	NACE
warehouse	7700/3	709/2	773
wholesale dealing in	6170	810/1	617.8
Teacher			
own account, not recreational activities	9330	872/5	935
training college	9310	872/3	931
undefined	9330	872/1	933
Teachers' Registration Council	9631/1	879/3	963
Teaching aid, electronic, manufacturing	3443	367/2	344
Teapot			
base metal, manufacturing	3167	399/6	316.7
ceramic, manufacturing	2489/3	462/3	248
precious metal, manufacturing	4910/1	392	491.2
Teasel			
growing	0100/1	001/1	01
rod (textile machinery accessory) manufacturing	3230/4	335	323.1
Technical			
college	9330	872/3	933
tallow	4116/3	221	411.4
toy, manufacturing	4941	494/1	494.1
white oil, manufacturing	1401	262	140.1
Telecommunication			
cable, manufacturing	3410	362	341
switchboard, manufacturing	3441	363	344
wire, manufacturing	3410	362	341
Telecommunications Headquarters, British Telecom	7902	708	790
Telegram Service	7902	708	790
Telegraph			
apparatus, manufacturing	3441	363	344
manager's office	7902	708	790
pole, manufacturing	4610/1	471/1	461.1
Telegraphic code expert	8395/4	865	839.3
Telemetering instrument, manufacturing	3442	354/2	344
Telemetric equipment, manufacturing	3443	367/2	344
Telephone			
answering service	8395/4	865	839.3
apparatus, manufacturing	3441	363	344
cleaning and sterilising service	9230	899/7	923
dial, manufacturing	3441	363	344
exchange	7902	708	790
exchange equipment, manufacturing	3441	363	344
handset, manufacturing	3441	363	344
hire (other than by public telephone undertakings)	8490	832/10	847
line installation (not by British Telecom)	5030	500	503.6
manager's office	7902	708	790
manufacturing	3441	363	344
service	7902	708	790
sterilizing	8395/4	899/7	839.3
Teleprinter, manufacturing	3441	363	344
Telescope, manufacturing	3732	354/1	373.2
Television			
cabinet, wooden, manufacturing	4671/4	472	467.5
camera lens, manufacturing	3733	354/1	373.3
camera, manufacturing	3443	367/2	344
camera tube, manufacturing	3453/1	364/1	345.1
closed-circuit equipment, manufacturing	3443	367/2	344
domestic hire	8460/1	821/3	846.2
EHT transformer, manufacturing	3453/2	364/3	345.1
picture tube, manufacturing	3453/1	364/1	345.1
receiver, manufacturing	3454/1	365/2	345.1
relay service	9741/1	881/2	974
scan coil, manufacturing	3453/2	364/3	345.1
service	9741/1	881/2	974
sets and equipment, retail dealing in	6480	821/3	648.8
studio	9741/1	881/2	974

Activity	SIC 1980	1968	NACE
transmitter, manufacturing	3443	367/2	344
Telewriter, manufacturing	3441	363	344
Telex			
machine, manufacturing	3441	363	344
service	7902	708	790
Temperance			
association	9611/1	899/3	961
buffet	6611/2	885	661
hotel	6650/2	884	665
Temperature measuring and control instrument (not electronic) manufacturing	3710	354/2	371.2
Temple (for worship)	9660	875	966
Tennis			
ball (finished) manufacturing	4942	494/3	494.2
ball core, manufacturing	4812/3	491/2	481.2
club	9791/1	882	978
court	9791/1	882	978
racket, manufacturing	4942	494/3	494.2
Tension strapping tool, manufacturing	3161/2	391	316.1
Tensional steel strapping, manufacturing	3164/5	399/12	316.4
Tent			
manufacturing	4556	422/2	455.4
pole, wooden, manufacturing	4650	479/3	465.1
Terminal			
equipment (telegraphic and data communication) manufacturing	3441	363	344
for electronic apparatus, manufacturing	3444	364/3	344
unit, computer, manufacturing	3302	366	330
Terneplate, manufacturing	2210	311/2	221.2
Terracotta ware, manufacturing	2489/3	462/3	248.6
Terrazzo work (building)	5040	500	504.5
Tesselated pavement tile, glazed, manufacturing	2489/1	462/2	248.3
Tesserae, earthenware, manufacturing	2489/1	462/2	248.3
Test			
tube, manufacturing	2479/3	463/1	247.7
wagon, railway, manufacturing	3620/2	385	362.2
well (petroleum) drilling	1300	104	502.3
Testing			
equipment, electronic, manufacturing	3442	354/2	344
machine and equipment, manufacturing	3286/1	339/9	328.9
or analysing laboratory	8370/2	879/2	837
Textile			
binding and mending	4370/2	423	437.4
bleaching	4370/2	423	437.1
calendering	4370/2	423	437.4
chemical auxiliaries, manufacturing	2567	271/3	256.6
converter	6160	812/2	616
doily, manufacturing	4557	422/1	455.1
dyeing	4370/2	423	437.2
embossing	4370/2	423	437.4
ending and mending	4370/2	423	437.4
fabric coated with plastic material, manufacturing	4831	492	438.3
fabric making machinery, manufacturing	3230/2	335	323.1
household, manufacturing	4557	422/1	455.1
lacquering	4370/2	423	437.4
machinery, manufacturing	3230	335	323.1
material cordage, manufacturing	4396	416	439.6
smallware (narrow fabric) manufacturing	4398/2	421/3	439.3
soap, manufacturing	2581	275	258.1
waste, dealing in	6220	832/7	622
Texturing and softening machinery (textile) manufacturing	3230/1	335	323.1
Thatching	0100/3	001/2	01

Activity	SIC 1980	1968	NACE
Theatre	9741/2	881/2	975
Theatre			
seat (upholstered) manufacturing	4671/1	472	467.4
ticket agency	9791/3	881/2	979
Theatrical			
agency	9791/3	881/2	979
costume, manufacturing	4539/3	449/4	453
costumier (hiring)	9791/3	821/2	979
Theodolite, manufacturing	3732	354/1	373.2
Theological college (if specialising in higher education course)	9310	872/3	931
Theosophical Society	9660	875	966
Thermal			
and sound insulating material, glass fibre, manufacturing	2479/4	463/1	247.5
insulation, contractor	5030	500	503.4
Thermo-forming machine, manufacturing	3275/2	339/9	324.3
Thermometer, manufacturing	3710	354/2	371.2
Thermoplastic asphalt tile, manufacturing	4833	492	438.2
Thermoplastic resins, manufacturing	2514	276/1	251
Thermosetting resins, manufacturing	2514	276/1	251
Thermostat, manufacturing	3710	354/2	371.2
Thinners for paint and varnish, manufacturing	2551	274	255
Thread			
guide (textile machinery accessory) manufacturing	3230/4	335	323.1
rubber, uncovered, manufacturing	4812/3	491/2	481.2
sewing and embroidery, cotton, manufacturing	4321/2	412	432.4
Threading			
die, manufacturing	3222/1	332/1	322.1
machine (metal-cutting) manufacturing	3221/1	332/1	322.1
tap, manufacturing	3222/1	390	322.2
Threads, wholesale dealing in	6160	812/2	616.5
Threshing			
by contractor	0100/3	001/2	01
machine, manufacturing	3211/2	331	321.1
Thyratron, manufacturing	3453/1	364/1	345.1
Thyristor, manufacturing	3453/1	364/1	345.1
Tic-tac man	9791/2	883	979
Ticket			
agency (travel)	7700/1	709/1	771
cutting and punching	4728	484/2	472.8
issuing machine, manufacturing	3301	338	330
machine hire	8430	832/10	843
printing	4754/3	489	473.2
punch, manufacturing	3301	338	330
writing	4754/5	489	473.4
Ticking, weaving	4322	413	432.5
Tie			
knitted, manufacturing	4363/2	417	436.2
silk, manufacturing	4322	413	433.5
Tiepin, manufacturing	3169/2	399/8	316.9
Tights, manufacturing	4363/1	417	436.1
Tile			
asbestos, woven, manufacturing	2440	429/1	244
asphalt, thermoplastic, manufacturing	4833	492	438.2
cork, manufacturing	4664/1	479/1	466.1
earthenware, glazed, manufacturing	2489/1	462/2	248.3
enamelled, glazed, manufacturing	2489/1	462/2	248.3
encaustic, manufacturing	2489/1	462/2	248.3
floor and wall (concrete/terrazzo) manufacturing	2437	469/2	243.2
flue, clay, manufacturing	2410	461/2	241
glass, manufacturing	2479/5	463/1	247.4
glazed, manufacturing	2489/1	462/2	248.3
hearth, clay, unglazed, manufacturing	2410	461/2	241
making machine, not plastics working, manufacturing	3275/5	339/9	325.3
other than floor tile, plastics, manufacturing	4834	496	483
paving, clay, unglazed, manufacturing	2410	461/2	241
plaster, manufacturing	2437	469/2	243.3
roofing, clay, unglazed, manufacturing	2410	461/2	241
slate, manufacturing	2450/2	469/2	245.2
vinyl asbestos, manufacturing	4833	492	438.2
wall, clay, unglazed, manufacturing	2410	461/2	241
Tiles			
wholesale dealing in	6130	831/2	613.2
wall or floor, ceramic, retail dealing in	6480	821/3	649.2
Tiling			
contractor (floors and walls)	5040	500	504.5
rubber, manufacturing	4812/3	491/2	481.2
Tillot and seal making	4754/5	489	473.4
Timber			
broker	6300	832/2	633
importer	6130	832/2	613.1
industrialised building component, manufacturing	4630	471/2	463
measurer	8395/4	865	839.3
merchant	6130	832/2	613.1
yard	6130	832/2	613.1
Time			
clock, manufacturing	3740	352	374
hire (computer)	8394	865	839.2
lock, manufacturing	3740	352	374
recorder, manufacturing	3740	352	374
switch, manufacturing	3740	369/5	374
Timer			
(industrial) manufacturing	3740	352	374
pocket, manufacturing	3740	352	374
Timetable, printing	4754/4	489	473.2
Timing belt, motor vehicle, manufacturing	4812/2	491/2	481.2
Tin			
can and box, manufacturing	3164/1	395	316.4
manufacturing	2247/1	323	224.1
mining	2100	109/2	212.1
ore concentrate, extraction and preparation	2100	109/2	212
printing	4754/5	489	473.4
Tinman's snips, manufacturing	3161/2	391	316.1
Tinned			
broth, manufacturing	4239/6	218/3	423.7
meat, manufacturing	4122/3	214/2	412.2
pudding, including rice pudding, manufacturing	4239/5	229/2	not classified
plate, sheet, strip (decorated, etc, for box and other container) manufacturing	3164/1	395	316.4
soup, manufacturing	4239/6	218/3	423.7
Tinplate			
wholesale dealing in	6120	832/1	612.6
manufacturing	2210	311/2	221.2
Tinted glass, manufacturing	2471/1	463/1	247.1
Tip			
cork, manufacturing	4664/1	479/1	466.1
for cutting tools, manufacturing	3222/1	390	322.2
Tipper, manufacturing	3255/1	337/1	325.5
Tipping gear (complete and parts, not hydraulic) (motor vehicle) manufacturing	3530	381	353

Activity	SIC 1980	1968	NACE
Tissue			
glass fibre, manufacturing	2479/4	463/1	247.5
paper (uncut) manufacturing	4710/5	481	471.3
Titanium			
dioxide, manufacturing	2516	277	251
manufacturing	2247/1	323	224.1
Title document printing	4754/3	489	473.2
Toast rack, base metal, manufacturing	3167	392	316.7
Toast-master (own account)	9890/2	899/7	984
Toaster, electric, manufacturing	3460	368	346
Tobacco			
broker	6300	812/1	617.6
for use in pipes and rolled cigarettes, manufacturing	4290	240	429
merchant, wholesale	6170	812/1	617.6
pouch, manufacturing	4959	499/2	495.3
processing machinery, manufacturing	3244/3	339/9	324.1
retail dealing in	6420	821/1	642.2
Tobacconist			
and newsagent, retail	6420	821/1	642.3
retail	6420	821/1	642.2
wholesale	6170	812/1	617.6
Tobacconists' sundriesman, wholesale	6170	812/1	617.6
Toe puff, manufacturing	4510	450	451.4
Toffee, manufacturing	4214/2	217/2	421.2
Toilet			
brush, manufacturing	4663	493	466.3
case, fitted, leather, manufacturing	4420/1	432	442.1
goods, retail dealing in	6430	821/4	644.2
paper (cut to size) manufacturing	4722	484/2	472.2
paper, (uncut) manufacturing	4710/5	481	471.3
preparations, manufacturing	2582	273	258.2
preparations, wholesale dealing in	6180	812/4	618.3
soap, manufacturing	2581	275	258.1
Toll bridge, road or tunnel	7610/1	709/1	761
Toluene, manufacturing	2512	271/2	251
Tomato, growing	0100/2	001/3	01
Toner			
photographic, manufacturing	2591	279/7	259.1
pigment, manufacturing	2516	277	251
Tongued wood, manufacturing	4610/2	471/1	461.2
Tonic wine, production	4261/1	239/2	425.1
Tool			
bar, agricultural machinery, manufacturing	3211/1	331	321.1
for mechanics or engineers, hire	8490	832/10	847
handle, wooden, manufacturing	4650	479/3	465.1
holder, manufacturing	3222/3	390	322.2
wooden, manufacturing	4650	479/3	465.1
Toolbag, leather, manufacturing	4420/1	432	442.1
Tools			
for construction, hire (without staff)	8420	500	842
hand, manufacturing	3161	391	316.1
machine and engineers, manufacturing	322	332 and 390	322
not machine tools, retail dealing in	6480	821/3	648.6
Tooth			
brush, not electric, manufacturing	4663	493	466.3
paste, manufacturing	2582	273	258.2
powder, manufacturing	2582	273	258.2
Toothpick, manufacturing	4959	499/2	495.3
Topmaking, wool	4310/1	414/1	431.2
Tops, dealing in	6110	832/4	611.6
Torch battery, manufacturing	3432/1	369/2	343.2
Torpedo, manufacturing	3290/2	342	328.9
Torsion bar spring, for motor vehicles suspension, manufacturing	3530	399/4	313.2
Totalisator	9791/2	883	979

Activity	SIC 1980	1968	NACE
Toughened glass, manufacturing	2471/2	463/1	247.6
Tour operator	7700/1	709/1	771
Touring			
caravan, manufacturing	3523	381	352
company (theatre)	9760	881/2	976
Tourist board or information service	9690/1	899/7	967
Tow			
flax, manufacturing	4340/1	412	434.1
jute, manufacturing	4350/1	415	435.3
man-made, manufacturing	2600	411	260
yarn of hard fibres, manufacturing	4396	416	439.6
Towel			
bath, manufacturing	4557	422/1	455.1
hire	9811	892	981
manufacturing	4557	422/1	455.1
paper, manufacturing	4722	484/2	472.2
rail (electric) manufacturing	3460	368	346
supply company	9811	892	981
Towelling, weaving	4322	413	432.5
Tower, manufacturing			
steel	3204/2	341/4	314.1
wooden	4630	471/2	463.1
Towing rope, manufacturing	4396	416	439.6
Town			
crier (own account)	9890/2	899/7	968
gas distribution	1620	601	162.2
gas production	1620	601	162.1
Toxic waste treatment service	9211	899/7	921
Toy			
animal, manufacturing	4941	494/1	494.1
balloon, rubber, manufacturing	4812/3	491/2	481.2
car, electric, manufacturing	4941	494/1	494.1
car, pedal, manufacturing	4941	494/1	494.1
furniture, manufacturing	4941	494/1	494.1
gun (not operated by compressed air) manufacturing	4941	494/1	494.1
mechanical, manufacturing	4941	494/1	494.1
metal, manufacturing	4941	494/1	494.1
musical instrument, manufacturing	4941	494/1	494.1
not rubber, manufacturing	4941	494/1	494.1
perambulator and pushchair, manufacturing	4941	494/1	494.1
plastics, manufacturing	4941	494/1	494.1
repairer	6730/3	821/4	675
rubber, manufacturing	4812/3	491/2	481.2
train, electric, manufacturing	4941	494/1	494.1
wheelbarrow, manufacturing	4941	494/1	494.1
Toy-car circuit, electric, manufacturing	4941	494/1	494.1
Toys			
and games, electronic (not linked with television set) manufacturing	4941	not classified	
retail dealing in	6540	821/4	654.3
wholesale dealing in	6190	812/4	619.5
Tracing			
cloth, manufacturing (textile finishing)	4370/2	423	437.4
cloth, weaving	4322	413	432.5
paper, manufacturing	4710/3	481	471.3
Track rod (motor vehicle) manufacturing	3530	381	353
Tracksuit, manufacturing	4535	444/1	453
Traction			
battery (rechargeable) manufacturing	3432/2	369/3	343.2
motor (with or without associated control equipment) manufacturing	3420/3	361	342
Tractor			
agricultural, hire (without driver)	8410	832/6	841
half track, manufacturing	3212	380	321.2
hoe, manufacturing	3211/1	331	321.1
plough, manufacturing	3211/1	331	321.1
shovel, manufacturing	3254/1	336	325.4
tyre, manufacturing	4811	491/1	481.1

Activity	SIC 1980	1968	NACE
wheeled, manufacturing	3212	380	321.2
winch, manufacturing	3254/1	336	325.4
Tractors			
agricultural, repairing	6149	832/5	614.6
dealing in	6149	832/5	614.6
Trade			
association	9631/2	899/6	963
journal, printing	4752/3	486	473.1
journal, printing—publishing	4752/2	486	473.1
journal, publishing	4752/1	486	474.4
protection society	9631/2	899/6	963
union	9631/3	899/6	965
Trades			
exhibition or fair	8395/2	864	839.1
Union Congress	9631/3	899/6	965
Tradesman's knife, manufacturing	3161/2	392	316.1
Trading stamp company	8395/4	865	839.3
Traffic			
control equipment (for roads and inland waterways) manufacturing	3433	367/1	343.1
indicator (for vehicle) manufacturing	3434	369/1	343.1
warden	9130	906/1	913
Trailer			
horse-drawn (not wooden) manufacturing	3650/2	399/12	365.2
motor-drawn, manufacturing	3522	381	352
Train			
electric, toy, manufacturing	4941	494/1	494.1
see under railway			
Trainer			
electronic, manufacturing	3433	367/2	344
racehorse or greyhound	9791/1	882	978
Training			
centre of Industrial Training Board	9330	872/5	933
school (Northern Ireland)	9120	872/5	912
Services Department (not Skillcentre) of the Manpower Services Commission	9111	901/6	911
stables	9791/1	882	978
Tramway			
rolling stock repairing	3620/3	385	362.3
service	7210/2	702/1	721.2
Transfer			
moulding press, for rubber or plastics, manufacturing	3275/2	399/9	324.3
printing	4754/4	489	473.2
Transformer			
(for electric apparatus) manufacturing	3444	364/3	344
(generator, transmission system and distribution) manufacturing	3420/1	361/1	342
industrial, manufacturing	3420/1	361/1	342
oil (at refineries) manufacturing	1401	262	140.1
oil (outside refineries) formulation	1402	263	140.2
Transistor, manufacturing	3453/1	364/1	345.1
Transit container, plastics closed, manufacturing	4835	496	483
Translation service	8395/4	865	839.3
Transmission			
belting, rubber or plastics, manufacturing	4812/2	491/2	481.2
chain, manufacturing	3261/1	349/2	326.1
equipment (telephone and telegraph) manufacturing	3441	363	344
line, construction	5020	500	502.7
Transmitter			
picture, manufacturing	3441	363	344
radio and television, manufacturing	3443	367/2	344
Transplanter, agricultural machinery, manufacturing	3211/1	331	321.1
Transport department (if a separate 'establishment' ancillary to the main activity of the business)	7230	704	723.2
Transporter, manufacturing	3255/2	337/2	325.5
Travel			
agent	7700/1	709/1	771
goods (leather or leather substitute) manufacturing	4420/1	432	442.1
goods, retail dealing in	6460	821/4	646.2
Travelling			
clock, manufacturing	3740	352	374
crane, manufacturing	3255/2	337/2	325.5
rug, making-up outside weaving establishment	4557	422/1	455.2
rug, woollen, manufacturing	4310/3	414/5	431.5
show	9791/3	881/2	979
trunk, wooden, manufacturing	4640/1	475/2	464.1
wave tube, manufacturing	3453/1	364/1	345.1
Trawl door, manufacturing	3289/1	370	361
Trawler, manufacturing	3610/1	370/1	361.1
Tray			
base metal, manufacturing	3167	399/12	316.7
plastics, manufacturing	4836	496	483
wooden, manufacturing	4650	479/3	465.1
Treacle, manufacturing	4200	216	420.3
Tree nursery (not fruit or ornamental trees)	0200	002	02
Treefelling (by forestry owners)	0200	002	02
Trellis work, manufacturing			
metal	3169/4	399/12	316.9
wooden	4630	471/2	463.2
Trencher, manufacturing	3254/1	336	325.4
Tribunal	9120	901/6	912
Trichologist	9820	889	982
Tricycle			
and parts, manufacturing	3634	382	363
children's, manufacturing	4941	494/1	494.1
motor and parts, manufacturing	3633	382	363
Trimming, woven, manufacturing	4398/2	421/3	439.3
Trimmings, manufacturing			
fur	4560	433	456.1
leather	4420/1	432	442.1
Trinitrotoluene (TNT) manufacturing	2565	279/3	256.5
Trinity House	7630	706	763
Tripe			
dealer, retail	6410	820/1	641.4
dressing	4126/2	214/2	412.5
Troop-carrier, motor vehicle, manufacturing	3510/2	381	351
Tropical helmet, manufacturing	4537/2	446/2	453
Trotting club	9791/1	882	978
Trouser			
suit, women's and girls', tailored (not retail bespoke) manufacturing	4533	443	453
work, manufacturing	4534	444/1	453
Trousers			
boys', tailored (not retail bespoke) manufacturing	4532	442	453
men's, tailored (not retail bespoke) manufacturing	4532	442	453
women's and girls', tailored (not retail bespoke) manufacturing	4533	443	453
Trowel, manufacturing			
garden	3161/1	391	316.1
not garden	3161/2	391	316.1
Truck, manufacturing			
horse-drawn not wooden	3650/2	399/12	365.2
manually propelled not wooden	3650/2	399/12	365.2
commercial vehicle	3510/2	381	351
wooden	4650	479/3	465.1
Trug, manufacturing	4664/2	475/1	466.2
Trunk			
handle, leather, manufacturing	4420/1	432	442.1
leather, manufacturing	4420/1	432	442.1

Activity	SIC 1980	1968	NACE
Truss			
rafter, manufacturing	4630	471/2	463.1
surgical, manufacturing	3720/3	353/1	372.4
Trustee	8150/2	862	813.2
Trustee Savings Bank	8140/3	861	812
Tub, manufacturing			
plastics	4835	496	483
wooden	4640/2	475/1	464.2
Tube			
blank, copper, manufacturing	2246/2	322	224.2
concrete, manufacturing	2437	469/2	243.2
container, plastics, manufacturing	4835	496	483
copper, manufacturing	2246/2	322	224.2
coupling and equipment (pneumatic) manufacturing	3283/3	333/4	328.3
electronic, manufacturing	3453/1	364/1	345.1
fittings, aluminium, manufacturing	2245/2	321	224.3
fittings, copper, manufacturing	2246/2	322	224.2
fittings, steel, manufacturing	2220	312	222
flexible, steel, manufacturing	2220	312	222
glass (for electric light) manufacturing	2479/2	463/1	247.4
mill plant, manufacturing	3286/2	339/9	322.1
paper, manufacturing	4728	484/2	472.8
round, steel, manufacturing	2210	311/2	221.1
shell, copper, manufacturing	2246/2	322	224.2
square, steel, manufacturing	2210	311/2	221.1
steel, manufacturing	2220	312	222
strip, steel, hot-rolled, manufacturing	2210	311/2	221.1
Tuberculosis sanatorium or hospital	9510	874/1	951
Tubing, glass, manufacturing	2479/3	463/1	247.4
Tubular			
container, glass, manufacturing	2478	463/2	247.7
container, metal, manufacturing	3164/1	395	316.4
rivet, manufacturing	3137/1	393	316.9
Tufted			
carpet, manufacturing	4384/2	419	438.1
fabric (other than household textile) manufacturing	4399/2	429/2	439.7
Tufting			
blankets	4557	422/1	455.2
household textiles	4557	422/1	455.1
machinery (carpet making) manufacturing	3230/2	335	323.1
Tug			
lessee or owner (inland waterways service)	7260/3	706	730
manufacturing	3610/1	370/1	361.1
owner or lessee for in-port service or salvage	7630	706	763
Tug-boat			
(for inland waterways) service	7260/3	706	730
for sea barge on domestic coastal route	7400/3	705	742
for sea barge or servicing off-shore well	7400/2	705	742
for servicing off-shore installation	7400/3	705	742
manufacturing	3610/1	370/1	361.1
Tumbler, manufacturing			
dryer, domestic	3460	368	346
glass	2479/1	463/1	247
Tun, wooden, manufacturing	4640/2	475/1	464.2
Tuner			
(audio separate) manufacturing	3454/1	365/2	345.1
radio and television (other than audio separates) manufacturing	3453/2	364/3	345.1
Tung oil, extraction	4116/2	221	411.3
Tungsten, manufacturing	2247/1	323	224.1
Tuning fork, manufacturing	4920/2	499/1	492.2
Tunnel			
oven refractory, manufacturing	2481	461/1	248.1
segment, cast iron, manufacturing	3111	313/3	311.1
steelwork, manufacturing	3204/2	341/4	314.1
Tunnelling			
contractor	5020	500	502.3
machine (mining) manufacturing	3251	339/1	325.1
Turbine for electricity generation, manufacturing	3420/1	361/1	328.2
Turbo-alternator, manufacturing	3420/1	361/1	342
Turf			
accountant	9791/2	883	979
commission agency	9791/2	883	979
Turkish			
baths	9820	899/7	982
delight, manufacturing	4214/2	217/2	421.2
Turned wood product, manufacturing	4650	479/3	465.1
Turning machine (metal-cutting) manufacturing	3221/1	332/1	322.1
Tweed, manufacturing	4310/3	414/5	431.5
Twill weaving	4322	413	432.5
Twin set, knitted, manufacturing	4363/2	417	436.2
Twine			
manufacturing	4396	416	439.6
paper, manufacturing	4728	484/2	472.8
wholesale dealing in	6190	812/4	619.6
Twist			
cord, fabric, manufacturing	4398/2	421/3	439.3
drill, manufacturing	3222/1	390	322.2
Twisting machinery (textile) manufacturing	3230/1	335	323.1
Tyne Improvement Commissioners	7610/2	706	762
Type			
metal, manufacturing	2247/1	323	224.2
setting machine, manufacturing	3276	339/2	327.2
Typewriter			
case, leather, manufacturing	4420/1	432	442.1
manufacturing	3301	338	330
ribbon, manufacturing	4954/2	495/2	259.3
Typewriters			
leasing of	8430	832/10	843
retail dealing in	6530	821/4	653.3
Typing service	8395/4	865	839.3
Tyre			
cord (cotton system) manufacturing	4321/2	412	432.4
dealer, retail	6510	894	651
fabric (woven from yarn spun on the cotton system) manufacturing	4322	413	432.5
inflator (cycle type) manufacturing	3634	382	363.2
manufacturing	4811	491/1	481.1
repair materials and kit, manufacturing	4811	491/1	481.2

U

Activity	SIC 1980	1968	NACE
Ulster College	9310	872/3	931
Ulsterbus	7210/2	702/1	721.2
Ultrasonic (metal working) machine tool, manufacturing	3221/1	332/4	322.1
Umbrella			
manufacturing	4539/2	449/3	453
repairer	6730/3	821/2	675
trimming (textile material) manufacturing	4398/2	421/3	439.3
Umbrellas, retail dealing in	6450	821/2	645.7
Underclothing, manufacturing			
children's	4536/3	445/3	453
knitted children's	4363/2	417	436.2
see also underwear			
Underskirt, manufacturing	4536/2	445/2	453
Undertaking (funerary)	9890/2	899/1	984
Underwater swimming suit, rubber or plastics, manufacturing	4812/3	491/2	481.2

Activity	SIC 1980	1968	NACE
Underwear			
children's, knitted, manufacturing	4363/2	417	436.2
children's, manufacturing	4536/3	445/3	453
knitted, manufacturing	4363/2	417	436.2
men's and boys', manufacturing	4535	444/2	453
paper, manufacturing	4722	445/2	472.2
women's and girls', manufacturing	4536/2	445/2	453
Underwriter			
fire, accident, health, marine, etc	8200/3	860	823
insurance	8200/1	860	821
life	8200/2	860	822
Lloyd's	8200/3	860	823
stock and share issues	8310	862	831
Unemployment benefit office	9190	901/6	919
Uniform			
(by men's tailors; not retail bespoke) manufacturing	4532	442	453
hat and cap, manufacturing	4537/2	446/2	453
helmet, manufacturing	4537/2	446/2	453
women's and girls' (not retail bespoke) manufacturing	4533	443	453
Union			
cloth, cotton/linen, manufacturing	4340/2	413	434.5
Trade	9631/3	899/6	965
Unionist association	9690/2	899/4	968
Unit			
construction and transfer machine (metal-working) manufacturing	3221/1	332/1	322.1
furniture (non-upholstered) manufacturing	4671/2	472	467.1
seating (upholstered) domestic, manufacturing	4671/1	472	467.4
trust	8150/2	862	813.2
Unitarian Church	9660	875	966
United			
Nations and affiliated organisations (not United Nations Association)	0000	899/5	000
Nations Association	9690/2	899/4	968
Reform Church	9660	875	966
Society for Christian Literature	9660	875	966
Universal			
joint (motor vehicle) manufacturing	3530	381	353
plate 150 mm and over, steel, manufacturing	2210	311/2	221.1
Universities' Central Council on Admissions	9310	872/3	931
University	9310	872/3	931
University			
canteen	6640/2	872/3	664
college	9310	872/3	931
extra-mural department (if separately identifiable)	9330	872/3	931
Grants Committee	9111	901/6	911
medical or dental school	9310	872/3	931
Unrecorded magnetic tape, manufacturing	2599	364/3	259.4
Unrendered and crude			
fat (from knackers) manufacturing	4126/3	899/7	412.4
fats, marine-animals, manufacturing	4116/1	221	411.1
fats, vegetable, manufacturing	4116/2	221	411.3
Unstitched rubber glove and gauntlet, manufacturing	4812/3	491/2	481.2
Unsupported rubber sheeting, piece goods, manufacturing	4812/3	491/2	481.2
Upholstered			
base for mattress, manufacturing	4671/5	472	467.8
chair, manufacturing	4671/1	472	467.4
furniture, manufacturing	4671/1	472	467.4
Upholsterers'			
springs, manufacturing	2234	399/4	223.4
trimming (textile material) manufacturing	4398/2	421/3	439.3
trimmings, wholesale dealing in	6160	812/2	616
Upholstery			
components from steel wire, manufacturing	2234	394	223.4
hair fibre and filling, manufacturing	4399/2	429/2	439.7
leather preparation	4410/1	431/1	441.3
manufacturing	4671/1	472	467.4
repairer	6730/3	821/3	675
spring, steel, manufacturing	2234	399/4	223.4
Upper leather, manufacturing	4410/1	431/1	441.3
Uranium			
enriched, manufacturing	1520	271/3	152
natural, production	1520	271/3	152
Urea			
(for use as fertiliser) manufacturing	2513	278	251
formaldehyde adhesive, manufacturing	2562	279/2	256.2
formaldehyde resins, manufacturing	2514	276/1	251
(not for use as a fertiliser) manufacturing	2512	271/2	251
Urinal (ceramic, fireclay etc) manufacturing	2489/2	462/2	248.5
Urologist			
hospital	9510	874/1	951
private practice	9530	874/1	953

V

Activity	SIC 1980	1968	NACE
V-jointed wood, manufacturing	4610/2	471/1	461.2
Vaccine, manufacturing	2570	272	257
Vacuum			
cleaner (industrial and commercial) manufacturing	3435	368	343.1
cleaner, domestic, manufacturing	3460	368	346
flask (complete) manufacturing	2479/5	463/2	247.4
flask inner, manufacturing	2479/5	463/1	247.2
forming machine, manufacturing	3275/2	399/9	324.3
jar, manufacturing	2479/5	463/2	247.4
pump, manufacturing	3283/1	333/3	328.3
treatment of wood	4620/2	471/1	462.4
Valet service	9812	893	981
Valuer			
any trade except real estate	8395/4	865	839.3
real estate	8340	863	834
Valve			
electronic, manufacturing	3453/1	364/1	345.1
engine (motor vehicle) manufacturing	3530	381	353
for hydraulic equipment, manufacturing	3283/2	333/4	328.3
for pneumatic control equipment, manufacturing	3283/3	333/2	328.3
Valves for tyres, manufacturing	3289/3	349/3	328.8
Van			
hire, self drive	8480/2	703	845
motor, manufacturing	3510/2	381	351
Vanadium, manufacturing	2247/1	323	224.1
Vane pump, manufacturing	3287	333/1	328.3
Vaporizing oil, manufacturing	1401	262	140.1
Variety			
agency	9791/3	881/2	979
artiste (own account)	9760	881/2	976
Varnish			
manufacturing	2551	274	255
printers', manufacturing	2552	279/5	255
Varnished tape (insulating) manufacturing	2569	491	438.3
Vase			
ceramic, manufacturing	2489/3	462/3	248
glassware, manufacturing	2479/1	463/1	247
plastics, manufacturing	4836	496	483

Activity	SIC 1980	1968	NACE
Vat			
dye, manufacturing	2516	277	251
wooden, manufacturing	4640/2	475/1	464.2
Vegetable			
dehydrating, for human consumption	4147/4	218/3	414.6
down, manufacturing	4399/2	429/2	439.7
fibre pulp, manufacturing	4710/1	481	471.1
growing (except potatoes)	0100/2	001/3	01
harvesting and sorting machinery, manufacturing	3211/2	331	321.1
juice, manufacturing	4283/2	232	414.4
oil refining	4116/3	221	411.4
pickling	4147/2	218/3	414.3
quick freezing	4147/1	218/2	414.1
tanning and dyeing extracts, manufacturing	2516	277	251
Vegetables, dealing in			
retail	6410	820/2	641.2
wholesale	6170	810/2	617.2
Vegetarian foods, retail dealing in	6410	820/1	642.3
Vehicle			
battery, manufacturing	3432/2	369/3	343.2
depot (Ministry of Defence)	9150	901/5	915
lamp (bulb and sealed beam unit) manufacturing	3470/1	369/4	347.1
transport (ship) manufacturing	3610/1	370/1	361
wooden, manufacturing	4650	479/3	465.1
Veiling			
not silk, manufacturing	4395	418	439.5
silk, manufacturing	4322	413	433.5
Vellum, manufacturing	4410/1	431/1	441.3
Velocity measuring instrument, manufacturing	3710	354/2	371.1
Velvet			
cutting or shearing	4370/2	423	437.4
dyeing	4370/2	423	437.2
manufacturing	4322	413	432.5
Velveteen			
cutting or shearing	4370/2	423	437.4
dyeing	4370/2	423	437.2
manufacturing	4322	413	432.5
Vending machine, manufacturing	3286/1	339/9	328.9
Veneer			
log sawing	4610/1	471/1	461.1
manufacturing	4620/1	471/1	462.1
press, manufacturing	3275/1	339/9	327.1
sheet, manufacturing	4620/1	471/1	462.1
Ventilating unit, manufacturing	3284/3	339/4	328.4
Ventriloquist	9760	881/2	976
Vermicelli, manufacturing	4239/7	229/2	417
Vermiculite expanded, manufacturing	2450/4	469/2	245.5
Vermin			
destroying (not agricultural)	9211	899/7	921
destroying and trapping on agricultural land	0100/3	001/2	01
Vernier, gauge, manufacturing	3710	390	371.5
Vertical boiler (not marine) manufacturing	3205/1	341/1	315.1
Vest			
knitted	4363/2	417	436.2
men's and boys', manufacturing	4535	444/2	453
women's and girls', manufacturing	4536/2	445/2	453
Vestment, clerical, (not retail bespoke) manufacturing	4532	442	453
Veterinarian, registered	9560/2	879/4	956
Veterinary			
biologicals, manufacturing	2570	272	257
equipment, manufacturing	3720/1	353/1	372.2
medicinal, feed additives, manufacturing	2570	272	257
pharmaceuticals, manufacturing	2570	272	257
surgeon	9560/1	879/4	956
surgery	9560/1	879/4	956
Viaduct steelwork, manufacturing	3204/2	341/4	314.1
Vial, manufacturing	2478	463/2	247.7
Victoria and Albert Museum	9770	899/4	977
Video			
recorders, retail dealing in	6480	821/3	648.8
tape recording, manufacturing	3452	365/1	345.2
Village general store (selling mainly foodstuffs)	6410	820/1	642.3
Vine yards	0100/2	001/3	01
Vinegar			
malt, spirit, wine, acetic acid, manufacturing	4239/9	218/3	423.3
processing machinery, manufacturing	3244/1	339/7	324.1
Vinyl			
acetate, manufacturing	2512	271/2	251
asbestos tile, manufacturing	4833	492	438.2
floorcoverings, homogeneous and printed, manufacturing	4833	492	438.2
floorcoverings, supported, manufacturing	4833	492	438.2
paint, manufacturing	2551	274	255
wallpaper, manufacturing	4721	484/1	472.1
Viola, manufacturing	4920/2	499/1	492.2
Violin			
case, not wooden, manufacturing	4959	499/2	495.3
etc., case, wooden, manufacturing	4671/4	499/2	467.5
manufacturing	4920/2	499/1	492.2
Viscometer, manufacturing	3710	354/2	371.2
Visible record computer (tabulator) manufacturing	3301	338	330
Visual display unit, computer, manufacturing	3302	366	330
Vitreous			
china sanitary ware, manufacturing	2489/2	462/2	248.5
enamel frits, manufacturing	2551	271/3	255
Vitrified bonded abrasives, manufacturing	2460	469/1	246.1
Vodka distilling	4240/2	239/1	424.2
Voile weaving	4322	413	432.5
Voltage regulator (for vehicle) manufacturing	3434	369/1	343.1
Voltmeter, manufacturing	3442	354/2	344
Volumetric glassware, manufacturing	2479/3	463/1	247.7
Vulcanising machines, rubber and plastics working, manufacturing	3275/2	339/9	327.1
Vulcanised fibre, manufacturing	4728	484/2	472.8

W

Activity	SIC 1980	1968	NACE
WRAC	9150	901/2	915
WRAF	9150	901/3	915
WRNS	9150	901/1	915
Wadding			
(from yarn spun on the cotton system) manufacturing	4322	413	432.5
(surgical) manufacturing	2570	279/6	257
Wafer, biscuit, making	4197	213	419.5
Wagon			
cover, manufacturing	4556	422/2	455.4
timber sawn, manufacturing	4610/1	471/1	461.1
Waistcoat			
boys', tailored (not retail bespoke) manufacturing	4532	442	453
men's, (not retail bespoke) manufacturing	4532	442	453
Walking stick, wooden, manufacturing	4650	449/3	465.1
Wall			
board, dealing in	6130	831/2	613.2
mountings, metal, manufacturing	3169/3	399/12	316.3

Activity	SIC 1980	1968	NACE
panels, structural, precast concrete, manufacturing	2437	469/2	243.2
tile, clay unglazed, manufacturing	2410	461/2	241
tile, glazed, manufacturing	2489/1	462/2	248.3
unit, manufacturing	4671/2	472	467.1
Wallace Collection	9770	899/4	977
Wallet, leather or leather substitute, manufacturing	4420/1	432	442.1
Wallets, retail dealing in	6460	821/4	646.2
Wallpaper			
and lining paper, manufacturing	4721	484/1	472.1
base, manufacturing	4710/3	481	471.3
retail dealing in	6480	821/3	649.1
Wardrobe			
manufacturing	4671/2	472	467.1
metal, manufacturing	3166/1	399/1	316.6
Warehouse	7700/3	709/2	773
Warm air generator, manufacturing	3284/2	339/4	328.4
Warp			
dressing, woollen	4310/2	414/5	431.3
knitted fabric, dyeing and finishing	4370/2	423	437
knitted fabric, manufacturing	4364	417	436.2
knitting	4364	417	436.2
sizing and dressing (worsted)	4310/2	414/2	431.3
starch, manufacturing	4180	229/2	418.4
Warping machinery, manufacturing	3230/2	335	323.1
Warship, manufacturing	3610/1	370/1	361.1
Wash			
and fat contracting (waste collecting)	6220	832/7	622
basin, plastics, manufacturing	4834	496	483
basin or sink, ceramic, fireclay, etc., manufacturing	2489/2	462/2	248.5
Washer, manufacturing			
leather	4420/2	432	442.3
metal	3137/1	393	313.1
rubber	4812/3	491/2	481.2
Washing machine, manufacturing			
domestic	3460	368	346
laundry	3275/6	339/9	327.3
textile	3230/3	335	323.1
Waste			
glass resulting from glass container, manufacturing	2478	463	247
glass resulting from glass product (other than glass container) manufacturing	2479/5	463	247
heat boiler, manufacturing	3205/1	341/1	315.1
paper sorting and dealing in	6220	832/7	622
rubber, dealing in	6220	832/7	622
string, dealing in	6220	832/7	622
textile; dyeing	4370/2	423	437.2
yarn, cotton, manufacturing	4321/1	412	432.3
Watch			
and clock movements, wholesale dealing in	6190	812/4	619.4
and clock repairer	6730/2	821/4	674
case, manufacturing	3740	352	374
glass, manufacturing	2479/5	463/1	247.4
manufacturing	3740	352	374
Watches and clocks			
manufacturing	3740	352	374
retail dealing in	6540	821/4	654.2
wholesale dealing in	6190	812/4	619.4
Watchmakers' jewels, manufacturing	4910/2	396	491.5
Watchstrap, leather or leather substitute, manufacturing	4420/1	432	442.1
Water			
authority (headquarters and water supply)	1700	603/1	170
butt, plastics, manufacturing	4836	496	483
closet bowl, ceramic, fireclay, etc., manufacturing	2489/2	462/2	248.5
company	1700	603/2	170
conservation	1700	603	170
heater (domestic, electric) manufacturing	3460	368	346
heater, gas, manufacturing	3165	399/9	316.5
ices, manufacturing	4213	215/3	421.3
meter, manufacturing	3710	354/2	371.1
proofed cover, canvas, manufacturing	4556	422/2	455.4
sensitive adhesive tape, manufacturing	2569	491	259.3
softening plant, manufacturing	3245/3	341/2	324.1
sports equipment, manufacturing	4942	494/3	494.2
stop and bar, plastics, manufacturing	4834	496	483
tower, of steel plate, manufacturing	3205/3	341/5	315.2
treatment chemical, manufacturing	2567	271/3	256.7
treatment plant, manufacturing	3245/3	341/2	324.1
tube boiler (not marine) manufacturing	3205/1	341/1	315.1
Watercress, growing	0100/2	001/3	01
Watering can, plastics, manufacturing	4836	496	483
Waterproof			
garment, manufacturing	4531	441	453
paper, manufacturing	4710/6	481	471.3
Waterproofing buildings	5010	500	501.4
Waterwings, rubber, manufacturing	4812/3	491/2	481.2
Wattmeter, manufacturing	3442	354/2	344
Wave-form generator, manufacturing	3442	354/2	344
Wax			
manufacturing	2567	279/1	256.7
model, manufacturing	4959	499/2	495.3
products, manufacturing	2599	279/1	259.4
Waxworks	9791/3	882	979
WC seat and cover unit, plastics, manufacturing	4834	496	483
Weather			
board, manufacturing	4610/2	471/1	461.2
protective industrial clothing, manufacturing	4531	441	453
Weatherboarding, plastics, manufacturing	4834	496	483
Weatherproof outerwear, manufacturing	4531	441	453
Weaving			
cotton and man-made fibres	4322	413	432.5
jute	4350/2	415	435.5
linen and union	4340/2	413	434.5
machinery (loom) manufacturing	3230/2	335	323.1
voile	4322	413	432.5
woollen cloth	4310/3	414/5	431.5
worsted	4310/3	414/3	431.5
Web equipment, making up	4556	422/2	455.4
Webbing			
non-elastic and non-elastomeric, manufacturing	4398/2	421/3	439.3
weaving	4398/2	421/3	439.3
Wedding photograph service	9890/1	899/2	983
Wedge (optical) manufacturing	3732	354	373.2
Weed killer, manufacturing	2568	279/4	256.8
Weft knitted fabric			
dyeing and finishing	4370/2	423	437
manufacturing	4363/3	417	436.2
Weighbridge, manufacturing	3285/1	339/5	328.9
Weighing machine, manufacturing	3285/1	339/5	328.9
Weight (for weighing machine) manufacturing	3285/1	339/5	316.9
Welded			
link chain, manufacturing	3137/3	399/12	313.4
steel tube, manufacturing	2220	312	222
Welding			
electrode, manufacturing	3435	332/3	223.4

Activity	SIC 1980	1968	NACE
equipment (electric) manufacturing	3435	332/3	343.1
machines (gas) manufacturing	3289/3	332/3	328.7
torch, manufacturing	3289/3	332/3	328.7
Welfare service	9611/1	899/3	961
Well			
and bulkhead glass, manufacturing	2479/2	463/1	247.4
drilling (petroleum)	1300	104	502.3
drilling equipment, manufacturing	3254/3	336	325.1
logging	1300	104	134
sinking (except gas or oil)	5020	500	502.3
Wellington boot, manufacturing	4510	450	481.2
Wesleyan Reform Union	9660	875	966
Wet			
fish, retail dealing in	6410	820/2	641.5
fish, wholesale dealing in	6170	810/2	617.9
mortars, ready-mixed, manufacturing	2436	469/2	243.6
Whale oil			
dealing in	6120	832/8	612.7
production	4116/1	221	411.1
refining	4116/3	221	411.4
Whalebone cutting and splitting	4959	499/2	495.3
Whaler, manufacturing	3610/1	370/1	361.1
Whaling	0300/1	003/1	03
Wharfinger	7630	706	763
Wheat			
flake, manufacturing	4160	211/2	416.1
milling	4160	211/1	416.1
offal, manufacturing	4160	211/1	416.1
starch, manufacturing	4180	229/2	418.1
Wheel			
abrasive, bonded, manufacturing	2460	469/1	246.1
and hub (motor vehicle) manufacturing	3530	381	353
chair, manufacturing	3650/1	494/2	365.2
diamond impregnated, manufacturing	2460	469/1	246.2
emery, manufacturing	2460	469/1	246.1
motor cycle, manufacturing	3633	382	363.2
pedal cycle, manufacturing	3634	382	363.2
Wheelbarrow			
hiring	8480/4	709/3	845
metal, manufacturing	3169/4	399/12	316.9
toy, manufacturing	4941	494/1	494.1
wooden, manufacturing	4650	479/3	465.1
Wheeled			
and half-track tractor parts, manufacturing	3212	380	321.2
tractors, dealing in	6149	832/6	614.6
tractor, manufacturing	3212	380	321.2
Whey (sweetened skimmed) production	4130/3	215/2	413.2
Whinstone quarry	2310/2	102/1	231.2
Whisky			
blending	4240/2	239/1	424.2
distilling	4240/2	239/1	424.2
White			
lead (in paste form) manufacturing	2551	274	255
lead (not in paste form) manufacturing	2511	271/1	251
metal, manufacturing	2247/1	323	224.2
salt, manufacturing	2330	109/3	233
spirit, manufacturing	1401	262	140.1
sugar, manufacturing	4200	216	420.2
Whitewash brush, manufacturing	4663	493	466.3
Whiting and prepared chalk, manufacturing	2450/1	469/2	245.1
Whitley Council (staff side)	9631/3	899/6	965
Wholesale			
dealer in cloth	6160	812/2	616.4
merchant (predominantly non-food, general or undefined)	6190	812/5	619.7
Wick (lamp, stove or candle) manufacturing	4398/2	421/3	439.7
Wicker			
basket, manufacturing	4664/2	475/1	466.2
furniture, manufacturing	4671/2	472	467.7
Wickerwork, manufacturing	4664/2	475/1	466.2
Wide cut gasoline, manufacturing	1401	262	140.1
Wig, manufacturing	4539/3	449/4	453
Willow growing	0100/1	001/1	01
Wilton carpet, manufacturing	4384/1	419	438.1
Winceyette weaving	4322	413	432.5
Winch, manufacturing	3255/4	337/4	325.5
Wind instrument, manufacturing	4920/2	499/1	492.2
Winding			
device, manufacturing	3255/4	337/4	325.5
machine (mining) manufacturing	3251	339/1	325.1
machinery (textile) manufacturing	3230/1	335	323.1
wire and strip, manufacturing	3410	362	341
Windlass, manufacturing	3255/4	337/4	325.5
Window			
blind and accessories, plastics, manufacturing	4836	496	483
cleaning	9230	899/7	923
cord, manufacturing	4396	416	439.6
dressing, freelance	8380	865	838
fittings, metal, manufacturing	3169/3	399/12	316.3
frame, plastics, manufacturing	4834	496	483
frame, metal, manufacturing	3142	399/2	314.2
frame, wooden, manufacturing	4630	471/2	463.2
furnishing fabric (knitted) manufacturing	4364	417	436.2
glass (cut to size) manufacturing	2471/2	463/1	247.6
glass (not cut to size) manufacturing	2471/1	463/1	247.1
ticket, manufacturing	4754/4	489	473.2
winding gear, not electric (motor vehicle) manufacturing	3530	381	353
Windscreen			
glass, manufacturing	2471/2	463/1	247.6
wiper, manufacturing	3434	369/1	343.1
wiper (non-electric) manufacturing	3530	381	353
Windsor			
Castle	9111	901/6	911
Great Park	9111	901/6	911
Wine			
and spirit merchant, wholesale	6170	810/1	617.5
and spirits, retail dealing in	6420	820/2	642.1
based on concentrated grape must, manufacturing	4261/1	239/2	425.1
from fresh grapes, manufacturing	4261/3	239/2	425
importer, wholesale	6170	810/1	617.5
making machinery, manufacturing	3244/1	339/7	324.1
making preparations (excluding yeast) manufacturing	2567	271/3	256.8
non-alcoholic, manufacturing	4283/1	232	428.2
rack, wooden, manufacturing	4650	479/3	465.1
vinegar, manufacturing	4239/9	218/3	423.3
Winkle gathering	0300/1	003/1	03
Winnower, manufacturing	3211/2	331	321.1
Wire			
aluminium, manufacturing	2245/2	394	224.3
and cable covering and sleeve plastics, manufacturing	4836	496	483
and cable drum, wooden, manufacturing	4650	479/3	465.1
and cable, insulated, manufacturing	3410	362	341
barbed, steel, manufacturing	2234	394	223.4
brush, manufacturing	4663	493	466.3
cable, steel, manufacturing	2234	394	223.4
carpet, ferrous, manufacturing	2234	394	223.4
coiling machine, manufacturing	3286/3	339/9	322.1
copper, uninsulated, manufacturing	2246/2	394	224.2
fabric, steel, manufacturing	2234	394	223.4
fencing, steel, manufacturing	2234	394	223.4
heavy, manufacturing	3137/2	394	313.1

Activity	SIC 1980	1968	NACE
iron, manufacturing	2234	394	223.4
nail, steel, manufacturing	2234	394	223.4
netting, steel, manufacturing	2234	394	223.4
piano, manufacturing	2234	394	223.4
product, copper, uninsulated, manufacturing	2246/2	394	224.2
rod, copper, manufacturing	2246/2	322	224.2
rod, steel, manufacturing	2210	311/2	221.1
rope, manufacturing	2234	394	223.4
rope making machine, manufacturing	3286/3	339/9	328.9
strand, aluminium, manufacturing	2245/2	394	224.3
weaving machine, manufacturing	3286/3	339/9	322.1
Wirebar, aluminium, manufacturing	2245/1	321	224.1
Wirebound box, wooden, manufacturing	4640/1	475/2	464.1
Wired glass, manufacturing	2471/1	463/1	247.1
Wires or rods (for gas welding, soldering or brazing) manufacturing	3289/3	332/3	223.4
Wiring			
accessories, manufacturing	3420/3	369/5	342
cable, general, manufacturing	3410	362	341
Witherite mine	2396	109/4	239.4
Withy growing	0100/1	001/1	01
Wolfram, manufacturing	2247/1	323	224.1
Women's			
and girls' dressing gown, manufacturing	4536/1	445/1	453
and girls' hat, felt, manufacturing	4537/1	446/1	453
and girls' leather garments, manufacturing	4533	443	453
and girls' light outerwear, manufacturing	4536/1	445/1	453
and girls' nightwear, manufacturing	4536/2	445/2	453
and girls' nightwear, knitted, manufacturing	4363/2	417	436.2
and girls' raincoat, manufacturing	4531	441	453
and girls' tailored blazer (not retail bespoke) manufacturing	4533	443	453
and girls' tailored coat (not retail bespoke) manufacturing	4533	443	453
and girls' tailored jacket (not retail bespoke) manufacturing	4533	443	453
and girls' tailored sportswear (not retail bespoke) manufacturing	4533	443	453
and girls' tailored trousers (not retail bespoke) manufacturing	4533	443	453
and girls' tailored trouser suit (not retail bespoke) manufacturing	4533	443	453
and girls' underwear, manufacturing	4536/2	445/2	453
and girls' uniform (not retail bespoke) manufacturing	4533	443	453
battledress, manufacturing	4533	443	453
clothing, tailored (not retail bespoke) manufacturing	4533	443	453
glove, manufacturing	4538	449/2	453
industrial overall, manufacturing	4534	444/1	453
knitted dress, manufacturing	4363/2	417	436.2
lightweight jacket, manufacturing	4536/1	445/1	453
outerwear, knitted, manufacturing	4363/2	417	436.2
Royal Voluntary Service	9611/1	899/3	961
sock, manufacturing	4363/1	417	436.1
stocking, manufacturing	4363/1	417	436.1
underwear, knitted, manufacturing	4363/2	417	436.2
Womens'			
outfitter, retail	6450	821/2	645
wear, retail dealing in	6450	821/2	645
Wood			
agent	6300	832/2	633
carving	4650	479/3	465.1
chip, manufacturing	4650	479/3	465.1
chipboard, agglomerated with non-mineral binding substances, manufacturing	4620/1	471/1	462.2
creosoting	4620/2	471/1	462.4
dealing in	6130	832/2	613.1
engraver (artist)	9760	879/5	976
flour, manufacturing	4650	479/3	465.2
grooving	4610/2	471/1	461.2
impregnation	4620/2	471/1	462.4
logging, etc., within forestry site	0200	002	02
marquetry, manufacturing	4620/1	471/1	462.1
panel, cellular, manufacturing	4620/1	471/1	462.1
paving block, manufacturing	4630	471/1	463.3
planing	4610/2	471/1	461.2
preservation	4620/2	471/1	462.4
pulp vessel, manufacturing	4728	484/2	472.8
sawing	4610/1	471/1	461.1
shavings, manufacturing	4650	479/3	465.1
spraying	4620/2	471/1	462.4
stain, manufacturing	2551	274	255
tar chemical, manufacturing	2567	271/2	256.7
treatment	4620/2	471/1	462.4
varnishing	4620/2	471/1	462.4
veneer, manufacturing	4620/1	471/1	462.1
wool, manufacturing	4650	479/3	465.3
worm preventative treatment service	9211	899/7	921
Wood-boring bit, manufacturing	3161/2	391	316.1
Wood-pulp, manufacturing	4710/1	481	471.1
Wooden			
box, manufacturing	4640/1	475/2	464.1
toy and game, manufacturing	4941	494/1	494.1
Woodpulp and paper making materials, dealing in	6120	832/8	612.7
Woodrot preventative treatment service	9211	899/7	921
Woodwind instrument, manufacturing	4940/2	499/1	492.2
Woodworking machinery, manufacturing	3275/1	339/9	327.1
Wool			
broker	6300	832/4	631
carbonising	4310/1	414/1	431.2
carding	4310/1	414/1	431.2
cleaning	4310/1	414/1	431.2
combing	4310/1	414/1	431.2
condensing	4310/1	414/1	431.2
cop, hank, warp etc., bleaching	4370/2	423	437.1
dealing in	6110	832/4	611.6
exchange	6300	812/2	616
extracting	4310/1	414/1	431.2
fellmongery, manufacturing	4410/2	431	431.1
felt and fur felt hood and capeline, manufacturing	4537/1	446/1	453
felt, pressed, manufacturing	4399/1	414/6	439.1
loose, dyeing	4370/2	423	437.2
merchant, wholesale	6160	832/4	616
opening and willeying	4310/1	414/1	431.2
printing	4370/2	423	437.3
recovery	4310/1	414/4	439.7
scouring	4310/1	414/1	431.2
sorting	4310/1	414/1	431.2
topmaking	4310/1	414/1	431.2
warehouse	7700/3	709/2	773
Woollen			
and worsted fabric bleaching, dyeing or otherwise finishing	4370/2	423	437
and worsted product, manufacturing	4310/3	414	431
bunting, manufacturing	4310/3	414/5	431.5
cloth, weaving	4310/3	414/5	431.5
coating, manufacturing	4310/3	414/5	431.5
damask, manufacturing	4310/3	414/5	431.5
draper, retail	6450	821/2	645.6
dress goods, manufacturing	4310/3	414/5	431.5

WOO-YOU

Activity	SIC 1980	SIC 1968	NACE
flag, manufacturing	4310/3	414/5	431.5
flock, dealing in	6110	832/4	611.6
rag, blending or sorting	6220	832/7	622
rag, carbonising	4310/1	414/4	431.2
rag, carding	4310/1	414/4	431.2
rag, garnetting	4310/1	414/4	439.7
rag, grinding or pulling	4310/1	414/4	439.7
suiting, manufacturing	4310/3	414/5	431.5
travelling rug, manufacturing	4310/3	414/5	431.5
waste, breaking	4310/1	414/4	439.7
waste, garnetting	4310/1	414/4	439.7
waste, grinding	4310/1	414/4	439.7
waste, opening and willeying	4310/1	414/4	439.7
yarn, carding	4310/2	414/5	431.3
yarn, condensing	4310/2	414/5	431.3
yarn, reeling	4310/2	414/5	431.3
yarn, sizing	4310/2	414/5	431.3
yarn, spinning	4310/2	414/5	431.3
yarn, twisting	4310/2	414/5	431.4
yarn, warping	4310/2	414/5	431.3
yarn, winding	4310/2	414/5	431.4
Woollens, wholesale dealing in	6160	812/2	616.6
Work			
holder (engineers' small tools) manufacturing	3222/3	390	322.2
trouser, manufacturing	4534	444/1	453
Workers' Educational Association	9330	872/4	933
Working men's club	6630	887	664
Works			
of art, retail dealing in	6480	821/3	649.6
salt	2330	109/3	233
school (if separately identifiable)	9330	872/3	933
Workshop wagon, railway, manufacturing	3620/2	385	362.2
Worsted			
bedford cord, weaving	4310/3	414/3	431.5
carding	4310/1	414/2	431.2
doubling	4310/2	414/2	431.3
spinning and twisting	4310/2	414/2	431
waste grinding	4310/1	414/4	431.2
weaving	4310/3	414/3	431.5
yarn, reeling	4310/2	414/2	431.3
yarn, warping	4310/2	414/2	431.3
yarn, winding	4310/2	414/2	431.4
Woven			
conveyor belting, manufacturing	4398/2	421/2	439.3
crepe, manufacturing	4322	413	432.5
elastic over 30 cm wide, manufacturing	4322	413	439.4
elastomeric over 30 cm wide, manufacturing	4322	413	439.4
felt, manufacturing	4399/1	414	439.1
fibre furniture, manufacturing	4671/2	472	467.7
glass fibre fabric, manufacturing	4322	413	432.5
machinery belting, manufacturing	4398/2	421/2	439.7
not wool, dress fabric, manufacturing	4322	413	432.5
plastic matting, manufacturing	4833	429/2	438.2
trimming, manufacturing	4398/2	421/3	439.3
Wrapping			
and packaging paper (including coated) manufacturing	4710/4	481	471.3
machinery, manufacturing	3244/2	339/8	324.2
paper, cut, packed, ready to use in sheets or rolls, manufacturing	4724/2	482/2	472.4
Wreck raising	7630	706	763
Wrecking bar, manufacturing	3161/2	391	316.1
Wrench, manufacturing	3161/2	391	316.1
Wrestling	9791/1	882	978
Wrist watch, manufacturing	3740	352	374
Writer to the Signet	8350	873	835

Activity	SIC 1980	SIC 1968	NACE
Writing			
ink, manufacturing	4954/2	495/2	259.3
paper, manufacturing	4710/3	481	471.3
paper pad, manufacturing	4723/1	483	472.3
Wrought			
iron, manufacturing	2210	311/1	221.1
steel tube, manufacturing	2220	312	222

X

Activity	SIC 1980	SIC 1968	NACE
X-Ray			
apparatus, industrial, manufacturing	3443	367/2	344
apparatus, medical, manufacturing	3443	367/2	344
diffraction or fluorescence apparatus, manufacturing	3442	354/2	344
Xerographic copying machine, manufacturing	3733	351	373.3
Xylene, manufacturing	2512	271/2	251

Y

Activity	SIC 1980	SIC 1968	NACE
YMCA—not hostel	9690/2	899/3	968
YMCA—hostel	9611/2	884	962
YWCA—not hostel	9690/2	899/3	968
YWCA—hostel	9611/2	884	962
Yacht			
club	9791/1	882	978
(other than sea-going luxury yacht) manufacturing	3610/2	370/1	361.3
sea-going luxury type (of gross 100 tons or more) manufacturing	3610/1	370/1	361.3
Yachts, wholesale dealing in	6149	812/4	614.7
Yarn			
agent	6300	832/4	631
bleaching, dyeing or otherwise finishing	4370/2	423	437
continuous filament (man-made fibres) manufacturing	2600	411	260
core-spun (cotton system) manufacturing	4321/1	412	432.3
cotton, manufacturing	4321/1	412	432.3
fibrillated, manufacturing	4350/3	415	435.3
finishing	4370/2	423	437.4
gassing	4370/2	423	437.4
jute, manufacturing	4350/1	415	435.3
mercerising	4370/2	423	437.4
polishing	4370/2	423	437.4
storing	4370/2	423	437.4
Yeast			
and vegetable extract, manufacturing	4239/4	229/2	423.8
preparation	4239/5	229/2	423.8
wholesale dealing in	6170	810/2	617.9
Yoghourt, manufacturing	4130/3	215/2	413.1
Youth			
centre	9690/2	899/3	968
club	9690/2	899/3	968
hostel	6670/3	884	667.1

Activity	SIC		NACE
	1980	1968	
Z			
Zephyr weaving	**4322**	413	432.5
Zinc			
compounds, manufacturing	**2511**	271/1	251
dealing in	**6120**	832/1	612.6
manufacturing	**2247/1**	323	224.1
oxide, manufacturing	**2511**	277	251
paint, manufacturing	**2551**	274	255

Activity	SIC		NACE
	1980	1968	
Zionist Organisation	**9690/2**	899/4	968
Zip			
fastener, metal, manufacturing	**3169/2**	399/8	316.9
(slide) fasteners, plastics, manufacturing	**4836**	496	483
Zirconium manufacturing	**2247/1**	323	224.1
Zoological gardens	**9770**	882	977

Annual Abstract of Statistics

The *Annual Abstract* is a selection of the most important statistics on the economic, industrial and social life of the United Kingdom. It presents the widest range of information of all Central Statistical Office publications, with data for periods of 10 years or more. Some 348 tables cover population, social conditions, employment, production, national income and expenditure, home finance, banking and insurance, and prices.

Price £17.50

Central Statistical Office publications are published by Her Majesty's Stationery Office.
They are obtainable from Government bookshops and through good booksellers

CENTRAL STATISTICAL OFFICE PUBLICATIONS

ANNUAL

Annual Abstract of Statistics — has some 350 tables generally giving data for the last eleven years covering just about every aspect of economic, social and industrial life.

Social Trends — provides a valuable insight into the changing patterns of life in Britain. The chapters provide analyses and breakdowns of statistical information on population, households and families, education and employment, income and wealth, resources and expenditure, health and social services, and many other aspects of British life and work.

Regional Trends — with over 130 tables and 50 maps and charts, brings together a wide range of government statistics on the various countries and regions of the United Kingdom.

United Kingdom National Accounts — The CSO Blue Book is the essential data source for everyone concerned with macro-economic policies and studies and shows how the nation makes and spends its money. It is issued in early September and covers all aspects of the United Kingdom economy giving data for the last eleven years or longer.

United Kingdom Balance of Payments — The CSO Pink Book is the basic reference book for balance of payments statistics, presenting all the statistical information, for the last eleven years or more, needed by analysts who seek to assess UK transactions with the rest of the world.

Key Data — with over 130 tables, maps and coloured charts covers a very wide range of social and economic data. Each table and chart is accompanied by a reference to sources.

MONTHLY

Economic Trends — a compilation of all the main economic indicators liberally illustrated with charts and diagrams. The largest section gives time series and graphs over the last five years or so. It is the primary publication for quarterly articles on national accounts and the balance of payments as well as others commenting on and analysing economic statistics. The *Economic Trends Annual Supplement* contains long runs of annual and quarterly figures for the key series of economic indicators.

Financial Statistics — gives data on the key financial and monetary statistics of the United Kingdom. Tables usually contain at least 18 monthly and 12 quarterly or 5 annual figures. The annual *Financial Statistics Explanatory Handbook* contains comprehensive notes and definitions for the tables.

Monthly Digest of Statistics — provides basic information on 20 subjects. Tables contain mostly runs of monthly and quarterly estimates for at least two years and annual figures for several more. The annual *Monthly Digest of Statistics Supplement of Definitions and Explanatory Notes* gives definitions for items and units in the *Digest*. It also applies to corresponding items in the *Annual Abstract* and *Regional Trends*.

OTHERS

Guide to Official Statistics (fifth edition) — an indispensible reference book for all users of statistics. Vital information about sources of government and important non-government statistics for the United Kingdom over the last five years are given.

United Kingdom National Accounts: Sources and Methods (third edition) — an essential reference book for everyone who makes use of national accounts data. It contains details of the concepts, definitions, statistical sources, methods of compilation and reliability of the various statistical sources which comprise the national accounts.

Statistical News — a quarterly journal providing a comprehensive account of current developments in British official statistics.

Standard Industrial Classification Revised 1980 — is a system of classification of establishments according to industry covering all economic activity.

Indexes to the Standard Industrial Classification Revised 1980 contains lists of characteristic activities for each heading of the classification as well as an alphabetical index of activities. The publication is also indexed to the previous 1968 classification and to the European standard industrial classification (NACE).

CSO publications are published by HMSO and available from the addresses given on the back cover.

SOCIAL TRENDS

For seventeen years Social Trends has provided a valuable insight into life in Britain and its changes

As much more than simply a source of updated information, *Social Trends* continues to provide an invaluable insight into changing patterns of British life.

Each *Social Trends* focuses on specific issues. The 17th edition includes two articles — one is on social trends since the second world war and the other looks at longitudinal perspectives of household formation and dissolution and housing tenure, complementing the information in Chapter 8 on Housing.

Social Trends remains necessary for those people involved in social policy both inside and outside Government, and has become an essential tool for market researchers, journalists and other commentators, teachers, advertisers, businessmen — for anyone who is interested in British society.

Regional Trends and the *Monthly Digest of Statistics* make ideal companions from the Central Statistical Office's comprehensive range of publications on Britain's society and economy.

Social Trends 17

For the sixth year running price held at £19.95

ISBN 011 6202440

Central Statistical Office publications are published by Her Majesty's Stationery Office.
They are obtainable from Government bookshops and through good booksellers.